Perl for Oracle DBAs

Perl for Oracle DBAs

Andy Duncan and Jared Still

O'REILLY®

Beijing · Cambridge · Farnham · Köln · Paris · Sebastopol · Taipei · Tokyo

Perl for Oracle DBAs
by Andy Duncan and Jared Still

Copyright © 2002 O'Reilly & Associates, Inc. All rights reserved.
Printed in the United States of America.

Published by O'Reilly & Associates, Inc., 1005 Gravenstein Highway North, Sebastopol, CA
95472.

O'Reilly & Associates books may be purchased for educational, business, or sales promotional
use. Online editions are also available for most titles (*safari.oreilly.com*). For more information,
contact our corporate/institutional sales department: (800) 998-9938 or *corporate@oreilly.com*.

Editor:	Deborah Russell
Production Editor:	Darren Kelly
Cover Designer:	Emma Colby
Interior Designer:	David Futato

Printing History:

August 2002:	First Edition.

ISBN: 0-596-00210-6

[M]

Table of Contents

Preface . . . . **ix**

Part I.   Introducing Perl for Oracle

1. Perl Meets Oracle **3**
What is Perl?   4
The Perl/Oracle Architecture   10
Perl for Oracle DBAs   15
For Further Information   24

2. Installing Perl **28**
Installing Perl   28
Installing Perl DBI   38
Running Perl DBI   48
Installing Cygwin   51

Part II.   Extending Perl

3. Perl GUI Extensions **65**
Perl/Tk   66
OraExplain   72
StatsView   74
Orac   82
DDL::Oracle   84
SchemaDiff   90
Senora   92

DBD::Chart   95

SchemaView-Plus   104

Open Source Perl IDEs   107

Open Source Perl GUI Debuggers   108

4. Perl Web Extensions **110**

Apache   111

Oracletool   118

Karma   127

5. Embedding Perl into Apache with mod_perl **136**

mod_perl   137

Apache::OWA   155

6. Embedded Perl Web Scripting **161**

Embperl   162

Mason   169

7. Invoking the Oracle Call Interface with Oracle::OCI **178**

What is Oracle::OCI?   179

What Is OCI?   180

Installing Oracle::OCI   185

Coding with Oracle::OCI   190

The Future of Oracle::OCI   198

8. Embedding Perl into PL/SQL **201**

Communication Between Perl and PL/SQL   202

Embedding Perl Within Oracle   204

Part III. The Perl DBA Toolkit

9. Installing the PDBA Toolkit **227**

Introducing the PDBA Toolkit   228

Toolkit Modules   232

Installing the PDBA Toolkit for Unix   257

Installing the PDBA Toolkit for Win32   261

Configuring the PDBA Toolkit   265

10. **Performing Routine DBA Tasks with the PDBA Toolkit** **279**
   Managing User Accounts   280
   Maintaining Indexes   297
   Killing Sniped Sessions   305
   Managing Extent Usage   312
   Extracting DDL and Data   315

11. **Monitoring the Database with the PDBA Toolkit** **328**
   Monitoring the Alert Log   328
   Monitoring the Databases   342

12. **Building a Database Repository with the PDBA Toolkit** **366**
   Repository Table Structure   367
   Installing the Repository   369
   Loading the Repository with Data   374
   Reporting on Database Changes   377
   Reporting on SQL Execution Plans   392

13. **Extending the PDBA Toolkit** **403**
   Modifying a Script in the Toolkit   404
   Modifying a Module in the Toolkit   421

Part IV. Appendixes

   A. **The Essential Guide to Perl** **439**

   B. **The Essential Guide to Perl DBI** **459**

   C. **The Essential Guide to Regular Expressions** **482**

   D. **The Essential Guide to Perl Data Munging** **521**

Index **575**

Preface

There are many books on Perl and many books on Oracle, but until now there have been no books dedicated to describing the relationship between these two popular technologies. Our aim is to bridge the gap between the world's leading data-processing language and the world's leading database. The Perl language was created with the goal of making "the easy things easy and the hard things possible." Oracle's ever-expanding purpose is to provide a complete database environment for the entire interconnected world. This mission makes Oracle a tough taskmaster—and thus an environment ideally suited to Perl, because being an Oracle database administrator is one of the toughest jobs around.

Oracle DBAs need enormous intelligence, infinite patience, and considerable courage. We think they also need Perl. The Perl open source language is a many-splendored thing; you can write scripts with it, develop GUIs with it, create web sites with it, generate XML with it—and you can probably hang your towels from it! Perl fills data warehouses and runs on virtually every operating system around. Perl is the toolkit without limitations, the salvation of your 24x7 lifestyle. If Gandalf the Wizard were to choose a scripting language, he would choose Perl.

Our mission in this book is to show you how Perl can revolutionize your life as an Oracle DBA. We'll focus on four aspects of the Perl/Oracle connection:

The Perl language itself
> We'll introduce you to the Perl language, with its rich history and culture, present some language basics, and shine some light on CPAN, the Comprehensive Perl Archive Network, the main distribution point for Perl modules.

The Perl/Oracle architecture
> We'll introduce you to the modules that allow Perl programs to communicate with Oracle databases.

Perl applications for Oracle DBAs
> We'll profile about a dozen of the best ready-made applications written in Perl for use by Oracle DBAs. These provide help with database administration,

monitoring, tuning, and daily troubleshooting. They also provide components you can use in your own Perl scripts, should you choose to add a little program development to your daily DBA routine.

The PDBA Toolkit

We'll present, for your enjoyment, an Oracle database administration toolkit we've written ourselves. The Perl Database Administration (PDBA) Toolkit contains nearly 100 Perl scripts and reusable modules that perform operations ranging from creating new Oracle users to monitoring the Oracle alert log to building a repository of database information for use in tuning and troubleshooting. All of this code is available on the O'Reilly web site (*http://www.oreilly.com/catalog/ oracleperl/pdbatoolkit*).

Audience for This Book

If you're an Oracle DBA who is trying desperately to keep up with the daily demands of administering, monitoring, and tuning your Oracle databases, this book is for you. We are Oracle DBAs ourselves, and we know how difficult your job can be. This book provides both information and software that we hope will ease your burden.

Although the primary audience is Oracle DBAs, many DBAs end up being developers from time to time, and there is no better language than Perl for writing those quick scripts. Anyone doing Perl development will find Chapters 7, 8, and 13, as well as the appendixes, particularly useful.

This book assumes no prior experience with Perl, though some knowledge of the language will help you get the most out of the material presented here. Although the book's appendixes explore the essential syntax of Perl, Perl DBI (DataBase Interface), Perl's regular expressions, and Perl's data-munging modules, a complete Perl tutorial is beyond our scope. Our goal here is to jump-start your explorations into the intersection where Perl meets Oracle. We'll provide plenty of suggestions for where to go next on your journey.

Which Platform and Version?

Both Perl and Oracle run on virtually every hardware platform and operating system. To demonstrate this ubiquity, we've used a wide variety of OS platforms and Oracle versions in the preparation of this book. Oracle versions range from Oracle7.3 through Oracle9*i*. OS platforms include Linux Red Hat 6, Linux SuSE 7.3, Solaris 8, Windows NT 4, Windows 2000, and others. We've focused on Unix and Win32 operating systems, but we've also included specific installation instructions for particular operating system variants when necessary.

Against this irresistible surge of platforms, our immovable rock is the Perl version we've used on all of these operating systems. Perl 5.6.1 was the latest stable Perl release available as we wrote this book and developed the toolkit software. We also used the most current stable version of Perl DBI, Version 1.20, in conjunction with Perl DBI's Oracle-specific driver module, *DBD::Oracle* (DataBase Driver for Oracle), Version 1.12.

 By the time you read this book, it's possible that the latest stable versions on the CPAN web site will have been upgraded, particularly if Perl itself is upgraded to Perl6, which was under development as we wrote this book. We'll be updating our toolkit as an open source project in order to cope with any such Perl enhancements.

Structure of This Book

This book is divided into four parts:

Part I, *Introducing Perl for Oracle*

- Chapter 1, *Perl Meets Oracle*, introduces the Perl language and explains why it is such a helpful language for Oracle database administrators. It also provides an overview of the main components of the Perl/Oracle architecture.
- Chapter 2, *Installing Perl*, describes how to install Perl on Unix and Win32 systems. It also describes how to install Cygwin, a Unix-like development environment you can install on your Win32 machine.

Part II, *Extending Perl*

- Chapter 3, *Perl GUI Extensions*, describes Perl/Tk, an extensive GUI-based toolkit for Perl, as well as a number of applications that provide Oracle DBAs with graphically oriented tools for performing database administration. These include OraExplain, StatsView, Orac, *DDL::Oracle*, SchemaDiff, Senora, *DBD::Chart*, SchemaView-Plus, and a variety of Perl GUI integrated development environments (IDEs) and debuggers.
- Chapter 4, , discusses the relationship between Perl and the Apache web server, and focuses on two Oracle applications that use a web browser as their user interface: Oracletool and Karma.
- Chapter 5, *Embedding Perl into Apache with mod_perl*, explains how the use of Apache's *mod_perl* module can greatly improve the performance of Perl web-based CGI (Common Gateway Interface) scripts used with Oracle. This chapter also covers several related Apache modules: *Apache::Registry*, *Apache::DBI*, and *Apache::OWA* (used to connect *mod_perl* to Oracle's PL/SQL Web Toolkit).
- Chapter 6, *Embedded Perl Web Scripting*, describes two applications, Embperl and Mason, that demonstrate the advantages of embedded scripting, a method that allows Perl code to be embedded within web pages. These tools provide a mechanism for filling your production web pages with dynamic Oracle data and

creating your own Oracle web tools, while separating content from design issues.

- Chapter 7, *Invoking the Oracle Call Interface with Oracle::OCI*, covers *Oracle:: OCI*, a Perl module that provides a more extensive interface to Oracle's Oracle Call Interface (OCI) than is possible with Perl DBI.

- Chapter 8, *Embedding Perl into PL/SQL*, discusses *extproc_perl*, a Perl module that communicates with the Oracle PL/SQL language's external procedure C library system (known as EXTPROC). This module and the others described here allow Perl code to be embedded directly in PL/SQL programs.

Part III, *The Perl DBA Toolkit*

- Chapter 9, *Installing the PDBA Toolkit*, introduces the components of the Perl Database Administration Toolkit (PDBA) and explains how to install it and build the toolkit's password server.

- Chapter 10, *Performing Routine DBA Tasks with the PDBA Toolkit*, describes the toolkit's Perl scripts that help DBAs perform day-to-day administration. We'll cover managing user accounts, maintaining indexes, killing sniped sessions, managing extent usage, and extracting DDL (Data Definition Language) and data.

- Chapter 11, *Monitoring the Database with the PDBA Toolkit*, describes the toolkit's Perl scripts that can be used to monitor both the Oracle alert log (containing database error and status messages) and the connectivity of the databases.

- Chapter 12, *Building a Database Repository with the PDBA Toolkit*, describes the toolkit's Perl scripts that allow you to build a repository in which to store information about the many changes made to an Oracle database's tables, indexes, roles, schemas, and other objects.

- Chapter 13, *Extending the PDBA Toolkit*, provides information that will be helpful if you decide to modify any of the scripts or modules in the toolkit. We'll take a detailed look inside one of the toolkit's scripts and modules and illustrate how you can change it to suit your specific database administration needs.

Part IV, *Appendixes*

- Appendix A, *The Essential Guide to Perl*, summarizes basic Perl syntax, including object-oriented features.

- Appendix B, *The Essential Guide to Perl DBI*, presents the main Perl DBI application programming interface (API) functions.

- Appendix C, *The Essential Guide to Regular Expressions*, describes the basics of regular expressions (regexes), patterns of literals and metacharacters used extensively by Perl for pattern matching.

- Appendix D, *The Essential Guide to Perl Data Munging*, summarizes the Perl data-munging modules that are helpful in formatting and transforming data for data warehouses and other such Oracle applications; it includes sections on numeric, date, conversion, and XML modules.

About the Perl DBA Toolkit and Examples

The full source code for the PDBA Toolkit is available on the O'Reilly web site at:

http://www.oreilly.com/catalog/oracleperl/pdbatoolkit

The toolkit is a fully open source-compliant project, and we welcome all contributions to extend it. In line with the OSI (Open Source Initiative) guidelines,[*] the PDBA Toolkit is freely available for download over the Internet under the Perl Artistic License.[†] We'll try our best to keep this code up to date as Perl and the many modules described in this book are upgraded. Our goal is to have you be able to download the latest and greatest version of the toolkit at all times as we seek constantly to improve it.

In addition to the toolkit programs, we have also provided a large number of stand–alone Perl programs in the book and on our site. We'll also try to keep this code up to date and available for download at the O'Reilly web page cited earlier.

Conventions Used in This Book

The following typographical conventions are used in this book:

Italic
> Used for filenames, directory names, and URLs. It is also used for emphasis and for the first use of a technical term.

Constant width
> Used for code examples.

Constant width bold
> Used occasionally in code examples to highlight statements being discussed.

> Indicates a tip, suggestion, or general note. For example, we'll tell you if a certain feature is version-specific.

---

[*] The Open Source Initiative (OSI) is a "non-profit corporation dedicated to managing and promoting the Open Source Definition for the good of the community" (see *http://www.opensource.org/*).

[†] The Perl Artistic License "state(s) the conditions under which a package may be copied, such that the copyright holder maintains some semblance of artistic control over the development of the package, while giving the users of the package the right to use and distribute the package in a more-or-less customary fashion, plus the right to make reasonable modifications" (see *http://www.perl.com/pub/a/language/misc/Artistic.html*).

Indicates a warning or caution. For example, we'll tell you if a certain operation has some kind of negative impact on the system.

Comments and Questions

We have tested and verified the information in this book and in the source code to the best of our ability, but given the number of tools described in this book and the rapid pace of technological change, you may find that features have changed or that we have made mistakes. If so, please notify us by writing to:

O'Reilly & Associates
1005 Gravenstein Highway
Sebastopol, CA 95472
(800) 998-9938 (in the U.S. or Canada)
(707) 829-0515 (international or local)
(707) 829-0104 (fax)

You can also send messages electronically. To be put on the mailing list or request a catalog, send email to:

info@oreilly.com

To ask technical questions or comment on the book, send email to:

bookquestions@oreilly.com

We have a web site for this book where you can find updated links to Perl and Oracle software discussed in this book, along with errata (previously reported errors and corrections are available for public view there). You can access this page at:

http://www.oreilly.com/catalog/perloracledba

To download the PDBA Toolkit, you can go directly to:

http://www.oreilly.com/catalog/oracleperl/pdbatoolkit

For more information about this book and others, see the O'Reilly web site:

http://www.oreilly.com

Acknowledgments

As you might expect, a tremendous number of people from the Perl and Oracle communities have helped us put this book together, including many of the creators of the actual tools discussed here. We cannot thank them enough (although we'll do our best). We also are very grateful to the whole O'Reilly editorial and production team.

From Andy

First of all I have to thank my wife and beg her not to throw me out of the house for having deserted our family (my son Ross, four-and-a-half, and daughter Ellie, two-and-a-bit) for the last six months while completing this *magnum opus*. I had thought my previous book, *Oracle & Open Source*, written with Sean Hull, was as tough as it would get on a family, but I was proved wrong. Daddy could often only be located by following the trail of pizza crumbs and Dr. Pepper cans from the fridge to the darkest recesses of the house where he hid, tip-tapping away on a variety of workstations. But all will be redeemed if you get as much out of this book as I have, in its long-fingered probings into the darkest recesses of Perl for Oracle DBAs. My wife Sue has been the magnificent rock upon which I built my effort, and without her and our beautiful children, you can just take everything else and give it all away. I am forever in their debt.

As with all O'Reilly books, this has also been an immense collaborative effort involving more than just the writing team of myself, Jared, and our omniscient editor, Debby Russell. I would like to thank Tim Bunce, the father of Perl DBI, for his help and support over the past five years, and everyone else who has helped us achieve our goal of producing this book, particularly our technical reviewers who did such a magnificent job under tight deadline pressure: Stephen Andert, Tim Bunce, Ben Evans, Lance Hollman, Thomas A. Lowery, Ilya Sterin, and Richard Sutherland.

Many others also helped us ensure that this book was both as accurate and as up-to-date as we could possibly make it. My deepest thanks to all of them: Dean Arnold, Jeffrey W. Baker, Doug Bloebaum, Ronald Bourret, Thomas Boutell, Hans-Bernhard Broeker, Alan Burlison, Damian Conway, Martin Drautzburg, Thomas Eibner, Kim Fowler, Andy Gillen, Lars Hecking, Russell Herbert, Roger Hipperson, Dan Horne, Jeff Horwitz, Sean Hull, Randy Kobes, Robert Lupton, Doug MacEachern, Edmund Mergl, Julian Moss, Alistair Orchard, Ian Pilgrim, Alan Ranger, Eric S. Raymond, Gerald Richter, Dave Rolsky, Dave Roth, Nick Semenov, Steve Shaw, Jonathan Swartz, Svante Sörmark, Jesse Reed Vincent, Adam vonNieda, and Ken Williams.

My future bar bill is now immense, possessing gravitational mass in its own right. However, before I finish, I have to thank our editor Debby Russell, who has done so much to support us and sculpt our natural techno-speak into what we hope you'll find to be an invaluable guiding light towards the Perl and Oracle mithril of a deep subterranean world. She also brought this book down from being a ridiculous 1,000-page cave troll into the more-or-less manageable wood-elf you hold in your hands without losing a single important point. And finally, I have to thank David Gray, for his album, *White Ladder*, without which the completion of my half of this book would have been simply impossible, Dr. Pepper or no Dr. Pepper.

From Jared

I must first thank my own personal goddess, my wife, Carla. Although her husband spent many early mornings, late nights, weekends, and even several days of vacation time over a period of months, sequestered away in his hobbit hole of a computer warren producing code and text, she remained supportive and understanding.

Next I must thank my coauthor Andy. A true human dynamo, Andy was a whirlwind of activity while we collaborated on this project, and a source of inspiration on several occasions. He and Debby Russell are responsible for bringing our massive first draft down to a manageable size.

Andy and I both owe a deep debt of gratitude to everyone who has assisted us in the creation of this book. Andy has already mentioned those who have given us direct help in this project. I would like to reiterate our thanks to Tim Bunce for his outstanding work on the Perl DBI and *DBD::Oracle* modules. I would take it even further and thank Larry Wall for the inspired moment when he first decided to create Perl.

Hats off to the entire open source community as well. Without the dedication and hard work of so many talented individuals, computing would be far less interesting. Trite? Maybe, but nonetheless sincere.

I'm grateful to my friends who listened patiently when they asked what "the book" was about when they learned I was working on one, even though they had never heard of Perl or Oracle, and for the fact they are still my friends, in spite of missed social occasions.

Finally, I thank my parents, Jerry and Betty. They had no idea that their combined genes would create progeny with a predilection for Perl, Unix, Linux, databases, and a fascination with ones and zeros arranged in meaningful patterns. Thanks Dad, thanks Mom.

Introducing Perl for Oracle

This first part of the book introduces Perl and the architecture that allows it to connect to the Oracle database. It consists of the following chapters:

Chapter 1, *Perl Meets Oracle*, introduces the Perl language and explains why it is such a helpful language for Oracle database administrators. It also provides an overview of the main components of the Perl/Oracle architecture.

Chapter 2, *Installing Perl*, describes how to install Perl on Unix and Win32 systems. It also describes how to install Cygwin, a Unix-like development environment you can install on your Win32 machine.

## CHAPTER 1

Perl Meets Oracle

Perl is the world's number one solution for transforming and gluing data together, and Oracle is the world's number one solution for storing that data. In this book we'll explore the interface between two of the finest American inventions since baseball and pretzels. We're going to grab that Oracle data, we're going to flip that Oracle data, and we're going to munge that Oracle data. And we're going to do it all in Perl!

The goal of this book is to explore the frontier connecting the Perl and Oracle worlds, having as much fun along the way as possible. There are many routes through this largely unexplored territory, and one we think is particularly important is the one focused on Oracle database administration. We are Oracle DBAs ourselves and we know the frustrations the job can bring. We've found Perl an enormous help to us in performing administrative tasks—both routine ones, like adding new users to the database, and more complex ones, like monitoring database connectivity in real time and tracking down database performance problems by comparing SQL execution plans. We want to share the information we've acquired over the years about Perl and its many Oracle applications. We also want to give you access to our own Oracle database administration scripts, which we've packaged up in the Perl Database Administration (PDBA) Toolkit described in this book and freely available on the O'Reilly web site.

This chapter sets the scene by introducing you to Perl and how it connects to Oracle. We'll look at the following:

Perl's origins and advantages
> We'll take a look at where Perl came from and what makes it such a popular and powerful language.

Perl/Oracle architecture
> We'll see how Perl connects to the Oracle database via the Perl DBI module, the *DBD::Oracle* program, and Oracle's own OCI product. These modules interact to allow Perl programs access to Oracle databases.

We'll discuss why Perl is a particularly appropriate language for Oracle DBAs to learn and use.

We'll also provide a list of additional Perl resources.

What is Perl?

Perl is a wonderful language with a rich history and culture. Many books have been written about its capabilities and roots. In this book we'll be focusing on how Perl and Oracle work together, and we'll only skim the surface of Perl's overall capabilities, giving you just enough detail so you'll appreciate what Perl can do for you.

In a nutshell, Perl is a freely available interpreted scripting language that combines the best capabilities of a variety of other languages. Despite borrowing other language capabilities, the whole of Perl is far greater than the sum of its parts. Perl was designed especially to be:

- Extremely fast, in order to be useful when scanning through large files
- Especially good at text handling, because data comes in many different forms and Perl has to handle them all
- Extensible, in order for Perl to expand users' horizons, not restrict them

A tutorial for basic Perl is outside the scope of this book. Fortunately, there are many excellent web sites and books containing the information you need to get going. We've collected references to what we consider to be the best Perl books and online documentation in the "For Further Information" section at the end of this chapter. The appendixes provide quick references to different aspects of Perl's capabilities. For online information, check out the main Perl portals at:

http://www.perl.com
http://www.perl.org
http://www.activestate.com (for Win32)

Before we get into the details of how Perl and Oracle interact, let's take a step back to look at where Perl came from.

The Origins of Perl

Larry Wall created Perl back in 1987 with the goal of making "the easy things easy and the hard things possible"—originally just for himself, but ultimately for a whole generation of developers. Larry had been working on a complex system and had been trying to get Unix's *awk* utility to do his bidding. He finally gave up on it and under the auspices of a secret project for the National Security Agency known as the "Blacker," he decided to create a new language by raiding a primeval soup of technologies and splicing together the genetic structures of *awk*, *sed*, *sh* and C, as well as *csh*, Pascal, and BASIC. The first release of Perl, Perl 1.0, arrived after a nine-month gestation period.

Perl was unlike any other computer language that had come before it, and this sea change was partially reflected in the name. The original name, "Pearl," stood for "Practical Extraction *And* Report Language," but in the spirit of this compact language, Larry wanted to save typing that extra fifth character. The name quickly morphed into *Perl*, which by now also stood for "Pathologically Eclectic Rubbish Lister." This self-irreverence further distinguished the language and gave it a certain counter-culture cachet.

Perhaps the most accurate summary of what Perl is best for can be found in the *README* file written by its author for Perl Version 1.0:

> Perl is a interpreted language optimized for scanning arbitrary text files, extracting information from those text files, and printing reports based on that information. It's also a good language for many system management tasks. The language is intended to be practical (easy to use, efficient, complete) rather than beautiful (tiny, elegant, minimal). It combines (in the author's opinion, anyway) some of the best features of C, sed, awk, and sh, so people familiar with those languages should have little difficulty with it. (Language historians will also note some vestiges of csh, Pascal, and even BASIC|PLUS.) Expression syntax corresponds quite closely to C expression syntax. If you have a problem that would ordinarily use sed or awk or sh, but it exceeds their capabilities or must run a little faster, and you don't want to write the silly thing in C, then perl may be for you. There are also translators to turn your sed and awk scripts into perl scripts. OK, enough hype.

The Unix world embraced the Perl language, and the fast-growing Perl development community gradually built their favorite language into the world's supreme text-processing engine. Over the next few years, Perl grew ever more powerful. Perl's regular expression handling was enhanced, the ability to handle binary files was added to the language, and the three main variable types were honed and sculpted. Soon the Perl Artistic License was adopted, and with the publication of the first edition of *Programming Perl*, the definitive guide to the language, the camel became the Perl trademark.[*]

Perl has become hugely popular, largely because of its extremely fast text processing and its ability to glue difficult things together with ease. With the explosion of the interactive Internet in the 1990s, Perl found itself superbly pre-adapted to become the new tool of an Internet generation. It glued those trillions of text packets into one big global village! And as the World Wide Web burst on the scene, Perl continued to evolve, emerging as the premier language for developing web applications. Perl 4 brought the release of modules allowing Perl to interact with Oracle (and other)

---

[*] The camel is a great image for Perl because it suggests a horse designed by more than one voice—perhaps a bit challenged in looks, but perfectly adapted for a difficult ecological niche.

databases. The current version of Perl, Perl 5, contains long-sought object-oriented features.

Perl on Win32

Although Perl's origins were in the Unix world, it was ported to Windows back in 1995 by Dick Hardt and Hip Communications, the forerunners of ActiveState. Windows NT administrators then discovered a whole new world of functionality via the Win32 modules supplied by ActiveState, and Perl became their dominant scripting language. Perl was a lifesaver for busy administrators performing large NT system updates. (Adding 100 users to a system via the repetitive and arthritic point-and-click method really is no fun!)

Win32 Perl became so popular that there was some danger that the Unix and Windows versions would diverge. But Larry Wall was not about to let this happen. Those not familiar with Perl may wonder why it matters. What difference would it make if the Unix and Win32 Perls were different? In fact, it is this hard-won unity that gives Perl its power. You can write a single script on one operating system, and as long as you don't use native methods, you can run it unchanged on every other kind of machine, from Linux to Windows NT to Solaris and back again. That is a huge advantage in our multiplatform, networked computing world.

CPAN (the Comprehensive Perl Archive Network)

Over the years, an enthusiastic and partisan army of Perl volunteers has extended Perl in a myriad of ways. CPAN (the Comprehensive Perl Archive Network), an online repository of Perl core files, documentation, and contributed modules, has become a model for an open source development community. Check out:

http://www.cpan.org

Literally thousands of Perl modules are now available on CPAN, providing virtually any application you can imagine—and many you haven't yet imagined. Just about every Perl module we describe in this book, from core modules like Perl and Perl DBI themselves to Oracle-specific database administration scripts like OraExplain and Orac, can be downloaded from CPAN.

New Perl modules go through an evolutionary process that begins with an individual developer's code, which he or she posts to CPAN. As others learn about the new module and start downloading and testing it, and relying upon it, it becomes more and more acceptable. If it's good enough, and if enough people and products rely upon it, the Perl gods ultimately might decide to include the new module in the next general Perl distribution.

Perl and the corporate world

When Java, Microsoft's Active Server Pages (ASP), and similar corporate tools came along, many people assumed that they would sweep the inelegant Perl away. However, this hasn't come to pass. Instead, Perl has grown exponentially both in market share and stature, especially since its 1994 Perl 5 adoption of reference technology, which greatly increased its scope in terms of both extensibility and object orientation. Tim Bunce's Perl DBI module, built on the object-oriented base, gave Perl the ability to interface with Oracle and other databases. The fact that Perl can now dynamically glue the Internet to the database has greatly increased corporate acceptance of the language.

The Perl Advantage

There are nearly as many reasons why people choose to use Perl as there are people who use Perl. Aside from the language's specific capabilities, we think there are a few key reasons for Perl's awesome acceptance among programmers and nonprogrammers alike:

Practicality
> Unlike some languages that have developed within the ivory towers of computer science departments, Perl is a practical language. It is unbound by dogma and driven by day-to-day practicalities. With its flexible syntax, it gives users enormous freedom to do what they want to do.

Bandwidth
> Perl is one of the most concise languages around. In ten lines of Perl code, you can achieve more than is possible in any other language. Disciplined use of Perl can thus reduce program maintenance costs (because there's less to maintain) and aid clarity (because there's less code to try to understand).

Range
> Literally thousands of Perl modules are available for download from CPAN, covering virtually every computing requirement imaginable. The abundance of prebuilt code modules makes Perl the number one choice for anyone with a wide range of programming needs—and that description fits most Oracle DBAs.

We believe that Perl's popularity is based to a large extent on the fact that it has resisted the temptation to try to become the most elegant language of its time. A linguist by training, Larry Wall took many lessons from the development of real-world natural human languages, and blended the necessary messiness of those languages into his evolving design for Perl. In the following sections we'll look at how the English language itself offers some important Perl analogies.

Perl's Three Virtues

In the original Camel Book—the latest edition is *Programming Perl* by Larry Wall, Tom Christiansen, and Jon Orwant, 3rd ed. (O'Reilly & Associates, 2000)—Larry Wall identified three characteristics of virtuous programmers; these have become the most basic Perls of Wisdom among the faithful:

Laziness

> From the Old English for "resistance to work," laziness is a virtue that makes you write labor-saving programs in order to avoid unnecessary effort. It also encourages good documentation to keep others from bothering you by asking impertinent questions.

Impatience

> From the Latin for "unwillingness to endure waiting," impatience pushes you into change and arises from the restless injustice felt when computer applications are inefficient. It makes you write programs that match and even anticipate your needs.

Hubris

> From the Greek for "excessive pride or wanton violence," hubris ensures that you create solutions that others say only good things about and that cut through any problem's resistance.

Flat learning curve

Although natural languages such as English are difficult and messy, even a baby can learn them. The messiness of such languages aids learning, develops expression, and allows the human mind to map complex real-world problems onto the symbolic logic of complex real-world languages. Perl tries to follow this pattern—it's very intentionally designed for humans rather than computers. You need only a little Perl to get going, just as a baby needs only a little language to ask for a chocolate ice cream. Indeed most of the fun of Perl is that you never stop learning about its new elements. This characteristic of Perl contrasts with some other languages where you have to learn virtually the entire shooting match before you can do the simplest thing, such as print:

```
"Hello World! :-)"
```

It also means that it's okay to know only parts of the whole language—every Perl programmer is on the same flat learning curve as every other Perl programmer, merely at a different position.

Expression

Perl is optimized for expressive power, rather than ease of operation. Once you've learned an element of Perl, such as the structure of hashes (described in Appendix A,

The Essential Guide to Perl), you can use this knowledge in many different ways to achieve many different ends. Again, this is similar to English, in which you can learn a rhetorical debating technique and then employ it in many different ways to get what you want.

There's more than one way to do it (TMTOWTDI)

In many computer languages, there's often a single acceptable way to do a certain thing—for example, communicate with a distant server. Perl is different. So is English. In real life, when you introduce yourself to other people, there are many different ways to successfully perform this occasionally tricky verbal task. It's the same in Perl. What counts is what works best for you, not some rigid adherence to a strictly enforced protocol. As with formal introductions, of course, there are certain conventions that most people use. There is peer pressure even among Perl programmers. But Perl itself doesn't care; if you want to do something different, you are free to do so.

Flexibility

English is a successful language mainly because it looks forward into the future, rather than backward towards its origins. It's built up from Latin, Greek, French, Anglo-Saxon, and many other elements. And if it needs to borrow the word "veranda" from the Portuguese in order to describe a covered porch, it just goes right ahead without worrying about whether doing so breaks some rule. Perl is the same: if it sees a great idea in Java, it just goes right ahead and borrows it, slipping it in so the join is invisible. Eventually, if it's a successful graft, even Java programmers may come to think that the idea originally came from Perl. It is this continuous evolution that transforms Perl from the ordinary into the extraordinary.

Ambiguity

English is also successful because it's so good at handling ambiguity. Although there are few cases, genders, or definitive word endings in the English language, local ambiguities are quickly resolved by the juxtaposition of certain other words, conventions, and punctuation. Perl is the same: some pieces of isolated code can be quite ambiguous, but the ambiguity is quickly resolved in the context of its word order, punctuation, and relationship to other code fragments. There are even pronouns in Perl, such as $_ and @_ for "it" and "they"!

Acceptance of the real world

In a pure computer language world, you could visit the local cinema in an infinite number of ways; for example, you could float up to 10,000 feet, disappear, and then rematerialize in your favorite seat to watch *The Lord of the Rings*. But the fact is that you'd most often walk or drive there. Similarly, Perl recognizes that most people tend to want to do things in familiar ways (e.g., opening a file, processing the lines in it, and then closing the file). So Perl will typically assume that you'll be following a natural order unless you tell it explicitly that you won't be.

Simplicity

Lawyers have taken the once straightforward English language and twisted it into the most tortuous logic the human mind could devise—unfortunately, this is the route most often taken by other computer languages. They start simply enough, but develop a rigid straitjacket of theoretical perfection before drowning in a bog of complexity. You'll be pleased to hear that Perl is much friendlier. There is no ideology that must be obeyed. A country run by Perl programmers would be a really cool place to live!

Cooperation and divergence

Natural languages have evolved with the involvement of different people over a long period of time—indeed, they continue to evolve. They're also continuously diverging into separate dialects and even other languages. Perl too began as an amalgam of different ideas, shepherded together by Larry Wall. It has since continued as a cooperative effort, with many contributing voices. The eventual creation of Perl 6 will be one vast community effort (something we hope you'll be part of).

But language fragmentation has been an ongoing problem for Perl. The solution has been a continuous release program over the last decade that has accommodated divergent tendencies. The CPAN architecture also offers a outlet for those with independent voices. The threatened Win32 divergence we discussed earlier in the "Perl on Win32" section could have had a dramatic impact on the unity of Perl—and all that implies in terms of portability and extensibility. Thankfully, as we described earlier, that threat came to a happy conclusion. And it's still true that if you write a Perl script on one operating system, then as long as you haven't used native methods and system commands, the script can be copied to any other machine and will work there identically, regardless of operating system.

The Perl/Oracle Architecture

How do Oracle DBAs, developers, and users take advantage of everything that Perl has to offer? The architecture illustrated in the figures in the following sections show how the various Perl and Oracle modules fit together to make the Perl/Oracle connection clean and efficient. In the following sections we'll take a look at the main components of this architecture:

- Perl DBI
- *DBD::Oracle*
- OCI

Perl DBI and *DBD::Oracle* are Perl modules available from CPAN. OCI is an Oracle Corporation product that comes with all versions of the Oracle database.

Perl DBI and DBD::Oracle

Perl DBI is a generic application programming interface (API). It is similar in concept to ODBC (Oracle DataBase Connectivity) and JDBC (Java DataBase Connectivity), but it has a Perl-based object-oriented architecture. Perl DBI's object-oriented architecture allows it to have a single routing point to many different databases (shown in Figure 1-1), each via a database-specific driver. Oracle uses the *DBD:: Oracle* driver, another Perl module that provides the actual communication to the low-level OCI code. It is OCI that makes the final connection to the Oracle database.

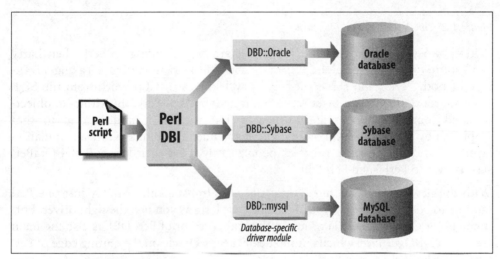

Figure 1-1. Perl DBI can interface to many databases

The beauty of Perl DBI is you can forget the details of the necessary connections beneath its simple API calls. The DBI package glides serenely over the surface of our databases, while the driver module, *DBD::Oracle*, does all the hard paddling beneath the surface.

Figure 1-2 shows how all the modules fit together on the Perl and Oracle sides.

The origins of Perl DBI

The origins of Perl DBI date back more than a decade. Way back in 1991, an Oracle DBA, Kevin Stock, created a database connection program called OraPerl that was released for Perl 4. Over time, similar Perl 4 programs appeared, such as Michael Peppler's Sybperl, designed for communication with the Sybase database. In a parallel development, starting around September of 1992, a Perl-based group was working on a specification for DBPerl, a database-independent specification for Perl 4.

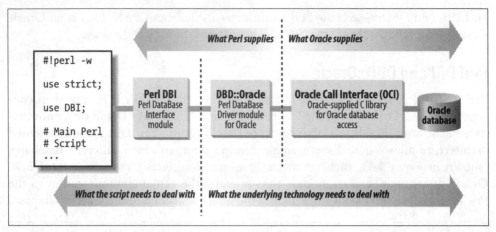

Figure 1-2. The Perl/Oracle architecture

Within two years they were just ready to start implementing DBPerl when Larry Wall started releasing the alpha version of the object-oriented Perl 5. Taking advantage of both Perl 5 and the earlier Call Level Interface (CLI) work from the SQL Access Group, the DBPerl team relaid the foundations of Perl DBI within an object-oriented framework, creating this new architecture in a similar form to that employed by the familiar API of ODBC. Meanwhile, Tim Bunce wrote an emulation layer for OraPerl Version 2.4 that let people easily move their legacy Perl 4 OraPerl scripts over to Perl 5 and Perl DBI.

With the new DBI architecture, you could now transparently employ just one Perl module to connect to every type of database, as long as you had the right driver. Fortunately for Oracle DBAs, Tim Bunce, the main creator of Perl DBI, is also the main creator of *DBD::Oracle*, which automatically keeps Oracle on the cutting edge of Perl DBI's development schedule.

The Perl DBI API

We won't try to describe all of the capabilities of Perl DBI here, but Table 1-1 provides a summary of the main calls (e.g., DBI class methods) to OCI. For additional background information about Perl DBI, see Appendix B, *The Essential Guide to Perl DBI*. And for much more information, consult the references listed under "Further Information on Perl DBI" at the end of this chapter.

Table 1-1. Main Perl DBI functions

DBI function	Description
available_drivers( )	Lists all of the available DBD drivers including *DBD::Oracle*
data_sources( )	Lists all of the databases available to *DBD::Oracle*
connect( )	Establishes an Oracle database connection

Table 1-1. Main Perl DBI functions (continued)

DBI function	Description
disconnect( )	Disconnects a login session from Oracle
err( )	Returns the relevant Oracle error code
errstr( )	Supplies an associated Oracle error message
prepare( )	Prepares a SQL statement for execution
execute( )	Executes a prepared statement
do( )	Prepares and executes a single SQL statement all together
bind_param( )	Binds a value to a prepared statement
commit( )	Commits a transaction
rollback( )	Rolls back a transaction
table_info( )	Fetches metadata information from a table
fetchrow_arrayref( )	Fetches a row of data into a referenced array
fetchrow_array( )	Fetches a row of data into an array
selectrow_array( )	Executes *prepare( )*, *execute( )* and *fetchrow_array( )* all in one call

The Oracle Call Interface

As we've said, Oracle Corporation's Oracle Call Interface (OCI) is the component in the Perl/Oracle architecture that makes the final connection to the Oracle database servers. This C-based API provides a comprehensive library used to connect into Oracle from the external world. Use of OCI lets your Perl programs take advantage of the following OCI capabilities:

- High performance
- Security features, including user authentication
- Scalability
- *N*-tiered authentication
- Full and dynamic access to Oracle objects
- User session handles
- Multi-threaded capabilities
- Support for accessing special Oracle datatypes such as LOBs (large objects)
- Transactions
- Dynamic connection and session management
- Asynchronous event notification
- Access to other databases
- Full character set support

For more about OCI, see Chapter 7, *Invoking the Oracle Call Interface with Oracle::OCI*, where we describe *Oracle::OCI*, a new Perl module that provides an even closer interface between Perl and Oracle. You can get complete information about OCI at Oracle Corporation's *http://technet.oracle.com* pages; in particular, see *http://technet.oracle.com/tech/oci/*.

In Table 1-2 we list the main OCI functions to give you a sense of the kinds of Oracle operations you can invoke from your Perl programs.

Table 1-2. Main OCI functions

OCI function	Description
OCIAttrSet( )	Sets handle attributes
OCIAttrGet( )	Gets attributes from a handle
OCIBindByName( )	Links variables to a SQL statement placeholder by name
OCIBindByPos( )	Links variables to a SQL statement placeholder by position
OCIDefineByPos( )	Links a typed select-list item with the output data buffer
OCIDescribeAny( )	Describes schema objects
OCIDescriptorAlloc( )	Allocates storage for descriptors and LOB locators
OCIDescriptorFree( )	Releases the resources taken by descriptors
OCIEnvInit( )	Allocates the initial OCI environment handle
OCIErrorGet( )	Returns a buffered error message
OCIHandleAlloc( )	Points to an allocated handle
OCIHandleFree( )	Explicitly releases a memory handle and its resources
OCIInitialize( )	Initializes the environment for OCI processes
OCILobRead( )	Reads specified LOB and FILE portions into a buffer
OCILobWrite( )	Writes a specified buffer into a LOB
OCILogoff( )	Ends a login session
OCILogon( )	Logs into the OCI session
OCIParamGet( )	Gets the descriptor of a parameter attached to a statement handle
OCIParamSet( )	Puts the object retrieval descriptor into an object retrieval handle
OCIServerAttach( )	Creates the pathway to a data source
OCIServerDetach( )	Detaches from a data source
OCISessionBegin( )	Begins a user session for a given server
OCISessionEnd( )	Ends a user session
OCIStmtExecute( )	Sends an application request to the server
OCIStmtFetch( )	Fetches data rows from previous queries
OCIStmtPrepare( )	Prepares a SQL statement for later execution
OCITransCommit( )	Commits a nominated transaction

At the most basic level, virtually all outside programs—from web applications to standalone GUI applications—interact with Oracle through this OCI program layer. Fortunately, the OCI libraries are automatically available in every Oracle database installation, so no special installation process is required. You'll generally discover the appropriate files under the *$ORACLE_HOME/lib* and *$ORACLE_HOME/ include* directories, on Unix systems, and under *%ORACLE_HOME%\lib* and *%ORACLE_HOME%\include* on Win32.

Perl for Oracle DBAs

Perl has become an increasingly popular tool for Oracle DBAs who need a quick way of handling the 101 different jobs a DBA is expected to do every day. Perl is operating system-independent, powerful, flexible, remarkably quick to code, and extremely fast in execution. These capabilities are especially important if you are working in a rapidly changing environment where one day you might be populating a data warehouse from a difficult data source, and the next you might be generating all of the information for a dynamic web application—and the whole time you're performing all of your usual administrative tasks. That certainly describes the diverse world of an Oracle DBA!

Of course, the focus of any Oracle site's business is data. And from the start, Perl was designed to be a data-processing engine, perhaps the finest and quickest in the world. It can find data, clean data, parse data, substitute data, print data, eat data, and spit data out from the other end in the exact format you require. It can do all of this with text data, binary data, and network data.

There are a variety of ways that Oracle DBAs can combine the power of Perl and Oracle. We describe four main paths in this book; the following list provides a road map:

Existing modules and applications
> All kinds of excellent Perl modules and complete open source applications are freely available for Oracle DBAs to use. The chapters in Part II of this book describe the Perl/Oracle applications that we consider the best of the bunch; these are listed in Table 1-3 and fall into several categories:

Perl GUI applications
> In Chapter 3, *Perl GUI Extensions*, we describe Perl/Tk, Perl's own tookit for developing graphical user interfaces, along with a variety of graphical Oracle applications and helper modules: OraExplain, StatsView, Orac, *DDL::Oracle*, SchemaDiff, Senora, *DBD::Chart*, SchemaView-Plus, as well as some Perl GUI integrated development environments (IDEs) and debuggers.

Perl web-based applications

In Chapter 4, , we discuss the use of Apache with Perl and Oracle and describe two particular applications, Oracletool and Karma. In Chapter 5 we show how using the Apache *mod_perl* module can greatly improve the performance of Perl web-based scripts. And in Chapter 6, *Embedded Perl Web Scripting*, we discuss two embedded Perl web scripting applications, Embperl and Mason.

Connectivity tools

In Chapter 2, *Installing Perl*, we describe how to install Perl DBI and *DBD::Oracle* to allow your Perl programs to interact with Oracle databases with great ease and efficiency. Later chapters describe some additional connectivity tools. In Chapter 7 we describe the new *Oracle::OCI* module that provides higher performance and a true one-to-one mapping with functions of the Oracle Call Interface. In Chapter 8, *Embedding Perl into PL/SQL*, we describe Perl's *extproc_perl*, Oracle's EXTPROC, and the other modules that allow Perl to be essentially embedded into Oracle's own PL/SQL language.

Database administration scripts

Just about every Oracle DBA has his or her own set of scripts they've written to make their daily lives easier. Many of these DBAs have been kind enough to share the wealth with their peers. Following this trend, we've packaged up our own set of scripts and modules into an open source collection we call the PDBA Toolkit. As a side benefit, the toolkit provides us with a living breathing entity whose code we can use to illustrate the use of Perl. We describe this toolkit in Part III of this book.

Data-processing scripts

Many Oracle DBAs spend at least part of their time dealing with data warehousing as well as database administration. They often need to clean and transform data that originates in other databases and applications and is now destined for Oracle. Perl, with its regular expressions and high performance, is one of the best solutions around for preparing data for use in data warehouse applications. *Data munging* is the term used to describe the data cleaning, formatting, and transformation often required by data warehouses. Appendix C, *The Essential Guide to Regular Expressions*, provides an essential guide to Perl regular expressions, and Appendix D, *The Essential Guide to Perl Data Munging*, summarizes the many Perl modules available to perform data-processing and data-munging operations on all kinds of data, including numeric, text, date, and XML formats.

Custom scripts

Helpful as all of these packaged solutions may be, DBAs often find it necessary to write their own custom queries and scripts to solve their immediate problems. Every DBA ends up needing to write quick 5- or 10-line *ad hoc* programs simply to glue things together in their databases. They also may find that the canned applications and tools available for Oracle are great, but not quite right for their needs. The nice thing about Perl is that it makes it easy for you to add, change, or customize. All of the applications we describe throughout this book are available in source form so you can modify them to suit your needs. Our own toolkit is designed specifically to accommodate such customization. The modular nature of the scripts, coupled with the documentation provided in Part III of this book (see Chapter 13, *Extending the PDBA Toolkit*, in particular) should make it easy for you. You'll also find the appendixes helpful in learning the basics of Perl.

Table 1-3 lists all of the applications and tools mentioned in this book. We tried to include the most up-to-date information possible in this book at the time of publication, but because most of these programs are continually being enhanced, make sure to check out the sites listed in the table for current information.

Table 1-3. Perl/Oracle applications and related tools

Application/tool	Chapter	Description/download site
ActivePerl	1	Precompiled binary Win32 Perl from ActiveState
		http://www.activestate.com
		http://aspn.activestate.com/ASPN/Downloads/
		http://aspn.activestate.com/ASPN/PPM/FAQ
		http://downloads.activestate.com/
Apache	4	Apache web server software
		http://www.apache.org/
		http://httpd.apache.org/
		http://httpd.apache.org/dist/httpd/
		http://httpd.apache.org/docs/windows.html
		http://httpd.apache.org/dist/httpd/binaries/win32/
		http://httpd.apache.org/docs/mod/directives.html
Apache *mod_perl*	5	Apache Perl integration
		http://perl.apache.org/
		http://www.cpan.org/authors/id/DOUGM/
		http://www.modperl.com/
		http://www.refcards.com/about/mod_perl.html
		http://theoryx5.uwinnipeg.ca/ppmpackages (Win32)
		http://theoryx5.uwinnipeg.ca/guide/
		http://mathforum.org/epigone/modperl
Apache::DBI	5	Caching Perl DBI connections with *mod_perl*
		http://www.cpan.org/authors/id/MERGL/
Apache::OWA	5	Linking Perl to Oracle's PL/SQL Web Toolkit
		http://sourceforge.net/projects/owa/
		http://owa.sourceforge.net/
		http://www.cpan.org/authors/id/S/SV/SVINTO
		http://www.cpan.org/authors/id/J/JI/JIMW/ (libapreq)
		http://technet.oracle.com
		http://technet.oracle.com/doc/windows/was.21/psqlwtlk.htm[a]

Table 1-3. Perl/Oracle applications and related tools (continued)

Application/tool	Chapter	Description/download site
CPAN (2000+ packages)	1	The Comprehensive Perl Archive Network
		http://www.cpan.org
		http://search.cpan.org
Cygwin (and DJGPP)	2	Unix-like environments for Win32
		http://www.cygwin.com/
		http://cygwin.com/cygwin-ug-net/using-cygwinenv.html
		http://www.delorie.com/djgpp/
DBD::Chart (see also, *zlib*, *gd*, and PNG)	3	SQL-like chart generation using Perl DBI
		http://www.presicient.com/dbdchart/
		http://www.cpan.org/authors/id/D/DA/DARNOLD/
		ftp://ftp.uu.net/graphics/jpeg
		http://www.ijg.org/
		http://www.cpan.org/authors/id/NI-S/ (Tk::JPEG)
DDL::Oracle	3	Perl package for specific Oracle DDL generation
		http://sourceforge.net/projects/ddl-oracle/
		http://www.cpan.org/authors/id/R/RV/RVSUTHERL/
Embperl (see also *HTML:: Template* and Mason)	6	HTML embedded Perl system
		http://perl.apache.org/embperl/
		http://www.cpan.org/authors/id/GRICHTER/ (*Apache::SessionX* and stable Embperl source)
		http://www.cpan.org/authors/id/A/AM/AMS/ (*Storable*)
		http://www.cpan.org/authors/id/JBAKER/ (*Apache::Session*)
		http://theoryx5.uwinnipeg.ca/ppmpackages (Win32)
Exception (see also Perl GUI debuggers)	B	Java-like try and catch structures in Perl
		http://www.cpan.org/authors/id/P/PJ/PJORDAN/
extproc_perl (see also Perl DBI)	8	Oracle Perl Procedure Library (Perl linkage to PL/SQL)
		http://www.smashing.org/
		http://www.cpan.org/modules/by-authors/Jeff_Horwitz
		http://technet.oracle.com
		http://download.oracle.com/otndoc/oracle9i/901_doc/appdev.901/a88876/adg11rtn.htm
		http://download.oracle.com/otndoc/oracle9i/901_doc/server.901/a90117/manproc.htm
		http://otn.oracle.com/deploy/security/alerts.htm (Oracle security alerts)
gcc (see also Unix freeware)	2	GNU C compiler
		http://www.gnu.org/
gd (see also PNG and *zlib*)	3	Graphics drawing packages with Perl
		http://www.cpan.org/authors/id/LDS/
		http://www.boutell.com/gd/ (gd)

Table 1-3. Perl/Oracle applications and related tools (continued)

Application/tool	Chapter	Description/download site
gdb (see also *gcc*)	8	GNU debugger (for particular usage with *gcc*) *http://www.gnu.org/software/gdb/*
HTML::Template (and Template Toolkit) (see also Embperl and Mason)	6	HTML embedded Perl system *http://www.cpan.org/authors/id/S/SA/SAMTREGAR/* *http://www.cpan.org/authors/id/ABW/* *http://www.openinteract.org/, http://openinteract.sourceforge.net/* *http://perl.apache.org/features/tmpl-cmp.html*
Karma	4	Web tool for Oracle DBAs *http://hypno.iheavy.com/karma/index.html* *http://www.cpan.org/authors/id/M/MA/MARKOV/ (MailTools)* *http://www.cpan.org/authors/id/KJALB/ (TermReadKey)* *http://www.cpan.org/authors/id/GBARR/ (libnet)*
LWP	5	Library for WWW access in Perl *http://www.cpan.org/authors/id/GAAS/ (LWP,URI,MIME::Base64,HTML::Parser, Digest::MD5)* *http://www.cpan.org/authors/id/S/SB/SBURKE/ (HTML::Tagset)* *http://www.cpan.org/authors/id/GBARR/ (libnet)* *http://www.cpan.org/authors/id/KWILLIAMS/ (HTML::SimpleParse)*
Linux packages	2	Linux application and package download sites *http://www.redhat.com/apps/download/* *http://www.suse.de/us/support/download/* *http://www.linux-mandrake.com/en/ftp.php3* *http://www.caldera.com/download/mirrors.html* *http://www.debian.org/distrib/ftplist* *http://www.turbolinux.com/download/* *http://www.slackware.com/packages/*
MSI (as standard from Win2000 onward)	2	Microsoft software package installer *http://download.microsoft.com/download/platformsdk/wininst/1.1/NT4/EN-US/ InstMsi.exe* *http://download.microsoft.com/download/platformsdk/wininst/1.1/W9X/EN-US/ InstMsi.exe*
Mason (see also *HTML:: Template* and Embperl)	6	HTML embedded Perl *http://www.masonhq.com/* *http://www.cpan.org/authors/id/J/JS/JSWARTZ/* *http://www.cpan.org/authors/id/DEWEG/ (Time::HiRes)* *http://www.cpan.org/authors/id/GSAR/ (MLDBM)* *http://www.cpan.org/authors/id/ILYAZ/modules/ (FreezeThaw)* *http://www.cpan.org/authors/id/A/AM/AMS/ (Storable)* *http://www.cpan.org/authors/id/D/DR/DROLSKY/ (Params::Validate)*
MySQL	D	Open source database *http://www.mysql.com/* *http://sourceforge.net/projects/mysql/* *http://www.cpan.org/authors/id/JWIED/ (DBD::mysql)*

Table 1-3. Perl/Oracle applications and related tools (continued)

Application/tool	Chapter	Description/download site
NMAKE (see also ActivePerl)	6	Pure Perl Win32 package compilation *http://download.microsoft.com/download/vc15/Patch/1.52/W95/EN-US/ Nmake15.exe*
OraExplain (see also Perl DBI)	3	Perl/Tk Oracle SQL tuning tool *http://www.cpan.org/authors/id/TIMB/*
Orac	3	Perl/Tk general Oracle DBA tool *http://www.cpan.org/authors/id/A/AN/ANDYDUNC/*
Oracle::OCI	7	Direct Perl interface to Oracle Call Interface *http://www.perl.com/CPAN/authors/id/TIMB/* *http://archive.develooper.com/oracle-oci@perl.org/* *http://www.cpan.org/authors/id/T/TB/TBONE/* (*Data::Flow*) *http://www.cpan.org/authors/id/HVDS/* (*C::Scan*) *http://technet.oracle.com* *http://technet.oracle.com/tech/oci/* *http://otn.oracle.com/tech/oci/htdocs/faq.html* *http://www.orafaq.org/faqoci.htm*
Oracletool	4	General web tool for Oracle DBAs *http://www.oracletool.com/* *http://www.cpan.org/authors/id/GAAS/* (*Digest::MD5*) *http://www.cpan.org/authors/id/D/DP/DPARIS/* (*Crypt::IDEA* and *Crypt::Blowfish*) *http://www.cpan.org/authors/id/LDS/* (*Crypt::CBC*)
PNG (see also *zlib* and *gd*)	3	Portable Network Graphics (GIF image alternative) *http://www.libpng.org/pub/png/* *http://www.cpan.org/authors/id/NI-S/* (*Tk::PNG*)
Perl	1	The main Perl portals and download sites *http://www.perl.com* *http://www.perl.org* *http://www.perl.com/CPAN/README.html* *http://www.perl.com/CPAN/src/stable.tar.gz* *http://learn.perl.org/* *http://history.perl.org/* *http://www.wall.org* *http://lists.perl.org/* *http://archive.develooper.com/*
Perl DBA Toolkit (see also *DDL::Oracle*)	9	Our Perl toolkit for Oracle DBAs *http://www.oreilly.com/catalog/oracleperl* *http://www.oreilly.com/catalog/oressentials/chapter/defrag.pdf* *http://www.cpan.org/authors/id/GBARR/* (*TimeDate*) *http://www.cpan.org/authors/id/S/SI/SIFUKURT/* (*Crypt::RC4*) *http://www.cpan.org/authors/id/M/MI/MIVKOVIC/* (*Mail::Sendmail*) *http://www.cpan.org/authors/id/SBECK/* (*Date::Manip*) *http://www.roth.net* (*Win32::Daemon*)

Table 1-3. Perl/Oracle applications and related tools (continued)

Application/tool	Chapter	Description/download site
Perl DBI and DBD::Oracle	1	Perl DBI portals and resources *http://dbi.perl.org* *http://dbi.perl.org/doc/faq.html* *http://xmlproj.dyndns.org/dbi/faq.html* *http://archive.develooper.com/dbi-users@perl.org/* *http://www.xray.mpe.mpg.de/mailing-lists/dbi/* *http://xmlproj.com/PPM/* (latest Win32 packages) *http://www.perl.com/CPAN/modules/by-module/DBI* *http://www.perl.com/CPAN/modules/by-module/DBD* *http://www.cpan.org/authors/id/TIMB/*
Perl DBI ProxyServer (version numbers may change; if so, try *http://search.cpan.org*)	2	Proxy serving for Perl DBI *http://search.cpan.org/doc/TIMB/DBI-1.20/lib/DBI/ProxyServer.pm* *http://search.cpan.org/doc/TIMB/DBI-1.20/lib/DBD/Proxy.pm* *http://www.cpan.org/authors/id/A/AM/AMS/* (*Storable*) *http://www.cpan.org/authors/id/JWIED/* (*Net::Daemon* and PlRPC—which contains *RPC::PlServer* and *RPC::PlClient*)
Perl GUI debuggers (see also Exception)	3	Perl GUI debug tools *http://members.tripod.com/~CurtMcKelvey/perldbgui/* (perldbgui) *http://www.cpan.org/authors/id/A/AE/AEPAGE/* (ptkdb) *http://sourceforge.net/projects/open-perl-ide/* (OpenPerlIDE)
Perl IDE tools	3	Perl GUI development tools *http://sourceforge.net/projects/open-perl-ide/* (OpenPerlIDE) *http://sourceforge.net/projects/kpad/* (KakePad) *http://www.xarka.com/optiperl/* (OptiPerl) *http://www.activestate.com/Products/Komodo/* (Komodo) *http://www.ultraedit.com/* (UltraEdit)
Perl SQL tools (see also Senora)	3	SQL*Plus-like Perl tools *http://www.perldoc.com/perl5.6.1/lib/DBI/Shell.html* *http://dbishell.sourceforge.net/* *http://piqt.sourceforge.net/* *http://sourceforge.net/projects/dsql/*
Perl XML (see later for specific XML Perl modules)	D	Perl XML resources *http://www.xml.com/pub/q/perlxml* *http://xmlxslt.sourceforge.net/* *http://perl.apache.org* *http://xml.sergeant.org/* *http://www.xmlsoft.org/* *http://www.xmlproj.com/perl-xml-faq.dkb* *http://www.perlxml.net http://www.cpan.org/modules/by-module/XML/* *http://sourceforge.net/projects/perl-xml:*

Table 1-3. Perl/Oracle applications and related tools (continued)

Application/tool	Chapter	Description/download site
Perl conversion modules	D	Perl's main data conversion modules
		http://www.gnu.org/software/recode/recode.html, ftp://ftp.gnu.org/gnu/recode/
		http://www.cpan.org/authors/id/CXL/ (*Convert::EBCDIC*)
		http://www.cpan.org/authors/id/COLINK/ (*Convert::SciEng*)
		http://www.cpan.org/authors/id/GENJISCH/ (*Convert::Translit*)
		http://www.cpan.org/authors/id/R/RR/RRWO/ (*Convert::Units*)
		http://www.cpan.org/authors/id/ANDK/ (*Convert::UU*)
		http://www.cpan.org/authors/id/E/ED/EDAVIS/ (*Convert::Recode*)
Perl date modules (and other required helper packages)	D	Perl's major date-handling modules
		http://www.cpan.org/authors/id/D/DE/DESIMINER/ (*Date::Business*)
		http://www.cpan.org/authors/id/STBEY/ (*Date::Calc* and *Date::Pcalc*)
		http://www.cpan.org/authors/id/H/HF/HFB/ (*Date::Christmas*)
		http://www.cpan.org/authors/id/M/MI/MIDI/ (*Date::Decade*)
		http://www.cpan.org/authors/id/RBOW/ (*Date::Easter*)
		http://www.cpan.org/authors/id/B/BB/BBEAUSEJ/ (*Date::Handler*)
		http://www.cpan.org/authors/id/M/MI/MIYAGAWA/ (*Date::Japanese::Era*)
		http://www.cpan.org/authors/id/JTOBEY/ (*Date::Simple*)
		http://www.cpan.org/authors/id/T/TM/TMTM/ (*Date::Range*)
		http://www.cpan.org/authors/id/SBECK/ (*Date::Manip*)
		http://www.cpan.org/authors/id/B/BZ/BZAJAC/ (*DateTime::Precise*)
		http://www.cpan.org/authors/id/GAAS/ (*Mime::Base64*)
		http://www.cpan.org/authors/id/D/DA/DANKOGAI/ (*Jcode*)
		http://www.cpan.org/authors/id/ADESC (*Devel::CoreStack*)
		http://www.cpan.org/authors/id/MSCHWERN (*Test::Harness* and *Test::Simple*)
Perl numeric modules	D	Perl's major numeric modules
		http://www.cpan.org/authors/id/L/LU/LUISMUNOZ/ (*Number::Encode*)
		http://www.cpan.org/authors/id/WRW/ (*Number::Format*)
		http://www.cpan.org/authors/id/S/SB/SBURKE/ (*Number::Latin*)
		http://www.cpan.org/authors/id/K/KE/KENNEDYH/ (*Number::Phone::US*)
		http://www.cpan.org/authors/id/W/WI/WIMV/ (*Number::Spice*)
		http://www.cpan.org/authors/id/L/LH/LHOWARD/ (*Number::Spell*)
Perl/Tk	3	Perl GUI toolkit (derived originally from Tcl/Tk)
		http://www.lehigh.edu/~sol0/ptk/ptk.html
		http://www.perltk.org/
		http://www.oreilly.com/catalog/mastperltk/
		http://www.cpan.org/authors/id/NI-S/
		http://www.cpan.org/authors/id/SREZIC/
SSL	5	Secure Sockets Layer for Perl and the Web
		http://www.openssl.org/ (*OpenSSL*)
		http://www.cpan.org/authors/id/C/CH/CHAMAS/ (*Crypt::SSLeay*)
		http://www.cpan.org/authors/id/SAMPO/ (*Net::SSLeay*)
		http://www.cpan.org/authors/id/A/AS/ASPA/ (*IO::Socket::SSL*)

Table 1-3. Perl/Oracle applications and related tools (continued)

Application/tool	Chapter	Description/download site
SchemaDiff	3	DDL::Oracle and Perl/Tk Oracle schema comparisons *http://sourceforge.net/projects/schemadiff/*
SchemaView-Plus (see also *XML::Dumper* and *XML:: Parser*)	3	Perl/Tk Oracle tool for viewing schema connections *http://www.cpan.org/authors/id/M/MI/MILSO* *http://dbman.linux.cz* (*dbMan*, earlier related tool)
Senora (see also Perl SQL tools)	3	DDL::Oracle-based SQL*Plus-like tool *http://sourceforge.net/projects/senora/*
StatsView (see also PNG, *zlib*, OraExplain)	3	Perl/Tk statistics for Oracle on Unix *http://www.cpan.org/authors/id/ABURLISON/* *http://www.gnuplot.info/* *http://sourceforge.net/projects/gnuplot/*
Unix freeware (also good sources for *gcc* binary packages; see also *gcc*)	2	Binary Perl packages for Unix *http://sunfreeware.com/* (Solaris) *http://ftp.univie.ac.at/aix/and ftp://aixpdslib.seas.ucla.edu/pub/* (AIX) *http://jazz.external.hp.com/src/index.html* (HP-UX) *http://freeware.sgi.com/index.html* (IRIX) *http://www.openbsd.org/ports.html* (OpenBSD)
XML::Dumper	3	Dump Perl data to structured XML *http://www.cpan.org/authors/id/E/EI/EISEN*
XML::Generator::DBI	D	DBI and XML linkage package *http://www.cpan.org/authors/id/M/MS/MSERGEANT* *http://www.cpan.org/authors/id/KMACLEOD/* (libxml-perl and *XML::Parser:: PerlSAX*) *http://www.cpan.org/authors/id/K/KR/KRAEHE/* (*XML::Handler::YAWriter*) *http://www.cpan.org/authors/id/GAAS/* (*MIME::Base64*)
XML::LibXML	D	Alternative Perl XML parser *http://www.cpan.org/authors/id/M/MS/MSERGEANT/* (*XML::LibXML* and *XML::Sax*) *http://www.xmlsoft.org* (libxml2)
XML::LibXSLT	D	Perl Extensible Stylesheet Language Transformations *http://www.cpan.org/authors/id/M/MS/MSERGEANT/* (*XML::LibXSLT*) *http://xmlsoft.org/XSLT/downloads.html* (*libxslt*) *http://www.w3.org/TR/xslt* *http://xmlsoft.org/XSLT/*
XML::Parser	3	Perl XML parser *http://sourceforge.net/projects/expat* (CXMLparser) *http://www.cpan.org/authors/id/C/CO/COOPERCL*
XML::XMLtoDBMS (see also *XML::Parser* and *XML::LibXML*)	D	The Perl port of XML-DBMS from Java *http://www.rpbourret.com/xmldbms/index.htm* (Perl port accessed from this page) *http://www.cpan.org/authors/id/GBARR/* (*TimeDate*)

Table 1-3. Perl/Oracle applications and related tools (continued)

Application/tool	Chapter	Description/download site
XML::XPath (see also *XML::Parser*)	D	Perl and XPath *http://www.cpan.org/authors/id/M/MS/MSERGEANT* *http://www.w3.org/TR/xpath*
zlib (see also PNG)	3	Gzip's back-end compression library *http://www.gzip.org/zlib/* *http://www.zlib.org* *http://www.gzip.org/* *http://www.info-zip.org/pub/infozip/* *http://www.pkware.com/*

[a] As with most *technet.oracle.com* pages, this requires password-protected membership, which can be freely acquired from *http://technet. oracle.com/membership/*.

For Further Information

We've collected what we consider to be the best online and offline resources for Perl in the following sections. If you run into problems or just want to expand your horizons, do check out the books, web sites, and mailing lists summarized here.

Further Information on Perl

Appendix A summarizes the essential elements of Perl's syntax, up to and including its object orientation. It also provides a full guide to the use of the very helpful *perldoc* command, which is the best way to access online manual page information on Perl once it has been installed.

Perl web sites

The following web sites provide good springboards into the world of Perl:

http://www.perl.com
    Contains everything you ever wanted to know about Perl.

http://www.perl.org
    Another central resource for Perl users.

http://learn.perl.org
    Site dedicated to people fresh to Perl.

http://history.perl.org
http://www.wall.org
    Information on the history of Perl.

Perl mailing lists

One of the wonderful benefits of open source tools like Perl is the large number of people out there willing to help you. There are literally hundreds of Perl mailing lists to choose from. Fortunately, there is one site for keeping tabs on all of them:

http://lists.perl.org
> An excellent central resource for tracking down virtually every kind of Perl mailing list you could possibly think of.

beginners-subscribe@perl.org
> Send a blank email here to get attached to the Perl beginners' mailing list.

beginners@perl.org
> Once registered, you can post your questions here.

beginners-unsubscribe@perl.org
> When you're ready to move on to other lists, you can unsubscribe by sending another blank email to the preceding address.

http://archive.develooper.com
> Before posting any questions, you may want to check the Perl archive first.

Perl books

There are enough books on Perl to fill the capacious saddles of several very large camels. Here we'll list just a few of our favorite general texts.

http://www.oreilly.com/catalog/lperl3 (the Llama book)
> *Learning Perl*, by Randal L. Schwartz and Tom Christiansen, 3rd ed. (O'Reilly & Associates, 2001)

http://www.oreilly.com/catalog/lperlwin (the Gecko book)
> *Learning Perl on Win32 Systems*, by Randal L. Schwartz, Erik Olson, and Tom Christiansen (O'Reilly & Associates, 1997)

http://www.oreilly.com/catalog/pperl3 (the Camel book)
> *Programming Perl*, by Larry Wall, Tom Christiansen, and Jon Orwant, 3rd ed. (O'Reilly & Associates, 2000)

http://www.roth.net/books/extensions2
> *Win32 Perl Programming: The Standard Extensions*, by Dave Roth, 2nd ed. (New Riders Publishing, 2001)

http://www.oreilly.com/catalog/perlnut
> *Perl in a Nutshell*, by Ellen Siever, Stephen Spainhour, and Nathan Patwardhan (O'Reilly & Associates, 1998)

http://www.oreilly.com/catalog/advperl (the Panther book)
> *Advanced Perl Programming*, by Sriram Srinivasan (O'Reilly & Associates, 1997)

http://www.effectiveperl.com (the Shiny Ball book)
Effective Perl Programming: Writing Better Programs with Perl, by Joseph N. Hall (Addison-Wesley, 1998)

http://www.oreilly.com/catalog/regex (the Owls book)
Mastering Regular Expressions: Powerful Techniques for Perl and Other Tools, by Jeffrey Friedl (O'Reilly & Associates, 1997)

http://www.manning.com/Conway/index.html (the Renaissance book)
Object Oriented Perl, by Damian Conway (Manning, 1999)

Further Information on Perl DBI

If you want to learn more about Perl DBI, first check out Appendix B. It's likely you'll need more detailed information, however, if you're planning to do anything complex. Here are some recommended resources.

Perl DBI web sites

The following sites are the best places to go for more information:

http://dbi.perl.org
Central home page for the Perl DBI project and the best place to start

http://dbi.perl.org/doc/faq.html
Central FAQ for Perl DBI

Perl DBI mailing lists

The DBI Users mailing list is the information backbone for the entire DBI community, and you'll find a great deal of help available there. However, it's generally considered good form if you at least search the DBI FAQ located at *http://dbi.perl.org/ doc/faq.html*, and possibly the following mail archives, before posting any new questions:

http://lists.perl.org/showlist.cgi?name=dbi-users
The folks at *perl.org* maintain the DBI Users mailing list, and you can register yourself with them at this web address.

dbi-users-subscribe@perl.org
To subscribe to the mailing list, send an empty email here.

dbi-users@perl.org
Once you've been successfully registered by *perl.org*, you can post your Perl DBI questions and comments via this email link.

dbi-users-unsubscribe@perl.org
To unsubscribe from the mailing list, post an empty email here.

http://archive.develooper.com/dbi-users@perl.org
> The main archive attached to the central DBI Users mailing list, organized by date and threaded topic.

http://www.xray.mpe.mpg.de/mailing-lists/dbi
> Another searchable archive for the DBI mailing list. Again, you may want to search through this archive before posting any new mailing list questions.

Perl DBI books

Two O'Reilly books complement the one you're reading right now. The first contains much more detail on the Perl DBI API; the second also describes Perl DBI, as well as many other open source technologies (including Tcl and Python) and their parallel use of OCI:

http://www.oreilly.com/catalog/perldbi
> *Programming the Perl DBI: Database Programming with Perl*, by Alligator Descartes and Tim Bunce (O'Reilly & Associates, 2000).

http://www.oreilly.com/catalog/oracleopen
> *Oracle & Open Source: Tools and Applications*, by Andy Duncan and Sean Hull (O'Reilly & Associates, 2001).

CHAPTER 2
Installing Perl

Now that you've learned how Perl can ease the burden of Oracle database administration, you're probably eager to get started. This chapter explains how to install Perl for use with Oracle. We'll cover the following steps:

Installing Perl
> If you're installing Perl on Unix, we recommend that you install directly from source. If you're installing Perl on Win32, we recommend that you use the prebuilt ActivePerl distribution, available from ActiveState; ActivePerl has become the *de facto* standard Perl version for the Win32 platform.

Installing Perl DBI
> Once you've installed Perl itself, you need database connectivity for it. We'll describe how to install Perl's generic DBI module, as well as *DBD::Oracle*, the Oracle-specific driver for Perl DBI.

Installing Cygwin
> Cygwin is a complete Unix-like development environment that you can install on your Win32 machine. It allows you to combine the benefits of access to Unix compilers, interpreters, and other tools (e.g., Perl, *gcc*) with the convenience of traditional Win32 software (e.g,. Microsoft Word, Excel). We'll explain how to install Cygwin and get the various Perl modules running on it.

Installing Perl

We described Perl's origins and advantages in Chapter 1, *Perl Meets Oracle*. In this section, we'll describe the basics of the installation process for Perl. To obtain Perl and to get more detailed information about this process, check out these web sites:

http://www.perl.com
http://www.perl.org
> Main Perl portals.

http://www.activestate.com

ActiveState Win32 Perl portal site. You'll find many other projects, including ActivePerl, under the main ActiveState portal; most ActiveState products tend to have fairly fluid web addresses, so we won't attempt to provide them here.

Installing Perl on Unix

There are three basic ways to get started with Perl on Unix and Linux systems, the third of which is best for reasons we'll explain shortly:

1. Find Perl already installed on your system.
2. Download a binary executable that will build Perl for you out of the box.
3. Configure and build Perl yourself from the source code.

On most Unix versions, if you install Perl as the *root* user and accept the default installation directories, it will generally embed itself into either one of the following directories:

/usr/bin
/usr/local/bin

In most cases, this is fine; however, you may wish to install it somewhere else, such as */u01/app/perl*.

There are several reasons why you might want to install Perl in a different location:

- If you're an Oracle DBA who is working on other people's systems, you may be denied access to the *root* user's system directories.
- You may have *theoretical* access, but jumping through the corporate hoops to get actual *physical* access on some production systems (and having to fill out all the necessary forms) may just not be worth it.
- Some versions of Perl, may already exist on your system and be used by everyone else. However, you want your own latest-and-greatest private Perl to do the work you need it to do, without upsetting the informational applecart. Those guys in marketing may be happy relying on that ancient Perl 4 workhorse, but we need something a bit more developed.

There are also several secondary reasons:

- Upgrading module versions, such as *DBD::Oracle*, when they become available, will be simpler if you're in complete control of the Perl installation location.
- Adding new modules also becomes easier if you don't need to ask people's permission to do it, or to work within their weekly downtime window (you can almost guarantee that window will be Wednesday morning at 3:00 AM).

- For similar reasons, upgrading Perl itself will also be painless. Your local neighborhood system administrators may even award you bonus points for keeping off their turf!

Although we'll assume in the following discussion that you're installing Perl in default locations as *root* (which is most often the case), we'll indicate the one place where you can change this default, if you want to install Perl under something more like the *oracle* or *oramon* user, in a nonstandard location.

> This chapter assumes that you want to create your own version of Perl—one that is distinct from the Perl executables provided automatically in Oracle releases beginning with Version 8.1.7. (Later in this chapter, in the section "Installing Perl from source" we'll explain why we recommend that you create your own version of Perl.) You need to be careful not to get these two versions of Perl confused (people installing Perl for the first time sometimes do this). One way to keep the versions straight is to ensure that your own independent version of Perl comes first in your system's generic *PATH* variable.

Finding Perl already installed on your system

If Perl exists somewhere on your system (i.e., the main *perl* executable program is available under your operating system, via the *PATH* environment variable), you can usually find it by running the following command:

```
$ perl -v
```

If you believe that Perl is on your machine, but this command fails to return anything, you may want to discover where Perl is living and then add it to your executables PATH. To find it, try one of the following commands:

```
$ type perl
$ which perl
$ whence perl
$ locate perl
```

If these fail to work, or if Perl is still unavailable on your flavor of Unix, try the ultimate blockbuster approach:

```
$ find / -name "perl*" -print 2>/dev/null
```

Click, whirr. Once you've found Perl, add its executable directory into your PATH and then run the *perl -v* command. What we're looking for is something like this:

```
$ perl -v

This is perl, v5.6.1 built for i686-linux

Copyright 1987-2001, Larry Wall

Perl may be copied only under the terms of either the Artistic License
or the GNU General Public License, which may be found in the
```

```
Perl 5 source kit.

Complete documentation for Perl, including FAQ lists, should be found
On this system using `man perl' or `perldoc perl'.  If you have access
to the Internet, point your browser at http://www.perl.com/, the Perl
Home Page.

$
```

Most Linux machines (depending on the release date of the Linux distribution) have Perl already on them. If you find Perl 5.6, or above, that's good enough. For some bizarre reason, many proprietary versions of Unix fail to come presupplied with Perl, but that's OK. It's much more fun to install from source! We'll show you how shortly.

Installing Perl from a prebuilt package

Some Oracle DBAs running Unix systems choose to install Perl from a prebuilt executable binary. In general, we recommend against this approach. Even if this option is available to you, it has several disadvantages in comparison to building Perl from source, mainly because prebuilt binaries may not match the configuration of your local system—for example:

- They may implicitly point to libraries that are not available on the particular machine.
- The original compiler options with which the package was created may not be supported on your current system.
- They may assume default paths that don't exist. For example, most of the pre-built Unix Perl packages assume that the main *perl* executable is going to live under */usr/local/bin*. This is especially problematic if, as we mentioned earlier, write access is unavailable to these kinds of directories.

Building from source, as we describe in the next section, is the best way to overcome local difficulties of these kinds.

If you do need to go down the prepackaged route, for whatever reason, be aware that most proprietary Unixes do have some great freeware sites. Although we think Perl is best if built from source on Unix, you need to build it with compilers, and if you haven't got one, these sites and their packages are invaluable for providing you with prepackaged compilers such as *gcc*. Some of the best sites we've found are:

For Solaris
  http://sunfreeware.com

For AIX
  http://ftp.univie.ac.at/aix
  ftp://aixpdslib.seas.ucla.edu/pub

For HP-UX
   http://jazz.external.hp.com/src/index.html#perl

For IRIX
   http://freeware.sgi.com/index.html

For OpenBSD
   http://www.openbsd.org/ports.html

For Linux
   Virtually every flavor of Linux also has its own home site, which is full of Unix freeware download opportunities. Here are just some of the possibilities:

   http://www.redhat.com/apps/download/
   http://www.suse.de/us/support/download/
   http://www.linux-mandrake.com/en/ftp.php3
   http://www.caldera.com/download/mirrors.html
   http://www.debian.org/distrib/ftplist
   http://www.turbolinux.com/download/
   http://www.slackware.com/packages/

You'll find the appropriate installation instructions at each site, and a web search should uncover any others. Here we'll run through the typical steps for Solaris. These are only guidelines; be sure that you obtain, and read carefully, the most up-to-date installation information for your own platform.

1. Download the latest Perl package for your version of Solaris from the web site.

2. Unzip the download (using either *gunzip* or *gzip -d*) as the root user.

3. Use *pkgadd -d* to add the package to your system.

For example, the following commands would install the standard Perl 5.6.1 package as the *root* user:

```
$ gzip -d perl-5.6.1-sol8-sparc-local.gz
$ pkgadd -d perl-5.6.1-sol8-sparc-local
```

These kinds of steps (as specified on the appropriate site FAQ or within any accompanying *README* files) will build a fully functioning Perl system for you, adding the Perl executable to a directory like */usr/local/bin/perl*. You'll follow similar steps for most of the other Unixes.

 Using some download browser screens, the prebuilt packages will occasionally download without the **.gz* suffix. This confuses the *gunzip* program. If this problem occurs, you can solve it by simply renaming the downloaded file with the additional **.gz* suffixed extension.

Installing Perl from source

This third option is the one we recommend for Unix. To use our PDBA Toolkit most effectively, we recommend that you install at least Perl 5.6 from source. It's true that you may have older versions of Perl on your system, or versions built from prepackaged executables. However, we need to lay a specific version of Perl DBI on top of Perl, and for that reason we must ensure that Perl 5.6 has been set up correctly for your machine. The best way of doing this is by building up from source.

Obtaining the required C compiler. You must have a C compiler before you can complete your Perl installation. Fortunately, Linux virtually always comes with a *gcc* C compiler already on board, and most proprietary Unix types often come with their own, which is usually called *cc*. Even if you already have a C compiler, though, you may want to get hold of *gcc* because most open source project installations are built and tested with it. Using *gcc*, rather than any other C compiler, automatically eliminates many compiler incompatibility problems.

The *gcc* compiler is the creation of the GNU project, which was started in 1984 by Richard M. Stallman with the goal of developing a completely free Unix-like operating system. This project culminated in the development of the various GNU/Linux operating systems, better known by their generic name "Linux" after their core kernel developed by Linus Torvalds. You can check out the GNU project's definition of the word "free," get information about *gcc*, and learn much more at:

http://www.gnu.org

Although *gcc* is usually the right choice, always read the appropriate *README* files within the *stable.tar.gz* Perl distribution for each operating system. For instance, here's what the *README.aix* file says about using *gcc*:

> Perl can be compiled with either IBM's ANSI C compiler or with *gcc*. The former is recommended, as not only can it compile Perl with no difficulty, but also can take advantage of features listed later that require the use of IBM compiler-specific command-line flags.

With AIX, you may have difficulties unless you do use the proprietary cc compiler, as the note suggests. Most HP platforms are also better served with HP's "official" C compiler, which you may have to purchase as an extra-cost item.

 If you enjoy a challenge, and you'd like to boot-strap *gcc* from its own source code using your own proprietary *cc* compiler as the bootstrapper, check out the GNU web site for details.

You won't need to compile *gcc* from source (unless you enjoy Catch-22-type challenges) because virtually every flavor of Unix has a *gcc* binary package built for it already by the open source community. You can get such packages from the freeware sites listed in the previous section.

For example, at the time this book went to press, the following sites contained the latest *gcc* package for three major commercial Unix flavors.

http://sunfreeware.com
  For Solaris

http://ftp.univie.ac.at/aix/aix432
  For AIX

http://jazz.external.hp.com/src/gnu/download2_95_2.html
  For HP-UX

You'll find appropriate *README* installation instructions at each site. Here, we'll run through the typical steps for Solaris. These are only guidelines. Be sure you obtain the most up-to-date installation information for your own platform, from the site where you get the *gcc* package:

1. Download the latest *gcc* package, for your version of Solaris, from the *sunfreeware.com* site.

2. Unzip the download using either *gunzip* or *gzip -d* as the *root* user. This file will be called something like *gcc-3.0.3-sol8-sparc-local.gz*.

3. Use *pkgadd -d* to add the package to your system.

For example, if you're logged on as the *root* user, the following commands will install the *gcc* package:

```
# gzip -d gcc-3.0.3-sol8-sparc-local.gz
# pkgadd -d gcc-3.0.3-sol8-sparc-local
```

The actual executable will usually get dispatched to */usr/local/bin/gcc*.

As a final compilation caveat, note that the default Perl installation process looks for a generic *cc* compiler, unless you alter this behavior by following the detailed instructions in the Perl *INSTALL* file. To make sure you still pick up *gcc* anyway, move your old *cc* compiler somewhere safe, such as *cc.old*, or place a new *cc* location higher up in your PATH. Now we symbolically link in the new *cc* file to point at the real *gcc* compiler, to achieve a situation similar to the following:

```
$ type cc
cc is /home/oracle/bin/cc
$ ls -l /home/oracle/bin/cc
/home/oracle/bin/cc -> gcc
$ type gcc
gcc is /usr/local/bin/gcc
```

Obtaining the source for Perl. Once the compiler is ready, it's time to get the Perl source code itself. To obtain the latest version, visit CPAN, the Comprehensive Perl Archive Network:

  http://www.perl.com/CPAN/README.html

This will probably direct you to download the most recent stable version of Perl—for example:

http://www.perl.com/CPAN-local/src/stable.tar.gz

Once you've obtained your own copy of *stable.tar.gz*, follow these basic steps to install Perl:

1. Download the zipped tar file (or "tarball," as we'll call it from now on) into a temporary directory accessible to the *root* user.

2. Unpack the main bundled file into its own directory:

```
# ls *.gz
stable.tar.gz
# gzip -d stable.tar.gz
# ls *.tar
stable.tar
# tar xvf stable.tar
```

3. Change into the new Perl directory once the extraction process has completed, and then carefully work through the instructions in the *README* and *INSTALL* files:

```
# ls
perl-5.6.1
# cd perl-5.6.1
# vi README INSTALL
```

4. These instructions ask us to run an intelligent and friendly configuration program, *Configure*, a sort of Hitchhiker's Guide to the Perl installation process. By now, this program has been run, quite literally, a few million times, so there are few installation issues the program has failed to cope with. You should have no problems running it, especially if you're happy with a totally default install. For re-installations, the following preparation step also ensures that no previously existing master configuration files will interfere with the process:

```
# rm -f config.sh Policy.sh
```

If you wish to install Perl as a non-*root* user within a nonstandard area, this is the place where we deviate from the path of *root* enlightenment. Pick your target installation directory (say, */u01/app/perl*) and then run the *Configure* program slightly differently, perhaps as an *oracle* or *oramon* user:

```
$ ./Configure -Dprefix=/u01/app/perl
```

This tells Perl all it needs to know. When you run *make install* shortly, */u01/app/perl* will become the parent directory where Perl will get installed.

To get back to the main flow, *root* users will simply run the following:

```
# sh Configure -de
```

(If you use *sh Configure -des*, the final "s" will take all the defaults for your system.)

5. Answering the configuration questions will only take a few minutes (if in doubt, simply accept the defaults supplied). Once this Q&A session is completed, we're ready to begin the build and installation stages. Make sure any configuration errors are dealt with before you proceed with each next step (although you're unlikely to encounter any unless your machine or workstation is fairly nonstandard). Run through the next few steps:

```
$ make
$ make test
$ make install
```

6. Once you've completed these, Perl should now be installed. Check it out with the *perl -v* command, as described earlier. Make sure it's the one you were expecting—at least the 5.6 version.

Installing Perl on Win32

For Win32, although you can build from source (if you have the relevant Win32 compilers, or you can use Cygwin (as described later in this chapter), most people use the prebuilt ActiveState binaries, and that's what we'll do here.

Follow these steps:

1. Consult the main portal page for ActiveState to see all of the latest information for installing ActivePerl (and many other products, including ActivePython and ActiveTcl):

    http://www.activestate.com

    You'll be able to go from there to pages like this:

    http://aspn.activestate.com/ASPN/Downloads/ActivePer
    http://aspn.activestate.com/ASPN/Downloads/ActivePerl/More

2. You can download the latest binary executable build of ActivePerl from a web address such as the following:

    http://downloads.activestate.com/ActivePerl/Windows/5.6

    The download file will be named something like the following:

    ActivePerl-5.6.1.628-MSWin32-x86-multi-thread.msi

3. You will need the appropriate MSI Microsoft Windows program installer. If it's not already available within your particular Win32 system (it comes as standard with Windows 2000), you'll need to obtain it. You'll generally find that the ActiveState site is the best place to direct you to the latest location and version for this purpose. We provide the current Microsoft addresses, but note that these do tend to move around a bit. If the following URLs are invalid, the ActiveState Perl download pages will contain the latest address:

http://download.microsoft.com/download/platformsdk/wininst/1.1/NT4/EN-US/
InstMsi.exe

For WinNT

http://download.microsoft.com/download/platformsdk/wininst/1.1/W9X/EN-US/
InstMsi.exe

For Win98 and Win95

Install the MSI Microsoft installer itself by double-clicking on it in Windows Explorer (this installation may be almost instantaneous).

4. Once the MSI program is confirmed as having been installed, double-click on the actual ActivePerl download, in Windows Explorer, as in Figure 2-1.

5. After answering some questions about where you want Perl to be installed and where you accepted the defaults, Win32 Perl is then installed directly onto your system, in the standard Win32 way.

Once the process is complete, you can then test your Perl installation with the *perl -v* test (also shown in Figure 2-1).

 Because of the standard security architecture of Win32 systems, network shares and shared drives in a cluster are sometimes unavailable to the SYSTEM user. Therefore, any Perl scripts running from a scheduler or as a service will require that Perl be installed on a local drive. The C:\ drive is often a safe bet (this is generally the default), and this is where we always install Perl.

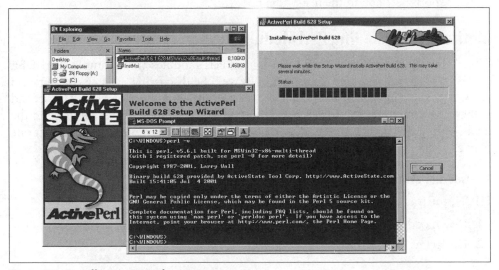

Figure 2-1. Installing ActivePerl

We hope you won't encounter any problems getting Perl installed. But if you do, and you can't get the necessary help from the *README* and *INSTALL* files or here in this book, go to the Perl information sources listed in Chapter 1.

Installing Perl DBI

Now that you've installed Perl itself, you need to set things up so your Perl programs can communicate with your Oracle database. The best way to do this is via the magic of the Perl DBI module and its Oracle-specific database driver, *DBD::Oracle*. These modules let us gain access to our target database through the Oracle Call Interface provided by Oracle Corporation. The architecture for this arrangement, which takes full advantage of the object-oriented features available within Perl 5, is shown in Figure 2-2. This figure also demonstrates how the same Perl DBI interface can be used, with other drivers, to connect to other databases, and how all of these drivers are hidden from your Perl scripts by the DBI package.[*]

This section focuses on the installation of Perl DBI. For more information about Perl DBI's capabilities, see Appendix B, *The Essential Guide to Perl DBI*, and the book and online references listed in Chapter 1. For complete online information, go to *http://dbi.perl.org*.

We'll show how to install the DBI modules for both Unix and Win32.

Before we get to the DBI and *DBD::Oracle* modules, however, we need to take a step back to discuss the methodology we'll be using for installing Perl modules onto Unix systems, both here and in the rest of the book.

Methods for Installing Perl Modules

There are two basic approaches to installing Perl modules (for example, Perl DBI, *DBD::Oracle*, and the many other modules we'll be discussing in later chapters) on Unix systems. The first is what some people call the *traditional method*. The second is the CPAN method. We recommend the traditional method, as we describe in the next section, but because the CPAN method is quite popular, we'll describe that one here as well.

The traditional method

Briefly, the traditional method consists of the following steps:

1. Download a module's tarball from *cpan.org*.
2. Unpack it.

---

[*] You can even access different database types within the same Perl script using DBI. Doing so can be especially useful when you want to transfer information from one database type to another without having to use Oracle's SQL*Loader product.

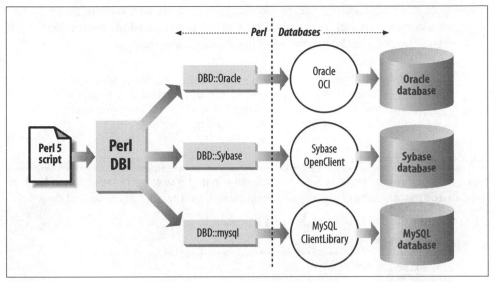

Figure 2-2. The Perl DBI architecture

3. Build it.

4. Test it.

5. Install it.

This process often requires specifying the following steps on the command line (once the module tarball has been downloaded from the CPAN site, *http://www.cpan.org*).

```
$ gzip SomeModule-1.00.tar.gz    # Unzip archive
$ tar xvf SomeModule-1.00.tar    # Unpack archive
$ cd SomeModule-1.00             # Enter archive
$ perl Makefile.PL               # Configure the build
$ make                           # Build, or compile, the module
$ make test                      # Test the module's compilation
$ make install                   # Install the tested module
```

There are a lot of keystrokes here. However, there is a way to cut down on this effort, and that's to use the *CPAN* module described in the next section.

The CPAN method

The *CPAN* module (a separate entity from CPAN itself) provides a streamlined way to install Perl modules. You can learn the details of this built-in module by running the following commands:*

```
$ perldoc perlmodinstall
$ perldoc CPAN
```

---

* The *perldoc* (Perl documentation) program itself is installed automatically with Perl, as part of the general Perl development environment.

If you have a valid Internet connection open, you will have two ways of using *CPAN*. You can use either an interactive shell or a direct command-line instruction. We'll load up two modules in the following sections using these methods.

 The *CPAN* module comes prebundled with Perl. When you run its shell (described in the next section) for the first time, it will ask you a one-time series of short configuration questions. Once you've completed these, you're ready to start installing online!

The interactive CPAN shell

First, we'll try the interactive *CPAN* shell, and install *Number::Format*, a helpful Perl module for manipulating number and string displays, particularly financial data:

1. We enter the shell via the following command:

```
$ perl -MCPAN -e "shell"
cpan shell -- CPAN exploration and modules installation (v1.59_51)
ReadLine support enabled

cpan>
```

2. We then install *Number::Format* with a straightforward instruction at the *cpan>* prompt. This sets off a train of events in which *CPAN* goes off to the nearest *cpan.org* mirrors, First, it interrogates the Comprehensive Perl Archive Network, as to whether our target module really exists. After validating this fact and a few other related pieces of information, it automatically downloads the latest existing tarball from the mirror and installs it for you. It does all this via some Perl magic of which Mithrandir himself would be proud:

```
cpan> install Number::Format
CPAN: Net::FTP loaded ok
Fetching with Net::FTP:
   ftp://ftp.demon.co.uk/pub/CPAN/authors/01mailrc.txt.gz
Going to read /home/andyd/.cpan/sources/authors/01mailrc.txt.gz
CPAN: Compress::Zlib loaded ok
Fetching with Net::FTP:
   ftp://ftp.demon.co.uk/pub/CPAN/modules/02packages.details.txt.gz
Going to read
   /home/andyd/.cpan/sources/modules/02packages.details.txt.gz
Fetching with Net::FTP:
   ftp://ftp.demon.co.uk/pub/CPAN/modules/03modlist.data.gz
Going to read /home/andyd/.cpan/sources/modules/03modlist.data.gz
Running install for module Number::Format
Running make for W/WR/WRW/Number-Format-1.44.tar.gz
Fetching with Net::FTP:
   ftp://ftp.demon.co.uk/pub/CPAN/authors/id/W/WR/WRW/Number-
Format-1.44.tar.gz
CPAN: MD5 loaded ok
Fetching with Net::FTP:
   ftp://ftp.demon.co.uk/pub/CPAN/authors/id/W/WR/WRW/CHECKSUMS
Checksum for
```

```
/home/andyd/.cpan/sources/authors/id/W/WR/WRW/Number-
Format-1.44.tar.gz ok
Scanning cache /home/andyd/.cpan/build for sizes

  CPAN.pm: Going to build W/WR/WRW/Number-Format-1.44.tar.gz

Writing Makefile for NumberFormat
  /usr/bin/make  -- OK
Running make test
No tests defined for NumberFormat extension.
  /usr/bin/make test -- OK
Running make install
Writing /usr/lib/perl5/site_perl/5.6.1/i686-
linux/auto/NumberFormat/.packlist
Appending installation info to /usr/lib/perl5/5.6.1/i686-
linux/perllocal.pod
  /usr/bin/make install  -- OK
cpan>
```

Although the preceding is a lot of output, it has taken our fingers relatively few keystrokes to get *Number::Format* installed. In addition to the interrogation shown here, notice the three build and installation steps we've highlighted—*make*, *make test*, and *make install*—all done automatically.

3. Once we've finished installing new packages, we simply quit out of the shell:

```
cpan> quit
Lockfile removed.

$
```

Number::Format (and any other requested modules) is now installed, as if you had done it by hand.

CPAN from the command line

Using *CPAN* directly from the command line is even easier than using the interactive *CPAN* shell. We'll use it to get another useful Perl module, the *Convert::EBCDIC* bundle, which deals with IBM mainframe EBCDIC data and its conversion to and from ASCII formats. Follow these steps:

1. This time, we'll install our target module directly, with a single command at the operating system prompt:

   ```
   $ perl -MCPAN -e "install 'Convert::EBCDIC'"
   ```

2. This runs through a processing operation that's similar to the shell method shown earlier:

   ```
   Going to read /home/andyd/.cpan/sources/authors/01mailrc.txt.gz
   CPAN: Compress::Zlib loaded ok
   Going to read
      /home/andyd/.cpan/sources/modules/02packages.details.txt.gz
   Going to read /home/andyd/.cpan/sources/modules/03modlist.data.gz
   Running install for module Convert::EBCDIC
   Running make for C/CX/CXL/Convert-EBCDIC-0.06.tar.gz
   CPAN: Net::FTP loaded ok
   ```

```
Fetching with Net::FTP:
  ftp://ftp.demon.co.uk/pub/CPAN/authors/id/C/CX/CXL/Convert-
EBCDIC-0.06.tar.gz
CPAN: MD5 loaded ok
Fetching with Net::FTP:
  ftp://ftp.demon.co.uk/pub/CPAN/authors/id/C/CX/CXL/CHECKSUMS
Checksum for /home/andyd/.cpan/sources/authors/id/C/CX/CXL/Convert-
EBCDIC-0.06.tar.gz ok
Scanning cache /home/andyd/.cpan/build for sizes

  CPAN.pm: Going to build C/CX/CXL/Convert-EBCDIC-0.06.tar.gz

Writing Makefile for ConvertEBCDIC
  /usr/bin/make  -- OK
Running make test
No tests defined for ConvertEBCDIC extension.
  /usr/bin/make test -- OK
Running make install
Writing /usr/lib/perl5/site_perl/5.6.1/i686-
linux/auto/ConvertEBCDIC/.packlist
Appending installation info to /usr/lib/perl5/5.6.1/i686-
linux/perllocal.pod
  /usr/bin/make install  -- OK
$
```

Convert::EBCDIC should now be fully installed. (We discuss both *Number::Format* and *Convert::EBCDIC* in Appendix D, *The Essential Guide to Perl Data Munging*.)

The traditional method

As you can see, the CPAN installation method is very convenient. However, like many Perl developers, we've chosen to use the older paradigm because it gives us better control and is more reliable.

Many of the modules we're going to discuss in this book have compilation routes that deviate from the norm. *CPAN* is a fire-and-forget missile. You press the button, and away it goes, but it always expects our target to be in view. If the target is elsewhere, it's intelligent enough to try to adapt, but it may still fail to do *exactly* what you wish, and consequently miss the mark. On the other hand, because of the greater number of steps required by the traditional method, we actually achieve better granularity when we use that method, and we find it particularly helpful when explaining Perl to others. We can hop between steps and offer you more advice on debugging, alternative location installations, and other compilation tips (particularly in places where the Perl module is a glue layer camouflaging the more difficult API of a passenger C library, which itself needs compilation).*

---

* You can think of the difference between the CPAN and traditional methods as analogous to the old conflict between what's called, in military circles, Sigint (Signals Intelligence) and Humint (Human Intelligence). Sigint, or *CPAN*, is easier to deploy and gather information from, whereas the traditional cloak-and-dagger Humint, pays for its greater management overhead with a greater depth of penetration.

Thus, from here on, we're going to sidestep the *CPAN* module and stick mainly to *la methode traditionelle* as we discuss Perl installation. However, if you ever get jealous of Win32 people using PPM (the Perl Package Manager, which we describe in the later section, "Installing Perl DBI on Win32"), nothing stops from you using *CPAN*; we promise to turn a blind eye, especially as we use PPM quite often.

Installing Perl DBI on Unix

In this section, we'll explain how to install Perl DBI using the following tarballs:

> *DBI-1.20.tar.gz*
> *DBD-Oracle-1.12.tar.gz*

The central locations for these are:

> *http://www.perl.com/CPAN/modules/by-module/DBI*
> *http://www.perl.com/CPAN/modules/by-module/DBD*

You can obtain the relevant interface and driver packages by clicking on and saving the files from the appropriate links. Save them to a Perl module repository.

Installing Perl DBI

Once you have the relevant downloads, you can begin the Perl DBI installation. Before starting, always scan through the relevant *README* files; the following instructions do change gradually over time. If any problems occur with your installation, you'll find that the solution is most likely buried deep within either the DBI or the *DBD::Oracle README* files. Follow these steps:

1. As a sanity check, make sure that the Perl version you installed earlier is set up correctly. Do this as the same user with which you installed Perl:

   ```
   $ type perl
   perl is hashed (/usr/bin/perl)
   $ perl -v
   This is perl, v5.6.1 built for i686-linux........
   ```

2. If this looks good, carry on with the Perl DBI installation by unpacking the tarball and checking the documentation:

   ```
   $ gzip -d DBI-1.20.tar.gz
   $ tar xvf DBI-1.20.tar
   $ cd DBI-1.20
   $ vi README
   ```

3. If you have no special requirements (as detailed in the *README* file), follow the standard Perl installation instructions.* If any step fails, you will need to sort out what's causing the problem before you can move on:

   ```
   $ perl Makefile.PL
   ```

---

* If you installed Perl earlier in a nonstandard directory as a non-*root* user, all subsequent module installations will automatically feed themselves into the correct library locations, and no further intervention will be required on your part.

This step may produce an informational note similar to the following:

```
*** Note:
      The optional PlRPC-modules (RPC::PlServer etc) are not installed.
      If you want to use the DBD::Proxy driver and DBI::ProxyServer
      modules, then you'll need to install the RPC::PlServer,
      RPC::PlClient, Storable and Net::Daemon modules. The CPAN
      Bundle::DBI may help you.
      You can install them any time after installing the DBI.
      You do *not* need these modules for typical DBI usage.
```

The *DBI::ProxyServer* and *DBD::Proxy* combination is an alternative approach to the one we describe in this section. It lets you avoid using *DBD::Oracle* on remote Oracle clients. We'll describe this approach, as well as the details of the *dbiproxy* daemon program, later in this chapter; the *dbiproxy* daemon is also displayed in Figure 2-4. To get *dbiproxy* to work, you'll need to install four more packages before installing DBI (remember that these are optional and unnecessary for typical DBI usage). You can always come back to these packages at a later time; for now, let's move on.

4. Having configured Perl DBI, let's build, test, and install it.

```
$ make
$ make test
$ make install
```

Perl DBI should now be installed. But we need to keep the bubbly on ice, for a little while longer. The next stage is to pair DBI up with its partner, the *DBD::Oracle* driver.

Installing DBD::Oracle

Follow these steps to install the *DBD::Oracle* module:

1. At this point, make sure you have a test Oracle database running, with the appropriate TNS listener up. Also, if you're the *root* user, make sure you have the usual Oracle environment variables set up: *ORACLE_HOME* and *ORACLE_SID* (you may choose to use *TWO_TASK*, instead of *ORACLE_SID*, depending on your setup). You particularly need *ORACLE_HOME* to locate the OCI code libraries. Note that *DBD::Oracle* is similar in concept to the Type II *fat* JDBC drivers for use with the *java.sql* database connectivity package in Java. It needs *at least* Oracle client libraries available, in order to compile successfully:[*]

```
$ ORACLE_HOME=/u01/app/oracle/product/8.1.5
$ export ORACLE_HOME
$ ORACLE_SID=orcl
$ export ORACLE_SID
```

---

[*] That is why DBI::ProxyServer and DBD::Proxy may be of interest for remote clients. They let you sidestep the requirement for Oracle client libraries at the remote end (see Figure 2-4).

2. To make sure the *DBD::Oracle* driver is working correctly (before its full installation in the *make test* step described later), you'll also need to set up the following special *ORACLE_USERID* environment variable. (Simply change the *scott/tiger@orcl* string on your own installation to a valid connection string on your own test database.)

```
$ ORACLE_USERID=scott/tiger@orcl
$ export ORACLE_USERID
```

3. As a final environmental gotcha, you may also need to have your *LD_LIBRARY_PATH* environmental value pointing to all of the right little places on various Unix flavors. This will help ensure that *DBD::Oracle* will pick up the correct Oracle libraries:

```
$ LD_LIBRARY_PATH=$LD_LIBRARY_PATH:$ORACLE_HOME/lib
$ export LD_LIBRARY_PATH
```

4. We're now ready to unpack *DBD::Oracle*:

```
$ gzip -d DBD-Oracle-1.12.tar.gz
$ tar xvf DBD-Oracle-1.12.tar
$ cd DBD-Oracle-1.12
$ vi README
```

5. As the Captain himself might have once said, "Transporter room, this is Kirk. Configure, build, and install":

```
$ perl Makefile.PL
$ make
$ make test
$ make install
```

If you do encounter any errors with this installation (particularly on the *make test* step), you must sort them out before running the final *make install* step—even if the errors appear to be nonfatal. That way, you'll have greater confidence when you're running production DBI scripts later on. Following this error hit list should remove most of the gremlins:

a. Ensure that *ORACLE_USERID* is set correctly, as described earlier.

b. Check that *LD_LIBRARY_PATH* can access the libraries residing in *$ORACLE_HOME/lib*.

c. Make sure your Oracle database is up and running with adequate memory available in the shared pool, particularly if you know that the machine's memory is tight.

d. Check that the correct Oracle listener is responding correctly. You can do this by connecting to it via a SQL*Plus session, from the same machine on which you're installing *DBD::Oracle*.

e. Scan through the *README* files again with a fine-toothed comb.

If you can't solve your problem (which should be a very rare case), you may be able to get help from the DBI users mailing lists or from the helpful information in the DBI FAQs. We explain how to access these at the end of Chapter 1.

Once you've successfully completed the *make install* step, you'll find plenty of up-to-date Perl DBI documentation automatically loaded onto your system. You can ensure that the documentation has been loaded by running the following pair of commands:

```
$ perldoc DBD::Oracle
$ perldoc DBI
```

Installing Perl DBI on Win32

In contrast to the Unix installation, installing Perl DBI using ActiveState's version of Perl is very straightforward. We recommend that for Win32 you use the PPM (Perl Package Manager) module, which installs automatically alongside ActivePerl with its utility *ppm* program (which runs it).

PPM simplifies the tasks of locating, installing, upgrading, and removing software packages on Win32. It determines whether the most recent version of a software package is installed, and can install or upgrade that package from a local or remote host. PPM is very similar to the interactive *CPAN* shell module described earlier. Although PPM is usually run via its *ppm* interactive shell program, it can also be used directly on the command line. PPM uses PPD (Perl Package Description) files containing an extended form of the Open Software Description specification,* for information about software packages. These description files are written in XML. For more information on PPM on Win32, run the very helpful *perldoc* command; we'll say more about *perldoc* in Appendix A, *The Essential Guide to Perl*:

```
DOS> perldoc PPM
```

We've chosen to use PPM ActivePerl packages, instead of hand-crafting Perl module installations, for the following reasons:

- Most Win32 users don't have a development environment in which to compile and test source code installations.

- Many Perl modules on Unix require the manual compilation of libraries such as *zlib* for compression, *expat* for XML parsing, or *gd* for dynamic image creation. All ActivePerl modules have precompiled these libraries for you into DLLs, where necessary, before you download them. These will save you a significant amount of work over compiling DLLs of your own.

- Just as compiling from source is the standard method for installing Perl on Unix, the *de facto* standard method on Win32 is to use PPM.

Running PPM

For a comprehensive guide to installing Perl modules on Win32, check out the following site:

---

* *http://www.w3.org/TR/NOTE-OSD.html*

http://aspn.activestate.com/ASPN/Products/ActivePerl/faq/ActivePerl-faq2.html

Unless you're accessing the Internet through proxies, as we'll discuss shortly, the following steps should take only a few minutes:

1. As with *CPAN*, make sure your PC is connected to the Internet before you run ActiveState's PPM. (Note that PPM itself was automatically installed when you loaded ActivePerl earlier.) If you're connected through a proxy, you'll need to set the Win32 environment variable *HTTP_proxy* to the name of your proxy server. You may also need to set the variables *HTTP_proxy_user* and *HTTP_proxy_pass*, if your server requires a username and password. If you need additional information, check out this web site: *http://aspn.activestate.com//ASPN/Products/ActivePerl/faq/ActivePerl-faq2.html#ppm_and_proxies*

2. Now start up an MS-DOS window and type the PPM command shown here at the command-line prompt:

   ```
   C:\> ppm
   ```

   This will bring up the PPM program prompt.

3. Install the ActivePerl DBI package as follows:

   ```
   PPM> install DBI
   ```

4. When this completes, type:

   ```
   PPM> install DBD-Oracle8
   ```

   This should load the latest Oracle *DBD::Oracle* package.

5. Alternatively, if Oracle8 (or later) is unavailable on your system, you may wish to load a slightly earlier *DBD::Oracle* package instead:

   ```
   PPM> install DBD-Oracle
   ```

6. Your Perl DBI installation process should now be complete. You can quit and prepare for the heady excitement of the "Hello World" example coming up.

Getting the latest PPD files

For the very latest Perl DBI and *DBD::Oracle* packages on Win32, you can go beyond ActiveState and turn to a knight in shining armor, Ilya Sterin. Ilya regularly provides the latest binary compilations at the *http://xmlproj.com/PPM* web page. Check this site first! If the PPD files you're looking for are there, you can run the following PPM commands to obtain the very latest DBI and *DBD::Oracle* downloads:

```
DOS> ppm
PPM> remove DBD::Oracle
PPM> remove DBI
PPM> set repository XMLPROJ http://xmlproj.com/PPM/
PPM> install DBI-1_20
PPM> install DBD-Oracle-1_12
PPM> quit
```

Running Perl DBI

Would this book be complete without a "Hello World" example? Of course not, so here goes! Our very simple Perl DBI script (in Example 2-1) will simply connect to the *orcl* Oracle database as the *scott* user, run through a straightforward SQL cursor on the DUAL table via a prepared statement, and then print out the result before logging off. We'll run the same script on both Unix and Win32 to demonstrate Perl's operating system independence:

Example 2-1. Our first Perl DBI script, HelloWorld.pl

```perl
#!perl -w
use strict;
use DBI;
# Connect to Oracle database, making sure AutoCommit is
# turned off and potential errors are raised.

my $dbh = DBI->connect( 'dbi:Oracle:orcl', 'scott', 'tiger',
                        { RaiseError => 1, AutoCommit => 0 } );
# Create the SQL.

my $sql = qq{ SELECT 'Hello World' FROM DUAL };

# Prepare the SQL and execute.

my $sth = $dbh->prepare( $sql );
$sth->execute();

# Fetch output rows into array, plus prepare a
# print formatter for the results.

while ( my($helloWorldString) = $sth->fetchrow_array) {

    # Print out the result.

    print $helloWorldString, "\n";
}
$dbh->disconnect();  # Disconnect
```

Example 2-1 may look a little scary, but after reading Appendix B, you'll quickly be able to reduce it to the following:

```perl
#!perl -w

use strict;
use DBI;

my $dbh = DBI->connect( 'dbi:Oracle:orcl', 'scott', 'tiger',
                        { RaiseError => 1, AutoCommit => 0 } );

print $dbh->selectrow_array(qq{ SELECT 'Hello World' FROM DUAL });

$dbh->disconnect();
```

Note the following about Example 2-1:

- If you know some Perl already, you may notice how we've only imported the DBI module, within the script, via Perl's *use* command. The Perl DBI package takes care of picking up *DBD::Oracle*, for us when we run the *DBI->connect* call. (The *dbi:Oracle:orcl* parameter string cleverly indicates that we want to use *DBD::Oracle* rather than any other database driver.)
- You may also wish to change the *orcl*, *scott*, and *tiger* information strings to something more appropriate for your own target database before running the program.

Before we run this script under either Unix or Win32, we need to do the following:

1. Make sure *ORACLE_HOME* is set within the command shell environment, to ensure that the *DBD::Oracle* driver can locate the OCI libraries.
2. Make sure the target database is up and ready.
3. Check that the relevant database listener is up and running; you can do this by trying to connect to the target database via a remote SQL*Plus session.

We should now be ready to run the *HelloWorld.pl* Perl script under both Unix and Win32.

Running a Perl Script on Unix

Follow these steps to run a Perl script on a Unix system:

1. Log in to Unix as the Oracle user. If necessary with your particular version of Unix, make sure that the *LD_LIBRARY_PATH* environment variable is set correctly by adding *$ORACLE_HOME/lib* to it.
2. Make sure the Perl executable program is within your PATH:

   ```
   $ type perl
   ```
   This should return something similar to the following:

   ```
   perl is hashed (/usr/bin/perl)
   ```
3. Ensure that you're in the directory where you've written the *HelloWorld.pl* script.
4. Now simply type:

   ```
   $ perl HelloWorld.pl
   ```
   (You may want to use the optional *-w* flag, as in *perl -w HelloWorld.pl*, to make explicit any warnings.)

   If you make the *HelloWorld.pl* file executable, you can also use the shebang syntax on line 1, *#!perl -w*, to run the program directly:

   ```
   $ chmod +x HelloWorld.pl
   $ ./HelloWorld.pl
   ```

5. The resulting output should be:

```
Hello World
```

OK, so it's lacking in wild inspiration, but from little acorns grow. You can see our output in Figure 2-3, along with the corresponding Win32 version.

Running a Perl Script on Win32

Follow these steps to run a Perl script on a Win32 system:

1. Go to the directory where you've created the *HelloWorld.pl* script (or copied it) from your Unix system.

```
C:\> cd Perl\eg
```

2. Enter the following:

```
C:\Perl\eg> perl HelloWorld.pl
```

(Some Win32 systems associate the *.pl* suffix with the Perl interpreter, which means that you may be able to drop the use of the explicit *perl* command.)

3. You should now see the following output generated:

```
Hello World
```

Again, this is demonstrated in Figure 2-3.

Now we can break out the bubbly!

DBI by Proxy

One of *DBD::Oracle*'s major limitations is its reliance on the presence of *at least* Oracle client libraries for successful compilation. Indeed, here's what the Version 1.12 *DBD::Oracle README* file has to say:

> Install enough Oracle software to enable *DBD::Oracle* to build. That usually includes Pro*C. That's not very specific because it varies so much between Oracle releases.

If you have an Oracle server but no client machines possessing on-board Oracle software, this is a problem. It's also a problem if you have a client firewall that *DBD::Oracle* fails to break through. Fear not, for there is a potential solution at hand—Jochen Wiedmann's amazing *DBI::ProxyServer* and *DBD::Proxy* module set, which comes automatically within the DBI tarball. For DBI 1.20, you can read about both modules here:

http://search.cpan.org/doc/TIMB/DBI-1.20/lib/DBI/ProxyServer.pm
http://search.cpan.org/doc/TIMB/DBI-1.20/lib/DBD/Proxy.pm

(Try searching on *http://search.cpan.org* if these version-specific documents have been superseded.)

The idea is to set up a proxy server daemon, *dbiproxy*, that runs on your Oracle server machine. On your remote clients, you use *DBD::Proxy* instead of *DBD::*

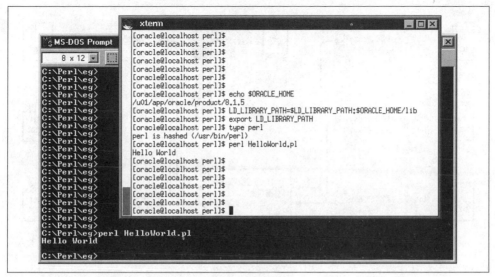

Figure 2-3. HelloWorld.pl running under Win32 and Unix

Oracle. This module connects across the network to the *dbiproxy* daemon, which passes through the SQL requests to a server-configured *DBD::Oracle* driver, thereby allowing proxy access to the Oracle database. This setup is displayed in Figure 2-4.

In order to use the ProxyServer system over a network, we need to install several Perl packages:

- *Storable* (as used by the following *PlRPC* packages); you can find this at *http://www.cpan.org/authors/id/KWILLIAMS*.
- *Net::Daemon.*
- *PlRPC* (which contains the *RPC::PlServer* and *RPC::PlClient* subpackages).

You can find these at *http://www.cpan.org/authors/id/JWIED*.

Installing Cygwin

Cygwin is a free, open source Win32 porting layer for Unix applications, originally developed by Cygnus Solutions (now a part of Red Hat, Inc.) The Cygwin library brings to Windows the Unix system calls and environment that Unix programs expect. This makes it fairly easy to port Unix applications to Win32 without having to make extensive changes to the source code.

Cygwin is an increasingly popular solution for Win32 users who want at least occasional access to the compilers, scripts, and favorite Unix commands (e.g., *grep*, *ps*, *sed*) that their Unix counterparts take for granted. Of course, Linux is often a viable choice for PC users, but many of those users aren't willing to give up Microsoft Word, Excel, and the other standard Windows programs. Cygwin is a nice compro-

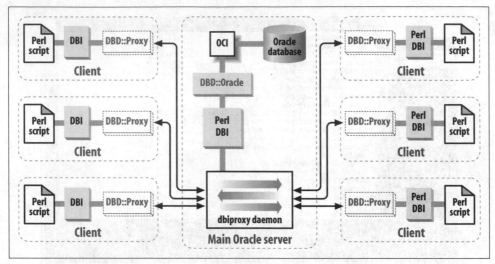

Figure 2-4. DBI:ProxyServer and DBD::Proxy architecture

mise. You can install it and have it available when you need to run a Unix program, without completely changing your environment. It's like having an extra driver in your bag of golf clubs; you may not need it all the time, but every now and then it is awfully useful!

If you're going to be using Perl on a Win32 platform, you may find Cygwin particularly useful. Because the *gcc* compiler comes with Cygwin, you'll be able to compile Perl, Perl DBI, and/or *DBD::Oracle* from source if you wish, rather than having to use the prebuilt binaries available from ActiveState. That way, you can customize Perl as needed to suit your own environment. And Cygwin also extends your reach; some of the Oracle applications we describe in this book, such as *Oracle::OCI* described in Chapter 7, *Invoking the Oracle Call Interface with Oracle::OCI*, or the latest XML parsers described in Appendix D (and many other open source applications as well), are yet to be available as Win32 executables. New Perl modules requiring C libraries don't tend to be available on ActivePerl for some time because of the required development lead-in time. You can keep ahead of the game with Cygwin.

You can learn much more about Cygwin at:

   http://www.cygwin.com

Installing Perl under Cygwin

First of all, visit the *http://www.cygwin.com* site and check out the latest download instructions for Cygwin. These are continuously updated to ease Cygwin's installation, which gets easier by the month. The following are the steps we took to install the latest version available to us:

---

1. Create a new directory on your PC that's ready for the Cygwin downloads:

```
C:\>mkdir cygwin
C:\>cd cygwin
C:\cygwin>
```

2. Download the setup program. Instead of downloading a single massive tarball, we chose to download *setup.exe*, a sort of traffic-cop program designed to direct the rest of the installation proper, in a manner conceptually similar to the Perl *configure* program. We got hold of *setup.exe* from this URL:

   http://www.cygwin.com/setup.exe

3. Run the setup program. Once we had downloaded *setup.exe*, we ran the program by double-clicking it inside the *C:\cygwin* directory in Windows Explorer. The first screen we saw is shown on the left in Figure 2-5.

4. We then pressed *Next->*, taking us to the screen on the right in Figure 2-5, which provided a range of three options. We decided to download our required packages from the Internet, and then install them later—you may prefer to install directly from the Internet. Choose the approach that suits you best.

5. We then moved progressively through the screens in Figures 2-6, choosing Internet Explorer *IE5* settings, to overcome any potential proxy difficulties. As before, you may prefer alternative options.

6. The next stage was the pop-up list of Cygwin mirrors, shown on the left side in Figure 2-7. All the Cygwin packages, shortly to be downloaded, come from one of these mirrors.

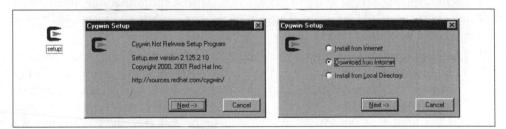

Figure 2-5. First steps—Setting up Cygwin

Figure 2-6. Determining download locations and options

7. After we chose a convenient mirror, the main package selection screen appeared. Note that the *setup.exe* program will *already* have worked out the absolute base set of packages you need to get Cygwin up and running. The rest are optional.

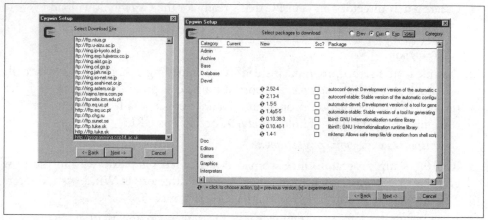

Figure 2-7. Choosing download packages

To get a real development environment going, we need more than the economy model cup-holder allocation of one for the driver. We need swing-out tables, portable showers, and a whole army of oil-damped cup-holders, all over the vehicle!

8. Click on the *Category* name tags of the main package selection screen shown in Figure 2-7. These include *Admin*, *Archive*, *Base*, *Database*, and *Devel*. Go ahead. Open them all up. In the early days, Cygwin used to be a single download, but it took 3.9812 eons to bring back the whole caboodle over a home Internet connection. A single rogue disconnection could lose the entire shooting match, forcing you to start all over again. Thankfully, the various bits and pieces of Cygwin are now available as separate items.

9. The packages we recommend you choose for a minimalist Perl-based development environment are detailed in Table 2-1. In compiling this list, we've tried to identify what's truly necessary and what's nice to have, balancing both against the restrictions of bandwidth. The safest bet, if you have both the time to spare and the hard disk capacity available, is to simply get *everything*. (If you don't have time or space for that now, though, you can always pick up the missed packages later on. Cygwin's *setup.exe* program is clever enough to determine what you've already got, and what you need. In addition, it will even flag the latest versions of programs as they become available on the Cygwin home site.)

Table 2-1. Cygwin packages for Perl development

Category	Packages required
Base	All
Devel	All
Editors	*vim*—*vi* Improved (not that we're die-hard *vi* fanatics, but we do need a text editor)

Table 2-1. Cygwin packages for Perl development (continued)

Category	Packages required
Graphics	All (for possible use with *DBD::Chart* and other Perl-based graphics packages that rely on these libraries)
Interpreters	Perl (fairly essential, this one)
Libs	All (although in a crunch you may want to come back later for the OpenGL, OpenSSL, and Tcl/Tk libraries; make sure you *do* get all the Win32 libraries)

10. To save further time and hard disk space, you may want to avoid selecting the source code options until you need to dig down into programs of interest later on.

11. Once you've selected what you want, click on *Next->* on the main packages selection screen in Figure 2-7, and let the download begin. At this point, you may need to go to your Win32 *Start* bar at the bottom of the screen in order to bring up the minimized Cygwin progress window—it may have disappeared behind all your other windows. Cygwin's *setup.exe* will now weave its gold and silvery magic, while we go for a nice hot cup of tea, or some other alkaloid-based stimulant.

12. Once we're back, and Cygwin has done its stuff, we just need to do a little housekeeping. Those who downloaded the packages, rather than installing directly, will have to rerun the first stages of the *setup.exe* process. This time, we install from locally supplied packages instead of downloading from the Internet. Installation should then take place, as shown in Figure 2-8.

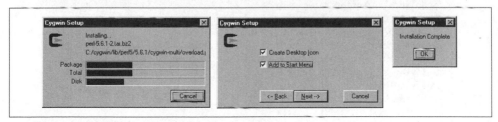

Figure 2-8. Completing the Cygwin installation

13. At some point, you should also have been asked if you wanted Cygwin to be added to the *Start* menu and a Cygwin shortcut placed on the desktop, as in the center screen of Figure 2-8. Once these options are installed, use either route to bring up a Cygwin shell window. For good measure, check to see if Perl has been installed as expected. You can do this with the following command:

```
$ perl -v
```

Perl should now be confirmed as available under Cygwin, and we should have a full GNU-like development environment for compiling both DBI and *DBD:: Oracle*.

Unix-like file security is only possible for Cygwin under NTFS partitions on the various Windows NT-related platforms. To effectively use file security commands such as *chmod*, you also need to add the *ntsec* flag to the *CYGWIN* environment variable—for example:

```
$ export CYGWIN="$CYGWIN ntsec"
```

You can read more about the *CYGWIN* variable and its many other options at *http://cygwin.com/cygwin-ug-net/using-cygwinenv.html*.

Installing Perl DBI under Cygwin

Follow these steps to install Perl DBI under Cygwin:

1. Download the latest Perl DBI and *DBD::Oracle* tarballs to *C:\cygwin* from:

   http://www.cpan.org/authors/id/TIMB

2. Now unpack the DBI tarball (once again, we used Version 1.20):

   ```
   $ gzip -d DBI-1.20.tar.gz
   $ tar xvf DBI-1.20.tar
   $ cd DBI-1.20
   ```

3. Next, compile DBI:

   ```
   $ make
   ```

4. You may get a few warnings with *make* under Cygwin, but everything should still be OK, as the *DBI.dll* file should get compiled as necessary. The final part of the output should look something like this:

   ```
   ...
   cp dbish blib/script/dbish
   /usr/bin/perl -I/usr/lib/perl5/5.6.1/cygwin-multi
   -I/usr/lib/perl5/5.6.1 -MExtUt
   ils::MakeMaker -e "MY->fixin(shift)" blib/script/dbish
   Manifying blib/man3/DBI.ProxyServer.3
   Manifying blib/man3/DBD.Proxy.3
   Manifying blib/man3/DBI.Format.3
   Manifying blib/man1/dbish.1
   Manifying blib/man3/DBI.Shell.3
   Manifying blib/man3/DBI.3
   Manifying blib/man3/DBI.FAQ.3
   Manifying blib/man3/Bundle.DBI.3
   Manifying blib/man3/Win32.DBIODBC.3
   Manifying blib/man1/dbiproxy.1
   Manifying blib/man3/DBI.W32ODBC.3
   Manifying blib/man3/DBI.DBD.3

   $
   ```

5. Now test and install:

   ```
   $ make test
   $ make install
   ...
   ```

```
Writing /usr/lib/perl5/site_perl/5.6.1/cygwin-multi/auto/DBI/.packlist
Appending installation info to /usr/lib/perl5/5.6.1/cygwin-multi/perllocal.pod

$
```

We're done!

Installing DBD::Oracle under Cygwin

The installation of *DBD::Oracle* is a little more involved than that of Perl DBI. Follow these steps:

1. Unpack as usual:

   ```
   $ cd C:/cygwin
   $ gzip -d DBD-Oracle-1.12.tar.gz
   $ tar xvf DBD-Oracle-1.12.tar
   $ cd DBD-Oracle-1.12
   ```

2. Read through some important *README* information, particularly the *README.wingcc* file:[*]

   ```
   $ vi README README.win32 README.wingcc
   ```

3. Create the *liboci.a* file, as instructed in *README.wingcc*, and place it somewhere such that Cygwin's *make* compilation utilities can find it later on, such as */usr/local/lib*. We did this via the following steps:

   ```
   $ cd C:/cygwin/DBD-Oracle-1.12
   $ dlltool --input-def oci.def --output-lib liboci.a
   $ ls -la liboci.a
   -rw-r--r--    1 andyd None       260806 Dec 28 14:40 liboci.a
   $ mv liboci.a /usr/local/lib
   ```

4. The required definitions archive is now available for other compilation tools, such as *make*, to view. Before beginning compilation, however, make sure that you can access all of the required Oracle client libraries, especially for the *make test* step. Change values where appropriate:

   ```
   $ ORACLE_HOME=C:/ORANT
   $ export ORACLE_HOME
   $ ORACLE_SID=orcl
   $ export ORACLE_SID
   $ ORACLE_USERID=scott/tiger@orcl
   $ export ORACLE_USERID
   ```

5. Because ActivePerl is the usual Win32 environment for DBI, Cygwin compilation can sometimes lag slightly behind other more typical Unix-style operating systems. For instance, the latest flavor of *DBD::Oracle* available at the time we carried out this installation was DBD-Oracle-1.12. This had slightly altered an older part of the *Makefile.PL* file from DBD::Oracle 1.08, a version we knew

---

[*] Those new to the *vi* editor can read some great help pages at *http://www.vim.org/html/quickref.html* and *http://www.vim.org/html/help.html*.

would compile without problems. The old code in *Makefile.PL* from *DBD:: Oracle* 1.08 was:

```
die qq{ The $ORACLE_ENV environment variable value ($OH) is not valid.
   It must be set to hold the path to an Oracle installation directory
   on this machine (or a compatible archtecture).
   See the README.clients file for more information.
   ABORTED!
} unless -d $OH;
```

This had become updated to:

```
die qq{ The $ORACLE_ENV environment variable value ($OH) is not valid.
   It must be set to hold the path to an Oracle installation directory
   on this machine (or a compatible archtecture).
   See the README.clients file for more information.
   ABORTED!
} unless (($os eq 'VMS') ? -d $OH : -d "$OH/lib/.");
```

Notice the more complex *unless* condition. Although the rest of our Cygwin compilation will look for important locations, such as */lib*, under *$ORACLE_ HOME/OCI80*, the code shown previously prechecks its location directly under *$ORACLE_HOME*, where it will fail to find it under certain Oracle versions. It then aborts the build operation. (This is version-specific however, and anything after Oracle8*i* Version 8.1.5 seems to revert back to the Unix-style directory structures.)

 You'll probably have no problems of your own. This is just an example of the kind of thing you have to look out for, especially if you use earlier versions of Oracle.

6. To get around this problem, we commented out the previous section in *Makefile. PL* and set it to this:

```
#die qq{ The $ORACLE_ENV environment variable value ($OH) is not valid.
#   It must be set to hold the path to an Oracle installation directory
#   on this machine (or a compatible archtecture).
#   See the README.clients file for more information.
#   ABORTED!
#} unless (($os eq 'VMS') ? -d $OH : -d "$OH/lib/.");
```

OK, this hack lacks splendor, but it does remove an immediate problem, and we're confident that it doesn't create other problems elsewhere. You may have your own little niggles to solve too, but ice-cool code warrior perseverance will see you through.

7. We can now begin the compilation run:

```
$ perl Makefile.PL
```

8. This produces rather "interesting" output:

```
Using DBI 1.20 installed in
/usr/lib/perl5/site_perl/5.6.1/cygwin-multi/auto/DBI
```

```
    Configuring DBD::Oracle ...

>>>       Remember to actually *READ* the README file!
          Especially if you have any problems.

Using Oracle in C:/ORANT
Can't stat C:/ORANT/rdbms: No such file or directory
I can't find the header files I need in your Oracle installation.
You probably need to install some more Oracle components.
I'll keep going, but the compile will probably fail.
See README.clients for more information.
Found OCI80 directory
Using OCI directory 'OCI80'
Using liboci.a  (did you build it?)
System: perl5.006001 cygwin_nt-4.0 loreley 1.3.2(0.3932)
2001-05-20 23:28 i686 unknown
Compiler:   gcc -O2 -DPERL_USE_SAFE_PUTENV -fno-strict-aliasing
-I/usr/local/inc
lude
Linker:     /usr/bin/ld
Sysliblist:

Warning: If you have problems you may need to rebuild perl with
-Uusemymalloc.
Checking if your kit is complete...
Looks good
LD_RUN_PATH=/usr/local/lib
Using DBD::Oracle 1.12.
Using DBI 1.20 installed in
/usr/lib/perl5/site_perl/5.6.1/cygwin-multi/auto/DBI
Writing Makefile for DBD::Oracle

***  If you have problems...
     read all the log printed above, and the README
     and README.help files.
     (Of course, you have read README by now anyway, haven't you?)
```

At first, this looks a little ugly, especially the fact that *C:/ORANT/rdbms* does not exist! Did we cause this with our hack? No, the preceding is absolutely fine and to be expected. We can ignore the *C:/ORANT/rdbms* problem—the compilation will later find everything it needs under *C:/ORANT/OCI80/include*. These kinds of warnings are only here because of the strange hybrid nature of a Unix-style Cygwin running on a Win32 box, with its own particular complexities.

9. We're now ready for compilation, with *make*—though did you also notice that reminder about *liboci.a*? Note also that the LD_RUN_PATH is set to */usr/local/lib*. This is where we should have placed *liboci.a*. Now let's go for the compilation:

    ```
    $ make
    ```

10. Again, we'll get more warnings than is usual under Unix, but as long as the *liboci.a* file is in */usr/local/lib* (or possibly */usr/lib*, if this should fail to work),

there should be no real worries, and the correct *Oracle.dll* file should be produced. It is possible, however, that you might encounter OCI8 problems because the latest Oracle client libraries may be unavailable. For example, if you get errors saying that certain OCI definitions are undeclared (such as *OCI_HTYPE_* and **OCI_DTYPE_** values), you should check to see if they're declared in *oci.h*, which should be under the following directory:

   $ORACLE_HOME/OCI80/include

If they're undeclared, you'll have two choices. You can either get more up-to-date Oracle client libraries or go back a step and run the following commands, which allow you to use the older Oracle7-style OCI libraries:

```
$ make clean
$ perl Makefile.PL -8
$ make
```

If the rogue definitions are declared in *oci.h*, you may need to check that the generated *Makefile* is including the appropriate C header file directories. More debug details should be available within the online *DBD::Oracle* documentation, which comes with the tarball.

11. Once we've got everything ship shape, we can then run the two final installation instructions:

```
$ make test
$ make install
```

We should then be able to run the program in Example 2-2, which is illustrated in Figure 2-9. We ran it with the following command:

```
$ perl cygwinDBI.pl
```

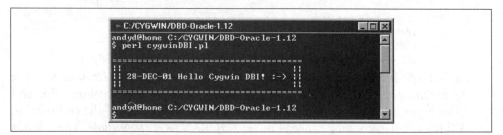

Figure 2-9. Perl DBI running under Cygwin

Example 2-2. Running DBI under Cygwin—cygwinDBI.pl

```
#!perl -w

use strict;
use DBI;

my $dbh = DBI->connect('DBI:Oracle:orcl', 'scott', 'tiger',
                       {RaiseError => 1, AutoCommit => 0} );
my $msg =
```

Example 2-2. Running DBI under Cygwin—cygwinDBI.pl (continued)

```
    $dbh->selectrow_array(
        "SELECT SYSDATE || ' Hello Cygwin DBI! :-)' message FROM DUAL"
                            );
# Lets have some formatting fun! :-)

my $msg_len = length( $msg );
$underline = '=' x ($msg_len + 6);

print "\n", $underline, "\n",
"|| ", ' ' x $msg_len, " ||", "\n",
"|| ", $msg, " ||", "\n",
"|| ", ' ' x $msg_len, " ||", "\n",
$underline, "\n\n";

$dbh->disconnect;
```

To further investigate some of the formatting operations shown in Example 2-2, try the following command to see the Perl online documentation (and see Appendix A for a full description of *perldoc*):

```
$ perldoc perlop
```

Now that Perl is well and truly on board, we're ready to sail out from the Perl havens and head towards an open sea of exploration and destiny. In the next few chapters, we'll examine a variety of Perl modules that extend the combined power of Perl and Oracle.

And Then There's DJGPP

In case Cygwin isn't enough for you and you're still feeling a little cramped creatively, yet another open source Win32 GNU compilation environment is available. This is DJGPP (which stands for DJ Delorie's GNU Programming Platform), a toolset related in spirit to Cygwin. You can learn more about it at:

http://www.delorie.com/djgpp/

There's even an online Perl document dedicated to building DJGPP Perl under DOS:

```
$ perldoc perldos
```

You may wish to give DJGPP a try; in Perl, there really is always more than one way to do it!

This second part of the book describes a wide variety of Perl modules and applications that Oracle DBAs will find helpful. It consists of the following chapters:

Chapter 3, *Perl GUI Extensions*, describes Perl/Tk, an extensive GUI-based toolkit for Perl, as well as a number of applications that provide Oracle DBAs with graphically oriented tools for performing database administration. In addition to Perl/Tk, this chapter covers OraExplain, StatsView, Orac, *DDL::Oracle*, SchemaDiff, Senora, *DBD::Chart*, SchemaView-Plus, and a variety of Perl GUI integrated development environments (IDEs) and debuggers.

Chapter 4, *Perl Web Extensions*, discusses the relationship between Perl and the Apache web server, and focuses on two Oracle applications that use a web browser as their user interface: Oracletool and Karma.

Chapter 5, *Embedding Perl into Apache with mod_perl*, explains how the use of Apache's *mod_perl* module can greatly improve the performance of Perl web-based CGI (Common Gateway Interface) scripts used with Oracle. This chapter also covers several related Apache modules: *Apache::Registry*, *Apache::DBI*, and *Apache::OWA* (used to connect *mod_perl* to Oracle's PL/SQL Web Toolkit).

Chapter 6, *Embedded Perl Web Scripting*, describes two applications, Embperl and Mason, that demonstrate the advantages of embedded scripting, a method that allows Perl code to be embedded within web pages. These tools provide a mechanism for filling your production web pages with dynamic Oracle data and creating your own Oracle web tools, while separating content from design issues.

Chapter 7, *Invoking the Oracle Call Interface with Oracle::OCI*, covers *Oracle::OCI*, a Perl module that provides a more extensive interface to *Oracle's OCI* than is possible with Perl DBI.

Chapter 8, *Embedding Perl into PL/SQL*, discusses *extproc_perl*, a Perl module that communicates with the Oracle PL/SQL language's external procedure C library system (known as EXTPROC). This module and the others described here allow Perl code to be embedded directly in PL/SQL programs.

## CHAPTER 3

Perl GUI Extensions

In Chapter 2, *Installing Perl*, we looked at standard Perl and its database connectivity module, Perl DBI. The command-line interface available in Perl and Perl DBI has served developers well for many years. But over time, people have become more accustomed to graphical user interfaces (GUIs), and there has been a movement towards GUI facilities for Perl. Oracle DBAs in particular appreciate applications that give them an easy-to-use graphical interface for managing their databases and a way to visually inspect difficult-to-interpret database data. In this chapter we'll look at Perl/Tk, an extensive GUI-based toolkit, as well as at a number of applications (many of them based on Perl/Tk) that provide Oracle DBAs with the graphical interfaces they find so useful. We'll cover:

Perl/Tk
   A popular toolkit often used to build GUIs in Perl for both Unix and Win32.

OraExplain
   A Perl/Tk SQL tuning tool for Oracle that explains SQL execution plans. OraExplain was the first major canned application that combined Perl DBI and Perl/Tk for Oracle. It also inspired many other Perl/Tk applications.

StatsView
   A statistics-gathering tool written in Perl/Tk for Oracle DBAs who also perform Unix system administration. This tool collects all kinds of useful statistics and then displays them in enhanced graphical format, courtesy of the *gnuplot* program.

Orac
   A GUI wrapper program built using Perl/Tk that provides a useful way to maintain a repository of configurable SQL scripts for interrogating and managing Oracle databases.

DDL::Oracle
   A nongraphical Perl package that reverse-engineers Data Definition Language (DDL) statements. This back-end Oracle package often drives Perl/Tk scripts in order to help them provide visual DDL aids for Oracle DBAs.

SchemaDiff

A Perl package built on *DDL::Oracle* and Perl/Tk that compares different Oracle schemas.

Senora

An interactive Oracle shell program that provides a flexible and extensible alternative to SQL*Plus.

DBD::Chart

A Perl driver interface that renders graphs and charts. *DBD::Chart* is another excellent supplementary module for visualizing complex information; it is often used to generate back-end images for use by Perl/Tk.

SchemaView-Plus

Another program built on Perl/Tk that compares different Oracle schemas. This program is also built on the Perl DBIx extension, *DBIx::SystemCatalog*.

Perl IDEs and GUI debuggers

Open source integrated development environments providing graphical interfaces for editing and debugging Perl code.

In the next chapter, we'll move on to look at the Perl extensions and applications that use the Web, rather than custom-built GUIs, as their user interface.

Perl/Tk

The Perl/Tk module, developed Nick Ing-Simmons, is one of the most popular and useful of the Perl extension modules. Perl/Tk is a toolkit that gives Perl the ability to create interactive and full-fledged GUI-driven applications. Writing GUIs can be complex, but Perl/Tk makes it easy by making available standardized libraries of reusable GUI code (widgets and controls) that you can select as appropriate.

For those interested in writing Oracle DBA GUI applications of their own, we'll try to cover all the bases in this chapter, but we'll mostly focus on the tools currently available for those simply looking for ready-to-use database administration and tuning programs. For more information on generic Perl/Tk issues, these are the online and book resources we consider to be best:

http://www.lehigh.edu/~sol0/ptk/ptk.html

Stephen Lidie's central portal, for all things Perl/Tk.

http://www.perltk.org

Didier Ladner's central Perl/Tk resource.

http://www.oreilly.com/catalog/mastperltk

For those who prefer information in book form, we thoroughly recommend *Mastering Perl/Tk*, by Nancy Walsh and Stephen Lidie (O'Reilly & Associates, 2002). As one of us helped technically review this book, we must admit a bias, but it's the definitive text.

For a quick example of what Perl/Tk can do for you, take a look at the widgets demonstration program in Figure 3-1, which comes automatically with the Perl/Tk installation.

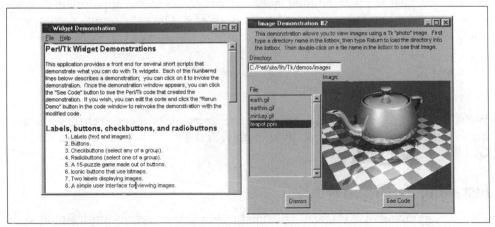

Figure 3-1. The Perl/Tk widget program's image interface

Installing Perl/Tk under Unix

As with virtually every other Perl module we'll discuss in this book, you can install Perl/Tk from the online CPAN system in the following way:

```
$ perl -MCPAN -e "shell"
cpan shell -- CPAN exploration and modules installation (v1.59_51)
ReadLine support enabled

cpan> install Tk <RETURN>
```

However, to gain far more control over the install and its tests, and to access all of the install information for the various Unix flavors, get hold of Perl/Tk's latest tarball from the following web site:

http://www.cpan.org/authors/id/NI-S

Once you've downloaded the CPAN source into the temporary directory of your choice, you can install Perl/Tk manually as follows (we've demonstrated this with the *Tk800.023.tar.gz* file):

```
$ gzip -d Tk800.023.tar.gz
$ tar xvf Tk800.023.tar
$ cd Tk800.023
```

Always comb religiously through the *README* and *INSTALL* files to make sure nothing special is required for your machine's setup:

```
$ vi README INSTALL
```

Once you're happy with your setup, you can proceed. Perl/Tk follows the usual pattern for installing most Perl modules. However, it is a large body of code, in comparison to most other Perl modules, so it often takes a few minutes to install, and you must ensure that the user running *make test* has access to the appropriate X Windows server, by running a command such as *xhost +*. Once the testing is complete, you'll also need to install Perl/Tk as *root*:

```
$ perl Makefile.PL
$ make
$ make test
$ make install
```

We're now all set! All that rigid command-line discipline is about to change. Assuming that the installation ran typically smoothly, Perl/Tk is now installed and ready to GUI.

Installing Perl/Tk on Win32

The corresponding ActiveState installation on Win32 is straightforward. Simply connect your PC to the Internet, as in Chapter 2, and then run through the following PPM commands, much as you did when installing Perl DBI and DBD-Oracle:

1. Fire up an MS-DOS command window and run PPM:

    ```
    C:\> ppm
    ```

2. Now install ActivePerl's remotely accessed Perl/Tk package by typing:

    ```
    PPM> install Tk
    ```

    This may take slightly longer to load than your average ActivePerl package, as it's very large, but should still only take a few minutes.

3. When the command completes, enter:

    ```
    PPM> quit
    ```

    Perl/Tk should now be installed.

Combining Perl/Tk and Perl DBI

To try Perl/Tk on for size, let's try searching for the widgets program demonstrated in Figure 3-1 as follows:

Unix

From the Perl/Tk installation location, look for the *../demos* directory, change directory into there, and then type *perl widget*.

Win32

Go to the *C:\Perl\bin* directory and type either *perl widget* or *widget.bat*.

Those of you who are rolling your own might like to run through Example 3-1. This follows the general Perl/Tk program algorithm shown in Figure 3-2.

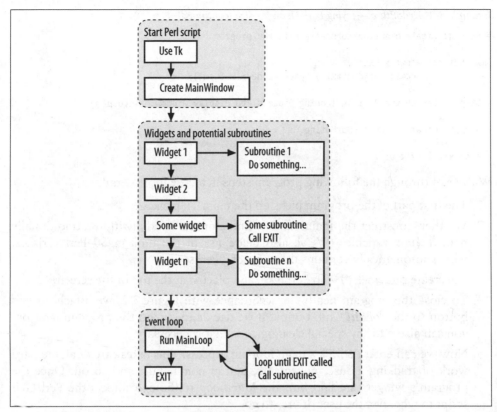

Figure 3-2. The basic structure of Perl/Tk programs

Example 3-1. HelloPtk.pl—trying Perl/Tk on for size

```perl
#!/usr/bin/perl

use strict;
use warnings;

# Step 1: Get hold of the main Perl/Tk package.

use Tk;

# Step 2: Create the Main Window.  Use the name of the program,
# held in the special Perl variable $0, to create the title.

my $mw = MainWindow->new(-title=>$0);

# Step 3: Pack a label onto the screen to hold our initial message.

$mw->Label(-text=> "Hello Perl/Tk", -anchor=>'center'
          )->pack(-side=>'top');
```

Example 3-1. HelloPtk.pl—trying Perl/Tk on for size (continued)

```
# Step 4: Create a button to neatly exit the program.

$mw->Button( -text=>'Exit',
            -command=>\&doExit )->pack(-side=>'bottom');

# Step 5: Launch the Perl/Tk looping process, to display window.MainLoop( );

# Step 6: Create an exit subroutine.

sub doExit { exit 0; }
```

We've run through the following program steps in a little more detail:

1. The first part of the program picks up the main Tk package.

2. We then construct the main window and store its handle within a traditionally named *$mw* variable. (We've also made use of the built-in *$0* Perl variable, which automatically contains the name of a Perl script.)

3. We create our label, "Hello Perl/Tk", and place it at the top of the screen.

4. To close the program neatly, in accordance with Figure 3-2, we attach an exit button to the *doExit( )* subroutine. If we decide to extend the program later on, you can also add any special cleanup code that is necessary.

5. Now we can enter Perl/Tk's main looping process. This takes care of all the hard work of tracking mouse movements, button commands, and so on. Once the program's widgets are laid out, the *MainLoop* traffic cop directs the Perl GUI script to wherever the user desires to go.

6. Finally, we code our special exit command. Although the exit subroutine is fairly basic in our prototype, you can place any necessary cleanup code here later on— for example, a graceful database disconnection. We run the program via the following command:

```
$ perl HelloPtk.pl
```

You can see *HelloPtk.pl* in action in Figure 3-3 on both Win32 and Unix.

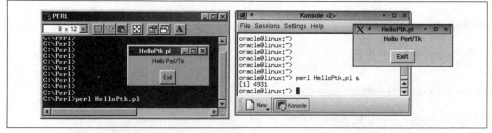

Figure 3-3. HelloPtk.pl under both Win32 and Linux

Exciting as *HelloPtk.pl* may be, both in looks and execution, the real fun begins when we start to combine Perl/Tk with Perl DBI. In Example 3-2 we've expanded

---

HelloPtk.pl to work out the time according to SYSDATE. You can see this program at work in Figure 3-4.

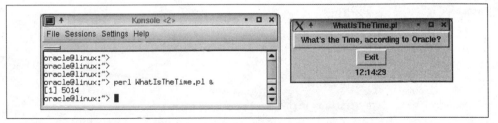

Figure 3-4. WhatIsTheTime.pl in action, under Unix

Example 3-2. WhatIsTheTime.pl—Combining Perl/Tk and Perl DBI

```perl
#!/usr/bin/perl

# Step 1: Get hold of the main Perl/Tk package, DBI, and set the
# Oracle Environment, plus set the database connection and SQL.

use Tk;
use DBI;
use strict;
use warnings;

my $dbh = DBI->connect( 'dbi:Oracle:orcl', 'scott', 'tiger',
                    { RaiseError=>1, AutoCommit=>0 } );
my $sql = qq{ SELECT TO_CHAR(SYSDATE, 'HH:MI:SS') FROM DUAL };

my $mw = MainWindow->new( -title=>$0);               # Set the main window up

# Step 2: Get the latest time from the Oracle database.

my oracleTime;

getTheOracleTime( );

# Step 3: Pack a simple button onto the screen, to ask Oracle for the
# current SYSDATE time.  Assign the appropriate callback.

$mw->Button(-text=>"What's the Time, according to Oracle?",
        -command=> \&getTheOracleTime )->pack(-side=>'top');

# Step 4: Pack a label onto the screen holding the SYSDATE time.

$mw->Label(-textvariable=> \$oracleTime, -anchor=>'center'
        )->pack(-side=>'bottom');
# Create another button to neatly exit the program.

$mw->Button( -text=>'Exit',
        -command=>\&doExit )->pack(-side=>'bottom');
```

Example 3-2. WhatIsTheTime.pl—Combining Perl/Tk and Perl DBI (continued)

```
# Launch the Perl/Tk looping process, to display the window! :-)

MainLoop();

# Step 5: Create the two required subroutines.

sub getTheOracleTime {
   my $sth = $dbh->prepare( $sql );
   $sth->execute();
   ($oracleTime) = $sth->fetchrow_array();
}
sub doExit {
   $dbh->disconnect();  # A clean and graceful disconnection 8-)
   exit;
}
```

In the following list we've indicated the main differences between this program and the original *HelloPtk.pl* skeleton:

1. We acquire Perl DBI, connect to the database, and create our SQL.

2. We call *getTheOracleTime()* to initialize the *$oracleTime* variable.

3. We create a button to call *getTheOracleTime()* and change the display.

4. We need to create a display label, referencing the *$oracleTime* variable. The text changes, as appropriate, whenever the call button is pressed.

5. Finally, we add the new *getTheOracleTime()* function and remember to disconnect cleanly from the database when the *doExit()* function is called.

6. We run the program by typing the following at the command line:

   ```
   $ perl WhatIsTheOracleTime.pl
   ```

Although this is a rather stripped-down example, it does show how easy it is to quickly combine Perl/Tk and Perl DBI in order to develop your own applications. Before you know it, you'll have built an entire collection of Perl/Tk widgets that do all sorts of wonderful things—and you'll fail to understand how you *ever* lived without them.

OraExplain

OraExplain, an Oracle tuning tool that DBAs can use to explain SQL execution plans and examine their SQL cache, was the first widely available tool that combined Perl/ Tk and Perl DBI. OraExplain was created by Alan Burlison, a Solaris kernel gatekeeper for Sun Microsystems, and Tim Bunce quickly added the original *ora_explain. pl* module to the *DBD::Oracle* driver download bundle. So when you obtain *DBD:: Oracle*, you'll get OraExplain automatically (at least if you're installing on Unix).

If you're on Win32 and using ActivePerl's DBD-Oracle8 package, you'll find that OraExplain fails to come with the download. However, you can get hold of the source bundle containing the precursor file, *ora_explain.PL,* from the following site:

http://www.cpan.org/authors/id/TIMB/

If you use WinZip or another decompression tool, you'll find the *ora_explain.PL* file within the main unload directory, as shown in Figure 3-5.

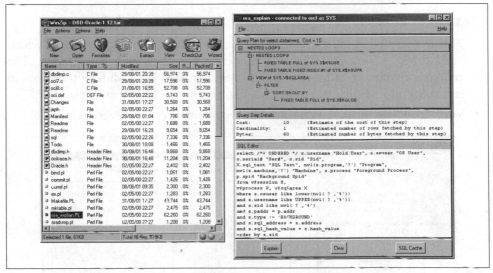

Figure 3-5. Finding and running OraExplain

Follow these installation steps:

1. Once you've extracted, or located, the *ora_explain.PL* precursor file, run the following command:

   ```
   $ perl ora_explain.PL
   ```

2. This extracts the actual *ora_explain* application. Now we can run it:

   ```
   $ perl ora_explain
   ```

   The rest of the steps should be fairly straightforward once you've connected to your target Oracle databases. Check out the program and consult the instructions provided with it if you need help.*

---

* The program may ask you to run the *utlxplan.sql* file, which is normally available from *$ORACLE_HOME/ rdbms/admin* (on Unix) or *%ORACLE_HOME%\rdbms\admin* (on Win32). This happens if the DBA user you've logged in as requires it to create the PLAN_TABLE object for EXPLAIN PLAN usage.

StatsView

After his triumph with OraExplain, Alan Burlison went on to create yet another superb Perl/Tk application, StatsView, a program designed for use by both system administrators and Oracle DBAs using Unix systems. If you serve both functions at your site, we feel confident that you'll love StatsView too. Although StatsView is aimed clearly at Solaris, the program's Oracle-based monitoring is equally applicable to other Unix operating systems, so we thought we'd install it on Linux to see how far we could push it.

Like many of the best things in life, StatsView comes with a few challenges:

- You have to preinstall the *gnuplot* command-driven plotting program, which itself relies on various C libraries, depending on how you configure it. The *gnuplot* program plots functions and data points in many different formats in either GIF or PNG image formats. See Figure 3-6 for a typical example.
- You'll also need an extra Perl/Tk module containing cutting-edge widgets.

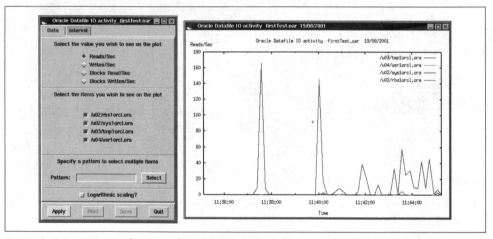

Figure 3-6. StatsView and some gathered tuning figures

Although installing StatsView requires some special challenges, it comes with a silver lining. In the course of getting StatsView to work, you'll have installed some of the best Perl and C libraries around for performing graphical information plotting on both Unix and Win32. Here's where you start going beyond Perl Imperial Trooper rank and start heading towards Perl Sith Lord status!

The first thing we need to do for StatsView is to get hold of the extended *Tk::GBARR* Perl/Tk module and layer it over the standard Perl/Tk Unix distribution. We'll describe that task and the other installation procedures in the following sections.

Installing Tk::GBARR

Although the main Perl/Tk download may seem to possess virtually all of the screen widgets you could possibly need, after a while you may require more specialized options. Many packages on CPAN provide additional functionality; check under the main */Tk* module directory on CPAN.

One of the most popular packages is Slaven Rezic's *Tk::GBARR* package, which contains many varied Perl/Tk widgets created by one of Perl/Tk's prime movers. Many of these widgets provide capabilities beyond those in standard Perl/Tk distributions. Most of the *Tk::GBARR* widgets, such as *Tk::ProgressBar*, do eventually become part of the standard distribution, but if you want to get ahead of the game, you can find *Tk::GBARR* at:

> *http://www.cpan.org/authors/id/SREZIC*

Follow these installation instructions:

1. Download and unpack the latest tarball from CPAN:

   ```
   $ gzip -d Tk-GBARR-2.05.tar.gz
   $ tar xvf Tk-GBARR-2.05.tar
   $ cd Tk-GBARR-2.05
   ```

2. Check for the latest notes, where to post potential errors, and so on, and then install the program in the usual manner. Once again, note that during the *make test* step you'll see lots of GUI examples popping up, albeit this time very briefly:

   ```
   $ vi README
   $ perl Makefile.PL
   $ make
   $ make test
   $ make install
   ```

3. Subject to our usual warnings that you must deal with any unlikely errors before going on, you can now consider *Tk::GBARR* to be installed, ready for use with StatsView.

Downloading StatsView

Get StatsView itself from the following location:

> *http://www.cpan.org/authors/id/ABURLISON*

Unpack it according to the standard cavalry drill:

```
$ gzip -d StatsView-1.4.tar.gz
$ tar xvf StatsView-1.4.tar
$ cd StatsView-1.4
```

The need for PNG

When we installed StatsView, we faced something of a dilemma. Although Stats-View assumes that *gnuplot* will use the GIF graphics file format, there are some reasons why you may prefer to use another format. GIF presents a problem because the Lempel Ziv Welch (LZW) algorithm that underlies the GIF format is patented (see the sidebar, "The LZW Patent Issue"). To avoid patent complications, many people prefer to use the freely available PNG* and JPEG† formats.

In fact, the PNG graphics format came about largely as a result of patent issues. Many people were interested in developing an alternative, freely available format that could be using in place of LZW. After an initial technical paper from Thomas Boutell describing a proposed format, a number of like-minded developers got together to work on the new format, culminating in Guy Eric Schalnat's creation of the *libpng* library.

To avoid patent issues ourselves, we'll load up the PNG library and its required compression companion, *zlib*, for use with *gnuplot*.

Installing zlib

Used by PNG to compress its graphics, *zlib* is an open data-compression library that has now been ported to virtually every kind of operating system. You can get hold of the latest *zlib* package, generally called *zlib.tar.gz*, from here:

> *http://www.gzip.org/zlib*
> *http://www.zlib.org*

Created originally for PNG, *zlib* is maintained by Jean-loup Gailly, the primary author of *gzip* (*http://www.gzip.org*), and *gzip* coauthor Mark Adler, the original author of Zip (*http://www.info-zip.org/pub/infozip*). Unsurprisingly, *zlib* is the back-end engine of the *gzip* program, decoupled and morphed into an independent library for other open source projects requiring compression (i.e., virtually everything using the Internet). *zlib* thus contains the same *lossless* deflationary compression algorithms employed by both Zip and *gzip*, and as originally used in PKWARE‡ (*http://www.pkware.com*). (For some help with compression terminology, see the sidebar, "Lossless versus Lossy," later in this chapter in the discussion of *DBD::Chart*.)

---

* You can find out much more about PNG (Portable Network Graphics) at the following page: *http://www.libpng.org/pub/png.*

† The Joint Photographic Experts Group designed this image standard, which is named for them. You can find out more at the following two sites: *http://www.ijg.org/*, and *http://www.jpeg.org.*

‡ PKWARE was founded in 1986 by Phil Katz, a pioneer of compression software, who developed the *.zip* file format in 1989. This inspired the Zip and GNU Zip (*gzip*) open source projects that use unpatented compression algorithms. These algorithms are an alternative to LZW, a patented algorithm used in the *compress* executables found with most proprietary Unix distributions. See the discussion in the sidebar, "The LZW Patent Issue."

To install *zlib*, run through the following steps to configure the *Makefile:*[*]

1. Decompress the original *zlib.tar.gz* tarball. This should unpack into a directory with a version number, such as *zlib-1.1.3* as follows:

```
$ gzip -d zlib.tar.gz
$ tar xvf zlib.tar
$ cd zlib-1.1.3
$ vi README
$ ./configure
```

Before compilation, make sure to read the *Makefile* to see whether you'd like to change any compile options:

```
$ vi Makefile
```

2. Once you're happy with *Makefile*, move straight into a tested compilation:

```
$ make test
```

You're trying to create an output response such as:

```
...
inflate with dictionary: hello, hello!
          *** zlib test OK ***
```

3. Now it's time to install:

```
$ make install
```

This copies *zlib.h* to */usr/local/include*, and the library archive *libz.a* to */usr/local/lib*. *zlib* is now accessible to other bodies of code that rely upon it, such as PNG.

Installing PNG

You can get hold of the latest *libpng* tarball from the following pages:

http://www.libpng.org/pub/png

1. We begin our dance with the usual introductions:

```
$ gzip -d libpng-1.0.12.tar.gz
$ tar xvf libpng-1.0.12.tar
$ cd libpng-1.0.12
$ vi README INSTALL
```

2. You'll find all sorts of *Makefile* versions in the */scripts* directory, for different Unix flavors. Choose your poison and copy it to the main download directory. Look it over carefully to ensure that it's right for your system:

```
$ cp scripts/makefile.linux makefile
$ vi makefile
```

3. Following the advice given within the file, we manually pointed the following variables at places matching our immediately previous installation of *zlib*:

---

[*] We install *zlib* and PNG automatically for Win32 later when we download ActivePerl's *GD.pm* module for use with *DBD::Chart*. This has the required binaries built in.

The LZW Patent Issue

Compression is the process that reduces the physical size of blocks of information. It is vital to storing and transmitting data, particularly graphics data and data being transferred over networks. A number of compression algorithms have been widely adopted. One of the most popular, the LZW (Lempel Ziv Welch) algorithm, is used in the GIF graphics file format, the Unix *compress* utility, and many other pieces of software.

LZW is named after its developers: Abraham Lempel and Jakob Ziv, who first proposed substitutional compression in 1977 and 1978, and Terry Welch who modified the LZ-78 variant to create the algorithm in 1984. Unisys acquired the patent on the compression algorithm that came to be known as LZW.

For many years, developers used the LZW algorithm freely. But on December 28, 1994 came an announcement by CompuServe that it would start trying to collect royalties on the use of the company's GIF graphics file format because of its underlying use of LZW. CompuServe and others had been under increasing pressure from Unisys, the LZW patent holder. With the popularization of the Web, use of GIF and other technologies using LZW were booming. Despite a lot of complaint and controversy among developers and users, Unisys' patent and licensing agreements held up. The company did compromise by not seeking fees on products using LZW that were delivered prior to 1995.

Ultimately, the LZW patent controversy led developers to seek out and develop their own compression algorithms and tools—for example, PNG and *zlib*.

```
ZLIBLIB=/usr/local/lib
ZLIBINC=/usr/local/include
```

Make sure you're also happy with the default installation file destinations:

```
prefix=/usr/local
INCPATH=$(prefix)/include
LIBPATH=$(prefix)/lib
```

4. Let's make and test PNG:

```
$ make test
```

Look for an output similar to the following:

```
...
 tIME = 7 Jun 1996 17:58:08 +0000
libpng passes test
```

5. Also check to make sure that the two PNG files produced by this installation, *pngtest.png* and *pngout.png*, are identical. You can view this PNG image in Figure 3-7; the image is also borrowed by the *Tk::PNG* installation we'll be doing later for Perl/Tk.

6. You'll find other assorted tests mentioned within the *INSTALL* file. Once you're happy with these, install PNG properly:

```
$ make install
```

All of the necessary libraries and include files should now go to */usr/local/include* and */usr/local/lib*, as with *zlib* earlier.

Figure 3-7. PNG, JPEG, and gd test images

Installing gnuplot

For all the latest information and downloads relating to *gnuplot*, check out:

http://www.gnuplot.info
http://sourceforge.net/projects/gnuplot

For GIF usage, *gnuplot* uses an old version of *gd*, which itself is no longer available from Thomas Boutell's *gd* site. This is because *gd* now only deals with PNG and JPEG images, which is why we're avoiding the use of GIFs with *gnuplot*.

In the future, the *gnuplot* team may be forced, for patent reasons, to withdraw the old *gd* downloads they maintain. They recommend that you switch to using PNG as soon as you can; most of the latest browser technologies now support PNG. (We'll be installing the more modern PNG-based *gd* program later, when we install Lincoln Stein's *GD.pm* program for use with Perl/Tk.)

1. Let's get straight into the installation game:

```
$ gzip -d gnuplot-3.7.1.tar.gz
$ tar xvf gnuplot-3.7.1.tar
$ cd gnuplot-3.7.1
```

2. Next, we check out the *0README* and *0INSTALL* files:

```
$ vi 0README 0INSTALL
```

3. Following their advice, we checked the *term/png.trm* file and found nothing problematic there. By default, the *gnuplot* compilation checks all the directories such as */usr/local/lib* and */usr/local/include*, where we'd installed our required PNG and *zlib* library files. We were able to configure without incident. Notice that we deliberately fail to include the old GIF-based *gd* program.

```
$ ./configure --without-gd --with-png
$ make
```

4. Optional tests are provided:

```
$ cd demo
$ ../gnuplot simple.dem
```

If the *../gnuplot simple.dem* step fails to work first time, and you're running an X11 display, it may be because *gnuplot* requires the currently uninstalled *gnuplot_x11* driver program. You may therefore have to update your PATH, unless you've previously installed an earlier *gnuplot* version:

```
$ PATH=`pwd`/..:$PATH
$ ../gnuplot simple.dem
```

(This test problem will resolve itself once you've fully installed *gnuplot*.)

5. Once *gnuplot* is executing successfully, you can run several other sample programs too from the same directory:

```
$ ../gnuplot fit.dem
```

6. Once you're happy with these demonstrations, install *gnuplot* under */usr/local/ bin*:

```
$ make install
```

Now we can get back to the StatsView installation directory.

Installing StatsView

Now we're back to more mainstream Perl territory. After the final *make install* step, StatsView produces a program called *sv*, which is placed into the */usr/local/bin* directory:

```
$ cd ..
$ perl Makefile.PL
$ make
$ make install
```

Now we can test this initial Linux-PNG setup in the following way:

1. First of all, the main */usr/local/bin/sv* program uses a Solaris-based *ps -ef* command to check whether the Oracle background processes are running. This command was unavailable on our Linux system, so we moved to */scripts* within the StatsView unload directory and copied the original *sv* program to a new one of our own, *lin_sv*.

```
$ cd scripts
$ cp sv lin_sv
```

We then edited this file to replace the *ps -ef* command with a *ps aux* one. You might like to try something similar on your own operating system, if you hit the same kind of OS-specific problem.

2. Before testing the program, also make sure that your target database is running with an appropriate listener.

3. Next, as the *root* user, create a statistical information storage directory:

```
$ pwd
$ mkdir StatsViewTest
```

4. Ensure that your environment is set correctly, especially *PATH*, to help *DBD:: Oracle* and your own system pick up the *sv* and *lin_sv* programs:

```
$ export ORACLE_HOME=/u01/app/oracle/product/8.1.5
$ export LD_LIBRARY_PATH=$ORACLE_HOME/lib
$ export PATH=.:/usr/local/bin:$PATH
```

5. Finally, we ran our slightly Linux-modified copy of the *sv* program:

```
$ cd scripts
$ ./lin_sv &
```

6. The first thing we did was set up a file for the monitor to store information in. We did this by clicking *Monitor*, then *Start*. On the resulting *Output* tab we selected an *Interval* of 10 seconds and a *Samples* rate of 60, and then pressed *Browse* to nominate a file in which to save the results (see Figure 3-8).

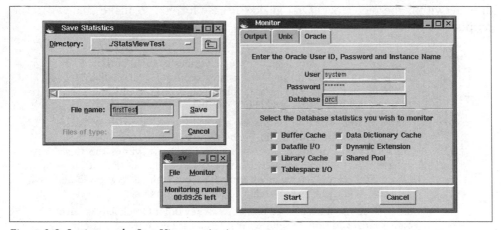

Figure 3-8. Setting up the StatsView monitoring process

7. We also chose all of these available monitoring options and then set the monitor going:

> Buffer Cache
> Datafile I/O
> Library Cache
> Tablespace I/O
> Data Dictionary Cache
> Dynamic Extension
> Shared Pool

After 10 minutes, the monitoring completed automatically. We then moved to the second stage of StatsView to graphically view the information collected:

1. Drill down onto the menu option, *File*, then *Open File...* to choose the nominated storage file.

2. Click down on whichever monitor option is of interest; we chose *Datafile I/O*. Now a *gnuplot* graph will appear (as in the earlier Figure 3-6).

Orac

Orac is a tool developed by one of your authors, Andy Duncan. It is based on Perl/Tk and its many widgets, and it employs Perl DBI to connect to the Oracle database. It is basically a GUI wrapper containing a large repository of prepared, configurable SQL scripts that allow Oracle DBAs to interrogate and manage their databases. Using Orac, users can rapidly apply these scripts to any target databases without having to copy them from one machine to another via complicated directory structure installs and environment variable setups. If these scripts are no longer up-to-date because of changes to the Oracle data dictionary, they can be modified or changed directly within the repository. Orac makes it easy for you to make changes to the scripts.

 Orac owes a great debt to many people besides its main author. Andy received early input from Dave Ensor, coauthor of *Oracle Design* (O'Reilly) and from Tim Bunce, chief creator of Perl DBI and coauthor of *Programming the Perl DBI* (O'Reilly).

Many of Orac's central scripts were based largely upon those packaged up by Brian Lomasky in his book, *Oracle Scripts*, for which he graciously gave permission for adaptation and use within the Orac program. As the program grew, Guy Harrison, author of the excellent *Oracle SQL: High Performance Tuning* (Prentice Hall), also allowed his very fine tuning scripts to be adapted for use within Orac.

Since Orac was first released on CPAN, many other Oracle DBAs have contributed additional useful scripts. Orac has become a real community effort.

Installing Orac

You can download the Orac tarball from here:

http://www.cpan.org/authors/id/A/AN/ANDYDUNC

Installing Orac on Unix

Once Orac has been downloaded, unpack it, and set the environment. Once this is completed, we can then simply run it with a single command:

```
$ gzip -d Orac-alpha-1.2.6.tar.gz
$ tar xvf Orac-alpha-1.2.6.tar
$ cd Orac-alpha-1.2.6
```

Before you actually run the program, make sure your environment can run both ordinary Perl DBI and Perl/Tk scripts. Ensure that *ORACLE_HOME* is set to make sure *DBD::Oracle* works correctly, underneath Perl DBI.

```
$ export ORACLE_HOME=/u01/oracle/8.1.5
```

Installing Orac on Win32

For Win32, simply unpack the tarball into its own directory with your favorite unzip program. If you have Perl DBI and Perl/Tk both working on your machine, Orac should be ready to fire up straight out of the box, once you've personalized it as described in the next section. (You may have to set *ORACLE_HOME* via the Registry, the system environment, or *AUTOEXEC.BAT* in order to get Perl DBI connecting to Oracle properly.)

Personalizing Orac

On a server system, Orac allows each of its users to save his or her own personalized options, such as font, background color, and so on. It then stores these in various locations depending upon the operating system:

Unix
    Your personal options are hidden within the *$HOME/.orac* directory.

Win32 (business systems with the USERPROFILE environment variable)
    Personal options are stored within the *%USERPROFILE%/orac* directory.

Win32 (home systems, without the USERPROFILE environment variable)
    Options are stored within the directory from which you launch Orac.

Alternatively, personal options can be stored in a named directory. To do this, set the following environment variable before running the program on Unix:

```
$ export ORAC_HOME=/my_personal_options_directory/orac_profile
```

To carry out a similar operation on Win32 (especially if you're on a non-*USERPROFILE* system like Win98), edit your *AUTOEXEC.BAT* file to preset your environment when booting up:

```
DOS> set ORAC_HOME=C:\Temp\Orac
```

Running Orac

Within the Win32 environment, double-click on the *orac_dba.pl* program icon, or on either Unix or Win32 command lines, run the following command:

```
$ perl orac_dbal.pl
```

Because Orac also works with other databases, the first time you log in to the program, choose Oracle as your default database. Following the subsequent user login dialog, you'll be given access to a wide range of menu-driven options designed for an Oracle DBA (see Figure 3-9) summarized in Table 3-1.

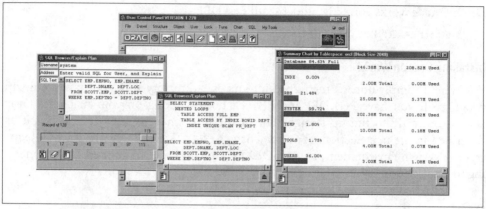

Figure 3-9. Some of the options under Orac

Table 3-1. Orac's main user options for Oracle DBAs

Main menu	Description
File	Provides individual user customizations and general program help.
Devel	Collection of GUI screens based on the *DDL::Oracle* API.
Structure	Options to access the current physical structure of the database.
Object	Daily DBA tasks and problem solving, such as DDL generation to create the entire database in a single script and PL/SQL debug options.
Lock	Investigates the various types of locking going on in a target database. Especially useful in panic stations.
Tune	Tuning options, including a SQL Cache Browser and physical IO graphs.
SQL	Gateway to Thomas Lowery's GUI shell program for direct database work.
My Tools	Facility for storing your own favorite DBA scripts and rerunning them as GUI reports driven by automatically generated buttons and menus.

DDL::Oracle

The *DDL::Oracle* back-end module developed by Richard Sutherland was initially designed to reverse-engineer Oracle DDL (Data Definition Language) from Oracle8*i* databases, although its functionality is expanding and the module now offers other additional features for Oracle DBAs. It currently resides on a SourceForge web site, but you can still get the latest tarball from the Perl CPAN site:

http://sourceforge.net/projects/ddl-oracle
http://www.cpan.org/authors/id/R/RV/RVSUTHERL

The *DDL::Oracle* object-oriented module is designed for use by other scripts (such as Orac or *debug.pl*, as we describe later), rather than as a standalone program. The SourceForge site also provides many of the facilities you'll find useful if you start using *DDL::Oracle* in a serious way with your own scripts (as we hope you will), including a mailing list:

ddl-oracle-users@lists.sourceforge.net

Installing DDL::Oracle on Unix

If you download *DDL::Oracle* directly, you can install it with the following steps:

```
$ gzip -d DDL-Oracle-1.10.tar.gz
$ tar xvf DDL-Oracle-1.10.tar
$ cd DDL-Oracle-1.10
$ vi README
```

The installation of *DDL::Oracle* follows the usual Perl pattern:

```
$ perl Makefile.PL
$ make
$ make test
$ make install
```

Once *DDL::Oracle* is installed, you can view its documentation from within the installation directory (see Appendix A, *The Essential Guide to Perl*, for much more information about the *perldoc* program):

```
$ perldoc DDL::Oracle
```

Using DDL::Oracle with Orac

You can use *DDL::Oracle* in many different ways, though mainly through other programs that make use of its facilities. The *DDL::Oracle* download bundle supplies a number of example scripts that can be used as templates for your own *DDL::Oracle*-scripts. We'll discuss some of these scripts—in particular, *defrag.pl,* in later sections, but first we'll show how *DDL::Oracle* is typically used within other programs. We'll start with Orac, which we introduced earlier in this chapter.

Example 3-3 shows how the Orac program uses *DDL::Oracle* to drive the *Devel* menu; note that all of the options you see here are direct mappings from *DDL:: Oracle*'s API. *DDL::Oracle* can create DDL for virtually every kind of object in the database and in many different ways (e.g., CREATE or DROP statements). To illustrate its use, we'll work through some cut-down code used to create the output in Figure 3-10.

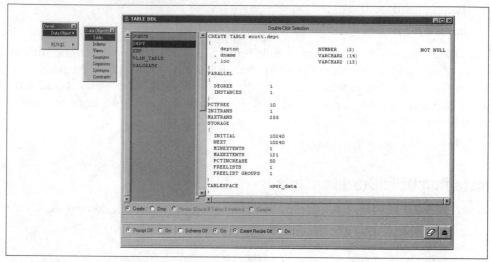

Figure 3-10. DDL::Oracle driving the Orac Devel menu

Example 3-3. Usage of DDL::Oracle within the Orac program

```perl
# Step 1: We bind the left-hand scroll list to the right-hand text
# screen.  If double-clicked, we go to the related subfunction.

$window->{text}->bind(
    '<Double-1>',    # Links a double-click to the command below
    sub{
            # Step 2: As soon as the user double-clicks, lock out
            # all other commands until we're done.

            $window->Busy(-recurse=>1);
            $self->{Main_window}->Busy(-recurse=>1);

            # Step 3: Here's the money shot.  Configure DDL::Oracle,
            # using its full API driven by other Perl/Tk buttons.
            DDL::Oracle->configure(
                        dbh      => $self->{Database_conn}, # database
                        resize   => $resize,                # handle
                        schema   => $schema,
                        prompt   => $prompt,
                        heading  => 0,
                        view     => $view,
                        blksize  => $Block_Size,
                        version  => $Oracle_Version
                    );

            # Step 4: Create a new DDL::Oracle object dependent
            # upon whatever live table or object was double-clicked.

            my $obj = DDL::Oracle->new(
                        type => $obj_type,
                        list => [[ $main::v_sys,
```

Example 3-3. Usage of DDL::Oracle within the Orac program (continued)

```
                              $window->{text}->get('active'),
                    ]] );
     my $sql;

     # Step 5: Depending upon the exact type of DDL required,
     # use DDL::Oracle to generate the DDL and fill $sql.

     if ( $action eq "drop" ){
         $sql = $obj->drop;
     } elsif ( $action eq "create" ){
         $sql = $obj->create;
     } elsif ( $action eq "resize" ){
         $sql = $obj->resize;
     } elsif ( $action eq "compile" ){
         $sql = $obj->compile;
     }

     # Step 6: Output the DDL text generated and then move
     # the cursor to the bottom of the text panel.

     $current_index = $text->index('current'); # Current mark

     $text->insert('end', $sql . "\n\n");
     $self->search_text(\$text, $current_index);
     $text->see( q{end linestart});

     # Step 7: Remove screen lock, to choose further options.

     $self->{Main_window}->Unbusy;
     $window->Unbusy;
 }         );
```

Here's what's going on in this code.

1. The code in Example 3-3 is basically a scroll widget bind command on the left side of the screen. This is filled with a table list, and the binding is attached to a text widget on the right side of the screen. Whenever an object such as the table SCOTT.DEPT is double-clicked, the defined subcommand runs. This fills up the text widget with DDL output.

2. Following the double-click operation, we lock the program. This turns the cursor into an hourglass or watch, depending on your operating system.

3. We then configure the new *DDL::Oracle* object. This derives its values from the radio buttons, seen displayed at the bottom of Figure 3-10. (The database handle provided by Perl DBI was previously stored in *$self->{Database_conn}* by the object-oriented *orac_Oracle.pm* module.)

4. Next, we find out what was actually double-clicked in the left-hand scrolling screen list generated earlier by a simple piece of SQL such as the SELECT TABLE_NAME FROM USER_TABLES statement.

5. Depending upon what kind of DDL we need, (determined from the higher Perl/Tk radio button set), we take the DDL text generated from $obj and store it in a simple Perl string variable, named $sql. (In this case, we wanted to view the DDL necessary to CREATE the DEPT table.)

6. The required DDL is then pasted to the right-hand text scroller.

7. On task completion, we unlock the screen to await further user instruction.

Installing DDL::Oracle on Win32

There is an ActivePerl package for *DDL::Oracle*. To obtain it, simply connect your PC to the Internet, as described in Chapter 2, and run *ppm*:

```
C:\>ppm
PPM interactive shell (2.1.5) - type 'help' for available commands.
PPM> install DDL-Oracle
Install package 'DDL-Oracle?' (y/N): y
Installing package 'DDL-Oracle'...
...
Writing C:\Perl\site\lib\auto\DDL\Oracle\.packlist
PPM> quit
```

As well as grabbing the *DDL::Oracle* module files, this ActivePerl installation also provides some of the most important sample scripts that come with Richard Sutherland's main source code download on Unix (see Table 3-2).

Table 3-2. DDL::Oracle download example scripts

Script	Purpose
ddl.pl	Generates various types of DDL for a single, named object.
copy_user.pl	Generates for new users, with identical privileges from other users.
defrag.pl	Creates command files to defragment Oracle tablespaces.
query.pl	Generates DDL for a specified list of objects.

Using DDL::Oracle as a Batch and List Processor

One important thing that differentiates *DDL::Oracle* from other available freely available tools is its batch orientation. If you're ever in a situation where you need to create many different scripts (for backups, performance tuning, or any other purpose) for your DBA work and you find yourself cutting and pasting from one script to another, you probably need *DDL::Oracle*. By using *DDL::Oracle* in batch mode, you can concentrate on solving your problem and let *DDL::Oracle* do the hard work on the back end, generating the actual DDL code required.

DDL::Oracle can also be used as a list processor. In this mode you can send it a list of objects or components for which to generate DDL—for example, all the tables in a particular tablespace. One of the most useful of the helpful sample scripts provided with the program is *defrag.pl*, which you can use for reorganizing these tablespaces. We'll take a quick look at this script in the next section.

defrag.pl

There are many different options for running *defrag.pl*, all of which you can read about by issuing this command:

```
$ perl defrag.pl --help
```

We ran the following command to generate defragmentation scripts for our USERS tablespace:

```
$ perl defrag.pl --user=system --password=manager --sid=orcl \
  --tablespace=USERS
...
defrag.pl completed successfully
on Sun Mar 24 12:34:49 2002
```

This operation created the following list of files:

defrag_USERS.sh
defrag_USERS.sh1
defrag_USERS.sh2
defrag_USERS.sh3
defrag_USERS.sh4
defrag_USERS.sh5
defrag_USERS_drop_all.sql
defrag_USERS_add_tbl.sql
defrag_USERS_add_ndx.sql
defrag_USERS_exp.par
defrag_USERS_imp.par

These scripts are essentially designed to export the target data, drop the objects, recreate the resized and defragmented objects, and then import the data once again. There are several different types of scripts:

Shell scripts

Let's look at a sample from the *defrag_USERS.sh2* script:

```
# Step 2 -- Use SQL*Plus to run defrag_USERS_drop_all.sql
#           which will drop all objects in tablespace USERS
sqlplus -s / << EOF
   SPOOL /u02/tools/DDL-Oracle-1.10/defrag_USERS_drop_all.log
   @ /u02/tools/DDL-Oracle-1.10/defrag_USERS_drop_all.sql
EOF
...
```

SQL scripts

Let's examine part of the *defrag_USERS_drop_all.sql* script mentioned:

```
PROMPT DROP TABLE demo.customer CASCADE CONSTRAINTS
DROP TABLE demo.customer CASCADE CONSTRAINTS ;
PROMPT DROP TABLE demo.department CASCADE CONSTRAINTS
DROP TABLE demo.department CASCADE CONSTRAINTS ;
...
```

Export/Import parameter files

Finally, here's a short sample from the *defrag_USERS_imp.par* file:

```
log          = /u02/tools/DDL-Oracle-1.10/defrag_USERS_imp.log
file         = /u02/tools/DDL-Oracle-1.10/defrag_USERS.pipe
rows         = y
commit       = y
ignore       = y
buffer       = 65535
analyze      = n
recordlength = 65535
full         = y
...
```

When you're ready to defragment, you simply execute the following command:

```
$ ./defrag_USERS.sh
```

This executes everything else needed to reorganize your tablespace. Defragtastic!

SchemaDiff

DDL::Oracle is a very helpful resource, and many of the new Oracle tools coming off the open source Perl conveyer belt from *SourceForge.net* and *FreshMeat.net* are based upon it. In this section we'll take a look at one of these tools, Alistair Orchard's SchemaDiff program, which you can use to compare different Oracle schemas.

Installing SchemaDiff

You can obtain SchemaDiff from:

http://sourceforge.net/projects/schemadiff

We downloaded *SchemaDiff-2.3.0.zip* and ran it on Win32, after having expanded it into the *C:\SchemaDiff* directory. (It works equally well on Unix.)

We already had the SCOTT user set up on the ORCL database. We decided to set up the IRISH user on the MYDB database with exactly the same structure. Once we'd done this, we ran the following SQL while logged on as IRISH:

```
DROP TABLE EMP;
CREATE TABLE EMP
       (EMPNO NUMBER(4) CONSTRAINT PK_EMP PRIMARY KEY,
        ENAME VARCHAR2(10),
```

```
            JOB VARCHAR2(9),
            SSN VARCHAR2(50),
            MGR NUMBER(4),
            HIREDATE DATE,
            SAL NUMBER(7,2),
            COMM NUMBER(7,2),
            DEPTNO NUMBER(2) CONSTRAINT FK_DEPTNO REFERENCES DEPT);
DROP TABLE EMP2;
CREATE TABLE EMP2
        (EMPNO NUMBER(4) CONSTRAINT PK_EMP2 PRIMARY KEY,
         ENAME VARCHAR2(10),
         JOB VARCHAR2(9),
         MGR NUMBER(4),
         HIREDATE DATE,
         SAL NUMBER(7,2),
         COMM NUMBER(7,2),
         DEPTNO NUMBER(2) CONSTRAINT FK_DEPTNO2 REFERENCES DEPT);
```

We wanted to check to see if SchemaDiff would notice that IRISH has the SSN (Social Security number) column added to the standard EMP table, and see if it would also spot the extra EMP2 table.

Running SchemaDiff

Let's see how SchemaDiff behaves with the database and user described in the previous section.

1. To get going, just start up the program:

   ```
   $ perl SchemaDiff.pl
   ```

   This will generate the left screen in Figure 3-11. Fill this in appropriately, connecting to the target databases as a DBA user.

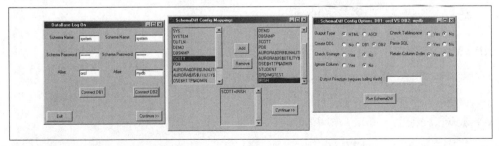

Figure 3-11. Setting up SchemaDiff

2. On the second screen, use the selection boxes to link the two target schemas, in this case SCOTT=IRISH.

3. The third screen now allows you to choose options for generating various report formats and DDL files to upgrade one schema or the other, depending on which you prefer to be dominant.

When running SchemaDiff, we opted for the HTML report option and for the DDL scripts to be written from the point of view of the IRISH schema. You can see part of the HTML summary in Figure 3-12, along with some of the DDL generated within the *IRISH.sql* file.

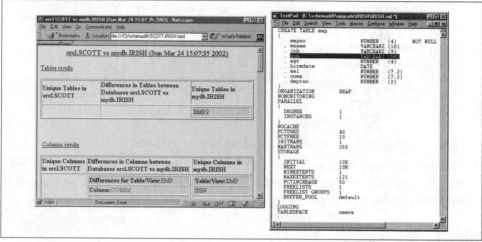

Figure 3-12. Typical SchemaDiff output

You'll find that plenty of other fine treasures can be hauled from SchemaDiff. Check out its Mother-of-Perl SourceForge foundry for the latest version.

Senora

Another helpful *DDL::Oracle*-based product is Martin Drautzburg's Senora, an alternative to Oracle's own SQL*Plus.

Installing Senora

You can get hold of Senora here:

http://sourceforge.net/projects/senora

We downloaded the *senora-0.4.tgz* tarball:

```
$ gzip -d senora-0.3.tgz
$ tar xvf senora-0.3.tar
$ cd senora
$ vi README.txt
```

To access Senora, type in something similar to this statement:

```
$ perl Senora.pm scott/tiger@orcl
```

You will now see a doppelganger screen that looks amazingly similar to something you may have seen somewhere before:

```
SEN*Ora: Release 0.4.0.0.4 - Production on Mon Dec 31 21:53:26 CET 2001

(c) Copyright 2001 Miracle Exploration.  No rights reserved.

Connected to:
Oracle8i Enterprise Edition Release 8.1.7.0.0 - Production
PL/SQL Release 8.1.7.0.0 - Production
...

0:scott@orcl>
```

Senora and SQL*Plus

The output in the previous section looks remarkably like SQL*Plus? Why, in the name of the two Larrys, would we bother changing to something new when SQL*Plus comes with all versions of Oracle (and is likely to be included at least until Kurt Vonnegut's Ice-9 has been invented, the whole world has become an icy lake and even the Oracle database has gone open source)? Well, Senora author Martin Drautzburg does put forward some arguments for consideration:

Extensibility

Like most of us, you may love SQL*Plus to bits, but even those devoted to SQL*Plus have to admit that it lacks extensibility. You have to get hold of tools like TOAD or SQL*Navigator to do anything beyond basic SQL*Plus—and even these tools are impossible to extend. If you don't want to pay for a commercial product, you just have to hope and pray that the noncommercial version of TOAD you download every month will now provide the features you need. And you may not yet be in a position to write your own tools with Perl/Tk. Senora fills the gap by giving you much of the browsing and analyzing capabilities of these tools without the need to acquire any other tool or hand over your credit card number.

Plug-ins

You can extend Senora by providing your own plug-ins, or maybe collecting other people's plug-ins from a growing Senora library. Who said the Napster spirit was dead? Most of Senora's core functionality is written as plug-ins providing additional commands to a basic Senora module. We've defined the main plug-ins in Table 3-3.

Unix-style options

Many appreciate Senora's Unix-style switches, provided via other plug-ins directly accessible from the Senora command line. This means you can have a single script with 10 different switch-dependent options, rather than 10 different scripts.

Flexible outputs

Senora also attempts to provide more flexible (and perhaps friendlier) report formatting than SQL*Plus, with columns tending to be only as wide as maximally necessary and linebreaks tending to come after blank lines, rather than splitting headers and columns.

Legacy scripts

Senora can run most existing SQL*Plus scripts, including those using @ and @@, DEFINE, ampersands (&), and bind variables.

Running Senora

Let's take a look at the plug-ins available through Senora (see Table 3-3) and then see how some of them work.

Table 3-3. Senora plug-ins

Senora plug-in	Description/commands/aliases
DataDictionary	Pulls the code of procedures or lists all objects according to a pattern:
	pull, ls, set ddView
Bind	Declares and prints out bind variables:
	print (p), variable (var)
Sqlplus	Provides many SQL*Plus-style cloned commands:
	show user (id), describe (desc|d), prompt, head, set server output (so), exec, define, list (l), spool (spo), column, show errors
SessionMgr	Connects and disconnects sessions:
	disconnect (dis), connect (conn|c), quit (exit|q)
MainLoop	Executes SQL scripts:
	set verify, startRel (@@), start (@)
Tuning	Provides many highly useful tuning output commands:
	show parameter (sp), ps, kept, xqueries (xq), waits, cstatement (cs), validate (vi), rollSegs, locks, space, hwm, stat, xplain, jobs
PluginMgr	Enables help and the addition of further plug-ins:
	help (he), register, set pluginCode

We particularly like the *ls* option provided by the *DataDictionary* plug-in, illustrated here:

```
0:scott@orcl> ls
Table/Bonus                          Table/Dept
Table/Emp                            Index/Pk_Dept
Index/Pk_Emp                         Table/Salgrade
```

The *DataDictionary* plug-in is standard with Senora. To add a new self-documented plug-in, you register it interactively via the shell command prompt. For example, the *Tuning.pm* module is an optional extra plug-in, and you can use the *PluginMgr* *register* command to set it.* You may also need to be connected as a DBA user when using the tuning options, because many of the commands—for example, *xqseries (xq),* which is illustrated here—access DBA-type tables:

```
$ perl Senora.pm system/manager@orcl
...
0:system@orcl> register Tuning
Tuning registered
0:system@orcl> xq
Order by "rds/xl" desc (top 10)

Username|reads|exec|loads|rds/Xl|cmd|statement                   |
---------------------------------------------------------------------
SYS     |1452 |389 |1    |3.73  |3  |select /*+ index(idl_ub1$ i_idl_u|
        :     :    :     :      :   : ub11) +*/ piece#,length,piece fr:
        :     :    :     :      :   :om idl_ub1$      where obj#=:1 and:
        :     :    :     :      :   : part=:2 and version=:3 order by :
        :     :    :     :      :   : piece#                          :
...
10 rows selected.
system@orcl>
```

We like Senora a lot, and we think you will too.

DBD::Chart

If you're an Oracle DBA who needs to visualize and report upon lots of complex information, particularly performance statistics, in graphical form, you will benefit from the amazing *DBD::Chart*. Just two of its many possibilities are displayed in Figure 3-13.

DBD::Chart provides a mechanism within Perl for rendering pie charts, bar charts, line, point, area, and candlestick graphs, and HTML image maps via the use of SQL. The neat thing about *DBD::Chart* is that it uses Perl DBI methods to create charts directly, rather than requiring you to invoke yet another programming interface. For example, a SELECT statement is used to output a particular chart type, and the WHERE clause is used to determine its dimensions.

If you tried to produce a chart without *DBD::Chart*, you'd have to select database row information into Perl arrays and then process the arrays separately to create the charts via a special Perl charting API. With *DBD::Chart*, you can do all this in one operation that is very SQL-like. For example, when you create a new chart, you do it with a CREATE statement just as if you're creating a table. When you insert information into the chart, you do this with an INSERT statement, as if you're adding a row to a table. This is a very neat idea. We particularly like it because virtually all of the dynamic charts we ever create come directly from databases.

---

* If you want to write your own Senora plug-ins, use the *Tuning.pm* file as a skeleton.

More SQL*Plus Clones

A number of other more generic SQL*Plus-like Perl DBI tools are available. You might want to check out the following:

http://www.perldoc.com/perl5.6.1/lib/DBI/Shell.html
> The *dbish* program is a command-line interface for Perl DBI itself; it comes with the Perl DBI download (so you probably already have it!). The program has evolved greatly over the years from the original *pmsql* script written by Andreas König. Its current incarnation has benefited from input from Tim Bunce, Jochen Wiedmann, Adam Marks, and most recently, Tom Lowery.

http://dbishell.sourceforge.net
> Vivek Dasmohapatra's *dbishell* database shell program includes specific support for Oracle, MySQL, Sybase, and PostgreSQL. It also provides a generic driver for every other DBI database type.

http://piqt.sourceforge.net
> Lorance Stinson's Perl Interactive Query Tool (PIQT) is similar to *dbishell*, but it has more of a Lisp-like syntax.

http://sourceforge.net/projects/dsql
> Daniel Tamborelli Alvarenga's SQL Query Tool works for MySQL, Oracle, PostgreSQL, SQL Server, ODBC, and all supported Perl DBI drivers.

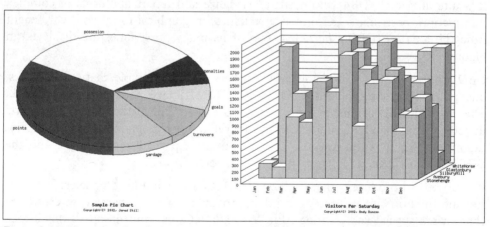

Figure 3-13. Two examples of what DBD::Chart can do

DBD::Chart is particularly useful with either Perl/Tk or Perl CGI, when run in conjunction with Perl DBI. (Image maps can also be linked to CGI programs, with HTML usage.) You can see from the following breakdown of the code used to generate the two images in Figure 3-13 just how close *DBD::Chart* is to ordinary DBI. (See Appendix B, *The Essential Guide to Perl DBI*, for a summary of the DBI API.)

1. Obtain Perl DBI and connect with the *DBD::Chart* driver:

```
use DBI;
use strict;
my $dbh = DBI->connect('dbi:Chart:', undef, undef,
                       { PrintError => 1, RaiseError => 1 });
```

2. We now can create a pie chart, with various rugby football information, in exactly the same way we might create an Oracle table with *DBD::Oracle*, and then select from it afterwards:

```
my @game_plan = qw(points possesion penalties goals turnovers yardage);
my @game_values = (70, 64, 18, 16, 19, 22);
$dbh->do('CREATE TABLE gamepie (
            Segment varchar(10),
            First integer)');
my $sth = $dbh->prepare('INSERT INTO gamepie VALUES(?, ?)');

for (my $i = 0; $i <= $#game_plan; $i++) {
    $sth->execute($game_plan[$i], $game_values[$i]);
}
$sth = $dbh->prepare(
    "SELECT PIECHART, IMAGEMAP FROM gamepie
       WHERE WIDTH=700 AND HEIGHT=600 AND
           TITLE = 'Sample Pie Chart' AND
           SIGNATURE = 'Copyright(C) 2002, Jared Still' AND
           3-D=1 AND
           COLORS=(red, white, blue, lyellow, lgray, pink)"
);
$sth->execute;
my $row = $sth->fetchrow_arrayref;
```

3. Having created the chart in memory via the use of SQL, we now output it to a PNG file. We then drop the memory structure, as if dropping a table:

```
open(PIE, '>gamepie.png');
binmode PIE;
print PIE $$row[0];
close PIE;

$dbh->do('DROP table gamepie');
```

4. We now create a three-axis bar chart. In this particular example, we'll cover ancient English sites of special interest (at least to one of the authors):

```
$dbh->do('CREATE TABLE spiritaxis (
    Month char(3),
    Visitors integer,
    Monument varchar(11))');

my @months = qw(Jan Feb Mar Apr May Jun Jul Aug Sep Oct Nov Dec);
my @monuments =
    qw(Stonehenge Avebury SilburyHill Glastonbury WhiteHorse);
    $sth = $dbh->prepare('INSERT INTO spiritaxis VALUES(?, ?, ?)');
    foreach my $month (@months) {
    foreach my $visitors (@monuments) {
```

```
        $sth->execute($month, 1 * int(rand(2000)), $visitors);
      }
    }
    $sth = $dbh->prepare(
        "SELECT BARCHART, IMAGEMAP
           FROM spiritaxis
          WHERE WIDTH=700 AND HEIGHT=600 AND
                TITLE = 'Visitors Per Saturday' AND
                SIGNATURE = 'Copyright(C) 2002, Andy Duncan' AND
                X-AXIS = 'Month' AND
                Y-AXIS = 'Visitors' AND
                Z-AXIS = 'Monument' AND
                COLORS=(white) AND
                SHOWGRID = 1"
                              );
    $sth->execute;
    $row = $sth->fetchrow_arrayref;
```

5. As before, we output the chart's memory structure into a file and then reclaim the memory by *dropping* the table:

```
open(BAR, '>spiritaxis.png');
binmode BAR;
print BAR $$row[0];
close BAR;

$dbh->do('DROP table spiritaxis');
```

DBD::Chart is an amazing piece of work. May it live long and prosper. In the following sections we'll explain how to install this tool.

Preparing DBD::Chart

DBD::Chart possesses an almost infinite number of uses, limited only by the SQL you can choose to fill it. It's available here:

> *http://www.presicient.com/dbdchart*
> *http://www.cpan.org/authors/id/D/DA/DARNOLD*

Although *DBD::Chart* itself is 100% pure Perl, it does rely on one other Perl module, *GD.pm*, which itself requires several other non-Perl C libraries. Fortunately, these libraries are all open source and either available to compile from source on Unix, or built into the precompiled *GD.pm* ActivePerl package.

Installing DBD::Chart on Unix

GD.pm relies upon three separate C libraries. Fortunately, we've already installed the ones required for *zlib* and PNG (see the earlier discussion under StatsView) so we only need one more library (we also recommend a JPEG library for completeness). Just to give you a sense of the scope of *DBD::Chart*, we've included every download in Table 3-4 for use with either Perl CGI or Perl/Tk. Collect your unclaimed tarballs, and then we'll work through the entire shooting gallery.

Table 3-4. DBD::Chart's related Unix downloads

Download	Download addresses	Example tarball
zlib	http://www.gzip.org/zlib/,http://www.zlib.org	zlib.tar.gz
PNG	http://www.libpng.org/pub/png	libpng-1.0.12.tar.gz
jpeg-6b	ftp://ftp.uu.net/graphics/jpeg,http://www.ijg.org	jpegsrc.v6b.tar.gz
gd	http://www.boutell.com/gd	gd-1.8.4.tar.gz
GD.pm	http://www.cpan.org/authors/id/LDS	GD-1.33.tar.gz
Tk::PNG[a]	http://www.cpan.org/authors/id/NI-S	Tk-PNG-2.005.tar.gz
Tk::JPEG	http://www.cpan.org/authors/id/NI-S	Tk-JPEG-2.014.tar.gz

[a] Although *Tk::PNG* and *Tk::JPEG* are only required for the use of *DBD::Chart* with Perl/Tk modules, we thought it would be useful to include them here as part of the full set.

JPEG

To complement our PNG library, we can load up JPEG support from the Independent JPEG Group (IJG). Although the lossless PNG graphics format is better for sharp letters and line drawings, JPEG's lossy nature allows you to create massively compressed files while still retaining a human perception of high quality (see the sidebar for a definitions of these terms).

This quality makes JPEG a very popular image content system for photographic usage on the Internet. Because the *Tk::JPEG* module is currently more widely available than *Tk::PNG*, particularly within ActivePerl, it's also a good format to use with Perl/Tk canvas applications. Let's take a look:

1. Read carefully through the *install.doc* document to ensure that the configuration provides all the options you require:

    ```
    $ gzip -d jpegsrc.v6b.tar.gz
    $ tar xvf jpegsrc.v6b.tar
    $ cd jpeg-6b
    $ vi README install.doc
    ```

2. You may be able to move straight into the following commands:

    ```
    $ ./configure
    $ make
    $ make test
    ```

The test step compares several JPEG files, which come with the download, with program compilations. Several of these test images should resemble the rose seen earlier in Figure 3-7, which is also borrowed by *Tk::JPEG* for its own testing. Note, however, that the various *.jpg* files will be of different physical sizes because of lossy compression.

Lossless versus Lossy

You will often hear the terms "lossless" or "lossy" used when referring to graphics images or compression algorithms. *Lossless* decompression preserves every part of an original file so it can be reproduced exactly as it was, no matter how small the compressed file gets. Think of lossless compression as being like a squashed-up handkerchief stuffed very small into a pocket; it can be uncompressed later as a complete, flat-ironed handkerchief. With *lossy* compression, on the other hand, the reduced storage technique throws away bits of the original file so when it is uncompressed it looks essentially the same, but lacks the completeness of the original.

The trick to saving room is to throw away only those bits that aren't essential later on. Think of someone making an annotated sketch of your monogrammed handkerchief. Embroiderers can take this sketch and stitch you another monogrammed hanky without needing to see the complete original. All they need are the cloth dimensions and the position, size, color, and shape of your initials. The stitch technique may be entirely different, but the difference may be visible only under a microscope. And the storage required for the embroidering instructions is massively reduced, or "lossy," leading to much cheaper information transmission for the price of an invisible reduction in similarity to the original.

3. Once the testing is complete, we can move on to the installation:

```
$ make install
$ make install-lib
```

Our default installation, on Linux, put the library and C header files into */usr/lib* and */usr/include* rather than */usr/local/*. You will want to be aware of this during installation, so we can pick up the library correctly later.

The gd library

Next we load up Thomas Boutell's *gd* library. The reason this library is required here is because it drives Lincoln Stein's *GD.pm* Perl package, which itself is relied upon by *DBD::Chart*. A splendid web of intrigue, indeed! Follow these steps:

1. Unpack the download:

```
$ gzip -d gd-1.8.4.tar.gz
$ tar xvf gd-1.8.4.tar
$ cd gd-1.8.4
```

2. The best help is available by browsing the download's *index.html* file. In accordance with the instructions provided, we changed the *Makefile* in several ways. We added the JPEG library to the main required libraries:

```
#LIBS=-lgd -lpng -lz -lm
LIBS=-lgd -lpng -lz -ljpeg -lm
```

Because the JPEG libraries and C header files had defaulted to be installed in */usr/lib* and */usr/include*, our *Makefile* had to be adjusted accordingly:

```
INCLUDEDIRS=-I. -I/usr/include/freetype2 -I/usr/include/X11 \
  -I/usr/X11R6/include/X11 -I/usr/local/include -I/usr/include
LIBDIRS=-L. -L/usr/local/lib -L/usr/lib -L/usr/lib/X11 -L/usr/X11R6/lib
```

(When you install JPEG on your own setup, your defaults may set to */usr/local/lib* and */usr/local/include*. If this happened, then the previous changes to INCLUDEDIRS and LIBDIRS will be unnecessary.)

3. We then tried:

```
$ make
$ make install
```

This installed the main *gd* library and header files in the following places:

```
/usr/local/lib/libgd.a
/usr/local/include/gd.h
```

4. When you install *gd*, you also obtain the *gddemo* program. If you run this program, you'll find that it creates a new PNG file, *demoout.png*, directly from a supplied one, *demoin.png*, which is a snazzy picture of a space shuttle:

```
$ ./gddemo
```

If this fails to work the first time, you may have to play around with the *LD_LIBRARY_PATH* variable, for example:

```
$ export LD_LIBRARY_PATH=$LD_LIBRARY_PATH:/usr/local/lib
```

The new file should be the original space shuttle, but overlaid with decorative imagery, as seen earlier on the right side of Figure 3-7.

GD.pm

Although he is better known for his work with *CGI.pm* and *mod_perl* (covered in the following chapters), Lincoln Stein has also created another great piece of work in *GD.pm*. This program provides a Perl front end to Thomas Boutell's *gd* C library. Follow these steps:

1. Because we're relying on the *gd* module's being available, this step differs from the standard vanilla Perl configuration:

```
$ gzip -d GD-1.33.tar.gz
$ tar xvf GD-1.33.tar
$ cd GD-1.33
$ perl Makefile.PL
```

The preceding step will ask various questions. Your mileage may vary. (Before completing the installation of *GD.pm*, you may wish to acquire FreeType and XPM (X PixMap) support. Information is available in the *GD.pm* download bundle. If you aren't interested, just say no):

```
Build JPEG support? [y]
Build FreeType support? [y]
Build XPM support? [y]
```

2. Next, compile and test the module:

```
$ make
$ make test
```

During the test stage, we're looking for output similar to the following:

```
...
All tests successful, 2 subtests skipped.
Files=1, Tests=10,
0 wallclock secs ( 0.49 cusr +  0.06 csys =  0.55 CPU)
```

3. You may also want to complete an optional step to provide a helpful *GD.html* documentation file in the current directory:

```
$ make html
```

4. We're now ready to:

```
$ make install
```

The *GD.pm* Perl package should now be loaded and ready to fire.

Completing the DBD::Chart installation

We can finally nail the main event:

```
$ gzip -d DBD-Chart-0.60.tar.gz
$ tar xvf DBD-Chart-0.60.tar
$ cd DBD-Chart-0.60
$ vi README
$ perl Makefile.PL
$ make
$ make test          # There may not be too much here just yet! 8-)
$ make install
```

DBD::Chart is now fully installed. If you want to test this program, the best way is to go to the */examples* directory, move all the current **.png* files to another directory, and then run all the example Perl programs to create new PNGs—for example:

```
$ cd examples
$ mkdir tmp_safe
$ mv *.png tmp_safe
$ perl simpcandle.pl
```

You should now find a handful of PNGs in the current directory, similar to those we first showed you in Figure 3-13. For specific *DBD::Chart* use with Perl/Tk programs, such as Orac, we also need to install the *Tk::JPEG* module. While we're at it, we'll also compile the *Tk::PNG* module here for Unix—it's bound to turn up as a package on ActivePerl sooner or later for Win32 users (it will make lossless PNG usage on Perl/Tk that much more attractive).

Tk::PNG

Follow these steps to install *Tk::PNG*:

1. Everything should run smoothly during this installation, because *TK::PNG* is expecting the *zlib* and PNG libraries to be just where we put them earlier. Well, that's the plan. For variations, scan the *README* file thoroughly for complete information:

   ```
   $ gzip -d Tk-PNG-2.005.tar.gz
   $ tar xvf Tk-PNG-2.005.tar
   $ cd Tk-PNG-2.005
   $ vi README
   $ perl Makefile.PL
   $ make
   ```

2. The *make test* step should pop up the PNG picture we showed back in Figure 3-7, as also used by the original *libpng* installation:

   ```
   $ make test
   ...
   All tests successful.
   Files=1, Tests=4,  2 wallclock secs
   ( 0.33 cusr +  0.03 csys =  0.36 CPU)
   ```

3. Now carry out the install:

   ```
   $ make install
   ```

Tk::JPEG

1. Let's wrap up by installing *Tk::JPEG*:

   ```
   $ gzip -d Tk-JPEG-2.014.tar.gz
   $ tar xvf Tk-JPEG-2.014.tar
   $ cd Tk-JPEG-2.014
   ```

2. As with the PNG installation, the *make test* step should pop up the JPEG picture of the rose, shown in Figure 3-7, as seen with the earlier installation of the JPEG libraries. If this occurs, the launchpad is ready:

   ```
   $ perl Makefile.PL
   $ make
   $ make test
   $ make install
   ```

Installing DBD::Chart on Win32

In absolute contrast with the Unix installation of *DBD::Chart*, the *DBD::Chart* installation on Win32 via ActiveState is a miniscule effort. The folks at ActiveState have locked up the hard work of installing the C libraries deep inside their *GD.pm* package.

To install *DBD::Chart* on Win32, follow these steps:

1. As earlier with the Perl/Tk download, connect your PC to the Internet and run the PPM program:

   ```
   C:\> ppm
   ```

2. Now install the ActivePerl GD and *Tk::JPEG* packages by typing:

   ```
   PPM> install GD
   PPM> install Tk-JPEG
   PPM> exit
   ```

   For those who have waded through the Unix install, we're embarrassed to say that this is really all you have to do to get *zlib*, PNG, JPEG, *gd,* and *GD.pm* onto Win32. When the revolution comes, there shall be a reckoning!

Loading DBD::Chart for ActivePerl

Although ActiveState may lack a *DBD::Chart* package in its library, the package is relatively straightforward to add because it's 100% pure Perl:

1. Get hold of the latest download file, such as *DBD-Chart-0.60.tar.gz*, from:

   http://www.cpan.org/authors/id/D/DA/DARNOLD

2. Unzip the tarball to the a temporary directory, such as:

   ```
   C:\DBD-Chart-0.60
   ```

3. Go to the main ..*DBD* directory where ActivePerl keeps its modules, and copy in *DBD::Chart*'s main *Chart.pm* module. For example:

   ```
   C:\DBD-Chart-0.60> cd C:\Perl\site\lib\DBD
   C:\Perl\site\lib\DBD> copy C:\DBD-Chart-0.60\Chart.pm .
   ```

4. Now create a new subdirectory under ..*DBD*, itself named *Chart*:

   ```
   C:\Perl\site\lib\DBD> mkdir Chart
   ```

5. Enter this subdirectory, and copy *Plot.pm* to it from the..*Chart* directory within the download area:

   ```
   C:\Perl\site\lib\DBD> cd Chart
   C:\Perl\site\lib\DBD\Chart> copy C:\DBD-Chart-0.60\Chart\Plot.pm .
   ```

This completes the Win32 installation of *DBD::Chart*. (We'll cover another way of installing larger pure-Perl modules, using *NMAKE,* in Chapter 6, *Embedded Perl Web Scripting*, where a slightly longer setup can save a lot of copying by hand.) To test our *Tk::JPEG* system, we fired up Orac to see if it could detect both *DBD::Chart* and *Tk::JPEG* as being successfully installed. The resulting, slightly lossy tablespace allocations chart is displayed in Figure 3-14.

SchemaView-Plus

SchemaView-Plus is another helpful Perl/Tk tool for Oracle DBAs that allows you to examine different database schemas and save them for future reference. It also

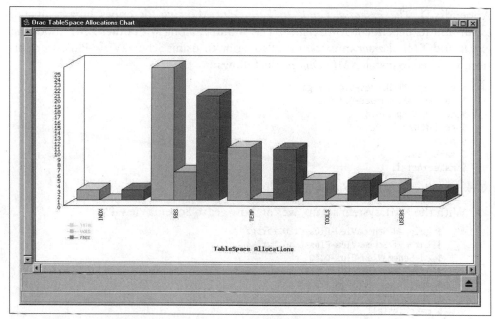

Figure 3-14. DBD::Chart examines tablespace allocations

provides insight into the world of Perl and XML data parsing. SchemaView-Plus was written by Milan Sorm, who also developed the dbMan application (see *http:// dbman.linux.cz*), also written in Perl/Tk. (The SchemaView-Plus tool also uses the Perl DBIx extension, *DBIx::SystemCatalog*.)

Installing SchemaView-Plus on Unix

In addition to downloading SchemaView-Plus itself, you'll need to obtain several additional modules. Table 3-5 lists the locations for the software you'll need to install.

Table 3-5. Description and downloads for SchemaView-Plus

C library/Perl module	Description/download address
expat	XML parser C library
	http://sourceforge.net/projects/expat
XML::Parser	Parses XML
	http://www.cpan.org/authors/id/C/CO/COOPERCL
XML::Dumper	Dumps Perl data to structured XML
	http://www.cpan.org/authors/id/E/EI/EISEN
SchemaView-Plus	Examines different database schemas
	http://www.cpan.org/authors/id/M/MI/MILSO

Appendix D, *The Essential Guide to Perl Data Munging*, describes how to install *expat* and its dependent *XML::Parser* Perl module, along with other XML modules; *expat* and *XML::Parser* must be installed prior to using SchemaView-Plus. In addition, we need to install *XML::Dumper* as follows:

```
$ gzip -d XML-Dumper-0.4.tar.gz
$ tar xvf XML-Dumper-0.4.tar
$ cd XML-Dumper-0.4
$ perl Makefile.PL
$ make
$ make test
$ make install
```

Now let's install SchemaView-Plus itself:

1. With the XML system set up, we can now get to SchemaView-Plus:

   ```
   $ gzip -d SchemaView-Plus-0.10.tar.gz
   $ tar xvf SchemaView-Plus-0.10.tar
   $ cd SchemaView-Plus-0.10
   $ perl Makefile.PL
   $ make
   $ make test
   $ make install
   ```

2. Make sure we can find the *svplus* program and set *ORACLE_HOME*:

   ```
   $ export PATH=/usr/local/bin:$PATH
   $ export ORACLE_HOME=/u01/app/oracle/product/8.1.5
   $ export LD_LIBRARY_PATH=$LD_LIBRARY_PATH:$ORACLE_HOME/lib
   $ svplus
   ```

Many different schema-related options are available via SchemaView-Plus, and walking through them when the program is installed is the best way to discover them. To give you a flavor of the program, we've included two screenshots in Figure 3-15, one for Unix and one for Win32.

Installing SchemaView-Plus on Win32

To install SchemaView-Plus on Win32, do the following:

1. Obtain the *XML::Dumper* package from over the Internet at ActiveState (*XML::Parser* comes preloaded with ActivePerl):

   ```
   C:\>ppm
   PPM> install XML-Dumper
   Install package 'XML-Dumper?' (y/N): y
   Installing package 'XML-Dumper'...
   ...
   Writing C:\Perl\site\lib\auto\XML\Dumper\.packlist
   PPM> quit
   ```

2. Next, download and extract SchemaView-Plus to a suitable directory.

3. Run the program like this:

   ```
   C:\SchemaView-Plus-0.10>perl bin/svplus
   ```

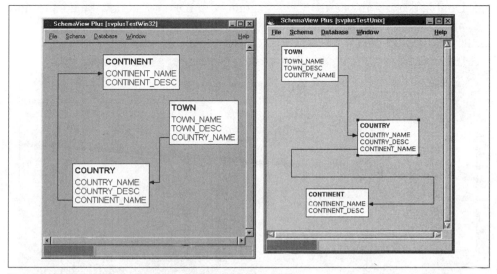

Figure 3-15. SchemaView-Plus examining table relationships

Open Source Perl IDEs

Even with all of the wonderful applications profiled in this book, you might still find that none are quite right for your own database administration needs. If you have a serious itch you really need to scratch, you might eventually decide that you need to do some coding of your own. Fortunately, this is becoming easier all the time.

Most Perl devotees are still wedded firmly to the command line and to the use of text editors like *vi* or *emacs* for development. However, for those accustomed to the typical Win32 code development style, Open Perl IDE offers an excellent development alternative. Open Perl IDE is an integrated development environment (IDE) for writing and debugging Perl scripts with any standard Perl distribution under Win32. This open source software is written in Delphi 5 Object Pascal and Perl. In addition to providing a complete development environment, it also offers excellent Perl code debugging facilities.

To install Open Perl IDE, follow these steps:

1. Go to:

    http://sourceforge.net/projects/open-perl-ide

    We downloaded the following file to its own newly created directory:

    `C:\OpenPerlIDE\Open_Perl_IDE_0.9.8.168a.zip`

2. Double-click on this and check the *readme.txt* file.

3. Unpack to the same directory.

4. Double-click on the *PerlIDE.exe* program. The IDE should now be up and running, as shown in Figure 3-16.

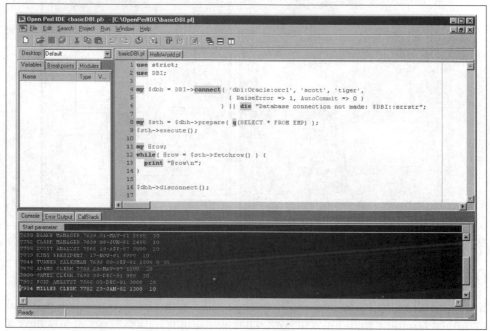

Figure 3-16. Open Perl IDE in action with Perl DBI

Other Perl IDEs you might want to consider include:

Kake Pad
    http://sourceforge.net/projects/kpad

OptiPerl
    http://www.xarka.com/optiperl

Komodo
    http://www.activestate.com/Products/Komodo

UltraEdit
    http://www.ultraedit.com

Open Source Perl GUI Debuggers

A number of excellent Perl GUI debuggers provide graphical interfaces for diagnosing problems in your Perl programs. The quickest way to get up to speed on the general topic of debugging in Perl is to type the following commands:

```
$ perldoc perldebug
$ perldoc perldiag
```

Perlish people tend to use command-line debug programs with major sprinklings of *print* statements. But several open source GUI debugger programs are out there that you might want to consider. We've listed the best-known in Table 3-6.

Table 3-6. Open source Perl GUI debugging programs

GUI	Description
perldbgui	A GUI for the standard Perl debugger:
	http://members.tripod.com/~CurtMcKelvey/perldbgui
ptkdb	This can work with Apache Perl scripts and is shown in Figure 3-17:
	http://www.cpan.org/authors/id/A/AE/AEPAGE
Open Perl IDE	This IDE, described in the previous section, can help write and debug Perl programs:
	http://sourceforge.net/projects/open-perl-ide

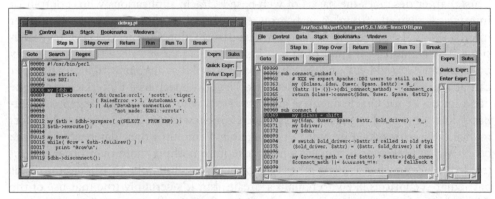

Figure 3-17. ptkdb—Stepping into the DBI module

CHAPTER 4
Perl Web Extensions

This chapter describes the basics of web-based Oracle applications whose output or interface is viewed through a web browser, rather than through the graphical user interfaces (GUIs) offered by the applications described in Chapter 3, *Perl GUI Extensions*. The advantage of employing a web solution is that you need to deploy it only once, at one web address, and thereby provide a tool that anyone with a web browser can access from anywhere on the network. Using the web as an interface can make life a lot easier for Oracle database administrators who may manage dozens of databases and who need to maintain a satellite's eye view of their operation and performance. DBAs have long dreamed of being able to monitor their databases from the beach via remote-control applications that require nothing more than browser control from a Palm pilot or some other type of PDA, a cellular phone, or a laptop. That particular scenario is likely to remain a dream, but it's certainly true that use of the Web adds a convenient dimension to database administration.

Many web-based database applications are implemented as Perl CGI scripts. CGI (Common Gateway Interface) programs are typically small programs (running on the web server) that have historically been used to provide dynamic content to web pages. The output of a CGI program is simply an HTML page that is read by a web browser. How do CGIs work? On the client side, the browser calls a CGI in the same way that it would call a static web page—by making a request for a file from the web server. By calling a CGI, though, the client is actually telling the server to run a small program. In the case of an Oracle CGI script, running that program pulls data from the Oracle database and thus produces the dynamic content for the web page. We won't attempt to describe the details of CGI in this book. If you are interested in learning more, we recommend the following classic text by Lincoln Stein, the creator of the *CGI.pm* module:[*]

---

[*] Lincoln is also the author of *Network Programming with Perl* (Addison-Wesley, 2000), and the coauthor, with Doug MacEachern, of *Writing Apache Modules with Perl and C* (O'Reilly & Associates, 1999).

Official Guide to Programming With Cgi.Pm, by Lincoln Stein (Wiley & Sons, 1998)

In this chapter we'll describe two excellent web-based applications for Oracle DBAs:

Oracletool
>One of the best tools around for Oracle DBAs is Adam vonNieda's Oracletool, which provides a web-based interface for database performance monitoring and a variety of other database administration tasks. Oracletool is implemented as a Perl CGI script.

Karma
>Another excellent web-based Perl application for Oracle database monitoring is Sean Hull's Karma. Karma is not strictly a Perl CGI script, but instead relies upon daemons to collect statistics and warnings for Oracle DBAs.

Something else we like about Oracletool and Karma is that you can play around with both of them on their home sites (listed later). If you're just interested in checking them out, and if the installation procedures described in the following sections seem like a little too much work at this point, feel free to examine the demonstrations provided on their sites. We're confident you won't be disappointed.

Before we look at the details of these applications, we'll take a step back and describe how to install and configure Apache, the leading web server in use today.

Apache

Apache is an open source web server—and the most popular web server in use today (including both open source and commercial web servers).[*] Apache is fast, efficient, easy to configure, and very stable on the widest variety of platforms. Apache[†] runs on virtually every operating system, including Win32, Linux, BSD, Solaris, and many other varieties of Unix. The main web site for Apache is:

>*http://www.apache.org/*

Apache and Perl are fast friends. This chapter focuses on Perl-based applications for Oracle that are implemented as CGI scripts or daemons. In Chapter 5, *Embedding Perl into Apache with mod_perl*, we'll discuss Apache's *mod_perl* module, which makes the Apache/Perl connection a more efficient one.

---

[*] According to Netcraft (*http://www.netcraft.com/survey/*), Apache's share of the web's active sites market was 64% as of March 2002. Following behind was Internet Information Server (IIS), placing second at 27%, and iPlanet, placing third at 2%.

[†] Apache 1.3.24 is the latest version as of this writing, with Apache 2.0 in alpha testing.

To obtain the downloads and information concerning Apache for Unix, Win32, and Oracle's use of Apache, check out the following URLs:

http://www.apache.org/
   Main Apache umbrella web site for all the Apache Software Foundation (ASF) related projects.

http://httpd.apache.org/
   Central site for the actual Apache web server, the ASF's core offering.

http://httpd.apache.org/dist/httpd/
   Main download page for Apache on Unix.

http://httpd.apache.org/docs/windows.html
   Page dedicated towards helping Win32 users of Apache.

http://httpd.apache.org/dist/httpd/binaries/win32/
   Download page for Win32 Apache.

http://www.oracle.com/ip/deploy/ias/index.html?web.html
   Oracle Corporation's use of Apache as the Oracle9*i* Application HTTP Server (iAS).

http://httpd.apache.org/docs/mod/directives.html
   The Apache Run Time Configuration Directives page.

Because Apache is supplied these days as part of your Oracle installation, you may simply choose to use that version because it's highly compatible with the Oracle development environment. The only problem is that it might be a fairly old version of Apache, depending on the Oracle version you're using, and it might therefore be difficult to modify in order to meet your own production standards or to blend in with non-Oracle toolsets. In case you need to customize Apache for your environment, we'll describe in the following sections how to install an independent Apache directly on both Unix and Win32. This way, you get the latest and greatest Apache, with complete freedom to modify it to meet your personal requirements.

Installing Apache on Unix

Download the latest stable version of Apache from:

   http://httpd.apache.org/dist/httpd/

Get the latest stable tarball (we used *apache_1.3.24.tar.gz*) and unpack it into a temporary working directory:

```
$ gzip -d apache_1.3.24.tar.gz
$ tar xvf apache_1.3.24.tar
$ cd apache_1.3.24
$ vi README INSTALL
```

The main installation instructions are within the *INSTALL* file where you're offered two options:

- The old-style compilation
- The out-of-the-box APACI (Apache AutoConf Interface) Install method

Unless you enjoy pain, we recommend that you go for APACI every time!

 Although we're installing Apache as *root*, it may not always be a good idea to run the resultant *httpd* servers as *root*. Most Unix systems immediately switch Apache to the *nobody* user in *nogroup* (a harmless person) once they've attached to port 80. However some may not and you may therefore risk superuser permissions being accessible over the Web. Alternatively, you may simply wish to run a thoroughly secure system. To achieve this goal, you may want to create a special user to run Apache, typically *webuser* in *webgroup*. Check out the *Group* and *User* directives on the Apache configuration directives page mentioned previously or via the two following references:

- *http://httpd.apache.org/docs/mod/core.html#group*
- *http://httpd.apache.org/docs/mod/core.html#user*

Let's run through the Unix installation instructions:

1. We're going to take the option to build Apache with Perl. To do this, find out where your Perl executable is living, and then configure Apache under APACI using this address, combined with the *--with-perl* directive. Also, let the *./configure* program know where you want to ultimately install Apache with the *-prefix=MyApacheDir* switch.[*] We'll assume for now that you're happy to install Apache in the usual place, */usr/local/apache*, as the *root* user:

   ```
   $ type perl
   perl is hashed (/usr/bin/perl)
   $ ./configure --prefix=/usr/local/apache --with-perl=/usr/bin/perl
   ```

2. We should now be ready to go straight into the installation:

   ```
   $ make
   $ make install
   ```

   You're looking for the following output:

   ```
   +----------------------------------------------------------+
   | You now have successfully built and installed the        |
   | Apache 1.3 HTTP server. To verify that Apache actually    |
   | works correctly you now should first check the           |
   | (initially created or preserved) configuration files     |
   ...
   +----------------------------------------------------------+
   ```

---

[*] In development mode, it's often a good idea to install Apache to a nondefault area; this helps you avoid overwriting a production version. It may also be necessary if you don't have *root* permission.

3. Finally, get the Apache *httpd* server itself up and running:

```
$ /usr/local/apache/bin/apachectl start
/usr/local/apache/bin/apachectl start: httpd started
```

You can test the successful installation by visiting *localhost* with your browser, as shown in Figure 4-1.

4. Now visit the *httpd.conf* configuration file and find out where the */cgi-bin/* directive will look for CGI scripts:

```
$ vi /usr/local/apache/conf/httpd.conf
```

The default should look like this:

```
ScriptAlias /cgi-bin/ "/usr/local/apache/cgi-bin/"
```

All CGI scripts should go in the */usr/local/apache/cgi-bin* directory.

5. Now search for the following line, dealing with *.cgi* scripts:

```
#AddHandler cgi-script .cgi
```

Uncomment this, and add a similar line to deal with *.pl* scripts:

```
AddHandler cgi-script .cgi
AddHandler cgi-script .pl
```

6. If you're not *root*, or you'd like a separate development port, you might like to change the Port value from 80, the default for the Internet, to some other value higher than 1024. A typical development port is:

```
Port 8080
```

To restart Apache, with the new configuration, run the following command:

```
$ /usr/local/apache/bin/apachectl restart
```

(You will find that the Apache logs go into the */usr/local/apache/logs* directory or in *<server_root>/logs*, depending upon how you've configured *httpd.conf*.)

You'll find a Perl CGI example script in Example 4-1.

Installing Apache on Win32

The process of installing Apache on Win32 platforms has improved by leaps and bounds in the last few years, and it's now a straightforward install. We downloaded this self-extracting file:

apache_1.3.24-win32-x86-no_src.msi

which we obtained from:

http://httpd.apache.org/dist/httpd/binaries/win32/

If you have the MSI installer program on your Windows box (as discussed in Chapter 2, *Installing Perl* on page 28), double-clicking on the Apache MSI file should result in a typical pain-free Windows-style installation. The main question you'll be asked is whether you want to run Apache as a Windows service or as a console appli-

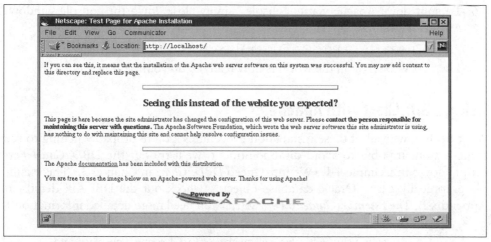

Figure 4-1. Hello Apache, the first screen arriveth

cation. We opted for the second choice because the Win32 version of *mod_perl* (which we'll be installing in Chapter 5) expects Apache to be run in console mode. Follow these steps:

1. As with the earlier Unix installation, we made some tiny changes to the *httpd.conf* file to enable the execution of our CGI Perl files before starting up Apache to test them. To gain direct access to *httpd.conf* from the Windows *Start* menu, click through the following:

   ```
   Start->Programs->Apache HTTP Server->Configure Apache Server->
   Edit the Apache httpd.conf Configuration File
   ```

2. Once inside *httpd.conf*, note the location of CGI's script *bin*:

   ```
   ScriptAlias /cgi-bin/ "C:/Program Files/Apache Group/Apache/cgi-bin/"
   ```

3. Now find the handler line dealing with *.cgi* scripts:

   ```
   #AddHandler cgi-script .cgi
   ```

4. Uncomment it to activate it and add a similar line to deal with *.pl* scripts:

   ```
   AddHandler cgi-script .cgi
   AddHandler cgi-script .pl
   ```

   At this point, you might want to review the discussion of the Port value in the Unix installation section, but on Win32 we're generally happy with the default HTTP value, unless we know something else is running on it:

   ```
   Port 80
   ```

5. Fire up Apache as a console application from the *Start* menu:

   ```
   Start->Programs->Apache HTTP Server->
   Start Apache in Console
   ```

6. To shut down Apache via its console, simply close down the console window. Any errors will have appeared in:

    C:\Program Files\Apache Group\Apache\logs**error.log**

The best web server in the world is now ready to do your bidding.

Using DBD::Chart with Apache

After dealing with all of these installation procedures, you're probably itching to see some action. In a bid to avoid disappointment, we'll try out the *DBD::Chart* Perl script shown in Example 4-1. (We introduced *DBD::Chart* in Chapter 3.) This example graphically charts Oracle database objects. (Check out the DBI API details in Appendix B, *The Essential Guide to Perl DBI*, if you need more detailed information.)

 If you're using ActivePerl, all of the Perl CGI scripts you place into Apache's *../cgi-bin/* directory, under Win32 must have the following first line:

    #!/perl/bin/perl

This tells the Apache web server to execute them with ActivePerl, which is generally available as:

    C:\Perl\Bin\perl.exe

If the ActivePerl *perl.exe* executable is in a different or nondefault location, alter the Apache directive appropriately.

Example 4-1. Oracle_objects.pl

```
#!/perl/bin/perl
use strict;
use DBI;
use Socket qw(:DEFAULT :crlf); # Built-in Perl module, provides $CRLF

# Step 1: Tell the calling browser a mime.types PNG is on its way.

print "Content-type: image/png$CRLF$CRLF";
# Step 2: Connect to Oracle and prepare the SQL.

my $dbh = DBI->connect( 'dbi:Oracle:orcl', 'system', 'manager',
                        { RaiseError => 1 } );

my $sth = $dbh->prepare( 'SELECT object_type, ' .
                         '        COUNT(*)' .
                         '  FROM dba_objects ' .
                         ' GROUP BY object_type' );
$sth->execute;
```

Example 4-1. Oracle_objects.pl (continued)

```
# Step 3: Create the DBD::Chart graph, and prepare to insert bars.

my $chart_dbh = DBI->connect('dbi:Chart:');
$chart_dbh->do(
  'CREATE TABLE bars (object_type CHAR(30), object_count FLOAT)' );

my $chart_sth = $chart_dbh->prepare('INSERT INTO bars VALUES(?, ?)');

while ( my @res = $sth->fetchrow) {

    # Step 4: Add an entry to chart.

    $chart_sth->execute( $res[0], $res[1] );
}

# Step 5: Prepare the Chart for output without the need for any
# temporary file storage of the default PNG output.

$chart_sth =
  $chart_dbh->prepare( "SELECT BARCHART " .
                       "  FROM bars " .
                       " WHERE WIDTH=900 " .
                       "   AND HEIGHT=300 " .
                       "   AND 3-D=1 " .
                       "   AND X-ORIENT= 'HORIZONTAL' " .
                       "   AND TITLE =  'Object Types' ");

# Step 6: Send the PNG on its way back to the browser, then clean up.

$chart_sth->execute;
my $row = $chart_sth->fetchrow_arrayref;
binmode STDOUT;
print $$row[0]; # PNG file sent here! :-)
$chart_dbh->do('DROP CHART bars');
$chart_dbh->disconnect;

$dbh->disconnect;
```

Here's what's going on in this script:

1. Before we pump out the PNG's binary image, we need to tell the calling browser to expect a *mime.types* PNG output.

   Note the *$CRLF* newline pair included here; it is used to separate the content-type declaration from the actual content. The *$CRLF* variable from Perl's built-in *Socket.pm* ensures that we get the right combination of \015\012 for Internet line endings. The \n character normally represents \012, and \r normally represents \015; however, this may vary from system to system. To be strict about what we output, we use Socket's *$CRLF*, which guarantees to be \015\012 (also known as

CRLF, for carriage return/line feed). Many systems also recognize \n as a CRLF, so web people often use the \n\n pair.*

2. We create the SQL to extract the required information from Oracle.

3. Next, we create the destination bar chart and get it ready for data entry.

4. Row by row, we fill up the bar chart with SELECT results.

5. We prepare to output the final dynamic chart using the DBI API.

6. We send the PNG directly to the browser. This is done entirely in memory, without the need for a transitional operating system file. Once we've sent the PNG on its way, we clean up and free our resources.

Store this Perl script in your CGI bin directory under either Unix or Win32:

```
/usr/local/apache/cgi-bin/
C:/Program Files/Apache Group/Apache/cgi-bin/
```

(Notice how Apache, even on Win32, still prefers the Unix-style forward slash, which is used internally by Win32 systems anyway.)

If you're using Unix, you will need to change the script's first line to call your local Perl version—for example:

```
#!/usr/bin/perl
```

Now call up the following address on your browser:

http://localhost/cgi-bin/Oracle_objects.pl

You should see something like Figure 4-2.

As we discussed in Chapter 3, *DBD::Chart* is a fine piece of work, one whose limitations are bounded only by feverish imagination. All we need now is a collection of SQL scripts, a CGI program providing a pick-list of these scripts, a wing, a prayer and a few parameter switches. If we had all of these, we could create a really lovely Oracle DBA tool. Or maybe we should just download a single canned application that does all of this for us? Read on....

Oracletool

Oracletool, developed by Adam vonNieda as a tuning, monitoring, and general database administration tool, is one of the best Perl CGI applications you'll find anywhere. Oracletool provides a simple web-based interface to many of the day-to-day maintenance tasks an Oracle DBA needs to keep a typical database in good working order. (It's also a very useful development utility.)

---

* This may actually be incorrect, though most browsers will be able to cope with it, even on DOS systems, because of the Internet rule of thumb: "Be strict about what you send out; be liberal about what you accept." See *http://www.faqs.org/rfcs/rfc2068.html* for a strict interpretation of Internet line endings.

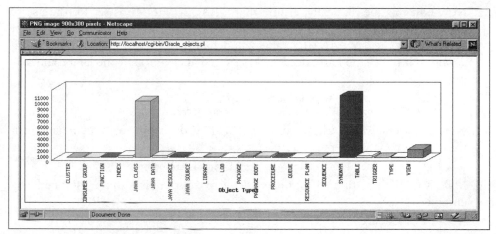

Figure 4-2. DBD::Chart and Apache

Oracletool provides a reasonable degree of security as a default, and also gives you the ability to configure more rigorous security. You can choose your level of security based on your own site's requirements. The faint of heart will be glad to hear that Oracletool does *not* modify your database. You can create a user with the SELECT ANY TABLE privilege, and rest assured that running Oracletool won't break your database. Not that you'll need to worry in any case—Oracletool is well written, and behaves consistently.

To learn more about Oracletool, visit the following page:

   http://www.oracletool.com/

In the following sections we'll show how to install Oracletool and try out a few of its options. There is much more to learn about Oracletool, however. You can find a more detailed discussion in *Oracle & Open Source*, and you can browse freely through the tool's many helpful menus and screens to explore its capabilities.

Installing Oracletool

The instructions for installing Oracletool are virtually identical under Unix and Win32. Get hold of the latest tarball, such as *oracletool-2.0.tar.gz*, and unpack it into a local directory. Good instructions come with the download. We'll provide the usual two summaries here.

Installing Oracletool on Unix

1. Copy the *oracletool.sam* file to your *../cgi-bin/* directory under Apache. Rename it to *oracletool.ini*. For instance:

   ```
   $ cp oracletool.sam /usr/local/apache/cgi-bin/oracletool.ini
   ```

2. Now edit this file. Basically, ensure that *ORACLE_HOME* is set for the use of Perl DBI and that *TNS_ADMIN* is set so Oracletool can get hold of your target databases.* (The *TNS_ADMIN* value will default to *$ORACLE_HOME/network/admin*, but there's no harm done making sure it's clear to anyone later maintaining the file.)

```
ORACLE_HOME = /opt/oracle/product/9.0.1
TNS_ADMIN = /opt/oracle/product/9.0.1/network/admin
```

3. Now copy *oracletool.pl* itself to your *../cgi-bin/* directory, without renaming it this time (unless you'd prefer a *.cgi* suffix):

```
$ cp oracletool.pl /usr/local/apache/cgi-bin/oracletool.pl
```

4. Make sure that the first line of the *oracletool.pl* script points to the right Perl executable:

```
#!/usr/bin/perl
```

5. We also had some problemettes connecting *orcl.world* and Oracletool to Oracle9*i*, on SuSE 7.3 Linux, but there are a range of connection options you can try near the top of *oracletool.pl*. For instance, we replaced the following line, which was deliberately stripping out *.world* suffixes:

```
my %hash =
    map { (split(/\.world/i,(split(':'))[-1]))[0] , undef }
        DBI->data_sources('Oracle')
```

We used one of the commented-out simpler alternatives. Problem solved:

```
my %hash =
    map { (split(':'))[-1] , undef } DBI->data_sources('Oracle')
```

6. Once you've solved any rare teething problems like this, you should secure *oracletool.pl* by changing its permissions, as with the Unix *chmod* command:

```
$ chmod 755 oracletool.pl
```

7. Now ensure that your Apache web server and target Oracle database are running. Type the following into your browser location field:

   http://localhost/cgi-bin/oracletool.pl

8. You'll be greeted with the screen sequence displayed in Figure 4-3.

Installing Oracletool on Win32

For Win32, follow these steps:

1. Copy the *oracletool.sam* file to your *..\cgi-bin* directory under Apache. Rename it to *oracletool.ini*:

```
C:> copy oracletool.sam
    C:\Program Files\Apache Group\Apache\cgi-bin\oracletool.ini
```

---

* Note that the parameters in *oracletool.sam* are not Perl variables; they are more in the style of Java *.ini* parameters. (See Table 4-1 for more initialization parameters.)

2. Now edit this file, in the same way as on Unix. Make sure *ORACLE_HOME* is set for the use of Perl DBI if your Win32 platform needs it, and that *TNS_ ADMIN* is set so Oracletool can get hold of your target databases:

```
ORACLE_HOME = C:\\ORANT        # You may not need to set this on Win32
TNS_ADMIN = C:\\ORANT\\NET80\\ADMIN
```

3. Now copy *oracletool.pl* itself to your *..\cgi-bin* directory:

```
C:> copy oracletool.pl
    C:\Program Files\Apache Group\Apache\cgi-bin\oracletool.pl
```

4. Make sure that the first line of the *oracletool.pl* script points to the right Perl executable. For Win32 using ActivePerl, that's usually:

```
#!/perl/bin/perl
```

5. If you're running on NTFS or a similarly secure NT-based filesystem, you should secure *oracletool.pl* by changing its permissions via your security system to have the equivalent of *755* status on Unix.

6. Now ensure that your Apache web server and target Oracle database are running. Then type the following into your browser location field to get to the screens displayed in Figure 4-3:

   http://localhost/cgi-bin/oracletool.pl

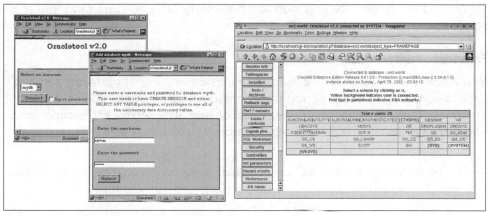

Figure 4-3. Logging into Oracletool on Win32 and Linux

Table 4-1. Main Oracletool initialization parameters

Parameter	Description
ORACLE_HOME	Enables Perl DBI to connect to Oracle
TNS_ADMIN	Tells Oracletool where to find your *tnsnames.ora* file
EXPIRATION	Cookie expiration time (defaults to one year)
ORACLENAMES	Uncomment if using Oracle*Names
DEBUG	Sends debug information to a nominated log file

Table 4-1. Main Oracletool initialization parameters (continued)

Parameter	Description
LOGGING	Similar to debug, but for standard logging information
LOG	Full path of log file required by DEBUG and LOGGING
AUTO_REFRESH	Determines screen refresh rate in seconds
LIMIT_SEARCH	Limits various searches (to keep resource use down)
ENCRYPTION_STRING	Used to encrypt passwords; should be made unguessable
ENCRYPTION_METHOD	Determines whether IDEA or Blowfish is used in level 2 security

Preferences and privileges

Once you've connected to a database, you can change the Oracletool look and feel by selecting one of the theme options from the *Preferences* menu. The following Oracle user privileges are also required to run Oracletool's selection reports:

Oracle7, Oracle8, Oracle8i
    SELECT ANY TABLE

Oracle9i
    SELECT ANY TABLE, SELECT ANY DICTIONARY

To obtain DBA reports, the user must also possess the DBA privilege. Once you're all sorted out, welcome to Oracletool!

Enhanced security

You'll notice that passwords are being stored inside cookies, which means you don't have to keep logging on. To protect these cookies, there are three levels of Oracletool security, and the program figures out ahead of time which extra Perl security modules you have installed. It then chooses the security level accordingly:

Level 0
    If you lack the security modules discussed as follows, you'll be at this security level. Passwords are stored in cookies, in plain text—for example:

        mydb.sessionid **system~manager**

Level 1
    The username, password, and encryption string are MD5-encoded into a single string. The default encryption string is stored within *oracletool.ini*:

        ENCRYPTION_STRING = **changeme**

    Obviously, you may wish to alter this string. We changed ours to *drinkme*, and this turned our cookie password string into:

        mydb.sessionid
        c3lzdGVt-bWFuYWdlcg%3D%3D-FbMoQ1xyHjwXuKU3aTIL3g%3D%3D

    The reason Oracletool did this was because two security modules, created by Gisle Aas, come preinstalled automatically with ActivePerl:

- *Digest::MD5*
- *MIME::Base64*

You'll have to install these manually with Unix. (See later for details.)

Level 2

This level uses the IDEA or Blowfish block ciphers (both use extremely secure algorithms). Oracletool defaults to the IDEA algorithm within *oracletool.ini*:

```
ENCRYPTION_METHOD = idea
```

If you'd like to use Blowfish instead, change *idea* to *blowfish* in *oracletool.ini*. You'll need the following modules for level 2 security:

- *Digest::MD5*
- *Crypt::IDEA* or *Crypt::Blowfish*, both by Dave Paris
- *Crypt::CBC*, by Lincoln Stein

As of this writing, some of the *Crypt-** modules mentioned previously, were not available under ActiveState; you should check out the current situation at:

http://aspn.activestate.com/ASPN/Downloads/ActivePerl/PPM/Packages

You can get the Unix packages via the three following addresses:

http://www.cpan.org/authors/id/GAAS/
http://www.cpan.org/authors/id/D/DP/DPARIS/
http://www.cpan.org/authors/id/LDS/

You can also find out your current security level from the main Oracletool menu by selecting the *About* option on the main menu

> Given a choice between *Crypt::IDEA* and *Crypt::Blowfish*, we recommend that you opt for the latter. Since around 1999, Version 1.01 of *Crypt::IDEA* has had some build problems with Perl, particularly with Perl 5.6.1 on some flavors of Linux (though it's possible that this been resolved with later versions of either Perl or *Crypt::IDEA*). This problem occurred because Perl used to "pollute" the namespace of C-based modules. The problem was fixed in Perl 5.6; however, some modules had come to rely upon this "feature."

Using Oracletool

We won't provide a detailed description of Oracletool here because ample documentation is available in your Oracletool download. Simply point your browser at the relevant directory where you unpacked Oracletool, and view the following file:

file:///C|/MyOracletoolUnpackDirectory/oracletool-2.0/doc/index.htm

We suggest that you wander through the different Oracletool DBA options and check out the program's many capabilities (one of them, the fragmentation monitoring option, is shown in Figure 4-4).

Oracletool was designed to be as concise and straightforward as possible. (One way it avoids "code bloat" is to limit itself to monitoring, rather than changing, its target databases.) To this end, Oracletool requires Perl DBI and *DBD::Oracle* as the only extra Perl modules beyond the standard module set for Perl 5.6.

The requirements code block for the 21,000+ line *oracletool.pl* file is simply:

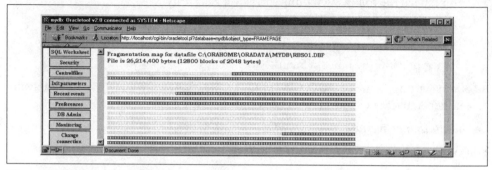

Figure 4-4. The Oracletool fragmentation feature

```
require 5.003;

use strict;
use CGI qw(:standard);    # CGI, File::Basename and FileHandle
use File::Basename;       # all standard built-in Perl modules! :-)
use FileHandle;

if (! eval "require DBI") {
    ErrorPage("It appears that the DBI module is not installed!");
}
```

Everything else is also contained within this single CGI script, except the initialization values held in *oracletool.ini*.

Not only does Oracletool currently offer a lot of features (for a summary of current features, see Table 4-2), but its author is continually adding even more capabilities. You can participate in its growth by emailing new ideas to Oracletool's creator via *adam@oracletool.com*.

Table 4-2. Major features of Oracletool 2.0

Feature	Description
Schema list	Drill-down screen used to examine each individual schema.
Session info	Various session-based reports and the ability to view sessions.
Tablespaces	Large tablespace report and access to tablespace allocations graph (see Figure 4-5).

Table 4-2. Major features of Oracletool 2.0 (continued)

Feature	Description
Datafiles	Datafiles report, plus access to a datafiles I/O chart.
Redo / Archives	Online redo log information, including archiving status.
Rollback segs	Access to various reports on rollback segments and transactions.
Perf / memory	Memory and SQL allocations, multithreaded server (MTS) use, and shared pool flushing.
Locks / contends	Checks on object lock contention and session wait information.
Explain plan	Online form to check SQL explain plans (Oracletool will install PLAN_TABLE for you automatically, if it is unavailable).
SQL Worksheet	Ability to enter and execute multiple SQL statements, online. SELECT statements produce formatted reports, and DML is executed.
Security	Reports on roles, profiles, auditing, and other security concerns.
Controlfiles	Various control file reports, including a breakdown of record types.
Init parameters	Report on all current *INIT.ORA* parameters, including descriptions.
Recent events	Various instance reports including log switches, and startup times
Preferences	Customization screens displayed for fonts and themes.
DB Admin	Many different reports and options, including: User administration Session administration Rollback segment administration Generate table DDL Invalid object administration Parameter administration Job Scheduler (DBMS_JOB) Space report by user Space report by tablespace / user Datafile fragmentation report Object extent report
Monitoring	Oracletool database monitoring system.
Change connection	Connection screen to other databases.
My Oracletool	Ability to add your own scripts to the Oracletool SQL repository.

In the following sections, we'll look at a few Oracletool features we especially like.

My Oracletool

The *My Oracletool* feature was recently added to Oracletool. Using this feature, you can add your own SQL scripts, store them within a target repository, and execute them later whenever you wish. One such script is shown in Figure 4-6.

Oracletool monitoring

Version 2.0 of Oracletool also added the ability to monitor databases by utilizing a PL/SQL-based framework. Oracletool checks for common database problems, such

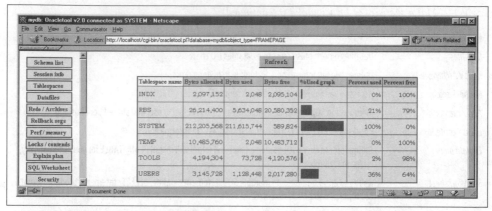

Figure 4-5. Oracletool's tablespace allocation

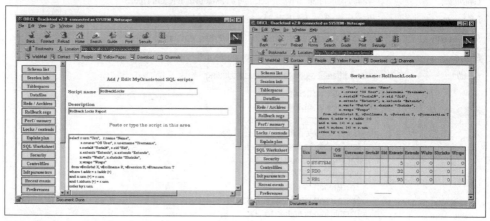

Figure 4-6. My Oracletool in action

as inadequate tablespace usage, resource contention, and so on. When these problems reach certain thresholds, a warning email is delivered to a configured pager's email address via a nominated email server. See Figure 4-7 for an example.

The way Oracletool is designed, the main server has certain PL/SQL procedures installed on it, and the target clients have other procedures installed. This framework is held together by database links. Because of this design, OS daemons are unnecessary. You schedule the monitoring tasks either via Oracle's built-in DBMS_ JOB package or via an OS *cron* script like this one:

```
#!/bin/sh

ORACLE_BASE=/u01/oracle
ORACLE_HOME=$ORACLE_BASE/8.1.7
TNS_ADMIN=$ORACLE_HOME/network/admin
PATH=$PATH:$ORACLE_HOME/bin
```

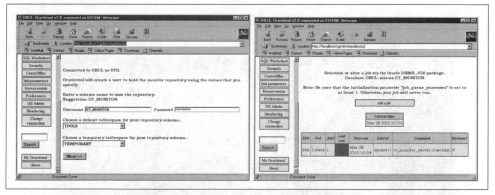

Figure 4-7. Setting up Oracletool monitoring

```
export ORACLE_BASE ORACLE_HOME TNS_ADMIN PATH

sqlplus -s ot_monitor/ot_monitor_password@server <<EOF
    exec ot_monitor_server.checkall;
EOF
```

The monitoring server must have a JServer release so that it is able to send emails via the DBMS_SMTP package; the result is that you must be running at least Oracle8*i*; note, however, that the clients need only be running Oracle8.

Karma

Sean Hull's Karma program takes Oracle database monitoring a step further. Like Oracletool, it is intended to help DBAs with their daily work. The program is especially helpful in automating the tracking of important, though tedious-to-collect information—information that you may need to know, but be too busy to gather personally. Karma's comprehensive configuration capabilities let you select the particular features and database events to monitor, how often to monitor them, and how strictly to monitor them. (See Figure 4-8 for a sample screen produced by Karma.) You can also break up your many databases into groups, each with its own monitoring criteria and thresholds. Karma's goal is to help Oracle DBAs collect numerous useful statistics automatically in the background. Karma offers the ability to notify the DBA by email when database problems occur, and it provides a single place to keep track of many different databases.

Because Karma collects a wider range of statistics than Oracletool's monitoring features do, and because it provides a full suite of online monitoring options, program installation and configuration are slightly more involved. Unlike Oracletool, Karma is not implemented as a CGI script. Instead, it runs a daemon, generating HTML pages in a specified location.

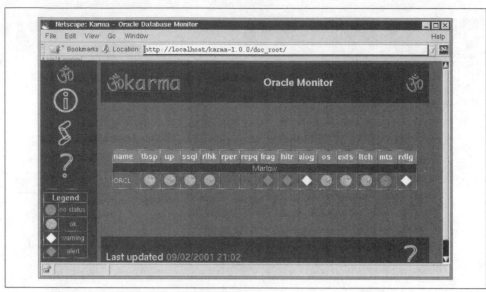

Figure 4-8. The main Karma page indicating alarms

For complete information about Karma, go to:

http://hypno.iheavy.com/karma/

The following sections describe the installation on both Unix and Win32. In both environments, note that you may also need several other modules, depending on your requirements:

http://www.cpan.org/authors/id/M/MA/MARKOV/
Graham Barr's and Mark Overmeer's *MailTools.pm* Perl module. This is needed by Karma if you'll be using the email notification facility.

http://www.cpan.org/authors/id/KJALB/
The CPAN home of Kenneth Albanowski's *TermReadKey.pm* package; it's necessary for collecting operating system statistics under Unix.

http://www.cpan.org/authors/id/GBARR/
Graham Barr's home CPAN directory containing some of Perl's most influential modules, including the *libnet* library required by *MailTools.pm*.

Installing Karma on Unix

We downloaded the following file from the Karma site provided earlier:

karma-1.0.0.tar.gz

For Unix, follow these instructions:

1. Unpack your Karma tarball under a suitable Apache *../htdocs* directory:

```
$ cd /usr/local/apache/htdocs
$ gzip -d karma-1.0.0.tar.gz
$ tar xvf karma-1.0.0.tar
$ cd karma-1.0.0
```

2. There are a variety of installation document files; the *QUICKSTART* document is especially designed for those who want to just get on with it:

```
$ vi README INSTALL QUICKSTART
```

3. When it's ready, Karma uses the *Makefile.PL* configuration method:

```
$ perl Makefile.PL
$ make
```

4. Check that the *make test* step produces output such as the following, before installing:

```
$ make test
PERL_DL_NONLAZY=1 /usr/bin/perl -Iblib/arch -Iblib/lib -I/usr/local/lib/perl5/5.
6.1/i686-linux -I/usr/local/lib/perl5/5.6.1 test.pl
...
ok 1
```

Now install:

```
$ make install
```

5. Before you run Karma, you may want to set the *KARMA_HOME* environment variable to ensure that the correct files are accessed by the daemon agents. You'll also need to set the Oracle environment:

```
$ export KARMA_HOME=/usr/local/apache/htdocs/karma-1.0.0
$ export ORACLE_HOME=/u01/app/oracle/product/8.1.5
$ export LD_LIBRARY_PATH=$LD_LIBRARY_PATH:$ORACLE_HOME/lib
```

Installing TermReadKey.pm

If you will later want to check the alert log file for each database via Karma, you need to install the *TermReadKey.pm* module to keep passwords secret. It provides Perl with various input controls for reading console input and allowing specialized input, such as reading in passwords without echoing them back. Follow these steps:

1. Unpack the tarball from the CPAN web site provided earlier:

```
$ gzip -d TermReadKey-2.14.tar.gz$ tar xvf TermReadKey-2.14.tar
$ cd TermReadKey-2.14
```

2. The command-line input effects are demonstrated by the *make test* step:

```
$ perl Makefile.PL
$ make
$ make test
...
This is ReadMode 2. It's just like #1, but echo is turned off. Great
for passwords.
You may enter some invisible text here:
You entered 'The Invisible Man'.
```

3. If the tests work OK, go for the install:

```
$ make install
```

Installing MailTools.pm

If you're thinking of using Karma's automatic email options, you'll need to install *MailTools.pm*. To do this, you also need Graham Barr's *libnet* library. We're after two Perl modules contained within this bundle, *Net::SMTP* and *Net::Domain*. The full libnet module collection is summarized in Table 4-3.

Table 4-3. Modules available within Perl's libnet library

Perl *libnet* module	Description
Net::FTP	File Transfer Protocol
Net::SMTP	Simple Mail Transfer Protocol
Net::Time	Daytime Protocol
Net::NNTP	Network News Transfer Protocol
Net::POP3	Post Office Protocol 3
Net::SNPP	Simple Network Pager Protocol

You can get hold of the latest bundle, such as *libnet-1.0704.tar.gz*, from:

http://www.cpan.org/authors/id/GBARR/

Once you've unpacked the tarball, the *perl Makefile.PL* step does more configuration than most Perl module construction kits, and the test step also requires access to a list of Internet hosts. Be prepared to answer plenty of questions, especially during the installation stage. You can, however, skip these tests if you wish:

```
$ perl Makefile.PL
$ make
$ make test
$ make install
```

We're now ready for *MailTools.pm* proper:

```
$ gzip -d MailTools-1.40.tar.gz
$ tar xvf MailTools-1.40.tar
$ cd MailTools-1.40
$ perl Makefile.PL
$ make
$ make test
$ make install
```

Configuring Karma

To test Karma and create errors (which we're hoping the program will email us about), we created a ridiculously small TEMP temporary tablespace:

```
CREATE TABLESPACE TEMP DATAFILE
   '/u04/temp1orcl.ora' SIZE 10240 REUSE AUTOEXTEND OFF
DEFAULT STORAGE
(
   INITIAL        4096
   NEXT           2048
   PCTINCREASE    0
)
TEMPORARY LOGGING ;
```

Because we're intending to use OS monitoring, we now need our own special user located directly within the target database, with a SELECT ANY TABLE privilege. We also need a small set of statistical collection tables. We can accomplish this by running two scripts provided by Karma, in the *../sql* directory:

> *karma_user.sql*
> *karma_objs.sql*

Running these two SQL scripts produces the following output, including the expected truncation error:

```
SQL> @karma_user
Enter value for karma_password: seadevil
User created.
Grant succeeded.
Grant succeeded.
SQL> connect karma/seadevil
Connected.
SQL> @karma_objs
Creating karma_os_stats table...
Table created.
Creating karma_alertlog_errors table...
Table created.
TRUNCATE TABLE karma_agent
               *
ERROR at line 1:
ORA-00942: table or view does not exist
Creating karma_agent table...
Table created.
1 row created.
SQL>
```

Follow these steps:

1. As the nominated Oracle user, we can now get the Karma OS monitor agent going. The following script prompted us for the *karma* user password, *seadevil*, which then kicked off a daemonized *karmagentd*. This woke up every 300 configured seconds to check the alert log file specified:

   ```
   $ karmagentd -u karma -t ORCL -a $ORACLE_HOME/rdbms/log/alert_orcl.log
   ```

2. The statistics collected by *karmagentd* are then made accessible to the Web by the *karmad* program itself. We'll be kicking this off shortly as the *root* user. But first, we need to make sure that our configuration is right. We do this by altering

the *karma.conf* file. The following example shows our *karma.conf* settings. These will check various database states and report back to us if warning or alert thresholds are crossed. Notice the *notify_email* tag, which tells Karma to whom to send emails. Additional help is available in the installation files.

```
karma:Marlow:ORCL:karma:seadevil
repqueue
reperror
Marlow:notify_email:full:oracle
notify_alert:10:fragmentation,a,b,c
notify_warning:15:hitratios,a,b,c
Marlow:refresh:5:75
Marlow:redolog:1:30:15
Marlow:rollback:1:0:0
Marlow:tablespace:1:85:95
Marlow:slowsql:1:100:200
Marlow:alertlog:1:60:86400
Marlow:hitratios:1:95:70
Marlow:fragmentation:1:0:0
Marlow:extents:1:2:1
Marlow:latch:1:0:0
Marlow:mts:1:50:75
Marlow:os:1:5:10
warn_blink:true
alert_blink:true
pref_group_sections:true
doc_root:/usr/local/apache/htdocs/karma-1.0.0/doc_root
```

3. We can then start up the main *karmad* program:

```
$ karmad -c $KARMA_HOME/karma.conf
```

4. Two mail messages are now generated automatically by the Karma system and sent to the *oracle* OS user. These allow us to focus on the requisite errors via the web pages that show these warnings:

```
Message 1:
From root  Sun Sep  2 21:00:16 2001
Return-Path: <root>
Received: (from root@localhost)
        by localhost.localdomain (8.8.7/8.8.7) id VAA01389;
        Sun, 2 Sep 2001 21:00:15 +0100
Date: Sun, 2 Sep 2001 21:00:15 +0100
From: root <root@localhost.localdomain>
Message-Id: <200109022000.VAA01389@localhost.localdomain>
Subject: ORCL:ALRT:fragmentation,hitratios,
To: oracle@localhost.localdomain
Status: RO
ORCL database **ALERT** - The following services have problems:
        fragmentation
        hitratios
&
Message 2:
From root  Sun Sep  2 21:00:16 2001
Return-Path: <root>
```

```
Received: (from root@localhost)
        by localhost.localdomain (8.8.7/8.8.7) id VAA01389;
        Sun, 2 Sep 2001 21:00:15 +0100
Date: Sun, 2 Sep 2001 21:00:15 +0100
From: root <root@localhost.localdomain>
Message-Id: <200109022000.VAA01389@localhost.localdomain>
Subject: ORCL:WARNING:alertlog, redolog
To: oracle@localhost.localdomain
Status: RO
ORCL database WARNING - The following services have problems:
        alertlog
        redolog
&
```

Checking on this later via the web browser, we'll also be able to find out something about our TEMP tablespace, with the information generated from our alert log file (see Figure 4-9).

Figure 4-9. Karma reporting on alert log errors

Installing Karma on Win32

At the time this book went to press, the full daemon *karmagentd* functionality of Karma had yet to be ported to a Win32 service. Even now, though, you can still do a lot with *karmad*:

1. Unzip the *karma-1.0.0.tar.gz* file into an unpack directory under Apache's *..\htdocs* directory, such as:

   C:\Program Files\Apache Group\Apache\htdocs\karma-1.0.0

2. You then need to check out the following set of files:

    README
    README.WIN32
    INSTALL
    QUICKSTART

3. We'll assume here that you don't have the compilation facilities on your Win32 box that are required for an automatic installation of Karma. We'll therefore explain how to perform a manual installation.

4. We unpack the *karmad* program from its wrapper:

    ```
    $ cd bin
    $ perl karmad.PL
    ```

    This should leave us with the Perl program, *karmad*.

As with Unix, you may wish to create a Karma user within the target database. The *../sql/karma.sql* script has been provided for this purpose. We're now ready to configure Karma for database action.

Configuring Karma on Win32

The *karma.conf* file itself contains plenty of help on how to configure Karma, though fortunately most of the configuration is fairly intuitive. The main configuration parameters we chose were:

```
karma:Henley-On-Thames:ORCL:karma:dalek
repqueue
reperror
Henley-On-Thames:refresh:5:75
Henley-On-Thames:redolog:1:30:15
Henley-On-Thames:rollback:1:0:0
Henley-On-Thames:tablespace:1:85:95
Henley-On-Thames:slowsql:1:100:200
Henley-On-Thames:alertlog:1:60:86400
Henley-On-Thames:hitratios:1:95:70
Henley-On-Thames:fragmentation:1:0:0
Henley-On-Thames:extents:1:2:1
Henley-On-Thames:latch:1:0:0
Henley-On-Thames:mts:1:50:75
Henley-On-Thames:os:1:5:10
warn_blink:false
alert_blink:false
pref_group_sections:true
#doc_root: Commented out to use default Present Working Directory
```

The database connection line at the top of the list is perhaps the most important thing to get right. We also decided to default the *..\doc_root* to the present working directory.

Running Karma on Win32

To get the basic *karmad* program running, change to the main Karma home directory, make sure your target Oracle database is accessible via its listener, and then run
the main Karma monitor program:

```
C:\> cd C:\Program Files\Apache Group\Apache\htdocs\karma-1.0.0
C:\> perl bin\karmad -c karma.conf
```

The daemonic *karmad* monitor periodically produces a series of HTML pages, which
you can access via a web server (you can also access them directly with a local
browser if you'd prefer). We liked the idea of the first option, so we started up
Apache and then visited the following page:

http://localhost/karma-1.0.0/doc_root/index.html

You can see the first result in Figure 4-10.

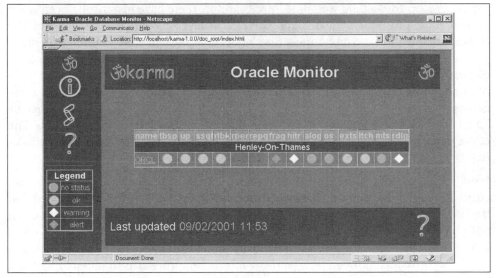

Figure 4-10. The main Karma screen on Win32

Extra Perl modules for Win32

If you do want to push Karma to get mail notification and OS monitoring, you'll
need to get hold of two more ActivePerl packages. Connect to the Internet and run
ActivePerl's PPM program to install the *MailTools* package. You may also want to
install *TermReadKey* in anticipation of the time that the daemon-based *karmagentd*
will be ported to a service under Win32:

```
C:\> ppm
PPM> install MailTools
PPM> install TermReadKey
PPM> exit
```

CHAPTER 5

Embedding Perl into Apache
with mod_perl

Although the Perl CGI methodology we discussed in Chapter 4, , is an easy and popular approach to building web-based applications, there have historically been some performance problems with this approach. Whenever a Perl CGI script is run, the rather sizeable Perl interpreter must first be brought into memory before it can interpret and execute your program. Unfortunately, that can be a very slow process. Fans of Java servlets have pointed to this performance issue in advocating that their technology be used instead of Perl. But Perl has not taken this challenge from Java evangelists lying down! Apache's *mod_perl* module provides an interface between Apache and Perl that allows Perl code to be cached in the web server's memory space. The effect is a substantial improvement in performance over standard Perl CGI applications.

How much is substantial? As with so many things, the only real benchmarks are either for highly oversimplified cases (with no real application) or for highly specialized cases (with little extensibility). For most real-world programs, however, we can tell you that *mod_perl* provides a raw speed increase of approximately 40 to 60%. But this is only part of the story. The really significant gain is the vastly increased scalability provided through *mod_perl* because the interpreter is in memory and can be shared between processes.

The *mod_perl* module binds the Perl interpreter directly into the heart of the Apache server, thus avoiding the overhead of loading the interpreter into memory for each script executed on the server. As well as doing memory caching, this module also allows you to extend the Apache server in the Perl language itself. With *mod_perl* in place, the entire server-side Apache API becomes available to Perl programs. In this chapter, we'll describe *mod_perl*, as well as several related Apache modules:

mod_perl
> The module that provides the interface between Apache and Perl.

Apache::Registry
> An Apache module that is provided as a standard part of the *mod_perl* download. It greatly improves the performance of your CGI Perl scripts by evaluating

your scripts into server subroutines that remain resident in the Apache server's memory.

Apache::DBI

This Apache module pools all of your database connections into memory. By providing persistent connections in this way, *Apache::DBI* greatly improves the performance of your Perl CGI scripts. This is a supplementary Apache module that you must obtain from CPAN.

Apache::OWA

To illustrate the effectiveness of *mod_perl*, we'll also show how it's used with the *Apache::OWA* Perl Apache module, which connects *mod_perl* to the PL/SQL Web Toolkit.

mod_perl

First created by Doug MacEachern in 1996, *mod_perl* is the main flower of the Apache Perl integration project. It brings the full power of the Perl language into the heart of the Apache HTTP server by linking the Perl runtime library into Apache's modular C language API. This is like being able to turn your Jeep into a jet-powered helicopter for the weekend, and then back again on Monday, at the flick of a switch.[*]

Once Apache is up and running with *mod_perl*, the Perl interpreter engine is up and running too, conveniently preloaded into constant memory. This means there's no restart overhead each time you run a Perl CGI script. The speed improvement brought to any Perl-based web site by the addition of *mod_perl*, and the scalability implications, are enormous. Important Apache *mod_perl* links include:

http://perl.apache.org:
Apache Perl integration project home page.

http://www.modperl.com:
Home page of Lincoln Stein and Doug MacEachern's helpful book, *Writing Apache Modules with Perl and C* (O'Reilly & Associates, 1999).[†]

http://www.refcards.com/about/mod_perl.html:
Andrew Ford's online reference cards for *mod_perl*, also supported by his book, the *mod_perl Pocket Reference* (O'Reilly & Associates, 2000).[‡]

---

[*] The same trick is repeated, later in this book, in Chapter 8, *Embedding Perl into PL/SQL*, when we embed Perl into a PL/SQL C library.

[†] The official O'Reilly page is *http://www.oreilly.com/catalog/wrapmod*.

[‡] *http://www.oreilly.com/catalog/modperlpr*

http://theoryx5.uwinnipeg.ca/guide

A good entry point to the University of Winnipeg's excellent pages on *mod_perl* and CGI scripting. This guide is particularly helpful in explaining the complex issue of porting CGI scripts to *Apache::Registry* and *mod_perl*.

http://mathforum.org/epigone/modperl

Ken William's superb *mod_perl* topics archive.

Installing mod_perl on Unix

Before you can test your *mod_perl* installation, you must make sure that the Perl *LWP.pm* module is available. Developed by Gisle Aas, this module provides a "Library for WWW access in Perl"; it consists of a wide range of related Perl modules designed to help simplify Perl Internet client connections. Not only is this module useful for our later *mod_perl* test, it's invaluable for many Perl Internet requirements. We'll come back to *LWP.pm* again and again as we discuss Perl and the Web in the next few chapters.

LWP-Library for WWW access in Perl

The main focus of *LWP* is to provide classes and functions allowing the creation of Internet Perl clients. The library also contains modules for more general use, even making it possible to create simple HTTP servers.

Fortunately for us, Gisle Aas has collated all of the related *LWP* modules into a single download, *libwww-perl-5.64.tar.gz* (or its latest derivative). However, *LWP* itself relies upon several other related modules, as detailed in the appropriate installation order, in Table 5-1. If you want to install these by hand, download the latest tarballs and process them in the usual *perl Makefile.PL* manner. Alternatively, we'll accept a little sneaky automation here. There is a very handy command you can run, which should load everything required for *LWP*, directly over the Internet, in just one line:

```
$ perl -MCPAN -e 'install Bundle::LWP'
```

An even sneakier routine loads the whole of *mod_perl* and many of its related modules:

```
$ perl -MCPAN -e 'install Bundle::Apache'
```

This will load every module you require, including *LWP*. However, we'll still go through the manual route; this way, we can describe all the bumps in the road and configure everything properly. The *CPAN* module is a great tool, but it can sometimes be unreliable, as we discussed in Chapter 2, *Installing Perl*, particularly when *CPAN* modules are not preconfigured by their authors in exactly the way that *CPAN* is expecting (many Internet modules fall into this category).

Table 5-1. Modules required to install LWP

Perl module	Description/download page
Digest::MD5	Perl interface to the MD5 message digest algorithm[a]
	http://www.cpan.org/authors/id/GAAS
HTML::Parser	HTML parser class module for Perl
	http://www.cpan.org/authors/id/GAAS
Libnet (e.g., libnet-1.0704.tar.gz)	Many related Perl modules
	http://www.cpan.org/authors/id/GBARR
MIME::Base64	Module for encoding and decoding of Base64 strings
	http://www.cpan.org/authors/id/GAAS
URI	Uniform Resource Identifiers module
	http://www.cpan.org/authors/id/GAAS
HTML::Tagset	Data tables handler useful for parsing HTML
	http://www.cpan.org/authors/id/S/SB/SBURKE
LWP (e.g., libwww-perl-5.64.tar.gz)	The complete library for WWW access in Perl
	http://www.cpan.org/authors/id/GAAS

[a]To learn more about Ronald L. Rivest's MD5 message digest algorithm, check out: http://theory.lcs.mit.edu/~rivest/homepage.html

Two other CPAN packages that people often use alongside *LWP* include:

Storable
> Persistent data storage used to make HTTP less stateless.
>
> *http://www.cpan.org/authors/id/A/AM/AMS*

HTML-SimpleParse
> A bare bones HTML parser.
>
> *http://www.cpan.org/authors/id/KWILLIAMS*

SSL—Secure Sockets Layer

If you need enhanced security at your site, you may also want to use the popular Secure Sockets Layer (SSL) program. Before you install *LWP* (or re-install it), be sure to check out the programs and Perl extensions listed in Table 5-2.

Table 5-2. Optional SSL modules for use with LWP

Perl module or C program	Description/download page
OpenSSL	Open Secure Sockets Layer program
	http://www.openssl.org
Crypt::SSLeay[a]	OpenSSL Perl glue providing *https* support to *LWP*
	http://www.cpan.org/authors/id/C/CH/CHAMAS
Net::SSLeay	Perl extension for using OpenSSL and *https* sockets
	http://www.cpan.org/authors/id/SAMPO

Table 5-2. Optional SSL modules for use with LWP (continued)

Perl module or C program	Description/download page
IO::Socket::SSL	SSL socket interface class
	http://www.cpan.org/authors/id/A/AS/ASPA

aSSLeay is named after the original "Secure Sockets Layer work by Eric A. Young."

Installing mod_perl

Before we begin our installation of *mod_perl*, we recommend that for security reasons you shut down all your Apache processes, and then save the entire Apache root structure, perhaps in a tarball, before continuing. We can always revert back to this saved structure later on, should *mod_perl* prove problematic.

To do the actual *mod_perl* installation on Unix, first download the latest and greatest goods by visiting Doug MacEachern's CPAN page:

http://www.cpan.org/authors/id/DOUGM

Then follow these steps:

1. Begin with the time-honored routine:

   ```
   $ gzip -d mod_perl-1.26.tar.gz
   $ tar xvf mod_perl-1.26.tar
   $ cd mod_perl-1.26
   $ vi README INSTALL
   ```

2. There exists a bewildering array of options you can use to build *mod_perl*. You'll find all of them detailed in the *INSTALL* file. We're just going to go for the simple install of compiling every option available, with the clever *EVERYTHING=1* switch:

   ```
   $ perl Makefile.PL EVERYTHING=1 APACHE_PREFIX=/usr/local/apache
   ```

3. The first thing *Makefile.PL* will try to do is find a source directory for Apache within the local vicinity. This should be available from the installation we performed in the previous chapter:

   ```
   Configure mod_perl with ../apache_1.3.24/src ? [y] y
   ```

   If a local Apache directory is unavailable, you'll be asked to supply one. Answer accordingly:

   ```
   Please tell me where I can find your apache src [] <your apache source>
   ```

   You'll then be asked if you want to build the *httpd* executable in the Apache source directory you nominated. We said yes:

   ```
   Shall I build httpd in ../apache_1.3.24/src for you? [y] y
   ```

   (On some Unix systems, including some Solaris flavors, it may be best to always use fully qualified path names, because of some problems with include paths. If *mod_perl* fails to build as expected, thoroughly check all the documentation that comes with *mod_perl* as well as the online resources mentioned at the start of this chapter, particularly the topics archive.)

4. Lots of information will then appear, but assuming no problems, we can go ahead with the compilation:

   ```
   $ make
   ```

5. The *make test* step is highly recommended if you've loaded *LWP*. In the following example, we include only a few lines of typical output, but much more than this should appear. Expect some tests to be skipped depending on your platform:

   ```
   $ make test
   ...
   internal/table......ok
   internal/taint......ok
   All tests successful, 6 tests skipped.
   Files=34, Tests=390, 23 wallclock secs
   (18.68 cusr +  1.75 csys = 20.43 CPU)
   ```

   If any tests should fail, re-run *make test*, but this time in verbose mode:

   ```
   $ make test TEST_VERBOSE=1
   ```

6. Before installing, go to */usr/local/apache/bin* directory and save the old *httpd* file (just in case):

   ```
   $ cd /usr/local/apache/bin
   $ mv httpd httpd.old
   ```

7. We can now do the install:

   ```
   $ make install
   ```

8. If you specified it earlier, you should also find a new *httpd* living under the Apache source directory, which you may have supplied on the *Makefile.PL* step. This will be approximately four times the size of your old *httpd*. Copy it to the main Apache executables' *bin*:

   ```
   $ cd ../apache_1.3.24/src
   $ cp httpd /usr/local/apache/bin
   $ cd /usr/local/apache/bin
   $ ls -la httpd*
   -rwxr-xr-x   1 root     root     1497133 Apr  1 15:47 httpd
   -rwxr-xr-x   1 root     root      410220 Apr  1 15:45 httpd.old
   ```

9. As a sanity check, to ensure that we've successfully loaded *mod_perl* into the *httpd* binary, try the following command:

   ```
   $ ./httpd -l
   Compiled-in modules:
     ...
     mod_auth.c
     mod_setenvif.c
     mod_perl.c      # Bingo!!! :-)
   ```

(If you didn't build Apache and *mod_perl* yourself, there is a chance that *mod_ perl* will be dynamically loaded (following the DSO build pattern). In this case, it won't show up on *httpd -l*, which shows only statically compiled-in modules.)

Specifying the mod_perl Apache library

After a refreshing rest, we can begin again by writing our first *mod_perl* server script module, *HelloApache.pm*. (We'll deal with the conversion of ordinary CGI scripts later.) First of all, we need to establish where our main *mod_perl* Apache library will be. We suggest that you create a *../lib/perl/Apache* directory:

```
$ cd /usr/local/apache
$ mkdir -p lib/perl/Apache
```

We now have two options for telling *mod_perl* where this library will be when Apache starts running. The first is to add the following line somewhere near the top of our *httpd.conf* configuration file:

```
PerlSetEnv PERL5LIB /usr/local/apache/lib/perl
```

However, because this approach adds a little overhead to each HTTP request, we recommend the second option instead. Go to your *conf* directory and edit a new Perl file:

```
$ cd /usr/local/apache/conf
$ vi startup.pl
$ chmod 755 startup.pl
```

Create the Perl script shown in Example 5-1 as your *superuser* (to ensure later security). Change directives, where appropriate, such as the location of the *perl* program in the shebang line (notice that we've commented out *Apache::DBI*, which we'll be covering later):

Example 5-1. startup.pl—Apache mod_perl initialization script

```
#!/usr/bin/perl
# Set up the include path to get our new lib/perl directory
BEGIN {
    use Apache();
    use lib Apache->server_root_relative('lib/perl');
}

# Insert the most required modules

use Apache::Registry();
use Apache::Constants();
#use Apache::DBI();        # We'll get to this later! :-)
use LWP();
use CGI qw(-compile :all);
use CGI::Carp();
1;                          # Must finish with a true value
```

On *httpd* startup, the preceding Perl script will be run and will therefore load everything important directly into memory (use *startup.pl* to add other modules later on). It is run by adding the following lines to *httpd.conf*:

```
PerlRequire conf/startup.pl
PerlFreshRestart On
```

 PerlFreshRestart On means that on every hit to Apache, its entire collection of compiled modules is dumped and reloaded. *PerlFreshRestart Off* means that modules are only loaded once, when the Apache child process fires up, for added performance. Having *PerlFreshRestart On* is a major performance cost but is pretty much essential while we're in development. Developing with *PerlFreshRestart Off* is a headache, because if you change a module and reload the page, you can't be sure whether you have the new modified version of your module, or some older cached copy that an Apache child still has hanging about.

Here's the bottom line: use *PerlFreshRestart On* for development, *Off* for production.

Now we can restart Apache, this time with the added zest of *mod_perl*:

```
$ /usr/local/apache/bin/apachectl restart
/usr/local/apache/bin/apachectl start: httpd started
```

This means we can also write our first new Apache module, to directly access the internal workings of the *httpd* server.

```
$ cd /usr/local/apache/lib/perl/Apache
$ vi HelloApache.pm
```

Now create the test package, as in Example 5-2:

Example 5-2. The HelloApache.pm module

```
package Apache::HelloApache;

use strict;
use Apache::Constants qw(:common);

sub handler {
    my $r = shift;
    $r->content_type('text/html');
    $r->send_http_header;
    my $host = $r->get_remote_host;
    $r->print(<<END);
<HTML><HEAD><TITLE>HelloApache</TITLE></HEAD>
<BODY><CENTER>
<H1>Hello $host</H1>
<H2>Okay, perhaps we should have said "Hello World!" but nobody
expects Perl Sith Lords to do the expected! :-)
<H2>
</CENTER></BODY></HTML>
END
```

Example 5-2. The HelloApache.pm module (continued)

```
   return OK;
}
1;                        # Must finish with a true value
```

Because this is a real live server upgrade, we need to tell *httpd* when to access this handler process. Again, edit *httpd.conf*:

```
<Location /hello/apache>
    SetHandler perl-script
    PerlHandler Apache::HelloApache
</Location>
```

Now restart Apache and point your browser to *http://localhost/hello/apache*:

```
$ /usr/local/apache/bin/apachectl restart
/usr/local/apache/bin/apachectl restart: httpd restarted
```

Ladies and Gentlemen, check out Figure 5-1. The *mod_perl* has landed.

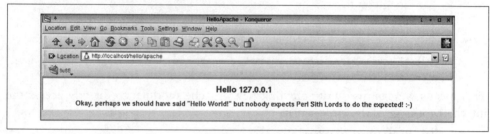

Figure 5-1. Our first Apache Perl module in sparkling form

Now, you may acknowledge that this is all very nice and agree that *mod_perl* works much more efficiently than the plain Perl CGI alternative. But you may also have 200 debugged Perl CGI scripts, all of which work brilliantly from a functional point of view, and you may have very little free time available to spend converting these scripts to Apache server modules. So even though your scripts are eating up too much CPU (and management is thinking of Java servlets), you probably have little inclination to plunge into a major conversion effort. What can you do? Read on.

Apache Perl Modules

Because you've embedded the Perl interpreter into the heart of the Apache server, the entire Apache server-side API is available to Perl programmers. The two modules listed here will provide you with the most bang for the buck in terms of managing your current collections of DBA CGI scripts:

Apache::Registry

> Fortunately, we can avoid rewriting all of our CGI scripts into Apache server functions like *HelloApache*. Like King Arthur's cavalry, *Apache::Registry* comes riding through the mist to our rescue. With *Apache::Registry*, we get most of the

benefits of *mod_perl* without having to change a single line of our current CGI scripts. We can then eventually choose to port these over to the new modular style in our own good time.

Apache::DBI

Using traditional Perl CGI scripts eats up memory, but there is another major cost as well, especially in conjunction with Perl DBI. That is the continuous creation stream of expensive database connections. The solution can be found in the mysterious connection pool of *Apache::DBI*.

We'll look at these two key modules in the following sections. All of the popular Apache *mod_perl* packages are summarized in Table 5-3.

Table 5-3. Main Apache mod_perl modules

mod_perl module	Description
Apache::Registry	Enhances the running of unaltered CGI scripts
Apache::Status	Embedded interpreter providing runtime status
Apache::Embperl	Embeds Perl within HTML
Apache::SSI	Server-side includes, implemented in Perl
Apache::DBI	Transparently maintains persistent DBI connections
Apache::Gateway	Implements an HTTP/1.1 gateway
Apache::GzipChain	Compresses web output on the fly
Apache::Filter	Filters document and script outputs
Apache::Sandwich	Automatically generates page headers and footers
Apache::TransLDAP	Translates URIs via LDAP lookups[a]
Apache::ASP	Implements a port of Active Server Pages to Perl[b]
Apache::AuthenDBI	Authenticates against a database via DBI
Apache::PHLogin	Authenticates against a PH database with the *Net::PH* module[c]
Apache::DBILogger	Logs requests to a database via Perl DBI
Apache::Session	Provides persistent session management facilities
Apache::Throttle	Content negotiation based on connection speed

[a] URI stands for Uniform Resource Identifiers (see *http://www.ics.uci.edu/pub/ietf/uri/* for more on related Internet definitions). LDAP stands for Lightweight Directory Access Protocol (see *http://www.openldap.org/* for the OpenLDAP project).

[b] Check out *http://www.nodeworks.com/asp/* for more details.

[c] The Ph (Phonebook) Nameserver is a database widely used as an online phonebook server for public organizations. See *http://www-dev.cso.uiuc.edu/ph/* for more details.

Apache::Registry

To take advantage of the performance advantages of *mod_perl*, you normally must rewrite your Perl CGI scripts in the form of server subroutines. *Apache::Registry*, which comes automatically with *mod_perl*, helps avoid this overhead.

As we mentioned, you may already have a large number of working scripts that you use in performing Oracle database administration. There is nothing really wrong with them; the only problem is the overhead of their full execution cycle every time they're requested. This makes them processor-intensive (i.e., slow). You'd rather avoid rewriting them all as *mod_perl* scripts, but you would like to make them run faster—this is where *Apache::Registry* comes in. It takes CGI script calls, in the form of *http://www.myhost.com/cgi-bin/cgi-script.pl*, and evaluates them into server subroutines, thereby turning plain old scripts into much quicker *mod_perl* objects. These server subroutines remain resident in the Apache server's memory. You will generally find that using *Apache::Registry* gives you a massive power enhancement.

You will need to check the *mod_perl* and *Apache::Registry* documentation, as this shortcut makes certain assumptions about your CGI coding standards. Scripts that you have coded in a quick-and-dirty way may end up failing the evaluation performed by *Apache::Registry*.[*]

By far the most common problem is using uninitialized "my" variables. What *Apache::Registry* really does is to grab the meat of a script and put it into a handler subroutine, which may fail to recognize uninitialized lexical variables. (See Appendix A, *The Essential Guide to Perl*, for a discussion of "my" variables.) Therefore, we need to hard-initialize all of our variables (e.g., specify *my $foo = 0;* instead of just *my $foo;*), to avoid the most common trap. Check out the following for much more detail:*http://theoryx5.uwinnipeg.ca/guide/*.

Note that each child process must compile at least once, so early requests may seem slow, but each subsequent request will be dealt with in Apache server memory and will seem very fast indeed. You will particularly notice this effect with large scripts or those with lots of module calls.

Follow these steps to use *Apache::Registry*:

1. We need to add a few more lines to our *httpd.conf* file:

   ```
   Alias /perl /usr/local/apache/perl
   <Location /perl>
       SetHandler perl-script
       PerlHandler Apache::Registry
       PerlSendHeader On
       Options +ExecCGI
   </Location>
   ```

2. Now create a corresponding *../perl* directory on the web server, into which we move our chosen CGI scripts (obviously, you may simply wish to point the */perl* alias, as above, directly towards your current CGI directory):

   ```
   $ cd /usr/local/apache
   $ mkdir perl
   ```

---

[*] Check out these pages for more information: *http://perl.apache.org/* and *http://perl.apache.org/dist/cgi_to_mod_perl.html*.

We'll use the code in Example 5-3 to demonstrate how *Apache::Registry* works. Notice that we can use all of the typical CGI environmental variables, such as *REMOTE_ADDR*.

Example 5-3. The HelloInquisition.pl program

```
#!/usr/bin/perl

use strict;
print "Content-Type: text/html\n\n";

print <<END;
<HTML><HEAD><TITLE>HelloInquistion</TITLE></HEAD>
<BODY><CENTER>
<H1>Hello $ENV{REMOTE_ADDR}, are you comfortable? 8-)</H1>
<H2>Nobody ever expects the HelloInquisition.pl Script!</H2>
</CENTER></BODY></HTML>
END
```

Make the script executable and restart Apache to pick up the *httpd.conf* change:

```
$ cd /usr/local/apache/perl
$ chmod 755 *.pl
$ /usr/local/apache/bin/apachectl restart
/usr/local/apache/bin/apachectl restart: httpd restarted
```

You can see the Perl script output in Figure 5-2.

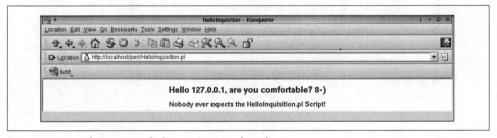

Figure 5-2. Apache::Registry linking CGI to mod_perl

Use of the *Apache::Registry* module helps overcome the performance problem that occurs when the Perl interpreter has to be re-executed every time a Perl script is called. But there is also another source of performance problems with CGI scripts more closely linked to database usage. We'll discuss that in the next section.

Apache::DBI

Each time you run a Perl CGI script that accesses a database, that script opens a new connection to the Oracle database at the beginning of the script, and then has to close it again at the end. This happens every single time you run the script, no matter how many thousands of people an hour are browsing the target page. This login process has a substantial overhead associated with it. It creates another performance issue for CGI scripts, one that even *Apache::Registry* can't overcome: even if the script is always in memory, it still has to open and close database connections.

Edmund Mergl has provided an excellent solution. His *Apache::DBI* module is an extension to Apache that's written in Perl (and thus requires the presence of *mod_perl*). Once you load *Apache::DBI*, it pools, or caches, all of the required database connections into memory, lending them out the same way that *ConnectionPool* classes do for Java. Whenever this module detects that a CGI script is opening or closing a database connection, it simply steps in and takes over from DBI, handing out and collecting its pooled Oracle connections as necessary, closing and opening them independently of the CGI scripts in current operation. These cached connections are known as *persistent connections* because the connection to the database is kept persistent between sessions. *Apache::DBI* does its work entirely in the background, so you'll be aware only that your web site has become much faster and far more scalable—even more important, your database is doing less work!

Unlike *Apache::Registry*, which comes preloaded with *mod_perl*, *Apache::DBI* is a supplementary module available from CPAN.* You can obtain it from:

> *http://www.cpan.org/authors/id/MERGL*

Follow these steps:

1. Simply install *Apache::DBI* the same way you'd install any other regular Perl module (notice that there is no *make test* step):

    ```
    $ gzip -d ApacheDBI-0.88.tar.gz
    $ tar xvf ApacheDBI-0.88.tar
    $ cd ApacheDBI-0.88
    $ vi README
    $ perl Makefile.PL
    $ make
    $ make install
    ```

2. Revisit *startup.pl* script and uncomment the earlier call to *Apache::DBI*:

    ```
    $ cd /usr/local/apache/conf
    $ vi startup.pl

    #!/usr/bin/perl
    ...
    use Apache::DBI(); # Uncomment this non-standard Perl Apache module! 8)
    ...
    1;
    ```

    Alternatively, add the following line to *httpd.conf*:

    ```
    PerlModule Apache::DBI
    ```

---

* The Apache module *Apache::AuthDBI* also comes with *Apache::DBI*, giving you two excellent modules for the price of downloading just one.

3. *Apache::DBI* transparently takes over the following DBI calls within scripts:

```
DBI->connect
DBI->disconnect
```

4. By taking over *DBI->connect* statements, to prevent them from connecting directly to a database each time, *Apache::DBI* lends scripts a preprepared database connection. It creates and deletes these connections, as necessary, in the background to maintain a pool of replacements. It also replaces the *DBI->disconnect* statement with a *do-nothing* statement, as follows:

```
sub disconnect {
    my $prefix = "$$ Apache::DBI          ";
    print STDERR "$prefix disconnect (overloaded) \n"
        if $Apache::DBI::DEBUG > 1;
    1;
};
```

Simply move your DBI web scripts to the target *../perl* area to gain its benefit.

Apache and ORACLE_HOME

Apache generally needs to know where your *ORACLE_HOME* is in order to get *DBD::Oracle* to work correctly. The easiest way of specifying any environment variable is to have a line such as the following in *httpd.conf*:

```
PerlSetEnv ORACLE_HOME /opt/oracle/product/9.0.1
```

(We use *PerlSetEnv*, rather than Apache's usual *SetEnv*, because it is guaranteed to take effect before all of the *mod_perl* and Apache handlers run; their Perl additions may later require values such as *ORACLE_HOME*.)

With persistent database connections now on board, let's give it a whirl. Try out the CGI script in Example 5-4. Notice that there's no explicit use of *Apache::DBI* within the script. It has been called off the bench in *startup.pl*, and *mod_perl* is holding it in memory for us under the floodlights, keeping it there until we send out the blade runners later on to shut down the Apache server daemons.

Example 5-4. WaitsMonitor.pl

```
#!/usr/bin/perl

use strict;
use DBI;
use CGI qw(:standard :netscape);
use CGI::Pretty qw(:html3);

# Link to Oracle, this time via Apache::DBI in the background,
# and set up our SQL to get our results.

my $url = 'dbi:Oracle:orcl.world';
my $user = 'system';
my $passwd = 'manager';
```

Example 5-4. WaitsMonitor.pl (continued)

```perl
my $dbh = DBI->connect($url, $user, $passwd, {RaiseError=>1, AutoCommit=>0});

my $sth = $dbh->prepare('select event Wait_Event, ' .
                        'total_waits Tot_Waits, ' .
                        'time_waited Times_Waited ' .
                        'from v$system_event ' .
                        'where event like \'%file%\' ' .
                        'order by total_waits desc ' ) ;

$sth->execute or die "Cannot execute";

# Get the fieldnames, and make them into table headers.
my $rs = $sth->{NAME};
my @col_head;
for (@$rs)
{
    push(@col_head, $_);
}

# Now get the data dough, and roll out the pastry
my @row;
my @rows;
while (@row = $sth->fetchrow_array)
{
    push(@rows, td(\@row));
}
$dbh->disconnect;

# Finished with DBI.  Now we sort out the CGI side of life.

my $title = "Welcome back to WaitsMonitor!";

# Create the HTML page.
my $current_time = localtime();
print header,
      start_html(-title=>$title, -bgcolor=>'white', -text=>'black'),
      center(h1($title),
              hr(),
              table({border=>'2'},
                    caption($current_time),
                    TR([th(\@col_head), @rows])
                  )),
      end_html;
```

Make the script executable:

```
$ cd /usr/local/apache/perl
$ chmod 755 WaitsMonitor.pl
```

You can see the results of this script's being called in Figure 5-3.

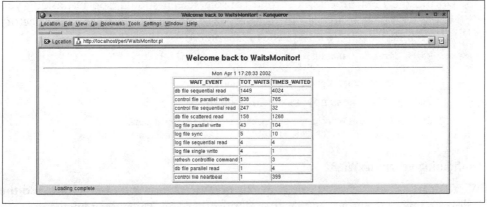

Figure 5-3. Apache::DBI saving us connection time

Installing mod_perl on Win32

Fortunately for those of us who have just waded through the Unix installation of *mod_perl*, there is a binary version of *mod_perl* that was built for Win32 and Perl 5.6 by the heroic Randy Kobes. Installing it is very straightforward:

1. Now is as good a time as any to load up your favorite optional Apache-related module from *ActiveState.com* (though it's also possible to do this later on):

   ```
   C:\Program Files\Apache Group\Apache\modules>ppm
   PPM interactive shell (2.1.5) - type 'help' for available commands.
   PPM> install ApacheDBI
   Install package 'ApacheDBI?' (y/N): y
   ...
   ```

2. We can also use PPM to install a more independent distribution of *mod_perl* (available from Canada's University of Winnipeg Department of Theoretical Physics). You will get all of the default Perl modules required by *mod_perl* with this download, and much more besides. (Notice the use of an HTTP address to pick up the PPD file, which itself points us towards the gzipped file on the web server that contains the necessary files):[*]

   ```
   PPM> set repository theoryx5
        http://theoryx5.uwinnipeg.ca/cgi-bin/ppmserver.pl?urn:/PPMServer
   PPM > install mod_perl
   PPM > set save
   ```

   The *set save* step ensures that *theoryx5* is available later for PPM downloads.

---

[*] The installation tarball can be downloaded directly from the University of Winnipeg site; if you'd like to view its constituents, check out *http://theoryx5.uwinnipeg.ca/ppmpackages*.

3. During the PPM process, a second console screen should pop up, asking you where you'd like to install the necessary *mod_perl.so* file. We used the directory for modules installed with Apache in Chapter 4:

```
Which directory should mod_perl.so be placed in?
   (enter q to quit) [C:/Apache/modules]
           C:/progra~1/apache~1/apache/modules
```

4. The *mod_perl.so* file is now safely shipped in:

```
C:\Program Files\Apache Group\Apache\modules>dir mod_perl*
MOD_PERL SO       208,896  14/03/02   1:39 mod_perl.so
```

Configuring Apache on Win32

We're nearly there. Before starting Apache on Win32, however, we need to add the following line to the *httpd.conf* file after all the other *LoadModule* statements:

```
LoadModule perl_module modules/mod_perl.so
```

Do this from the Win32 Start menu as follows:

```
Start → Programs → Apache HTTP Server → Configure Apache Server →
Edit the Apache httpd.conf Configuration File
```

Also make sure you add the following line after the *AddModule* section:

```
AddModule mod_perl.c
```

Keep *httpd.conf* open at this point, and move onto the next stage.

Testing on Win32

As with Unix, we need to load up the Count of Monte Cristo's chest of Apache jewels every time we fire up the server.

1. Modify the original *startup.pl* file from Unix and insert it into the *C:\Program Files\Apache Group\Apache\conf* directory. Note especially the first line, which directs Apache to use ActivePerl's Perl executable:

```
#!/perl/bin/perl
# Set up the include path to get our new lib/perl directory
BEGIN {
    use Apache();
    use lib Apache->server_root_relative('lib/perl');
}

# Insert our A-Team modules

use Apache::Registry();
use Apache::Constants();
use Apache::DBI();
# use LWP();                 Uncomment if LWP loaded! :-)
use CGI qw(-compile :all);
use CGI::Carp();
1;
```

On server startup, this will locate our nominated Apache/Perl library and load all of our *Apache::** modules into the requisite memory areas.

2. Now create the actual directories necessary to store the Apache modules; *startup.pl* will point at these when it's fired up:

```
C:\Program Files\Apache Group\Apache\lib>mkdir perl
C:\Program Files\Apache Group\Apache\lib>cd perl
C:\Program Files\Apache Group\Apache\lib\perl>mkdir Apache
```

3. Now add the following to *httpd.conf* to ignite this process later on:

```
PerlRequire conf/startup.pl
PerlFreshRestart On
```

We can now write our first Win32 Perl Apache module.

HelloWin32.pm

Move to our new *perl\Apache* directory:

```
C:\ cd C:\Program Files\Apache Group\Apache\lib\perl\Apache
```

We can create our new module, shown in Example 5-5, which does some checking on tablespace fragmentation via a subroutine called from the Apache handler process. (It's easy to forget, but what we're doing here really is *quite* amazing. We're right in the heart of the Apache server, changing it directly to make it do exactly what we want it to do. Could any other web server give you this kind of flexibility with something as relatively easy to use as Perl?)

Example 5-5. HelloWin32.pm

```perl
package Apache::HelloWin32;

use strict;
use DBI;
use Apache::Constants qw(:common);
use CGI qw(-compile :all);

sub handler {

    my $r = shift;
    $r->content_type('text/html');
    $r->send_http_header;
    my $host = $r->get_remote_host;
    my $table = tabspace_frag();
    $r->print(<<END);
<HTML><HEAD><TITLE>Hello Win32</TITLE></HEAD><BODY>
<H1>Hello $host - Let's do something half useful</H1><HR>
$table
</BODY></HTML>
END

    return OK;
}
```

Example 5-5. HelloWin32.pm (continued)

```perl
sub tabspace_frag {
    my $url = 'dbi:Oracle:orcl';
    my $user = 'system';
    my $passwd = 'manager';

    my $dbh = DBI->connect($url, $user, $passwd, {RaiseError=>1});

    my $sth = $dbh->prepare( 'SELECT ts.name tspace, ' .
                                    'tf.blocks blocks, ' .
                                    'sum(f.length) free, ' .
                                    'count(*) pieces, ' .
                                    'max(f.length) biggest, ' .
                                    'min(f.length) smallest, ' .
                                    'round(avg(f.length)) average, ' .
                                    'sum(decode(sign(f.length-5), ' .
                                    '-1,f.length,0)) dead ' .
                               'FROM sys.fet$ f, sys.file$ tf, ' .
                                    'sys.ts$ ts ' .
                              'WHERE ts.ts# = f.ts# ' .
                                'AND ts.ts# = tf.ts# ' .
                              'GROUP BY ts.name,tf.blocks');
    $sth->execute;

    # Get the fieldnames, and make them into table headers.
    my $rs = $sth->{NAME};
    my @col_head;
    for (@$rs)
    {
        push(@col_head, $_);
    }
    # Now get the data, to fill the table with shortly.
    my @row;
    my @rows;
    while (@row = $sth->fetchrow_array)
    {
        push(@rows, td(\@row));
    }
    $dbh->disconnect;

    # Now we sort out CGI and return to handler.

    # Create the HTML page.
    return center(table({border=>'2'},
                        caption("Tablespace Fragmentation"),
                        TR([th(\@col_head), @rows])));
}
1;  # This is a package, therefore truth required
```

Before we complete our test run, we need to make one final addition to the *httpd.conf* configuration file before running the server:

```
<Location /hello/win32>
    SetHandler perl-script
```

```
    PerlHandler Apache::HelloWin32
</Location>
```

We can now set Apache running:

```
Start-> Programs-> Apache HTTP Server-> Start Apache in Console
```

You can see the spectacular results in Figure 5-4.

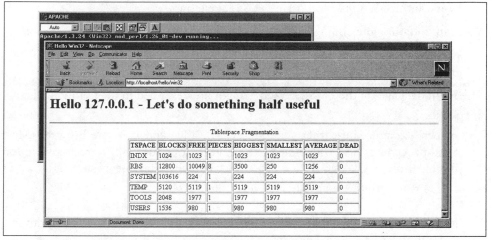

Figure 5-4. HelloWin32.pm attempting to be half useful

Apache::OWA

Apache::OWA was written by Svante Sörmark and was named originally after the Oracle Web Application server, which has since morphed into Oracle *iAS*. *Apache:: OWA*'s mission is to give Apache direct access to Oracle Corporation's PL/SQL Web Toolkit. These packages ship automatically with later Oracle servers, from Oracle Version 8.1.7 onward, and they allow PL/SQL programs to create web content.

Although this module is not obviously aimed squarely at Oracle DBAs, we've included it for several reasons:

- Many DBAs have database administration tools that are driven by the PL/SQL Web Toolkit or have tools that they would like to access over the Web. If that is true at your site and you either don't have access to a web application server or you want to bypass the complexities of working within your particular server setup, *Apache::OWA* may be a good option. Essentially, this module will provide you with the necessary access to the PL/SQL Web Toolkit and save you from having to do all of the necessary configuration on your own. You'll end up being able to combine Oracletool, Karma, your own Perl and PL/SQL Web Toolkit DBA scripts, and perhaps some Perl-based system administration web pages too—all within one personalized centrally controlled environment.

- Many Oracle DBAs are also Web Application Server administrators, and for those folks *Apache::OWA* may be a critically important tool.

- This module is a great piece of work. In just a few hundred lines of Perl code, *Apache::OWA* is one of the greatest examples of Oracle-accessing code we've seen. If you're thinking of writing your own Apache Perl modules at any point—for example, to drive your own web and data needs, we highly recommend that you use the *OWA.pm* file work as a code skeleton.[*]

You can find out more about *Apache::OWA* from the following web sites:

http://sourceforge.net/projects/owa
http://owa.sourceforge.net

The main packages in the PL/SQL Web Toolkit are described in the following list.

HTP
> HyperText procedures that generate HTML and send it to the browser. Most HTP procedures bear the name of the HTML construct they're responsible for. For example, HTP.ANCHOR creates HTML anchor statements such as:
>
> ```
> <A HREF="http://www.oreilly.com">Input text...</A>
> ```

HTF
> HyperText functions that help corresponding HTP procedures by wrapping input with various HTML constructs.

OWA_UTIL
> A collection of utility procedures and functions divided into three groups:
>
> *HTML utilities*
>> A typical procedure here would retrieve the values of CGI environment variables or perform a URL redirection operation.
>
> *Dynamic SQL utilities*
>> These produce web pages with dynamically generated SQL.
>
> *Date utilities*
>> These simplify date handling.

OWA_OPT_LOCK
> This package imposes optimistic locking strategies in order to prevent lost updates.

OWA
> Holds internal procedures called by the Oracle PL/SQL Agent itself.

---

[*] Richard Sutherland's *DDL::Oracle* tool (described in Chapter 3, *Perl GUI Extensions*) is also an excellent code template.

OWA_PATTERN

These pattern-matching utilities perform string matching and substitution with regular expression functionality. Many of the regex definitions used here are the same as those defined in Appendix C, *The Essential Guide to Regular Expressions*.

OWA_TEXT

This set of utilities is used by OWA_PATTERN to manipulate large data strings. They have also been externalized for direct implementation.

OWA_IMAGE

A set of utilities for manipulating HTML image maps.

OWA_COOKIE

Datatypes, procedures, and functions for manipulating HTML cookies.

For more information about these packages, check out *http://technet.oracle.com*—in particular, pages like the following:

http://technet.oracle.com/doc/windows/was.21/psqlwtlk.htm

Installing Apache::OWA on Unix

Before installing *Apache::OWA*, you should be aware that this module relies upon the presence of another module called *Apache::Request*, which lives on CPAN under the name *libapreq*. You can get this module from:

http://www.cpan.org/authors/id/J/JI/JIMW

Apache::Request was developed by Jim Winstead and mimics the abilities of *CGI.pm* to deal with *GET* and *POST* program parameters. However, it does this in a quicker way for Apache/Perl modules, giving *Apache::OWA* more execution speed. To improve performance even more, we recommend that you install *Apache::DBI* for use with *Apache::OWA*.

The Perl modules contained within the generic *Apache::Request* library make use of the underlying *libapreq* C library. They're installed as follows:

```
$ gzip -d libapreq-1.0.tar.gz
$ tar xvf libapreq-1.0.tar
$ cd libapreq-1.0
$ vi README INSTALL
$ perl Makefile.PL
$ make
$ make test
$ make install
```

(Make sure to check out the *README* and *INSTALL* files with *libapreq*, particularly on Solaris 8 and Red Hat Linux. There were some issues noted with Version 0.31, although Version 1.0 should have resolved them.)

We can now download and install Apache::OWA proper. We got hold of the *Apache-OWA-0.7.tar.gz* tarball from the following site:

> *http://www.cpan.org/authors/id/S/SV/SVINTO*

Apache::OWA bends the old conventions a little by naming its unpack directory differently from the download tarball, but hey, we like a little individuality to break up these installation runs. Also note that the *make test* step was a little skimpy with our tarball, though this may have changed by the time you come to download your own latest version. Let's work through the steps:

```
$ gzip -d Apache-OWA-0.7.tar.gz
$ tar xvf Apache-OWA-0.7.tar
$ cd OWA
$ vi README
$ perl Makefile.PL
$ make
$ make test     # May be a little skimpy, just yet! :-)
$ make install
```

That should be it. Now let's try the same under Win32.

Installing Apache::OWA on Win32

Once again, those great folks at ActiveState have done us proud. Just start up a command console while connected to the Internet, and then click in about 50 letters. We'll highlight the places you actually *have* to type:

```
C:\Perl\site\lib\Apache> ppm
PPM interactive shell (2.1.5) - type 'help' for available commands.
PPM> install libapreq
Install package 'libapreq?' (y/N): y
...
Writing C:\Perl\site\lib\auto\libapreq\.packlist
PPM> install Apache-OWA
Install package 'Apache-OWA?' (y/N): y
...
Writing C:\Perl\site\lib\auto\Apache\OWA\.packlist
PPM> quit
```

Configuring Apache::OWA

Those who have wrestled in the past with the various Oracle Webserver products and their sometimes cumbersome administration suites will appreciate how minutely scaled the same process is for *Apache::OWA* in comparison. It's the size of *The Incredible Shrinking Man* at the end of the film, when he escapes from the spider (i.e., very small indeed). We simply edit *httpd.conf*, to create a DAD (Database Access Descriptor). Follow these steps:

1. For applications with little need for authentication, all you'll require is the following. This calls procedures in the *orcl* database, living under *scott's* schema:

```
<Location /scott/ >
    SetHandler perl-script
    PerlHandler Apache::OWA
    PerlSendHeader ON
    PerlSetVar DAD orcl:scott:tiger
</Location>
```

2. When we create the *scott.HelloApacheOWA* procedure, in Example 5-6, we'll call it from a browser as follows:

   http://localhost/scott/HelloApacheOWA

   If by using the same URL we decide instead to call a similarly named procedure under another schema (e.g., *webaccess*, we'd do it like this):

```
<Location /scott/ >
    SetHandler perl-script
    PerlHandler Apache::OWA
    PerlSendHeader ON
    PerlSetVar DAD orcl:scott:tiger
    PerlSetVar SCHEMA webaccess
</Location>
```

3. Alternatively, if we set the correct public synonyms and execute permissions, and we want all of our users to log in to the web pages with their individual Oracle username and passwords, we'd do it like this:

```
<Location /owa_db_auth/ >
    AuthName owa_db_auth
    AuthType Basic
    PerlAuthenHandler Apache::OWA
    PerlSendHeader ON
    Require valid-user
    PerlSetVar DB orcl
    PerlSetVar SCHEMA webaccess
    PerlSetVar DB_AUTH true
</Location>
```

(Other more complex security possibilities are documented within the *Apache:: OWA* download.)

As an example of how *Apache::OWA* works, let's take the first simple configuration we worked through preceding, and insert it into our *httpd.conf* file. We created the *HelloApacheOWA* procedure in Example 5-6, under *scott*:

Example 5-6. HelloApacheOWA.sql

```
create or replace procedure HelloApacheOWA as
    cursor curs_dept is
        select deptno, dname, loc
          from dept
         order by deptno;
begin
    htp.htmlOpen;
    htp.headOpen;
    htp.title('Apache::OWA, Perl Apache Module for Oracle PL/SQL');
```

Example 5-6. HelloApacheOWA.sql (continued)

```
    htp.headClose;
    htp.bodyOpen( cattributes => ' bgcolor="WHITE" ' );
    htp.centerOpen;
    htp.header(1, 'Hello Apache::OWA! :-)');
    htp.hr;

    htp.tableOpen( cattributes => ' border="2" width="80%" ' );
    htp.tableRowOpen;
    htp.tableHeader( 'Department Number' );
    htp.tableHeader( 'Department Name' );
    htp.tableHeader( 'City Location' );
    htp.tableRowClose;

    for rec_dept in curs_dept loop
        htp.tableRowOpen;
        htp.tableData(rec_dept.deptno);
        htp.tableData(rec_dept.dname);
        htp.tableData(rec_dept.loc);
        htp.tableRowClose;
    end loop;

    htp.tableClose;
    htp.hr;
    htp.centerClose;
    htp.bodyClose;
    htp.htmlClose;
end;
```

When we call this procedure via the browser, it generates the output in Figure 5-5. At this point, you may already be thinking of a hundred ways you could expand your own usage of *mod_perl* and *Apache::OWA* to create the mother of all remote DBA web toolkits, driven by Perl and PL/SQL. Go for it!

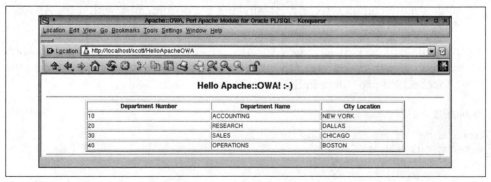

Figure 5-5. Apache::OWA calls PL/SQL

## CHAPTER 6

Embedded Perl Web Scripting

In the last two chapters, we've looked at several categories of Perl web-based Oracle applications: those that use standard Perl CGI scripts and those that use the Apache *mod_perl* module to make those scripts run more efficiently. With both approaches, though, the developer needs to worry about the design of the web pages displayed by the application. Interesting as web page design can be, you may feel that as an Oracle DBA you have enough responsibilities on your plate. You may need to fill web pages with data—product lists, employee data, and all kinds of other information—but you may not have a keen interest in how to lay out that data on the pages themselves. In this chapter, we'll look at another approach to dynamic web programming, one that completely separates database issues and web page design issues. This approach is to use embedded scripting, and it can be an elegant solution, as long as the embedded language is a simple and straightforward one.

This embedded approach is also known as *templating*, because the presentation layer—or site design—is the template to which is added the application or code development layer (that layer contains the business-specific detail).

There are various web programming solutions loosely based on the idea of embedding code into HTML pages, and then preprocessing it. With Java, for example, you use Java Server Pages (JSPs). Microsoft's version of this technology is known as Active Server Pages (ASPs). There are also several excellent Perl embedded scripting solutions that we'll describe in this chapter:

Embperl
> An embedded scripting language that's useful for building up *mod_perl* web sites from collections of small reusable components. It uses a C-library back end to assist with its processing.

Mason
> Another embedded scripting language. Similar to Embperl in its functionality and use of *mod_perl*, but built purely in Perl. It uses an object-oriented style of component programming.

Embperl

Gerald Richter's Embperl program is a popular solution for those who want to separate web page design from data coding issues while taking advantage of Perl's ability to generate dynamic content without having to worry about web page design issues. As its name suggests, Embperl provides the ability to embed Perl within your HTML presentation layer templates.*

The Embperl 2.0 release promises extensive new capabilities, offering such features as XML and XSLT integration. Although Embperl is implemented primarily in Perl, it also has a C back end for speedier processing. For detailed information, go to:†

> *http://perl.apache.org/embperl*
> *http://www.cpan.org/authors/id/GRICHTER*

In the following sections we'll describe how to install Embperl on Unix and Win32 systems. The Apache configuration and execution of Embperl is virtually identical on the two systems, so once we're installed on both systems we'll run through a single configuration sequence.

Installing Embperl on Unix

This section describes how to install Embperl and its associated modules on Unix platforms.

 Although you can use Embperl under vanilla CGI Apache, we strongly recommend that you use *mod_perl*. Not only is the performance difference astonishing, but *mod_perl* also allows you to use a wide range of Apache modules, including the highly useful *Apache::Session* and *Apache::DBI*. And without *Apache::Session* (as we describe below), you will get no session persistence between HTTP requests.

1. If you're installing Embperl on Unix, you need to obtain a few additional modules to get its full application benefit. (Embperl is also expecting you to have preloaded *mod_perl*, which provides it with many of its extended options. We'll also assume this, for the rest of this installation.)

   Storable.pm
   > Raphael Manfredi's popular advanced module for storing various persistent data structures in Perl (and required by *Apache::Session*). In the later section, "Embperl Forms Handling and Apache::Session," we'll explain the

---

* This approach is similar to what is done with PHP (*http://www.php.net*) and PL/SQL Server Pages (PSPs).

† As a rule of thumb, only the latest stable releases make it to CPAN, whereas beta versions are generally available on the other site.

---

advantages of storing persistent web data. Download and install the tarball from the following Perl 5 Porters site:

http://www.cpan.org/authors/id/A/AM/AMS

Apache::Session

Jeffrey Baker's Apache Perl module. This interface between Apache and the *Storable.pm* module is used to store persistent web data. Download and install it from:

http://www.cpan.org/authors/id/JBAKER

Apache::SessionX

This is a subsidiary module developed by Gerald Richter to complement Embperl by creating an extended persistence framework for Embperl's session data between HTTP requests (thus extending *Apache::Session*). Download and install the latest version from the CPAN site at:

http://www.cpan.org/authors/id/GRICHTER

2. For testing purposes, Embperl also requires that LWP and all of its precursor modules be installed; Chapter 5, *Embedding Perl into Apache with mod_perl*, contains the full details about LWP installation.

3. Once you've installed these required modules, you can install Embperl itself. During the installation you need to supply the location of your Apache source directory. Embperl can then get hold of the relevant Apache code headers, and configure itself against *mod_perl*. For example:

```
$ perl Makefile.PL
Build with support for Apache mod_perl?(y/n) [y]y
Use ../apache_1.3.24/src as Apache source(y/n) [y]y
...
```

4. Once Embperl has been configured, complete the installation as follows:

```
$ make
$ make test
$ make install
```

We can now head on down to Embperl's configuration.

Installing Embperl on Win32

Installing Embperl on Win32 is remarkably easy because of the good work of those physics philosopher-kings at the University of Winnipeg. The gig's all been tied up with super-strings and made as simple as falling off a p-brane bubble quark. When it's installing, take a look at all of those modules you get. It's just like Christmas:

```
PPM> set repository theoryx5
      http://theoryx5.uwinnipeg.ca/cgi-bin/ppmserver.pl?urn:/PPMServer
PPM> set save
PPM> install Storable
Install package 'Storable?' (y/N): y
Installing package 'Storable'...
```

```
...
PPM> install Apache-Session
Install package 'Apache-Session?' (y/N): y
Installing package 'Apache-Session'...
...
PPM> install Apache-SessionX
Install package 'Apache-SessionX?' (y/N): y
Installing package 'Apache-SessionX'...
...
PPM> install Embperl
Install package 'Embperl?' (y/N): y
Installing package 'Embperl'...
...
PPM> quit
```

And that's it. We're now ready to configure and deploy Embperl, a process that is virtually identical on both Win32 and Unix.

Deploying HTML::Embperl

There are many different ways to deploy Embperl, and all of them are discussed in depth within the documentation. For starters, take a look at the information obtained from the following command:

```
$ perldoc Embperl
```

Our favorite way of deploying Embperl is to ask the Apache web server to call it. Apache can be called with any files bearing a particular suffix (such as *.epl*) in the same way that you can configure Apache to call Perl if it finds scripts ending with *.cgi*. You do this in *httpd.conf* by adding a handler (in our case a *PerlHandler*) and associating a file type with a nominated suffix in the following way. Here we have chosen the typically generic Embperl *.epl* suffix:

```
PerlModule Embperl
EMBPERL_DEBUG 2285
<Files *.epl>
    SetHandler  perl-script
    PerlHandler Embperl
    Options     ExecCGI
</files>

AddType text/html .epl
```

1. Once we restart Apache, every time anybody calls up a web page from this server, suffixed with *.epl*, Embperl will be called to deal with it.

2. There are many different *EMBPERL_DEBUG* levels, and we've chosen an output level initially recommended by the Embperl download installation files. While you're getting used to Embperl, you may want to try these settings as a starting point, and then alter them to create varying output within Apache's generated logs as you progress.

We started, as illustrated in Example 6-1, with our first Embperl .*epl* file, which checks up on who is accessing which object within the Oracle database. A bit later we'll run through how Embperl interprets this information.

Example 6-1. ObjectAccess.epl—Embperl and Oracle

```
<html><head>
<title>Embperl Object Access Checker</title>
</head><body><center>

<h1>Hello Embperl, Let's Check Object Access! 8-)</h1><hr>

[-

$url = 'dbi:Oracle:orcl';
$user = 'system';
$passwd = 'manager';

use DBI ;

# Connect to the database
$dbh = DBI->connect($url, $user, $passwd, {RaiseError=>1});

# Prepare the SQL to check up on object access
$sth = $dbh->prepare ('select s.osuser "OS User", ' .
                      's.username "Username", ' .
                      's.serial# "Serial#", ' .
                      's.sid "Sid", ' .
                      'a.owner||\'.\'||a.object "Object Name", ' .
                      '\'=> \'||a.type "Lock Mode" ' .
                      'from v$session s, v$access a ' .
                      'where a.sid = s.sid ' .
                      'order by 6,1,2,3,4,5');
# Execute the Query
$sth->execute;

# Get the Column Headers
$head = $sth->{NAME} ;
# Fetch the data into the drillable data_ref array reference
$data_ref = $sth->fetchall_arrayref ;
-]

<table border="2">
<tr><th>[+ $head->[$col] +]</th></tr>
<tr><td>[+ $data_ref->[$row][$col] +]</td></tr>
</table>
<hr></center></body></html>
```

Store *ObjectAccess.epl* within the *../htdocs* directory alongside ordinary flat HTML files, and then fire up Apache. Our new Embperl file produced the subsequent browser output in Figure 6-1. So *that's* the culprit!

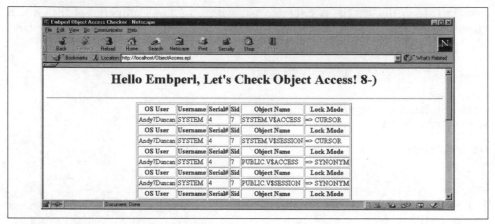

Figure 6-1. Our first Embperl execution

Looking at Embperl Syntax

Now let's look at what is going on in Example 6-1. There are three main ways to actually embed Perl within Embperl templates; these different approaches are summarized in Table 6-1. In the following sections we'll focus on how Embperl syntax differs from standard Perl syntax.

Table 6-1. Embedding Perl within the Embperl template

Format	Description	Example
[- ... -]	**Code execution:** The code between the *[-* and the *-]* is executed, without any HTML being generated. This approach is mainly for assignments, function calls, creating database connections, and so on, as in Example 6-1.	*[-* *$dbh = DBI->connect(* *$url, $user, $passwd)* *-]*
[+ ... +]	**Code output:** The code is executed as with the previous example, except this time the last thing evaluated is streamed back to the HTML output.	*<tr><th>* *[+ $head->[$col] +]* *</th></tr>*
[! ... !]	**One-time execution:** The code is executed as with *[- ... -]*, but only for the first request, which is useful for variable or subroutine initialization and other one-off executions	*[!* *Sub session_start {* *$start_time = localtime; }* *!]*

Controlling template-driven program flow

To exercise structured program flow within Embperl, you can employ another square-bracketed syntactical element:

[$ <conditional element> <optional conditional construct> $]

This is perhaps best explained by working through the examples in the following numbered list:

1. Suppose you want to set up a conditional *if* chain to do different things with HTML. Depending upon how you're being sent data, you do it like this:

```
[$ if $ENV{REQUEST_METHOD} eq 'GET' $]
    <h2> I see you've called me with a GET request! :-) </h2>
[$ elsif $ENV{REQUEST_METHOD} eq 'POST' $]
    <h2> Thanks for calling me with a POST request! 8-) </h2>
[$ else $]
    <h1> You've created a new Request Method, Congratulations! $-) </h1>
[$ endif $]
```

Notice that although this code looks similar to ordinary Perl, brackets such as (...), are missing from the main *if* condition, and no curly brackets like {...} are used to wrap statements. Also notice that whereas in ordinary Perl you would use a left-facing bracket, }, to end the complete *if* statement, in Embperl you use *endif* instead. This is a keyword that traditional Perl would fail to recognize.

 We have been told that Embperl 2.0 will be more closely aligned with standard Perl.

2. You can also use *while* loops, for example, to display the Apache server's current environment:

```
[$ while ($env_variable_name, $env_value) = each (%ENV) $]
    [+ $env_variable_name +] = [+ $env_value +] <br>
[$ endwhile $]
```

Again notice the use of *endwhile* rather than a left-facing curly bracket, }.

3. Similarly, you can also employ *do...until* loops:

```
[-
@crew = ('Kirk', 'McCoy', 'Spock', 'Beam Me Up');
$tribble = 0;
-]
[$ do $]
    [+ $crew[ $tribble++ ] +]
[$ until $tribble > $#crew $]
```

Notice how the tribbles keep growing in number.

4. You can also use *foreach* loops:

```
[-
$warp_factor = 1;
@federation_planet = ('Earth', 'Vulcan',
                      'Solaria', 'Aurora', 'Terminus', 'Trantor');
-]
[$ foreach $thataway ( @federation_planet ) $]
Head for Federation Planet [+ $thataway +],
    Mr Sulu, Warp Factor [+ $warp_factor++ +]
[$ endforeach $]
```

Strict variable naming

As with standard Perl, variables pop into existence as soon as you mention them, but if you'd rather enforce stricter discipline and pre-declare global variable names, you can use *var*:

```
[$ var $klingon @vulcan %romulan $]
```

This is equivalent to the Perl *strict* pragma shown here:

```
use strict;
use vars qw ($klingon @vulcan %romulan) ;
```

Useful table tricks

The eagle-eyed among you may have spotted something strange about the following lines in Example 6-1:

```
<tr><th>[+ $head->[$col] +]</th></tr>
<tr><td>[+ $data_ref->[$row][$col] +]</td></tr>
```

There is only one table header element, and one detail element, yet the screen in Figure 6-1 is filled to overflowing with the milk and honey of multiline and multi-column results. What's going on? A little bit of magic.

First, the special *$col* variable works out just how many element are within the array referenced by *$head*, which was created by the *$head* = *$sth->{NAME}* code line. The special *$row* variable does exactly the same for the *$data_ref* reference value.

Next, Embperl iterates through the whole of the arrays accessed by these variables, until *$col* and *$row* return *undef* values (i.e., they run out of milk and honey). You may want to avoid questioning too much how Embperl does this; otherwise the fairy dust may lose its sparkle. The Pandora's box of source code is available though, if you're prepared to open it.

Embperl Forms Handling and Apache::Session

One of the major benefits of the Web is its stateless protocol, HTTP, which makes your processing extremely lightweight at both the server and browser ends. Unfortunately, the stateless protocol can also be a great disadvantage when compared with a stateful client-server model, for example. The problem is that you keep losing all of your user information every time users change pages. This can be financially challenging if your site runs shopping-cart applications!

Embperl can perform many of the regular *<hidden>* type shenanigans to overcome this limitation, but it can also make use of *Apache::Session* to draw an Excalibur sword of stateful data from a dry stone of statelessness. It stores this rich vein of information between page requests via the following special Perl hash variables:

%udat

Stores individual user data. Every time an individual comes back to your server, via his browser, to hit different pages, you can access all of his previously input data (if your Embperl script stored it neatly away when you last had access to it).

%mdat

Stores data for a nominated module or page.

%fdat

Stores all of the data associated with a form.

%idat

Stores all of the data input so far on a particular form, which is very useful for those of us who relish sticky widgets.

Mason

Jonathan Swartz, aided and abetted by Dave Rolsky, has created another fine Perl templating package in *HTML::Mason*. Unlike Embperl, which has a C-based back end, Mason is built purely with Perl, and this implementation tends to reduce potential complexities during installation.

You can download the latest package from CPAN and learn much more about Mason at the following sites:

> *http://www.masonhq.com*
> *http://www.cpan.org/authors/id/J/JS/JSWARTZ*

The following sections describe how to install Mason on Unix and Win32 and then work through an example.

Installing Mason on Unix

We need to pre-install the following Perl modules for Mason on Unix platforms:

Time::HiRes

Douglas E. Wegscheid's module helps Mason deal with POSIX commands such as *usleep()* and *ualarm()* at subsecond levels.

> *http://www.cpan.org/authors/id/DEWEG*

MLDBM

Gurusamy Sarathy's Multi-Level DBM module serializes multilevel hashes, and all the data their references point to, into single BLOBs of data; these can then be stored by any one of the different Perl modules listed here. You can learn more at:

> *http://www.cpan.org/authors/id/GSAR*

Data::Dumper

This comes automatically with Perl now, and saves Perl hash structures in neatly formatted platform-independent files, useful for printing or evaluating.

FreezeThaw

Converts Perl data structures to and from strings suitable for storage.

http://www.cpan.org/authors/id/ILYAZ/modules

Storable

As discussed earlier with Embperl, this module uses a C back end to greatly speed information storage and retrieval and thus make your Perl data structures persistent. We recommend that you load *Storable*, because it is significantly faster than either *Data::Dumper* or *FreezeThaw*.

http://www.cpan.org/authors/id/A/AM/AMS

Params::Validate

This validates method or function call parameters, and can also determine their type and class hierarchy relationships.

http://www.cpan.org/authors/id/D/DR/DROLSKY

Now follow these steps:

1. Once the main modules above are installed, we can get to the main event:

   ```
   $ gzip -d HTML-Mason-1.04.tar.gz
   $ tar xvf HTML-Mason-1.04.tar
   $ cd HTML-Mason-1.04
   ```

2. You may wish to set an environmental variable, APACHE, to direct the Mason configuration to pick up an Apache server with *mod_perl* attached[*]—for example:

   ```
   $ export APACHE=/usr/local/apache/bin/httpd
   ```

3. Alternatively, just insert the full *httpd* file path when *Makefile.PL* asks for it:

   ```
   $ perl Makefile.PL
   ...
   ```

4. For testing purposes, specify the full path to an *httpd* with *mod_perl* enabled. The path defaults to *$ENV{APACHE}*, if present.

   ```
   [/usr/local/apache/bin/httpd] ('!' to skip):
   ...
   $
   ```

5. Mason's *make test* step will also keep stopping and restarting *httpd*—for example:

   ```
   $ make
   $ make test
   ```

---

[*] As with Embperl, Mason can be operated without *mod_perl*, but you will achieve much better performance if you do use it.

```
...
Testing whether Apache can be started
Waiting for httpd to start.
Killing httpd process (746)
Waiting for previous httpd to shut down
...
$ make install
```

Installing Mason on Win32

To install Mason on Win32 platforms, simply connect to the Internet, call up PPM, and install *HTML::Mason* direct from the University of Winnipeg. (You'll notice on the actual install that you'll get a lot of other modules delivered.)

```
PPM> set repository theoryx5
      http://theoryx5.uwinnipeg.ca/cgi-bin/ppmserver.pl?urn:/PPMServer
PPM> install HTML-Mason
Install package 'HTML-Mason?' (y/N): y
Installing package 'HTML-Mason'...
...
```

You then can install the following additional modules from the ActiveState site:

```
PPM> install Time-HiRes
Install package 'Time-HiRes?' (y/N): y
Installing package 'Time-HiRes'...
...
PPM> install MLDBM
Install package 'MLDBM?' (y/N): y
Installing package 'MLDBM'...
...
PPM> quit
```

Installing Params::Validate

There is a slight complication with Mason on Win32: it requires the *Params:: Validate* module. This module may not be available from either the University of Winnipeg, which specializes in difficult-to-install XS modules, or ActiveState itself. Fear not, for *HTML::Mason* is a pure Perl module, so in the worst case we can create our own PPM installation with it very easily. Here's how:

1. First, get the latest tarball from Dave Rolsky's site:

   http://www.cpan.org/authors/id/D/DR/DROLSKY

2. Unpack it to its own directory, using *gzip* or WinZip. Go to this directory and run the following command:

   ```
   C: \Params-Validate-0.14>perl Makefile.PL
   ```

3. Now, while steadying your hand with a single malt whisky, download the latest *NMAKE* self-inflating program from Microsoft into the *C: \Params-Validate-0.14*

directory. The latest incarnation of *NMAKE* should always be pointed to by the current ActiveState PPM FAQ. The one we used was:

> *http://aspn.activestate.com/ASPN/PPM/FAQ*

This pointed us towards the *NMAKE* download at the following address:

> *http://download.microsoft.com/download/vc15/Patch/1.52/W95/EN-US/ Nmake15.exe*

4. Once you've got this, inflate it:

```
C: \Params-Validate-0.14>Nmake15.exe
...
   Inflating: NMAKE.ERR
   Inflating: NMAKE.EXE
   Inflating: README.TXT
```

5. Now run the *NMAKE.EXE* program, which will read the *Makefile* created earlier by the *perl Makefile.PL* step:

```
C: \Params-Validate-0.14>nmake
...
cp lib/Attribute/Params/Validate.pm blib\lib\Attribute\
      Params\Validate.pm
cp lib/Params/Validate.pm blib\lib\Params\Validate.pm
```

6. You can even run tests if you want to:

```
C: \Params-Validate-0.14>nmake test
...
noop.t t\03-attribute.t t\04-defaults.t t\05-noop_default.t
Using C:/Params-Validate-0.14/blib
t\01-validate.......ok
t\02-noop..........ok
...
```

7. We're now ready to install *Params::Validate* via the PPM program:

```
C: \Params-Validate-0.14>ppm install
...
Installing C:\Perl\site\lib\Attribute\Params\Validate.pm
Installing C:\Perl\site\lib\Params\Validate.pm
Writing C:\Perl\site\lib\auto\Params\Validate\.packlist
C: \Params-Validate-0.14>
```

Mason is now ready for launch on Win32.

Configuring Mason for Apache

There is plenty of excellent documentation on configuring Mason for use with Apache. Simply point your browser at the HTML documents that come with the Mason download:

```
../htdocs/index.html
```

To configure Mason, visit the following page:

```
../htdocs/Mason.html#configuring_mason
```

In this section, we'll illustrate a fairly simple setup—we'll treat all the files found with the *.mcomp* suffix as special Mason templates files. We added the following to our *httpd.conf* file, including two alternative commented-out lines for Win32:

```
PerlSetVar MasonCompRoot /usr/local/apache/htdocs
PerlSetVar MasonDataDir /usr/local/apache/mason
#PerlSetVar MasonCompRoot "C:/Program Files/Apache Group/Apache/htdocs"
#PerlSetVar MasonDataDir "C:/Program Files/Apache Group/Apache/mason"
PerlModule HTML::Mason::ApacheHandler
<FilesMatch "*.mcomp">
    SetHandler perl-script
    PerlHandler HTML::Mason::ApacheHandler
</FilesMatch>
AddType text/html .mcomp
```

Let's see what's going on here:

1. The *MasonCompRoot* directive tells Apache where our Mason component root will be (in this case, it's the same as our default document root).

2. The *MasonDataDir* directive tells Apache where Mason will be storing transitory and permanent data information. Although this directory and its subdirectories will be created automatically on server startup, we'll take the trouble to create the Mason directory manually here just to show how it's done:

   ```
   $ cd /usr/local/apache
   $ mkdir mason
   ```

3. The *PerlModule* directive assigns Mason the requisite Apache handler.

4. The *FilesMatch* block next tells Apache to look out for *.mcomp* files and to direct them toward Mason's Apache handler, if it should find them.

5. We also need to let Apache know that *.mcomp* files are to be ultimately treated as *.html* files, with the *AddType* line.

Now that we've loaded Mason, let's take a look at using it. Like Embperl, Mason is component-based, a mixture of Perl and HTML that gives you powerful direct access into the heart of the Apache server. We've briefly summarized its major features in Table 6-2.

Table 6-2. Mason's main object features

Mason API	Description
Request	Provides a gateway to all of Mason's extra features beyond syntactic tags
Component	Allows you to examine components currently loaded into memory
Parser	Translates components into Perl subroutines
Interpreter	Defines how Mason components are loaded and then executed
ApacheHandler	Connects Mason to *mod_perl*, in response to HTTP requests

Next, we'll work through Mason's inline use of Perl (here's where it comes closest in functionality to Embperl). The three inline methods are all used in Example 6-2, which is executed and displayed in Figure 6-2.

Example 6-2. hello.mcomp

```
<html><head><title>Hello HTML::Mason</title></head><body>
<center>

<p><h1>HTML::Mason :-)</h1><hr>

<%perl>
my $noun = 'World';
my @time = split /[\s:]/, localtime;
</%perl>

<h2>Hello <% $noun %>,
% if ( $time[4] < 12 ) {
   Good morning.
% } elsif ( $time[4] < 18 ) {
   Good afternoon.
% } else {
   Good evening.
% }
</h2><br>
<h3><% scalar(localtime) %></h3>

<hr></center></body></html>
```

Figure 6-2. Hello Mason!

Table 6-3 provides examples of the three types of inline Perl available with Mason.

Table 6-3. Embedding Perl within the Mason template

Format	Description	Example
<% ... %>	The single piece of Perl within the braces is evaluated and returned to the browser.	*Hello, <% $user_login %>!*
% ...	Any line beginning with % is treated as a Perl line to be executed.	*% if (/Hello/) {*

Table 6-3. Embedding Perl within the Mason template (continued)

Format	Description	Example
<%perl> ... *</%perl>*	For code blocks, use this syntax, and everything between the tags is executed as Perl code. The tag is case-insensitive so *<%PERL> ... </%PERL>* is equally valid.	*<%perl>* *my $dbh = DBI->connect($url, $user, $passwd);* *</%perl>*

For a database-related example, we've provided *MasonBlock.mcomp* in Example 6-3. Once again, set *mod_perl* running, along with the target database, and call up the page as in Figure 6-3.

Incidentally, one of the things we especially like about Mason is the comprehensive error browser reporting it provides. This feature greatly aids the development of code, especially when it's all spaghettified across the *httpd* server, *mod_perl*, Perl itself, and the Oracle database!

Example 6-3. MasonBlock.mcomp—Combining Mason with DBI

```
<html><head><title>Hello HTML::Mason and DBI</title></head><body>
<center>
<p><h1>Chiseling into DBI with HTML::Mason 8)</h1><hr>

<%perl>

use DBI;

my $url = 'dbi:Oracle:orcl';
my $user = 'system';
my $passwd = 'manager';

my $dbh = DBI->connect($url, $user, $passwd, {RaiseError->1});

my $sth = $dbh->prepare(
   'select tablespace_name tabSpace, ' .
         'segment_type segType, ' .
         'owner, ' .
         'segment_name segName, ' .
         'blocks, ' .
         'bytes, ' .
         'extents, ' .
         'next_extent nextExt ' .
    'from dba_segments ' .
   'where owner != \'SYS\' ' .
   'order by 1, 2, 3, 4');
$sth->execute;
my $rs = $sth->{NAME};

</%perl>
```

Example 6-3. MasonBlock.mcomp—Combining Mason with DBI (continued)

```
<table border="2">
<tr>
% for my $heading (@$rs)
% {
    <th><% $heading %></th>
% }
</tr>

% while (my @row = $sth->fetchrow_array)
% {
<tr>
%    for my $data (@row)
%    {
        <td><% $data %></td>
%    }
</tr>
% }
<caption>DBA Segments</caption></table>

% $dbh->disconnect;

<hr></center></body></html>
```

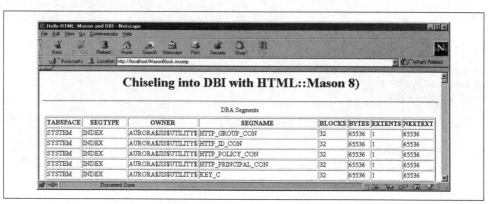

Figure 6-3. Mason, Oracle, and DBI

If you still hunger for more Perl HTML templating, you may to try out Sam Tregar's *HTML::Template* module. This module is based on the use of extended HTML tags. *HTML::Template* aims for a more lightweight, streamlined interface than those offered by Embperl and Mason, while also stressing the separation of design and content production. You may also be tempted by the larger solutions of Andy Wardley's *Template Toolkit* or Matt Sergeant's XML-based *AxKit* (you'll find more on XML in Appendix D, *The Essential Guide to Perl Data Munging*). Check out the following:

> *http://www.cpan.org/authors/id/S/SA/SAMTREGAR*
> *http://www.cpan.org/authors/id/ABW*

http://www.openinteract.org
http://openinteract.sourceforge.net
http://www.cpan.org/authors/id/M/MS/MSERGEANT
http://perl.apache.org/features/tmpl-cmp.html

CHAPTER 7

Invoking the Oracle Call Interface with Oracle::OCI

Back in Chapter 1, *Perl Meets Oracle*, we introduced the Oracle Call Interface (OCI), the low-level application programming interface (API) provided by Oracle Corporation that allows the outside world access to the Oracle database engine. The 3GL language most often used to interact with OCI is C, although it is also possible to use higher-level languages like Perl to communicate with the database via OCI.

Although it is possible to access OCI directly, doing so is quite complicated, and most DBAs and developers (who fear being lost in a swirling river of pointers, linked lists, and casts) prefer a simpler and more convenient interface such as Perl DBI, which we introduced in Chapter 2, *Installing Perl*. Perl DBI is actually not database-specific. It can be used to communicate with Oracle, SQL Server, MySQL, and a variety of other databases. When communicating with Oracle, Perl DBI requires the Oracle-specific driver, *DBD::Oracle*, also described in Chapter 2.

The Perl DBI connection to OCI via *DBD::Oracle* is a useful one, and for many years it has represented the only convenient way that Perl programs could communicate with Oracle. The main design goal of Perl DBI is to provide a consistent, easy-to-use interface to a variety of databases. It isn't especially optimized for any specific database. As a result, the Perl DBI interface to OCI is rather limited; it allows access to only a subset of the extensive functionality of OCI. Back in Chapter 2 we described how Perl DBI allows Perl programs to include appropriate API calls to OCI for certain common database operations. But what if the calls available through Perl DBI are insufficient? Developers and DBAs wanting more sophisticated access to database operations—for example, specialized data loading, use of multiple database connections, and so on—have been faced with a choice between sticking with Perl (and limiting what they could do) and being forced to use C (in order to have full access to everything OCI has to offer). But now there's a new game in town—the Perl module *Oracle::OCI*.

What is Oracle::OCI?

Oracle::OCI takes Perl/Oracle connectivity to a new level. It combines the power of a typical C programming environment with a much friendlier Perl interface. *Oracle:: OCI* gives you access to every bit of functionality available in OCI, and it operates seamlessly with any version of the Oracle database. It lets you do the more complex direct data loading, threading, and large object (LOB) handling that until now has required C programming. *Oracle::OCI* communicates with Oracle at a very low level, which also gives it excellent performance. If you've ever wanted to get that 15-hour batch extract program down to 5 hours, *Oracle::OCI* may be just the thing you've been looking for. There is a price for this power, however. When you use *Oracle:: OCI*, you must code in such a way that there is close to a line-by-line correspondence between your Perl script and OCI, with *Oracle::OCI* acting as the router in between.

In this chapter we'll first look at the Oracle Call Interface itself and what it provides. Then we'll explain how to install *Oracle::OCI* and use it to get the most effective and efficient connectivity between your Perl programs and the Oracle database. Next we'll look at several examples of the code you might write to issue OCI calls from Perl to Oracle. We'll compare the line-by-line *Oracle::OCI* approach to the Perl DBI approach and, finally, we'll suggest a way you can mix and match the two approaches.

Let's start by looking at Figure 7-1, which illustrates the various modules now providing connections to the Oracle database. This figure shows the full set of modules and how they relate, assuming that you have all of them. Most people don't yet have the *Oracle::OCI* module, and they rely entirely on the Perl DBI and *DBD::Oracle* link. This situation may change in the future, however, and *Oracle::OCI* may become integral for everyone. Figure 7-2 compares the two architectures (*Oracle::OCI* vs. Perl DBI/*DBD::Oracle*).

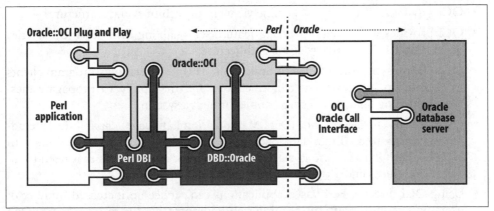

Figure 7-1. The Perl triumvirate: Perl DBI, DBD::Oracle, and Oracle::OCI

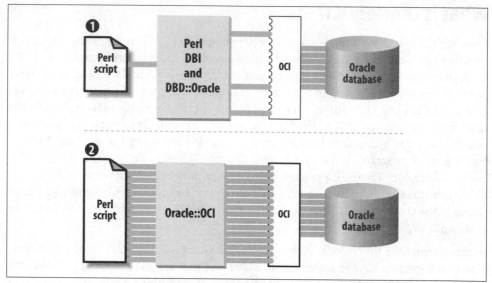

Figure 7-2. Comparing the Oracle::OCI and the Perl DBI/DBD::Oracle architectures

What Is OCI?

As we've discussed, Oracle's Oracle Call Interface is the comprehensive API that is used to connect internally to the Oracle database server. Here is a sampling of what OCI has to offer. *Oracle::OCI* allows Perl programs to access all of these capabilities; in a few cases, we'll note what *Oracle::OCI*'s interface offers us over that provided historically by Perl DBI:

- OCI provides tight low-level control over all aspects of program flow, from server connections to the management of networked transactions, all accomplished in a highly efficient and scalable way.

- OCI's dynamic structures can define virtually any arbitrary data structure.

- OCI provides a complete metadata feature set, enabling drill-down discoveries on the database's entire structural architecture.

- OCI offers asynchronous event notification. This feature allows program clients to register an interest in such notifications and the ability to propagate messages, enabling domino effects to ripple through a system.

- OCI gives us enhanced DML (Data Manipulation Language) capabilities, including the ability to do direct data loading (this is similar to what can be done with SQL*Loader). This feature is particularly useful for applications that need to fill data warehouses under tight time constraints.

- Using OCI directly, Perl-based applications can service an increased number of users and requests without requiring an additional hardware investment. OCI does this by reducing SQL round-trips, using piggy-backing processes, and sharing logins and transactions. User handling can be considerably simplified.

- OCI can manipulate large objects in chunks and streams. Although binary large object (BLOB) features are available within standard Perl DBI, if you need fine-grained LOB access via Perl, *Oracle::OCI* is the way to go. For instance, if a BLOB contains XML data (as many applications now do), *Oracle::OCI* provides the perfect way to parse this data. (For more information, see the discussion of data munging with XML in Appendix D, *The Essential Guide to Perl Data Munging*.)

- OCI offers us a back-stage pass into Oracle's tactical core. For instance, it can perform such complex underlying activities as cache pinning, advanced queuing, and parallel server management.

- OCI provides access to the latest Oracle object development techniques and many of its data transformations—for example, string substitution, decoding, and so on. These aren't available using a more generic API, such as basic Perl DBI or ODBC.

- OCI provides all of the capabilities summarized here with high performance and thread safety as a consequence of its fine-tuned low-level optimization.

The interleaved relationship between *Oracle::OCI* and Perl DBI/*DBD::Oracle* (illustrated earlier in Figure 7-1) also allows us to mix the calls to either API and to reuse handles and object instances. This is impossible in languages other than Perl. You'd either have to use reams of pure OCI or choose an alternative interface at a much higher level (for example, ODBC). There is no way to work on the middle ground in between the two. In Perl, however, you can get the best of both worlds.

Most DBAs will never need the low-level capabilities offered by OCI and available via the *Oracle::OCI* interface. If you are in this category, you can safely ignore this chapter. However, if you *do* need to include any of the functionality listed previously in your own applications, and Perl DBI falls just short of your personal summit (or if you are just curious about what all the excitement is about), then please read on.

Why Oracle::OCI Instead of C?

Let's assume that you're convinced now that OCI is a great thing. But why choose *Oracle::OCI* to build your applications? Why not just use C, the traditional choice of the professional? To convince the jury, let's take a brief look at what we needed to be able to do in order to write effective OCI programs before *Oracle::OCI* arrived on the scene:

1. We had to be fully competent in our chosen 3GL. For example, in C, you had to be comfortable with pointers, voids, casts, and the asterisk-laden shooting match, which is what drove many wizened C programmers over to Perl in the

first place.* (Witnessing a thousand lines of difficult C code being shrunk to ten of Perl for the first time, without spotting the dreaded *malloc* anywhere, was divine revelation for many.)

2. You probably had to write huge source code files for even trivial jobs. (Even logging on, within OCI, can take pages of code, as we'll witness shortly.) The point of Perl DBI was to be the tip of an iceberg, to hide the gory details of OCI behind a simple API. It was also able to provide easy Perl-based access to all of the other hundreds of Perl modules available out there (e.g., *Apache::DBI, DBD::Chart, Perl/Tk,* etc.). When encountering a situation that really did require that low-level OCI functionality, many people who had become downright comfortable with Perl had to throw all of that advantage away, and begin again with their dusted-down Kernighan and Ritchie.†

3. You needed to compile the source files down to object code with a native compiler, and link it to the OCI libraries, thereby making the final application machine-dependent. This seemed a shame, because OCI is the most widely available interface for connecting Oracle to the outside world. And porting 3GL code to other systems, even if you're a believer in strict ANSI C, is more than a trivial afterthought (especially if like Gulliver on his travels, you get your Big-Endians mixed up with your Lilliputians).

The 3GL compilation process is illustrated in Figure 7-3. It works, but it's certainly not ideal. It would be nice to overcome this one-way track to binary-only solutions. It would be great if we could write shorter, machine-independent OCI programs, in clear understandable Perl code.

That's what this chapter is all about.

For More Information on OCI

We've introduced OCI, but there is much more to learn. At last count (in OCI 8.1), there were 530 distinct functions! We have found the following resources to be the most useful; note that most of these references are to the very helpful Oracle Technology Network (OTN).

 The guiding aim of the *Oracle::OCI* project is to keep synchronized with OCI itself and thus to ensure that the official Oracle Corporation OCI documentation always remains simultaneously the documentation for *Oracle::OCI*.

---

* At least one of your authors still has nightmares about linked lists.

† The classic text for C is *The C Programming Language*, by Brian W. Kernighan and Dennis M. Ritchie (Prentice Hall); it is surely one of the finest technical books of all time.

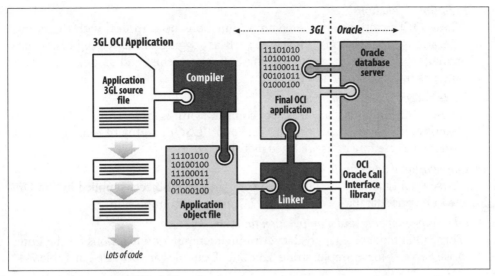

Figure 7-3. Constructing 3GL OCI applications

http://technet.oracle.com:
> Main technical reference for all Oracle products. Once you've set up a free login user, search with the string "OCI" and you should get access to a great many useful references.

http://technet.oracle.com/tech/oci:
> Good general reference kick-off point for drilling down into OCI.

http://otn.oracle.com/tech/oci/htdocs/faq.html:
> Comprehensive FAQ.

http://www.orafaq.org/faqoci.htm:
> Another more independent, FAQ.

OCI Functions

Basically, if there is an OCI function supplied by Oracle Corporation within your local version of OCI (the one that comes with your database), then you can assume that once we build *Oracle::OCI*, there will be a corresponding function available for use within Perl. See Figure 7-2 for a diagrammatic representation of this one-to-one mapping.

OCI functions can be broken down into four main categories as follows. Because there are so many OCI functions, we haven't attempted to list them all. For all but the second category (where there are only four functions in all), we've simply provided examples of the most common functions. Check out the documentation listed in the previous section for much more.

OCI relational functions

These OCI functions are the common functions used to deal with the normal operations of a relational database, such as logging on, executing statements, managing database access, processing SQL statements, and so on. We provide some examples of these in Table 7-1.

OCI external procedure functions

These OCI functions are used to connect with *extproc_plsql*, a module we describe in Chapter 8, *Embedding Perl into PL/SQL*, and with other external C libraries. These functions are listed in Table 7-2.

OCI navigational and type functions

These OCI functions are used to navigate between objects supplied by the Oracle Enterprise database server. Table 7-3 provides examples.

OCI datatype mapping and manipulation functions

These OCI functions supply data attribute manipulation functions for the Enterprise Server—for example, string handling. Examples are provided in Table 7-4.

Table 7-1. OCI relational functions

Functional area	Example function
Advanced Queuing	*OCIAQListen* listens on queues for agents
Handles and descriptors	*OCIDescriptorAlloc* allocates and initializes a LOB locator
Bind and define	*OCIStmtGetBindInfo* gets the bind and indicator variables
Direct path loading	*OCIDirPathFinish* finishes and commits loaded data
Connect and authorize	*OCIEnvCreate* creates and initializes an OCI environment
Large objects	*OCILobFileOpen* opens LOB files
Statement handling	*OCIStmtFetch* fetches rows from queries
Thread management	*OCIThreadCreate* creates new threads
Transactions	*OCITransRollback* rolls back transactions
Miscellaneous	*OCIBreak* carries out an immediate asynchronous break

Table 7-2. OCI external procedure functions

OCI function	Description
OCIExtProcAllocCallMemory	Allocates memory for external procedures
OCIExtProcRaiseExcp	Raises PL/SQL exceptions
OCIExtProcRaiseExcpWithMsg	Raises exceptions along with a message
OCIExtProcGetEnv	Gets the handles detailing the OCI environment

Table 7-3. OCI navigational and type functions

Functional area	Example function
Flush and refresh	*OCICacheRefresh* refreshes pinned persistent objects
Mark cache objects	*OCIObjectMarkDelete* marks an object as deleted

Table 7-3. OCI navigational and type functions (continued)

Functional area	Example function
Get object status	*OCIObjectExists* checks if an instance of an object exists
General navigation	*OCIObjectGetObjectRef* returns a reference to a given object
Pin, unpin, and free	*OCIObjectPin* pins objects in the cache
Type information	*OCITypeByName* gets Type Descriptor Objects (TDOs) by name

Table 7-4. OCI datatype mapping functions

Functional Area	Example function
Collectors and iterators	*OCIIterDelete* deletes an iterator
Date functions	*OCIDateAddDays* adds or subtracts days
Number functions	*OCINumberAbs* works out an absolute value
Raw functions	*OCIRawAllocSize* allocates raw memory
REF functions	*OCIRefIsEqual* compares two REFs for equality
String functions	*OCIStringAssignText* assigns text to a string
Table functions	*OCITableFirst* returns the first index of a table

Installing Oracle::OCI

In order to install *Oracle::OCI* itself, you will need to obtain some additional precursor modules from CPAN. We'll describe those and then explain how to install and run *Oracle::OCI*.

Installing Oracle::OCI on Win32

There is quite a bit of compilation needed for *Oracle::OCI*, and at the time of writing there are no PPM files available to help us (basically because of a necessary bootstrapping process we'll describe later). However, we're confident that the Win32 Perl DBI community will oblige, sooner rather than later. If you're prepared to get your compilers dirty on Win32, the steps will be logically the same as for Unix, so simply follow the Unix installation steps we've provided, and adapt the instructions for your particular compiler type.

At the present time, *Oracle::OCI* is still something of an experimental Perl development. For now, if you're running Win32, your options are to try installing *Oracle::OCI* with Cygwin, as we discussed in Chapter 2, or to create your own versions with commercial Win32 compilers.

The best place to keep track of new developments is the main DBI page at *http://dbi. perl.org*, where you should look for the FAQ work of Ilya Sterin. Ilya regularly creates both XML and Oracle PPD files independently of *ActiveState.com*; he's often on the leading edge of the technical frontier. You can also look for Ilya's DBI FAQ at *http://xmlproj.com/dbi/faq.html* or his Perl Oracle PPM packages for Win32 at *http://xmlproj.com/PPM*.

Precursor Modules

You will need to install these modules in the following order:

Data::Flow
> Following original inspirational work by Ilya Zakharevich, Terrence Brannon took over the *Data::Flow* module, which is a Perl extension for simple recipe-controlled builds of data. You can obtain it from:
>
> > *http://www.cpan.org/authors/id/T/TB/TBONE*

C::Scan
> *C::Scan* also follows in the footsteps of original work by Ilya Zakharevich. *C::Scan* is designed to scan C language files for easily recognized constructs. You'll require its latest incarnation, especially modified for use with Perl 5.6, at Hugo van der Sanden's CPAN site. (Note that future versions may once again be taken over by their original creator, whose CPAN site listing follows). For *Oracle::OCI* 0.06, we required at least *C::Scan* Version 0.74:
>
> > *http://www.cpan.org/authors/id/HVDS*
> > *http://www.cpan.org/authors/id/ILYAZ*

Setting the Oracle::OCI Environment

To make sure that the latest downloaded version of *Oracle::OCI* works, you'll probably also need the latest Perl DBI and *DBD::Oracle* modules installed. All three modules are tightly interwoven, as we saw earlier in Figure 7-1. We'll explain how to do those installations shortly.

Oracle::OCI is unlike any other typical Perl module installation we've seen in this book. The main difference is the tarball, which is actually a toolkit for building *Oracle::OCI*, rather than being *Oracle::OCI* itself. Why is the software built in this way? The project's aim is to match your own database's OCI setup as closely as possible. The toolkit therefore examines your own exact OCI situation and configures accordingly. Doing so ensures that every single OCI function that's available on your own system will be available later within a brand-new *Oracle::OCI* module tailored exactly for your system. Let's go to work.

Installing Oracle::OCI on Unix

The first step in understanding how to install *Oracle::OCI* is to get our heads around its central concept. It's not a Perl module in its own right—one you can simply unpack and install, as if you're taking a nice shiny laptop out of a box and plugging in the wires. Instead, *Oracle::OCI* is a toolkit for building a nice shiny Perl module. What this toolkit does is examine your local version of OCI and then do a one-to-one mapping of all of its functions in order to build a blueprint of the *Oracle::OCI* system you will eventually require. This blueprint is then used to pull all the bits and pieces together, constructing the module that *will* be installed. The world's most highly personalized Perl module is essentially built before your very eyes, and you then simply install *this* module. It's magic!

 The following installation notes were prepared using the latest version of *Oracle::OCI* available to us. However, this project is an *extremely* fast-moving one. Always check out the latest *README* file coming with your own latest *Oracle::OCI* download. This file will contain the most up-to-date installation instructions, and these are expected to get much easier over time. Tim Bunce is likely to be developing this Perl module rapidly over the next few years.

Follow these steps to install *Oracle::OCI* on Unix systems:

1. First of all, you might want to alter the *boot* and *h2xs* scripts so they have the correct version of Perl on their first shebang line. For instance, *Oracle::OCI-0.06* had the following Perl command at the top of the *boot* file:[*]

   ```
   #!/opt/perl5/bin/perl -w
   ```

   We changed ours to:

   ```
   #!/usr/bin/perl -w
   ```

   The following form may be more of a universal solution:

   ```
   #!perl -w
   ```

   (However, make sure to first check step 3, which follows, before doing these hacks.)

2. If you experience connection errors on the build, you might want to update the first few lines of the *01base.t* and *05dbi.t* test programs. You'll find that these are dynamically linked to the main unpack directory, and you'll need to get the right *ORACLE_SID* and *ORACLE_USERID* variables set for your environment before installing *Oracle::OCI*:

   ```
   $ export ORACLE_SID=orcl.world
   $ export ORACLE_USERID=scott/tiger
   ```

3. Once everything's looking good, just run the *boot* program:

   ```
   $ ./boot
   ```

---

[*] For more on *h2xs*, which is beyond the scope of this book, we highly recommend Chapter 18, *Extending Perl: A First Course*, in Sriram Srinivasan's finely honed masterpiece, *Advanced Perl Programming* (O'Reilly & Associates, 1997), *http://www.oreilly.com/catalog/advperl/*.

Alternatively, if you don't want to hack the *#!* lines as in step 1, simply run this program as follows:

```
$ perl boot
```

This will build and test everything, and will prepare your proper OCI configuration system (to be installed later).

4. You may experience some difficulties during the build. We can't predict everything that might go wrong. Because the errors can be varied, we think the best way of tackling any problems is to use the resources detailed in the next section. We also think that getting your hands dirty in the OCI code mines, while clutching an elven ring, should steer you clear of the really ugly cave trolls. Here are some of those we encountered:

- On SuSE Linux 7.3, we got some *ORACLE not available* errors, with Oracle9*i*. Setting *TWO_TASK* to *orcl.world* cleared these.

- We kept getting *./boot* test compilation errors, related to various OCI pointer types, possibly errors only introduced since the introduction of Oracle9*i*. We added the following lines to *getptrdef.h*, and this cured the problem:

```
#define ora_getptr_OCIAnyDataSetPtr ora_getptr_generic
#define ora_getptr_OCIAnyDataPtr ora_getptr_generic
#define ora_getptr_OCICPoolPtr ora_getptr_generic
#define ora_getptr_OCIXADTablePtr ora_getptr_generic
#define ora_getptr_OCIXADFieldPtr ora_getptr_generic
```

Once the *boot* command does fire correctly, you're looking for output like this:

```
chmod 755 blib/arch/auto/Oracle/OCI/OCI.so
...
t/01base...........ok
t/05dbi............ok
All tests successful.
Files=2, Tests=119, 11 wallclock secs (0.81 cusr+0.07 csys = 0.88 CPU)
...
```

5. Now we get to the fun part. After the first compilation stage, we should now possess a pre-installation *Oracle::OCI* module, ready to load up and install as in the usual Perl manner. It should be quietly awaiting instruction within the *../Oracle/OCI* directory. Go here, and inscribe the following spells onto the command line to repeat the wizardry:

```
$ cd Oracle/OCI
$ perl Makefile.PL
$ make
$ make test
...
All tests successful.
...
```

6. The final step should produce plenty of output:

```
$ make install
```

For Further Help with Oracle::OCI

Here are some suggestions for things to check and do if you have trouble with *Oracle::OCI*:

1. There's some great help on the *Oracle::OCI* mailing lists. To join the mighty throng, send an email to:

   oracle-oci-help@perl.org

2. There is also a mail archive, which is especially useful for dealing with installation problems when slight tweaks are required for different flavors of Unix. Check out:

   http://archive.develooper.com/oracle-oci@perl.org

3. Oracle Corporation occasionally moves their installation directories around just to keep us on our toes. For example:

   - You might want to look out for situations where *Oracle::OCI* is expecting to see *$ORACLE_HOME/network/public*, but the files it's looking for are actually in *$ORACLE_HOME/rdbms/public*
   - C header files expected in *$ORACLE_HOME/rdbms/demo* may also be hiding in *$ORACLE_HOME/plsql/public*

4. You may get lines such as the following:

   ```
   Error: invalid argument declaration
   'void * argv[ ]' in OCI.xs, line 666
   ```

   Find the offending line in the *OCI.xs* file, and then add the relevant function to the following piece of code in the *boot* file, which deliberately excludes such problematic items:

   ```
   oci_skip => [ sort keys %{ { ... } } ]
   ```

5. For errors such as:

   ```
   Error: 'OCIFooBar *' not in typemap in
   OCI.xs, line 777
   ```

   You might want to add an extra line to the *extra.typemap* file:

   ```
   OCIFooBar *    T_PTROBJ
   ```

You might also want to check the *README.build* file, which may hold the exact answer to your problem. However, as *Oracle::OCI* matures, expect it to become as pain-free as *DBD::Oracle* and Perl DBI are now.

Coding with Oracle::OCI

In the following sections, we're going to present essentially the same example coded three different ways; each creates a simple table description:

1. Example 7-1 shows how the example looks using pure *Oracle::OCI* code. You'll notice that this is a lot more code than a typical Perl DBI script. Essentially, we use OCI functions on a one-to-one basis, so even just logging in to a database can take a whole page of code, whereas DBI does it in one line.

2. Example 7-2 shows how much shorter the example can be if you use pure Perl DBI, where a single DBI function takes the place of as many as ten *Oracle::OCI* functions.*

3. Example 7-3 shows a blended approach. We combine, in a single Perl script, both Perl DBI and *Oracle::OCI*. Where we can use DBI commands within *Oracle::OCI*, we do so to save typing pages of code. The only places where we actually need to use one-to-one OCI mappings are the cases where we journey *beyond* Perl DBI.† (The earlier Figure 7-1 shows the relationship between Perl DBI and *Oracle::OCI*.)

Pure Oracle::OCI Code

This first example (Example 7-1) shows pure unadulterated *Oracle::OCI* code. Notice how just logging on takes over a page of code. (We'll work through the steps after the example.)

Example 7-1. rawOCI.pl—Oracle::OCI in action

```
#!/usr/bin/perl -w

# Pure-ish Oracle::OCI

use strict;

use DBI qw(neat);
use Oracle::OCI qw(:all);

# Step 1: Get the environment right, and set up your target
# database and user, before we initialize.
$ENV{ORACLE_SID} ||= 'ORCL';
my $dbuser = $ENV{ORACLE_USERID} || 'scott/tiger';
```

---

* Basically, this is what DBI has been doing for us all along. It's just that we've had no need to worry about it before; it's all been kept under the covers.

† We're only doing this because we're hunting for that last iota of extra functionality or performance. In general, we let the standard Army infantry of Perl DBI make up the bulk of the Normandy invasion forces. We bring in the Airborne troops of *Oracle::OCI* just do that little bit extra at the end.

Example 7-1. rawOCI.pl—Oracle::OCI in action (continued)

```perl
# The following call to new_ptr() and bless are 'scaffolding'
# which this version of Oracle::OCI requires, but these will not be
# needed in future versions.  This will reduce the clutter
# and bring the code much closer to the equivalent OCI C code! :-)

sub new_ptr {
    my $class = shift;
    my $modifiable = do { my $foo = shift || 0 };
    return bless \$modifiable => $class;
}

# Initialize the environment via OCI.

my $envhp = new_ptr('OCIEnvPtr');

OCIInitialize (OCI_OBJECT, 0, 0, 0, 0);
OCIEnvInit($envhp, OCI_DEFAULT, 0, 0);

# Step 2: Allocate the various handles.
# Get the Error Handle

OCIHandleAlloc ($$envhp, my $errhp=0, OCI_HTYPE_ERROR, 0, 0);
bless $errhp => 'OCIErrorPtr';

# Get the Server Contexts etc.

OCIHandleAlloc ($$envhp, my $svrhp=0, OCI_HTYPE_SERVER, 0, 0);
bless $svrhp => 'OCIServerPtr';
OCIHandleAlloc ($$envhp, my $svchp=0, OCI_HTYPE_SVCCTX, 0, 0);
bless $svchp => 'OCISvcCtxPtr';

# Step 3: Now Attach and set the attribute server context
# within the Service context, before logging on.
OCIServerAttach ($svrhp, $errhp, 0, 0, OCI_DEFAULT);
OCIAttrSet
   ($$svchp, OCI_HTYPE_SVCCTX, $$svrhp, 0, OCI_ATTR_SERVER, $errhp);

OCIHandleAlloc($$envhp, my $authp=0, OCI_HTYPE_SESSION, 0, 0);
bless $authp => 'OCISessionPtr';

my ($user, $pass) = split /\//, $dbuser;
my @user_buf_len = oci_buf_len($user);
my @pass_buf_len = oci_buf_len($pass);

OCIAttrSet  ($$authp, OCI_HTYPE_SESSION, @user_buf_len,
            OCI_ATTR_USERNAME, $errhp);

OCIAttrSet  ($$authp, OCI_HTYPE_SESSION, @pass_buf_len,
            OCI_ATTR_PASSWORD, $errhp);

# Finally, meine kleine Freunden, we begin a session...
```

Example 7-1. rawOCI.pl—Oracle::OCI in action (continued)

```perl
my $status = OCISessionBegin ($svchp, $errhp, $authp,
                              OCI_CRED_RDBMS, OCI_DEFAULT);
warn get_oci_error($errhp, $status) unless $status == OCI_SUCCESS;

OCIAttrSet ($$svchp, OCI_HTYPE_SVCCTX, $$authp, 0,
            OCI_ATTR_SESSION, $errhp);

# Step 4: Now prepare the description of the target table,
# and start some data processing.
OCIHandleAlloc($$envhp, my $dschp, OCI_HTYPE_DESCRIBE, 0, 0);
bless $dschp => 'OCIDescribePtr';

my $tablename = $ARGV[0];
OCIDescribeAny ($svchp, $errhp, oci_buf_len($tablename),
                OCI_OTYPE_NAME, 1, OCI_PTYPE_TABLE, $dschp);

# Get the parameter descriptor.

OCIAttrGet ($dschp, OCI_HTYPE_DESCRIBE, my $parmp, 0, OCI_ATTR_PARAM,
            $errhp, 'OCIDescribePtr');

# Get the table list, number of columns and description.

OCIAttrGet ($parmp, OCI_DTYPE_PARAM, my $collst, 0,
            OCI_ATTR_LIST_COLUMNS, $errhp, 'OCIParamPtr');

OCIAttrGet ($parmp, OCI_DTYPE_PARAM, my $numcols, 0, OCI_ATTR_NUM_COLS,
            $errhp, 'OCIParamPtr');
my $errstr;

# Describe the target table.

printf ("\n------------------\n");
printf ("TABLE : %s \n", $tablename);
printf ("------------------\n");

my %col_attr = (
   OCI_ATTR_NAME       =>  "ColName",
   OCI_ATTR_IS_NULL    =>  "NULL?",
);

foreach my $colnum (1..$$numcols) {

   my $col_parmdp_int = 0;
   my $col_parmdp = bless \$col_parmdp_int => 'OCIParamPtr';
   OCIParamGet($collst, OCI_DTYPE_PARAM, $errhp, $col_parmdp, $colnum);

   my $describe_attr = {
      OCI_ATTR_NAME       =>  0,
      OCI_ATTR_IS_NULL    =>  1,
   };
   printf "\n";
```

Example 7-1. rawOCI.pl—Oracle::OCI in action (continued)

```
   foreach my $attr (sort keys %$describe_attr) {
      my $type = $describe_attr->{$attr};
      no strict 'refs';
      $status = OCIAttrGet( $col_parmdp, OCI_DTYPE_PARAM,
                            oci_buf_len(my $tmp, 90),
                            &$attr, $errhp, $type);
      warn "$attr: ".get_oci_error($errhp, $status, 'OCIAttrGet')
         if $status;

      warn get_oci_error($errhp, $status)
         if $status;

      printf "%-20s: %s\n", $col_attr{$attr}, neat($tmp);
   }
}

# Step 5: Logout and detach from the server.
OCIHandleFree($$dschp, OCI_HTYPE_DESCRIBE);
OCISessionEnd($svchp, $errhp, $authp, 0);
OCIServerDetach($svrhp, $errhp, OCI_DEFAULT );

# Step 6: Clean up memory and deallocate handles.
OCIHandleFree($$svrhp, OCI_HTYPE_SERVER);
OCIHandleFree($$svchp, OCI_HTYPE_SVCCTX);
OCIHandleFree($$errhp, OCI_HTYPE_ERROR);
OCIHandleFree($$authp, OCI_HTYPE_SESSION);  # Bye, Bye !!! :-)
```

You can see that this is quite a bit of work. Let's go through the code and examine what it is we're doing:

1. We first ensure that our passwords and all the other usual suspects are sorted out before initializing the OCI environment.

2. Having initialized, we can now allocate all of our various memory handles.

3. We attach to the server, log in, and establish various attributes.

4. Now we can do some processing. In this case, we describe the various columns of a target table. We format and print the results as we go.

5. In the final stages, we end the session and then detach from the server.

6. We can now deallocate all of the memory handles.

Once completed, we can run the script with the target table supplied:

```
$ perl rawOCI.pl DEPT
```

We received the following output:

```
-------------------
TABLE : DEPT
-------------------

NULL?                : 0
```

```
ColName              : 'DEPTNO'

NULL?                : 1
ColName              : 'DNAME'

NULL?                : 1
ColName              : 'LOC'
```

Pure Perl DBI and DBD::Oracle

We did an awful lot of work in Example 7-1—two pages of code just to get a few simple column descriptions! What if we'd done something similar in Perl DBI instead? We'll do just that in Example 7-2.

Example 7-2. rawDBI.pl

```perl
#!/usr/bin/perl -w

use strict;

# Pure-ish DBI

use DBI qw(neat);

# Step 1: Get the environment right, and set up your target
# database and user.
$ENV{ORACLE_SID} ||= 'ORCL';
my $dbuser = $ENV{ORACLE_USERID} || 'scott/tiger';

# Steps 2 & 3: We initialize and log onto the database.
my ($user, $pass) = split /\//, $dbuser;
my $dbh = DBI->connect("dbi:Oracle:", $user, $pass,
                        {RaiseError => 1});

# Step 4: Now prepare the description of the target table.
my $sth = $dbh->prepare("select * from $ARGV[0]");
$sth->execute;

# Describe the target table.

printf ("\n------------------\n");
printf ("TABLE : %s \n", $ARGV[0]);
printf ("------------------\n");

my %col_attr = (
   NAME => "ColName",
   NULLABLE => "NULL?",
);

foreach my $colnum (0..($sth->{NUM_OF_FIELDS} - 1)) {

   printf "\n";
   foreach my $attr (sort keys %col_attr) {
```

Example 7-2. rawDBI.pl (continued)

```
    my $tmp = $sth->{ $attr }->[$colnum];
    printf "%-20s: %s\n", $col_attr{$attr}, neat($tmp);
  }
}
$sth->finish;

# Steps 5 & 6: Logout, clean-up and check out.
$dbh->disconnect;  # Bye, Bye !!! 8)
```

There's much less work involved using just Perl DBI and *DBD::Oracle*, especially with logging on and logging off. Just for the record, we obtained the following results:

```
$ perl rawDBI.pl DEPT

------------------
TABLE : DEPT
------------------

ColName              : 'DEPTNO'
NULL?                : ''

ColName              : 'DNAME'
NULL?                : 1

ColName              : 'LOC'
NULL?                : 1
```

So what's the point of *Oracle::OCI*—the same result for four times the effort? Has the stardust of Perl lost its magic? No, it has become more powerful than you can imagine. What we're trying to do is get the finely-grained OCI stuff we mentioned earlier without having to do it all in hundreds of lines of C. We'll see how shortly.

Mixing and Matching Oracle::OCI, Perl DBI, and DBD::Oracle

When you need certain OCI functionality that isn't available in Perl DBI, the most effective thing to do is to mix and match. Where we can save code using Perl DBI, we can do that, and where we really need OCI functionality, we can do that too—all within the same script. As the earlier Figure 7-1 showed, the various interface modules—*Oracle::OCI*, Perl DBI, and *DBD::Oracle*—are all tightly integrated. When you set up a *$dbh* database handle with Perl DBI, for example, you get access to all of the memory handles *Oracle::OCI* also requires. Take a look at Example 7-3 to see how we use the best of both the DBI and OCI worlds. In fact, this is why we think *Oracle::OCI* may potentially become the very best way of accessing the entire OCI API in *any* language. (See the section called "The Future of Oracle::OCI" at the end of this chapter.)

Example 7-3. blendOciDbi.pl—Combining DBI and Oracle::OCI

```perl
#!/usr/bin/perl -w

use strict;

# Blended DBI and OCI

use DBI qw(neat);
use Oracle::OCI qw(:all);
# Step 1: Get the environment right, and set up your target
# database and user.
$ENV{ORACLE_SID} ||= 'ORCL';
my $dbuser = $ENV{ORACLE_USERID} || 'scott/tiger';

# Steps 2 & 3: We initialize and log onto the database.
my ($user, $pass) = split /\//, $dbuser;
my $dbh = DBI->connect("dbi:Oracle:$ENV{ORACLE_SID}", $user, $pass);

# Step 4: Now prepare the description of the target table, this time
# using OCI, after we've established our connection with DBI.
# Notice the frequent use of the Perl DBI $dbh variable.
my $tablename = $ARGV[0];

bless $dbh => 'OCIEnvPtr';
OCIHandleAlloc($dbh, my $dschp, OCI_HTYPE_DESCRIBE, 0, 0);
bless $dschp => 'OCIDescribePtr';
OCIDescribeAny ($dbh, $dbh, oci_buf_len($tablename), OCI_OTYPE_NAME,
                1, OCI_PTYPE_TABLE, $dschp);

# Get the parameter descriptor.

OCIAttrGet ($dschp, OCI_HTYPE_DESCRIBE, my $parmp, 0, OCI_ATTR_PARAM,
            $dbh, 'OCIDescribePtr');

# Get the table list, number of columns and description.

OCIAttrGet ($parmp, OCI_DTYPE_PARAM, my $collst, 0,
            OCI_ATTR_LIST_COLUMNS, $dbh, 'OCIParamPtr');

OCIAttrGet ($parmp, OCI_DTYPE_PARAM, my $numcols, 0,
            OCI_ATTR_NUM_COLS, $dbh, 'OCIParamPtr');
my $errstr;

# Describe the target table.

printf ("\n------------------\n");
printf ("TABLE : %s \n", $tablename);
printf ("------------------\n");

my %col_attr = (
   OCI_ATTR_NAME      =>   "ColName",
   OCI_ATTR_IS_NULL   =>   "NULL?",
);
```

Example 7-3. blendOciDbi.pl—Combining DBI and Oracle::OCI (continued)

```perl
my $status;
foreach my $colnum (1..$$numcols) {

    my $col_parmdp_int = 0;
    my $col_parmdp = bless \$col_parmdp_int => 'OCIParamPtr';
    OCIParamGet($collst, OCI_DTYPE_PARAM, $dbh, $col_parmdp, $colnum);

    my $describe_attr = {
        OCI_ATTR_NAME        => 0,
        OCI_ATTR_IS_NULL     => 1,
    };

    printf "\n";
    foreach my $attr (sort keys %$describe_attr) {
        my $type = $describe_attr->{$attr};
        no strict 'refs';
        $status = OCIAttrGet( $col_parmdp, OCI_DTYPE_PARAM,
                              oci_buf_len(my $tmp, 90),
                              &$attr, $dbh, $type);
        warn "$attr: ".get_oci_error($dbh, $status, 'OCIAttrGet')
            if $status;
        warn get_oci_error($dbh, $status) if $status;
        printf "%-20s: %s\n", $col_attr{$attr}, neat($tmp);
    }
}
```

 # Steps 5 & 6: Logout, clean-up and check out.
```perl
$dbh->disconnect;  # Bye, Bye !!! >=8+)
```

When we ran the code in Figure 7-3 in *blendOciDbi.pl*, we received this output:

```
$ perl  blendOciDbi.pl DEPT


------------------
TABLE : DEPT
------------------

NULL?              : 0
ColName            : 'DEPTNO'

NULL?              : 1
ColName            : 'DNAME'

NULL?              : 1
ColName            : 'LOC'
```

With more than 530 OCI functions to choose from, we're confident you'll find exactly what you're looking for when you combine Perl DBI and Oracle::OCI. For instance, the following bioinformatics code snippet takes LOB processing a helpful bit further than DBI can go. We fetch a LOB locator with DBI, and then process its genetic information with *Oracle::OCI*:

```
my $lob_locator = $dbh->selectrow_array("select my_lob " .
                                        "from human_genome " .
                                        "where id = 'insulin' " .
                                        "for update",
                                        { ora_auto_lob => 0 });
# Start Oracle::OCI
OCILobGetLength($dbh, $dbh, $lob_locator, my $lob_len = 0);
OCILobTrim($dbh, $dbh, $lob_locator, $lob_len - 2);
# Update the Bioinformatics genetic code inside the LOB
my ($offset, $amount, $buffer) = ($lob_len/2, 44, '');
OCILobRead($dbh, $dbh, $lob_locator, $amount, $offset,
           oci_buf_len($buffer, 200, \$amount), 0, 0, 0, 0 );
$buffer =~ s/ATGC/ACTG/g;
OCILobWrite($dbh, $dbh, $lob_locator, $amount, $offset,
            oci_buf_len($buffer), OCI_ONE_PIECE, 0, 0, 0, 1 );
# Back to DBI
...
```

The Future of Oracle::OCI

We're sure that within a few years *Oracle::OCI* will be an advanced, mature set of packages used by every Perl Oracle user around. Author Tim Bunce actually predicts that *Oracle::OCI* will eventually hold the complex code, but that simpler modules will be layered on top to provide specific functionality. For example, future modules may include the following:

Oracle::LOB
> For dealing with large binary objects

Oracle::DirectPath
> For speeding data loads

Oracle::Collection
> For collections, index-by tables (associative arrays), and nested tables

Oracle::Transaction
> For finely grained remote transactions

Oracle::PLSQL

Another extremely interesting development in the world of OCI will be *Oracle:: PLSQL*. At the time we were writing this book, this module was planned but did not yet exist. We expect this module to provide fantastic connectivity between PL/SQL and Perl. In this way, it will tie in neatly with the *extproc_plsql* module we describe in Chapter 8. Using the upcoming *Oracle::PLSQL*, PL/SQL functions could be mapped directly to Perl functions, and vice versa, in a way similar to what's happened with

SQLJ and Java. We expect that eventually there could be room enough for this symbiosis of Perl and PL/SQL to manage all of the following Oracle features:

- Transparent use of the UTL_FILE built-in package between PL/SQL and Perl
- Advanced Queuing
- Replication
- Standby databases
- Parallel servers
- Gathering and processing of performance statistics
- Building of custom tools with the DBMS_DEBUG built-in package

For instance, Tim Bunce predicts snippets of code, such as the following example, which works with binary files to load their information into the *$buffer* variable:

```
use DBI;
$dbh = DBI->connect('dbi:Oracle:', $user, $pass, { ora_autolob => 0 });
$bfile =
    $dbh->selectcol_array(
        "select bfile from mylobs where id=? for update", undef, 1);

use Oracle::PLSQL;

$dbms_lob = new Oracle::PLSQL DBMS_LOB => \$dbh;
$dbms_lob->fileexists($bfile) or die "File missing";

$length = $dbms_lob->filelength($bfile);
$dbms_lob->filegetname($bfile, $diename, $filename);
$dbms_lob->fileopen($bfile, $dbms_lob->{file_readonly});
$dbms_lob->read($bfile, 40, 1, $buffer);
$dbms_lob->fileclose($bfile);
```

Stay tuned to the *Oracle::OCI* dial for further information.

Contributing to the Oracle::OCI Project

Most Oracle DBAs probably already have their hands full and won't be interested in adding to their workload. But if you do want to help with the *Oracle::OCI* project, we recommend that you get hold of the latest download and start trying to make it work for your own needs. It can take a while to get the hang of it, but for practice you might want to try to replicate the OCI demonstration programs provided by Oracle Corporation, listed in the next section. For further information on the project, visit Tim Bunce's CPAN site where you'll find numerous presentation downloads on DBI, *DBD::Oracle*, and *Oracle::OCI*:

http://www.perl.com/CPAN/authors/id/TIMB

Demo Programs

If you want to cut your teeth on some hard-core OCI programming, check out the code examples provided by Oracle Corporation detailing in-depth usage of OCI calls, available automatically within your current Oracle installation.* These C files, and supporting SQL files, generally appear in the *../rdbms/demo* or *../oci/samples* directories. A variety of helpful information is included within the header parts of these files; for example, you'll find out what accompanying SQL files need to be pre-installed, and so on. We've listed the OCI 8.1 demonstration programs in Table 7-5.

Table 7-5. OCI demonstrations from Oracle Corporation

C programs	Description
cdemo1.c..cdemo5.c	Basic SQL processing
cdemo81.c, cdemo82.c	Basic Oracle8 SQL session and object processing
cdemobj.c	REF selection and navigational interface
cdemocor.c..cdemocor1.c	Demonstrate a prefetching user interface
cdemodp.c..cdemodp_lip.c	Loading data through direct path API
cdemodr1.c..cdemodr3	Returning values and LOBs, etc.
cdemodsa.c, cdemodsc.c	Used for describing tables
cdemoext.c	OCI extraction
cdemofil.c	OCI file handling
cdemofo.c	OCI callbacks for application failover
cdemofor.c	OCI formatting
cdemolb2.c, cdemolb2.c, cdemolbs.c, cdemoplb.c	Working with LOBs
cdemorid.c	DML prefetches
cdemort.c	Type information
cdemoses.c	Session management
cdemosyev.c	System event registration
cdemothr.c	OCI threading
cdemoucb.c, cdemoucbl.c	User callbacks

---

* These are not guaranteed to appear, nor guaranteed to work, by Oracle Corporation, but you'll generally find them and they do generally work. They provide excellent templates on which to build your own code, especially if you wish to help develop Oracle::OCI.

## CHAPTER 8

Embedding Perl into PL/SQL

PL/SQL is Oracle's own programming language. It©'s a powerful procedural language that is tightly integrated with SQL ("PL/SQL" stands for "Procedure Language extension to Structured Query Language"). It offers a full range of datatypes, conditional and sequential control, looping, exception handling, modular code constructs, user-defined datatypes (such as objects), and a lot more. It's likely that you have a whole raft of PL/SQL programs that you use daily to perform Oracle database administration.

With all of its advantages, PL/SQL has a few limitations as well. There are things PL/SQL programmers want to do that turn out to be impossible, or at least inefficient, to do with PL/SQL alone. As you might suspect, we think Perl is the ideal supplement to PL/SQL. By calling Perl modules from your PL.SQL programs (more accurately, by embedding Perl within PL/SQL), your PL/SQL programs acquire many additional capabilities:

Mailing and the Internet
> It is sometimes difficult to email or connect to the Internet from within PL/SQL, but there are hundreds of helpful connectivity options available through Perl.

Encryption
> PL/SQL offers very little built-in security, but Perl provides access to many different types of encrypted security systems. (Later in this chapter we'll show how we use the MD5 message digest algorithm from within PL/SQL via *Digest::MD5*.)

Operating system commands
> Every now and again—perhaps while running complex backup maneuvers—we run into situations where we'd like to be able to run system commands directly via the operating system. Perl provides this ability (though, as we'll see, we will have to be careful how we use it).

Access to C libraries

Perl has literally hundreds of modules providing API access to the world's most popular C libraries. Allowing PL/SQL to access these via Perl extends PL/SQL's functional horizons.

Regular expressions

Although Oracle is catching up with regular expressions, particularly with some of the PL/SQL Web Toolkit packages, such as OWA_PATTERN and OWA_TEXT, Perl's regular expression engine is generally held to be the world's most powerful. It would be nice to get access to it via PL/SQL.

Overall performance

Before external procedures arrived on the scene, it was a laborious process (usually necessitating wrestling with the DBMS_PIPE built-in package), to get PL/SQL to talk to the outside world. It involved complex listener setups, excellent 3GL language skills, plus a good sense of humor and a large *Simpsons* video collection for post-installation de-stress relaxation.*

With external procedures now capable of linking to Perl, we save a lot of effort, and our programs run much faster.

Communication Between Perl and PL/SQL

The way you combine Perl and PL/SQL, and get the most out of these two excellent languages, is with Perl's *extproc_perl* module, created by Jeff Horwitz. PL/SQL is able to communicate with this library via its external procedure C-library system, which is known as *EXTPROC*.

What are External Procedures?

External procedure is a generic term for a server-side program that you can compile into the native "shared library" format of the operating system. Under Unix, a shared library is a shared object or *.so* file. Under Win32, it's a DLL (dynamically linked library). You can write an external procedure in any language you wish, as long as your compiler, interpreter, and/or linker will generate the appropriate shared library format that is callable from the language you have used. Historically, most external procedures called from PL/SQL have been C programs, but Perl is now becoming a popular option. This is because it is now possible to embed Perl directly within a C library via Doug MacEachern's *ExtUtils::Embed* module, as shown in Figure 8-1.

---

* It actually was possible to involve Perl in these older solutions, as we did at the following web page, but we believe that *extproc_perl* is a much better solution: *http://www.cybcon.com/~jkstill/util/debug_pipe/debug_pipe.html*.

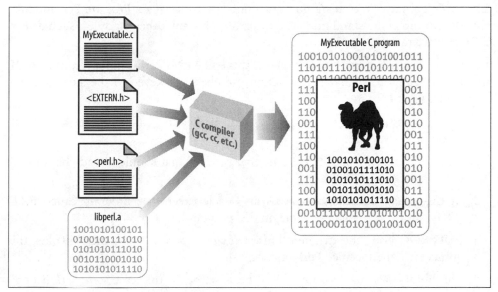

Figure 8-1. Embedding Perl directly within a C library

Embedding Perl in C

The *ExtUtils::Embed* module was actually developed as a way of embedding the Perl interpreter within C, via Apache, specifically for *mod_perl*. Our ability to use it with PL/SQL is really a byproduct of that development. To find out more about its use, run the following command:

```
$ perldoc perlembed
```

Instead of having to work out all the information necessary to embed Perl into C, all we have to run now is a command such as the following:

```
$ cc - o myCexecutable myCexecutable.c \
    `perl -MExtUtils::Embed -e ccopts -e ldopts`
```

This determines everything your C program will need in order to embed Perl, including the three main C-related files held under the Perl library tree: *EXTERN.h*, *perl.h*, and *libperl.a*. It's a particularly good technique, because the embedded Perl interpreter is still able to read and interpret independent Perl scripts, a fact we rely on with our embedded Perl system, as we'll explain later in this chapter. Although the two header include files are important, it's the *libperl.a* archive which is the really crucial file to include; this archive contains the core of Perl's interpreter C code.

Calling the Embedded Perl C Library from PL/SQL

Once we've compiled our new library with its embedded Perl system (we'll show how to do that shortly), we can start using it like any other efficient C-based

EXTPROC library. (We create our new one with a special *ExtProc.pm* Perl module; this sits on top of the standard Perl interpreter, plus any other modules, such as Perl DBI, that we require.)

Let's look at what happens when you call this embedded Perl C library from PL/SQL in order to call a particular Perl function; numbers are keyed to the step numbers shown in Figure 8-2.

1. The process starts with a PL/SQL client application calling a special PL/SQL "module body."

2. PL/SQL looks for a special Net8 listener process* that should already be running in the background.

3. At this point, the listener spawns an Oracle executable program called *EXT-PROC* (note the uppercase name on this program).

4. *EXTPROC* loads the dynamic library (*extproc_perl.so*), and then invokes this library with the specified Perl function call.

5. The library then interrogates a Perl boot script (in this case, *ora_perl_boot.pl*) and looks for the requested function.

6. On finding it, it executes the Perl function code, deals with any parameters, and then returns the results all the way back to the calling PL/SQL client.

7. The *extproc_perl.so* C library returns these results via the *EXTPROC* process.

8. The *EXTPROC* process channels these results into the PL/SQL Runtime Engine.

9. And finally, the PL/SQL Runtime Engine returns these results to the calling PL/SQL application code.

Embedding Perl Within Oracle

Running *extproc_perl* is mainly about getting the Oracle external procedures system working correctly. One of the best general guides we've found for these installation procedures is Chapter 23 of *Oracle PL/SQL Programming*, 3rd ed. (now covering Oracle9*i*) by Steven Feuerstein with Bill Pribyl (O'Reilly & Associates, 2002). For further information on Oracle's external procedures, the best online information source is perhaps *http://technet.oracle.com*. Although the pages are very fluid (you may need to browse around a bit), we found the following pages useful when we were investigating the subject:

http://download.oracle.com/otndoc/oracle9i/901_doc/appdev.901/a88876/adg11rtn.htm
Oracle9*i* Application Developer's Guide—Fundamentals for Release 1, Chapter 10, *Performing Routine DBA Tasks with the PDBA Toolkit.*

---

* Net8 is known as Oracle Net in Oracle8*i* and later releases and SQL*Net in Oracle7 and earlier releases.

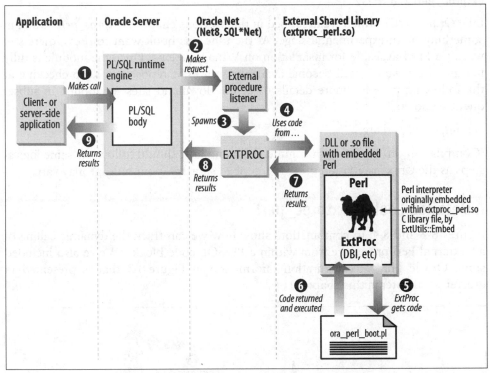

Figure 8-2. extproc_perl in action

http://download.oracle.com/otndoc/oracle9i/901_doc/server.901/a90117/manproc.htm
  Oracle9i Database Administrator's Guide for Release 1, Chapter 5, *Embedding Perl into Apache with mod_perl.*

EXTPROC security

Before you get too deeply into the details of *extproc_perl*, we recommend that you check out the following page for possible security alerts about *EXTPROC*, the actual program spawned by the Oracle external procedure listener processes:

  http://otn.oracle.com/deploy/security/alerts.htm

Because of the nature of what *EXTPROC* does—using external libraries to access the inside of the Oracle database—we have to be vigilant in our use of the *EXTPROC* system provided by Oracle. We recommend that you carefully follow the guidelines provided in any relevant security advisories you find on the web page we've referenced previously.

extproc_perl and Win32

Like *Oracle::OCI*, which we described in the previous chapter, *extproc_perl** is still in something of an experimental stage. At the time this book went to press, there still wasn't a PPM available for installation on Win32 systems. Once the module is fully mature, we're sure it will become available on a PPM repository. Keep checking at the following page for more details or at the download sites mentioned in subsequent sections:

> *http://dbi.perl.org*

(Compilation on Win32, with commercial compilers, should follow the same logical steps as the Unix installation process described shortly—your mileage may vary.)

A Detailed Look at extproc_perl

Figures 8-3 and 8-4, in combination, show how we can track the dynamic calling of an external Perl procedure from within a PL/SQL code block. (We've also included some Oracle library configuration information in Figure 8-3 that is presented in greater detail later in this chapter.)

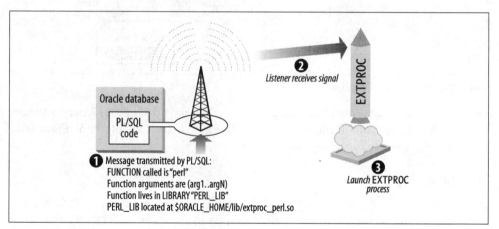

Figure 8-3. PL/SQL's active linkage to extproc_perl #1

Let's see what's going on here:

1. From deep within the database, the PL/SQL program broadcasts to the *EXTPROC* listener. It sends out targeting information, stored within library and function declarations, so the listener can locate the correct code within the external procedure. It also sends any required parameters.

2. The listener picks up the signal from the PL/SQL engine.

---

* Also known as the "Oracle Perl Procedure Library."

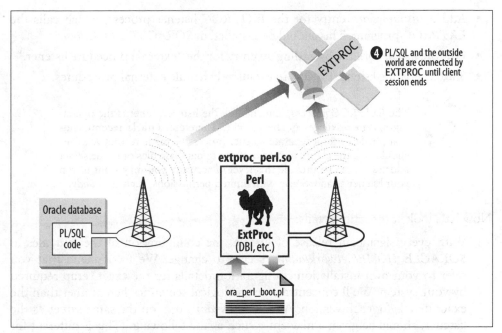

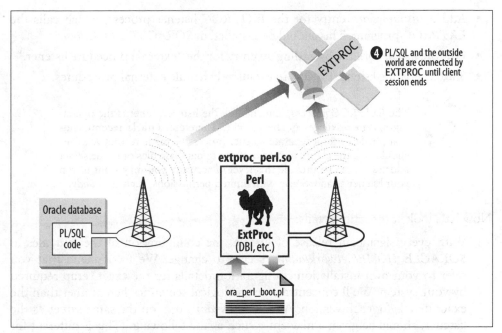

4 PL/SQL and the outside world are connected by EXTPROC until client session ends

Figure 8-4. PL/SQL's active linkage to extproc_perl #2

3. It then launches the *EXTPROC* rocket program (or spawns it, as the manuals say, which is too Borg for those of us who are followers of the One True Kirk.)

4. Once *EXTPROC* is deployed, it takes over mission control, and coordinates the entire operation between the PL/SQL ground station and the external C program agents. It maps shared code pages into the address space of the user process and maintains this link until the client session completes. It then retracts its panels and splashes back down, to be sent up again on later missions. While on station, *EXTPROC* deals with all requests by the client session for external procedural help.

Downloading extproc_perl

You can download the latest stable version of *extproc_perl* from here:

http://www.smashing.org
http://www.cpan.org/modules/by-authors/Jeff_Horwitz

Setting Up External Procedures

Setting up external procedures is not simple. You will need to do quite a bit of work to get the setup right. We've summarized the main steps here; in the following sections we'll show the details for each point:

- Add a *tnsnames.ora* entry for the *EXTPROC* listener process, which calls the *EXTPROC* program. This should be installed in *$ORACLE_HOME/bin*.
- Edit the *listener.ora* file by adding an entry for the "external procedure listener."
- Start a separate listener process to exclusively handle external procedures.

> The *EXTPROC* process, launched by the listener, inherits the operating system privileges of the listener. Therefore, Oracle recommends that privileges for a separate listener process be made restrictive. They should lack the ability to read or write to database files or to the server address space. To provide this level of security, you may want to run your listener as an OS user with limited permissions, such as *nobody*.

Now let's look at the setup details:

1. With every significant release of Oracle, the configuration of the *.ora* files in *$ORACLE_HOME/network/admin* seems to change. We recommend that you refer to your own installation configuration details for the exact setup required by your system. We'll concentrate on the logical semantics here, rather than the exact details for each version. A typical *tnsnames.ora*, on the same server as the listener, should be given a new entry such as the following. (This is different for Oracle9*i*; see the discussion later for details):

    ```
    extproc_connection_data =
    (DESCRIPTION =
        (ADDRESS = (PROTOCOL=IPC)(KEY=extproc_key))
        (CONNECT_DATA = (SID = extproc_agent)
    )
    ```

    In some examples, the basic entry name, *extproc_connection_data*, is fixed. However, even if this is the case in your version of Oracle, it may need a suffix if your *sqlnet.ora* contains a default domain name such as:

    ```
    NAMES.DEFAULT_DOMAIN=ORACLE.OREILLY.COM
    ```

    You may need to change the server *tnsnames.ora* entry name to match the domain name entries as follows:

    ```
    extproc_connection_data.ORACLE.OREILLY.COM = ...
    ```

2. However, the key you specify (in this case *extproc_key*) must also match the KEY you specify in the *listener.ora* file. In addition, the SID name you specify (in this case *extproc_agent*) must match the SID entry in the *listener.ora* file. (You may just want to call everything *extproc* to keep it simple.) In the following, we've attached entries to a new listener entry in order to run up a separate listener purely for external procedures:

    ```
    EXTERNAL_PROCEDURE_LISTENER =
    (ADDRESS_LIST =
        (ADDRESS = (PROTOCOL=ipc)
    ```

```
            (KEY=extproc_key)
    )
)

SID_LIST_EXTERNAL_PROCEDURE_LISTENER =
(SID_LIST =
    (SID_DESC = (SID_NAME=extproc_agent)
                (ORACLE_HOME=/u02/app/oracle/product/8.0.4)
                (PROGRAM=extproc)
    )
)
```

3. Note the following conditions for the preceding *listener.ora* example:

   - The *EXTPROC* program is conventionally referred to as *extproc* in lower case.
   - The *ORACLE_HOME* must be set to the Oracle software home.
   - The *EXTPROC* executable must exist in *$ORACLE_HOME/bin*.
   - However, in Oracle9*i*, most things are automatic with *PLSExtProc*. With a small change to *DBD::Oracle*, described later, this is fine. Let's examine two snippets from the two main Oracle9*i* *.ora* files. First, *listener.ora*:

```
(SID_DESC =
  (SID_NAME = PLSExtProc)
  (ORACLE_HOME = /opt/oracle/product/9.0.1)
  (PROGRAM = extproc)
)
```

   And now, *tnsnames.ora*:

```
EXTPROC_CONNECTION_DATA.LOCAL =
  (DESCRIPTION =
    (ADDRESS_LIST =
      (ADDRESS = (PROTOCOL = IPC)(KEY = EXTPROC))
    )
    (CONNECT_DATA =
      (SID = PLSExtProc)
      (PRESENTATION = RO)
    )
  )
```

4. Once ready, we can start up a separate listener as a low-privilege user:

```
$ lsnrctl start EXTERNAL_PROCEDURE_LISTENER
```

Once the listener is running successfully, we can skip the following section. However, it may prove useful if you encounter any listener problems.

Debugging External Procedure Listeners

You'll be among friends if your listener setups refuse to work first time around. This badge of honor even has a special debug routine to help you; look for the following file under *ORACLE_HOME*:

   dbgextp.sql

Before you install this file, be sure to read it; it contains some good documentation regarding how you can make use of it with debugging programs.

Now follow these steps:

1. In a perfect world, you should get no errors when you execute the *STARTUP_ EXTPROC_AGENT* procedure. Notice that in addition to CONNECT and RESOURCE, other important privileges granted to the new user include both CREATE ANY LIBRARY and DROP ANY LIBRARY:

```
SQL> connect system/manager
SQL> create user extproctest identified by extproctest;
SQL> grant connect, resource to extproctest;
SQL> grant create any library, drop any library to extproctest;
SQL> connect extproctest / extproctest
SQL> @?/plsql/demo/dbgextp.sql
SQL> call DEBUG_EXTPROC.STARTUP_EXTPROC_AGENT( );
Call completed.
```

2. If *STARTUP_EXTPROC_AGENT* refuses to fire, this will indicate that the *.ora* files have a configuration problem of some kind. Once everything's ship shape, drop this test user:

```
SQL> connect system/manager;
SQL> drop user extproctest cascade;
```

 The DEBUG_EXTPROC package can be made to work with popular C program debug utilities. If you don't have a debugger on your system and you're using *gcc*, you will be able to use the excellent *gdb* debugger, which is designed to work hand-in-glove with *gcc*. See *http:// www.gnu.org/software/gdb/*.

Building a New Perl

Before doing anything else, you will need to establish whether you're using a Perl distribution with a shared *libperl*. This is a pre-condition for *extproc_perl*. In the following sections we'll see how to find this out and how to build a new Perl if you need to do so.

The need for a shared libperl

To find out if you are using a Perl distribution with a shared *libperl*, you can issue the following:

```
$ perl -MConfig -e 'print "$Config{useshrplib}\n"'
false
```

Alas, *false* was the wrong answer. But, every cloud has a mithril silver lining. Because we're pointing Perl directly into the heart of the Oracle database, we'll do as Jeff Horwitz actually recommends and build a special version of Perl, just for Oracle's use. This way, we can do all the things we need to do without clobbering anyone or anything else along the way.

We're also going to make use of a *DBD::Oracle* patch, supplied within the *extproc_ perl* download, to rebuild Perl DBI. This makes it doubly sensible to break out a fresh Perl to play with.

Because Oracle lacks support for the dynamic loading of shared objects from external procedures, Perl's DynaLoader is compromised. We have to load shared objects from targeted modules at runtime, and this static architecture requires XS hooks, special pleading, and a delegation of Papal Nuncios from Rome. Building a brand new Perl is definitely the way to go!

Building Perl for the oracle user

In this section, we'll work through how to build a brand new Perl for the *oracle* user. You may want to breeze through Chapter 2, *Installing Perl*, again to remind yourself about the basics of Perl installation, but we'll do an abbreviated installation run right here and now, and assume that the *oracle* user's HOME directory is:

```
/opt/oracle
```

If security is an issue, you may wish to create this new Perl for whichever user you run your listeners with (see our earlier note on listener security):

1. Once the Perl installation user is chosen, you may want to create a new directory in the *$HOME* directory (to store the forthcoming downloads) and a related *perl/bin* directory (where we'll ultimately install Perl):

   ```
   $ cd $HOME
   $ mkdir perldown
   $ mkdir -p perl/bin
   ```

2. Next, get and unpack *stable.tar.gz* from *http://www.perl.com/CPAN/src*:

   ```
   $ cd ../perldown
   $ gzip -d stable.tar.gz
   $ tar xvf stable.tar
   $ cd perl-5.6.1
   ```

3. Configure in a shared *libperl* and a Perl home of */opt/oracle/perl*:

   ```
   $ rm -f config.sh Policy.sh
   $ sh Configure -Dprefix=/opt/oracle/perl -Duseshrplib
   ```

   The configurator will ask lots of questions, depending on your setup. We have to be careful here and resist pumping the *RETURN* key like a Motörhead drummer. You must say "no" to the following question:

   ```
   Many scripts expect perl to be installed as /usr/bin/perl.
   I can install the perl you are about to compile also as /usr/bin/perl
   (in addition to /opt/oracle/perl/bin/perl).
   Do you want to install perl as /usr/bin/perl? [y] n
   ```

   This is an exception; aside from the use of a shared *libperl*, we do intend to build a totally regular, though local, Perl.

4. Once Perl is configured, run *make*:

```
$ make
```

5. You may find time to make a nice hot cup of tea, while the Perl monkey spends a couple of minutes churning the compilation organ. When it's completed, check it over:

```
$ make test
... All tests successful.
u=0.93  s=0.12  cu=64.77  cs=8.81  scripts=249  tests=12503
```

6. Now let's go create (note that for once we can avoid doing this as *root*):

```
$ make install
```

7. At some point during this installation, you may get the following warning:

```
Warning: perl appears in your path in the following locations
beyond where we just installed it:    /usr/bin/perl
```

This is kind of like a private sentry turning back a known Four Star General because of a forgotten password; it's a good thing. To get around this, we must make sure our local hero Perl comes ahead of any others when we compile our library. Once the compilation has finished, you'll still see the older Perl before our nice new sparkling one:

```
$ type perl
perl is hashed (/usr/bin/perl)
```

We can get round this immediately by resetting *PATH*:

```
$ export PATH=$HOME/perl/bin:$PATH
$ type perl
perl is /opt/oracle/perl/bin/perl
```

(We'll also have to do this more permanently via whatever profiling system we're using, to ensure that our *oracle* user always gets the right Perl.)

8. Now, the proof of the Christmas pudding is in the eating, so let's see if we've acquired the use of a shared *libperl*. Go to it, Red:

```
$ perl -MConfig -e 'print "$Config{useshrplib}\n"'
true
```

Way to go!

Next, we can move on and install Perl DBI and *DBD::Oracle* over the fresh new Perl.

Perl DBI and DBD::Oracle

As Figure 8-5 shows, once PL/SQL calls the embedded Perl interpreter via external procedures, it's pretty much out on a limb in the outside world. Therefore, although we can return ordinary values to the host database, we need to use DBI (using its own form of SQL) if we wish to loop back. This loopback behavior is displayed in Figure 8-6. (Notice that we can connect to other databases as well, although we have to establish a proper connection in these cases.)

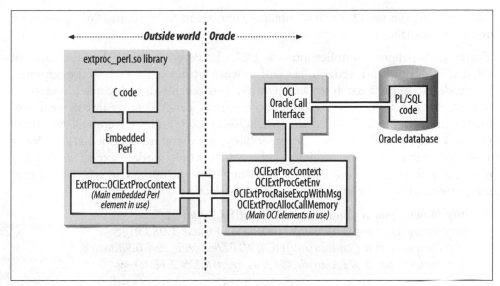

Figure 8-5. The basic circuitry of extproc_perl

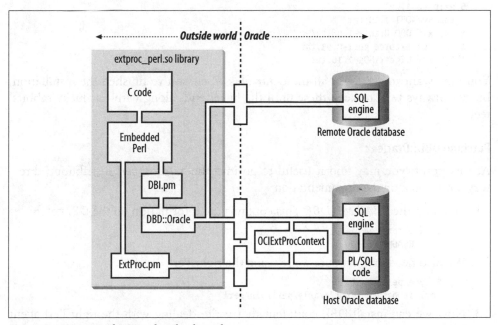

Figure 8-6. Using Perl DBI in loopback mode

The importance of OCIExtProcContext

The *OCIExtProcContext* structure from OCI, originally set up when *extproc_perl* is first called, gives DBI the ability to remain within the current PL/SQL transaction.

This prevents the need for a new database connection to be set up. (We'll say more about this shortly.)

There is a slight complication to DBI, however, caused by the use of *OCIExtProcContext*. In order to get DBI to work within our Oracle Perl interpreter, we needed to apply a patch to *DBD::Oracle*. This patch will be included in versions of *DBD::Oracle*, from 1.13 onward, but the *extproc_per-0.93.tar.gz* tarball we downloaded had the patch designed for *DBD::Oracle 1.08*, and we were still on *DBD::Oracle* 1.12. To deal with this incompatibility, we therefore obtained *DBD::Oracle* 1.08, just to make sure the patch we had access to would work as expected. To complete our tarball set, we obtained the following files, including *Digest::MD5* for testing purposes, and copied them to */opt/oracle/perldown*:

> *http://www.cpan.org/authors/id/TIMB/DBI-1.20.tar.gz*
> *http://www.cpan.org/authors/id/TIMB/DBD-Oracle-1.08.tar.gz*
> *http://www.cpan.org/authors/id/JHORWITZ/extproc_perl-0.93.tar.gz*
> *http://www.cpan.org/authors/id/GAAS/Digest-MD5-2.16.tar.gz*

Before we went into combat, we extracted the Perl ammunition:

```
$ gzip -d *.gz
$ tar xvf DBI-1.20.tar
$ tar xvf DBD-Oracle-1.08.tar
$ tar xvf extproc_perl-0.93.tar
$ tar xvf Digest-MD5-2.16.tar
```

You may want to get rid of all these *.tar* files when you've finished the installation, but we always tend to keep these until the bitter end, along with our lucky rabbits' feet.

Patching DBD::Oracle

At this point, you may find it useful to go into the *extproc_perl* distribution directory, and check on the documentation:

1. Open up the *README.DBI*. This contains the information on the DBI patch:

   ```
   $ cd extproc_perl
   $ vi README.DBI
   ```

2. We also need to make sure we're using the right Perl:

   ```
   $ type perl
   perl is hashed (/opt/oracle/perl/bin/perl)
   ```

3. Now we can install DBI, confident that we're dealing with the right Perl agent (those agents can get tricky when you've got more than one of them):

   ```
   $ cd ../DBI-1.20
   $ vi README
   $ perl Makefile
   $ make
   $ make test
   $ make install
   ```

```
...
Writing
    /opt/oracle/perl/lib/site_perl/5.6.1/i686-linux/auto/DBI/.packlist
```

Now the patch comes into play. Go to *DBD::Oracle*'s installation home:

```
$ cd ../DBD-Oracle-1.08
```

4. It's time to start up our target Oracle database and make sure its listeners are fired up. Make sure that *ORACLE_HOME*, *ORACLE_SID*, and *ORACLE_USERID* are all set, as per the *DBD::Oracle README* file:

```
$ export ORACLE_USERID=scott/tiger@orcl.world
$ env | grep ORACLE
ORACLE_SID=orcl.world
ORACLE_USERID=scott/tiger@orcl.world
ORACLE_HOME=/opt/oracle/product/9.0.1
```

The *DBD::Oracle* patch is worth a look if you have time. You'll notice a sustained use of *OCIExtProcContext* and other OCI code elements, as from Figures 8-5 and 8-6. We've detailed a snippet or two here:

```
...
 #ifdef OCI_V8_SYNTAX
+    SV **svp;
+    struct OCIExtProcContext *this_ctx;
...
+       if (sv_isa(*svp, "ExtProc::OCIExtProcContext")) {
+           IV tmp = SvIV((SV*)SvRV(*svp));
+           this_ctx = (struct OCIExtProcContext *)tmp;
+       }
...
```

5. To patch *DBD::Oracle*, carry out the following steps:

```
$ cp dbdimp.c dbdimp.old
$ chmod 644 dbdimp.c
```

6. Now move down a directory, as the patch is designed to be applied from the parent directory:

```
$ cd ..
$ cp extproc_perl/DBD-Oracle.patch .
$ patch -p0 < DBD-Oracle.patch
patching file `DBD-Oracle-1.08/dbdimp.c'
$ cd DBD-Oracle-1.08
$ ls -la dbdimp.* | grep -v '.h'
-r--r--r--   1 oracle   oinstall    57336 Apr  7 12:02 dbdimp.c
-r--r--r--   1 oracle   oinstall    56354 Apr  7 12:01 dbdimp.old
```

Note the slightly larger *dbdimp.c* file.

7. Oracle9*i* users and anyone else with a *PLSExtProc* listener instance may want to make a very small manual change to the *dbdimp.c* file before compiling. Look for the following line:

```
if (!strncmp(dbname,"extproc",7)) is_extproc = 1;
```

Change this to:

```
if (!strncmp(dbname,"PLSExtProc",10)) is_extproc = 1;
```

This will ensure that the correct database context is called later on.

8. We can now install *DBD::Oracle* as usual:

```
$ perl Makefile.PL
$ make
$ make test
$ make install
```

You may also want to install other modules at this point—for example, *Digest::MD5* or anything else from CPAN that catches your fancy. Because we're embedding Perl into a C library, we have to embed everything along with it that we might need later. Fortunately, the main module that makes *extproc_perl* possible, *ExtProc.pm*, will always be installed automatically.

Connecting back to the host database

As far as the host database goes, when you call the external procedure you remain permanently connected to the database as the PL/SQL client user. However, to use DBI for host callbacks, you can make use of the *OCIExtProcContext* object, as noted earlier. Fortunately, *ExtProc.pm* has made this easy. You simply use it to grab the database context from within the bootstrap *.pl* script file and then use the following code to phone home:

```
use DBI;
use ExtProc;

# Pick up the current OCI context

my $context = ExtProc::context;

# Call back to the host database

my $dbh = DBI->connect( "dbi:Oracle:extproc", "", "",
                        { 'context' => $context });
```

Here's what's going on:

1. Notice that there is no user or password required with the *DBI->connect* statement. You're still technically logged into the database as the user who's running the actual PL/SQL and are still part of the current transaction.

2. Notice as well the database SID, *extproc* within the DBI driver setup string (you may wish to change this to *PLSExtProc*, depending on your setup):

```
dbi:Oracle:extproc
```

If you choose a more standard connection, such as *dbi:Oracle:orcl*, you'll create a *proper* DBI connection, which incurs significant overhead. You'll also need to supply a user and password. Using *dbi:Oracle:extproc* is also much faster, as it's tuned directly into OCI.

3. Alternatively, if you wish to connect to a remote database or to connect as another database user, just connect with DBI normally and follow its standard *scott/tiger@my_remote_database_sid* pattern. For example:

```
my $dbh =
    DBI->connect( "dbi:Oracle:my_remote_database_sid", "scott", "tiger",
                  { RaiseError=>1, AutoCommit=>0 } );
```

Installing extproc_perl

We can now move on to the actual installation of *extproc_perl*. Switch over to the */extproc_perl* directory and ritually scan the installation files:

```
$ cd ../extproc_perl
$ vi README INSTALL
```

Note that the *INSTALL* file is the one you want to be checking here, rather than *README*.

ora_perl_boot.pl

Before configuration, we created a bootstrap Perl script file, *ora_perl_boot.pl*; at runtime, the C library will scan this file for functions. *ora_perl_boot.pl* contains the subroutines we'll be calling later from within PL/SQL. The name of this file on the configuration step will default to:

```
$ORACLE_HOME/lib/ora_perl_boot.pl
```

This seems to be a sensible name. We don't actually have to create this bootstrap file right now (see the note later in this section), but it seems a good time to illustrate doing so. In addition, although test routines are not necessary right now, this also seems as good a time as any to write some in a new *$ORACLE_HOME/lib/ora_perl_boot.pl* file. (See Example 8-1, and notice our alternative use of *PLSExtProc* in Test 4, for database context.)

Example 8-1. The ora_perl_boot.pl bootstrap file

```perl
sub localtime { # Test 1 - What's the time Mr Wolf? :-)

    my $x = localtime(time);
    return $x;
};

sub ls { # Test 2.  ==> Hey, this could be rather dangerous! <==

    my ($lsarg) = @_;
    $lsarg ||= '.';

    my $ls = '/bin/ls -l';
    my $lsret = qx( $ls $lsarg );
    return $lsret;
}
```

Example 8-1. The ora_perl_boot.pl bootstrap file (continued)

```perl
sub md5hex { # Test 3 - A little enigmatic encryption :)

    my ($data) = @_;

    use Digest::MD5;

    my $ctx = Digest::MD5->new;
    $ctx->add($data);
    my $digest = uc($ctx->hexdigest);
    return $digest;
}

sub tab_keyword { # Test 4 - Using DBI call-back context

    # Pick up the current OCI context and recall host.

    use DBI;
    use ExtProc;

    my($keyword) = @_;

    my $context = ExtProc::context;
    my $dbh = DBI->connect( "dbi:Oracle:PLSExtProc", "", "",
                            {RaiseError=>1, context => $context});

    # Viewing all SYSTEM tables, formatted

    my $sth = $dbh->prepare( "SELECT table_name " .
                             "FROM user_tables ");
    $sth->execute;

    $sth->bind_columns(\$table_name);

    my $return_string;

    my $counter = 0;

    while ($sth->fetch) {

        $table_name = lc($table_name);
        $table_name =~ s/($keyword)/uc($1)/ieg;  # Hey, Regular
                                                 # Expressions!!! 8-)
        $counter++;

        if ($counter > 4) {
            $counter = 1;
            $return_string .= "\n";
        }
        $return_string .= sprintf("%-30s ", $table_name);
    }
```

Example 8-1. The ora_perl_boot.pl bootstrap file (continued)

```
$dbh->disconnect;
return $return_string;
}
```

 You can create this boot file after the installation if you wish. As long as the subsequent installation knows where to expect to find it, that's good enough. You can also change the boot file after the installation to add extra subroutines, extra parameters, and so on. The only restriction is that you must use basic Perl, pre-installed modules, or pure Perl modules. If you wish to use a new optional module—for example, *Oracle::OCI*—you must rebuild the *extproc_perl.so* library with the *Oracle::OCI* module explicitly mentioned in the build process. Everything you wish to use has to be included within the *extproc_perl.so* library file, although rebuilding this is fairly painless once you've successfully set up the *EXTPROC* listener process.

Example 8-1 is not a polished subroutine collection. At this point, we'd recommend that you go back and check the *ls()* subroutine in the example. You could almost drive a Saturn V rocket through its security (or lack of it)! (See Figure 8-7 a bit later for more details.) You will need to watch out for this kind of thing if you employ the rocket thrust power of *extproc_perl*. For more on Perl security, check out:

```
$ perldoc perlsec
```

Installation steps

Follow these steps to install *extproc_perl*:

1. Depending on the Oracle version, some header files may be missing from the locations where *extproc_perl* (originally developed on Solaris) expects to find them. You may have to symbolically link them in where appropriate. For now, though, let's assume that all the files are where we need them:

   ```
   $ perl Makefile.PL
   ```

   This step will ask several questions. Because of the restriction on dynamically loaded Perl modules, we have to specifically embed Perl modules statically within our external procedure library via the *extproc_perl* configuration process. The *Makefile.PL* configurator will automatically suggest several modules you might like to include. In addition to these, we'll also add the DBI, *DBD::Oracle*, and *Digest::MD5* modules, which we'll be testing later via subroutine *md5hex()* in the boot file:

   ```
   Modules to include in this
       build [IO Socket attrs]: IO Socket attrs Digest::MD5
       DBI DBD::Oracle <RETURN>
   ```

2. We also accepted the default name and location for the bootstrap file:

```
Path to bootstrap
    file [/opt/oracle/product/9.0.1/lib/ora_perl_boot.pl]: <RETURN>
```

3. It's time to compile:

```
$ make
```

We hope you have as much fun as we did with the *make* step!

4. We can now create our special library file, which also automatically installs the essential *ExtProc.pm* Perl module:

```
$ make install
...
*** You should now copy extproc_perl.so to a convenient location.
...
```

So, Mr. Bond, did we cut the library file from the Monte Carlo card pack?

```
$ ls -la *.so
-rwxr-xr-x   1 oracle oinstall 13008 Apr  7 12:18 extproc_perl.so
```

You win again, Mr. Bond, but we'll be back! Having created a shiny *extproc_perl.so* library, we place it where Oracle can find it later. *$ORACLE_HOME/lib* seems the most natural place:

```
$ cp extproc_perl.so $ORACLE_HOME/lib
```

Now there's just one more hurdle before the home stretch; we'll discuss it in the next section.

There are two built-in *extproc_perl* functions detailed in the *README. special* file. The first is *_version*, which supplies the current *extproc_perl* version, and the second is *_flush*, which destroys the current Perl interpreter and all the Perl data; a new interpreter is started for the next query. (You'll see *_flush* in action at the end of the chapter in Figure 8-9.)

Deploying extproc_perl

All of the operating system elements are now in place for being able to use *extproc_perl*. The final task is the creation of the actual *PERL_LIB* library within the database and its associated *perl* function. We'll do this in Example 8-2; you can change this code and add more parameters to suit your own environment, either now or at a later time.

Example 8-2. Creating the PERL_LIB library and perl function

```
CREATE OR REPLACE LIBRARY PERL_LIB IS
   '/opt/oracle/product/9.0.1/lib/extproc_perl.so'
/

show error library perl_lib
```

Example 8-2. Creating the PERL_LIB library and perl function (continued)

```
CREATE OR REPLACE FUNCTION perl (
    sub IN VARCHAR2, arg1 in VARCHAR2 default NULL,
    arg2 in VARCHAR2 default NULL, arg3 in VARCHAR2 default NULL,
    dummy in VARCHAR2 default NULL
) RETURN STRING AS
EXTERNAL NAME "ora_perl_sub"
LIBRARY "PERL_LIB"
WITH CONTEXT
PARAMETERS (
    CONTEXT,
    RETURN INDICATOR BY REFERENCE,
    sub string,
    arg1 string,
    arg1 INDICATOR short,
    arg2 string,
    arg2 INDICATOR short,
    arg3 string,
    arg3 INDICATOR short,
    dummy string,
    dummy INDICATOR short
);
/
show errors function perl;

create public synonym perl for perl;

grant execute on perl to public;
```

Testing extproc_perl

To recap, here's what we've done to get ready to run *extproc_perl*:

- The external procedure listener is running and ready to spawn *EXTPROC*.
- The *PERL_LIB* library has been created, along with the related *perl* function, and has been made available to public.
- The *extproc_perl.so* library has been compiled and is accessible to *EXTPROC*.
- The *ora_perl_boot.pl* bootstrap file has been put in place; it is waiting now for calls from the *perl* function via *extproc_perl*.

Oh, what a tangled web we've woven—but one with a huge potential problem. Let's do some testing. You can see our first two tests being called in Figure 8-7; note the security implications of our *ls* subroutine. Figure 8-8 shows our third test; note how the addition of the *md5hex* encryption subroutine adds a necessary degree of security.

Figure 8-9 shows our final context link back to Perl DBI, and the use of regular expressions. This Perl routine's purpose is to list all of the tables in USER_TABLES

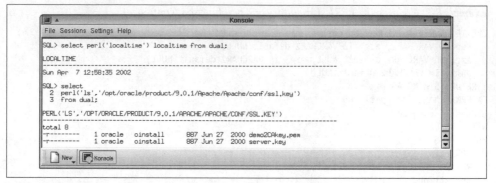

Figure 8-7. extproc_perl—tests 1 and 2

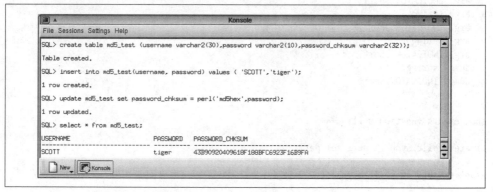

Figure 8-8. extproc_perl—test 3

and to highlight a chosen string—in this case, *COL*. Notice the use of *_flush*, the built-in function that clears out the Perl interpreter beforehand.

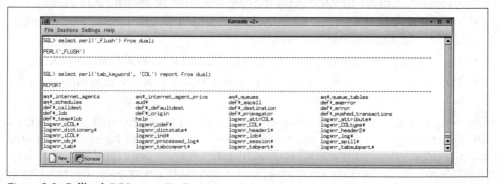

Figure 8-9. Callback DBI, using ExtProc context

As Laurence Olivier might have said, we'll leave it to your imagination to fill in the many and varied possibilities of using *extproc_perl*. Suffice it to say that through *extproc_perl* you now have the entire range of Perl and CPAN modules to play with—including mailing, regular expressions, FTP, Telnet, *IO::Socket*, and all the other golden gems of Perl Internet functionality. If you're interested in encryption and related security operations, you'll find that you now have a full range of Perl security modules available, including *Authen::ACE*, *Crypt::Beowulf*, the various message digest algorithms, and the *Crypt::Twofish2* encryption module. You can see the ever-growing list of Perl security modules at *http://search.cpan.org/Catalog/Security/*.

The Perl DBA Toolkit

This third part of the book describes the Perl Database Administration (PDBA) Toolkit, a set of Perl scripts and reusable modules that we've developed to help Oracle DBAs perform both routine database administration and more advanced monitoring and tuning. It consists of the following chapters:

Chapter 9, *Installing the PDBA Toolkit*, introduces the components of the Perl Database Administration Toolkit and explains how to install it and build the toolkit's password server.

Chapter 10, *Performing Routine DBA Tasks with the PDBA Toolkit*, describes the toolkit's Perl scripts that help DBAs perform day-to-day administration. We'll cover managing user accounts, maintaining indexes, killing sniped sessions, managing extent usage, and extracting DDL (Data Definition Language) and data.

Chapter 11, *Monitoring the Database with the PDBA Toolkit*, describes the toolkit's Perl scripts that can be used to monitor both the Oracle alert log (containing database error and status messages) and the connectivity of the databases.

Chapter 12, *Building a Database Repository with the PDBA Toolkit*, describes the toolkit's Perl scripts that allow you to build a repository in which to store information about the many changes made to an Oracle database's tables, indexes, roles, schemas, and other objects.

Chapter 13, *Extending the PDBA Toolkit*, provides information that will be helpful if you decide to modify any of the scripts or modules in the toolkit. We'll take a detailed look inside one of the toolkit's scripts and modules and illustrate how you can change them to suit your specific database administration needs.

## CHAPTER 9

Installing the PDBA Toolkit

In earlier chapters we looked at a number of applications that Perl programmers have developed to help you perform Oracle database administration tasks. In this part of the book we'll introduce our own toolkit of scripts and modules written in Perl. These scripts are also aimed at Oracle DBAs and focus on areas of database administration that aren't covered in the other applications we've examined. You will find all of the toolkit code freely available on the O'Reilly web site (see the Preface for details).

Rather than being a ready-made application, you can think of the Perl DBA Toolkit (PDBA, for short) described in this chapter and the following ones as a collection of resources. You can run the scripts as is, or you can build on them in any way you wish. Think of the scripts provided in the toolkit as a handy collection of sailing knots and rigging splices that you can use for tying various Perl modules together into the best Oracle DBA solution for your own needs.

In this chapter, we'll cover these topics:

Introducing the toolkit and its core modules
> We'll explain the contents of the toolkit and describe the functionality of the common modules that are used by many of the Perl scripts described in subsequent chapters.

Installing the toolkit
> We'll describe how to install the toolkit on Unix and Win32 systems.

Configuring the toolkit
> After installation, we'll explain how you can configure the toolkit with users, passwords, and other system-specific characteristics to meet your own site's needs.

Subsequent chapters describe different components of the toolkit in greater detail.

One part of the toolkit, the PDBA repository, requires special installation procedures; those are covered in Chapter 12, *Building a Database Repository with the PDBA Toolkit*, not in the general installation procedures described in this chapter. If you do not need the capabilities provided by the repository, you can simply skip that chapter and the repository installation.

Introducing the PDBA Toolkit

Your authors have been Oracle DBAs for many years. Over that time we've encountered our share of frustration with database problems and inadequate tools. We've also ended up writing literally thousands of *ad hoc* scripts to diagnose and fix problems on the fly. We've checked database connectivity, monitored the Oracle alert log, wrestled with password management, rebuilt indexes, and endured the drudgery of creating thousands of user accounts. We've used many programming languages and applications. Some we've loved and others we've hated. Some did the trick, but at a huge cost in money and complexity. Then we discovered Perl and realized how helpful it could be in developing those quick scripts so essential to an Oracle database administrator. Perl—and the modules that connect it to Oracle—gave us the keys to the kingdom!

The Perl DBA Toolkit is our own ongoing open source contribution to the world of Perl and Oracle. We have pooled our own script libraries and modules in order to build a cohesive Perl tool library for you to use in performing Oracle database administration tasks. Many of the scripts included here are integrated versions of those we've used on a regular basis in our DBA activities over the years. Others have been on our wish lists for a very long time, and this book has finally inspired us to transfer these wishes into reality.

It's up to you how you want to use this toolkit. It serves as a complete, standalone application, and it also provides a helpful template for you to use in doing Perl programming of your own. In building this toolkit, we've tried to demonstrate the flexibility and power of this amazing language by putting together, for your enjoyment, a living, breathing network of Perl coding examples (in addition to providing a huge array of Oracle database administration operations, of course).

The toolkit contains two distinct types of programs:

Perl scripts
> Standalone scripts, written in Perl, that perform some distinct function; examples include adding a new user to the database, rebuilding an index, or populating the toolkit repository with data from the Oracle data dictionary.

Supporting modules
> Underlying modules, also written in Perl, that provide more basic functionality that is shared by multiple scripts; examples include finding and loading various types of configuration files and processing command-line arguments.

Tables 9-1 through 9-5 list the toolkit scripts that are installed automatically, along with the supporting modules (listed in Table 9-6) when you install the toolkit. All toolkit scripts are shown here except for a few additional scripts used only for setting up the repository (described in Chapter 12) and for demonstration purposes.

 We describe the routine database administration scripts (Chapter 10, *Performing Routine DBA Tasks with the PDBA Toolkit*) before the monitoring scripts (Chapter 11, *Monitoring the Database with the PDBA Toolkit*) and repository scripts (Chapter 12) because they provide general-purpose functionality. However, if you use the monitoring and/or repository functionality of the toolkit, we recommend that you install and run those scripts before using any other toolkit scripts. Essentially, the monitoring scripts provide a first perimeter of security for your database, and the repository scripts provide a second. For the safest possible database operation, it's best to install and run these scripts before undertaking routine database administration.

Table 9-1 lists the scripts that are associated with the password server described in Chapter 13, *Extending the PDBA Toolkit*. (See the sections "Password Server Configuration," and "Password Client Configuration," later in this chapter.)

Table 9-1. Chapter 9 scripts—Password encryption

Script	Description
pwd.pl	Password server daemon that encrypts passwords via a TCP socket; works remotely with the other Perl scripts via the toolkit module set.
pwc.pl	Client that remotely retrieves encrypted passwords from the password server, easing the secure database access overhead imposed by other scripts.
pwd_service.pl	Installs the password server as a service on Win32.

Table 9-2 summarizes the database administration scripts found in Chapter 10. These scripts perform a wide variety of DBA tasks, including managing user accounts (e.g., creating new users from the command line, creating new users via duplicated accounts, creating multiple accounts with automatically mailed passwords), maintaining indexes, killing sniped database sessions, managing extent usage, and extracting DDL and data (e.g., creating delimited data dump files for SQL*Loader transfer).

Table 9-2. Chapter 10 scripts—Routine database administration

Script	Description
ddl_oracle.pl	Generates the DDL necessary to recreate schemas, tables, indexes, views, PL/SQL, materialized views, and other objects.
sqlunldr.pl	Dumps entire schemas to comma-delimited files and generates the SQL*Loader scripts necessary to reload them. Also dumps LONG RAW and BLOB objects, converting them to hex format via the Oracle HEX_TO_RAW function in the SQL*Loader control file in order to convert the data back into binary format.

Script	Description
create_user.pl	Creates Oracle users from the command line. You can create a user and assign passwords, tablespaces, and privileges, all with one easy command-line call. Best of all, you can use this script to preconfigure different groups of runtime privileges.
drop_user.pl	Drops a database user by first dropping all of the users' tables and indexes before dropping the account. Doing so avoids most of the resource-intensive SQL recursion incurred when dropping an account containing many tables and indexes.
dup_user.pl	Duplicates an account, with the source user's system privileges, object privileges, roles, and quotas assigned directly to the target user.
my_script.pl	This is a demonstration script used in the explanation of the *PDBA::OPT* module.
mucr8.pl	When creating a large number of users, this utility creates them all with a single operation. Configurable permissions are granted, and the passwords automatically generated get emailed back to the new account owners.
kss.pl	Kills sniped sessions. (We'll explain what these are, and why you would want to kill them, in Chapter 10.)
kss_NT.pl	Win32 version of *kss.pl*.
kss_service.pl	Used to create an appropriate snipe-killing service on Win32.
idxr.pl	Determines if an index should be rebuilt and, if so, rebuilds it. Checks on a per-schema basis, and is configured to check indexes based on days since the index was last analyzed. A configurable time limit is imposed, which allows index rebuilds to fit within a predefined time schedule.
maxext.pl	Monitors the size and number of extents in tables and indexes. If they're nearing a maximum allowed or if the object will be unable to extend because of limited free space, it notifies the DBA. This script is most useful for databases that use dictionary-managed extents.

Table 9-3 lists the monitoring scripts described in Chapter 11. These will help you maximize the availability of your databases by alerting you to problems—both error conditions reported in the Oracle alert log and problems with database connectivity.

Table 9-3. Chapter 11 scripts—Database monitoring

Script	Description
chkalert.pl	Daemon that monitors Oracle alert logs for error conditions and notifies the DBA via either email messages or pager calls. Oracle's *alert.log* files contain important error messages as well as a log of database startup and shutdown messages.
chkalert_NT.pl	Win32 version of *chkalert.pl*.
chkalert_service.pl	Utility script that creates a Win32 service for *chkalert_NT.pl*.
dbup.pl	Working alongside *chkalert.pl*, a highly configurable database connectivity monitor that checks to see if databases are up and available.
dbup_NT.pl	Win32 version of *dbup.pl*.
dbup_service.pl	Creates the Win32 service for *dbup_NT.pl*.
dbignore.pl	Utility script used with *dbup.pl* to temporarily disable connectivity checks on an individual database (e.g., while maintenance is being performed).

Table 9-4 summarizes the PDBA repository scripts contained in Chapter 12. These scripts compare different database schema versions over time, detecting database changes (official or otherwise). They also store SQL execution plans within a library cache; doing so allows the scripts to compare the current execution plan with plans previously collected; this way, the scripts can report on changed execution plans and the reasons behind the changes.

Table 9-4. Chapter 12 scripts—repository and DDL "time travel"

Script	Description
baseline.pl	Creates the baseline for the PDBA repository (described inChapter 12), establishes "time travel" control of DDL (Data Definition Language), and stores the entire database structural change record across time boundaries.
spdrvr.pl	Perl driver for SQL*Plus that reports on information created by *baseline.pl.*
sxp.pl	Collects and stores SQL statements from the data dictionary and generates accompanying execution plans for later comparison with other plans.
sxpcmp.pl	Examines the current SQL statements, generating execution plans.
sxprpt.pl	Generates reports based on the stored SQL and execution plans.

Table 9-5 lists the scripts described in Chapter 13. In particular, you'll find in that chapter a line-by-line examination of the *dba_jobsm.pl* script, providing a detailed example of how the PDBA Toolkit is used in a Perl script.

Table 9-5. Chapter 13 scripts—extending the PDBA Toolkit

Script	Description
dba_jobs.pl	Reports on the status of jobs in a database.
dba_jobsm.pl	Reports on the status of jobs in multiple databases.
null_test.pl	Test script used in explanation of extending the PDBA Toolkit.

Supporting Modules

We've written most of the PDBA Toolkit's functionality in the form of encapsulated Perl modules. These modules are called by many of the scripts in the toolkit. Our purpose was to both encourage code reuse and simplify the creation of new scripts. Table 9-6 provides a summary of the modules; we'll discuss them in some detail in the following sections.

Note that these modules are also available for use in scripts you develop yourself. You will find that taking advantage of this ready-made code will speed your own development process. If you decide to create your own scripts, you'll find that using these modules will dramatically reduce the amount of code you'll need to write yourself.

Table 9-6. PDBA Toolkit supporting modules

Module	Description
PDBA::CM	Connection manager that simplifies Perl-to-Oracle connectivity.
PDBA::ConfigFile	Finds and opens configuration files.
PDBA::ConfigLoad	Finds, opens, parses, and loads configuration files into memory.
PDBA::DBA	Designed for DBA-specific tasks; many are data-dictionary related.
PDBA::Daemon	Runs Perl script daemons on Unix.
Win32::Daemon	This module, by Dave Roth, is included here because it is so important to toolkit daemon services on Win32 systems.
PDBA::GQ	Generic query module that simplifies single-table queries.
PDBA::LogFile	Creates and locks log files; used by many scripts in the toolkit to perform logging actions.
PDBA::OPT	Processes command-line arguments unhandled by calling scripts.
PDBA::PWC	Password client module.
PDBA::PWD	Password server module.
PDBA::PWDNT	Password server modules for Win32.
PDBA::PidFile	Used to control script execution.
PDBA	Modular collection of widely used methods.

Toolkit Modules

The supporting modules listed in Table 9-6 are described in the following sections. Over the next few chapters we'll work through the scripts supported by these modules.

PDBA::CM (Connection Manager)

The *PDBA::CM* module is the connection manager for the toolkit. This module makes connections to Oracle databases via the Perl DBI and *DBD::Oracle* modules. *PDBA::CM* also allows you to predefine Oracle environment variables; we'll explain how in the installation instructions for this module later in the chapter.

Why is CM necessary? To see why, we'll first see how Perl DBI makes the connection to Oracle without CM. Because we're only interested in connecting to Oracle databases, we can safely override or "subclass" the Perl DBI *connect* method with the *PDBA::CM* module. This provides our own Oracle-optimized method. Why would we want to do that? If you choose to configure the optional *PDBA::CM* configuration file, you can let it set up the Oracle environment for you.

First let's look at what's involved in setting up the environment on your own. Before running an ordinary standalone Perl script for Oracle, you would usually need to set up the environment as shown in the following example:

```
$ export ORACLE_SID=mydb
$ export ORACLE_HOME=/u01/app/oracle/product/8.1.7
$ export ORACLE_BASE=/u01/app/oracle/
$ export TNS_ADMIN=/u01/app/oracle/product/8.1.7/network/admin
```

A regular Perl DBI script then connects to the target database like this:

```
my $db = $ENV{ORACLE_SID}
my $username = 'scott';
my $password = 'tiger';
my $dbh = DBI->connect('dbi:Oracle:' . $db, $username, $password,
                       { RaiseError => 1, AutoCommit => 0 });
```

By using *PDBA::CM* and setting its configuration file, you avoid this environmental overhead:

```
my $db = 'orcl';
my $username = 'scott';
my $password = 'tiger';
my $dbh =
    new PDBA::CM (DATABASE=>$db, USERNAME=>$username, PASSWORD=>$password);
```

Here are the main differences between using *CM* and configuring on your own:

1. There was no manual work needed to set the Oracle environment; this is a blessing when you are faced with many scripts that need to be run for different remote databases.

2. The *CM* module makes use of its own configuration file, which lets it determine at runtime what ORACLE_HOME, ORACLE_BASE, and the other variables should be set to.

3. By subclassing DBI, we include all of its functionality, via Perl's object orientation, for the price of a single new method and a single call at the top of your scripts:

   ```
   use PDBA::CM;
   ```

   The module calls *DBI::init_rootclass* to set up *PDBA::CM* as a DBI root class. (For more detail on this, examine the script *t/subclass.t* in the DBI distribution.)

We'll look at a few special cases in the following sections.

Special login cases for SYSDBA and SYSOPER

As we describe in Appendix B, *The Essential Guide to Perl DBI*, if you need to connect via Perl DBI as SYSDBA or SYSOPER, you must explicitly indicate it. Here's how SQL*Plus does it:

```
sqlplus "system/manager as sysdba"
```

To do this in Perl DBI, you alter the login sequence as follows:

```
$dbh = DBI->connect('dbi:Oracle:' . $db, $username, $password,
                    {RaiseError => 1, AutoCommit => 0, ora_session_mode => 2});
```

What is happening here?

1. By setting the *ora_session_mode* to 2, you tell DBI that this is a SYSDBA account.

2. To log in as SYSOPER, you set *ora_session_mode* to 4.

In our *PDBA::CM*, you only need to set the *MODE* attribute to one of two valid values:

```
$dbh = new PDBA::CM (DATABASE=>$db, USERNAME=>$username, PASSWORD=>$password,
                     MODE=>'SYSOPER'); # Or SYSDBA! :-)
```

RaiseError and AutoCommit

All connections to Oracle databases established via the *CM* module set the class attribute *RaiseError* to 1, and *AutoCommit* to 0. This is done for the following reasons:

- If *RaiseError* is set to its DBI default of 0, fatal errors must be explicitly trapped:

  ```
  my $sth = $dbh->prepare('select * from dual') or die "$DBI::errstr\n";
  ```

  With *RaiseError* set to 1, you avoid this code overhead on all method calls, but the exception is still raised if there is a problem with any method:

  ```
  my $sth = $dbh->prepare('select * from dual');  # Raises error on failure! :-)
  ```

- If *AutoCommit* is set to 1, or true, as a DBI default to match ODBC, this commits all database transactions automatically. We want to avoid this behavior in the toolkit, so we turn it off by setting *AutoCommit* to 0, or false.

PDBA::DBA (DBA Methods)

The *PDBA::DBA* module stores methods that can be used by the toolkit to simplify routine Oracle database administration tasks. Although each of these individual tasks might be perfectly straightforward, as such tasks accumulate most DBAs end up spending much too much valuable time writing one-off scripts. *PDBA::DBA* aims to remedy this situation.

Creating user accounts

One good example of a typical one-off DBA task is the creation of a new user account. You may already possess several tools for creating new users. User creation can be a rather cumbersome process. Depending on the target application, there are often numerous privilege sets that need to be assigned to various application roles. To complicate matters, users may need multiple roles assigned in ways that are difficult to predict ahead of time. You'll start developing a particularly bad headache when you're responsible for several applications. Worse still, this labor-intensive work is quite prone to human error.

Our *PDBA::DBA* module can automate all of these complexities and remove the chance for error. Here's an example of how you can use this module's *new* method to duplicate a user account.

```
$ dup_user.pl -machine turing -database orcl -username scott \
  -new_username scott -source_user samantha
```

This example creates user *scott* in the database *orcl*. A password is generated for the new *scott* account, and the account receives the same privileges as the source user—in this case, *samantha*.

You can also use *PDBA::DBA* directly within Perl scripts of your own:

```
my $newUser = new PDBA::DBA(
    DBH => $dbh,
    OBJECT_TYPE => 'user',
    OBJECT => 'alicia',
    PASSWORD => 'generate',
    DEFAULT_TABLESPACE => 'users',
    TEMPORARY_TABLESPACE => 'temp',
    PRIVS => ['create session', 'resource', 'connect', 'oem_monitor'],
    QUOTAS => { users => 'unlimited', tools => '10m', indx => 'unlimited'}
);
eval { $newUser->create };
if($@) { warn "error creating user: $DBI::errstr\n" }
else    { print "Password: $newUser->{PASSWORD}\n" }
```

The main *PDBA::DBA* methods are summarized in Table 9-7.

Table 9-7. Main PDBA::DBA module methods

Method	Description
new	Used to instantiate a new *PDBA::DBA* object.
create	Used to create various objects in an Oracle database.
drop	Used to drop various objects in the Oracle database.
info	Gathers information on target objects within the database.

PDBA::ConfigFile (Configuration File Handler)

The *PDBA::ConfigFile* module plays a very important part in the PDBA Toolkit. It facilitates the creation of powerful and robust scripts that are driven by a configuration file. If you need to change a script's purpose, all you need do is change the configuration file.

Simplifying configuration

First let's look at a script that uses a configuration file, on execution, *without PDBA:: ConfigFile*:

```
$ myscript1.pl -conf $HOME/pdba/myconfig.conf
```

The bare bones *myscript1.pl* script is shown in Example 9-1.

Example 9-1. myscript1.pl—Opening a configuration file with standard Perl

```perl
#!/usr/bin/perl

use Getopt::Long;
my %optctl=();
GetOptions(\%optctl, "conf=s");
my $configFile='';
my $fh;

if ( exists $optctl{conf} ) {
  $configFile = exists $optctl{conf};

  # Exit, if you can't read the file.

  unless( -r $configFile ){
    die "cannot read the config file, $configFile - $!\n";
  };
  $fh = new IO::File;
  $fh->open($configFile) || die "Cannot open $configFile - $!\n"

} else { die "please specify a configuration file!\n"; }
```

There are a number of drawbacks to this approach:

Code volume

> You will need to type in a fair amount of code every time you need to use a configuration file.

Maintenance

> It's difficult to modify the configuration code block when it's embedded in several scripts.

Flexibility

> *myscript1.pl* only looks for the configuration file in the full path location specified by the command line. It would be nice if you could just supply a file name, and let Perl go find it, wherever it is. That's what we've done with *PDBA::ConfigFile*.

Here's an example of doing much the same thing with *PDBA::ConfigFile*:

```
$ myscript2.pl -conf myconfig.conf
```

This executes *myscript2.pl* in Example 9-2. Notice that there is a lot less script code.

Example 9-2. myscript2.pl—Opening a configuration file with PDBA::ConfigFile

```perl
#!/usr/bin/perl

use PDBA::ConfigFile;
use Getopt::Long;
my %optctl=();
```

Example 9-2. myscript2.pl—Opening a configuration file with PDBA::ConfigFile (continued)

```
GetOptions(\%optctl, "conf=s");
my$configFile='mytest.conf';
my $fh;

unless ( $fh = new PDBA::ConfigFile( FILE => $configFile ) ){
  die "failed to open $configFile\n";
}
```

Automatic file searching

In cases where you don't specify a full OS path, *PDBA::ConfigFile* checks in several places for your config file:

1. The first place it looks is the current directory.

2. Next is the home directory, as specified by the HOME environment variable.

3. Next up is *PDBA_HOME*, assuming that you've set up this environment variable.

4. *PDBA::ConfigFile* then searches through the directories in your PATH.

5. You can also search a specific set of directories:

   ```
   unless ( $fh = new PDBA::ConfigFile(
     FILE => $configFile,
     PATH => ENV{$HOME} . PDBA->pathsep() . "$ENV{ORACLE_HOME}/conf"
   )){ die "failed to open $configFile\n" }
   ```

   PDBA::ConfigFile returns a value of *undef* if the configuration file remains unfound, a behavior used to trap errors, as with the *die* call above. (The *pathsep* method allows the proper parsing of the PATH variable, depending on whether you're running via Unix or Win32. We'll say more about this later on.)

PDBA::ConfigLoad (Configuration File Loader)

The *PDBA::ConfigLoad* module finds your configuration file and loads it for you. In doing this, it assumes that the configuration information is structured as Perl code. This provides several advantages:

- It entails much less script programming.

- You will have an easier time understanding the structure of the configuration data.

- The reduction in complexity makes scripts much more maintainable.

Let's consider the example of an old-fashioned configuration file:

1. You want there to be a defaults list when you're creating users or objects for a specific database.

2. The configurations must be capable of specifying defaults for different databases.

3. There must be a generic default for unspecified databases.

Let's examine what these requirements entail in a typical configuration file in Example 9-3.

Example 9-3. Old-fashioned colon-separated configuration file

```
# tables: object type:database:tablespace:pctfree:pctused:initial:next
table:default:users:60:10:128k:128k
table:dw:dwload:10:5:128m:128m
# indexes: object type:database:tablespace:pctfree:initial:next
index:default:indx:5:128k:128k
index:dw:load_idx:5:4m:4m
# users: object type:database:tablespace:temp tablespace:privs:quotas
# privs must be separated by commas
# quotas must be in tablespace/space usage pairs, all comma separated
user:default:users:temp:connect,resource:users,10m,indx,5m
user:dw:dw_users:dw_temp:create session,dw_user:dw_users,200m,dw_indx,100m
```

As Morpheus might have said to Neo in *The Matrix*, "Do you think that's easy to read, or modify?" If you were to use this configuration file, you'd also need to write some complex code to parse it. Contrast this to the Perl configuration script in Example 9-4. Each component is clearly labeled, as in a *tnsnames.ora* file structure, and when you need to add to this configuration file, it's a simple matter of pasting in appropriate values.

Example 9-4. New-fangled Perl script configuration file

```
package dbparms;
use vars qw(%defaults);

%defaults = (
  table => {
    default => { tablespace => 'users',   pctfree => 60,  pctused => 10,
                 initial => '128k',       next => '128k'
    },
    dw => {      tablespace => 'dw_load', pctfree => 10,  pctused => 5,
                 initial => '128m',       next => '128m'
    },
  },

  index => {
    default => { tablespace => 'index',   pctfree => 5,
                 initial => '128k',       next => '128k'
    },
    dw=> {       tablespace => 'load_idx', pctfree => 5,
                 initial => '4m',         next => '4m'
    },
  },

  user => {
    default => { default_tablespace => 'users',
                 temporary_tablespace => 'temp',
                 privs => ['connect', 'resource'],
```

Example 9-4. New-fangled Perl script configuration file (continued)

```
                quotas => { users => '10m', indx => '5m' }
      },
    dw=> { default_tablespace => 'dw_users',
           temporary_tablespace => 'dw_temp',
           privs => ['create session', 'dw_user'],
           quotas => { dw_users => '200m', dw_indx => '100m' }
      },
    },
);
```

Loading a Perl configuration script

Coincidentally, it's also easier to load into a Perl script using *PDBA::ConfigLoad*:

```
use PDBA::ConfigFile;
my $nf = new PDBA::ConfigLoad( FILE => 'nf.conf' );
unless ( $nf ) { die "failed to load\n " }
```

That's all there is to it. Three lines of Perl makes your configuration file loaded and ready to use. The data structure for your configuration files is defined and documented, and there's an added silver-lining benefit as well; it's also now a simple matter to check your configuration file for syntactical correctness. Here's how:

```
perl -cw myconfig.conf   # -c, checks syntax, -w, looks for warnings
```

Because this is a Perl script, Perl will throw an error if the file fails to compile.

So how do you access all of these configuration parameters? It's easier than you might think. The following script will print some of the values loaded in the previous example:

```
$dwprivs = join(', ', @{$dbparms::defaults{user}->{dw}{privs}});
%dwquotas = %{$dbparms::defaults{user}->{dw}{quotas}};

print qq {

user defaults for dw:

default tablespace  : $dbparms::defaults{user}->{dw}{default_tablespace}
temporary tablespace: $dbparms::defaults{user}->{dw}{temporary_tablespace}
};

print "privs: $dwprivs\n";
print "\ntablespace quotas\n";
for my $tbs ( keys %dwquotas ) {
   print "\ttbs: $tbs   quota: $dwquotas{$tbs}\n";
}
```

Here's the output from the preceding script, using the configuration file in Example 9-4:

```
user defaults for dw:

default tablespace  : dw_users
```

```
temporary tablespace: dw_temp
privs: create session, dw_user

tablespace quotas
    tbs: dw_users   quota: 200m
    tbs: dw_indx    quota: 100m
```

(Appendix A, *The Essential Guide to Perl*, walks through the concepts that underly the discussion in this section; see particularly its discussions of anonymous arrays and references.)

Referring to configuration variables by package name

Take another look at our first line in Example 9-4:

```
package dbparms;
```

By packaging the configuration variables in this way, we also remove the possibility of overwriting variables in the main script, because they're in a different namespace. In Perl's *use strict* mode, every variable has to be referred to by its package name, *dbparms*, and its variable name. For example, the *%defaults* hash is accessed by *%dbparms::defaults*. (Again, refer to Appendix A if you are confused by all this.)

PDBA::Daemon and Win32::Daemon (Background Programs)

The *PDBA::Daemon* module (and its Win32 partner, *Win32::Daemon*) create background, server-like programs. These are programs that you start once; they then continue to run in the background without any necessary user interaction, and they continue to run until you explicitly tell them to stop. These background programs differ for Unix and Win32:

Unix
> Unix background programs are often referred to as *daemons*. The term comes from an ancient Greek definition of *daemon* as a guardian spirit.

Win32
> Background processes on Win32 are more often known as *services*.

We'll look first at creating a daemon process in Unix and later turn our attention to Win32.

PDBA::Daemon: Creating a Unix daemon process in Perl

There are a few basic rules you will need to follow when creating simple daemon processes on Unix:

1. Close unnecessary open files, including STDIN and STDOUT.
2. Disassociate the daemon from the original process group.

3. Disassociate the daemon from the controlling terminal.

4. Make sure that the daemon issues a *chdir* to a directory that will remain mounted.

This is all done easily, within a few lines of Perl:

```perl
if ($pid = fork) { exit 0 }   # exit parent
    if (defined($pid )) {
        close STDOUT;
        close STDIN;
        chdir('/');
        croak  "Cannot detach from terminal" unless $sess_id = POSIX::setsid( );
        return $pid;
    }
    if (++$tries>5 ) { die "fork failed after $tries attempts: $!\n" }
    else {
        sleep 3;
        redo;
    }
}
```

Let's see what's going on here:

1. The call to *fork* is how Perl starts a new process. In this case, the *parent* process exits while the *child* continues running in the background.

2. The next section closes STDIN and STDOUT and then changes to the *root* directory. (It is important that daemons run on file systems that are unlikely to be dismounted. For instance, if your daemon were started in */u01/oracle/app/perl/bin* and left there, it becomes difficult to unmount that file system for necessary maintenance.)

3. The final task is to disassociate the daemon from the controlling process group. This is done via the Perl POSIX module using the *setsid* function.

> Although daemons require only a small amount of Perl code, there's a lot of Unix magic going on behind the scenes. If you are interested in discovering the Unix system internals underlying daemons, you might want to read *The Magic Garden Explained*, by Berny Goodheart and James Cox (Prentice Hall, 1994).

Let's demonstrate a short daemon script in Example 9-5.

Example 9-5. daemon_test.pl—Example Perl daemon

```perl
#!/usr/bin/perl

use warnings;
use PDBA::Daemon;
use IO::File;

my $logFile = '/tmp/daemon_test.log';
```

Example 9-5. daemon_test.pl—Example Perl daemon (continued)

```perl
my $lh = new IO::File;

$lh->open("+> $logFile" ) || die "unable to create log file $logFile - $!\n";

&PDBA::Daemon::daemonize;

for ( my $i = 0; $i < 5; $i++ ) {
    my ($sec,$min,$hour) = localtime(time);
    my $output = sprintf("%02d:%02d:%02d\n", $hour,$min,$sec);
    $lh->printflush($output);
    sleep 5;
}
$lh->close;
```

You can check this background daemon's progress, once it has been started, by tailing its log file as follows:

```
$ ./daemon_test.pl
$ tail -f /tmp/daemon_test.log
21:43:39
21:43:44
...
```

A little code, and one call to *PDBA::Daemon::daemonize*, and you have an independent Perl daemon up and running. This is an extremely useful feature, as we'll see later.

Win32::Daemon: Creating a Win32 daemon in Perl

Win32 also has background processes, better known as *services*. Win32 services are implemented differently than Unix daemons. Therefore, our standard daemon creation operation via *PDBA::Daemon* needs adjustment. Enter the *Win32::Daemon* module, a brilliant piece of software created by Win32 Perl guru Dave Roth of Roth Consulting. This module creates system services written entirely in Perl and is available from *http://www.roth.net*. We'll show you how to install it later in this chapter.

 Unlike Unix systems, Win32 platforms typically have a service control application. Each Perl service must continually respond to signals from this, like the High King of the Nazgûl periodically checking the fiery Red Eye's beam from Barad-dûr.

Win32 service scripts look substantially different from daemonized Unix scripts, as Example 9-6 shows.

Example 9-6. Win32 service script

```perl
use Win32;
use Win32::Daemon;  # http://www.roth.net! :-)
```

Example 9-6. Win32 service script (continued)

```perl
use IO::File;

my $attempts;
Win32::Daemon::StartService( );
sleep( 1 );

my $lh = new IO::File;
my $logFile = "c:/temp/daemon_test.log";
$lh->open($logFile) || die;

LOG($lh, "Service Starting - State is: " . $State);

while( SERVICE_START_PENDING != Win32::Daemon::State( ) )
   LOG($lh, "Waiting for service - state is: " . $State . "..." );
   sleep( 1 );
   if ( $attempts++ > 15 ) {
      LOG("Failed to start service in " . $attempts . " attempts");
      Win32::Daemon::State(SERVICE_STOPPED);
      Win32::Daemon::StopService( );
      exit 2;
   }
   $State = Win32::Daemon::State( );
}

Win32::Daemon::State(SERVICE_RUNNING);
$State = Win32::Daemon::State( );
LOG($lh, "Service Started - State is: " . $State);

while (1) {                              # Main loop! 8-)
   # check for Win32 Service state
   my $PrevState = SERVICE_RUNNING;
   while( SERVICE_STOPPED != ( $State = Win32::Daemon::State( ) ) ) {
      if( SERVICE_RUNNING == $State ) {
         LOG($lh, "Service running");
            last;
      } elsif( SERVICE_PAUSE_PENDING == $State ) {
         # "Pausing...";
         LOG($lh, "Pausing Service");
         Win32::Daemon::State( SERVICE_PAUSED );
         $PrevState = SERVICE_PAUSED;
         next;
      } elsif( SERVICE_CONTINUE_PENDING == $State ) {
         # "Resuming...";
         LOG($lh, "Resuming Service");
         Win32::Daemon::State( SERVICE_RUNNING );
         $PrevState = SERVICE_RUNNING;
         last;
      } elsif(
         SERVICE_STOP_PENDING == $State  or
         SERVICE_CONTROL_SHUTDOWN == $State ) {
         # "Stopping...";
         LOG($lh, "Stopping Service");
```

Example 9-6. Win32 service script (continued)

```
            # Tell the OS that the service is terminating...
            Win32::Daemon::State(SERVICE_STOPPED);
            Win32::Daemon::StopService();
            exit 8;
            last;
        } else {
            # We have some unknown state...
            # reset it back to what we last knew the state to be...
            LOG($lh, "Unknown State of : " . $State . " - exiting...");
            Win32::Daemon::State(SERVICE_STOPPED);
            Win32::Daemon::StopService();
            exit 8;
            last;
        }
        sleep 1;
    }
    LOG($lh, "Main Loop");
    sleep 1;
}
########################
sub LOG {
    my($lh) = shift;
    my @msg = @_;
    my( $sec, $min, $hour, $mday, $mon, $year, $wday, $yday, $isdst );
    # mon = 0..11 and wday = 0..6
    ($sec, $min, $hour, $mday, $mon, $year, $wday, $yday, $isdst) =
        localtime(time);
    # change $mon to 1-12 and $wday to 1-7;
    $mon++; # to get it to agree with the cron syntax
    $day++;
    $year += 1900;    # Y2K fix
    $lh->printflush("%04d/%02d/%02d %02d:%02d:%02d: %s\n",
                    $year,$mon,$mday,$hour,$min,$sec,@msg);
}
```

As you can see, setting up Win32 services is an involved process—and remember that *Win32::Daemon* has sheltered you from the really gory internals!

Using Unix Daemons and Win32 services in Perl

Now that you have some grasp of Unix daemons and Win32 services, let's consider why you would want to use them in the first place. In this chapter, we'll focus on how they can help to automate as many Oracle DBA tasks as possible:

* When we're using daemons and services, we can be instantly notified of problems, even during evenings and weekends. That way, we can fix them immediately (rather than end up walking unaware into user firestorms the next day).

* We'd like to avoid reading log files by eye. We'd much rather a Perl robot did this for us. (Perl robots are *very good* at reading log files; they don't get tired or bored and don't inadvertently skip over a page.)

- We can manage more databases than we could otherwise, and do a better job of it.
- We can free up more time to do interesting things (often involving even more Perl!).

Running Unix daemons and Win32 services also helps us maintain those two commandments tattooed in deep purple on a DBA's soul:

- Thou shalt monitor the *alert.log* file for serious problems.
- Thou shalt ensure that databases can be connected to over the network.

Unless it's an acceptable plan to manually check *alert.log* for each database, you'll want to automate these processes. To do this, many shops run *cron* or *at* scripts, with names like *every10* or *LifeSaver*. These run every few minutes, attempting database connections, and they notify the DBA if problems occur. In Chapter 11 we'll present a better method of checking the alert logs, using Perl of course. It's a better method because it allows you to determine which errors are of importance to you, paging the DBA only when necessary. It will be flexible, will be easy to set up, and will avoid the straitjacket of a rigidly bound *cron* schedule.

PDBA::GQ (Generic Query)

DBAs often open cursors to single tables (such as DBA_TABLES), read in some rows from it, get the column values, and then process the data in some way. If you do this routine often enough, you'll soon tire of its repetitive nature, even if you're just cutting and pasting queries from prestored SQL scripts. The *PDBA::GQ* module is designed to streamline this task. The module's main methods are listed in Table 9-8.

Table 9-8. PDBA::GQ module methods

Method	Description
new	Instantiates a new GQ query object
next	Retrieves the next row from a query object
all	Retrieves all the rows from a query object
getColumns	Returns a hash reference of column names for a query object[a]

[a]See Appendix A for a description of anonymous hash references.

The standard DBI query method often uses bind variables in the following way:

```
my $sql = q{
    select object_name, created, last_ddl_time
    from dba_objects
    where owner = ?
        and object_type = ?
};
my @bindparms = qw(SCOTT TABLE);
```

```
    my $sth = $dbh->prepare($sql);
    mu $rv = $sth->execute( @bindparms );
    while ( my $hashRef = $sth->fetchrow_hashref ) {
        print "Object: $hashRef->{OBJECT_NAME}\n";
        print "Created on : $hashRef->{CREATED}\n";
        print "Last DDL Time : $hashRef->{LAST_DDL_TIME}\n";
    }
```

PDBA::GQ can help simplify that approach as follows:

```
    my @bindparms = qw(SCOTT TABLE);
    my $dbaObj = new PDBA::GQ {
        $dbh, "dba_objects",
        {
            WHERE => "owner = ? and object_type = ?",
            BINDPARMS => \@bindparms
        }
    };
    while ( my $row = $dbaObj->next ) {
        print "Object: $row->{OBJECT_NAME}\n";
        print "Created on : $row->{CREATED}\n";
        print "Last DDL Time : $row->{LAST_DDL_TIME}\n";
    }
```

Note how the *PDBA::GQ* module saves us several steps from the previous code snippet:

- The *prepare* and *execute* methods are called automatically on object creation.
- All column names are made available without explicit specification.
- Column names are still available via the regular *fetchrow_hashref* mechanism.

PDBA::GQ uses several Perl DBI methods for returning data from Oracle (all of these are fully described in Appendix B).

fetchrow_hashref

> Offers a straightforward interface at the sacrifice of a little speed. Because of its ease of operation, we've used *fetchrow_hashref* as the query method in *PDBA:: GQ*'s *next* method.

fetchall_arrayref

> Used in *PDBA::GQ*'s *all* method to retrieve all the rows from a SQL query in one go; especially helpful when we're loading small sets of reference data.

The default return value for *PDBA::GQ*'s *all* method is a reference to an array of hash references. Example 9-7 uses this approach. The memory structure is displayed in Figure 9-1.

Example 9-7. GQ::all—Returning a reference to array of hashrefs

```
my $vobj = new PDBA::GQ(
    $dbh,
    'v$parameter',
    { WHERE => q{name like 'job%'} }
```

Example 9-7. GQ::all—Returning a reference to array of hashrefs (continued)

```
);
# Default is reference to an array of hash references.
my $arrayref = $vobj->all;
# Print it out.
for my $row ( @$arrayref ) {
    print "PARM: $row->{NAME} VALUE: $row->{VALUE}\n";
}
```

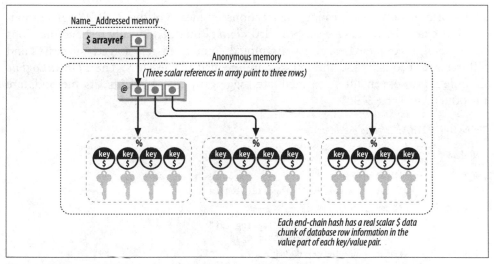

Figure 9-1. An array reference to a list of hashes

We can change this default memory structure by using the *[ ]* anonymous array notation. Example 9-8 shows the same query, this time with data returned as a reference to an array of array references. (Again, for more about this and other Perl DBI topics, see Appendix B.)

Example 9-8. GQ::all—returning a ref to array of array refs

```
my $vobj = new PDBA::GQ(
    $dbh,
    'v$parameter',
    { WHERE => q{name like 'job%'} }
);
# Send an empty array reference, as an argument to indicate
# the requested return type of data.
my $arrayRowRef = $vobj->all([]);
my $colNames = $vobj->getColumns;
# Print it out.
for my $row ( @$arrayRowRef ) {
    print "PARM: $row->[$colNames->{NAME}] VALUE: $row->[$colNames->{VALUE}]\n";
}
```

With the *array-to-array* method, you generally refer to the exact position of an element within an array. However, the *getColumns* method loads up a hash array, with the column names as keys and the array elements as values. This allows you to refer to the column names, even though your data is stored in an array. It's a kind of magic!

PDBA::LogFile (Logfile Handler)

Many of our toolkit utilities log their actions by means of the *PDBA::LogFile* module. For example, we have a script called *dbup.pl* that periodically tests connections to all configured databases. Every attempted connection gets logged, successes and failures are recorded, and the failures are emailed to the DBA. The *PDBA::LogFile* module's purpose in life is to facilitate logging by PDBA scripts; its methods are introduced in Table 9-9.

Table 9-9. PDBA::LogFile methods

Method	Description
new	Creates a new log file object:
	`$logFh = new PDBA::LogFile($log);`
makepath	Creates a path to the logfile:
	`$log="$ENV{HOME}/pdba/log/log.txt";`
	`PDBA::LogFile->makepath($log);`
print	Performs buffered prints to the logfile:
	`$logFh->print("test line\n");`
printflush	Performs nonbuffered prints to the logfile:
	`$logFh->printflush("test line\n");`

Logfiles are often locked, so if another instance of a utility is run, it avoids writing over the logfile in use. Therefore, if you are planning several utility instances, it's often best if each gets its own logfile. To open and lock a logfile, here's what you need to do:

```
use PDBA;
use PDBA::LogFile;

my $logFile = PDBA::pdbaHome . '/logs/test.log';
my $logFh = new PDBA::LogFile($logFile);

if( ! $logFh ) {
    die "failed to open log file for writing - $!\n"
}
```

It's a lot simpler than you may have imagined. Here's part of what was going on behind the scenes in *PDBA::LogFile*, when the logfile was created:

```
if ( -r $logFile and -w $logFile ) {
    # This should never happen, but we'll check anyway.
```

```
        $self->open($logFile) || return undef;
        $self->close;

        # Try to open existing log file.
        # file must be opened with intent to write
        $self->open("+<$logFile" ) || return undef;

        # Lock file, recreate and relock, and print PID to file.
        if ( flock $self, LOCK_EX|LOCK_NB ) {
            $self->open("+>>$logFile" ) || return undef;
            print "LogFile 4 : $logFile\n" if $debug;
            if ( flock $self, LOCK_EX|LOCK_NB ) {
                $self->autoflush;
                return 1;
            } else { return undef }
        } else { $self->close; return undef }

    } else { # Lock file does not exist.
        $self->open("+>>$logFile" ) || return undef;
        # Get an exclusive lock on the file.
        if ( flock $self, LOCK_EX|LOCK_NB ) {
            print "LogFile 7 : $logFile\n" if $debug;
            return 1
        }
        else { return undef }
    }
```

Setting up logfiles is one of those necessary but code-intensive tasks that most of us don't care to spend a lot of time on: we'll take the modular use of *PDBA::LogFile* every time! *PDBA::LogFile* also avoids assuming anything about logfile location. This means we can do OS-portable log creation using the built-in *File::Spec* and *File::Path* modules:

```
use PDBA;
use PDBA::LogFile;
use File::Spec;
use File::Path;

my $logFile = PDBA::pdbaHome . '/logs/test.log';
my ($volume, $directories, $file) = File::Spec->splitpath($logFile);
my $path = $volume . $directories;

# Create the path.
File::Path::mkpath($path, 0, 0750);
# Make sure it's there.
-d || -w || -r || -x $path || die "dir $path not usable\n";
my $logFh = new PDBA::LogFile($logFile);

if( ! $logFh ) { die "could not open log file for writing - $!\n" }

for ( my $i = 1; $i<10; $i++ ) {
    $logFh->printflush("test line # $i\n");
    sleep 5;
}
```

Path creation is made even simpler by adding a *makepath* method to *PDBA::LogFile* as shown in Example 9-9.

Example 9-9. Simplified logfile creation

```
use PDBA::LogFile;

my $logFile = PDBA::pdbaHome . '/logs/test.log';
PDBA::LogFile->makepath($logFile);
my $logFh = new PDBA::LogFile($logFile);

if( ! $logFh ) { die "could not open log file for writing - $!\n" }

for ( my $i = 1; $i<10; $i++ ) {
   $logFh->printflush("test line # $i\n");
   sleep 2;
}
```

On Unix, *makepath* creates directories with default file permissions of read, write, and execute for the owner; read and execute for the group, and nothing for others. On Win32, *makepath* also tries to set permissions, but doing so depends on the file system security setup.

PERMS attribute

To set permissions to other values, use the PERMS attribute with an octal permissions value. The following example will prevent anyone other than the system administrator and the file owner from viewing the contents of the log directories:

```
my $logFile = PDBA::pdbaHome . '/logs/test.log';
PDBA::LogFile->makepath($logFile, PERMS => 0700 );
```

The two print methods, *print* and *printflush*, both create a timestamp, which is prefixed on each printed line. Both methods print by calling methods in the *IO::File* superclass. The output from Example 9-9 would look like this:

```
20011021233514:test line # 1
20011021233516:test line # 2
...
20011021233530:test line # 9
```

 The *printflush* method is preferred for logging operations, as its output is unbuffered and immediately logged, but you may require *print* if you need to buffer disk IO.

PDBA::OPT (Option Handler)

The *PDBA::OPT* module is used in conjunction with the password-control modules (*PDBA::PWC*, *PDBA::PWD*, and *PDBA::PWDNT*) described in the following sections. The role of *PDBA::OPT* is to scan the command line for options that may be intended for the password server, rather than for Oracle itself. *PDBA::OPT* then feeds the security information found on the command line to the *PDBA::PWC* module to retrieve a password. The following sections describe the basics of how the various password modules work. See Chapter 11 for an extended example of how *PDBA::OPT* supports the alert log monitoring scripts provided in the toolkit.

PDBA::PidFile (Program Id Handler)

A popular mechanism for preventing programs from being run concurrently is to create a baton file that is then immediately locked. Subsequent attempts to run the same program try to lock the baton file as well. If a program is unable to lock the file, that program exits gracefully with an appropriate message. If the program *is* able to lock its baton file, processing continues as in the following code snippet, which uses the *PDBA::PidFile* module to control script execution:

```
use PDBA::PidFile;
my $lockFile = '/tmp/myapp_pid.lock';
my $fh = new PDBA::PidFile( $lockfile, $$ );

if ( ! $fh ) {
    die "could not lock PID file\n";
}
```

One approach might be a daemon for monitoring *alert.log*. Let's look at the requirements:

- You only want this program to run on one instance at one time.
- To ensure that it's always running, you run it once per hour via the system scheduler:
  - If the script is unable to create and lock a baton file via *PDBA::PidFile*, the script simply exits.
  - If the previous monitor script dies for some reason, then the next time the scheduler tries to start another instance, *PDBA::PidFile* successfully creates and locks the baton, and normal processing continues.

Example 9-10 shows how *PDBA::PidFile* accomplishes these goals.

Example 9-10. Locking portion of PDBA::PidFile module

```
sub lockFile {
  my $self=shift;
  my ( %options ) = @_;

  my $lockFile = $options{file};
  croak "lockFile requires a file name\n" unless $lockFile;

  my $pid = $options{pid};
  croak "lockFile requires a PID\n" unless $pid;
```

Example 9-10. Locking portion of PDBA::PidFile module (continued)

```
   if ( -r $lockFile and -w $lockFile ) {
      $self->open($lockFile) || return undef;
      ($lockPid) = <$self>;
      $self->close;

      # try to open existing lock file
      # file must be opened with intent to write
      $self->open("+<$lockFile" ) || return undef;

      # lock file, recreate and relock
      # print PID to file
      if ( flock $self, LOCK_EX|LOCK_NB ) {
         $self->open(">$lockFile" ) || return undef;

         # return pid from file if you can't lock
         if ( flock $self, LOCK_EX|LOCK_NB ) {
            $self->printflush($pid) ;
            return $pid;
         }
         else { return undef }
      } else { return $lockPid }
   } else { # lock file does not exist

      $self->open(">$lockFile" ) || return undef;
      $self->printflush($pid);

      # get an exclusive lock on the file
      if ( flock $self, LOCK_EX|LOCK_NB ) { return $pid }
      else { return undef }
   }
}
```

PDBA::PWD (Password Daemon)

The *PDBA::PWD* module provides the core functionality in the *pwd.pl* script that we use to centralize password management in the toolkit.

Password management is a recurrent issue for DBAs. There is a trend today in many large Oracle sites towards OS authentication, in which the Oracle database allows all authentication to be enforced by the operating system. But this type of authentication may not be feasible in some environments. Many corporate security policies may prohibit the use of *OPS$* Oracle accounts, and many DBAs dislike OS authentication, preferring the forced use of passwords because that approach gives DBAs greater control over database security.

Despite the recent advent of single sign-on systems, Public Key Infrastructures (PKI),[*] and other advanced security schemes, database accounts protected by passwords are

---

[*] For a discussion of the very real risks of PKI, see *http://www.counterpane.com/pki-risks.html*.

likely to be with us for some time to come. Unfortunately, there are some inherent problems with the use of passwords—for example:

Process monitoring
> Passwords entered on command lines are visible to utilities such as the *ps* program.

Maintenance overhead
> Passwords that are hard-coded into scripts make code maintenance difficult.

Username rigidity
> Inflexible privilege assignment leads to extra work when people join or leave development teams. If getting help from DBAs takes extra time or effort, users may compromise security by swapping usernames and passwords among themselves.

User resistance
> If site policy requires regular password changes, you may find yourself flooded with users who have forgotten the new passwords they've been forced to create.

Password security overload
> If password policy prohibits the use of dictionary words and previous passwords, and insists upon vowel number replacement,* people will inevitably come up with password schemes designed to aid memory. Unfortunately, these are rapidly figured out by cracker systems. As a challenge, see if you can guess the third password in this list:
>
> ```
> P4SSWORDON3
> P4SSWORDTWO
> ?
> ```
>
> *P4SSW0RDTHR33* just got you access to the Human Resources payroll table.

Batch job password problems

Even totally secure password systems may encounter difficult management situations. Batch table loads, index rebuilds, billing statement runs, and a host of other long-running jobs are usually run at night. Unless someone is going to run these jobs manually and input all the passwords as necessary, these jobs need an automated method for inputting correct passwords.

To deal with this situation, some DBAs create protected files that contain passwords accessible to scripts requiring passwords. Unfortunately, this solution produces its own problems:

---

* Vowel number replacement refers to the practice of replacing vowels in words with numeric digits that resemble the vowel—for example, the word *PASSWORD* becomes *P4SSW0RD*. The numeric digit *4* replaces the letter *A*, and the numeric digit *0* replaces the letter *O*.

External password visibility

System administrators often have the ability to read any file on a Unix or Win32 server. When your passwords are stored in a local file or are hard-coded in scripts on every system that has an Oracle database, this increases the risk to your databases by exposing those passwords to people who may not have been granted access to them.

File distribution

You often need to distribute copies of this hard-coded file to all of your servers; once again, this complicates password management in a distributed environment.

The *PDBA::PWD* module lessens these problems. It's a TCP socket server, written in Perl, and modeled after the non-forking server found in the excellent *Perl Cookbook*, by Tom Christiansen and Nathan Torkington (O'Reilly & Associates, 1998). Account passwords remain stored in a single Fort Knox file, and passwords are encrypted over the network.

PDBA::PWC (Password Client)

We've also provided a client module, *PDBA::PWC*, used to communicate with the password server. The *pwc.pl* script can retrieve passwords on the command line or, even better, Perl scripts can import the *PWC* module and in this way avoid making passwords visible to operating systems.

PDBA::PWDNT (Password Client for NT)

The *PDBA::PWDNT* module is the Win32 version of *PDBA::PWC*. It makes use of the *Win32::Daemon* module that allows it to be installed as a Win32 service.

PDBA (PDBA Utilities)

The *PDBA* module is a collection of utilities. These are used throughout the other modules, as well as in the individual scripts included in the toolkit. *PDBA* simplifies the process of writing portable scripts—or at least minimizes the changes necessary when porting scripts across platforms. Table 9-10 lists the methods provided in PDBA. The following sections describe their use.

Table 9-10. PDBA methods

Method	Description
email	Sends emails from Perl scripts
pathsep	Determines the correct separator to use in *PATH* variables
osname	Returns the platform as either Unix or MSWin32
pdbaHome	Returns the value of *PDBA_HOME*

pathsep

Back in the IBM PC dark ages, someone decided that PATH entries in MS-DOS would be separated by semicolons (;). This presented a problem to folks used to the colon character (:) employed by Unix. Today, *PATH* variables are seldom used in Perl scripts, but when they are, the *pathsep* method comes in really handy. By using *pathsep* rather than literal characters, we make the path separator transparent, and we always end up getting the right one:

```
use PDBA;
my @pathDirs = split(PDBA->pathsep(),$ENV{PATH});
my $fullPath='';
my $file='test.conf';
for my $dir ( @pathDirs ) {
    $fullPath = $dir . PDBA->pathsep() . $file;
    # if file exists and is readable, we're done
    last if -r $fullPath;
    $fullPath = '';
}
# raise an error if not found
unless( $fullPath ) { die "could not find config file $file\n" }
```

This code snippet works on either Win32 or Unix without hard-coding.

osname

We sometimes need to let our code know which platform it's being executed on. In such cases, you will find the *osname* method very helpful. For example:

```
use PDBA;
my $pathsep = ';';
if ('Unix' eq PDBA->osname() ) { $pathsep = ':' }
return $pathsep;
```

pdbaHome

The *pdbaHome* method determines the location of *PDBA_HOME*. On Win32, *PDBA_HOME* is stored in the Windows Registry. On Unix, it simply needs to be set as an ordinary environment variable. The following code snippet illustrates the use of *pdbaHome:*

```
use PDBA;
my @searchPaths = ( './', '../', PDBA->pdbaHome() );
```

There's a lot going on internally here to determine the correct value for *PDBA_ HOME*:

```
sub pdbaHome {
    if ( 'Unix' eq PDBA->osname() ) {
        if (exists $ENV{PDBA_HOME}) {return $ENV{PDBA_HOME}}
        else{return $ENV{HOME} }
    } else {
        eval q{use Win32::TieRegistry ( Delimiter=>q{/}, ArrayValues => 0 )};
```

```
        if ($@) {
            die "could not load Win32::TieRegistry in PDBA\n";
        } else {
            no warnings;
            $pdbaKey= $Registry->{"LMachine/Software/PDBA/"};          # :-)
            use warnings;
            $ENV{PDBA_HOME}  = $pdbaKey->{'/PDBA_HOME'};
            unless ( $ENV{PDBA_HOME} ) { die "PDBA_HOME not set in registry\n" }
            return $ENV{PDBA_HOME};
        }
    }
}
```

There is a default for *PDBA_HOME* on Unix, but not on Win32:

- On Unix, if you examine the code for *pdbaHome*, you'll see that the return value defaults to *$ENV{HOME}* if *PDBA_HOME* is unset.

- In contrast, on Win32 the *PDBA_HOME* registry value is mandatory, because some Win32 platforms lack a suitable default value for *PDBA_HOME*.

By wrapping the *use Win32::TieRegistry* portion inside an *eval{}* block, Perl avoids compiling this code unless it is being executed on a Win32 platform. This feature allows us to write a script that can be executed on both Unix and Win32 platforms.

email

We've centralized a simple-to-use *email* method in the *PDBA* module. There are several reasons why you'll find this method helpful:

- You'll often want to notify someone via email if a Perl monitor detects a problem.

- You may want a facility for notifying Oracle account owners of various information regarding the administration of your databases and their accounts.

The *email* method shown here in use is based on the *Mail::Sendmail* module developed by Milivoj Ivkovic:[*]

```
use PDBA;
my @addresses = ('scott.tiger@oracle.com','tony.tiger@oracle.com');
my $message = "yes, we're almost there";
my $subject = "are we there yet?";

if ( PDBA->email(\@addresses, $message, $subject) ) {
    print "Mail sent\n";
} else {
    print "Mail unsent\n";
}
```

---

[*] For more information, see *http://alma.ch/perl/mail.htm#Mail::Sendmail*

To conclude, the *PDBA* module is our workhorse module, the spider module in the center of the toolkit's web. Therefore, in addition to the methods described in this section, it contains additional private methods designed only for internal use by other modules in the PDBA Toolkit. This module is the one we're most likely to update as we continue the development of this toolkit. If you wish to explore it further, check out the comprehensive documentation available via the *perldoc PDBA* command.

Installing the PDBA Toolkit for Unix

There are three basic steps involved in installing the toolkit on Unix systems:

Set the environment
> We need to ensure that the Unix environment has been correctly prepared for installation.

Load the modules and scripts
> Once the environment is set, we can install the main body of code.

Edit the configuration files
> Once the code is installed, we can configure, secure, and store all of our database connection parameters.

You will need to follow the steps in this section to install the PDBA Toolkit on your Unix platform so the scripts introduced in later chapters will work properly.

Setting the PDBA Environment

PDBA_HOME is the default directory for the PDBA Toolkit and all of its associated files. However, as we mentioned earlier in the discussion of the *PDBA* module, it may not be necessary to set *PDBA_HOME* on Unix. If you create an account dedicated to running the PDBA Toolkit, you may be happy enough storing its configuration files under the HOME structure of that account. Recall from our earlier discussion that this is where *PDBA* will look for them if *PDBA_HOME* has not been set. For instance, for new user *oramon* in the */home* directory, the default location will be under */home/oramon/pdba*.

Setting PDBA_HOME from the command line

If you do wish to explicitly control the location of *PDBA_HOME*, it's as easy as this:

```
$ export PDBA_HOME=/u01/my_pdba_home_dir
```

To avoid typing this line as part of every login, edit your *.profile* file or equivalent, and add *PDBA_HOME* to the usual suspects required for the toolkit's installation. They are:

ORACLE_HOME
ORACLE_SID (or *TWO_TASK*)
TNS_ADMIN

 It is possible to create the entire PDBA Toolkit, while logged in as the *root* account, but we'd like to recommend another approach. The toolkit modules and scripts should be installed as *root* or as the user who owns the Perl installation. (For instance, you may have installed a local Perl for user *oracle*.) However, the configuration files should be installed in a user account, such as *oramon*, *oracle*, or *pdbauser*. Toolkit scripts should be executed under that account as well to keep your system administrator happy.

Installing the PDBA Perl Modules and Scripts

Before actually installing the toolkit there are some other tasks you will need to deal with:

Install additional Perl modules
> The PDBA Toolkit is dependent on other Perl modules that must first be installed.

Determine installation locations
> Decide if the default locations for the supporting modules and the scripts are acceptable. Determine alternate locations as needed.

We'll first install the additional Perl modules needed for the PDBA Toolkit.

Installing additional modules

There are three external Perl modules we need to load. We've kept this list of extras to a minimum in order to keep installation as simple as possible. However, as we developed this toolkit, we did try to follow the maxim of Perl programmers everywhere: "Laziness is a virtue." Put another way, Perl programmers are advised to avoid reinventing the wheel whenever possible and to make use of existing code wherever they can.

These are the necessary modules; all of which can be installed from CPAN:

http://www.cpan.org/authors/id/GBARR
> Graham Barr's *TimeDate* date parser.

http://www.cpan.org/authors/id/S/SI/SIFUKURT
> Kurt Kincaid's *Crypt::RC4* cryptographic module.

http://www.cpan.org/authors/id/M/MI/MIVKOVIC
> Milivoj Ivkovic's OS-independent *Mail::Sendmail* email sender (described earlier).

When connected to the Internet, the easiest way of installing these modules is this:

```
$ perl -MCPAN -e "shell"
cpan> install Date::Format
cpan> install Crypt::RC4
cpan> install Mail::Sendmail
cpan> quit
Lockfile removed.
```

 Installing *Date::Format* automatically picks up the rest of the *TimeDate* bundle.

Determining installation locations for Perl modules

Now we can go ahead with the toolkit installation. First you need to download the toolkit. You can download *PDBA-1.0.tar.gz*, or its latest derivative, from our O'Reilly site:[*]

http://www.oreilly.com/catalog/oracleperl/pdbatoolkit

You now need to make two important decisions:

- Where do we want the PDBA supporting modules to go?
- Where do we want the PDBA scripts to go?

We generally want all of our Perl modules to be stored within the default Perl library tree. However, if you wish to install these modules elsewhere—perhaps to control access—use the PREFIX switch. For example, the following will install everything under *~/oramon/pdba*:

```
$ perl Makefile.PL PREFIX=/home/oramon/pdba
```

This will mean that the modules get installed in directories that normally are invisible to Perl. The installer will take care of this by adding a code line near the top of PDBA executable shell scripts, as in the following:

```
use lib qq{/home/oramon/pdba/lib/site_perl/5.6.1/};
```

Later on, this specification will tell Perl where to find the PDBA modules as Perl requires them. However, we recommend that you accept the default Perl library locations just to keep everything simple.

Determining installation locations for Perl scripts

The recommended location for the Perl scripts isn't as obvious. Perl's *ExtUtils:: MakeMaker* generally places scripts within the */usr/bin* location. However, we (or

---

[*] We will be regularly updating the PDBA Toolkit as an evolving open source project, although you may wish to load *PDBA-1.0.tar.gz* first, just to get the hang of its installation.

your system administrator) may prefer */usr/local/bin*. A slight command-line modification changes the target script directory as follows:

```
$ perl Makefile.PL INSTALLSCRIPT=/usr/local/bin
```

Installing the PDBA scripts in */usr/local/bin* has the added advantage of separating the executable scripts from the OS binaries found in */usr/bin*. This makes your scripts less vulnerable during system upgrades or rebuilds. Making them publicly available under */usr/local/bin* still avoids a security risk (as the configuration files contain the confidential information). This information may be easily protected inside a user account such as *oramon*.

INSTALLSITELIB

Installation variations are possible too. For example, you might wish to put the modules in */home/oramon/pdba* and the executable scripts in */usr/local/bin*. But beware! You might think the following would suffice:

```
$ perl Makefile.PL PREFIX=/home/oramon/pdba INSTALLSCRIPT=/usr/local/bin
```

Alas, this produces unintuitive results. Rather than placing executables in */usr/local/bin*, you'll find them lurking in */home/oramon/local/bin*. This is because *PREFIX* takes precedence over *INSTALLSCRIPT*. We must instead substitute *INSTALLSITELIB* for *PREFIX*:

```
$ perl Makefile.PL INSTALLSITELIB=/home/oramon/pdba INSTALLSCRIPT=/usr/local/bin
```

For more on this and other *MakeMaker* variations, try the following command:

```
$ perldoc ExtUtils::MakeMaker
```

Ready to install

From now on, we'll assume that the PDBA Toolkit is being built by the *oramon* account. Follow these steps:

1. Go to the *PDBA_HOME* directory:
   ```
   $ chdir $PDBA_HOME
   ```

2. Unpack the tarball:
   ```
   $ gzip -d PDBA-1.0.tar.gz
   $ tar xvf PDBA-1.0.tar
   ```

3. Now we configure and compile in the traditional manner:
   ```
   $ cd PDBA-1.0
   $ perl Makefile.PL INSTALLSCRIPT=/usr/local/bin
   $ make
   ```

Let's test the compilation. This requires setting the *ORACLE_USERID* environment variable to a user with the SELECT ANY TABLE privilege:

```
$ export ORACLE_USERID=system/manager
$ make test
```

4. To install the PDBA Toolkit under the Perl library tree, you'll need to log in as *root*:

```
$ su - root
# cd /home/oramon/PDBA-1.0
```

5. Now finish the job:

```
# make install
```

You'll see output that looks something like this:

```
Installing /usr/lib/perl5/site_perl/5.6.1/PDBA/CM.pm
...
Installing /usr/share/man/man3/PDBA::CM.3pm
...
Installing /usr/bin/pwd.pl
Writing /usr/lib/perl5/site_perl/5.6.1/i586-linux/auto/PDBA/.packlist
Appending installation info to /usr/lib/perl5/5.6.1/i586-linux/perllocal.pod
```

Installing PDBA Unix Configuration Files

We'll store our Unix configurables via the highly sophisticated flat-file method,[*] albeit one with a special twist. While PDBA modules and scripts are now installed in the proper locations, the configuration files remain within the build directory. Let's find them a proper home:

```
$ cd $PDBA_HOME/PDBA-1.0
```

Of course, the final location of the files will depend on how you set *PDBA_HOME*:

- If *PDBA_HOME* is set to */u01/app/pdba*, for example, this is where the files will get stored.
- If *PDBA_HOME* is not set, the configuration files will get stored in *$HOME/ pdba*.

To install the default configuration files, you simply need to execute this command:

```
$ perl cp_config
```

The *cp_config* script checks any potential *PDBA_HOME* value, determines what to do, and then installs the files accordingly (as described earlier). To configure these files, skip the Win32 installation, and go directly to the section "Configuring the PDBA Toolkit," later in this chapter, as configuration is similar for both platforms.

Installing the PDBA Toolkit for Win32

Before we discuss toolkit installation on Win32 systems, we need to make sure that the *PDBA_HOME* environment variable is in an accessible place. On Win32, only

---

[*] If it's good enough for Apache, it's good enough for us!

one mechanism ensures the availability of this variable—the Windows Registry. Although we'll use the Registry just once, we must make sure that *PDBA_HOME* can be accessed by programs running through the Windows Scheduler, through the Windows services system, or just as plain old scripts.

 We recommend that the PDBA Toolkit and all its configuration files be stored on the *C:* drive, because of the way that Windows security works. Programs executing from drives other than *C:* may lack access to drives other than *C:* when running via the Windows Scheduler. Likewise, Perl scripts running as Win32 services may fail to work properly when executed from a network drive.

You will need to follow the steps in this section to install the toolkit on your Win32 platform so the scripts introduced in later chapters will work properly.

PDBA Registry Settings

Follow these steps to provide the proper registry settings:

1. Visit our O'Reilly site and download *PDBA.ppd*. Save this to a suitable place such as *C:\TEMP*. (You only need this temporarily and can delete it afterwards):

   http://www.oreilly.com/catalog/oracleperl/pdbatoolkit

2. Now install PDBA via ActivePerl's PPM program:[*]

   ```
   DOS> ppm
   PPM> install --location=c:\temp PDBA
   Install package 'PDBA?' (y/N): y
   ...
   Installing C:\Perl\site\lib\PDBA\CM.pm
   ...
   Installing C:\Perl\site\lib\PDBA\util\pdba.reg
   ...
   Installing C:\Perl\bin\pwc.pl
   ...
   Writing C:\Perl\site\lib\auto\PDBA\.packlist
   PPM>
   ```

   (Notice the *--location* PPM argument used to locate the *PDBA.ppd* file. (Note that there are two dashes in the option, not one.)

3. Once you've installed PDBA via PPM, you'll need to track down the *pdba.reg* file. If your Perl installation is on drive *C:*, its file path will be:

   C:\Perl\site\lib\PDBA\util\pdba.reg

---

[*] You could also download *PDBA_1_00_Win32.tar.gz*, uncompress it, and install it manually, copying the files to the appropriate locations. PPM is much easier, though, and less error-prone.

4. Edit this file with a right-click, and check to make sure you're happy with the default for *PDBA_HOME*, which we've preset to:[*]

   ```
   C:/pdba
   ```

5. Change it if you wish and then exit from the file. To update the Registry, double-click the *pdba.reg* file via Windows Explorer.

6. This installs the key *[HKEY_LOCAL_MACHINE/Software/PDBA]* with a *PDBA_HOME* entry assigned to *C:/pdba* (or whatever you've changed it to). Registry work is now over. Sighs of relief, as we go back to our lives, citizens.

7. Finally, you need to copy the supplied configuration files from their installed location to the directory indicated by *PDBA_HOME*. You can do this by simply using the Windows Explorer to cut-and-paste the files from their current location. Alternately, you can use the *copy* command from the command prompt window. Assuming that the PDBA Toolkit was installed on drive *C:*, the configuration files will be located in the *C:\Perl\site\lib\PDBA\conf* directory, as in Figure 9-2. Assuming that *PDBA_HOME* is set to *C:\pdba*, the following command will locate the configuration files at their final destination:

   ```
   DOS> copy C:\Perl\site\lib\PDBA\conf\*.conf C:\pdba
   ```

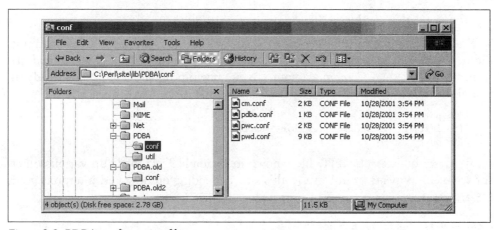

Figure 9-2. PDBA configuration files

Installing Additional Perl Modules

A few additional modules are required for the toolkit to work properly:

---

[*] You may be curious about the use of the forward slash, /, rather than the standard Windows backslash, \. The backslash has a special meaning in Perl, changing the meaning of following characters. Perl therefore requires two backslashes, \\, to really mean a single one, \. Because the Windows kernel uses a forward slash internally as the separator, using it in Perl works just fine.

TimeDate
>   Graham Barr's *TimeDate* date parser.

Crypt::RC4
>   Kurt Kincaid's *Crypt::RC4* cryptographic module.

Mail::Sendmail
>   Milivoj Ivkovic's OS-independent email sender.

Win32::Daemon
>   Dave Roth's invaluable module that allows us to create Win32 services in Perl.

Install the first three from ActiveState via PPM:

```
DOS> ppm
PPM> install TimeDate
PPM> install Crypt-RC4
PPM> install Mail-Sendmail
```

The last module, *Win32::Daemon*, was described earlier in the section "PDBA:: Daemon and Win32::Daemon." This module allows Perl to act as a service on Win32, the same way it can run as a daemon on Unix. The URL for *Win32::Daemon* is:

>   *ftp://ftp.roth.net/pub/ntperl/Daemon/20000319/Bin/*

The latest version, as this book went to press, was *daemon_5006.Zip*. Download this file to a suitable location, such as *C:\temp*, and extract the *Win32-Daemon.ppd* file from the archive into *C:\temp* via your favorite unzip program. You're now ready to install the module via PPM:

```
DOS> ppm
PPM> install --location=c:\temp Win32-Daemon
PPM> quit
```

As we describe later, this PPD file (shown in Example 9-11) loads up various other software components from Dave Roth's site, depending on how Perl interprets your OS architecture.

Example 9-11. Win32-Daemon.ppd

```
<SOFTPKG NAME="Win32-Daemon" VERSION="0,2000,06,20">
    <TITLE>Win32::Daemon</TITLE>
    <ABSTRACT>The Win32::Daemon extension for Win32 X86. Allows Perl
            to be a Win32 service.</ABSTRACT>
    <AUTHOR>Roth Consulting (http://www.roth.net/)</AUTHOR>
    <IMPLEMENTATION>
            <OS NAME="MSWin32" />
            <ARCHITECTURE NAME="MSWin32-x86-object" />
        <CODEBASE
HREF="http://www.roth.net/perl/packages/x86/Win32/Daemon_5005_AS.tar.gz" />
    </IMPLEMENTATION>
    <IMPLEMENTATION>
            <OS NAME="MSWin32" />
```

Example 9-11. Win32-Daemon.ppd (continued)

```
        <ARCHITECTURE NAME="MSWin32-x86" />
      <CODEBASE
HREF="http://www.roth.net/perl/packages/x86/Win32/Daemon_5005.tar.gz" />
    </IMPLEMENTATION>
    <IMPLEMENTATION>
        <OS NAME="MSWin32" />
        <ARCHITECTURE NAME="MSWin32-x86-multi-thread" />
      <CODEBASE
HREF="http://www.roth.net/perl/packages/x86/Win32/Daemon_5006.tar.gz" />
    </IMPLEMENTATION>
    </SOFTPKG>
```

You're done with the installation! All of the Perl modules and scripts needed for the toolkit are now installed. Onward and upward to the toolkit configuration.

Configuring the PDBA Toolkit

PDBA Toolkit configuration works the same way for both Unix and Win32. As we mentioned earlier, it's based upon a flat-file system.

 From this point on, we'll refer to the file locations as *PDBA_HOME/ file_name.conf*, regardless of platform.

We'll begin with the actual *PDBA* module and then continue with Connection Manager, the Password Server, and then the Password Client, each with its own configuration file, as shown in Figure 9-2.

PDBA Module Configuration

The *PDBA* module requires little configuration. It needs to know just two things:

- Which mail server to use
- Where it should say the emails are being sent from

The configuration file is *PDBA_HOME/pdba.conf*. The default contents are shown in Example 9-12.

Example 9-12. pdba.conf —Default values

```
package pdbaparms;
use vars qw( %parms );
%emailParms = (
   # required for sending mail
mailServer => 'sherlock.jks.com',
   # who should mail be from?
   # does not need to be a valid address
```

Example 9-12. pdba.conf —Default values (continued)

```
    fromAddress => 'oracle@jks.com',
);
```

Simply adjust the values to those for your own site. The *mailServer* parameter needs to be a valid mail server, but *fromAddress* can be a purely informational *FROM:* address. For example, if your domain is *mydomain.com*, you may want to simply set it to *oracle@mydomain.com*. Or you can set it to a real address, if you prefer, to make potential replies easier. For instance, you could change the two key lines like this:

```
    mailServer => 'mail.mydomain.com',
    ...
    fromAddress => 'oracle@mydomain.com',
```

When you're finished, check the file for syntactic correctness with the *-cw* switches:

```
    $ perl -cw pdba.conf
```

PDBA::CM Module Configuration

We've included the *PDBA::CM* (Connection Manager) module in the toolkit as an optional convenience, although we hope you'll want to set it up. The default *PDBA_HOME/cm.conf* is shown in Example 9-13.

Example 9-13. cm.conf —CM configuration file

```
package cmconf;
use vars qw(%env);
%env = (
    default => {
        ORACLE_HOME => '/u02/app/oracle/product/8.1.7',
        ORACLE_BASE => '/u02/app/oracle',
        TNS_ADMIN => '/u02/app/oracle/product/8.1.7/network/admin'
    },

    ts99 => {
        ORACLE_HOME => '/u02/app/oracle/product/8.1.7',
        ORACLE_BASE => '/u02/app/oracle',
        TNS_ADMIN => '/u02/app/oracle/product/8.1.7/network/admin'
    },
);
```

New database connection attempts made via *PDBA::CM* check for this file as follows:

1. If it exists, the contents are checked for the target database.

2. If the database entry exists, *cm.conf* values are used to set *ORACLE_HOME*, *ORACLE_BASE*, *TNS_ADMIN*, and any other required environment variables.

3. If a database entry is not specified, the *default* values are used.

Setting the environment variables in this way means you get them right every time you connect to a target database—and you don't have to remember them. This is useful for scripts running from a system scheduler. The usual method used to run an ordinary Perl script is to wrap it. The wrapper sets the environment and then executes the script. Example 9-14 may look familiar to *cron* users. When running a script via the Unix *cron* scheduler, you normally must explicitly set all Oracle environment variables in the script. This is because scripts that run via *cron* do not inherit the environment variables that are normally set when logged into an interactive Unix account.

Example 9-14. mybatch.sh—Setting up a Perl script in a wrapper script

```
#!/bin/ksh

# Set the environment
export ORACLE_SID=ts01
export ORAENV_ASK=NO
. /usr/local/bin/oraenv $ORACLE_SID

# Execute the script
mybatch.pl -database -username ayn -password rand
```

Using *PDBA::CM*'s configuration file eliminates the need for this kind of logic. You simply run the Perl script *mybatch.pl* directly via the system scheduler. For most situations, you set up *cm.conf* with just the default values and it works fine. You need only add specific database parameters as necessary. For Win32 users who need a simple default, edit the supplied *cm.conf* file to make it look like Example 9-15:

Example 9-15. cm.conf —Basic CM configuration file

```
package cmconf;
use vars qw(%env);
%env = (   default => {
      ORACLE_HOME => 'c:/oracle/ora81',
      ORACLE_BASE => 'c:/oracle',
      TNS_ADMIN => 'c:/oracle/ora81/network/admin'
   },
);
```

Note that by default *PDBA::CM* ignores the *cm.conf* file if ORACLE_HOME is set. You can override that behavior with the *FORCE_CONFIG* attribute. You can also tell *PDBA::CM* to look beyond *PDBA_HOME* for a configuration file via *PATH* and *FILE*:

```
my $dbh = new PDBA::CM (
    DATABASE => $db,
    USERNAME => $username,
    PASSWORD => $password,
    FORCE_CONFIG=> 1,                    # Use the config file! :-)
```

```
    PATH => '/u02/app/oracle/config',
    FILE => 'oracle_cm.conf'
);
```

Password Server Configuration

The password server configuration file, *PDBA_HOME/pwd.conf*, contains five data structures:

$port
> Sets the TCP port for the password server

%pwd
> Sets the passwords for the password server

%users
> Sets up password server users

%encryption
> Encrypts passwords

%instanceAuth
> Sets up per-account authorization

We'll describe these in the following sections.

$port: Setting the TCP port for the password server

First you need to set the TCP port to be used by the password server. The setting in the file is currently 1579. You can change this to any other setting as follows:

```
package pwd;
use vars qw($port %pwd %instanceAuth %users %encryption );
$port=1579;
```

 Ports < *1024* will require special OS or *root* permissions.

%pwd: Setting the passwords for password server

This is where the passwords for each account are specified by machine or database server name, Oracle instance name, and account name, in a manner similar to the *tnsnames.ora* file structure. Example 9-16 is taken directly from the *pwd.conf* file included in the PDBA distribution. It contains passwords for the *sys* and *system* users, for the databases *ts98* and *ts99* on the *watson* server, and for database *ts01* on the *sherlock* server.

Example 9-16. pwd.conf

```
%pwd = (
    sherlock => {
        ts01 => { system  => 'hoser',
                  sys      => 'hosehead' }
    },
    watson => {
        ts99 => { system  => 'wazzup',
                  sys      => 'wizard' },

        ts98 => { system  => 'whynot',
                  sys      => 'bcuz' }
    }
);
```

This type of data structure is known as a *hash of hashes* (see Appendix A). The *%pwd* Perl hash contains a list of hash keys, in this case *sherlock* and *watson*. Each of these contains another Perl hash. Inside these hashes are the actual accounts and passwords. Here's what you need to do:

- If you're ready to edit your *pwd.conf* file, go ahead and change the server names, accounts, and passwords to those appropriate for your site.

- If you do edit the file, be sure to check it with *perl -cw pwd.conf* when done.

The method used to access this data may appear initially to be somewhat daunting, but scrutiny reveals that it's only a loop extracting servers, instances, usernames, and passwords, as Example 9-17 shows.

Example 9-17. pwd.pl—Accessing data elements

```
1 use PDBA::ConfigFile;
2
3 unless ( new PDBA::ConfigLoad( FILE => 'pwd.conf', PATH => './' ) ) {
4    die "could not load pwd.conf\n";
5 }
6
7 $t=0;
8 for my $server ( keys %pwd::pwd ) {
9    print "\t" x $t, "server: $server\n";
10   $t++;
11   for my $instance ( keys %{$pwd::pwd{$server}} ) {
12       print "\t" x $t, "instance: $instance\n";
13       $t++;
14       for my $user ( keys %{$pwd::pwd{$server}->{$instance}} ) {
15           print "\t" x $t, "username: $user",
16               "password: $pwd::pwd{$server}->{$instance}{$user}\n";
17       }
18       $t--;
19   }
20   $t--;
21 }
```

Here's what is going on.

1. Line 8 extracts the server names from the *%pwd* hash via the built-in Perl function *keys*. (Recall how each server has its own hash inside *%pwd*.)

2. Line 11 extracts instances.

3. Line 14 uses *%{}* to de-reference yet another nested hash, this time for each server.

4. The account names and passwords are finally revealed in lines 15 and 16.

Fortunately, *PDBA::PWD* takes care of all these technical difficulties. The only place this password structure is used is within the *PDBA::PWD* module. Retrieving a single password in a real-life script is actually fairly simple, as you can see here:

```
my $password = $pwd::pwd{$server}->{$instance}{$user};
```

%users: Setting up password server users

The password server is only available for clients specified in the *%users* hash. These require a password. In case you're thinking "Oh great, another password to remember, let's use *P4SSW0RDF1V3* or something," keep in mind that this one greatly reduces the number of other passwords you need to remember. Attempts to retrieve a password without a correct username and password will return no data. There are no informational messages declaring that the password or username is incorrect. Simply change the content for your own users in *pwd.conf* as follows:

```
%users = ( andyd => 'perlgeek',   # Needs to get out more! :-)
           jkstill => 'getalife',  # Gotta turn off that computer! 8-)
           scott => 'tiger' );
```

%encryption: Encrypting passwords

Most folks have become increasingly security-conscious lately, and rightly so. Sending clear text passwords over a network is now considered unacceptable practice, because the routing of TCP/IP packets over a multiply-redundant network makes it easy for unauthorized persons to compromise security. With that in mind, we designed the *PDBA::PWD* module to ensure that passwords are transmitted in encrypted form. To assist in the encryption, we've chosen the RC4 encryption algorithm available via the *Crypt::RC4* Perl module. It is fast, easy to install, and available for both Unix and Win32 platforms.* All you need do is specify a string to use as the encryption key. This is done via the *%encryption* hash in *PDBA/pwd.conf*, shown in Example 9-18.

---

* Once you're used to *Crypt::RC4*, you may wish to modify our toolkit to gain even greater security with ever more secure Perl modules; see *http://search.cpan.org/Catalog/Security*.

Example 9-18. pwd.conf —The %encryption hash

```
%encryption = (
    # don't change this
    level => 'simple',
    # make your key at least 56 characters
    key => 'One Ring to bring them all and in the darkness bind them',

    # don't change this
    maxKeyLen => 56
);
```

There are three pieces of data in the *%encryption* hash, and the only one you need to be concerned with for now is *key*. Here are the requirements for *key*:

- It needs to be a phrase and can be practically anything you want.
- Nonsense key phrases are best—anything that is difficult to guess.
- The key is used to encrypt passwords sent over the network.
- If you make the key longer than 56 characters, it will be truncated to a length of 56.
1. It can be shorter than 56 characters, but for best results make it at least 56.

You may recognize our own key as being from J.R.R.Tolkien's *The Lord of The Rings*. It is too predictable for an actual encryption key, but demonstrates that the key can be anything you like. Change the key, and then check the configuration file with *perl -cw pwd.conf*.

%instanceAuth: Setting up per-account authorization

The *%instanceAuth* hash provides an optional security feature. It can be used to limit which users are able to retrieve passwords for a particular account. If you have some sensitive accounts, you can limit access to them with *%instanceAuth*. Any accounts unspecified will be available to all authorized users. If the *%instanceAuth* structure is missing completely, all users found in *%users* have access to all passwords for all accounts.

Consider Example 9-19: it's a subset of the servers found within Example 9-16. In the *%pwd* hash, there are two servers, with three Oracle instances, and two accounts in each instance, *sys* and *system*. This is a total of six passwords, and we want to filter their access as follows:

- You want to allow *andyd* and *jkstill* to have access to the *system* account on *ts01*.
- Only *andyd* is to have access to the *sys* account on *ts01*.
- Only *scott* and *andyd* are to have access to the *sys* account on *ts99*.
- All authorized users of the password server, as found in the *%users* hash, are to have access to the supplied accounts *sys* and *system* in the *ts98* instance, as well as to the *system* account in *ts99*.

The entries in *%instanceAuth* shown in Example 9-19 create the required filter. The only entries needed are for accounts where you wish to limit the users who can retrieve passwords.

Example 9-19. pwd.conf—Using the %instanceAuth structure

```
%instanceAuth = (

    sherlock => {
       ts01 => { system  => [ qw(andyd jkstill) ],
                 sys     => [qw(andyd)] }
    },

    watson => { ts99 => {
                 sys  => [qw( scott andyd )] }
    }
);
```

Let's see what's going on here.

1. The lowest-level entry in the *%instanceAuth* structure is something called an "anonymous array"—that is, it exists in Perl memory as an array, but it has no name. (You can read up on anonymous arrays in Appendix A.)

2. You can tell it's an anonymous array because the data is in square brackets *[]*, indicating an array, but there is no name associated with it.

3. If this level of security is unnecessary, just delete all of the data inside the *%instanceAuth* hash so it looks like this:

    ```
    %instanceAuth = ( );
    ```

   You must keep *%instanceAuth*, though, even if it is undefined. If you delete it entirely, a warning will be raised when you check the file via the command *perl -cw pwd.conf*.

Securing pwd.conf

The *PDBA/pwd.conf* file is sensitive, so you need to set Fort Knox file permissions enabling only authorized users to read or edit it. On Unix, this is done via *chmod*:

```
$ chmod 640 pwd.conf
$ ls -la pwd.conf
-rw-r-----    1 oramon  dba    8508 Apr 14  07:27 pwd.conf
```

Setting the permission to 0640 allows users belonging to the DBA group to view the file, while only the file owner can edit it. Win32 security is different. Setting the proper permissions on Win32 is a point-and-click operation that works as follows:

1. Find the target file in Windows Explorer and right-click on it.

2. If you have network security on your system, you'll see a *Security* tab. Click on it.

3. The *File Permissions* dialog should appear, like the one in Figure 9-3. In this example, everyone on the network has access to *PDBA_HOME/pwd.conf*.

4. Allowing all users on the network to have read access should be avoided for a file containing passwords. You may want to highlight users or groups that should no longer have access to the file (such as *Everyone*). Click on *Remove* so they no longer have access to this file.

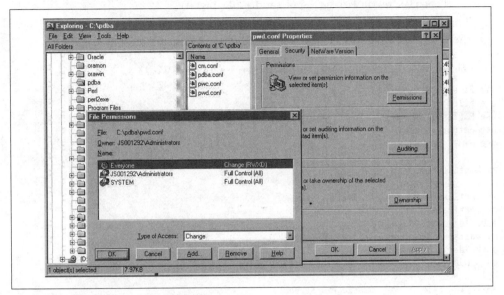

Figure 9-3. Setting file security on Win32

Running the password server on Unix

Those on Unix are now ready to run the password server via the command line as follows:

```
$ pwd.pl
```

That's all there is to it. The password server has landed. You can verify its operation via a *ps* command, using either the *-fea* or *-aux* switches, depending on your own Unix flavor:

```
$ ps -fea | grep pwd | grep -v grep
oramon   25771    1  0 08:12 ?       00:00:00 perl /usr/bin/pwd.pl
$ ps -aux | grep pwd | grep -v grep
oramon   25771 0.0  0.8  5668 4540 ?      S    08:12 0:00 perl /usr/bin/pwd.pl
```

Running the password server on Win32

Running the password server on Win32 is slightly more involved. You need to install the *pwd.pl* script as a service. Thanks to the *Win32::Daemon* module, this is straightforward.

1. The first thing to do is to locate the script *pwd_service.pl*. This is used to install *pwd.pl* as a service or to remove it. If Perl is installed on *C:*, the path will be:

   ```
   C:\Perl\site\lib\PDBA\util\pwd_service.pl
   ```

2. Once the script has been located, you open a command prompt window to execute the script and install the password server service. The following command will install the service.

   ```
   C:\Perl\site\lib\PDBA\util\pwd_service.pl -install
   ```

3. This will automatically detect where *Perl.exe* and *pwd.pl* are located and use them to install the service. Example 9-20 reproduces the relevant script portion.

Example 9-20. pwd_service.pl—Install password server service on Win32

```
use File::Basename;
use File::Spec;
use English;
use Getopt::Long;
use Win32::Daemon;

my %optctl=();

my $perlExe = $EXECUTABLE_NAME;
my $perlPath = dirname($perlExe);
# build a path to pwd.pl
my @dirs = File::Spec->splitdir($perlPath);
push @dirs, qw(pwd.pl);
my $pwdPath = File::Spec->catfile(@dirs);

%Hash = ( name    => 'Oracle_PWD_Server',
          display => 'Oracle_PWD_Server',
          path    => $perlExe,
          user    => '',   # Unnecessary, for this particular application.
          pwd     => '',   # Unnecessary, for this particular application.
          parameters => $pwdPath );
unless ( GetOptions(\%optctl, "install!", "remove!" ) ) {
   usage(1);
}
if ( $optctl{remove} ) {
   if( Win32::Daemon::DeleteService( $Hash{name} ) ) {
      print "Successfully removed.\n";
   } else {
      print "Failed to remove service: " . GetError() . "\n";
   }
}
print "finished.\n";

sub GetError {
   return( Win32::FormatMessage( Win32::Daemon::GetLastError() ) );
}
```

If you should happen to have a nonstandard installation of Perl, you can use Table 9-11 (password server parameters) as a guide in editing the attributes of the %Hash data structure in *pwd.pl*.

Table 9-11. Parameters for installing the password server on Win32

Attribute	Description
name	The name of the service. We've set it to *Oracle_PWD_Server*.
display	The name to display in the Win32 Service Manager.
path	The full path to the Perl executable—for example, *C:\Perl\bin\perl.exe*.
user	Who the user is to run as (unnecessary for this application).
pwd	Password for user (unnecessary for this application).
parameters	The full pathname to the *pwd.pl* script—for example, *C: \Perl\bin\pwd.pl*.

Starting the service

Now all you need do is run *Win32 Service Manager* to start the service. There are two different paths, shown in Table 9-12, depending on which Win32 platform you're on.

Table 9-12. Installing the password server on Win32

Win32 version	Start menu instructions
NT 4.0	Start->Settings->Control Panel. Then double-click on the Services icon. Highlight the *Oracle_PWD_Server* service and click *Start*.
Windows 2000	Start->Programs->Administrative Tools->Services. Highlight the *Oracle_PWD_Server*, right-click on it, and press *Start*.

Password Client Configuration

We're in the home stretch now. All that's left is to set up the password client *pwc.pl* and give it a whirl. As with the password server, the client program uses a configuration file. Unlike the server, the configuration file is optional. We hope you'll want to use it though, as it makes the client program considerably easier to use. Bring up *PDBA_HOME/pwc.conf* in your favorite editor and take a look at it. The contents of the file, as it appears in the PDBA distribution, are shown in Example 9-21.

Example 9-21. pwc.conf—Password client configuration

```
package pwc;
use vars qw(%optctl);
%optctl = ( host => 'sherlock',
            port => 1579,
            machine => 'watson',
            instance => 'ts98',
            username => 'sys',
            my_username => 'scott',
```

Example 9-21. pwc.conf—Password client configuration (continued)

```
      my_password => 'tiger',
      key => 'One Ring to bring them all and in the darkness bind them');
```

All of the command-line options except *-conf* can be specified in this file, thus avoiding long command-line entries and the use of clear text passwords (which is what we were trying to avoid in the first place). It assumes that the configuration file name is *PDBA_HOME/pwc.conf*, unless another name is specified directly on the command line with the *-conf filename* option. Typing *pwc.pl -help* on the command line displays all of the options as a useful reminder of what you'll need to input. Table 9-13 summarizes these options.

Table 9-13. Command-line options for pwc.pl

Argument	Value
conf	Tells *pwc.pl* the name of the configuration file to use.
host	Win32 or Unix server on which the password server is running.
port	Host port being used by the password server. This will be the same value specified for *port*, in *PDBA_HOME/ pwd.conf*.
machine	Name of the physical host the database instance is on.
instance	Database instance.
username	Username for which you are requesting the password.
my_username	Your password server username.
my_password	Your password server password.
key	Key used to encrypt/decrypt passwords sent over the network. Your password server authentication is encrypted as well. Include this value in quotes if spaces or special characters are included.

Note the following:

- Any options not specified in this file will need to be included on the command line.

- Arguments specified on the command line override those in the configuration file.

One common approach is to create a configuration file specifying the password server and port, your username and password, and the key used to encrypt data across the network. With those options present in the configuration file, you would only need to specify the configuration file, database server machine, database instance, and account name on the command line. For example, your command line would look something like this when you're retrieving the password for account *system* in instance *vdr* on database server *elfenwood*:

```
$ pwc.pl -machine elfenwood -instance VDR -username system -conf pwc.conf
```

To connect to a different host's password server, you would modify the command line as follows:

```
$ pwc.pl -host mycroft -machine elfenwood -instance VDR \
    -username system -conf pwc.conf
```

Example 9-22 is an example of connecting to an alternate password server. In this case the password server on Unix server *sherlock* was unavailable, so a connection was made to the alternate password server on the Win32 server *mycroft*.

Example 9-22. Connecting to an alternate password server

```
%oramon > pwc.pl
              Uncaught exception from user code:Couldn't connect to sherlock:1579 : IO::
Socket::INET: Timeout at ...

%oramon >
%oramon >
 pwc.pl -host mycroft
whyn0t %oramon >
```

Let's see what's happening in Example 9-22.

1. Notice in the example that the password *whyn0t* was returned for the *sys* user in database instance *ts99* on the database server *watson*. You might find the password, originally found in Example 9-16, a little hard to pick out, because neither a line feed nor a carriage return is displayed, just the password. (Obviously, you can adapt your client scripts so passwords are not revealed in this way; we've done it only to demonstrate the concept.)

2. You can copy the configuration file to any file name you like, and use it that way. This would be useful if you wanted to keep different configuration files for each database server or to organize them by username.

3. Be sure that you avoid changing the password client package line near the top of the package, *package pwc;*, as that line is required for this configuration file to work properly.

4. Secure *PDBA_HOME/pwc.conf* to protect it from unauthorized users, as we showed with *pwd.conf* earlier.

The *pwc.pl* script is useful in demonstrating how to use the password server in your own scripts. It is also useful as a standalone script for retrieving passwords at the command line. On Unix systems, it may even be used to retrieve passwords and use them directly as input. This example demonstrates its use in logging in to SQL*Plus without any need to type the password:

```
sqlplus system/$(pwc.pl -machine sherlock -database ts01 -username system)
```

This uses the Korn shell's *$()* subshell mechanism, returning the output of *pwc.pl* to the current shell.

Alas, we do not know of an equivalent subshell mechanism on the Win32 platform.

Using PDBA::PWC in your own Perl scripts

The password client module is available for use in your own Perl scripts as well. Here are the basic pieces you'll need to include in order to connect to the password server:

```
use PDBA::PWC;

my $client = new PDBA::PWC(
    host => $remote_host,
    port => $remote_port
);
$client->authenticate(
    username => $myusername,
    password => $mypassword,
    key => $key,
    debug => $optctl{debug}
);
my $password = $client->getPassword(
    machine => $machine,
    instance => $instance,
    username => $username,
    key => $key
);
```

This completes the toolkit installation. In the following chapters, we'll see what it can do for us.

Performing Routine DBA Tasks with the PDBA Toolkit

The Perl DBA Toolkit we introduced and installed in Chapter 9, *Installing the PDBA Toolkit* contains dozens of Perl scripts that you can use to simplify—and even automate—the many routine tasks that Oracle DBAs wrestle with every day. We use these scripts daily in our own database administration work, and we think you will find that they make your work much more efficient.

This chapter focuses on the repetitive operations that Oracle DBAs tend to perform over and over again. In the following chapters we'll focus on a few more specialized tasks: in Chapter 10 we'll show how you can monitor your database using the toolkit scripts, and in Chapter 11, *Monitoring the Database with the PDBA Toolkit* we'll build a repository for storing database information.

If you have installed the PDBA Toolkit as described in Chapter 9, all of the scripts mentioned in this chapter will be on your system. If you're running on a Unix system, you'll find them in */usr/local/bin*, and if you're using Win32, you'll find them in *C:\Perl\bin* (unless you chose alternative locations during the installation). We'll examine the scripts in the following categories:

Managing user accounts
> We'll use the *create_user.pl*, *create_user.conf*, *drop_user.pl*, *dup_user.pl*, *mucr8. msg*, and *mucr.pl* scripts and files to create single users and groups of users, to drop users, and to perform account maintenance.

Maintaining indexes
> We'll use the *idxr.pl* and *index_frag_test.sql* scripts and files to inspect, tune, and rebuild database indexes.

Killing sniped sessions
> We'll use the *kss.pl*, *kss.conf*, and *kss_NT.pl* scripts and files to kill sniped sessions and manage user connection resources.

Managing extent usage
> We'll use the *maxext.pl* script to determine extents, manage statistics, and reorganize objects.

Extracting DDL and data

We'll use the *sqlunldr.pl, exp_exclude.conf,* and *ddl_oracle.pl* scripts and files to extract data and DDL statements in a portable way and to transfer objects and data transparently across systems.

Managing User Accounts

Managing user accounts can consume quite a bit of database administration time, especially if the DBA doesn't have the proper tools to simplify the job. Even when account management is performed infrequently,[*] it can be resource-intensive. Any new account you create must have the proper privileges to log on to the database and be able to create database objects as necessary. And for any new account, you will need to make sure you're granting only the necessary privileges on requisite database objects—and not granting any privileges the user should *not* have.

Dropping database accounts may also be a bit of a chore, but for different reasons. Dropping an account with a large number of objects can cause an extreme amount of activity in the Oracle data dictionary. This can result in contention with other processes in the data dictionary and may result in failure of the DROP USER command.

This section introduces scripts and configuration files you can use to simplify account management. We'll provide ways for you to:

- Create predefined PDBA roles.
- Create users simply from the Unix or Win32 command line.
- Duplicate existing accounts within the database.
- Drop existing accounts (first removing the account's tables and indexes to prevent data dictionary contention).

Creating Accounts the Old Way

Oracle DBAs often create new users by means of shell scripts such as the one shown in Example 10-1.

Example 10-1. Creating users with a shell script

```
#!/usr/bin/ksh

DBAUSER=system
DBAPASSWORD=manager
DEFTBS=users
TMPTBS=temp
```

---

[*] It may even be that managing accounts is least organized when done infrequently; in such cases, there is less impetus to organize the tasks.

Example 10-1. Creating users with a shell script (continued)

```
ROLES="connect,resource"

for var in username password database
do
    print "please enter the value for $var : \c"
    read answer
    eval "$var=$answer"
done

sqlplus <<EOF
$DBAUSER/$DBAPASSWORD@$database
CREATE USER $username IDENTIFIED BY $password
DEFAULT TABLESPACE $DEFTBS
TEMPORARY TABLESPACE $TMPTBS;
GRANT $ROLES TO $username;
EOF
```

While this method is effective if you're creating a simple account, more work is often needed to tailor specific accounts. For example, if you're creating a user within a particular application suite, there are likely to be specific roles and privileges that must be granted users so they will be able to gain access to the application's data. Here is a typical scenario:

1. You're asked to create a data entry account for someone new working on a Human Resources package. For this clerical role you've already created an appropriate role, hr_clerk. Let's assume this new *carla* account was created in the database via the script in Example 10-1. We must now relog into SQL*Plus and execute the following:

   ```
   SQL> GRANT HR_CLERK TO CARLA;
   ```

2. Because *carla* does not need to be able to create database objects, we revoke RESOURCE to prevent inadvertent misuse of database resource.

3. You may recall that granting a user RESOURCE means that Oracle auto-grants an UNLIMITED TABLESPACE privilege to *carla*. So now we have to issue a countermanding REVOKE UNLIMITED TABLESPACE.

Let's just stop here, because this kind of manual DBA work can quickly spiral out of control, especially with multiple users on multiple applications coming and going across the entire company.

Fortunately, Perl provides an easier way, and we've packaged some helpful Perl account maintenance scripts in our toolkit for you to use.

Creating a Single Account with create_user.pl

The toolkit script *create_user.pl* and its associated configuration file *create_user.conf* give you a lot of flexibility in creating new user accounts from the command line. In

comparison with the rather cumbersome way we created *carla* for use with the HR_
CLERK role in the earlier example, we can now issue a single command. There is no
need to perform the extra manual work of logging onto SQL*Plus for fine tuning.
Let's look at some examples..

Scenario #1

First, we're going to create a single user account.

1. Here *carla* is created with a single script, *create_user.pl*, and the generated password is printed to the screen.
2. The *-verbose* option shows all the CREATE and GRANT steps taken:

```
$ create_user.pl -machine sherlock -database ts01 -username jkstill \
-new_username carla -new_password generate -pdbarole app_clerk -verbose

creating user 'carla'

default tablespace  : users
temporary tablespace: temp
grants: create session hr_clerk
quotas:

user 'carla' created
password BNHV815
$
```

Scenario #2

After creating *carla*, we learn that a developer needs access to a production database
in order to troubleshoot a newly discovered problem. The developer's access needs
to be the same as it is in his development database. First let's see how you'd fix
things without the toolkit. (Later, we'll show how you'd do it with the toolkit, which
manages the whole operation more simply with configurable and pre-stored elements that replace manual investigative hunches with precise and reliable information.)

1. Although you're opposed to developers possessing accounts on production databases, through gritted teeth you agree to create *alicia* on production with the
   same privileges she has in development.
2. Using the trusty old shell script method, you create the basic *alicia* account, then
   log in to the development database to determine her exact privilege set (you
   might use an application such as Orac or Oracletool to work this out). You then
   manually grant the discovered privileges to production, in a process that is both
   tedious and error-prone.

The toolkit comes to the rescue. Fortunately, you've predefined all of the privileges
needed for the databases you administer in the toolkit's *create_user.conf* file. Instead,

you can simply run a command line similar to what you did to create *carla*'s account, with some changes for the user name and privileges granted. Example 10-2 shows how it's done.

Example 10-2. Create a developer account with create_user.pl

```
%oramon> create_user.pl -machine sherlock -database ts01 \
  -username jkstill -new_username alicia -new_password generate \
  -pdbarole developer -verbose
creating user 'alicia'

default tablespace  : users
temporary tablespace: temp

grants:  connect resource plustrace javauserpriv javadebugpriv
 select_catalog_role

revokes:  unlimited tablespace

quotas:
  indx:  5m
  users:  unlimited

user 'alicia' created
password: CBLD1749
```

With a single command you create the new *alicia* account and grant the following roles to it:

> CONNECT
> RESOURCE
> PLUSTRACE
> JAVAUSERPRIV
> JAVADEBUGPRIV
> SELECT_CATALOG_ROLE

In addition, you set the user quotas on the USERS and INDX tablespaces. Let's take a closer look now at *create_user.conf* and *create_user.pl*.

The create_user.conf configuration file

Make sure that the *create_user.conf* file is in your *PDBA_HOME* directory:

1. If it's missing from *PDBA_HOME* (perhaps because you are logged on as a new user), copy it from the *PDBA* installation directory. For Unix, type:

   ```
   $ cp /u01/build/PDBA-1.00/routine_tasks/create_user.conf $PDBA_HOME
   ```

   On Win32, type:

   ```
   DOS> copy C:\Perl\site\lib\PDBA\conf\create_user.conf C:\PDBA
   ```

2. Now open the file with your favorite text editor. The working contents of the file will look similar to Example 10-3. This example also gives us a good opportunity to show how Perl's *qw{}* quote word constructor is used.[*]

Example 10-3. create_user.conf

```
package cuconf;
use vars qw{ %roles %tablespaces };

%roles = (
   developer =>  {
      grants => [ qw{ connect
                      resource
                      plustrace
                      javauserpriv
                      javadebugpriv
                      select_catalog_role }],

      revokes => [ 'unlimited tablespace'],

      quotas => { users => 'unlimited', indx => '5m', },
   },
   app_clerk => {
      grants => ['create session', 'hr_clerk'],
      revokes => [],
      quotas => {},
   },
   app_admin => {
      grants => ['create session','hr_admin',],
      revokes => [],
      quotas => {},
   },
   backup => {
      grants => [qw{ connect exp_full_database imp_full_database }],
      revokes => [],
      quotas => {},
   },
   dba => {
      grants => [qw{connect dba}],
      revokes => [],
      tablespaces => { default => 'tools', temporary => 'temp2', },
      quotas => {},
   },
   sysdba => {
      grants => [ qw{connect dba sysdba} ],
      revokes => [],
      quotas => {},
```

---

[*] For much more on the *qw{}*, *q{}*, and *qq{}* quote constructions in Perl (these essentially allow us to use less punctuation within our code), check out *perldoc perlop*.

Example 10-3. create_user.conf (continued)

```
    },
);

%tablespaces = ( default  => 'users', temporary => 'temp', );
```

create_user.conf defines a number of logical roles; we'll refer to these as *PDBA roles*, to differentiate them from standard Oracle database roles. Near the top of the *%roles* hash in Example 10-3, you'll find the role DEVELOPER. Each PDBA role is a privilege group assigned as a single entity. (Example 10-2 shows account *alicia*, as created using the PDBA role DEVELOPER.)

If you compare the granted privileges listed for DEVELOPER in Example 10-3, you'll see that they match the screen in Example 10-2.

Notice also the UNLIMITED TABLESPACE revoke, reversing its automatic assignment to those granted RESOURCE. The *create_users.conf* configuration file directed this operation without your needing to remember. You can extend this approach to any combination of grants, revokes, and quotas.

New entries can be added to *%roles*. For example, you might need to create lots of inventory testers on your application. You could then add the following PDBA role:

```
inventory_tester => {
    grants => [ qw{
        connect
        resource
        plustrace
        select_catalog_role
        inventory_user }],

    revokes => ['unlimited tablespace'],

    quotas => { users => '10m', indx => '5m', },
},
```

Let's see what's going on here:

1. In addition to the standard database roles of CONNECT, RESOURCE, PLUS-TRACE, and SELECT_CATALOG_ROLE, the application-specific role of INVENTORY_USER is included.

2. Because RESOURCE was granted, UNLIMITED TABLESPACE is specified under *revokes*, ensuring its immediate removal from any new account.

3. Finally, any user created under *inventory_tester* will receive *quotas* of 10 and 5 megabytes on the USERS and INDX tablespaces, respectively.

To create a more limited production version of INVENTORY_TESTER, you can limit the *grants* to CREATE_SESSION and the database role INVENTORY_USER:

```
inventory_production => { grants => ['create session','inventory_user'}],
                         revokes => [],
                         quotas => {}, },
```

Tablespaces

When you are creating an account, it is good practice to specify a default tablespace for the user's object creation needs, and a temporary tablespace for disk sorts and related operations. Specifying tablespaces in this way avoids having the generic SYSTEM tablespace being assigned for both purposes (this also avoids point deductions by the Big DBA in the sky, who generally frowns upon disk sorts in the SYSTEM tablespace's data dictionary area and the potential for SYSTEM to run out of room).

Going back to Example 10-3, you'll notice that the DBA PDBA role has the following clearly specified *tablespaces*:

```
tablespaces => { default => 'tools', temporary => 'temp2', },
```

Every other account makes use of another special hash, *%tablespaces*:

```
%tablespaces = ( default => 'users', temporary => 'temp', );
```

This ensures that every new user created gets USERS and TEMP as its default tablespaces; this avoids having us clobber SYSTEM!

We can also override all these configured tablespaces, as we'll find out shortly.

create_user.pl

Now let's examine the *create_user.pl* script, which does the actual user account creation. The script's options are listed in Table 10-1.

Table 10-1. Command-line options - create_user.pl

Option	Description
-machine	Server where target database resides.
-database	Target database.
-username	DBA account that is creating the new account.
-password	DBA's account password (optional if password server used).
-new_username	New user account to be created.
-new_password	Password for new account. (Specifying a value of *generate* causes automatic password generation; see Example 10-2.)
-pdbarole	PDBA role to assign to the new account.
-default_tbs	Overrides the default tablespace value in *create_user.conf*.
-temp_tbs	Overrides the temporary tablespace value in *create_user.conf*.
-verbose	Outputs every user creation step to the screen.
-list_roles	Prints the list of available PDBA roles and privileges.

The password generation code for the *-new_password* switch is found in the *PDBA::DBA* module and is shown in Example 10-4. This code simply selects several characters of the alphabet, based on the current time value of seconds as returned by *SYSDATE* and a *MOD* value of *v$timer.hsecs*.

Example 10-4. Generating passwords in PDBA::DBA.pm

```
my $Alphabet = 'ABCDEFGHIJKLMNOPQRSTUVWXYZ';
my $PasswordGenSql = qq {select
    substr('$Alphabet',MOD(TO_CHAR(SYSDATE,'SS'),25)+1,1)||
    substr('$Alphabet',MOD(substr(mod(hsecs,99999999)+?,5,2),25)+1,1)||
    substr('$Alphabet',MOD(substr(mod(hsecs,99999999)+?,6,2),25)+1,1)||
    substr('$Alphabet',MOD(substr(mod(hsecs,99999999)+?,7,2),25)+1,1)||
    mod(hsecs,9999) as password
    from v\$timer
};
sub genPassword {
    my $newPassword;
    my $sthPasswordGen = $dbh->prepare( $PasswordGenSql );
    $sthPasswordGen->bind_columns( undef, \$newPassword );
    my $seed = (localtime(time))[0];
    use DBI qw{:sql_types};
    $sthPasswordGen->bind_param( 1, $seed, SQL_INTEGER );
    $sthPasswordGen->bind_param( 2, $seed, SQL_INTEGER );
    $sthPasswordGen->bind_param( 3, $seed, SQL_INTEGER );
    $sthPasswordGen->execute( );
    $sthPasswordGen->fetch( );
    return $newPassword;
}
```

This routine lacks true randomness but possesses sufficient uniqueness for the assignment of new account passwords. Users should, of course, be told to change these passwords upon receipt.

The *list_roles* switch reveals all of the roles, types, and privileges as follows:

```
$ create_user.pl -list_roles
ROLE: app_clerk
    TYPE: grants
        PRIV: create session
        PRIV: hr_clerk
    TYPE: quotas
    TYPE: revokes
...
ROLE: dba
    TYPE: grants
        PRIV: connect
        PRIV: dba
    TYPE: quotas
    TYPE: revokes
    TYPE: tablespaces
        PRIV: default: tools
        PRIV: temporary: temp
```

The *-default_tbs* and *-temp_tbs* switches assign specific tablespaces by overriding *create_user.conf*. The following creates a new DBA user, *homer*, with default and temporary tablespaces of USERS and TEMP, respectively:

```
$ create_user.pl -machine sherlock -database ts01 \
    -username system -password manager \
```

```
-new_username homer -new_password doh \
-pdbarole dba -default_tbs users -temp_tbs temp
```

Creating a Single Account With dup_user.pl

At times, you may wish to simply duplicate a user account by copying all of the characteristics of one user to another user. However, the source account may come with a large number of directly granted privileges. Duplicating accounts like this is difficult; you will need to untangle all of the source account's privileges, no matter how twisted they've become. Moreover, you must log in as the owner of original objects and re-grant these privileges. In Figure 10-1 we've illustrated a new account's receiving direct privileges from the GL, AP, and HR accounts.

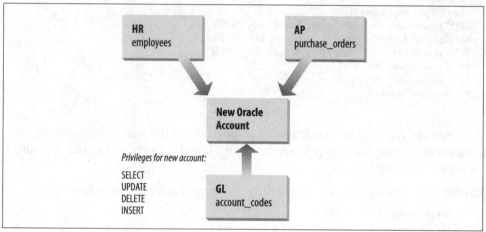

Figure 10-1. Multiple direct grants to a new account

If your new account name were *rowan*, here's what you'd need to do to assign the correct database privileges:

```
CONNECT HR/password
GRANT SELECT,UPDATE,INSERT,DELETE ON EMPLOYEES TO ROWAN;
CONNECT GL/password;
GRANT SELECT,UPDATE,INSERT,DELETE ON ACCOUNT_CODES TO ROWAN;
CONNECT AP/password;
GRANT SELECT,UPDATE,INSERT,DELETE ON PURCHASE_ORDERS TO ROWAN;
```

This may look fairly painless. However, if the source account has many such privileges, this process can become very complex. This inspired us to create the *dup_user. pl* script. It fully duplicates a complete Oracle user, including all roles, directly granted privileges, system privileges, default and temporary tablespace assignments, and tablespace quotas. Its options are summarized in Table 10-2.

Table 10-2. Command-line options—dup_user.pl

Option	Description
-machine	Server where the target database resides.
-database	Target database.
-username	DBA account.
-password	DBA account password (optional if password server in use.)
-source_username	Account to duplicate.
-new_username	User account to create.
-nosystemprivs	Avoids assigning source system privileges to target.
-systemprivs	Assigns source system privileges to target (the default).
-noobjectprivs	Avoids assigning source object privileges to target.
-objectprivs	Assigns source object privileges to target (the default).
-noroles	Avoids assigning source roles to target.
-roles	Assigns source roles to target (the default).

We'll demonstrate the use of *dup_user.pl* on our test database by creating a duplicate of *scott* who has been granted a few extra privileges:

```
SELECT GRANTEE, 'ROLE' PRIVTYPE, GRANTED_ROLE PRIVNAME,
       NULL OWNER, NULL TABLE_NAME
  FROM DBA_ROLE_PRIVS
 WHERE GRANTEE = 'SCOTT'
 UNION
SELECT GRANTEE, 'SYSPRIV' PRIVTYPE, PRIVILEGE PRIVNAME,
       NULL OWNER, NULL TABLE_NAME
  FROM DBA_SYS_PRIVS
 WHERE GRANTEE = 'SCOTT'
 UNION
SELECT GRANTEE, 'TABPRIV' PRIVTYPE, PRIVILEGE PRIVNAME,
       OWNER, TABLE_NAME
  FROM DBA_TAB_PRIVS
 WHERE GRANTEE - 'SCOTT'
 ORDER BY 1, 2, 3, 4, 5;


           PRIV
GRANTEE    TYPE    PRIV NAME              OWNER       TABLE NAME
---------- ------- --------------------- ----------- --------------------
SCOTT      ROLE    CONNECT
                   RESOURCE
                   SELECT_CATALOG_ROLE
           SYSPRIV CREATE SESSION
                   CREATE TRIGGER
           TABPRIV DELETE                 JKSTILL     LCL_1
                   EXECUTE                JKSTILL     TRUNCATE_TEST_NAMES
                   SELECT                 JKSTILL     LCL_1
                   UPDATE                 JKSTILL     LCL_1
```

We'll use *dup_user.pl* to create SCOTT_DUP, a duplicated clone of SCOTT. Note the following:

1. The script must log in to the test database as JKSTILL, and grant privileges on the LCL_1 table and TRUNCATE_TEST_NAMES procedure.

2. For this to work, the Password server (see the discussion in Chapter 9) must be running and configured with passwords from accounts holding necessary privileges.

3. JKSTILL's password on the *ts01* database is also required.

Here's the command line needed to create the duplicate account:

```
$ dup_user.pl -machine sherlock -database ts01 -username jkstill \
    -source_username scott -new_username scott_dup
```

The data dictionary confirms SCOTT_DUP's creation, with SCOTT's privileges:

```
PRIV
GRANTEE     TYPE     PRIV NAME            OWNER       TABLE NAME
----------  -------  -------------------  ----------  -------------------
SCOTT_DUP   ROLE     CONNECT
                     RESOURCE
                     SELECT_CATALOG_ROLE
            SYSPRIV  CREATE SESSION
                     CREATE TRIGGER
            TABPRIV  DELETE               JKSTILL     LCL_1
                     EXECUTE              JKSTILL     TRUNCATE_TEST_NAMES
                     SELECT               JKSTILL     LCL_1
                     UPDATE               JKSTILL     LCL_1
```

Creating Multiple Accounts with mucr8.pl

Most requests for new accounts come one at a time. However, you may occasionally have to deal with the need to create a large number of new accounts all at once. For example, you may be asked to migrate an existing application to Oracle or to install a new company-wide application. Whatever the reason, creating hundreds of new users can be a heavy piece of work, and it's essential to create an accurate list of all the new account names. This will be our starting point in this section. But entering many account names by hand is a time-consuming and potentially error-prone process. So let's first try to obtain the list, with permission, from such places as:

- The project manager of the company-wide application.

- The company personnel records (although it's often rightly difficult to obtain this sensitive information).

The information we'll need is the following:

The account name
The user's email address

The user's first name (optional)

The user's last name (optional)

The essential elements are the account name and the email address, though the first and last names are useful for constructing account names if specific account names remain unavailable. Once we have the list, we could employ single-user creation tools executed inside a Unix *for* loop.

However, our cross-platform *mucr8.pl* (Multi User Create) toolkit script provides functionality well beyond this. Here's what we do:

1. We'll start by getting a copy of the *mucr8.conf* file and placing it into your PDBA_HOME directory (you may have already done this in Chapter 9). (We also need the *create_user.conf* configuration file that was configured earlier in this chapter in the "Creating A Single Account" section.)

2. On Unix, copy configuration files from the PDBA installation directory:

   ```
   $ cp /u01/build/PDBA-1.00/routine_tasks/mucr8.conf $PDBA_HOME
   ```

   On Win32, type:

   ```
   DOS> copy C:\Perl\site\lib\PDBA\conf\mucr8.conf C:\PDBA
   ```

3. Now open up *mucr8.conf* within a text editor, as shown in Example 10-5.

Example 10-5. mucr8.conf

```
package mucr8;

use PDBA;
use vars qw( %conf %tags ) ;

%conf = (
   messageFile => PDBA->pdbaHome . '/mucr8.msg',
   fieldSeparator => ':',
   usernamePosition => 0,
   emailAddressPosition => 1
);

%tags = (
   '<<APPLICATION>>' => '$optctl{application}', # Used later,
   '<<DATABASE>>' => '$optctl{database}',       # in messages!  :-)
   '<<USERNAME>>' => '$newUsername',
   '<<PASSWORD>>' => '$newUser->{PASSWORD}'
);
1;
```

The *%conf* hash sets up script controls, and *%tags* personalizes the email messages sent to each new account. There are four keys in *%conf*:

messageFile

    Points to the message file emailed to users. This file contains tags used as placeholders for runtime data, which we'll discuss shortly.

fieldSeparator

Separates fields in the list file data used by *mucr8.pl*.

usernamePosition, emailAddressPosition

Numeric positions of data within the text record; for example:

```
rogerwil:rogerw@yourdomain.com:Wilco:Roger
```

The *rogerwil* username is held in field 0, the email address in field 1.

mucr8.msg

The *mucr7.msg* file contains the text that will be automatically emailed to the owners of new Oracle accounts. It makes use of << >> tags to customize the message, as we'll explain shortly.

On Unix, copy the *mucr8.msg* file from the directory from which PDBA was installed:

```
$ cp /u01/build/PDBA-1.00/routine_tasks/mucr8.msg $PDBA_HOME
```

On Win32, the copy operation is very similar:

```
DOS> copy C:\Perl\site\lib\PDBA\conf\mucr8.msg C:\PDBA
```

Take a look at *mucr8.msg* in Example 10-6.

Example 10-6. mucr8.msg

```
An account has been created for you on one of the company Oracle databases in support of
the following application:

Application: <<APPLICATION>>

The information you need to logon to this database is as follows:

Username   : <<USERNAME>>
Password   : <<PASSWORD>>
Database   : <<DATABASE>>

If you are unsure why you received this email or are having difficulty, please contact the
Help Desk at 555-346-2852.

Thank You,
Your DBA Team
```

At runtime, the *mucr8.pl* script replaces the <<*>> tags with the attributes assigned in *mucr8.conf* within the *%tags* hash (shown in Example 10-5). These replace the corresponding tag values found in *mucr8.msg*. The following cut-down code from *mucr8.pl* accomplishes this:

```
open(MSG,"< mucr8.msg")  # Open the email message file.

my @mailMsg = <MSG>;       # Slurp the message file into @mailMsg array.
close MSG;
```

```
# Create a scalar variable, $msg, made up of all elements from the
# @mailMsg array, slurped in earlier.

my $msg = join('',@mailMsg);
# Loop through all tags defined in the %tags hash, found in mucr8.conf.
foreach my $tag ( keys %mucr8::tags ) {

    # For each tag from %tags, replace the tag found in the message
    # file with the value specified from %tags.

    eval '$msg =~ ' . "s/$tag/" . (eval $mucr8::tags{$tag}) . "/gm" ;
}
```

If the tag found in *mucr8.msg* is <<USERNAME>>, it's replaced by the variable *$newUsername* from the *mucr8.pl* script, and so on. Any of the attributes associated with a new user object may also be used as replacement text message values. Here are some you may find useful:

Scalars

> OBJECT
>> Name of the created user.
>
> PASSWORD
>> Scalar containing the password assigned.
>
> DEFAULT_TABLESPACE
>> Default tablespace.
>
> TEMPORARY_TABLESPACE
>> Corresponding temporary tablespace.
>
> PROFILE
>> Assigned profile, if any.

Array references

> PRIVS
>> Reference to an array of privileges granted.
>
> REVOKES
>> Reference to an array of privileges revoked.

Hash references

> QUOTAS
>> Hash reference to the account quotas.

You add the scalars to the *mucr8.conf* like this:

```
'<<DEFAULT_TBS>>' => '$newUser->{DEFAULT_TABLESPACE}',
```

The following array reference lists privileges in the *mucr8.conf* file:

```
'<<PRIVS>' => q{join(',' @{$newUser->{PRIVS}})},
```

The following hash reference fills the *<<QUOTAS>>* key in any message:

```
'<<QUOTAS>>' =>
    q{join(',',map { $_ . ' => ' . $newUser->{QUOTAS}{$_}}
    keys %{$newUser->{QUOTAS}})},
```

The variable information from an example email using *<<PRIVS>>* and *<<QUOTAS>>* might look like this:

```
...
Application: ACCT and HR

The information you need to log on to this database is as follows:

Username    : brubble
Password    : KAEE7858
Database    : ts01

Grants      : connect,resource,plustrace,javauserpriv,javadebugpriv,select_catalog_
role
Quotas      : indx => 5m,users => unlimited
...
```

Running mucr8.pl

Creating actual database accounts in a test database may make our discussion easier to understand, so let's try out the *mucr8.pl* script. Create a file called *myusers.txt* with the following lines:

```
brubble,<your email address here>
fflintstone, <your email address here>
```

(Change the email addresses to some valid and observable test values.) Table 10-3 summarizes the *muc8.pl* command-line options.

Table 10-3. Command-line options—mucr8.pl

Option	Description
-machine	Server where the target database resides.
-database	Target database.
-username	DBA account.
-password	DBA password (optional if Password server in use).
-filename	File name containing the new account information.
-application	Informational only; allows the use of this value within the email message file to specify the application.
-pdbarole	Which PDBA role to assign to the new account.
-default_tbs	Overrides default tablespace.
-temp_tbs	Overrides temporary tablespace.
-verbose	Outputs all of the user creation steps to the screen.
-message_file	Name of the email message file sent to new account owners. This overrides the file name in *mucr8.conf*.

Table 10-3. Command-line options—mucr8.pl (continued)

Option	Description
-logfile	Log of operations. Defaults to *mucr8.log*.
-field_separator	Field separator for list file. Overrides *mucr8.conf* value.
-mail_password	Causes *mucr8.pl* to email account information to users.
-dryrun	Prints an operational dry run. Logging is turned off, email is unsent, and the new accounts remain untouched.

Account creation dry run

We'll try the new *-dryrun* option in our first example. Example 10-7 shows a dry run for our friends Barney Rubble and Fred Flintstone.

Example 10-7. A mucr8.pl dry run

```
mucr8.pl -machine sherlock -database ts01 -username jkstill \
  -filename myusers.txt -pdbarole developer -verbose \
  -application 'ACCT and HR' \
  -dryrun

dry run only

default tablespace: users
temp    tablespace: temp
grants:  connect resource plustrace javauserpriv javadebugpriv
 select_catalog_role
  indx:  5m
  users:  unlimited

user: fflintstone           email: fred.flintstone@yourdomain.com
user: brubble               email: barney.rubble@yourdomain.com
```

Here's what's going on in Example 10-7:

1. Because the *-dryrun* option was specified, account creation failed to take place. Only a report of the future task is shown on the screen.

2. Next, having checked the output, we actually create the accounts:

   ```
   $ mucr8.pl -machine sherlock -database ts01 -username jkstill \
     -filename myusers.txt -pdbarole developer -verbose \
     -application 'ACCT and HR'
   user: brubble               password: KAEE7858
   user: fflintstone           password: KBPF7869
   ```

3. As you can see, the only output when creating accounts for real includes the username and password. You may wish to record these, even though the passwords have been mailed to the user. They're also recorded in *mucr8.log*, so make sure that this file is secure or simply delete it afterwards.

If you run a test with PDBA role DEVELOPER, you may encounter errors against databases with some Java components missing. If so, use the CONNECT PDBA role, which has minimal privileges; it should work on most databases.

Dropping Oracle Accounts

You can drop most user accounts easily using Oracle's SQL*Plus, as in the following example:

```
SQL> DROP USER username CASCADE;
```

However, account removal can become complex. When an Oracle account owns a large number of objects, removing that account with DROP USER can cause a great deal of recursive data dictionary SQL. This can be a major resource drain, and take excessive time to complete. To avoid this situation, some DBAs drop all account tables before executing DROP USER *username* CASCADE. In the toolkit, we've provided a Perl script that allows you to do this automatically—*drop_user.pl*. Table 10-4 summarizes the command-line options for this script.

Table 10-4. Command-line options—drop_user.pl

Option	Description
-machine	Server where the target database resides.
-database	Target database.
-username	DBA account.
-password	DBA password (optional if password server in use).
-drop_username	Name of the user to drop.
-force	Drops user without verification (the default is to ask).

The *drop_user.pl* script allows you to change your mind; before actually dropping the user, it will ask you to verify that you really do want to drop that user. In the following example we use *drop_user.pl* to erase the newly created account for Barney Rubble:

```
$ drop_user.pl -machine sherlock -database ts01 -username system \
    -drop_username brubble

dropping user 'brubble'

Really drop user brubble?: Y/N: y
user brubble successfully dropped
```

Because the *-force* option was not specified, *drop_user.pl* required verification. Any response starting without Y (or y) results in *drop_user.pl* exiting without dropping the account.

Maintaining Indexes

Indexes on tables are required in any database to help enforce integrity constraints and, more importantly, to increase database performance. If you don't maintain your indexes, there will be a measurable and noticeable effect on performance. In this section we'll provide some index maintenance scripts aimed at helping Oracle DBAs keep their databases running efficiently.

Looking at Oracle Space Problems

When table space is freed due to DML deletes or updates within previously full index blocks, Oracle ordinarily fails to reuse this space except under special circumstances. Oracle reuses such an index block only when it becomes completely empty, and this situation naturally leads to *b*-tree* index fragmentation. If unattended, indexes eventually become like Tom and Jerry's favorite snack—except Swiss cheese is supposed to be full of holes. An exaggerated example using *index_frag_test.sql* illustrates the point.

On Unix, you'll find this script in the PDBA installation directory:

```
$ ls /u01/build/PDBA-1.00/routine_tasks/index_frag_test.sql
```

On Win32, type:

```
DOS> type C:\Perl\site\lib\PDBA\sql\index_frag_test.sql
```

This test script is shown in Example 10-8.

Example 10-8. index_frag_test.sql

```
DROP TABLE IDX_FRAGMENT;
PROMPT creating test table IDX_FRAGMENT
CREATE TABLE IDX_FRAGMENT (PK NUMBER NOT NULL, TESTDATA VARCHAR2(2000));

PROMPT inserting test data into IDX_FRAGMENT
DECLARE
    Maxcount CONSTANT INTEGER := 1000;
    Insert_Str VARCHAR2(2000);
BEGIN
    Insert_Str := RPAD('X',1000,'X');
    FOR N IN 1 .. maxcount
    LOOP
        INSERT INTO IDX_FRAGMENT(PK,TESTDATA )
        VALUES(N, Insert_Str);
    END LOOP;
    COMMIT;
END;
/
PROMPT creating primary key IDX_FRAGMENT_PK
ALTER TABLE IDX_FRAGMENT ADD CONSTRAINT IDX_FRAGMENT_PK PRIMARY KEY(PK);

PROMPT creating index IDX_FRAGMENT_IDX
```

Example 10-8. index_frag_test.sql (continued)

```
CREATE INDEX IDX_FRAGMENT_IDX ON IDX_FRAGMENT(TESTDATA, PK) PCTFREE O;

COL SEGMENT_NAME FORMAT A30 HEAD 'SEGMENT NAME'
COL EXTENT_ID FORMAT A10 HEAD 'EXTENT ID'
COL BYTES FORMAT 999,999,999 HEAD 'BYTES'
COMPUTE SUM OF BYTES ON REPORT
BREAK ON REPORT


-- show number of extents, and then number of rows in table
SELECT SEGMENT_NAME, DECODE(EXTENT_ID,0,'0',TO_CHAR(EXTENT_ID)) EXTENT_ID,
       BYTES
  FROM DBA_EXTENTS
 WHERE OWNER = USER
   AND SEGMENT_NAME = 'IDX_FRAGMENT_IDX'
 ORDER BY TABLESPACE_NAME, SEGMENT_TYPE, SEGMENT_NAME;

SELECT COUNT(*) IDX_FRAGMENT_ROW_COUNT FROM IDX_FRAGMENT;

PROMPT delete every 5th row from the table and reinsert it
DECLARE
    Maxcount CONSTANT INTEGER := 1000;
    insert_str VARCHAR2(2000);
BEGIN
    insert_str := RPAD('X',1000,'X');
    FOR N IN 1 .. Maxcount
    LOOP
       -- DELETE EVERY 5TH ROW
       IF MOD(N,5) = 0 THEN
          -- DELETE THE ROW
          DELETE FROM IDX_FRAGMENT WHERE PK = N;
          -- PUT IT BACK
          INSERT INTO IDX_FRAGMENT(PK,TESTDATA )
          VALUES(N, Insert_Str);
       END IF;
    END LOOP;
    COMMIT;
END;
/
SELECT SEGMENT_NAME, DECODE(EXTENT_ID,0,'0',TO_CHAR(EXTENT_ID)) EXTENT_ID,
       BYTES
  FROM DBA_EXTENTS
 WHERE OWNER = USER
   AND SEGMENT_NAME = 'IDX_FRAGMENT_IDX'
 ORDER BY TABLESPACE_NAME, SEGMENT_TYPE, SEGMENT_NAME;

SELECT COUNT(*) IDX_FRAGMENT_ROW_COUNT FROM IDX_FRAGMENT;
```

In a nutshell, *index_frag_test.sql* creates a two-column table with 1000 rows, each row averaging 1002 bytes. We're going to fragment this index to make our point.

Both columns help create an IDX_FRAGMENT_IDX index, creating 12.6 rows per index block on our 8K block database. Let's take a look at the output. We'll pick up the important lines afterwards:

```
01:  creating test table IDX_FRAGMENT
02:  inserting test data into IDX_FRAGMENT
03:  creating primary key IDX_FRAGMENT_PK
04:  creating index IDX_FRAGMENT_IDX
05:
06:  Index created.
07:
08:  SEGMENT NAME                  EXTENT ID        BYTES
09:  ----------------------------  ----------  ------------
10:  IDX_FRAGMENT_IDX                  0            131,072
11:  IDX_FRAGMENT_IDX                  1            131,072
12:  IDX_FRAGMENT_IDX                  2            131,072
13:  IDX_FRAGMENT_IDX                  3            131,072
14:  IDX_FRAGMENT_IDX                  4            131,072
15:  IDX_FRAGMENT_IDX                  5            131,072
16:  IDX_FRAGMENT_IDX                  6            131,072
17:  IDX_FRAGMENT_IDX                  7            131,072
18:  IDX_FRAGMENT_IDX                  8            131,072
19:  IDX_FRAGMENT_IDX                  9            131,072
20:  IDX_FRAGMENT_IDX                 10            131,072
21:                                             ------------
22:  sum                                         1,441,792
23:
24:  11 rows selected.
25:
26:  IDX_FRAGMENT_ROW_COUNT
27:  ----------------------
28:                    1000
29:  1 row selected.
30:
31:  delete every 5th row from the table and reinsert it
32:
33:  PL/SQL procedure successfully completed.
34:
35:  SEGMENT NAME                  EXTENT ID        BYTES
36:  ----------------------------  ----------  ------------
37:  IDX_FRAGMENT_IDX                  0            131,072
38:  IDX_FRAGMENT_IDX                  1            131,072
39:  IDX_FRAGMENT_IDX                  2            131,072
40:  IDX_FRAGMENT_IDX                  3            131,072
41:  IDX_FRAGMENT_IDX                  4            131,072
42:  IDX_FRAGMENT_IDX                  5            131,072
43:  IDX_FRAGMENT_IDX                  6            131,072
44:  IDX_FRAGMENT_IDX                  7            131,072
45:  IDX_FRAGMENT_IDX                  8            131,072
46:  IDX_FRAGMENT_IDX                  9            131,072
47:  IDX_FRAGMENT_IDX                 10            131,072
48:  IDX_FRAGMENT_IDX                 11            131,072
49:  IDX_FRAGMENT_IDX                 12            131,072
```

```
50:   IDX_FRAGMENT_IDX            13                131,072
51:   IDX_FRAGMENT_IDX            14                131,072
52:   IDX_FRAGMENT_IDX            15                131,072
53:   IDX_FRAGMENT_IDX            16                131,072
54:   IDX_FRAGMENT_IDX            17                131,072
55:   IDX_FRAGMENT_IDX            18                131,072
56:   IDX_FRAGMENT_IDX            19                131,072
57:   IDX_FRAGMENT_IDX            20                131,072
58:   IDX_FRAGMENT_IDX            21                131,072
59:   IDX_FRAGMENT_IDX            22                131,072
60:                                             ------------
61:   sum                                        3,014,656
62:
63:   23 rows selected.
```

Viewing the code output shows that:

- At line 24, IDX_FRAGMENT_IDX gets created with a total of eleven 128K extents.

- At line 31, a procedure deletes every fifth table row before immediately reinserting it. The index impact can be seen at line 63. Even though the index is still pointing to the same 1000 rows, it now requires more than twice as much space to do so; 3,014,656 bytes.

- If this were a million-row index, the additional space required would cause many more index buffer gets and disk reads. The holes in the index would have a noticeable impact on performance.

The *idxr.pl* script described in the next section will help you maintain your indexes for peak performance.

Rebuilding Indexes with idxr.pl

To assist you in rebuilding an index and improving the efficiency of index operations, we've included the script *idxr.pl* in the toolkit. This script uses Oracle's ALTER INDEX REBUILD statement. Some of its features include:

Compute index statistics
    You can generate statistics for the index at the time of the rebuild.

Control over length of runtime
    You can specify a limited runtime. The script runs within a maintenance window, rebuilding as many indexes as possible in that time frame.

Incremental index rebuilds
    Based on LAST_ANALYZED dates, and runtime windows, you control how many *idxr.pl* executions are necessary to completely rebuild indexes.

Index optimal height calculation
    The optimal index height is calculated from index statistics. If the actual height is greater than the calculated value, the index will be rebuilt.

Percent of deleted rows threshold

A threshold based on the percentage of deleted rows in the index can be used to force the index to be rebuilt.

The *idxr.conf* configurationfile contains only a few parameters, as shown in Example 10-9.

Example 10-9. idxr.conf

```
package idxr;

use PDBA;
use vars qw{ %config };

%config = (
    # don't check indexes that have been analyzed more recently
    # than a specified number of days. The reason for this is
    # that large systems may have many thousands of indexes, more
    # than can be done in a single pass.  It may take several passes
    # if you have an hour each night to run this, and it takes 20
    # hours to validate structure, rebuild and analyze your indexes,
    # you would set mostRecentlyAnalyzed to 20 and maxRunTime to 60

    # specifify maxRunTime in minutes
    maxRunTime => 60,
    # don't check indexes that have
    # been analyzed more recently than
    # mostRecentlyAnalyzed, expressed in days
    mostRecentlyAnalyzed => 0,
    # rebuild the index if percent of deleted
    # rows is greater than this
    pctDeletedThreshold => 10,
    logFile => PDBA->pdbaHome . q{/logs/idxr.log},
);
1;
```

Three parameters determine the runtime characteristics of the script, and one locates the log file:

maxRunTime

Time in minutes that *idxr.pl* is allowed to run. This time won't be exact, because it is rechecked after each index rebuild. If 60 minutes are set, and a rebuild requiring 10 minutes starts at 58 minutes, the script exits at 68 minutes.

mostRecentlyAnalyzed

This parameter determines how old an index must be before it will be considered for rebuilding. If this parameter is set to 3, and the script is set to run on a Sunday, indexes analyzed more recently than the previous Thursday will be ignored. Suppose that:

- You have 500 indexes, and it takes 20 hours to rebuild them all.
- You have a one-hour maintenance window each evening.

With these constraints in mind, you set *mostRecentlyAnalyzed* to 20 and *maxRunTime* to 60. All of your indexes will be gradually rebuilt over a 20-day period.

logFile

Sets the location of the output log file.

pctDeletedThreshold

If the deleted row percentage in the index exceeds the value of this parameter, the index is rebuilt.

Fragmentation

The *idxr.pl* script also determines whether the height of the *b*-tree* index has exceeded its optimal value. We've ignored the standard formulas for this value and adapted our SQL from a popular paper on Oracle fragmentation.[*] The relevant portion of *idxr.pl* is reproduced in Example 10-10. The script's command-line options are summarized in Table 10-5.

Example 10-10. Determining optimal b*-tree height

```
sub getStat {
  my ($self, $dbh) = @_;

  my $statSql = q{
    SELECT
        NAME INDEX_NAME
      , DECODE (
          SIGN(
            CEIL(
              LOG(
                BR_BLK_LEN/(BR_ROWS_LEN/BR_ROWS),
                LF_BLK_LEN/((LF_ROWS_LEN - DEL_LF_ROWS_LEN)
                /(LF_ROWS - DEL_LF_ROWS))
              )
            ) + 1 - HEIGHT
          )
          , -1, 'YES'
          , 'NO'
        ) CAN_REDUCE_LEVEL
        ,DEL_LF_ROWS*100/DECODE(LF_ROWS, 0, 1, LF_ROWS) PCT_DELETED
      FROM INDEX_STATS
      WHERE LF_ROWS <> 0
      AND DEL_LF_ROWS <> 0
      AND DEL_LF_ROWS_LEN <> 0
      AND LF_ROWS_LEN <> 0
      AND BR_ROWS <> 0
      AND BR_ROWS_LEN <> 0
```

---

[*] See "How To Stop Defragmenting and Start Living: The Definitive Word On Fragmentation" by Bhaskar Himatsingka and Juan Loaiza at *http://www.oreilly.com/catalog/oressentials/chapter/defrag.pdf*

Example 10-10. Determining optimal b*-tree height (continued)

```
    };
    my $statSth = $dbh->prepare($statSql);
    $statSth->execute;
    my $row = $statSth->fetchrow_hashref;

    return $row ? $row : undef;
}
```

Here are the steps that determine whether an index should be rebuilt:

- Run ANALYZE INDEX VALIDATE STRUCTURE for each index. (If you have index partitions and subpartitions, these will be analyzed too.)
- Retrieve ANALYZE figures from the INDEX_STATS system view.
- If the CAN_REDUCE_LEVEL row from the *getStat* method is YES, or the deleted rows percentage exceeds *pctDeleteThreshold*, then rebuild.
- If *-compute_statistics* was specified, then rebuild and compute statistics.

Table 10-5. Command-line options—idxr.pl

Option	Description
-machine	Server where the target database resides.
-database	Target database.
-username	DBA account.
-password	DBA password (optional if Password server in use).
-conf	Configuration file. This defaults to *idxr.conf*.
-target_schema	Target schema on which to rebuild indexes.
-compute_statistics	Compute statistics when rebuilding index. (Adds very little overhead.)

Testing idxr.pl

We'll demonstrate the use of *idxr.pl* with the following test:

1. A single-column test table HASH_TEST is created with a HASH PARTI-TIONED index of HASH_TEST_PK.

2. We insert 100,000 table rows and then immediately delete 20,000 of them.

3. For our test we set the *mostRecentlyAnalyzed* parameter in *idxr.conf* to 0. This will cause *idxr.pl* to consider all indexes as candidates for rebuilding regardless of age. We also set the *pctDeletedThreshold* parameter in *idxr.conf* to 10 so that candidate indexes with more than 10% deleted rows will be rebuilt.

4. Because this deletion exceeds the deleted rows percentage of 10% in the index hash partition, the index partitions should all be rebuilt:

   ```
   $ idxr.pl -machine sherlock -database ts01 \
       -username system -target_schema jkstill
   ```

All the output from *idxr.pl* is directed to a log file, so nothing should appear on the screen while it's running. The results of the test are seen here:

```
20020217105027:starting
20020217105027:maxRunSeconds:3600
20020217105027:sysDate:2002/02/17 10:50
20020217105027:globalName:TS01.JKS.COM
20020217105027:schema:JKSTILL
20020217105027:checking indexes analyzed more than 0 days ago
20020217105028:checking INDEX CHILD_PK_IDX
20020217105028:checking INDEX DM_UNQ
20020217105028:checking INDEX IDX_FRAGMENT_IDX
...
20020217105030:checking INDEX PARTITION HASH_TEST_P1
20020217105032:Rebuilding INDEX PARTITION HASH_TEST_P1
20020217105032:Attempting to Rebuild Index online
20020217105032:Rebuilt INDEX PARTITION HASH_TEST_P1 online
...
20020217105035:checking INDEX PARTITION HASH_TEST_P8
20020217105035:Rebuilding INDEX PARTITION HASH_TEST_P8
20020217105035:Attempting to Rebuild Index online
20020217105036:Rebuilt INDEX PARTITION HASH_TEST_P8 online
20020217105036:exiting
```

Because we specified that all indexes of any age having more than 10% deleted rows should be rebuilt, all of the indexes were rebuilt in this test.

Tracking

An internal *idxr.pl* feature tracks how long the script has been running. We've used a form of *closure* to determine when the maximum runtime is breached. In standard Perl terms, a closure is simply a subroutine reference that preserves the value of a lexically scoped variable between calls. In this case, it's simply an anonymous code block that accomplishes the same thing.

The closure is formed by curly braces *{}* on lines 10 and 29 of Example 10-11. The lexically scoped or *my* variables of *$maxRunSeconds* and *$startTimeSeconds* are enclosed within this block. When the *startTimer* method is called at line 1, it sets the value of *$maxRunSeconds*. Even when the *startTimer* method returns, the value of *$maxRunSeconds* is maintained because the code block containing it is never actually exited.

After each index is rebuilt, the *checkTimer* method at line 21 is used to determine if the maximum allowable runtime has been reached. If so, the number of actual seconds elapsed is returned; otherwise, zero is returned. If a nonzero value is returned by *checkTimer* at line 3, messages are logged indicating the actual runtime, and the index rebuild loop is exited via the *last* statement. The script then exits.

Example 10-11. Closure in idxr.pl

```
1 my $maxRunSeconds = idxrp->startTimer($idxr::config{maxRunTime});
2
3 if ( my $runSeconds = idxrp->checkTimer ) {
4     $logFh->printflush("Max seconds $maxRunSeconds reached\n");
5     $logFh->printflush("Actual runtime was $runSeconds seconds\n");
6     last;
7 }
8
9 {
10     my $maxRunSeconds = undef;
11     my $startTimeSeconds = time;
12
13     sub startTimer {
14         my ($self, $maxMinutes) = @_;
15         $maxRunSeconds = $idxr::config{maxRunTime} * 60;
16         $startTimeSeconds = time;
17         return $maxRunSeconds;
18     }
19
20     sub checkTimer {
21         my $self = shift;
22         my $currTimeSeconds = time;
23         my $runSeconds = $currTimeSeconds - $startTimeSeconds;
24         if ( $runSeconds >= $maxRunSeconds ) {
25             return $runSeconds;
26         } else { return 0 }
27     }
28 }
```

Killing Sniped Sessions

A sniped session occurs when a user has exceeded his idle time. The situation has been noted in the database, and the user's actual database session has been suspended. However, the user is still consuming a dedicated server resource that has not yet been allocated to someone else. This situation can have an adverse effect on overall database performance.

Limiting Resource Consumption

Oracle provides the ability to limit resource consumption via the user PROFILE, a collection of limits holding resource hogs in check. We've found that some of these limits are very useful, particularly IDLE_TIME. The IDLE_TIME limit disconnects user sessions if they remain unused for too long. When a session is disconnected in this manner, Oracle changes the status of the session to SNIPED in the V$SESSION system view. We've used this limit effectively—especially in data warehouse applications where a session may be consuming large swathes of memory even it is when idling.

Here's how you create a PROFILE called IDLE_LIMIT with an IDLE_TIME of 1 minute.* We'll assign it to *scott*:

```
SQL> create profile idle_limit limit idle_time 1;
SQL> alter user scott profile idle_limit;
```

This following displays all non-default profile parameters:

```
SELECT *
  FROM DBA_PROFILES
 WHERE PROFILE != 'DEFAULT'
   AND LIMIT != 'DEFAULT';


PROFILE     RESOURCE_NAME                        RESOURCE  LIMIT
----------  -----------------------------------  --------  ----------
IDLE_LIMIT  IDLE_TIME                            KERNEL    1

1 row selected.
```

This next example shows all users with nondefault profile assignments:

```
SELECT B.USERNAME, A.RESOURCE_NAME, A.LIMIT
  FROM DBA_PROFILES A, DBA_USERS B
 WHERE A.PROFILE = B.PROFILE
   AND A.PROFILE != 'DEFAULT'
   AND A.LIMIT != 'DEFAULT';


USERNAME    RESOURCE_NAME   LIMIT
----------  --------------- ----------------
SCOTT       IDLE_TIME       1
SCOTT_DUP   IDLE_TIME       1

2 rows selected.
```

When a session has been idle for longer than IDLE_TIME, Oracle changes the session status to SNIPED. The user typically notices this session suspension in the following way when he tries to run some more SQL commands, perhaps after a very long lunch break:

```
SQL> select USER from dual;
select USER from dual
*
ERROR at line 1:
ORA-02396: exceeded maximum idle time, please connect again
```

Even though the session has timed out, memory resources are still being consumed, as you can see in Example 10-12. The *ps -fp18471* command shows that the Oracle dedicated session server is still in place. The SQL used to select this information from the V$SESSION view is shown in Example 10-13.

---

* You can create an idle limit of 1 minute, but Oracle interprets it as 2 or 3 minutes, the lowest IDLE_TIME value it recognizes. The actual value depends upon the OS platform.

Example 10-12. Status of timed-out session in V$SESSION

```
13:24:31 SQL> /
                            SRVR
USERNAME SID SERIAL# STATUS    PID LOGON TIME       IDLE TIME
-------- --- ------- -------- ------ ----------------- -----------
SCOTT     16    1321 INACTIVE  18471 02/17/02 13:23:53 00:00:00:41

1 row selected.

13:24:33 SQL> /
                            SRVR
USERNAME SID SERIAL# STATUS    PID LOGON TIME       IDLE TIME
-------- --- ------- -------- ------ ----------------- -----------
SCOTT     16    1321 SNIPED    18471 02/17/02 13:23:53 00:00:02:10

1 row selected.

13:26:02 SQL> !ps -fp18471
UID      PID  PPID C STIME TTY    TIME CMD
oracle 18471 18470 0 13:23 ?  00:00:00 oraclets01 (DESCRIPTION=(LOCAL=YES)

13:26:11 SQL>
```

Example 10-13. Displaying status of sessions

```
SELECT S.USERNAME, S.SID, S.SERIAL#, S.STATUS,
       TO_CHAR(LOGON_TIME, 'MM/DD/YY HH24:MI:SS') LOGON_TIME,
       SUBSTR('0'||TRUNC(LAST_CALL_ET/86400),-2,2)  || ':' ||
       SUBSTR('0'||TRUNC(MOD(LAST_CALL_ET,86400)/3600),-2,2) || ':' ||
       SUBSTR('0'||TRUNC(MOD(MOD(LAST_CALL_ET,86400),3600)/60),-2,2)||
       ':' ||
       SUBSTR('0'||MOD(MOD(MOD(LAST_CALL_ET,86400),3600),60),-2,2)
       IDLE_TIME
  FROM V$SESSION S, V$PROCESS P
 WHERE S.USERNAME = 'SCOTT' AND P.ADDR(+) = S.PADDR
 ORDER BY USERNAME, SID;
```

Notice in Example 10-12 that this is a database using dedicated server processes. Avoid killing sniped sessions with the *kss.pl* script in a database using Oracle's Multi-Threaded Server (MTS), because in such situations the script will disconnect all sessions that are using the same MTS dispatcher.

On a busy database with frequently created sessions, lapsed memory resource consumption may be tolerable. Sniped sessions are reused by newly logged-in sessions, minimizing resource wastage. However, on databases with infrequently created sessions, snipes can remain with us for quite some time. We've seen this happen in data warehouses with plenty of memory wastage, so we decided to go snipe hunting*— and lo, the *kss.pl* (Kill Sniped Sessions) script was born.

---

* For information on snipe hunting, please see *http://www.snipehunter.com*.

To make use of Oracle PROFILE allocations, your database must have the following parameter set in the *INIT.ORA* file: RESOURCE_LIMIT = TRUE. Using a PROFILE will have no effect otherwise. This parameter can also be set at runtime with the command:

```
SQL> ALTER SYSTEM SET RESOURCE_LIMIT = TRUE;
```

When removing a session from Oracle, the ALTER SYSTEM KILL SESSION command is often sufficient. In the toolkit, we've taken it one step further, though, and we actually kill* the session's dedicated server process. We then use ALTER SYSTEM KILL SESSION if the session still exists with a status of KILLED.

So why the literal overkill? On numerous occasions over the years—and through several versions of Oracle—we've run into serious problems when killing sessions. Nearly every time, the standard method works just fine, but every once in a while it fails. The sessions may possess a status of KILLED, but they're never actually removed. When this happens, and the session is holding a vital table lock, it seems that nothing less than a plasma cannon† is sufficient to remove these poltergeist sessions (or a database bounce, but we'd rather avoid going there). We've seen this happen on every version of Oracle from 7.0.16 through to 8.1.6 and on both Unix and Win32. It's sporadic enough that we've never learned how to reproduce it, but regular enough so we've learned how to cope with it. We cope by killing the dedicated server process on Unix (or the thread on Win32). We've never experienced a hanging session using this method. Remember, though, that this method is inappropriate for Multi-Threaded Servers (MTS), where you would end up disconnecting a great many other sessions by killing the MTS dispatcher.

Enough rationale. Now it's time to set up *kss.pl* and run it. Because this script runs as a daemon on Unix and a service on Win32, we'll show you how to set it up for both.

Installing kss.pl on Unix

Installing this script on Unix systems is easy. Simply make sure the *kss.conf* file is in the right place. If it is still uninstalled, copy it in like this from the toolkit installation directory:

```
$ cp /u01/build/PDBA-1.00/routine_tasks/kss.conf $PDBA_HOME
```

That's it—we're done! Running the *kss.pl* daemon is equally simple. Here's the command we used on our Linux server; Table 10-6 summarizes the command-line options:

```
$ kss.pl -machine sherlock -database ts01 -username system
```

---

* On Unix, we kill the Oracle thread using *kill -9*. On Win32 we use *orakill*.

† For definitive information on plasma cannons, the following web site may be helpful: *http://www.schlockmercenary.com/d/20000829.html*

Without the password server (see Chapter 9), add the password argument:

```
$ kss.pl -machine sherlock -database ts01 -username system \
    -password manager
```

Table 10-6. Command-line options—kss.pl

Option	Description
-machine	Server where the target database resides
-database	Target database
-username	DBA account
-password	DBA password (optional if password server in use)

 The *kss.pl* script must run as the owner of the Oracle processes. This is necessary to enable the use of the *kill* command on dedicated Oracle server processes.

Installing kss_NT.pl on Win32

Follow these steps on Win32 systems:

1. Make sure that the *kss.conf* configuration file is installed in PDBA_HOME, as with the other configuration files described previously in this chapter.

2. Install *kss_NT.pl* as a Win32 service using *kss_service.pl*.

3. If you are using the password server (see Chapter 9), install *kss_NT.pl* like this:

   ```
   DOS> C:\Perl\site\lib\PDBA\util\kss_service.pl \
       -machine database_server -database database_name \
       -username DBA account
   ```

4. Without the password server, you need to include the relevant password:

   ```
   DOS> C:\Perl\site\lib\PDBA\util\kss_service.pl \
       -machine database_server -database database_name \
       -username DBA_account -password DBA_password
   ```

5. We used the following to install *kss_NT.pl* on our Windows 2000 server:

   ```
   DOS> C:\Perl\site\lib\PDBA\util\kss_service.pl \
       -machine mycroft -database ts20 -username system
   ```

6. To start the server you need to navigate to the *Services* administration application. The specifics will vary, depending on your Win32 platform:

   • Windows 2000: Click through *Start → Settings → Control Panel*, double-click on *Administrative Tools*, and double-click on *Services*. Scroll down to the *Oracle_SID_kss_monitor* service and highlight it. Click on *Action → Start* from the menu to start the service.

   • Windows NT: Click through *Start → Setting → Control Panel*, double-click on *Services*. Scroll down to *Oracle_SID_kss_monitor*, highlight it with the mouse, and click the *Start* button.

The service appears on Windows 2000, as shown in Figure 10-2.

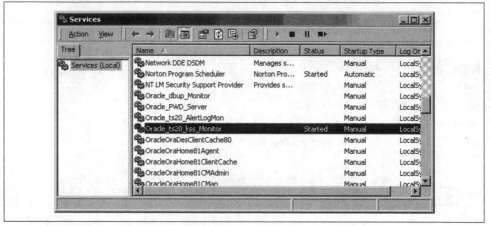

Figure 10-2. The kss service on Windows 2000

Configuring kss.pl

The configuration file for the *kss.pl* script requires little editing. The contents of *kss. conf* are shown in Example 10-14. Note the following about this example:

- The only parameter that should be edited is *sleepTime*. The default is 180, which is the number of seconds between each snipe check. Avoid setting it too low; if you do, the monitor will consume unnecessary resources, just as snipes do.

- The remaining parameters (*killSql*, *snipeSql* and *killCmd*) should stay as they are for the foreseeable future. They work fine for both Unix and Win32. (The *killCmd* parameter uses *PDBA->osname* to determine whether the Unix *kill* or Win32 *orakill* commands should be used. The others will only need changing if Oracle itself changes significantly.)

Example 10-14. kss.conf

```
package kss;

use PDBA;
use File::Spec;
use vars qw(%config);

%config = (
   sleepTime => 180,
   killSql => q(ALTER SYSTEM KILL SESSION '<<SID>>,<<SERIAL>>'),
   snipeSql => Q( SELECT S.USERNAME USERNAME, S.SID SID, S.STATUS STATUS,
                      S.SERIAL# SERIAL, P.SPID SPID
                  FROM V$SESSION S, V$PROCESS P
```

Example 10-14. kss.conf (continued)

```
                WHERE S.USERNAME IS NOT NULL
                AND P.ADDR(+) = S.PADDR
                AND S.STATUS = 'SNIPED'
                ORDER BY USERNAME, SID
   ),
   killCmd => PDBA->osname( ) eq 'unix'
      ? q(/bin/kill -9 <<PID>> >/dev/null 2>&1)
      : File::Spec->catfile( PDBA->oracleHome, 'bin','orakill')
        . q{ <<ORACLE_SID>> <<PID>> },
);
1;
```

After starting the *Oracle_ts20_kss_monitor* service, on Win32, we created an IDLE_ LIMIT profile with a one-minute threshold for IDLE_TIME. The profile was then assigned to *scott*. Example 10-15 shows the action taken by *kss_NT.pl* after *scott*'s session timed out. At marker *20020217184600* the thread for *scott*'s session is first killed with Oracle's *orakill* utility, then terminated with ALTER SYSTEM KILL SESSION.

Example 10-15. scott session cleaned up by kss_NT.pl

```
20020217184355:attempting to load Win32::Daemon
20020217184356:Service Starting - State is:
220020217184356:Service Started - State is: 4
20020217184356:password retrieved for user system
20020217184356:Service running
20020217184359:SCANNING
20020217184359:SLEEP: 30
20020217184429:Service running
20020217184430:SCANNING
20020217184430:SLEEP: 30
20020217184500:Service running
20020217184500:SCANNING
20020217184500:SLEEP: 30
20020217184530:Service running
20020217184530:SCANNING
20020217184530:SLEEP: 30
20020217184600:Service running
20020217184600:SCANNING
20020217184600:STATUS:SCOTT:8:9:1384
20020217184600:OSKILL:SCOTT:8:9:1384:D:\oracle\ora81\bin\orakill ts20 1384
20020217184600:DBKILL:SCOTT:8:9:1384:alter system kill session '8,9'
20020217184600:SLEEP: 30
20020217184630:Service running
20020217184630:SCANNING
20020217184630:SLEEP: 30
20020217184700:Service running
```

Managing Extent Usage

An *extent* in Oracle parlance is the size of the chunks of storage that are allocated to a table or index upon creation or when that table or index needs to be extended to accommodate more data. Extent management was always a problem in older versions of Oracle because it could never be precisely controlled.

With the advent of locally managed tablespaces (LMTs) in Oracle8*i*, Oracle has greatly simplified space management. LMTs allow DBAs to control the extent sizes allocated for tablespace objects, regardless of their STORAGE specifications. This eliminates the fragmentation that can occur in dictionary-managed tablespaces when objects are created with different extent sizes. Such fragmentation is impossible when LMTs are used. With LMTs, the extent size can be controlled so that all tablespace extents are the same size. In this section, we'll look at the benefits of LMTs and then see how the toolkit script *maxext.pl* can make this feature even more effective.

Locally Managed Tablespaces (LMTs)

If CREATE TABLE statements request an extent greater than the tablespace's uniform extent size, they receive multiple smaller extents, satisfying the total storage amount requested. This is illustrated in Example 10-16. There, a tablespace is created with locally managed extents of 128K. Even though the requested extent size for EMPTEST is 512K, the space is allocated in 128K chunks. USER_EXTENTS shows four allocated chunks of 128K each.

Example 10-16. Extent allocation in a locally managed tablespace

```
CREATE TABLESPACE USERS DATAFILE '/u01/oradata/ts01/users.dbf' SIZE 20M
EXTENT MANAGEMENT LOCAL UNIFORM SIZE 128K;

CREATE TABLE EMPTEST ( FNAME VARCHAR2(20), LNAME VARCHAR2(20) )
TABLESPACE USERS STORAGE( INITIAL 512K NEXT 512K );

BREAK ON TABLESPACE_NAME SKIP 1 ON SEGMENT_TYPE SKIP 1 ON SEGMENT_NAME SKIP 1 ON REPORT
COMPUTE SUM OF BYTES ON REPORT

SELECT TABLESPACE_NAME, SEGMENT_TYPE, SEGMENT_NAME,
       DECODE(EXTENT_ID,0,'0',TO_CHAR(EXTENT_ID)) EXTENT_ID, BYTES
  FROM USER_EXTENTS
 WHERE SEGMENT_NAME = 'EMPTEST'
 ORDER BY TABLESPACE_NAME, SEGMENT_TYPE,
         SEGMENT_NAME, TO_NUMBER(EXTENT_ID);

TABLESPACE TYPE   NAME       ID    BYTES
---------- ------ ---------- --   ------------
USERS      TABLE  EMPTEST    0       131,072
                             1       131,072
                             2       131,072
```

Example 10-16. Extent allocation in a locally managed tablespace (continued)

```
                               3        131,072
********** ****** **********        ------------
sum                                   524,288
4 rows selected.
```

Even though fragmentation is eliminated, storage still needs monitoring. In Example 10-16 a table is created, with four empty extents. If no more tablespace extents are available, does this require an increase in tablespace size?

Increasing tablespace size may be unnecessary. Even if your table sits within a full tablespace, the table itself contains no data. If you could determine whether all tablespace objects have a sufficient number of unused blocks to satisfy application data needs for six months, for example, there would be no immediate need to increase tablespace size. To figure this out, we will need to check the individual objects to determine if their free space is sufficient. The statistics of interest in determining if an object will soon need more space are the following:

EXTENTS
Total number of extents allocated for an object.

FREE_BLOCKS
Number of blocks on the freelist. Either these blocks are filled below the PCT-FREE threshold, or the space used has fallen below the PCTUSED threshold after having been above PCTFREE at some point. Free blocks also include UNUSED_BLOCKS, discussed next.

UNUSED_BLOCKS
Number of blocks allocated to an object which have never contained any data. All unused blocks are also FREE_BLOCKS.

MAX_EXTENTS
Maximum number of extents an object may be allocated.

MAX_BYTES_FREE
Largest chunk of free space in the object's allocation.

NEXT_EXTENT
Size of the next extent for the object.

TOTAL_BLOCKS
Total number of database blocks consumed by an object.

Examining Object Space with maxext.pl

The *maxext.pl* script in our toolkit determines if an object may be running out of space. It follows the steps illustrated in Figure 10-3 and listed here:

- It checks to see if there are any more segments in DBA_SEGMENTS.

- If so, it checks to see if the current segment is nearing its maximum number of extents or will be unable to extend .
- If either of the previous conditions is true, it checks the number of UNUSED_BLOCKS with DBMS_SPACE.UNUSED_SPACE.
- It sends a warning to the DBA if UNUSED_BLOCKS is below the threshold.

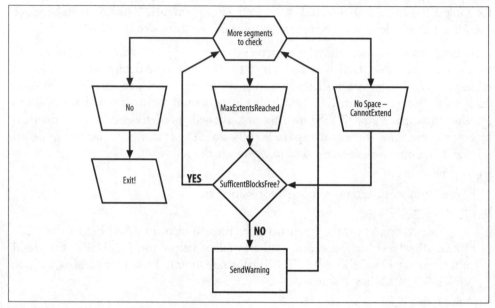

Figure 10-3. Flowchart of maxext.pl operations

In *maxext.pl* we rely upon UNUSED_BLOCKS, rather than FREE_BLOCKS, because the amount of space available in a used freelist block is unknown. It can be calculated, but we prefer to rely on the ratio of UNUSED_BLOCKS / TOTAL_BLOCKS to determine if a tablespace or tablespace object needs space attention. Before running *maxext.pl*, make sure that you have a copy of the *maxext.conf* file stored in *PDBA_HOME*, as for the other configuration files described earlier in this chapter. There are only a few parameters in this configuration file that you will need to edit, shown in the following list. The entire file *maxext.conf* is reproduced in Example 10-17.

Example 10-17. maxext.conf

```
package maxext;
use vars qw{ %config @emailAddresses };

%config = ( minExtentsCanExtend => 3, minPctBlocksUnused => 10, );
@emailAddresses = ( 'dba@yourdomain.com', 'dba2@yourdomain.com', );
```

minExtentsCanExtend

Set this to the minimum number of extents by which an object should be able to extend. In the preceding configuration file, this is set to 3, and a table has 98 extents allocated and a MAXEXTENTS value of 100; in this case, a value of 3 will cause a check to be made with DBMS_SPACE. This is because it is only possible for two more extents to be allocated to the table.

minPctBlocksUnused

Percentage of unused blocks that an object should have before a warning is sent to the DBA. If an index has 100 total blocks, and 11 of those are unused blocks, no warning will be issued because 11% of unused blocks is greater than the 10% minimal threshold set.

@emailAddresses

Array of email addresses to which reports should be mailed.

There are only a few command options for *maxext.pl*, summarized in Table 10-7.

Table 10-7. Command-line options—maxext.pl

Option	Description
-machine	Server where the target database resides.
-database	Target database.
-username	DBA account.
-password	DBA password (optional if password server in use).
-email	Send email to DBAs if a report is generated.
-silent	Only send email, and process without printing output.

The results of running *maxext.pl* can be seen in Example 10-18. We forced these tables to appear in the report by setting the *minPctBlocksUnused* parameter to 100 in the *maxext.conf* file.

Example 10-18. Results from maxext.pl

```
%oramon > maxext.pl -machine sherlock -database ts01 -username \
  system -email
RPT:
Database Objects That Cannot Extend                         Page:       1
Database: TS01.JKS.COM                        Date: 2002/05/20 01:12
                                                     NUMBER
                                                    EXTENTS     NEXT
OWNER      NAME         TYPE      AVAILABLE  EXTENT SIZE MAX BYTES FREE
========= ============ ======== ========== =========== ================

JKSTILL    BIG_TABLE    TABLE     UNLIM        65536            0
JKSTILL    FILL_ER_UP   TABLE     UNLIM        65536            0

%oramon >
```

Extracting DDL and Data

Oracle supplies the Export (*exp*) and Import (*imp*) utilities to export Oracle database objects and then import them back into Oracle databases. The Export utility extracts not only the data for these objects but the DDL (Data Definition Language) to create them.

These venerable utilities work well enough, but sometimes fall short in a number of important ways:

Performance
> Exports are fairly quick, but imports can be unbearably slow. Importing more than 10 gigabytes of data can be too time-consuming to consider.

Portability
> The Import file format is proprietary to Oracle. This makes it virtually impossible to load other databases with exported data. We suppose that's fair enough, because Oracle Corporation is, after all, in the business of Oracle databases. What's really frustrating though, is Import's inability to work with Oracle's own superb high-speed data handler, SQL*Loader.

Limited DDL extraction
> It's possible to extract most (but not all) of the DDL from an export file via the *indexfile* feature of *imp*. The following command, for example, extracts most of the DDL from an export file, but fails to retrieve stored procedures:
> ```
> $ imp userid=scott/tiger file=mydata.dmp indexfile=myddl.sql
> ```

Compatibility
> The Oracle export utility is highly version-dependent. Trying to export data from an 8.0.5 database with an 8.1.7 export utility results in the error message:
> ```
> EXP-00037: Export views not compatible with export version.
> ```

We've included two Perl/DBI scripts in the toolkit to help fill these gaps. Using *sqlunldr.pl* and *ddl_oracle.pl* you can dump all schema data to comma-delimited files, generate SQL*Loader control and parameter files, and then generate DDL for all user tablespaces and schemas.

Extracting Data With sqlunldr.pl

Sometimes you need raw portable data—to populate another database, build a customer's spreadsheet, or perform some other data operation. Unfortunately, Oracle's Export utility is the wrong mousetrap. One popular solution to such problems is to build SQL*Plus dump scripts. This approach works for single tables, but grows cumbersome when dumping entire schemas or even a handful of selected tables. What's needed is a single dump utility that creates portable output. It would also be nice if the data field separators were configurable and if enclosed quote characters were both configurable and optional. The *sqlunldr.pl* script fits the bill on all counts. Here are some of its main features. In the following sections we'll include several examples that show you to use this script.

SQL*Loader support
> Generates parameter and control files for SQL*Loader.

Configurable characters
> The default for field separation is a comma. The default for enclosing fields is the double quote. Each is configurable via the command line.

LONG column support
> Long columns of arbitrary length are supported.

Binary data support (with limitations)
> Binary data of LONG, CHAR, VARCHAR, and VARCHAR2 types can be dumped as hexadecimal by the script and reloaded into binary format. This feature is limited to data 32K in length. Note that the Oracle function UTL_RAW. CAST_TO_VARCHAR2 converts data from hex to binary within the SQL*Loader control script, which is also limited to strings of 32K.

Binary data limits
> The *sqlunldr.pl* script only partially supports LOB (large object) data. Both CLOB (character large object) and BLOB (binary large object) columns may be dumped to output files, but you will need to manually edit the generated SQL*Loader control *.ctl* script to load the data. Binary data is subject to the 32K-byte limit because of the Oracle software predefined limitation. This is probably fine for 95% of systems, however.

The script's command-line options are summarized in Table 10-8.

Table 10-8. Command-line options—sqlunldr.pl

Option	Description
-machine	Server where the target database resides.
-database	Target database.
-username	DBA account.
-password	DBA password (optional if password server in use).
-owner	Owner of tables to dump.
-directory	Directory in which to unload data. Defaults to *<owner>.dump*.
-dateformat	NLS_DATE_FORMAT—for example, *-dateformat 'mm/dd/yyyy'*
-header	Includes the column names as the first line of output.
-noheader	Outputs without column names.
-table	Dumps tables. May be repeated as often as necessary —for example, *-table emp -table dept -table salary*
-schemadump	Dumps entire schema. Makes *sqlunldr.pl* ignore *-table*.
-rowlimit	Limits number of rows output for each table to *N* rows.

Table 10-8. Command-line options—sqlunldr.pl (continued)

Option	Description
-fieldsep	Separates row fields, defaults to comma. If used, you probably need to escape the character—for example, -fieldsep |.
-quotechar	Character used to enclose each field. Defaults to a double quote. A literal value of none will disable quotes.
-longlen	Maximum length of LONG datatypes you expect to encounter. Defaults to 65535.
-bincol	Columns of binary data which should be translated to hex format before dumping. Maximum length is 32767 bytes. Specified as <table>=<column1, column2,...>, etc.

Dumping and reloading SCOTT's schema

In this first example, we'll use *sqlunldr.pl* to dump the entire *scott* schema. This time we can ignore the *-dateformat* option, as we'll simply reload the data straight back into the same database. However, we'd need this option if the data were to be loaded into a database with a different NLS_DATE_FORMAT. Here's the command to dump the *scott* schema:

```
$ sqlunldr.pl -machine watson -database ts99 -username system \
    -owner scott -noheader -schemadump
```

Once this entirely portable command completes, you'll find all the output in the *scott.dump* directory. Example 10-19 displays the output on a Unix system.

Example 10-19. Dumping the SCOTT schema with sqlunldr.pl

```
%oramon> sqlunldr.pl -machine watson -database ts99 -username system \
  -owner scott -noheader -schemadump
Table: EMP
Table: BONUS
Table: SALGRADE
Table: DEPT
Table: BINCOL_TEST
%oramon> ls -l scott.dump
total 704
-rw-r--r--   1 jkstill   dba            141 May 20 01:17 bincol_test.ctl
-rw-r--r--   1 jkstill   dba             85 May 20 01:17 bincol_test.par
-rw-r--r--   1 jkstill   dba             56 May 20 01:17 bincol_test.txt
-rw-r--r--   1 jkstill   dba            129 May 20 01:17 bonus.ctl
-rw-r--r--   1 jkstill   dba             67 May 20 01:17 bonus.par
-rw-r--r--   1 jkstill   dba              0 May 20 01:17 bonus.txt
-rw-r--r--   1 jkstill   dba            123 May 20 01:17 dept.ctl
-rw-r--r--   1 jkstill   dba             64 May 20 01:17 dept.par
-rw-r--r--   1 jkstill   dba            104 May 20 01:17 dept.txt
-rw-r--r--   1 jkstill   dba            167 May 20 01:17 emp.ctl
-rw-r--r--   1 jkstill   dba             61 May 20 01:17 emp.par
-rw-r--r--   1 jkstill   dba         661709 May 20 01:17 emp.txt
-rw-r--r--   1 jkstill   dba            132 May 20 01:17 salgrade.ctl
-rw-r--r--   1 jkstill   dba             76 May 20 01:17 salgrade.par
-rw-r--r--   1 jkstill   dba             89 May 20 01:17 salgrade.txt
%oramon>
```

Let's see what's going on in this code:

1. We'll delete all the table rows from SCOTT's schema in our test database:

```
SQL> DELETE FROM BONUS;
SQL> DELETE FROM SALGRADE;
SQL> DELETE FROM EMP;
SQL> DELETE FROM DEPT;
SQL> COMMIT;
```

2. We're now ready to reload the data via SQL*Loader using the control and parameter files generated by *sqlunldr.pl*. Here's how to reload DEPT:

```
$ cd scott.dump
$ sqlldr parfile=dept.par
```

3. We're asked for SCOTT's password. After we supply it, SQL*Loader reloads the DEPT table and generates *dept.log*. The contents of this log should be similar to what's shown in Example 10-20. We can now reload the other tables:

```
$ sqlldr parfile=emp.par
$ sqlldr parfile=salgrade.par
$ sqlldr parfile=bonus.par
```

*Example 10-20. SQL*Loader log file—dept.log*

```
Table DEPT, loaded from every logical record.
Insert option in effect for this table: INSERT


  Column Name                    Position   Len  Term Encl Datatype
------------------------------ ---------- ----- ---- ---- ----------------
DEPTNO                             FIRST     *    ,  O(") CHARACTER
DNAME                               NEXT     *    ,  O(") CHARACTER
LOC                                 NEXT     *    ,  O(") CHARACTER


Table DEPT:
  4 Rows successfully loaded.
  0 Rows not loaded due to data errors.
  0 Rows not loaded because all WHEN clauses were failed.
  0 Rows not loaded because all fields were null.

Space allocated for bind array:                  49536 bytes(64 rows)
Space allocated for memory besides bind array:       0 bytes

Total logical records skipped:          0
Total logical records read:             4
Total logical records rejected:         0
Total logical records discarded:        0

Run began on Sun Feb 24 17:18:17 2002
Run ended on Sun Feb 24 17:18:24 2002

Elapsed time was:     00:00:07.40
CPU time was:         00:00:00.10
```

Dumping binary data

Now we'll look at a more complex example. We'll create a table with one column of plain text, convert it to unreadable binary form, and then dump the table with *sqlunldr.pl*. We'll then delete all of the data from the table, reload it with the generated SQL*Loader scripts, and then validate it. Example 10-21 shows a test of this operation.

Example 10-21. Binary data test

```
1 DROP TABLE BINCOL_TEST;
2 CREATE TABLE BINCOL_TEST
3    (CLEAR_TEXT VARCHAR2(10), BINARY_DATA VARCHAR2(10));
4
5 INSERT INTO BINCOL_TEST(CLEAR_TEXT) VALUES('Post-Dated');
6 INSERT INTO BINCOL_TEST(CLEAR_TEXT) VALUES('Check');
7 INSERT INTO BINCOL_TEST(CLEAR_TEXT) VALUES('Loan');
8 COMMIT;
9
10 VAR xorstr VARCHAR2(10)
11
12 BEGIN
13    :xorstr := RPAD(CHR(127),10,CHR(127));
14 END;
15 /
16
17 UPDATE BINCOL_TEST
18    SET BINARY_DATA =
19        UTL_RAW.CAST_TO_VARCHAR2(
20           UTL_RAW.BIT_XOR(
21              UTL_RAW.CAST_TO_RAW(CLEAR_TEXT),
22              UTL_RAW.CAST_TO_RAW(SUBSTR(:xorstr,1,LENGTH(CLEAR_TEXT)))
23           )
24        );
25 COMMIT;
26 SET TERM OFF
27 SPOOL BINCOL_TEST.LOG
28 SELECT * FROM BINCOL_TEST;
29 SPOOL OFF
30 SET TERM ON
31
32 ED bincol_test.log
33 SELECT UTL_RAW.CAST_TO_VARCHAR2(
34         UTL_RAW.BIT_XOR(
35            UTL_RAW.CAST_TO_RAW(BINARY_DATA),
36            UTL_RAW.CAST_TO_RAW(:XORSTR)
37         )
38      )
39   FROM BINCOL_TEST;
```

You'll find the example scripts *bincol_test.sql* and *bincol_test2.sql* in the following locations, so you can run these tests yourself if you wish:

Unix (assuming a build directory of /u01/build)
    /u01/build/PDBA-1.00/routine_tasks

Win32
    c:\Perl\site\lib\PDBA\sql

Let's see what's going on in this example:

1. In lines 2–3 in Example 10-21 we create BINCOL_TEST.

2. In lines 5–7 we insert "Post-Dated Check Loan" into three of its rows.

3. In lines 10–15 we build a 10-character string, *:xorstr*, from ASCII character 127 elements. In lines 17–24, *:xorstr* is used with the Oracle built-in functions UTL_RAW.CAST_TO_VARCHAR2, UTL_RAW.CAST_TO_RAW, and UTL_RAW.BIT_XOR to create binary data that is unreadable by humans.[*]

4. In line 27 the data is spooled to a file, and in line 32 the output is sent to our favorite *vi* text editor. (Notice that in line 26 the console output was turned off. This stops the binary data displaying to our SQL*Plus session, possibly making it unreadable.)

5. Here is the result of this edit, as it would appear viewed safely in *vi*.

```
CLEAR_TEXT   BINARY_DATA
----------   -----------
Post-Dated   /^P^L^KR;^^^K^Z^[
Check        <^W^Z\^T
Loan         3^P^^^Q
```

6. After closing the editor, the SQL script continues. Lines 33–39 convert the newly created binary data back into human-readable form, and if you're running this test yourself, the output should be similar to that shown here:

```
PL/SQL procedure successful completed.
3 rows updated.
Commit complete.
UTL_RAW.CAST_TO_VARCHAR2(UTL_RAW.BIT_XOR(UTL_RAW.CAST_TO_RAW(BINARY_DATA),UTL_RA
--------------------------------------------------------------------------------
Post-Dated
Check
Loan
SQL>
```

7. We're now ready to dump the data, delete the rows from BINCOL_TEST, reload from the output of *sqlunldr.pl*, and then validate the results. Use *sqlunldr.pl* to dump the table:

```
$ sqlunldr.pl -machine watson -database ts99 -username system \
    -owner scott -noheader -table bincol_test \
    -bincol bincol_test=binary_data
```

---

[*] Except half-Vulcans and machine-code gods, of course.

8. Now we'll delete the test rows from BINCOL_TEST:

```
$ SQLPLUS SCOTT/TIGER
SQL> DELETE FROM BINCOL_TEST;
SQL> COMMIT;
SQL> EXIT
```

9. We can now reload the table from the *sqlunldr.pl* dump. The data will be in directory *scott.dump*, one level below your current directory. Go there and examine the files *bincol_test.par*, *bincol_test.ctl*, and *bincol_test.txt*. You can see how they appeared in our tests in Example 10-22. Notice that the binary data contained in BINCOL_TEST.BINARY_DATA has been converted to hexadecimal format. When loaded back, the Oracle built-in procedure UTL_RAW.CAST_TO_VARCHAR2 will convert it back into binary.

Example 10-22. Files generated by sqlunldr.pl

```
%oramon > cat bincol_test.par
userid = scott
control = bincol_test.ctl
log = bincol_test.log
bad = bincol_test.bad

%oramon > cat bincol_test.ctl
load data
infile 'bincol_test.txt'
into table BINCOL_TEST
fields terminated by ',' optionally enclosed by '"'
(
CLEAR_TEXT,
BINARY_DATA "utl_raw.cast_to_varchar2(:BINARY_DATA)"
)

%oramon > cat bincol_test.txt
"Post-Dated","2F100C0B523B1E0B1A1B"
"Check","3C171A1C14"
"Loan","33101E11"
%oramon >
```

10. We can now reload the data using SQL*Loader and the parameter files generated by *sqlunldr.pl*:

```
$ cd scott.dump
$ sqlldr parfile=bincol_test.par
```

11. The most important line to observe in *bincol_test.log* is the one saying *3 Rows successfully loaded*:

```
SQL*Loader: Release 8.1.7.0.1 - Production on Sun Feb 24 16:43:54 2002
(c) Copyright 2000 Oracle Corporation.  All rights reserved.
...
Table BINCOL_TEST:
  3 Rows successfully loaded.
  0 Rows not loaded due to data errors.
```

```
0 Rows not loaded because all WHEN clauses were failed.
0 Rows not loaded because all fields were null.
```

12. Now log back into SQL*Plus and run the script *bincol_test2.sql*. The output should be identical to that shown earlier. We can now drop the test table from SCOTT's account:

```
$ SQLPLUS SCOTT/TIGER
SQL> DROP TABLE BINCOL_TEST;
SQL> EXIT
```

Extracting DDL with ddl_oracle.pl

Although Perl-based Oracle tools like Orac and Oracletool supply options to regenerate DDL, and although the *DDL::Oracle* module was designed to explicitly perform this operation (we describe all of these applications in Chapters 3 and 4), it would sometimes be convenient to extract DDL from a database in one easy operation. We could then recreate all the objects in user and application schemas. Oracle's Export utility does extract all of this information, but often in unusable form.

It is possible to use the *indexfile=myddl.sql* construct with the Export utility to extract the DDL for tables, indexes, and constraints from an Oracle export file, but this utility fails to cover packages, procedures, functions, and triggers. To fill the gap, we've developed the *ddl_oracle.pl* script to generate the DDL to recreate the following schema database elements; in the list we've noted any exceptions to what can be generated:

Tablespaces
Generates DDL to recreate all tablespaces except the SYSTEM tablespace.

Rollback segments
Generates DDL to recreate all rollback segments.

Public database links
Generates DDL to recreate all public database links.

Public synonyms
Generates DDL to recreate public synonyms with the exception of public synonyms referring to a configurable list of user accounts. This exception prevents the inclusion of public synonyms created as part of a standard database.

User profiles
Generates DDL to recreate all user profiles with the exception of DEFAULT.

Roles
Generates DDL to recreate all database roles with the exception of a configurable list of roles. This exception prevents the script from recreating roles created as part of a standard database.

User accounts
Generates DDL to recreate all user accounts with the exception of those found in a configurable list of user accounts.

Schemas

Generates DDL to recreate all schema objects, including PL/SQL, with the exception of objects belonging to users in a configurable list.

Grants from schemas

Generates DDL to recreate all grants made from all user accounts.

Before going any further, let's examine the configurationfile *exp_exclude.conf*. This file is simply a list of user accounts and roles that we don't care to preserve in DDL files, often because they are created for us when creating a new database.

The file included in the PDBA distribution is shown in Example 10-23. Most of the generic Oracle database users and roles are included.

Example 10-23. exp_exclude.conf

```
package expexclude;
use vars qw{ @users };

@users = qw{ SYS                      SYSTEM
             OUTLN                    DBSNMP
             TRACESVR                 ORDSYS
             ORDPLUGINS               MDSYS
             AURORA$JIS$UTILITY$      OSE$HTTP$ADMIN
             AURORA$ORB$UNAUTHENTICATED };

@roles = qw { CONNECT                 RESOURCE
              DBA SELECT_             CATALOG_ROLE
              EXECUTE_CATALOG_ROLE    DELETE_CATALOG_ROLE
              EXP_FULL_DATABASE       IMP_FULL_DATABASE
              RECOVERY_CATALOG_OWNER  AQ_ADMINISTRATOR_ROLE
              AQ_USER_ROLE            SNMPAGENT
              OEM_MONITOR             HS_ADMIN_ROLE
              JAVAUSERPRIV            JAVAIDPRIV
              JAVASYSPRIV             JAVADEBUGPRIV
              JAVA_ADMIN              JAVA_DEPLOY
              PLUSTRACE               TIMESERIES_DEVELOPER
              TIMESERIES_DBA          CTXAPP };
1;
```

Make sure that the *exp_exclude.conf* file is in your PDBA_HOME directory, as with other configuration files described earlier in this chapter. There's no need to edit *exp_exclude.conf* unless you need to edit the roles or user lists. For instance, if you want OUTLN included in DDL generation, remove it from *@users*. Most of the DDL generation is accomplished via Richard Sutherland's *DDL::Oracle* module, which we discussed in Chapter 3, *Perl GUI Extensions*. If that application is not available on your system, you will need to install it (making sure to use at least Version 1.10). Here's a Perl one-liner to determine what version of *DDL::Oracle* you are using:

```
perl -e "use DDL::Oracle 1.10; print qq{OK!\n}"
```

If the proper version is installed, you'll see *OK!* printed on the screen; otherwise, you'll need to install the latest version. This is easier for Win32 users. Simply start the ActiveState PPM package manager and install directly as follows:

```
C:\> ppm
PPM> install DDL::Oracle
```

Unix users will need to download the latest version and install it. If you want to do a manual install (as we described in Chapter 2, *Installing Perl*), you can get the file at *http://search.cpan.org/search?dist=DDL-Oracle*. For a direct CPAN install, do the following:

```
$ perl -MCPAN -e "shell"
cpan> install DDL::Oracle
...
Running make for R/RV/RVSUTHERL/DDL-Oracle-1.10.tar.gz
...
```

Although we make use of *DDL::Oracle* to generate much of the DDL output from *ddl_oracle.pl*, we don't use it for all of the DDL. Let's see why.

One of the goals of the script was to be able to generate a single file of all object grants made on a schema's objects from the perspective of the *grantor*, or owner, of the objects. If the SCOTT schema owns 10 tables and SCOTT has issued SELECT grants on all of his tables to the JONES, ADAMS, and CLARK accounts, we wanted a single script to contain all of those grants. This way, the DBA needs to issue only a single Oracle logon to the SCOTT account so that the DDL script containing those grants can be run.

The *DDL::Oracle* module generates grants from the perspective of the *grantee*, or recipient of the granted privileges. In the case of generating the DDL required to grant SELECT privileges to the JONES, ADAMS, and CLARK accounts, this would require three separate logons by the SCOTT account to create those grants.

In our script, we crafted our own DDL generation for certain aspects to get just the output we wanted. For example, we did this in generating the DDL to create users and roles, and in generating the GRANT statements by grantor rather than grantee.[*]

The command line for *ddl_oracle.pl* is rather basic, with the usual command-line options summarized in Table 10-9.

Table 10-9. Command-line options—ddl_oracle.pl

Option	Description
-machine	Server where the target database resides.
-database	Target database.

---

[*] If you want to see the details of this, examine the *%ddl* hash and the *ddl*, *_userPrivs*, *_rolePrivs*, and *_grantorPrivs* methods in the *PDBA::DBA* toolkit module.

Table 10-9. Command-line options—ddl_oracle.pl (continued)

Option	Description
-username	DBA account.
-password	DBA password (optional if password server in use).
-conf	Config file. The default is *exp_exclude.conf.*

Running *ddl_oracle.pl* is very simple, as shown here:

```
$ ddl_oracle.pl -machine watson -database ts99 -username system
Building List
working on profiles
working on public database links
working on public synonyms
working on rollback segments
working on tablespaces
working on users
working on SCOTT
working on COMMON
working on JKSTILL
working on PDBA_ROLE
...
```

The output consists of a number of SQL scripts; each script name is prefixed with a number, which indicates the order in which the scripts need to be run (assuming that all are to be used). An abbreviated version of the *1_create.sql* script is shown in Example 10-24. See Table 10-10 for all of the script names.

Table 10-10. SQL scripts generated by ddl_oracle.pl

SQL Script	Description
1_create.sql	Used to call all of the other scripts. See Example 10-24.
2_tbs_ddl.sql	DDL for all tablespaces other than SYSTEM.
3_rbs_ddl.sql	DDL for all rollback segments.
4_pub_db_link.sql	DDL for all public database links.
5_pub_synonyms.sql	DDL for all public synonyms for all objects other than those owned by accounts in the *@users* array of *exp_exclude.conf.*
6_user_profiles.sql	DDL for all user profiles except for DEFAULT.
7_role_ddl.sql	DDL for all database roles except those listed in the *@roles* array of *exp_exclude.conf.*
8_user_ddl.sql	DDL to create all accounts not listed in *@users*. Includes grants for all privileges, roles, profiles, and quotas.
9_schema_<USER>. sql	One file generated for each account. Includes the DDL for all database objects owned by the account: tables, indexes, constraints, views, sequences, stored procedures, stored functions, packages, etc.
10_grant_<USER>.sql	One of these files generated for each account. It includes all grants made by the grantor to other accounts and roles.

The output is designed so it could be run sequentially by running *1_create.sql*, but you'll rarely do things this way. By grouping objects and privileges by owner, it's a bit easier for you to recreate a single schema. This approach also reduces the number of files you must deal with.

Example 10-24. The 1_create.sql script

```
@@2_tbs_ddl.sql
@@3_rbs_ddl.sql
@@4_pub_db_link.sql
@@5_pub_synonyms.sql
@@6_user_profiles.sql
@@7_role_ddl.sql
@@8_user_ddl.sql

PROMPT connecting to SCOTT - please enter the password
CONNECT SCOTT
@@9_schema_scott.sql
@@10_grant_scott.sql

PROMPT connecting to PDBAREP - please enter the password
CONNECT PDBAREP
@@9_schema_pdbarep.sql
@@10_grant_pdbarep.sql
...
```

CHAPTER 11

Monitoring the Database with the PDBA Toolkit

So far we have looked at a variety of scripts in the Perl DBA Toolkit and have seen how they can help make our lives as Oracle DBAs more productive. In this chapter we're going to focus on two particularly urgent areas of DBA activity:

Alert log monitoring

> The Oracle database alert log is an important source of information about error conditions, and DBAs need to keep a careful eye on this file. However, finding the time to do manual monitoring is difficult for most DBAs. In this chapter, we'll create an alert log monitor that detects Oracle errors and messages and emails them to specific addresses, all in real time. The primary scripts used to do this monitoring are *ckalert.pl*, *ckalert_NT.pl*, and *ckalert.conf*.

Connectivity monitoring

> DBAs also need to constantly monitor all of their Oracle databases to ensure that connections to these databases can be established. If a database goes down, the DBA needs to find out about the problem—and fix it—ideally before users are even aware that their connectivity has been affected. In this chapter we'll describe a toolkit connectivity monitor that does this real-time monitoring using the scripts *dbup.pl*, *dbup_NT.pl*, and *dbup.conf*.

Monitoring the Alert Log

When an Oracle database is created, a file commonly referred to as the *alert log* is created. As errors and other conditions occur during processing, messages are logged to this file. Basically, every important event that occurs causes a record to be written to the alert log: when the database starts up, when it shuts down, and everything in between (e.g,. creating tablespaces and datafiles, performing privileged operations). Every important error message ends up in the alert log; in some cases, a message directs the DBA to a trace file that contains more detailed alert information.

It is the responsibility of the DBA to monitor the alert log on a regular basis so as to deal with any problems or potential security issues before they affect the database or its users. The sooner you find out about error conditions, the better; unlike wine and cheese, database problems don't improve with age. Monitoring the alert log can be a challenge, however: there is an alert log for every database, and busy DBAs have many other things to do that are more pressing than manually scanning alert log files. As somewhat dyed-in-the-wool geeks,* your authors find that the thought of spending valuable daily minutes manually poring over database alert logs sends shivers up and down our workstations. Frankly, trawling through alert logs makes for a great insomnia cure, but it's hard to fit into the day.

To automate this tedious process and help DBAs keep close watch over their databases, we've written a collection of scripts designed to monitor the Oracle alert logs in real time and to report directly to the DBA the instant a database problem is detected. These scripts let you configure what to look for in the alert log and the email addresses to which to send messages. In addition, they allow messages to be mailed individually or batched up (depending on platform) and to be sent either immediately or at particular time intervals.

Where is the Alert Log?

The location and name of the file containing the alert log are operating system and version-dependent; they may also be subject to local DBA standards or the caprice of a third-party application's enforcing its own standards for the location of the alert log.

Given a database of the name *orcl*, the alert log may normally be found at either of these locations on Unix systems:

```
$ORACLE_HOME/admin/orcl/bdump/alert_orcl.log
$ORACLE_BASE/admin/orcl/bdump/alert_orcl.log
```

On Win32 systems it would likely be found at:

```
%ORACLE_HOME%\admin\orcl\bdump\orclALRT.log
```

Monitoring with chkalert.pl

The *chkalert.pl* script is at the center of the toolkit alert-monitoring application. This Perl script provides the following capabilities:

Constant monitoring
    Monitors the alert log for errors and collects these into an array that is emailed automatically to the addresses you've specified.

Multiple email address
    Emails error messages to multiple email addresses if you configure them.

---

* If you think this is synonymous with "aging geeks," you're right. Your authors readily admit to being over 18 years old.

Message throttling

Controls the rate at which that email is sent; this is very helpful in cases where a large number of error messages occur simultaneously. (This feature is only available on Unix systems.)

Flexible configuration of errors to check

Allows you to specify the errors the script should check for in the alert log. You specify errors via a list of Perl regular expressions (giving you the ultimate in flexibility).

This script runs in the background as a daemon on Unix. A version of it, *ckalert_NT. pl*, runs as a service on Win32.

One particularly important feature of *chkalert.pl* is the set of configurable controls it provides in an effort to prevent error messages from overwhelming your mail server. You may wonder what terrible circumstances would generate so many error messages that it could bring a mail server to its knees! Actually, this happens more than you would imagine. A relatively common example is an imperfectly tested program that ignores error messages and continues to attempt the same operation over and over. For example, consider a PL/SQL routine that collects records from an OLTP system and inserts them into a data warehouse. After a month of record-breaking sales, the warehouse table chews through all the available space allocated for that month—suddenly, you'll run into a brick wall in the form of an Oracle error such as the following:

```
ORA-1653 unable to extend table MY_TABLE by 16 in tablespace OLTP_DATA.
```

A reasonable and well-behaved PL/SQL routine would catch this error and abort the process, notifying someone of the problem. However, if a miscreant piece of code fails to catch an exception of this kind, it can easily generate thousands of error messages in a very short time. This can keep a mail server very busy!

The problem is compounded when the receivers of such emails are running a mail filter, such as *procmail*, which spawns a new process for each email received. This can easily cause your company's mail server to suddenly display poorer performance than the old Commodore 64 you still have in your closet (don't try to deny it).

As you can well imagine, system administrators are somewhat less than amused by such denials of service, especially when they occur in the wee hours of the morning. And let's face it, things like this *always* occur in the wee hours of the morning. We like our own sysadmins, and try to avoid giving them reasons to feel otherwise about us, so we use *chkalert.pl* to keep mail server disasters from occurring.

Although in almost every other case we provide a single script that operates on both Unix and Win32 platforms, that isn't the case here. We originally designed the *chkalert.pl* script to run on Unix and subsequently created a modified version that works on Win32. When dealing with background daemons for Unix or services for Win32, the code base becomes quite unwieldy if it tries to do both jobs. So in this case we achieved much better performance out of maintaining separate Unix and Win32 versions.

In the installation procedures described later in this chapter, we cover Unix installation followed by Win32 differences. Because most aspects of installation and configuration are the same for the two platforms, we recommend that if you are running on Win32, you nevertheless read the Unix section first.

Installing and Configuring chkalert on Unix

If you followed the installation instructions in Chapter 9, *Installing the PDBA Toolkit*, the Unix version of the alert-monitoring script, *chkalert.pl*, will already be installed on your system. You'll find it in the same location as the other executable scripts, most likely in */usr/local/bin*. (As long as *PATH* includes the script installation directory, your system will find it.) Once underway, the Perl daemon carries out the following tasks (all of which can be configured)

chkalert.conf

The first installation step is to locate and update the *chkalert.conf* configuration file used by the *chkalert.pl* script. The configuration file contains settings for the parameters used to control alert monitoring at your site. Default settings are provided in the configuration file that is included in the toolkit when you first install it. You can then edit this file as desired. We perform this editing process as follows:

1. Change directory to wherever you unzipped the PDBA Toolkit archive, and then move into the *../chkalert* directory. For example, if you unpacked *PDBA-1.00.tar.gz* into */tmp*, you would move to */tmp/PDBA-1.00/chkalert*:

   ```
   $ cd /tmp/PDBA-1.00
   $ cd chkalert
   $ pwd
   /tmp/PDBA-1.00/chkalert
   ```

2. If you don't already have the *chkalert.conf* file in *PDBA_HOME* (perhaps you have installed it as another user), make sure you do, and then *cd* to *PDBA_HOME*:

   ```
   $ ls $PDBA_HOME/chkalert.conf
   ls: chkalert.conf: No such file or directory
   $ cp chkalert.conf $PDBA_HOME
   $ cd $PDBA_HOME
   ```

3. Make sure you can write to the file, and then begin to edit its configuration. (The *chkalert.conf* filename is specified in *chkalert.pl*, so please don't change the name of the file.)

```
$ chmod u+w chkalert.conf
$ cp chkalert.conf chkalert.old  # Once bitten, twice shy! :-)
$ vi chkalert.conf
```

There are just a few parameters you'll need to modify. We've reproduced the configuration file from the PDBA distribution in Example 11-1. Following the example we describe the main parameters you can specify in the file.

Example 11-1. Configuration for chkalert.pl—chkalert.conf

```
package chkalert;
use vars qw{ %ckConf };

%ckConf = (
   # recipients of email for alert log errors
   dbaAddresses => [qw{ scott@tiger.com 7775551212@mobile.att.net }],
   # mail addresses for debugging
   debugDBA => [qw{someone@somewhere.com}],
   oratabFile => '/etc/oratab',
   # or whatever the location of your oratab file is
   # it consists of the instance name, Oracle_Home and
   # a flag field of Y or N.

   alarmTime => 300,
   # this is the number of seconds to wait before sending
   # a batch of error messages as email
   # this is batched to prevent large numbers of email

   maxLogLines => 100,
   # this is the override for alarmTime.  If maxLogLines
   # of messages are received, mail them now

   watchdogLength => 5,
   # this is the max size of the array used to
   # determine if too much mail is being sent too fast

   watchdogTime => 10,
   # this is the elapsed number of seconds between email
   # batches that is used to determine if mail is being
   # sent too quickly

   # if the time between the first and last times in the
   # watchdog buffer is <
   # ( watchdog[watchdogLength] - watchdog[0] )
   # * ( watchdogLength * watchdogTime )
   # then the mail delivery is throttled back until things slow down

   throttleDelaySeconds => 10,
   # how many seconds to delay between email batches
   # when many errors are being generated
```

Example 11-1. Configuration for chkalert.pl—chkalert.conf (continued)

```
    # this is to protect the system from being choked
    # with procmail processes if you are using it

    # what is the name of this server?
    serverName => 'sherlock.jks.com',

    # list of errors to check for
    # must be a comma separated list of regular expressions
    # e.g.  errorList = ^ORA-, ^TNS-, crash
    # the qw operator may also be used
    errorList => qw{^ORA- ^TNS- crash},
);
1;
```

Here are the configuration file parameters:

dbaAddresses

Address list to which email is sent when errors are detected. Notice that the list is included inside paired square brackets, *[]*, indicating an anonymous array reference (see Appendix A, *The Essential Guide to Perl*, for a description of anonymous arrays). The *qw* (quote word) Perl operator also avoids the need to use quote punctuation, which simplifies editing.

debugDBA

Has the same form as *dbaAddresses*, but consists of a list of addresses for use when debugging the application. You will only need one address for this entry.

oratabFile

An all-important directive that locates the crucial *oratab* file. We won't try to guess the location of this file, as it can differ widely on various Unix flavors. Simply insert the location of your own *oratab* file so *chkalert.pl* can find the proper ORACLE_HOME for each target database.

alarmTime

Number of seconds you want *chkalert.pl* to hold onto error messages before mailing them. Sometimes errors come in large grape-like bunches, so you may wish to avoid separate emails being sent out for each one (especially if the email destination *happens* to be your pager and it's 2:00 AM on Sunday morning). One piercing scream from a pager is enough to wake most of us. If you really do want to receive a separate email for each error, possibly because you own shares in the phone company, read on.

maxLogLines

Maximum number of lines *chkalert.pl* should buffer before mailing them out. This overrides *alarmTime*. At its default setting of 100, if 100 error messages appear in the alert log before *alarmTime* times out, this overrides the timer and causes the messages to be mailed immediately. The timer simply resets to 0 when this happens. To see error messages immediately, just set *maxLogLines* to a value of 1. An email is then sent the moment the monitor detects an error.

watchdogLength , watchdogTime, throttleDelaySeconds

These closely related parameters prevent *chkalert.pl* from overwhelming a mail system in the event of a runaway error's flooding the alert log:

Whenever error messages are mailed out, the time is recorded in an array called *@watchdog*. The number of entries in *@watchdog* is controlled by the parameter *watchdogLength*. The parameter *watchdogTime* is the number of seconds and is used as a control to determine whether *chkalert.pl* should slow down mail deliveries.

Whenever error messages get mailed, *chkalert.pl* compares the current time with the oldest timestamp in *@watchdog*. If the difference in seconds between these is less than *(watchdogLength * watchdogTime)*, *chkalert.pl* inserts a *sleep* of *throttleDelaySeconds* between each mailing until the incoming error message rate slows down.

For example, if your database starts throwing errors into the alert log faster than a Tribble population can munch its way through a star cruiser shipment of Quadrotriticale,[*] this could send your mail server into a reproductive frenzy trying to keep up. The script tries to prevent that from happening. Let's assume these values are set as in Example 11-1, and that *chkalert.pl* finds that the first batch of error messages got sent out less than 50 seconds ago and this is the fifth batch since then. A 10-second wait will be inserted between mailings, giving the mail server time to breathe.

serverName

Name of the database server. This name is used purely for informational purposes whenever error messages are emailed.

errorList

Allows us to specify exactly what we want *chkalert.pl* to consider as an error. This is a list of regular expressions contained within either a comma-separated list or a list specified by Perl's *qw* operator. (See Appendix C, *The Essential Guide to Regular Expressions*, for more information.)

Running chkalert.pl

We're now ready to run *chkalert.pl* to see how it works. Let's test it first, on a copy of an alert log in which we've generated our own error messages:

1. Our test database is *ts01*, and we copy its alert log to */tmp*:

    ```
    cp $ORACLE_HOME/admin/ts01/bdump/alert_ts01.log /tmp
    ```

---

[*] *Star Trek*, season 2, episode 15. See *http://www.scifi.com/startrek/episodes/102.html*.

2. We can now start running *chkalert.pl* against this test log copy:

```
$ chkalert.pl -debug -database ts01 -alertlog /tmp/alert_ts01.log
oratab: ts01:/u02/app/oracle/product/8.1.7:Y
ORACLE_HOME: /u02/app/oracle/product/8.1.7
DATABASE: ts01
ALERT LOG: /tmp/alert_ts01.log
DBA's    : someone@somewhere.com
```

3. In another shell, we add an error message onto the end of our test log:

```
$ echo "ORA-20000: this is a chkalert test error" >> /tmp/alert_ts01.log
```

The content of the message is unimportant, as long as it begins with *ORA-*. The output in the first window should now gain an extra line:

```
$ chkalert.pl -debug -database ts01 -alertlog /tmp/alert_ts01.log
oratab: ts01:/u02/app/oracle/product/8.1.7:Y
ORACLE_HOME: /u02/app/oracle/product/8.1.7
DATABASE: ts01
ALERT LOG: /tmp/alert_ts01.log
DBA's    : someone@somewhere.com
ORA-20000: this is a chkalert test error
```

4. We've now confirmed that monitoring is properly configured, so let's ensure that the mailing works. Stop *chkalert.pl* with a Ctrl-C, and then restart it with a new *-sendmail* switch added:

```
$ chkalert.pl -debug -sendmail -database ts01 \
    -alertlog /tmp/alert_ts01.log

oratab: ts01:/u02/app/oracle/product/8.1.7:Y
ORACLE_HOME: /u02/app/oracle/product/8.1.7
DATABASE: ts01
ALERT LOG: /tmp/alert_ts01.log
DBA's    : someone@somewhere.com
```

5. Add another fake error message to the end of the test alert log, and then sit back with your feet up, sipping a quick coffee. The default configuration waits five minutes before sending out the following *Alarm Time* message:

```
ORA-20000: this is a chkalert test error

Alarm Time: 2002/12/02 - 14:26

SUBJ: ts01 Database - Alert Log Errors -
ORA-20000: this is a chkalert test error encountered  in ts01 at 2002/12/02 - 14:
26
sending email
```

After *chkalert.pl* says it's sent the email, check to see that we've actually received it. If not, you may need to verify that the mail server specified in *$PDBA_HOME/pdba.conf* is valid. (If necessary, see Chapter 9 for details on the mail server configuration.)

Testing with a real alert log

This time we'll execute *chkalert.pl* against a real alert log without the previous *-debug* option. This forces *chkalert.pl* to run as a daemon process:

```
$ chkalert.pl -sendmail -database ts01 \
    -alertlog $ORACLE_HOME/admin/ts01/bdump/alert_ts01.log
DATABASE: ts01
ALERT LOG: /u02/app/oracle/product/8.1.7/admin/ts01/bdump/alert_ts01.log
DBA's    : oradba@yourdomain.com 7775551212@mobile.att.net
```

We're set. If you've included your cell phone or pager number as one of the email addresses and if the database has a sudden problem at 2:00 AM, you'll get the call first so you can deal with it. You'll then be able to stroll casually into your office at 8:45 AM without anyone ever knowing there *was* a problem. No more angry mobs ambushing you in the car park, no more smirkers loafing round the coffee machine waiting for the DBA to fix the database, no more sudden surprises.*

Just to maintain this blissful nirvana moment and help ensure that *chkalert.pl* is always running, you might want to schedule it to start periodically via your system scheduler (often *cron* on Unix systems).

When *chkalert.pl* starts, it creates a lock on a temporary baton file of the form */tmp/ chkalert.$ORACLE_SID*. Subsequent attempts to run *chkalert.pl* on the same database will fail when the file lock operation is attempted. This is harmless, because *chkalert.pl* merely exits when it's unable to lock the temporary baton file.

If you need to terminate the *chkalert.pl* daemon, it's easily done via *chkalert.pl*'s own *-kill* option. When *chkalert.pl* starts, it creates a temporary file containing its own process ID—sort of like an Apache *.pid* file. The *-kill* option tells *chkalert.pl* to open that file, in read-only mode, and use its artificial intelligence, glowing red eyes, and liquid metal, to locate the PID of the running process. Once tracked down, the process is terminated.

The file containing the process ID is always named *chkalert.<database>*. On our Unix server for instance, the database is named *ts01*. When *chkalert.pl* is started, a file named *chkalert.ts01* is created. On Unix systems this file is created in the */tmp* directory, and on Win32 servers it's created in *C:\TEMP*. The contents of this file are fairly simple:

```
$ cat /tmp/chkalert.ts01
15575
```

The following is an example of stopping a currently running *chkalert.pl* daemon. All of the command-line options are summarized in Table 11-1:

```
oramon > chkalert.pl -database ts01 -kill
DATABASE: ts01
```

---

* OK, so we're the first to agree that restful slumber's being broken is a long way from being good, but performance reviews where share options may go up, rather than down, should provide adequate compensation.

```
ALERT LOG: /u02/app/oracle/product/8.1.7/admin/ts01/bdump/alert_ts01.log
DBA's    : someone@somewhere.com 7775551212@mobile.att.net
chkalert process 3790 killed
```

Table 11-1. Command-line options—chkalert.pl

Option	Description
-alertlog	Full path to the database alert log file
-database	ORACLE_SID of database to check
-debug	Runs in console mode and prints debugging messages
-kill	Used with -database option to stop the chkalert.pl daemon
-sendmail	Error messages mailed to DBA addresses in configuration file

Installing and Configuring chkalert_NT.pl for Win32

So far, we've been focusing on how to do alert monitoring on Unix systems. The methods for handling background processes differ significantly for Win32, and as we mentioned, there is a separate script for Win32. That script, *chkalert_NT.pl*, was installed along with the rest of the toolkit. This script is dependent on the *Win32:: Daemon* Perl module, also installed in Chapter 9, which allows *chkalert_NT.pl* to run as a service. These are the main configuration steps. Note that in many cases, the installation is the same for Unix and Win32, so we'll refer to the earlier Unix discussion where appropriate:

1. When the PDBA Toolkit was installed, a number of configuration files were installed along with it in a temporary location. Copy the *chkalert_NT.conf* file from this temporary location to the PDBA_HOME directory. As in Chapter 9, we'll assume that Perl is installed on your *C:* drive and that PDBA_HOME is set to *C:\PDBA*. You'll need to alter the following command appropriately if your installation is different:

   ```
   C:> copy C:\Perl\site\lib\PDBA\conf\chkalert_NT.conf C:\pdba
   ```

2. Now edit* *PDBA_HOME\chkalert_NT.conf* and set the required parameter values, as discussed earlier for Unix *chkalert.pl* configuration (see the parameters in Example 11-1, such as *dbaAddresses* and *serverName*). Example 11-2 is an example of how this file will appear with comment lines removed.

3. We recommend that you leave the default values of *alarmTime, maxLogLines, watchdogLength, watchdogTime,* and *throttleDelaySeconds.* Changing the watchdog values currently has no effect on Win32 platforms. They have been retained for future use when the *alarm()* call may be available in Perl on Win32. In the

---

* Both authors of this book are Bruce-Willis-style die-hard *vi* fanatics. We won't give it up. We used *gvim*, the windowing version of *vim*, an improved version of the *vi* text editor, for much of the code editing in this book. It's available at *http://www.vim.org*.

meantime, the watchdog functionality found in *chkalert.pl* on Unix systems is not available in *chkalert_NT.pl*.

4. Because *alarm()* is unavailable, keep the default *alarmTime* parameter.

5. You must also leave *maxLogLines* set to 1 on Win32; the timeout method for periodic mailing of error messages is not available on Win32.

Example 11-2. Editing chkalert_NT.conf on Win32 platforms

```
package chkalert;
use vars qw{ %ckConf };
%ckConf = (
  dbaAddresses => [qw{yourname@yourdomain.com 8885551234@mobile.att.net}],
  debugDBA => [qw{someone@somewhere.com}],
  alarmTime => 5,
  maxLogLines => 1,
  watchdogLength => 5,
  watchdogTime => 10,
  throttleDelaySeconds => 10,
  serverName => 'mail.yourdomain.com',
  errorList => qw{^ORA- ^TNS- crash},
);
1;
```

6. To install the *chkalert_NT.pl* service, navigate to the install directory:

```
C:> cd C:\perl\site\lib\pdba\util
```

7. Now run the *chkalert_service.pl* utility. The following command assumes that our database server is Oracle 8.1.x on Drive *D:* and that the target database is *ts20*. Your mileage may vary. (The following command must be entered on one line; we've split it only for formatting purposes):

```
C:> chkalert_service.pl -install -database ts20 -alertlog \
        d:\ora81\admin\bdump\ts20\ts20alrt.log
```

8. If you need to remove the service, replace *-install* with *-remove*:

```
C:> chkalert_service.pl -remove -database ts20 -alertlog \
        d:\ora81\admin\bdump\ts20\ts20alrt.log
```

Table 11-2 summarizes the command-line options for *chkalert_service.pl*.

Table 11-2. Command-line options—chkalert_service.pl

Option	Description
-install	Installs the alert log monitor service
-remove	Removes the alert log monitor service
-database	Supplies the SID of the database
-alertlog	Provides the full path to the alert log

Starting the service

Now that *chkalert_NT.pl* has been installed, we fire up the Win32 Service Manager to start the service. You can navigate to this tool with one of the following sets of keystrokes. (Note that Service Manager works much the same on the two platforms.)

Windows NT
> *Start → Settings → Control Panel*, click *Services*

Windows 2000
> *Start → Settings → Control Panel*, click *Administrative Tools*, click *Services*

Figure 11-1 is an example of what you should see in Service Manager after successfully installing *chkalert_NT.pl*. The new service appears as *Oracle_ts20_AlertLogMon*. Simply click on the *Start* button, and your alert log monitor should be off and running. (If this install fails to go smoothly the first time around, check Chapter 9 for all the modules required by *chkalert_NT.pl*.)

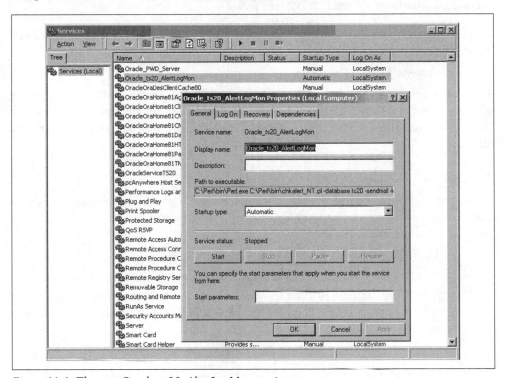

Figure 11-1. The new Oracle_ts20_AlertLogMon service

If the install should have the temerity to run imperfectly first time out, you may see a screen like that shown in Figure 11-2. You will need to go to the command line to try to sort it out. Check to see if Perl can compile the script:

```
C:> perl -cw c:\perl\bin\chkalert_NT.pl
```

You can see the results of that in the following:

```
Can't locate Win32/Daemon.pm in @INC (@INC contains: C:/Perl/lib
C:/Perl/site/lib .) at c:\perl\bin\chkalert_NT.pl line 10.
BEGIN failed--compilation aborted at c:\perl\bin\chkalert_NT.pl line 10.
```

It appears that we missed installing the *Win32::Daemon* module. Should something like this happen, go back and review the installation instructions in Chapter 9 to make sure that all the required elements were installed.

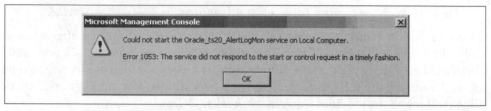

Figure 11-2. Oracle_ts20_AlertLogMon service failure

After re-installing *Win32::Daemon* to its former glory (we kept removing it in our test runs), the compile was successful, producing this output:

```
c:\perl\bin\chkalert_NT.pl syntax OK
```

If you continue to experience difficulties in running the service, make sure that the fully qualified file name, specified for the alert log during *chkalert_service.pl* installation, is correct. If it is incorrect, it won't cause an error until you attempt to restart the service.

Testing Oracle_SID_AlertLogMon

Now that we have the *Oracle_SID_AlertLogMon* service running, we can verify that it's working as expected. Carry out this test only while a test database is down, as we need to directly edit its alert log.

1. Use your favorite text editor to edit the database's alert log:

   ```
   C:> vi c:\oracle\admin\ts20\bdump\ts20alrt.log  # Just say vi! :-)
   ```

2. Navigate to the last line of the file. We've displayed a fragment of our own alert log seen here. The last line begins with *ORA-20000*. Add a similar line at the end of your own alert log.

   ```
      Current log# 3 seq# 918 mem# 0: D:\ORACLE\ORADATA\TS20\REDO03.LOG
      Successful open of redo thread 1.
      Tue Aug 21 21:45:02 2001S
      MON: enabling cache recovery
      Tue Aug 21 21:45:02 2001
      ARC0: Beginning to archive log# 2 seq# 917
      ARC0: Completed archiving log# 2 seq# 917
      Tue Aug 21 21:45:07 2001
      SMON: enabling tx recovery
      Tue Aug 21 21:46:28 2001
   ```

```
Completed: alter database open
ORA-20000: chkalert test error
```

3. Enter a RETURN at the end of the line, and then save the file.

4. When *chkalert_NT.pl* was installed earlier, the logging feature was turned on. To access this log, we navigate to the *C:\temp* directory in Explorer.

5. Sort the entries by date so the newest files appear at the top of the window. You just need to click twice on the *Modified* column in the file detail pane. (Note that this is not a double-click. The first click will sort the files by date in ascending order, and the second click will sort by date in descending order.) Your display should be similar to that shown in Figure 11-3.

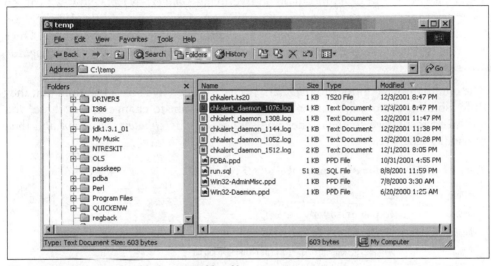

Figure 11-3. Locating the chkalert_NT.pl log file

6. The logging files are created with the process ID embedded in them. If we start and stop the alert checking service a few times, we'll therefore see several files of the form *chkalert_daemon_PID.log*. Choose the newest one, and open it with your favorite editor. Here's ours; notice that the *ORA-20000* error appears in the middle of the file.

```
Waiting for service...Service started, ready to change stateService state changed
to SERVICE_RUNNUNG
Options loaded from command line
DATABASE: ts20
ALERT LOG: d:\oracle\admin\ts20\bdump\ts20alrt.log
DBA's    : someone@somewhere.com 7775551212@mobile.att.net
Top of main loop
Top of main loop
Top of main loop
Error: ORA-20000: chkalert test error
Top of MailMsgs
Mail To: someone@somewhere.com:7775551212@mobile.att.net
```

```
Mail Subject: Alert Log Errors in ts20 on sherlock.jks.com
Mail Message:
ORA-20000: chkalert test error encountered  in ts20 at 2001/12/03 - 20:47
Top of main loop
Top of main loop
Top of main loop
Stopping Service
exiting - files cleaned up
```

7. The log file should prove two things:
   - The fake error was detected.
   - The fake error was mailed to the configured email addresses.

8. That's it. We're done installing and verifying *chkalert_NT.pl*. Now we can go back to the Services Manager application and stop the *Oracle_PID_AlertLogMon* service. We should also remove the fake error message from the alert log. Once this is done, restart the database and then restart the *Oracle_PID_AlertLogMon* service.

The command-line options for *chkalert_NT.pl* are listed in Table 11-3; note that they differ somewhat from the earlier Unix list. If you want to change any of these, you will need to remove the alert checking service, modify *chkalert_service.pl* and then reinstall the service.

Table 11-3. Command-line options—chkalert_NT.pl

Option	Description
-alertlog	Full path to the database alert log file
-database	ORACLE_SID of the database to check
-debug	Indicates debugging messages to be included in log file
-logging	Turns on the logging feature
-sendmail	Error messages mailed to the configured DBA addresses

Monitoring the Databases

Another very high priority for Oracle DBAs is the monitoring of database connectivity. You need to constantly poll all of the databases at your site to make sure they are up and running. If a database is unavailable for any reason, you must be proactive and check out the problem as soon as possible. It is definitely *not* good practice to wait until your users discover a connectivity problem before you take care of it. It's far better to deal with such problems as soon as they occur in order to minimize the impact on users. Much as we dislike the dissonant refrains of a pager in the small hours, we still prefer that to having users inform us of database problems as we stroll innocently into the office the next morning! As databases grow more critical to business, the importance of uptime continues to grow too. It's clear that we need a tool to help us maintain 24x7 connectivity, or at least edge us closer to this ideal state.

We've included a collection of database monitoring scripts in our PDBA Toolkit that will help you keep track of database connectivity and alert you when something goes wrong. The scripts described in the following sections continually poll databases to make sure they're up and running. When a database is unavailable, the on-call DBA is immediately emailed and paged, and every member of the DBA team also receives an email. Using our scripts, you can configure the emailing and timing to meet your specific needs.

Monitoring Database Connectivity with dbup.pl and dbpu_NT.pl

We've written a pair of connectivity monitoring scripts: *dbup.pl* for Unix and *dbup_ NT.pl* for Win32. Both are highly configurable and offer these features:

Database uptime
> You specify the time periods that a specific database should be up. If the database goes down outside these hours, the DBA gets emailed but is not paged.

DBA rotation
> You can create an on-call rotation for DBAs, and you can specify a default DBA to cover any exposed gaps you may choose to leave. We'll show a sample DBA schedule later.

Supervisor notification
> You may optionally page a supervisor (or anyone else) when a database fails, regardless of the DBA that is on call. You can also email the supervisor.

Connection test interval
> You can configure the intervals between database connection attempts.

Delayed paging
> You can also delay paging during off-duty hours. The configuration parameter *hoursToPageImmediate* determines the hour range when paging is suspended. The parameter *maxConnectRetries* determines the number of connection attempts before the on-call DBA is paged. This prevents the DBA or supervisor from being paged during the night if database connectivity is restored within a preset number of reconnection attempts. This is useful for situations that disrupt database connectivity for a few minutes without causing a true problem— for example, evening reboots that occur on a standard schedule. Email and event logging still take place.

Impressing your system administrators
> OK, this is hardly built into the system, but it does tend to happen anyway. When one of your database servers decides to head for the land of dreams, you're naturally going to get paged when the connectivity monitor cannot connect to the database server. If you configure *dbup.pl* to connect to each database every five minutes, it won't be long before you're aware that the database server

itself is down. Sysadmins are always somewhat amazed to find out that you know about a server outage before they do. We've found this goes a long way towards maintaining cordial relations with our own systadmins.

Installing Additional Modules

In order to properly manipulate dates in our *dbup.pl* monitoring script, we've chosen to use Sullivan Beck's *Date::Manip* module, an incredibly flexible pure Perl module used for parsing and comparing dates. It allows you to specify a date in literally hundreds of formats, recognizing them automagically and parsing them into its own internal operational format.* This module allows *dbup.pl* to handle the time intervals you specify.

Because the *Data::Manip* module is not part of the regular Perl distribution, you will need to install it before continuing with the configuration of *dbup.pl*.

Installing Date::Manip on Unix

Download the latest version of *Date::Manip* from a CPAN site near you:

  http://www.cpan.org/authors/id/SBECK

Follow the usual drill to unpack its tarball and install it, or alternatively use the CPAN shell as follows:

```
$ perl -MCPAN -e "shell"
cpan> install Date::Manip
cpan> quit
```

Installing Date::Manip on Win32

Connect to the Internet and perform the usual ActivePerl maneuver:

```
C:> ppm
PPM> install Date::Manip
PPM> quit
```

Up until now, most of the Win32 Perl modules we've installed via PPM have been fairly simple to install. *Date::Manip* is a bit more complex. We don't have to compile anything, but we do need to do some editing, as we'll describe in the next section.

TZ—Time Zones

The *Date::Manip* module needs to be able to get time zone information from the machine it's running on. This is not a problem on Unix platforms, which give up time zone data quite readily. However, obtaining this information on Win32 is a

---

* Appendix D, *The Essential Guide to Perl Data Munging*, also describes *Date::Calc*, a more rapid, less diverse, C-based date-manipulation module.

little more involved. The *Date::Manip* documentation describes a number of methods for setting the attributes of the time zone environment variable, *TZ*, but we've found only one reliable way on Win32 platforms, and that's to use the *Date::Manip* configuration file, *Manip.cnf*. This file is not normally configured when you install the *Date::Manip* module with PPM. Follow these steps to obtain and edit this file:

1. Copy a *Date::Manip* configuration file to *PDBA_HOME*. There are two ways to obtain this file. The first and easiest way is to copy it from the PDBA Toolkit distribution as we've already included it for you there:

   ```
   C:> copy C:\perl\site\lib\PDBA\conf\Manip.conf C:\pdba
   ```

2. The other way is to download the *Date::Manip* tarball from CPAN. The current version of *Date::Manip*, as of this writing, was 5.40. If the version installed on your system is different, you may wish to install the configuration file from the latest version of *Date::Manip*, which can be found at *http://www.cpan.org/ authors/id/SBECK*. Open the archive file, locate the file *Manip.cnf*, and save it to *PDBA_HOME* as shown in Figure 11-4.

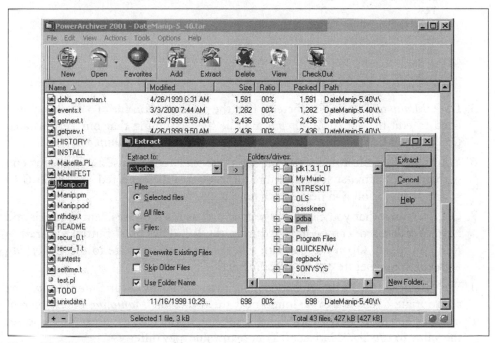

Figure 11-4. Extracting Manip.cnf from the archive

3. Rename the file from *Manip.cnf* to *Manip.conf*. (This is simply to stay consistent when naming configuration files and thus avoiding later confusion.) You can rename the file by right-clicking on the file in Windows Explorer, and clicking on *Rename*. Alternatively, do this from the command line:

   ```
   C:> move C:\pdba\Manip.cnf C:\pdba\Manip.conf
   ```

4. Next up sports fans, edit the file:

```
C:> vi C:\pdba\Manip.conf
```

There are two entries for *TZ* that you may need to edit: *TZ* and *ConvTZ*. The following example shows where they're usually located in the *Manip.conf* file. If your time zone* happens to be PST (Pacific Standard Time), you can save the file the way it came out of the box (which is nice, if you live in Oregon, USA, but less nice if you live in Oxfordshire, England). If you're not sure of your exact time zone, you can check the full documentation for yourself via *perldoc Date:: Manip*, on both Unix and Win32. Once you do have the time zone data set correctly, save the file and close the editor.

```
############################## CONFIG VARIABLES##############################
# See Date::Manip man page for a description of all config variables.
EraseHolidays    =
PersonalCnf      = Manip.cnf
PersonalCnfPath  = t:.
Language         = English
DateFormat       = US
TZ               = PST
ConvTZ           = PST
Internal         = 0
FirstDay         = 1
WorkWeekBeg      = 1
WorkWeekEnd      = 5
...
```

5. *Date::Manip* must be told where to find the configuration file. To do this, you'll need to edit the actual *Manip.pm* module file. Assuming that our Perl installation is under *C:\Perl*, this will be found as *C:\Perl\lib\Date\Manip.pm*.

6. You won't be able to edit this file with *Notepad.exe* because the file lines end with an *<LF>* Unix-style line terminator instead of the expected MS-DOS *<CR> <LF>* combination. Oh dear, you'll have to use *vi*!

7. OK, we admit that you can use *Wordpad.exe*, as it's more resilient, but *vi* is still best. *Wordpad.exe* can be accessed from the Windows *Start* button via *Start → Run*, Wordpad. Open the file with *File → Open* and navigate to the *C:\Perl\lib\ Date* directory before opening *Manip.pm*.

8. We just need to edit the global configuration file location for *Date::Manip*. The appropriate directive can be found near the top of the *Manip.pm* file by searching for *GlobalCnf*. We've highlighted this line in the following example and set the value to *c:/pdba/Manip.conf*. Your own value may differ.

```
##########################################################################
# CUSTOMIZATION
##########################################################################
```

---

* You can learn more about the time zones defined in *Date::Manip* by reading section 5 of RFC 822 on the "Standard for ARPA Internet Text Messages" at *http://www.faqs.org/rfcs/rfc822.html*

```
#
# See the following POD documentation section CUSTOMIZING DATE::MANIP
# for a complete description of each of these variables.

# Location of the global config file.  Tilde (~) expansions are allowed.
# This should be set in Date_Init arguments.
$Cnf{"GlobalCnf"}="c:/pdba/Manip.conf";
$Cnf{"IgnoreGlobalCnf"}="";
...
```

9. We now need to save the file, and be sure to save it as a text file. *Wordpad.exe* has the disconcerting habit of adding a *.txt* file extension to any file when you do this, but save it that way anyway.

10. We have to ensure that the file name is correct. The *Manip.pm* file has a read-only attribute, so change this before renaming the file. Open a command window and adapt the following commands, depending on what your edited file is called:

```
C:> attrib -r C:\perl\site\lib\Date\Manip.pm
C:> del C:\perl\site\lib\Date\Manip.pm
C:> move C:\perl\site\lib\Date\Manip.pm.txt C:\perl\site\lib\Date\Manip.pm
C:> perl -cw C:\perl\site\lib\Date\Manip.pm
```

Notice our use of the *perl -cw* switch. The *-c* switch causes Perl to check the syntax of a script without actually executing it, and the *-w* switch enables warnings that will catch many common errors. Using these switches ensures that the changes we made to the file are syntactically correct. Checking regularly when making changes to Perl files can save many headaches later down the road.

The *Date::Manip* Win32 configuration is now complete.

Using the PDBA::OPT and PDBA::PWC Modules

When we installed the PDBA Toolkit, it included a number of background modules, all of which are described in Chapter 9. These modules provide code that is used to support the operations of many of the Perl scripts in the toolkit. Two modules that are particularly important to the connectivity monitoring discussed in the following sections are the *PDBA::OPT* and *PDBA::PWC* modules. The purpose of the *PDBA::OPT* module is to scan the command line for options that may be intended for the password server; it then feeds the security information found on the command line to the *PDBA::PWC* module, which retrieves a password.

In the following sections, we'll delve into the guts of the toolkit in order to explain why you need *PDBA::OPT* and *PDBA::PWC* and how they work. Most readers won't need to know this information. But if you are interested in how we've put the toolkit together and may want to extend it some day, read on.

The password server

You may recall that back in Chapter 9 we set up the password server and experimented with the password client *pwc.pl*, which makes use of the *PDBA::PWC* module. This script can be used on the command line to retrieve passwords from the server, and the same interface is used in most of our toolkit scripts. Fortunately, the *pwc.conf* configuration file allows us to make use of the password server while keeping the number of command-line options to a minimum.* The password server is required if you wish to use the *dbup.pl* connectivity monitor. It's the *PWD::OPT* module that works behind the scenes to allow us to eliminate a great deal of related code. Here's how it works:

1. *Getopt::Long* is a standard Perl module used for parsing command line arguments. We need to configure the *Getopt::Long* module to allow extra command-line options, which it doesn't recognize by default. Here's an excerpt from *dbup.pl* with the new *Getopt::Long* configuration clearly shown:

```
use Getopt::Long;
our %optctl=();

# passthrough allows additional command line options
# to be passed to PDBA::OPT if needed
Getopt::Long::Configure(qw{pass_through});
GetOptions( \%optctl, "conf=s",   "debug!",
                      "kill!",    "mail!",
                      "daemon!",  "h|z|help" );
```

The *Getopt::Long::Configure(qw{pass_through})* statement tells *Getopt::Long* to ignore any extra command-line arguments it may soon see via *@ARGV*. These will be passed onto *PDBA::OPT*.

2. The *dbup.pl* script loops through a hash data structure, *%dbup::uptime*, which lists the databases to which *dbup.pl* should attempt to connect. For each target database, it calls the *PDBA::OPT* module. This module, in turn, uses *pwc.conf* to help connect to the password server. Here's a simplified example of the call to *PDBA::OPT*:

```
for my $db ( keys %dbup::uptime ) {
    my $password =
        PDBA::OPT->pwcOptions ( INSTANCE => $db,
                                MACHINE => $dbup::uptime{$db}->{machine},
                                USERNAME => $dbup::uptime{$db}->{username});
}
```

What isn't apparent in this short example is the volume of hard work that *PDBA::OPT* is doing in the background. It looks up the *pwc.conf* configuration file, loads its entire contents, and then makes sure that any parameters input via

---

* The only options normally needed at the command line in order to use the password server are *-machine*, *-database*, and *-username*, which we'll cover soon.

the command line take precedence over those just found in *pwc.conf*. With the required information, *PDBA::OPT* then retrieves the necessary password from the password server.

We've reproduced the working portion of *PDBA::OPT* in Example 11-3. Configuration is unnecessary because it uses the password client setup we created in Chapter 9. It's important, though, to understand how *PDBA::OPT* makes use of command-line parameters to override values found in the *pwc.conf* file. We'll work through the important code lines after Example 11-3.

Example 11-3. PDBA::OPT

```
1    package PDBA::OPT;
2
3    $VERSION = '1.00';
4
5    use strict;
6    no strict 'vars';
7
8    use Getopt::Long;
9    use PDBA::ConfigFile;
10   use Carp;
11   %optctl = ();
12
13   sub pwcOptions {
14
15       my $self = shift;
16       my %args = @_;
17
18       Getopt::Long::Configure(qw{pass_through});
19
20       use PDBA::PWC;
21
22       $optctl{pwc_conf} = 'pwc.conf';
23
24       # specified directly on the command line
25       GetOptions(\%optctl,
26           "pwc_host=s",       # remote password server host
27           "pwc_port=i",       # port to connect to
28           "pwc_machine=s",    # database server
29           "pwc_instance=s",   # database instance
30           "pwc_username=s",   # database username
31           "pwc_conf=s",       # configuration file
32           "pwc_key=s",        # encryption key
33           "pwc_my_username=s", # your password server username
34           "pwc_my_password=s", # your password server password
35           "pwc_debug!"        # turn debug on
36       );
37
38       # overrides from the config file
39       if ( exists( $optctl{pwc_conf} ) ) {
40           use PDBA::ConfigFile;
```

Example 11-3. PDBA::OPT (continued)

```
41        unless ( new PDBA::ConfigLoad( FILE => $optctl{pwc_conf} ) ) {
42            croak "could not load config file  $optctl{pwc_conf}\n";
43        }
44
45        for my $key ( keys %pwc::optctl ) {
46            $optctl{'pwc_' . $key} = $pwc::optctl{$key}
47                unless exists $optctl{'pwc_' . $key};
48        }
49    }
50
51    # overrides from args passed to pwcOptions
52    # just a bunch of ifs
53    if (defined($args{HOST})){ $optctl{pwc_host} = $args{HOST} }
54    if (defined($args{PORT})){ $optctl{pwc_port} = $args{PORT} }
55    if (defined($args{MACHINE}))
56        { $optctl{pwc_machine} = $args{MACHINE} }
57    if (defined($args{INSTANCE}))
58        { $optctl{pwc_instance} = $args{INSTANCE} }
59    if (defined($args{USERNAME}))
60        { $optctl{pwc_username} = $args{USERNAME} }
61    if (defined($args{CONF})){ $optctl{pwc_conf} = $args{CONF} }
62    if (defined($args{KEY})){ $optctl{pwc_key} = $args{KEY} }
63    if (defined($args{PWD_USERNAME}))
64        { $optctl{pwc_my_username} = $args{PWD_USERNAME} }
65    if (defined($args{PWD_PASSWORD}))
66        { $optctl{pwc_my_password} = $args{PWD_PASSWORD} }
67    if (defined($args{DEBUG})){ $optctl{pwc_debug} = $args{DEBUG} }
68
69    if (
70        ! defined( $optctl{pwc_host})
71        || ! defined( $optctl{pwc_port})
72        || ! defined( $optctl{pwc_machine})
73        || ! defined( $optctl{pwc_instance})
74        || ! defined( $optctl{pwc_username})
75        || ! defined( $optctl{pwc_key})
76        || ! defined( $optctl{pwc_my_username})
77        || ! defined( $optctl{pwc_my_password})
78    ) {
79    croak qq/usage: $0 with PDBA::OPT
80    --pwc_host <password server>
81    --pwc_port <tcp port>
82    --pwc_machine <database server>
83    --pwc_instance <database instance>
84    --pwc_username <database username>
85    --pwc_conf <configuration file - optional but recommended >
86    --pwc_key <encryption key>
87    --pwc_my_username <password server username>
88    --pwc_my_password <password server password
89  /;
90    }
91
92    my $remote_host=$optctl{pwc_host};
```

Example 11-3. PDBA::OPT (continued)

```
93      my $remote_port=$optctl{pwc_port};
94      my $machine=$optctl{pwc_machine};
95      my $instance=$optctl{pwc_instance};
96      my $username=$optctl{pwc_username};
97      my $myusername=$optctl{pwc_my_username};
98      my $mypassword=$optctl{pwc_my_password};
99      my $key=$optctl{pwc_key};
100
101     $optctl{pwc_debug} =
102         exists $optctl{pwc_debug} ? $optctl{pwc_debug} : 0;
103
104     my $client = new PDBA::PWC(
105         host => $remote_host,
106         port => $remote_port
107     );
108
109     $client->authenticate(
110         username => $myusername,
111         password => $mypassword,
112         key => $key,
113         debug => $optctl{pwc_debug}
114     );
115
116     # get response
117     my $password = $client->getPassword(
118         machine => $machine,
119         instance => $instance,
120         username => $username,
121         key => $key,
122         debug => $optctl{pwc_debug}
123     );
124
125     return $password;
126 };
127 1;
```

Configuring Getopt::Long for pass-through mode

Let's look at the code and see what's going on here. In the example, at line 18, you'll see *Getopt::Long* configured into pass-through mode. This prevents it from complaining about unrecognized *@ARGV* options. Line 25 is the *GetOptions* call used to retrieve additional arguments from the command line, which may be used to override parameters in *pwc.conf*.

Let's consider an example to see how this works. The script *my_script.pl* relies on *PDBA::PWC* to retrieve passwords from the password server so a database connection can be made. A typical call to the script might look like this:

```
$ my_script.pl -machine sherlock -database ts01 -username scott
```

The script relies on the password server on Unix server *watson* to retrieve the password for user *scott* on database *ts01*. The *ts01* database is itself housed on Unix server *sherlock*. The password server running on *watson* is normally transparent to the user. This is because the nitty-gritty details are hidden away in the *pwc.conf* configuration file, and *PDBA::OPT* is taking care of all of that for you.

What happens though, if the server *watson* is inaccessible for some reason? We still need to run our script, but because the password server is unavailable, we'll see an error like the code snippet here:

```
Uncaught exception from user code:
        Couldn't connect to watson:1579 : IO::Socket::INET: Timeout
    ...
        PDBA::OPT::pwcOptions('PDBA::OPT', 'INSTANCE', 'ts01', 'MACHINE',
'sherlock', 'USERNAME', 'scott') called at ./my_script.pl line 39
```

Further investigation reveals that the server itself is down and won't be up for another two hours. But we do know that an identically configured password server is *also* running on server *mycroft* as shown in Figure 11-5. Because *PDBA::OPT* allows us to override the parameters in *pwc.conf* with those stipulated on the command line, you rerun the command to execute *my_script.pl*, this time redirecting *PDBA::OPT* to connect to the password server on *mycroft*:

```
$ my_script.pl -machine sherlock -database ts01
        -username scott -pwc_host mycroft
```

This successfully outputs:

```
GLOBAL_NAME: TS01.JKS.COM
```

The script *my_script.pl* is a simple one; all it does is retrieve the GLOBAL_NAME of the database from the system view GLOBAL_NAME. The important point, however, is that it succeeded in doing so.

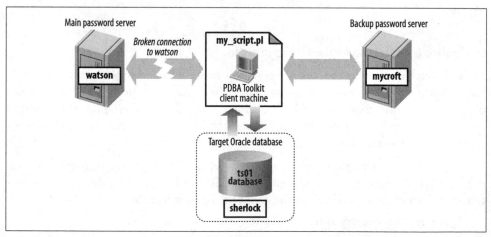

Figure 11-5. Use of an alternative password server

Loading the password client parameters

At line 41, in Example 11-3, the parameters from *pwc.conf* are loaded. These are used to load the *%optctl* hash with keys that begin with *pwc_*, in lines 45–48. This code will only set parameters that have not already been set with command line parameters.

In lines 53–67, the hash reference *$args* is checked for explicit overrides passed to *PDBA::OPT* by the caller. If any values are found, they replace the corresponding keys in the *%optctl* hash. For example, the following code fragment always directs *PDBA::OPT* to try to connect via the password server on host *moriarty*, regardless of what is contained in *pwc.conf* or directed to by the command-line option *-pwc_host*.

```
my $password = PDBA::OPT->pwcOptions (
    INSTANCE => $db,
    MACHINE => $dbup::uptime{$db}->{machine},
    USERNAME => $dbup::uptime{$db}->{username},
    HOST => 'moriarty' );
```

In lines 92–127 these final values are used to set up a session with the password server and retrieve the requested password.

Although we've provided quite a bit of detail here, you'll be relieved to hear that most Oracle DBAs never need to worry about this level of detail. As we mentioned earlier, we've exposed this implementation information for those who might want to modify our scripts or create your own. (We'll say more about doing that in Chapter 13.) Table 11-4 contains a listing of all command-line overrides available to *PDBA::OPT*.

Table 11-4. Command-line overrides for PDBA::OPT

Option	Description
-pwc_host	Password server host
-pcw_port	TCP connection port
-pcw_machine	Database server
-pcw_instance	Database Instance
-pcw_username	Database username needing retrieved password
-pcw_conf	Password client configuration file
-pcw_key	Password server encryption key
-pcw_my_username	Password client username
-pcw_my_password	Password client password
-pcw_debug	Turns on debug code

Configuring dbup.pl and dbup_NT.pl

After our skirmish with the black box forces of *PDBA::OPT*, let's get back to the task at hand. We need to periodically check our database connectivity and get notified immediately if there's a problem. Fortunately, we have the technology. We'll discuss the Unix and Win32 configurations together because although the two scripts differ internally, they are configured identically. However, there is a bit of preparation that is platform-specific.

Win32 preparation

Before configuring *dbup_NT.pl* on Win32, you need to do the following:

1. First, place a copy of the supplied *dbup.conf* config file into PDBA_HOME:

    ```
    C:> copy C:\perl\site\lib\PDBA\conf\dbup_NT.conf C:\pdba
    ```

2. Now we have to install the *dbup* service. As luck would have it, you should find a pre-supplied Perl script, *dbup_service.pl*, available for just this purpose. Navigate to the directory where the PDBA utilities are living and run the install script:

    ```
    C:> dbup_service.pl -install
    Install
    Successfully added.
    Finished.
    ```

Unix preparation

Change to the directory where the PDBA Toolkit was installed. Make sure that the configuration file exists in PDBA_HOME if you've changed Unix users and it's not already there:

```
$ cd /u01/build/PDBA-1.00
$ cp dbup2/dbup.conf $PDBA_HOME
```

Configuration on both platforms

The only real difference between the two systems is that *dbup_NT.conf* has had each line terminated with *<CR><LF>*, enabling us to edit this config file with *Notepad. exe*. The first section of the file is displayed in Example 11-4.

Example 11-4. dbup.conf

```
# this line is required
package dbup;
use PDBA;

use vars qw( $dateFormat $ignoreFile
             %parms %uptime %addresses
             %onCallList @supervisors );

# format of date in ignoreFile
$dateFormat = "%Y/%m/%d-%H:%M:%S";
$ignoreFile = 'dbignore.conf';
```

Here's what's happening in this code:

1. The first code line establishes the Perl package name as *dbup*.

2. The *use vars* statement prevents runtime warnings from occurring whenever a variable is referenced only once.

3. *$dateFormat* and *$ignoreFile* are used later on to notify the monitor whenever you wish to remove a specific database from these regular connectivity checks until a specified date and time.

The rest of the module is then loaded. Example 11-5 shows some operational parameters that we may need to edit.

Example 11-5. Operational parameters—dbup.conf

```
%parms = (
    mailServer => 'mail.yourdomain.com',
    fromAddress => 'oracle@yourdomain.com',

    # how often to check database connectivity
    # measured in seconds
    # low value used for testing
    # connectInterval => 30,
    connectInterval => 300,
    # hours are 0 - 23
    # these are the hours to page immediately without
    # retrying the connection.  outside of these hours,
    # retry a configurable number of times before paging

    hoursToPageImmediate => [6..18],
    # use a limited range for testing during the day
    #hoursToPageImmediate => [19..20],
    # don't page DBA during lunch. :)
    #hoursToPageImmediate => [6..11, 13..18],

    # how many times to retry a connection when the time
    # is outside the range of hoursToPage
    maxConnectRetries => 3,
    # *everything* is logged
    # will use PDBA_HOME
    logfile => PDBA->pdbaHome() . q{/logs/dbup.log},
);
```

The following summarizes these parameters; some of them may be familiar from our earlier discussion of alert monitoring:

mailServer

You need to change the default value of *mail.yourdomain.com* to your local mail server. If your domain is *acme.com*, this might be *mail.acme.com*. Talk to your friendly sysadmin about this if you're unsure.

fromAddress

Used in the *sent from* part of the mail header for all mail dispatched from *dbup*. This needn't necessarily be a real email address. Continuing with the domain of *acme.com*, you could set this to *oracle_dba@acme.com*.

connectInterval

Determines how much time, in seconds, passes between database connection attempts. The default of 300 allows five minutes between attempts, though on Unix you may wish to alter this value. On Win32, we set it to a lower value, such as 180, which is explained in the following note. Keep in mind that when a database is down, we'll be emailed, or paged whenever a connection attempt fails. The lower the value for *connectInterval*, the more often this will happen until the situation is remedied.

 Win32 services are stopped and started via the Service Manager. This presents a problem with *dbup_NT.pl* if the *connectInterval* parameter is set too high. The monitor runs in a loop, and at the end of each iteration a *sleep* call is made, for a period of *$dbup::parms::connectInterval* seconds. The *dbup* service fails to respond to the Service Manager's request for termination until the *sleep* call is completed. If *connectInterval* is set to 600, the service will ignore termination requests for 10 minutes. We therefore recommend a lower value, such as 180.

The next two parameters work in concert, determining if the on-call DBA will be paged immediately or if the page call will be deferred:

hoursToPageImmediate

In Example 11-5, *hoursToPageImmediate* is set to a value of [6..18]. These numbers refer to a 24-hour clock. From 6:00 AM, until 6:59 PM (18:59), the DBA is paged immediately if a connection error occurs.

maxConnectRetries

If a connection error does occur outside of the *hoursToPageImmediate* time frame, *dbup* makes *maxConnectRetries* reconnect attempts before paging the DBA. We particularly appreciate this feature when servers are rebooted in the middle of the night after a minor hardware glitch, and paging is avoided because the target server and all its databases are back up within a few minutes. All *failures-to-connect* are still recorded in the log, however, and an email is sent regardless of whether the on-call DBA was paged.

Let's thank the two Larrys for small mercies. Because this is Perl, we're allowed enormous flexibility in defining the *hoursToPageImmediate* hourly range. You may have noticed a commented-out section in Example 11-5, where we'd previously specified the DBA paging hours as [6..11, 13..18]. If you feel that you deserve a two-hour lunch window between 11:00 AM and 1:00 PM, when the *dbup* secretary should place all calls on hold, the opportunity is there!

---

logfile

Full path file name for the log of all *dbup* operations. The default displayed in the example should work fine as is, unless you wish to place the log somewhere else. Because the config files are executed as code in the *PDBA::ConfigLoad* module, you can use the *PDBA->pdbaHome* method to place the file, as shown in Example 11-5.

Examining uptime requirements

Let's examine Example 11-6 to determine the database uptime requirements.

Example 11-6. Database uptime requirements—dbup.conf

```
%uptime = (
    ts01 => {
        machine => 'sherlock',
        upDays => [0..6],
        upHours => [0..23],
        username => 'system',
        alertLevel => 3 },
    ts20 => {
        machine => 'mycroft',
        upDays => [0..6],
        upHours => [0..23],
        username => 'system',
        alertLevel => 3 },
    ts99 => {
        machine => 'watson',
        upDays => [1..5],
        upHours => [6..18],
        username => 'system',
        alertLevel => 2 },
);
```

The *%uptime* hash specifies five parameters for each database needing testing:

machine

Name of the server hosting the database.

upDays

This value range specifies the weekdays that the database is in live production mode. The values are *0..6*, which means from Sunday through Saturday. Let's look at a few examples; see the following section for more details:

A value of [0..6] means that the database is required 7 days a week.

A value of [1..5] means that the database is required Monday through Friday.

A value of [1..3, 5,6] tells *dbup* that this database needs to be up Monday through Wednesday, and then Friday through Saturday.

upHours

> Just as you can specify weekday requirements, you can also set the daily hours of required uptime. Let's look at a few examples; see the following section for more details:
>
> > A value of [0..23] indicates a database that's required 24 hours a day.
> >
> > A value of [8..17] means that the database is only required to be up from 8:00 AM until 6:00 PM; this sets the time of operation from 8:00 AM to 5:59 PM (the granularity of this parameter is 1 hour, and at 6:00 PM the hour becomes 18:00). In practice we'd set these parameters to [6..18] (see the next section).

username

> Database account used to attempt the database connection.

alertLevel

> A strictly informational field. When the on-call DBA is paged, it includes a line detailing *alertLevel*. For example, we use alert levels of 1 through 3, with 3 being Ace-high. We'll see an email like this on our cell phones:

```
2002/12/29 - 03:45 DB Down: ts20
From: oracle@jks.com
To: dba@yourcompany.com
Failed to connect to database ts20 at 2002/12/29 - 03:45
 Alert Level: 3
```

> If we see this one, we know that we'd better stop hugging that pillow, get out of bed, and take care of that database right away!

Looking at upDays and upHours parameters

Before moving on, let's take a moment to discuss how DBA paging is impacted by the *upDays* and *upHours* parameters. If *dbup.pl* or *dbup_NT.pl* is unable to connect to a database outside of the time specified by these parameters, the on-call DBA avoids being paged. This is useful for systems without 24x7 uptime requirements.

Let's see what the best parameter settings would be for this type of system. Given a database requiring uptime from Monday through Friday and from 8:00 AM until 6:00 PM each day, we'd set the *upHours* parameter to [6..18]. This specification has the effect of notifying the on-call DBA of any problems at 6:00 AM, allowing time to rectify those problems before 8:00 AM when users will typically expect the database to be available. This also allows an extra hour after the 6:00 PM end of uptime. At this point, the DBA can correct any errors that might have occurred during that dangerous time of day when machine operators are ending their shifts (and possibly rushing to go home and introducing errors in the process).

Setting up pager and email addresses

Example 11-7 shows the section of the configuration file that is used to set up the pager and email addresses for the DBA Manager, the Operations Manager, and the DBAs themselves.

Example 11-7. Email addresses—dbup.conf

```
%addresses = (

    'dbamgr' => {
        pager => '7775551212@mobile.att.net',
        emailWork => 'atwork@yourdomain.com',
        emailHome => 'athome@yourdomain.com' },

    'opsmgr' => {
        pager => '7775551212@mobile.att.net',
        emailWork => 'atwork@yourdomain.com',
        emailHome => 'athome@yourdomain.com' },

    'dba_1' => {
        pager => '7775551212@mobile.att.net',
        emailWork => 'atwork@yourdomain.com',
        emailHome => 'athome@yourdomain.com' },
    'dba_2' => {
        pager => '7775551212@mobile.att.net',
        emailWork => 'atwork@yourdomain.com',
        emailHome => 'athome@yourdomain.com' }
);

# these need to be the names of standard address
# entries in the %addresses hash.
# if these exist, supervisors will be paged at
# all times a DBA is paged, and will be sent
# all mail sent to the oncall DBA
# if you don't want this feature to be enabled,
# set it to an empty list.
# e.g.
#   @supervisors=();
# or just comment it out.
@supervisors = ('opsmgr','dbamgr');
```

Note the following guidelines:

- There should be a single entry for each of the *dbamgr* and *opsmgr* entries.
- The DBA entries may be repeated for as many DBAs as you want to include.
- If you don't want the Operations or DBA Managers to be paged in the event of database failure, just leave those entries as they are. We'll demonstrate shortly how to disable them.

Each entry has three parameters—one for a pager and two more for emails.

pager

> Email address for a pager or cell phone. This must be a valid email address—simply using a phone number will not work, as all communications from *dbup* are done via email. Many cellular phone companies offer an email address for cellular phones, similar to those shown in Example 11-7.

emailWork

> Valid email address for the nominated person's workplace.

emailHome

> Valid email address for the nominated person's home email.

Be aware of the following rules:

- The *pager* parameter is strictly unnecessary. If you wish to disable it, just set the value to an empty pair of quotes:

  ```
  pager => '',
  ```

- The *emailWork* and *emailHome* parameters are required. Set them both to the same email address if necessary.

The last entry in the *%addresses* section is the *@supervisors* array. This determines which extra entries will be paged and emailed, in addition to the on-call DBA, in case of database failure. You disable this feature by commenting out the line with a hash # character or by creating an empty list:

```
@supervisors=( );
```

Who's on Third?

The last thing we need to do before putting our connectivity monitor into action is to determine which DBA is on-call during any given week. Example 11-8 contains the start and the end of the default entries you'll find in the *%onCallList* hash, in the *dbup* configuration file. These abbreviated entries cover the time period from October 3, 2001, through October 2, 2002; each date is a Wednesday. If your schedule requires a different day as the switchover day of the on-call week, you need to edit these dates. Be sure to retain the *YYYYMMDD* format as shown.

Example 11-8. DBA on-call schedule—dbup.conf

```
%onCallList = (
  '20011003' => 'dba_1',
  '20011010' => 'dba_2',
  '20011017' => 'dba_1',
  '20011024' => 'dba_2',
  ...
  '20020911' => 'dba_2',
  '20020918' => 'dba_1',
  '20020925' => 'dba_2',
  '20021002' => 'dba_1',
  'default' => 'dba_1' );
```

Note the following about this example:

1. Simply change our *dba_1* and *dba_2* values to those corresponding to the DBAs specified within the section shown in Example 11-7.

2. The final entry in the *%onCallList* hash is *default*. This is the DBA (or manager) who is paged when dates fall outside the date range specified.

3. There is some latitude possible when setting the *%onCallList* hash. If you use a single physical pager for the on-call DBA, and pass it around among those in the DBA group, you can delete all of the dated entries and leave just the default entry. This entry will thus always be the one paged in the case of a database failure. Even though only one DBA entry in the configuration file will now be paged, email will still be sent to all entries in the *%addresses* hash. Example 11-9 is an example of just such a setup.

Example 11-9. Configuring for a single pager—dbup.conf

```
%addresses = (
    'dbamgr' => { pager => '7775551212@mobile.att.net',
                  emailWork => 'atwork@yourdomain.com',
                  emailHome => 'athome@yourdomain.com' },

    'dba_1' => { pager => '7775551212@mobile.att.net',
                 emailWork => 'atwork@yourdomain.com',
                 emailHome => 'athome@yourdomain.com' },

    'dba_2' => { pager => '7775551212@mobile.att.net',
                 emailWork => 'atwork@yourdomain.com',
                 emailHome => 'athome@yourdomain.com' },

    'dbaPager' = > { pager => '7775551212@mobile.att.net',
                 emailWork => 'oracle@yourdomain.com',
                 emailHome => 'oracle@yourdomain.com' }
);
@supervisors = ('dbamgr');
%onCallList = ('default' => 'dbaPager');
```

Now that we're finished editing the *dbup* configuration file, we can check it for syntax. On Unix, specify:

```
$ perl -cw $PDBA_HOME/dbup.conf
```

On Win32 you'll need to specify the full path to the file:

```
C:\> perl -cw c:\pdba\dbup_NT.conf
```

If the syntax is valid, Perl responds with *dbup.conf syntax OK* (or a similar message). If invalid, you need to correct the error in your configuration file before continuing.

Running the Connectivity Monitor

We're now ready to run the fully loaded *dbup* monitor. For Unix, simply enter the following at the command line:

```
$ dbup.pl -daemon
```

For Win32, we'll need to start the Windows Service Manager application and then the *Oracle_dbup_Monitor* service, as shown earlier for *chkalert_NT.pl*.

Testing the monitor

Now we'll actually run the *dbup* monitor under varying conditions and examine the logfile output. The tests shown in this section were run under a Windows 2000 system. The configuration file we'll use is the one shown in Example 11-10. The only changes made for testing purposes were the substitution of real phone numbers and email addresses. Of the three databases to be checked, one of them, *ts20*, will be unavailable. We'll examine the log entries on a standard 24x7 schedule and then modify the entry for *ts20* to ensure that the required uptime is Monday through Friday. We'll then look again at the log entries.

Example 11-10. Test configuration—dbup.conf

```
package dbup;
use PDBA;
use vars qw( $dateFormat $ignoreFile
             %parms %uptime %addresses
             %onCallList @supervisors );
$dateFormat = "%Y/%m/%d-%H:%M:%S";
$ignoreFile = 'dbignore.conf';
%parms = ( mailServer => 'watson.jks.com',
           fromAddress => 'oracle@jks.com',
           connectionTimeout => 10,
           connectInterval => 120,
           hoursToPageImmediate => [0..23],
           maxConnectRetries => 3,
           logfile => PDBA->pdbaHome() . q{/logs/dbup.log} );

%uptime = (
   ts01 => { machine => 'sherlock',
             upDays => [0..6],
             upHours => [0..23],
             username => 'system',
             alertLevel => 3 },

   ts20 => { machine => 'mycroft',
             upDays => [0..6],
             upHours => [0..23],
             username => 'system',
             alertLevel => 3 },

   ts99 => { machine => 'watson',
```

Example 11-10. Test configuration—dbup.conf (continued)

```
                upDays  => [0..6],
                upHours => [0..23],
                username => 'system',
                alertLevel => 2 },
);

%addresses = (
   'dbamgr' => { pager => '7775551212@mobile.att.net',
                 emailWork => 'myboss@thecompanycom',
                 emailHome => 'myboss@herhome.com' },

   'jkstill' => { pager => '7775551213@mobile.att.net',
                  emailWork => 'jkstill@somewhere.com',
                  emailHome => 'jkstill@somewhere.com' },

   'andyd' => { pager => '7775551214@mobile.att.net',
                emailWork => 'andyd@somewhere.com',
                emailHome => 'andyd@somewhere.com' }
);

#@supervisors = ('opsmgr','dbamgr');

%onCallList = ( '20011107' => 'andyd',
                '20011114' => 'jkstill',
                '20011121' => 'andyd',
                '20011128' => 'jkstill',
                '20011205' => 'andyd',
                '20011212' => 'jkstill',
                '20011219' => 'andyd',
                '20011226' => 'jkstill',
                'default' => 'jkstill' );
1;
```

We let the *Oracle_dbup_Monitor* service run for about five minutes before stopping it. Example 11-11 displays the contents of the log file.

Example 11-11. dbup test #1

```
20011209163103:Service Starting - State is: 2
20011209163103:Service Started - State is: 4
20011209163103:Service running
20011209163103:Main Loop
20011209163104:Check database: ts01
20011209163105:Connection to ts01 successful
20011209163105:Check database: ts99
20011209163105:Connection to ts99 successful
20011209163105:Check database: ts20
20011209163106:Database ts20 down during required uptime
20011209163106:On call DBA is: andyd
20011209163106:Sent email to andyd@somewhere.com, jkstill@somewhere.com
20011209163106:Database ts20 is down - paging DBA: andyd
20011209163107:Sent page to 7775551214@mobile.att.net
```

Example 11-11. dbup test #1 (continued)

```
20011209163307:Service running
20011209163307:Main Loop
20011209163308:Check database: ts01
20011209163308:Connection to ts01 successful
20011209163308:Check database: ts99
20011209163308:Connection to ts99 successful
20011209163308:Check database: ts20
20011209163309:Database ts20 down during required uptime
20011209163309:On call DBA is: andyd
20011209163309:Sent email to andyd@somewhere.com, jkstill@somewhere.com
20011209163309:Database ts20 is down - paging DBA: andyd
20011209163310:Sent page to 7775551214@mobile.att.net
20011209163510:Stopping Service
```

Let's examine a few of the high points found in the logfile.

1. At 04:31:06 PM, on December 9, 2001, *dbup* found that *ts20* was unavailable.

2. Because the *dbup_NT.conf* file determined that this database was on a 24x7 schedule, the on-call DBA was paged at 04:31:07 PM.

3. Two minutes later, the database was still unavailable, so the on-call DBA was again paged at 04:33:10 PM.

4. At this point, the *Oracle_dbup_Monitor* service was stopped.

We then changed the following *dbup_NT.conf* file, indicating that we only required the *ts20* database to be up from Monday through Friday. The *Oracle_dbup_Monitor* service was restarted, allowed to run for five minutes, and then stopped:

```
ts20 => { machine => 'mycroft',
        upDays => [1..5],
        upHours => [6..18],
        username => 'system',
        alertLevel => 3 },
```

The results of this change are seen in Example 11-12.

Example 11-12. dbup test #2

```
20011209164456:Service Starting - State is: 220011209164456:Service Started - State is:
420011209164456:Service running20011209164456:Main Loop20011209164457:Check database:
ts0120011209164458:Connection to ts01 successful
20011209164458:Check database: ts99
20011209164458:Connection to ts99 successful
20011209164458:Check database: ts20
20011209164459:Database ts20 down during off hours
20011209164459:On call DBA is: andyd
20011209164500:Sent email to andyd@somewhere.com, jkstill@somewhere.com
20011209164700:Service running
20011209164700:Main Loop
20011209164701:Check database: ts01
```

Example 11-12. dbup test #2 (continued)

```
20011209164701:Connection to ts01 successful
20011209164701:Check database: ts99
20011209164701:Connection to ts99 successful
20011209164701:Check database: ts20
20011209164702:Database ts20 down during off hours
20011209164702:On call DBA is: andyd
20011209164703:Sent email to andyd@somewhere.com, jkstill@somewhere.com
20011209164903:Stopping Service
```

Please note the following highlights from Example 11-12:

1. At 04:44:59 PM, and again at 04:47:02 PM, *ts20* was unavailable.

2. Because this occurred outside of the required uptime for this database, the on-call DBA was emailed, but not paged.

3. If *ts20* remains unavailable after 06:00 AM on one day of required uptime, the on-call DBA is paged.

We've found this utility to be very useful, and we hope you do too. The ability to catch database connectivity problems before they have an effect on the users of the live database goes a long way toward maintaining good customer relations.

Command-line options

Only a few command-line options are available for *dbup.pl* and *dbup_NT.pl*; they are summarized in Table 11-5.

If you change an option for Win32, you must remove the *Oracle_dbup_Monitor* service via *dbup_service.pl*, edit *dbup_service.pl*, and then re-install the service at the command line to put the changes into effect. The reason for this is that the monitor is started and stopped via the Win32 Service Manager, and any command-line arguments to the *dbup* monitor are stored in the Win32 Registry. You may take comfort in the fact that the defaults are probably fine for most systems.

Table 11-5. Command-line options—dbup.pl and dbup_NT.pl

Option	Description
-conf	Name of the configuration file. This defaults to *dbup.conf*. You do not need to specify a full path locator.
-daemon	On Unix, causes *dbup.pl* to run in the background as a daemon. This option is not available for *dbup_NT.pl* on Win32.
-debug	On Unix, causes additional information to be placed in the logfile. If you are running in console mode, informational debug messages will be printed to the terminal. On Win32 systems, this option causes additional information to be placed in the logfile only.
-mail	Causes mail to be sent to the DBAs.
-nomail	Prevents email from being sent to the DBAs. (The default between *-mail* and *-nomail* is *-mail*.)
-help	Prints a help message on the terminal console.

CHAPTER 12

Building a Database Repository with the PDBA Toolkit

This chapter focuses on another important Oracle database administration requirement: the need to keep track of the many changes made to an Oracle database—changes to tables, indexes, roles, schemas, and other database objects. As part of building the Perl toolkit, we decided to create a *repository*, a central place in which to store all kinds of database changes. By centralizing the storage of changes in this way, we can easily perform such administrative tasks as tracking table changes over time, restoring last week's user passwords, recreating database roles as they appeared last month, determining the effect of major index changes on SQL execution plans, and comparing a schema against itself from a month ago. By providing a way to go back in time to compare today's database with last week's or last month's, we can often determine why programs that ran efficiently last week are now crawling—we can achieve something that looks a lot like time travel!

 Using the PDBA repository does impose some additional overhead on your use of the toolkit. You will need to install it separately and perform some customization, as described in this chapter. If you don't want to use the repository—at least at this point in time—you can simply skip this chapter. (But we hope you'll consider coming back to it in the future: using the repository does provide Oracle DBAs with very helpful information.)

The repository uses the Oracle data dictionary as the source of much of its information, freezing certain dictionary images on a regular basis and storing them over time. This chapter describes how to install the repository scripts and tables, load the repository with data, and use it to report on a variety of different kinds of database changes. We'll divide the discussion as follows:

Structure of the repository

We will introduce the tables required to hold database information in the repository.

Installing the repository

> We'll describe how to install the repository for both Unix and Win32 systems (in both standard form and for Oracle's locally managed tablespaces—LMTs).

Loading the repository with data

> We'll show how to collect the baseline data needed for the repository via the *baseline.pl* script and run some tests on the archived dictionary data.

Reporting on database changes

> We'll show a number of different reports illustrating how you can use the *spdrvr. pl* script to detect changes in database parameters and objects such as indexes and sequences over time.

Reporting on SQL execution plans

> We'll also show reports illustrating how you figure out why database performance problems are occurring by retrieving SQL from a previous period and comparing the old execution plan against the latest version. We'll describe the *sxp.pl*, *sxpcmp.pl*, and *sxprpt.pl* scripts.

Repository Table Structure

The toolkit repository contains two sets of tables. The first is a set of tables containing information we copy from the Oracle data dictionary on a regular basis. We don't copy the entire dictionary, by any means, but we do copy the most interesting and changeable data. The second set of tables is our own group of specialized tables containing information that allows us to track SQL and generate explain plans.

Tables from the Oracle Data Dictionary

Table 12-1 lists the repository tables that mirror the contents of certain Oracle data dictionary tables, and summarizes the types of database objects stored in those tables. The names of the tables are derived from the names of the corresponding data dictionary tables. For example, our PDBA_INDEXES table pulls data from the Oracle's DBA_INDEXES data dictionary view. In the later section, "Reporting on Database Changes," we'll show how we use the data in these tables to analyze changes to database objects.

The repository itself is compatible with the data dictionary provided in Oracle Versions 8.0 and later.

Table 12-1. Main PDBA repository tables

Table	Contents
PDBA_INDEXES	Index information, statistics, storage information, and a number of other parameters.
PDBA_IND_COLUMNS	Index columns, statistics, storage information, and other related items.
PDBA_PARAMETERS	V$PARAMETER initialization parameters.

Table 12-1. Main PDBA repository tables (continued)

Table	Contents
PDBA_PROFILES	DBA_PROFILES data.
PDBA_SNAP_DATES	Database dictionary image and the date it was taken. The primary key of this table is used as a foreign key in most of the other tables in the repository; in this way, it ties information into the proper databases.
PDBA_SYS_PRIVS	System privileges, as granted to users and roles.
PDBA_TAB_PRIVS	Object and stored procedure privileges.
PDBA_ROLE_PRIVS	Role grants from DBA_ROLE_PRIVS.
PDBA_ROLES	Role definitions from DBA_ROLES.
PDBA_SEQUENCES	DBA_SEQUENCES sequence definitions.
PDBA_TABLES	Tables, table statistics, table storage information, and related information.
PDBA_TAB_COLUMNS	Table columns, column statistics, and related information.
PDBA_TABLESPACES	DBA_TABLESPACES definitions.
PDBA_USERS	Usernames, passwords, default tablespaces, temporary tablespaces, creation dates, and other information from DBA_USERS.

Specialized Repository Tables

In addition to the tables described in the previous section that mirror the Oracle data dictionary tables, the repository contains another set of more specialized tables. The purpose of these tables is to track the SQL found in the V$SQLTEXT data dictionary table and generate execution plans from that SQL. In these tables we'll store Oracle SQL and EXPLAIN PLAN information so we can perform comparisons on it at a later date. We'll describe the scripts that perform these comparisons in the later section, "Reporting on SQL Execution Plans."

Use of the data in these tables will help to answer a common complaint from users—that their SQL, which worked perfectly last week, has slowed down significantly. This isn't necessarily a figment of our users' imaginations! It's often obvious to all, including the troubleshooting DBA, that something *has* changed in the database since last week. It just isn't always clear *what* has changed:

> Was an index dropped?
> Was a new index created?
> Were statistics available on this table last week?
> What did the execution plan look like last week?

All of these things can have a major impact on SQL execution and overall database performance.

Having read Stephen Hawking's *Universe in a Nutshell* (Bantam Press, 2001), we know that travelling backwards in time is impossible (unless you're Mr. Spock), so the last two questions in the list are usually quite difficult to answer. We've often thought, though, that if we *could* answer them, it would be very interesting. At last, such a thing is possible. All we need is the SXP (Sql eXplain Plan) repository tables, which track the objects listed in Table 12-2.

Table 12-2. SQL explain plan repository tables

Table	Contents
PDBA_SXP_DATES	Database dates for SQL statements.
PDBA_SXP_EXP	Execution plans for SQL statements.
PDBA_SXP_SQL	Actual SQL statements.

Installing the Repository

Before installing the repository, we need to create two tablespaces. We've included templates of the necessary scripts for both Oracle 8.0 and 8.1 (and higher). The only difference between them is that version 8.1 uses Oracle's *locally managed tablespaces* (LMTs).

 LMTs provide several advantages—in particular, the removal of object extent management from the Oracle data dictionary and the elimination of wasted space due to fragmentation. If you don't need these features or if they seem overkill for your site, however, use the 8.0 script.

The location of the scripts depends on your operating system:

Unix
> Unix users will find the scripts by doing a *chdir* to the directory where the PDBA archive was installed, and then doing a *chdir* to the *pdbarep* directory. Ours was installed in */u01/build*:
>
> $ cd /u01/build/PDBA-1.00/pdbarep

Win32
> Win32 users will find the scripts in the *c:\perl\site\lib\PDBA\sql* directory.

 All of the repository scripts run identically on both Win32 and Unix. There is no need for separate versions.

It is very likely that you won't be able to use the repository creation scripts on your own system without first editing them. Your filesystem layout is probably different from ours, so you'll need to edit the datafile paths. For example, let's take the *pdba_tbs8i.sql* script and modify it for Oracle8i use on Win32. Example 12-1 shows what the file looks like initially.

Example 12-1. Unix version—pdba_tbs81.sql

```
-- pdba_tbs8i.sql
-- create tablespaces for PDBA repository
-- as Locally Managed Tablespaces
create tablespace pdba_data
datafile '/u01/oradata/ts01/pdba_data_01.dbf' size 20m
extent management local uniform size 128k
/
create tablespace pdba_idx
datafile '/u01/oradata/ts01/pdba_idx_01.dbf' size 20m
extent management local uniform size 128k
/
```

These datafile names won't work on Win32, so we need to change them to something more appropriate, as shown in Example 12-2.

Example 12-2. Win32 version—pdba_tbs81.sql

```
-- pdba_tbs8i.sql
-- create tablespaces for PDBA repository
-- as Locally Managed Tablespaces
create tablespace pdba_data
datafile 'E:\oradata\ts01\pdba_data_01.dbf' size 20m
extent management local uniform size 128k
/
create tablespace pdba_idx
datafile 'F:\oradata\ts01\pdba_idx_01.dbf' size 20m
extent management local uniform size 128k
/
```

 Storing all of the SQL from Oracle's SQL cache can consume a fair amount of disk storage on databases with a large SQL cache. It's good practice to be generous with the amount of space allotted to the PDBA repository if your database caches a large number of SQL statements. We've used up to 100 megabytes of storage storing all the SQL from a database that had approximately 65,000 cached SQL statements in memory, athough this may be an extreme example.

Now we're ready to install the repository:

1. The first step is to actually create the PDBA tablespaces. If your repository is to be installed on Oracle8i or later, use the *pdba_tbs8i.sql* script; on Oracle 8.0, choose *pdba_tbs.sql*. (We'll install our repository with version 8.0.)

2. To create the tablespaces, log in to the database as a DBA user. (Although sys should rarely be used and is unnecessary for creating tablespaces, we do recommend it here; we'll explain why in step 5.)

3. Once logged into the sys account, you can start installing the repository. The following shows our successful tablespace creation on the 8.0.5 database, *ts99*. You should see similar results when creating your own tablespaces:

```
SQL> set echo on
SQL> @pdba_tbs
SQL> -- pdba_tbs.sql
SQL> -- create tablespaces for PDBA repository
SQL>
SQL> create tablespace pdba_data
        datafile '/u05/oradata/ts99/pdba_data_01.dbf' size 2
        default storage ( initial 128k next 128k
                        pctincrease 0 maxextents unlimited )
    /
Tablespace created.
SQL> create tablespace pdba_idx
        datafile '/u06/oradata/ts99/pdba_idx_01.dbf' size 20m
        default storage ( initial 128k next 128k
                        pctincrease 0 maxextents unlimited )
    /
Tablespace created.
```

4. After tablespace creation is complete, it's time to create the PDBAREP repository owner. Run the *pdbarep_user.sql* script as follows:

```
SQL> set echo on
SQL> @pdbarep_user
SQL> create user pdbarep identified by pdbarep
        default tablespace pdba_data
        temporary tablespace temp
    /
User created.

SQL> alter user pdbarep quota unlimited on pdba_data;

User altered.

SQL> alter user pdbarep quota unlimited on pdba_idx;

User altered.
```

Now run *pdbarep_grants.sql* to give PDBAREP permission to create objects and gain other vital database permissions:

```
SQL> @pdbarep_grants
```

5. This is where we have to be the sys user. To function properly, PDBAREP must have SELECT privileges on a pair of data dictionary views that are normally invisible to users. These are V_$PARAMETER and V_$INSTANCE, more commonly known via synonyms as V$PARAMETER and V$INSTANCE. Only sys can grant the necessary permissions.

6. We simply execute the script to grant the proper privileges, and then exit SQL*Plus. (A lot of output will be generated.)

```
SQL> connect sys/change_on_install
SQL> @pdbarep_grants
...
```

7. Now log back into the database as PDBAREP. The password is set to PDBAREP; this password must be changed as soon as the installation completes.

8. To ensure that the direct grants to see the data dictionary views succeeded, try to view them with the DESCRIBE command.

   If you see results similar to those in Example 12-3, you're ready to create the repository tables and indexes.

Example 12-3. Access to V\$PARAMETER and V\$INSTANCE

```
pdbarep@ts99 SQL> desc v$parameter
 Name                            Null?    Type
 ------------------------------- -------- --------------------
 NUM                                      NUMBER
 NAME                                     VARCHAR2(64)
 TYPE                                     NUMBER
 VALUE                                    VARCHAR2(512)
 ISDEFAULT                                VARCHAR2(9)
 ISSES_MODIFIABLE                         VARCHAR2(5)
 ISSYS_MODIFIABLE                         VARCHAR2(9)
 ISMODIFIED                               VARCHAR2(10)
 ISADJUSTED                               VARCHAR2(5)
 DESCRIPTION                              VARCHAR2(64)

pdbarep@ts99 SQL> desc v$instance
 Name                            Null?    Type
 ------------------------------- -------- --------------------
 INSTANCE_NUMBER                          NUMBER
 INSTANCE_NAME                            VARCHAR2(16)
 HOST_NAME                                VARCHAR2(64)
 VERSION                                  VARCHAR2(17)
 STARTUP_TIME                             DATE
 STATUS                                   VARCHAR2(7)
 PARALLEL                                 VARCHAR2(3)
 THREAD#                                  NUMBER
 ARCHIVER                                 VARCHAR2(7)
 LOG_SWITCH_WAIT                          VARCHAR2(11)
 LOGINS                                   VARCHAR2(10)
 SHUTDOWN_PENDING                         VARCHAR2(3)

pdbarep@ts99 SQL>
```

9. While still logged in as PDBAREP, run the script *pdbarep_create.sql*. This is the final step in the creation of the PDBA repository.

   ```
   SQL> @pdbarep_create
   ```

   There's a lot of output here. As long as there are no errors, the output will consist of a series of lines of text such as *Table created*, *Index created*, *Sequence created*, and *Trigger created*.

10. If you encounter errors, these will be recorded in the *pdbarep_create.log* file. Once the script completes, you should examine this file for any errors. Should you need to correct any problems, and rerun the creation script, you may wish to run *pdbarep_drop.sql* first to drop objects successfully created. This makes it easier to examine *pdbarep_create.log* later for errors:

```
SQL> @pdbarep_drop
SQL> @pdbarep_create
```

If you don't drop existing objects before rerunning the creation script, the log file will be cluttered with errors such as *ORA-955: name is already used by an existing object*. This clutter makes it difficult to find the important errors that we really need to be concerned about.

11. The final step is to copy the configuration file *pdbarepq.conf* to PDBA_HOME. You may need to make a minor edit to this file, but only if you wish to change the date format shown in the repository reports from *YYYY/MM/DD HH24:MI: SS*. We'll show you how to change this default shortly.

On Unix, navigate to the PDBA installation directory, and copy the file:

```
$ cd /u01/build/PDBA-1.00
$ cd pdbarep
$ cp pdbarepq.conf $PDBA_HOME
```

On Win32, do the equivalent:

```
C:> cd c:\perl\site\lib\PDBA\conf
C:> copy pdbarepq.conf c:\pdba
```

12. If you wish to change the date format that will be used in the repository reports, you'll need to edit *pdbarepq.conf* and find the following lines near the top of the file:

```
# uncomment the appropriate line for your preferred date format
#
$calendar = 'International';   # YYYY/MM/DD HH24:MI:SS
#$calendar = 'American';       # MM/DD/YYYY HH24:MI:SS
#$calendar = 'European';       # DD/MM/YYYY HH24:MI:SS
```

If you want to change the default date format to either *European* or *American*, comment out the *International* line and uncomment appropriately, as for *European* here:

```
# uncomment the appropriate line for your preferred date format
#
#$calendar = 'International';   # YYYY/MM/DD HH24:MI:SS
#$calendar = 'American';       # MM/DD/YYYY HH24:MI:SS
$calendar = 'European';        # DD/MM/YYYY HH24:MI:SS
```

If you're running the *DBD::Oracle* module on Win32 (as discussed in Chapter 2, *Installing Perl*), you will need to make sure that you have a version installed that was compiled with Oracle libraries of Version 8 or higher. The repository relies on certain features that were introduced in Oracle8, such as the CLOB (character large object) datatype. ActiveState is often several versions behind the latest Unix release of *DBD::Oracle*. However, if you visit Ilya Sterin's PPD site (also described in Chapter 2), you'll usually find the very latest DBD-Oracle PPDs and binary downloads.

Loading the Repository with Data

It won't be long until we see the fruits of our labors. Once you install the repository and build the tables, you'll be all set to track database changes. The next time someone changes a column or an index outside of your established change control procedures, you'll know what the database looked like before inside the original Oracle data dictionary.

In this section we'll demonstrate how to load baseline data dictionary data into the PDBA repository using the *baseline.pl* script, and we'll run some tests on that data. As changes are made to the database objects and new baseline data is collected from the data dictionary, we'll show the effects of running several reports comparing current objects with the previous incarnations of those objects. We'll pay special attention to the repository reporting script *spdrvr.pl* (a unique hybrid of Perl and Oracle's SQL*Plus).

Collecting Baseline Data

To kick things off, we need to collect our first baseline set of data. We'll collect it from the data dictionary in database *ts99* on server *watson* using the *baseline.pl* script, and we'll place it in our repository. The command-line options for *baseline.pl* are listed in Table 12-3.

Table 12-3. Command-line options—baseline.pl

Option	Description
-machine	Target database server
-database	Target database
-username	DBA account user name
-password	DBA's password (optional if password server in use)
-rep_machine	Repository database server
-rep_database	Repository database

Table 12-3. Command-line options—baseline.pl (continued)

Option	Description
-rep_username	Repository owner
-rep_password	Repository owner's password (optional if Password server in use)

Invoke the *baseline.pl* script as follows:

```
$ baseline.pl -machine watson -database ts99 -username system \
    -rep_machine sherlock -rep_database ts01
```

Notice the absence of passwords in this example. Here we're making use of the password server to fill in the blanks for us. Otherwise, we would have needed the *-password* and *-rep_password* options, with the appropriate passwords. When you run *baseline.pl*, the output should be similar to that shown in Example 12-4.

 We strongly encourage you to make use of the password server for use with the repository. While this server is optional for collecting data dictionary information for insertion into the repository, it will be required for scripts that parse and store SQL from the V$SQLTEXT system view.

Example 12-4. Output from baseline.pl

```
%oramon>  baseline.pl -machine sherlock -database ts01 -username system \
-rep_machine sherlock -rep_database ts01 -rep_username pdbarep
Retrieving baseline data for database ts01
Working on Baseline for Table: PDBA_PROFILES
.
Working on Baseline for Table: PDBA_ROLE_PRIVS
..
Working on Baseline for Table: PDBA_ROLES
.
Working on Baseline for Table: PDBA_PARAMETERS
...
Working on Baseline for Table: PDBA_TAB_COLUMNS
.......................................................................................
......
Working on Baseline for Table: PDBA_TABLESPACES
.
Working on Baseline for Table: PDBA_SYS_PRIVS
.....
Working on Baseline for Table: PDBA_TAB_PRIVS
....................................................................
Working on Baseline for Table: PDBA_USERS.
Working on Baseline for Table: PDBA_TABLES
.......
Working on Baseline for Table: PDBA_INDEXES
.................
Working on Baseline for Table: PDBA_SEQUENCES.
Working on Baseline for Table: PDBA_IND_COLUMNS
...........................
```

Viewing Repository Data

We can now view some of our collected data via the *spdrvr.pl** script. Enter the following command to produce a report showing the table information collected from the data dictionary:

```
$ spdrvr.pl -machine sherlock -database ts01 -username pdbarep \
    -rep_report table_rpt -rep_instance ts99% -rep_shema scott
```

Notice the use of the SQL wildcard % for the *-rep_instance* argument. The argument in this case refers to the database's global name, so we used the wildcard character instead of a full global name. Alternatively, if the database global name had been *TS99.OREILLY.COM*, we could have specified this command instead:

```
$ spdrvr.pl -machine sherlock -database ts01 -username pdbarep \
    -rep_report table_rpt -rep_instance ts99.oreilly.com -rep_shema scott
```

The *spdrvr.pl* script will take care of converting the name to the correct case. The output should be similar to that shown in Example 12-5.

Example 12-5. Output from the initial table report

```
%oramon> spdrvr.pl -machine sherlock -database ts01 -username pdbarep \
-rep_report table_rpt -rep_database ts99% -rep_schema scott
RPT: start pk    1000000
RPT: start date  2001/10/05 18:29:05
RPT:   end pk    1000000
RPT:   end date  2001/10/05 18:29:05

PDBAREP Table report for                              Page:        1
TS99.JKS.COM


                                                        NUMBER
OWNER            TABLE NAME   SNAPSHOT DATE       BLOCKS OF ROWS
---------------  -----------  --------------------  -----------  -----------
SCOTT            BONUS        2001/10/05 18:29:05

                 DEPT         2001/10/05 18:29:05

                 DUMMY        2001/10/05 18:29:05

                 EMP          2001/10/05 18:29:05

                 SALGRADE     2001/10/05 18:29:05

5 rows selected.
```

---

* The name *spdrvr.pl* is shorthand for SQL*Plus Driver.

Reporting on Database Changes

The remaining sections in this chapter describe the various kinds of reports you can produce once you have collected the necessary baseline database data. This section focuses on database changes resulting from changes to database objects and parameters. The next section focuses on changes to the SQL execution plan.

After collecting our first set of baseline data, we made some changes to the database, collected additional baseline data, made some more changes, and then collected even more baseline data. We did this for several weeks.

Database Changes

The details and times of the changes made to the database are summarized in Table 12-4.

Table 12-4. Baseline changes made to the test database

Date	Changes made since previous baseline
5 Oct	Initial baseline data collected for database *ts99*
13 Oct	Added a few hundred rows to SCOTT.EMP
	Analyzed tables for SCOTT
	Changed values for database initialization parameters: SHARED_POOL_SIZE, DB_BLOCK_BUFFERS, and JOB_QUEUE_PROCESSES
19 Oct	Added a few hundred rows to SCOTT.EMP
	Added an EMAIL column to SCOTT.EMP
	Updated the value in the EMP table
	Dropped the column LOSAL from SALGRADE
	Analyzed tables for SCOTT
	Created a new user, PDBAREP, and granted it several privileges
	Granted SELECT on V_$INSTANCE, to SCOTT
28 Oct	Added a few hundred rows to SCOTT.EMP
	Created an index on SCOTT.EMP
	Analyzed tables for SCOTT
	Gave SCOTT UNLIMITED quota on USERS tablespace
	Dropped index IDXTEST_3_1_IDX
8 Nov	Added a few hundred rows to SCOTT.EMP
	Analyzed tables for SCOTT
	Revoked SELECT privileges on JKSTILL.LCL_1 from SCOTT
	Granted SELECT, INSERT on JKSTILL.PRIMES table to SCOTT

Reporting on Parameter Changes with spdrvr.pl

Now let's see how we can use the repository to engage in a form of time travel. Although less exciting than as H.G. Wells envisioned it, you'll effectively be able to go back in time to find elusive missing columns and corner privilege revocations. Pretend for a moment that the date is October 15. We've just become aware that the initialization file for one of our databases was recently modified and that, coincidentally, the server is now a little low on memory. We know that everything was correct a week ago, on October 8, but how do we determine what the settings were back then?

Without our repository, there would be no easy way to determine the correct values, except by restoring a tape backup of the file as it appeared last week. This would probably be neither practical nor desirable.

 Of course, if you are using a version control system, you'll be able to detect every authorized database change to your database and therefore be able to track official changes. However, experience teaches us, in vivid Technicolor, that such a system is of little use if people bypass it, ignore it, and then deny they've done anything when things go awry. "What? Me? That index? I was fishing. Honest."

But with the repository, you can find these values as they appeared prior to the change. Because you know that the values from October 8 are correct, let's see which parameters have been changed since then. Let's produce a report detailing the difference. We can do that with the *-rep_report parameter_diff_rpt* command:

```
$ spdrvr.pl -machine sherlock -database ts01 -username pdbarep \
    -rep_report parameter_diff_rpt -rep_instance ts99.jks.com \
    -rep_start_date '10/08/2001' -rep_end_date '10/15/2001'
```

Even though the first baseline was actually run on October 5, the *spdrvr.pl* script determines which baseline to use by searching for the most recent baseline date that is less than or equal to the date specified. The same type of operation takes place with the end date specified in the example by the following switch:

```
-rep_end_date
```

When using this switch, and its complement *-rep_start_date*, be sure to use a date format matching the setting in the *pdbarepq.conf* configuration file. If the *parameter_diff_report* were run with the *International* date format, the command line would look like this:

```
$ spdrvr.pl -machine sherlock -database ts01 -username pdbarep \
    -rep_report parameter_diff_rpt -rep_instance ts99.jks.com \
    -rep_start_date '2001/10/08' -rep_end_date '2001/10/15'
```

The output from the *parameter_diff_report* report appears in Example 12-6. Note that data appears only when there are differences within values associated with the database parameters, as stored in PDBA_PARAMETERS. If, for example, there have been no changes to the Oracle initialization parameters between October 5 and October 13, there will be nothing to report. A parameter comparison on these two dates will reveal that nothing has changed.

Example 12-6. Output from the parameter_diff_rpt report

```
PDBAREP Parameter Differences report Page: 1
as of 2001/10/13 03:09:37 compared to 2001/10/05 18:29:05
TS99.JKS.COM  2002/05/19 21:55:40
                                          S S
                                          E Y
                                          S S
                                        D M M M A
                                        E O O O D
PARAMETER            DESCRIPTION    VALUE  F D D D J
-------------------  -------------- ---------- - - - - -
db_block_buffers     Number of database b 1000   N N N N N
                     locks cached in memo
                     ry
job_queue_processes  number of job queue  2     Y N I N N
                     processes to start
shared_pool_size     size in bytes of sha 3145728 N N N N N
                     red pool


3 rows selected.

PDBAREP Parameter Differences report            Page:      1
as of 2001/10/05 18:29:05 compared to 2001/10/13 03:09:37
TS99.JKS.COM  2002/05/19 21:55:40
                                          S S
                                          E Y
                                          S S
                                        D M M M A
                                        E O O O D
PARAMETER            DESCRIPTION    VALUE  F D D D J
-------------------  -------------- ---------- - - - - -
db_block_buffers     Number of database b 500    N N N N N
                     locks cached in memo
                     ry
job_queue_processes  number of job queue  0     Y N I N N
                     processes to start
shared_pool_size     size in bytes of sha 2097152 N N N N N
                     red pool

3 rows selected.
```

On the other hand, suppose that sometime between October 5 and October 13 you changed the database initialization parameters DB_BLOCK_BUFFERS, JOB_QUEUE_PROCESSES, and SHARED_POOL_SIZE. When you run the *parameter_diff_rpt* report, it would show the values of these parameters as they appeared on

October 13, followed by the values as they appeared on October 5. Looking again at Example 12-6, you'll see that the report appears in two parts:

- The first part shows the parameters on October 13.
- The second part shows that the parameters were indeed different on October 5 and October 13. The values of the parameters were all increased after October 5.

We now know what the correct settings were eight days ago, and we can change them back to the former values if necessary.

The *pdbarepq.conf* configuration file contains templates of the SQL for each of the available repository reports. The command-line options of *spdrvr.pl* are used with these templates to generate the actual SQL used. Typical PDBA-generated SQL used to create this kind of report is shown in Example 12-7.

Example 12-7. Sample query for spdrvr.pl

```
select
  s.global_name cinstance
, p.name parm_name
, p.description parm_description
, p.value parm_value
, decode(
    nvl(p.isdefault,'FALSE'),
    'FALSE','N',
    'TRUE','Y',
    substr(nvl(p.isdefault,'F'),1,1)
) isdefault
, decode(
    nvl(p.isses_modifiable,'FALSE'),
    'FALSE','N',
    'TRUE','Y',
    substr(nvl(p.isses_modifiable,'F'),1,1)
) isses_modifiable
, decode(
    nvl(p.issys_modifiable,'FALSE'),
    'FALSE','N',
    'TRUE','Y',
    substr(nvl(p.issys_modifiable,'F'),1,1)
) issys_modifiable
, decode(
    nvl(p.ismodified,'FALSE'),
    'FALSE','N',
    'TRUE','Y',
    substr(nvl(p.ismodified,'F'),1,1)
) ismodified
, decode(
    nvl(p.isadjusted,'FALSE'),
    'FALSE','N',
    'TRUE','Y',
    substr(nvl(p.isadjusted,'F'),1,1)
) isadjusted
```

Example 12-7. Sample query for spdrvr.pl (continued)

```
from pdba_parameters p, pdba_snap_dates s
where s.global_name like 'TS99.JKS.COM'
and s.pk = 1000000
and s.pk = p.snap_date_pk
minus
select
    s.global_name cinstance
  , p.name parm_name
  , p.description parm_description
  , p.value parm_value
  , decode(
      nvl(p.isdefault,'FALSE'),
      'FALSE','N',
      'TRUE','Y',
      substr(nvl(p.isdefault,'F'),1,1)
  ) isdefault
  , decode(
      nvl(p.isses_modifiable,'FALSE'),
      'FALSE','N',
      'TRUE','Y',
      substr(nvl(p.isses_modifiable,'F'),1,1)
  ) isses_modifiable
  , decode(
      nvl(p.issys_modifiable,'FALSE'),
      'FALSE','N',
      'TRUE','Y',
      substr(nvl(p.issys_modifiable,'F'),1,1)
  ) issys_modifiable
  , decode(
      nvl(p.ismodified,'FALSE'),
      'FALSE','N',
      'TRUE','Y',
      substr(nvl(p.ismodified,'F'),1,1)
  ) ismodified
  , decode(
      nvl(p.isadjusted,'FALSE'),
      'FALSE','N',
      'TRUE','Y',
      substr(nvl(p.isadjusted,'F'),1,1)
  ) isadjusted
from pdba_parameters p, pdba_snap_dates s
where s.global_name like 'TS99.JKS.COM'
and s.pk = 1001570
and s.pk = p.snap_date_pk
order by 1,2;
```

More Report Examples

On October 25, we decided to run some additional reports to see what might have
changed in the *ts99* database since the time that we started capturing repository

metadata.* Example 12-8 shows different variants on the commands you can specify in order to view the data in different ways.

Example 12-8. Reports on database changes as of October 19

```
$ spdrvr.pl -machine sherlock -database ts01 -username pdbarep \
   -rep_report table_rpt -rep_instance ts99% -rep_schema scott \
   -rep_end_date '10/25/2001'

$ spdrvr.pl -machine sherlock -database ts01 -username pdbarep \
   -rep_report column_diff_rpt -rep_instance ts99% -rep_schema scott \
   -rep_end_date '10/25/2001'

$ spdrvr.pl -machine sherlock -database ts01 -username pdbarep \
   -rep_report table_privs_diff_rpt -rep_instance ts99% \
   -rep_grantee scott -rep_end_date '10/25/2001'

$ spdrvr.pl -machine sherlock -database ts01 -username pdbarep \
   -rep_report user_rpt -rep_instance ts99%
```

The reports *table_rpt*, *column_diff_rpt*, and *table_privs_diff_rpt* produce the outputs summarized here:

 Tables and indexes need to be periodically analyzed via the ANALYZE command to provide statistics for Oracle's cost-based optimizer (CBO). The CBO is the part of the database engine that determines how best to join indexes and tables when querying the database.

table_rpt

In Example 12-9 we see that the number of employees in the EMP table has dramatically increased since the time when the repository was first populated. By implication, we can also tell that EMP was *unanalyzed* (not processed with the ANALYZE command) when its first baseline was taken, because BLOCKS and NUMBER OF ROWS have no values for October 5.

Example 12-9. The table_rpt report, as of October 19

```
%oramon> spdrvr.pl  -machine sherlock -database ts01 -username pdbarep \
-rep_report table_rpt -rep_database ts99% -rep_schema scott

PDBAREP Table report for                               Page:        1
TS99.JKS.COM
                                                 NUMBER
OWNER   TABLE NAME SNAPSHOT DATE         BLOCKS OF ROWS
------  ---------- --------------------  ------ -------
```

---

* Metadata is data about data. An example of metadata is the statistics stored in the Oracle data dictionary when the ANALYZE TABLE command is use. It is data about the data in the specified table.

Example 12-9. The table_rpt report, as of October 19 (continued)

```
SCOTT   BONUS     2001/10/05 18:29:05
                  2001/10/13 03:09:37        0        0
                  2001/10/19 04:11:23        0        0
        DEPT      2001/10/05 18:29:05
                  2001/10/13 03:09:37        1        4
                  2001/10/19 04:11:23        1        4

        DUMMY     2001/10/05 18:29:05
                  2001/10/13 03:09:37        1        1
                  2001/10/19 04:11:23        1        1


        EMP       2001/10/05 18:29:05
                  2001/10/13 03:09:37        3      224
                  2001/10/19 04:11:23       29    1,792


        SALGRADE  2001/10/05 18:29:05
                  2001/10/13 03:09:37        1        5
                  2001/10/19 04:11:23        1        5

15 rows selected.
```

column_diff_rpt

In Example 12-10, the Column Differences report, we find that two column changes have been made between October 5 and October 19. The EMAIL column has been added to the EMP table during this time, and the column LOSAL no longer appears in SALGRADE.

Example 12-10. The column_diff_rpt report as of October 19

```
%oramon> spdrvr.pl  -machine sherlock -database ts01 -username pdbarep \
  -rep_report column_diff_rpt -rep_database ts99% -rep_schema scott \
  -rep_end_date '2001/10/19'


PDBAREP Table Column Differences report              Page:        1
as of 2001/10/19 04:11:23 compared to 2001/10/05 18:29:05
                              TS99.JKS.COM  2002/05/19 22:19:51
                            COL        DATA     DATA   DATA
OWNER  TABLE NAME  COLUMN    ID DATA_TYPE LENGTH PRECISION SCALE NULL
------ ----------- -------- ---- ---------- ------ --------- ------ ----
SCOTT  EMP         EMAIL      9 VARCHAR2      40                     Y

1 row selected.

PDBAREP Table Column Differences report              Page:        1
as of 2001/10/05 18:29:05 compared to 2001/10/19 04:11:23
TS99.JKS.COM  2002/05/19 22:19:51


                            COL        DATA     DATA   DATA
OWNER  TABLE NAME  COLUMN    ID DATA_TYPE LENGTH PRECISION SCALE NULL
------ ----------- -------- ---- ---------- ------ --------- ------ ----
```

Example 12-10. The column_diff_rpt report as of October 19 (continued)

```
SCOTT   SALGRADE    LOSAL       2 NUMBER          22                    Y

1 row selected.
```

table_privs_diff_rpt

In Example 12-11 we're surprised to see that scott has been granted SELECT privilege on V_$INSTANCE. Although this view contains non-sensitive information, we believe in granting direct privileges on dictionary objects *only for DBAs.* Maybe in another life we'll reconsider our conservative views! Based on this report, you decide to chat with scott, to find out how he stumbled upon this privilege.

Example 12-11. The table_privs_diff_rpt as of October19

```
%oramon> spdrvr.pl   -machine sherlock -database ts01 -username pdbarep \
  -rep_report table_privs_diff_rpt -rep_database ts99% \
  -rep_grantee scott -rep_end_date '2001/10/19'

PDBAREP Table Privileges Differences report          Page:        1
as of 2001/10/13 03:09:37 compared to 2001/10/05 18:29:05
TS99.JKS.COM  2002/05/19 22:46:27
GRANTEE      TABLE NAME        PRIVILEGE  OWNER     GRANTOR  GRANTABLE
------------ ----------------- ---------- --------- -------- ---
SCOTT        V_$INSTANCE       SELECT     SYS       SYS      NO

1 row selected.

no rows selected
```

spdrvr.pl Implementation

Before we look further at the kinds of reports you can produce with the *spdrvr.pl* script, let's dig down and take a quick look at its implementation and see why, despite our abiding love for Perl, we've also used SQL*Plus in our implementation.

Have you ever had a household tool you love so much that you find yourself exploring the house from attic to basement, looking for ways to make use of it? That's the way we feel about Perl. However, as Clint Eastwood said once of a man's belief in himself, we've got to recognize its limitations. A screwdriver may sometimes get called up for reserve duty as a chisel, but that usage *will* impact its longevity as a screwdriver. And if you trim the hedges around your home with a circular power-saw, people are going to talk.

We've come to realize, somewhat sadly, that Perl does indeed have its limits. The most glaring one we've noticed emerges when we're writing *ad hoc* SQL reports. Perl is a good choice when writing reports that demand lots of computation, but it fails to do things easily that long-time users of SQL*Plus take for granted. Here are a few examples:

Column breaks and report breaks

The SQL*Plus BREAK command formats reports to make them easier to interpret:

```
break on username skip 1 page on table name skip 1
```

Column and report totals

SQL*Plus calculates totals with simplicity:

```
break on custid skip 1 on invoice_id skip 1 on report
compute sum of invoice_amt on custid
compute sum of invoice_item_amt on invoice_id
compute sum of invoice_amt on custid
```

Report headers and footers

The SQL*Plus *ttitle* and *btitle* commands can create report headers and footers:

```
ttitle 'PDBAREP Parameter Differences report ' RIGHT 'Page: ' SQL.PNO -
   skip 'as of <<END_DATE>> compared to <<START_DATE>>' -
   right uinstance '  ' usysdate skip 2
```

All of the above features can be duplicated in Perl, but it takes a while. And being the virtuously lazy programmers we are, we can't really justify writing all the necessary code when SQL*Plus already handles these features so well.* What we've done, therefore, is to create a Perl/SQL*Plus hybrid that uses the best features from each tool to accomplish our goal. In this case, the goal is to produce nice reports with a minimum amount of effort. Before we begin, let's take a look at some of the pros and cons of both tools:

- With SQL*Plus we get nicely formatted reports that are easy to produce.

- With Perl we can make up for some of the serious cross-platform liabilities of SQL*Plus, take advantage of Perl's strong command-line processing, use Perl's many modules, and easily redirect output. Perl also possesses a command-line interface that is infinitely flexible.

Predefined spdrvr.pl Reports

The *spdrvr.pl* repository script allows you to invoke a number of predefined database reports simply by specifying the appropriate command-line options. Several reports are predefined for you.

---

* You might want to take a look at the Senora tool described in Chapter 3, *Perl GUI Extensions*; this tool, which is based on *DDL::Oracle* (also described in Chapter 3), provides a SQL*Plus clone written entirely in Perl, along with several other interactive Perl DBI tools such as *dbish*.

column_diff_rpt

Report on differences in table columns in the repository. This report may be delimited by a date range. If dates are not supplied, the oldest and newest dates from the repository will be used.

column_rpt

Report on table columns in repository.

index_column_diff_rpt

Report on differences in index columns in the repository. This report may be delimited by a date range. If dates are not supplied, the oldest and newest dates from the repository will be used.

index_column_rpt

Report on indexed columns in the repository.

index_rpt

Report on indexes in the repository.

master_priv_rpt

Report on database privilege grants in the repository.

parameter_diff_rpt

Report on database initialization parameter differences in the repository. This report may be delimited by a date range. If dates are not supplied, the oldest and newest dates from the repository will be used.

parameter_rpt

Report on database initialization parameters in the repository.

profile_rpt

Report on profiles in the repository.

role_privs_diff_rpt

Report on differences in role privileges in the repository.

role_privs_rpt

Report on role privileges in the repository.

role_rpt

Report on database roles in the repository.

sequence_rpt

Report on sequences in the repository.

sys_privs_diff_rpt

Report on differences in system privileges in the repository.

sys_privs_rpt

Report on system privileges in the repository.

table_privs_diff_rpt

Report on differences in table privileges in the repository.

table_privs_rpt
> Report on table privileges in the repository.

table_rpt
> Report on tables in the repository.

tablespace_rpt
> Report on tablespaces in the repository.

user_rpt
> Report on users in the repository.

Command-line Options for spdrvr.pl

You can request the reports listed in the previous section by including the appropriate command-line options when you invoke the *spdrvr.pl* repository script. Tables 12-5 and 12-6 summarize these options.

Common command-line options

You will need to include most of the options in Table 12-5 regardless of what report you want to produce. You can obtain a list of available reports and their required command-line options by typing:

```
$ spdrvr.pl -report_list
```

We'll show the output from this command a little later in this section.

Table 12-5. Common command-line options—spdrvr.pl

Option	Description
-machine	Server where the repository database resides.
-database	Database where the PDBAREP user is installed.
-username	Repository schema owner.
-file	Optional parameter that specifies output to a file.
-verbose	Optional parameter that prints the SQL as it is executed.
-report_list	Outputs a list of available reports to the console
-rep_report	Specifies which report to run.
-rep_database	Specifies which database (*global_name*) to report on.

The arguments for *-machine*, *-database*, *-username*, and *-rep_report* are always required. The argument for *-rep_database* is optional but recommended. The use of *-rep_database* really depends on the nature of the report. If you want to find out what changes have been made to a table on a specific database between two dates, you'll need to specify which database the report should be querying on. If you omit this option, any tables from other databases with the same name will be included in the output. (This is probably not what you want.)

Let's suppose you want to run the report *table_rpt* for the database *ts99.jks.com* and that the repository owned by *pdbarep* is in database *ts01* on server *sherlock*. The minimal command line needed to run this report would be:

```
$ spdrvr.pl -machine sherlock -database ts01 -username pdbarep \
    -rep_instance 'ts99%' -rep_report table_rpt
```

To include only tables with "PSAP" as the first four characters of their name, within accounts that begin with "SAP," the command line would look like this:

```
$ spdrvr.pl -machine sherlock -database ts01 -username pdbarep \
    -rep_instance 'ts99%' -rep_report table_rpt \
    -rep_schema 'sap%' -rep_table_name 'psap%'
```

Report-specific command-line options

Table 12-6 lists the report-specific command-line options. For example, you might use the *-rep_privilege* option if you are requesting the *table_privs_rpt* report, but that option would have no effect on the *parameter_rpt* that lists database initialization parameters.

Table 12-6. Report-specific command-line options—spdrvr.pl

Report	Specific parameters
-rep_end_date	End date for report (unnecessary for some reports).
-rep_grantee	Grantee of privileges. Use this option to report on the privileges granted to a particular user or role.
-rep_grantor	Grantor of privileges. This will limit the report to privileges granted by this user.
-rep_granted_role	Roles granted. This will limit the report to a role or roles that have been granted.
-rep_index_name	Index to report on.
-rep_object_owner	Owner of database object to report on.
-rep_object_name	Name of database object to report on.
-rep_pagesize	Controls the SQL*Plus *pagesize*.
-rep_parm_name	Name of database parameter to report on.
-rep_parm_value	Value of database parameter value to report on.
-rep_privilege	Database privileges granted.
-rep_profile	Database profile name to report on.
-rep_resource_type	Profile resource type to report on.
-rep_resource_name	Profile resource name to report on.
-rep_role	Role to report on.
-rep_schema	Schema to report on.
-rep_sequence_name	Name of sequence to report on.
-rep_start_date	Start date for report (unnecessary for some reports).
-rep_table_name	Table to report on.

Table 12-6. Report-specific command-line options—spdrvr.pl (continued)

Report	Specific parameters
-rep_table_owner	Table owner to report on.
-rep_tablespace_name	Tablespace to report on.
-rep_username	Username to report on.

No single report makes use of all of these switches, although some are used in several reports.

Using the -report_list option

The first time you run the *spdrvr.pl* script, you should use the *-report_list* option, which prints out a list of currently configured reports along with the report-specific command-line options that may be used with it:

```
$ sprdrvr.pl -report_list
```

Go ahead and try it. The output should be similar to that displayed in Example 12-12 (although we've cut down the actual output, as it can run to several pages).

Example 12-12. Partial output from "spdrvr.pl -report_list"

```
column_diff_rpt :
  report on differences in table columns in repository
  may be delimited by a date range.
  if dates not supplied, the oldest and newest dates
  from the repository will be used
  may be limited by the following tags:
  <<GLOBAL_NAME>>    -rep_instance
  <<OWNER>>          -rep_schema
  <<TABLE_NAME>>     -rep_table_name
  <<START_DATE_PK>> -rep_start_date
  <<END_DATE_PK>>   -rep_end_date

master_priv_rpt :
  report on privileges granted in repository
  may be limited by the following tags:

  <<GLOBAL_NAME>>    -rep_instance
  <<GRANTEE>>        -rep_grantee
  <<PRIVILEGE>>      -rep_privilege
  <<OBJECT_OWNER>>   -rep_object_owner
  <<OBJECT_NAME>>    -rep_object_name
  <<GRANTED_ROLE>>   -rep_granted_role

parameter_diff_rpt :
  report on database parameter differences in repository
  may be delimited by a date range.
  if dates not supplied, the oldest and newest dates
  from the repository will be used
```

Example 12-12. Partial output from "spdrvr.pl -report_list" (continued)

```
    may be limited by the following tags:

    <<GLOBAL_NAME>>      -rep_instance
    <<START_DATE_PK>>    -rep_start_date
    <<END_DATE_PK>>      -rep_end_date

  sys_privs_diff_rpt :
    report on differences in system privileges in repository
    may be limited by the following tags:

    <<GLOBAL_NAME>>      -rep_instance
    <<GRANTEE>>          -rep_grantee
    <<PRIVILEGE>>        -rep_privilege
    <<START_DATE_PK>>    -rep_start_date
    <<END_DATE_PK>>      -rep_end_date

  table_rpt :
    report on tables in repository
    may be limited by the following tags:

    <<GLOBAL_NAME>>      -rep_instance
    <<OWNER>>            -rep_schema
    <<TABLE_NAME>>       -rep_table_name
```

Options and Tags

Each command-line option shown in Example 12-12 is associated with a tag enclosed in a double set of angle brackets: <<TAG>>. The *column_diff_rpt* report has these tags associated with the following command-line options:

```
    <<GLOBAL_NAME>>      -rep_instance
    <<OWNER>>            -rep_schema
    <<TABLE_NAME>>       -rep_table_name
    <<START_DATE_PK>> -rep_start_date
    <<END_DATE_PK>>   -rep_end_date
```

These tags are used internally within *spdrvr.pl* to replace values in a SQL script, values that will later get sent to SQL*Plus. The tags are divided into two types, date and text, as discussed in the following sections.

Date options

The *-rep_start_date* and *-rep_end_date* command-line options are the only date-style options. The tags usually associated with these options are <<START_DATE_PK>> and <<END_DATE_PK>>.

-rep_start_date
> Used to specify a particular date on the command line; however, this is used internally by *spdrvr.pl* to look up the primary key of the row in *PDBA_SNAP_*

DATES, the one corresponding to the requested date. The value of that primary key is used to replace the value of *<<START_DATE_PK>>* in the actual query.

If *-rep_start_date* date is missing from the repository, the most recent date, up to the date specified, is used. Using the following dates, the first date in PDBA_SNAP_DATES is October 5, the second is October 13, and the third is October 19. If you specified the report to start from October 15, the *spdrvrl.pl* script would find no data collected for that date, and would then choose the closest date that's *less* than October 15, which is October 13. (We promise that this will make more sense when you run the actual reports.):

```
GLOBAL_NAME      SNAP_DATE
---------------  --------------------
TS99.JKS.COM     2001/10/05 18:29:05
TS99.JKS.COM     2001/10/13 03:09:37
TS99.JKS.COM     2001/10/19 04:11:23
TS99.JKS.COM     2001/10/28 23:13:25
TS99.JKS.COM     2001/11/08 12:18:36
```

If you specified a date *less* than any in the repository, the *first* available date in the repository will be used, which is October 5. This will also be used if *-rep_start_date* is not specified.

-rep_end_date

Works in similar fashion. If you specify an end date of October 25, the *actual* end date used will be October 19, as this is the latest one that's *less* than the date specified. If the specified date is greater than the latest one in the repository, or if the *-rep_end_date* switch remains unused, the latest repository date will be used in reports; that is, November 8.

This logic may seem rather convoluted, but trust us, it does make reports easier to run. Let's look at an example. Suppose that midway through November you suspect that changes have been made to the HELP_DESK schema. You know that last month everything worked fine—but now there's a problem. To figure out what's going on, you won't need to check every date in the repository. You can simply enter the approximate range and let *spdrvr.pl* determine the *actual* dates. The following reports *all* changes:

```
$ spdrvr.pl -machine sherlock -database ts01 -username pdbarep \
    -rep_report column_diff_rpt -rep_instance ts99% \
    -rep_schema help_desk \
    -rep_start_date '2001/10/01' \
    -rep_end_date '2001/11/12'
```

The actual report dates used would be October 5 and November 8.

Text options

Most of the command-line options on the *spdrvr.pl* script are text options. These include all the database objects—users, tables, tablespaces, indexes, and so on. We can be somewhat inexact in specifying these text strings. Most of the SQL queries found in *pdbarepq.conf* use the *LIKE* operator, rather than the = equality operator. This allows the use of the % wildcard for text-based columns, used in WHERE clauses.

The following command requests a report on *which* roles have been granted to *which* users, where the grantee's name begins with an *S*:

```
spdrvr.pl -machine sherlock -database ts01 \
  -username pdbarep -rep_database ts99% \
  -rep_report role_privs_rpt -rep_grantee s%
```

If you wish to see the actual SQL generating the report, add the *-verbose* option to the command line. In our example, the SQL looks like this:

```
select
    s.global_name cinstance
  , p.grantee
  , p.granted_role
  , p.admin_option
  , p.default_role
  , s.snap_date
from pdba_role_privs p, pdba_snap_dates s
where s.global_name like 'TS99%'
and p.grantee like 'S%'
and s.pk between 1000000 and 1006331
and s.pk = p.snap_date_pk
order by global_name, grantee, granted_role, snap_date;
```

Notice how the switches *-rep_database ts99%* and *-rep_grantee s%* uppercase their corresponding values in the SQL statement. (The % wildcard may be used in any of the non-date command-line arguments.)

Reporting on SQL Execution Plans

If you've been a DBA for more than 15 nanoseconds, you've no doubt received an urgent phone call that goes something like this:

> "I have a *critical* SQL statement that's running *very* slowly! You *need* to fix the database!"

The next sentence is almost always: "It worked *fine*, last week!"

As you try desperately to determine why this critical piece of SQL is suddenly running slower than a three-toed sloth taking a nap, you may think to yourself:

> "It would be nice if I could see the execution plan for this SQL from when it *was* working properly."

We've had that exact same thought any number of times ourselves. And so the SXP portion of the PDBA repository was born.

SXP (SQL EXecution Plan) Scripts and Tables

The scripts and tables that make up SXP come in threes—we've designed a triumvirate of tables described earlier in this chapter in Table 12-2 (and shown graphically in Figure 12-1) used to store SQL and its corresponding execution plans, and we've designed a triumvirate of Perl scripts that populate these tables and report on the results. The scripts are:

sxp.pl
> Collects SQL statements from the V_$SQLTEXT data dictionary view and stores them unformatted within the PDBA_SXP_SQL table. The script logs in as the user who originally parsed the SQL, and generates an execution plan for the statement with the EXPLAIN PLAN SQL statement. The resulting execution plan is then stored in the PDBA_SXP_EXP repository table.

sxprpt.pl
> Generates reports on the stored SQL and execution plans.

sxpcmp.pl
> Examines the current SQL statements, as contained in V_$SQLTEXT, generating execution plans for each statement. When a matching SQL statement is found in the repository, the execution plans are compared. If the plans differ, the SQL statement and its varying execution plans are included in the report.

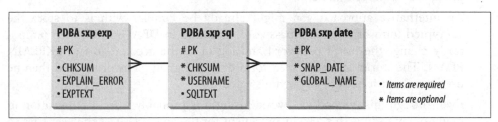

Figure 12-1. The SPX table system

SXP Limitations

Helpful as the SXP scripts are, they do have a few limitations:

Type of SQL
> Only SELECT, INSERT, DELETE, and UPDATE statements are retrieved from the SQL cache. PL/SQL anonymous blocks, packages, procedures, and functions are ignored.

Formatting of SQL
> The only interface to the cached SQL statements is through either the V_$SQL-TEXT or V_$SQLTEXT_WITH_NEWLINES system views. The SQL in these Oracle views is broken into 64-character chunks, often with breaks appearing right in the middle of words. We've chosen to store the SQL as a single line of

text, as that's the way it appears after joining the various 64-character chunks together.

As it appears in these views, the SQL is often non-executable, because of comments included in them. Including an embedded comment in a single line of SQL often renders the rest of the statement as a comment too.

To generate an execution plan for the SQL, it must first be preformatted. We do this via the *PDBA->formatSql* method. The goal of this method is to format the SQL and get it into an executable form that's suitable for use with SQL's EXPLAIN PLAN statement. Most of the time it succeeds, but sometimes it fails, for reasons we'll explain shortly. When that happens, the error is reported and skipped over by the SXP scripts.

Limit on users

As with many EXPLAIN PLAN tools, the SQL generated by the SYS user is ignored.

Passwords

To generate an execution plan for a SQL statement, it's necessary to log in as the *same* user who parsed the SQL. In addition, the password for that user must be set up in the password server. If the password is unavailable, the SXP scripts report an error and continue on to the next user. If the wrong password is supplied, the scripts terminate.

An alternative approach you might already be familiar with is to store the encrypted form of the user's password, as found in DBA_USERS, then temporarily change the user's password and log in to the account to run EXPLAIN PLAN. The stored and encrypted form of the original password would then be used to restore it back to its previous value.

Even though this method will work,[*] using it is probably a security violation in many organizations. It's also inconvenient for the actual user: if the user tries to log on to his own account, he may find himself locked out because of a temporarily changed password. If at all possible, we'd rather avoid the extra work involved in dealing with the complaints that we're likely to hear if this kind of thing occurs!

Collecting SQL with sxp.pl

With those caveats out of the way, let's go about the business of actually using this utility. You'll use the *sxp.pl* script to collect SQL from the database and store it in the repository.

---

[*] We sometimes use this method to log in to a user's account for administrative reasons. This is usually in an emergency, however, and is therefore outside the scope of our automated tool.

We suggest that you restrict your initial excursions into the Oracle SQL cache, using only test or development databases until you're familiar with the process. Querying the V_$SYSTEM view can be a resource-intensive task, and doing so multiple times, while you learn to use these tools on a production database, may lead to unfriendly relations with regular users.

On our test database, this script runs in less than a minute. We also employ this tool on several production databases where it can take several minutes* to complete.

You can enter the following command to collect SQL from database *ts01* on server *sherlock*. (Coincidentally, this is the same database on which the repository resides.) Table 12-7 lists the command-line options for this script.

```
$ sxp.pl -machine sherlock -database ts01 -username system \
    -rep_machine sherlock -rep_database ts01 \
    -rep_username pdbarep
```

Table 12-7. Command-line options—sxp.pl

Option	Description
-machine	Server where the target database resides
-database	Target database
-username	DBA account
-password	Password for the DBA account (optional)
-rep_machine	Server where the repository database resides
-rep_database	Database the PDBA repository is in
-rep_username	Repository schema owner
-rep_password	Repository owner password (optional)

Unique constraint error

Example 12-13 contains the actual output from *sxp.pl*, as it was run on one of our test databases. You'll notice that there is an Oracle error:

```
ORA-00001: unique constraint (PDBAREP.PDBA_SXP_UK_IDX) violated
```

This error occurred about halfway through processing. This happens occasionally when there are syntactically identical SQL statements in the database cache that have been formatted somewhat differently. When *sxp.pl* encounters these paired statements, they're reformatted identically for our EXPLAIN PLAN statement. That

---

* One of these databases had a very large SQL cache and resulted in 122,829 new entries in the PDBA_SXP_ SQL table, requiring 98 MB of storage and taking more than 20 minutes to complete. We've hit the old quantum mechanics limit again. It's impossible to measure an event without causing an effect within the area under test. *Who shall guard the guards?* (We avoid running *sxp.pl* on that database too often!)

results in *sxp.pl* trying to save the same SQL statement twice during the same session. This was a design decision on our part. Rather than search the PDBA_SXP_SQL table looking for duplicates each time we save SQL to the repository, we simply let the database catch it with a unique constraint. The *sxp.pl* script traps this error, reports it, and continues onto the next SQL statement.

Example 12-13. Output from sxp.pl

```
%oramon> sxp.pl -machine sherlock -database ts01 -username system \
-rep_machine sherlock -rep_database ts01 -rep_username pdbarep
........DBD::Oracle::st execute failed: ORA-00001: unique constraint
(PDBAREP.PDBA_SXP_SQL_UK_IDX) violated (DBD ERROR: OCIStmtExecute) at
/usr/local/bin/sxp.pl line 283.
...no password available from PWD for ORADES
.... %oramon>
```

Password and privilege messages

You'll note another message in the *sxp.pl* output, but this one is simply informational:

```
    no password available from PWD for ORADES
```

This means that there are SQL statements within the cache for the user ORADES, but that their password was not available from the password server, and thus processing moved onto the next user.

Another error that may appear is:

```
    ORA-01039: insufficient privileges on underlying objects of the view
```

We encounter this error when attempts are made to generate execution plans for a SELECT statement on a view. Although the user may have SELECT privileges on the view, Oracle requires that we also have SELECT privileges on the view's underlying tables in order to generate an execution plan. There is nothing we can do about that, so we report the error and move onto the next SQL statement.

Reporting Execution Plans

The *sxprpt.pl* script reports on the SQL and execution plans now stored within the PDBA repository. Table 12-8 lists the command-line options for this script.

Table 12-8. Command-line options—sxprpt.pl

Option	Description
-machine	Server where the target database resides
-database	Target database
-username	DBA account
-password	Password for the DBA account (optional)
-verbose	Prints parameters and the SQL used to query the repository

Table 12-8. Command-line options—sxprpt.pl (continued)

Option	Description
-rpt_machine	Server where the repository database resides
-rpt_start_date	Optional date on which to begin reporting
-rpt_end_date	Optional date on which to end reporting

Now that we have some data loaded into the repository, let's get a report of what's in there. Because our test database already contains a number of data collections, we'll limit the report by specifying a date range constraint in the following command:

```
$ sxprpt.pl -machine sherlock -database ts01 \
    -username pdbarep -rpt_database 'ts01%' \
    -rpt_start_date '11/25/2001' -rpt_end_date '11/27/2001'
```

The resulting report will contain the following:

- The username of the account that parsed the SQL originally
- A checksum for the SQL text
- A reformatted version of the SQL
- The execution plan for the SQL

If all goes well, there will be:

- A copy of the execution plan
- The checksum for the execution plan

In the event that an error occurs while generating the execution plan, the error will be displayed instead of the execution plan.

Checksums

This might be a good time to explain the way checksums work within our scripts. Whenever a SQL statement or execution plan is stored in the repository, the Perl security module *Digest::MD5* is drafted into action to generate a unique 32-character "message digest" of the data. Because this digest will be unique for each SQL statement and execution plan, it serves as a unique key that we can use to search for identical SQL statements and compare execution plans. Using a checksum results in better performance—much smaller indexes and faster search times.

Example SPX Report

For your edification and delight, we've reproduced a portion of an SPX report from one of our test databases. In Example 12-14 you'll note that the first SQL statement failed to parse because of Oracle error *ORA-00936*. This error was the result of the SQL formatting problem mentioned earlier. (This is not a very common error, but worth being aware of.)

The second SQL statement in Example 12-14 also failed during the generation of the execution plan. This was because the user had insufficient privileges on a view's underlying objects. In this case, the PDBAREP user has the SELECT privilege granted on the system view ALL_TABLES, but lacks privileges on the data dictionary tables used in that particular view.

The third and fourth SQL statements shown in Example 12-14 were both successfully submitted to the Oracle parser for the generation of execution plans via the EXPLAIN PLAN statement.

Example 12-14. Example report—sxprpt.pl

```
Instance: TS01.JKS.COM
sqlUsername: PDBAREP

SQL Check Sum: 3413C8988F25F181D463272348F404D4
SnapShot Date: 11/27/2001 12:57:01
SQL Text:
SELECT TO_CHAR(SYSDATE
   ,'MM/DD/YY') TODAY
   ,         TO_CHAR(SYSDATE
   ,'HH:MI AM') TIME
   ,
--DATABASE||' Database' DATABASE
   ,
--rtrim(database) passout       name||' Database' DATABASE
   ,       lower(rtrim(name)) passout
FROM    v$database

Explain Check Sum:
Explain Plan:

Explain Error: ORA-00936: missing expression (DBD ERROR: OCIStmtExecute)
   at ./sxp.pl line 345. eval {...} called at
========================================================================
Instance: TS01.JKS.COM
sqlUsername: PDBAREP

SQL Check Sum: 3A0D45C0E2E730555B413F17A7E41E95
SnapShot Date: 11/25/2001 12:56:24
SQL Text:
SELECT Table_Name
FROM ALL_TABLES
WHERE OWNER = :f1
ORDER BY Table_Name

Explain Check Sum:
Explain Plan:

Explain Error: ORA-01039: insufficient privileges on underlying objects
   of the view (DBD ERROR: OCIStmtExecute) at
========================================================================
```

Example 12-14. Example report—sxprpt.pl (continued)

```
Instance: TS01.JKS.COM
sqlUsername: PDBAREP

SQL Check Sum: 07BF585D872E136C7341FF573CAD8FCD
SnapShot Date: 11/27/2001 12:57:01
SQL Text:
select      s.global_name cinstance
   , t.owner
   , t.table_name
   , t.column_name
   , t.column_id
   , t.data_type
   , t.data_length
   , t.data_precision
   , t.data_scale
   , t.nullable
from pdba_snap_dates s
   , pdba_tab_columns t
where s.global_name like '%'    and t.owner like '%'
and t.table_name like '%'
-- here is how to get a range of dates
and s.pk = 1009436
and s.pk = t.snap_date_pk
minus
select      s.global_name cinstance
   , t.owner
   , t.table_name
   , t.column_name
   , t.column_id
   , t.data_type
   , t.data_length
   , t.data_precision
   , t.data_scale
   , t.nullable
from pdba_snap_dates s
   , pdba_tab_columns t
where s.global_name like '%'    and t.owner like '%'
and t.table_name like '%'
-- here is how to get a range of dates
and s.pk = 1000000
and s.pk = t.snap_date_pk
order by 1,2,3,4
```

Explain Check Sum: 3D9734F45B31736AB7DF5B69FB8DA713

Explain Plan:

POS	OPERATION	OBJECT_NAME	COST	TOTAL ROWS	BYTES	OPTIMIZER
29	SELECT STATEMENT		29	5K	294203	CHOOSE
1	MERGE JOIN		29	5K	294203	
1	TABLE ACCESS FULL	PDBA_SNAP_DATES	1	7	84	ANALYZED
2	SORT JOIN		28	793	32513	
1	TABLE ACCESS FULL	PDBA_TAB_COLUMNS	4	793	32513	ANALYZED

Example 12-14. Example report—sxprpt.pl (continued)

```
Explain Error:
===============================================================================
Instance: TS01.JKS.COM
sqlUsername: PDBAREP

SQL Check Sum: 3BE4FE5486D11246DA2A358A27A0CE92
SnapShot Date: 11/27/2001 12:57:01
SQL Text:
select *
from PDBA_SNAP_DATES
where  snap_date < trunc(to_date('01/01/1700'
   ,'mm/dd/yyyy')+1)
order by snap_date

Explain Check Sum: 2C7545806582F6D3EC95AA2F48212C6D
Explain Plan:                                     TOTAL
POS OPERATION            OBJECT_NAME      COST  ROWS  BYTES OPTIMIZER
-----------------------------------------------------------------------
  2 SELECT STATEMENT                        2    1    24    CHOOSE
  1  TABLE ACCESS ROWID  PDBA_SNAP_DATES    2    1    24   ANALYZED
  1   INDEX RANGE SCAN   PDBA_SNAP_DATES_UK_IDX 1 1    0   ANALYZED
Explain Error:
```

Comparing execution plans

Now let's take a look at the *sxpcmp.pl* script. This script scans the SQL buffer via the V_$SQLTEXT view and prepares execution plans and SQL checksums in the buffer. Next, it searches the PDBA repository for a SQL statement with a matching checksum. If more than one match is found in the repository, the most recent one is used. This behavior may be modified with the *-rep_report_date* option. (See Table 12-9 for all of the command-line options.) If a matching SQL statement is found, the script compares the checksums for the current execution plan and the stored execution plan. If these match, nothing is reported and the next SQL statement is checked. If the checksums for the execution plans don't match, this indicates that some database change has taken place, thus altering the way the SQL executes. The SQL and both execution plans are reported.

Table 12-9. Command-line options—sxpcmp.pl

Option	Description
-machine	Server where the target database resides
-database	Target database
-username	DBA account
-password	Password for the DBA account (optional)
-rep_machine	Server where the target repository resides
-rep_database	Repository database
-rep_username	DBA account password

Table 12-9. Command-line options—sxpcmp.pl (continued)

Option	Description
-rep_password	Password for the DBA account (optional)
-rep_report_date	Date of SQL data to which to compare current SQL. Defaults to the most recent copy of an identical SQL statement.

Example 12-15 contains a sample report generated from *sxpcmp.pl*. The command used to generate this report looks like this:

```
$ sxpcmp.pl  -machine sherlock -database ts01 \
    -username system -rep_machine sherlock \
    -rep_database ts01 -rep_username pdbarep \
    -rep_report_date '12/15/2001'  > sxpcmp.txt
```

Looking at the output

It's a good idea to redirect the output of *sxpcmp.pl* to a file, as we've done via this command, because a fair number of pop-up warnings may end up cluttering the screen on a run through a complex database. Typically, all of the warnings are sent to STDERR, so redirecting STDOUT to a file will often provide a cleaner report.

Example 12-15. Output from sxpcmp.pl

```
Active SQL From Data Dictionary Matching SQL In Repository    Page:    1
But With Different Execution Paths

Database: TS01.JKS.COM                         Date: 12/16/2001
14:49:56
========================================================================
SQL Username: SCOTT
SQL Check Sum: 75125F4AD88511A11D3C12AF83BE8F4C
SnapShot Date: 12/15/2001 14:27:57
SQL Text:

select /*+ index(e emp_deptno) */  *
from dept d
, emp e
where d.deptno = e.deptno
Current Explain Plan:
                                        TOTAL
POS OPERATION             OBJECT_NAME COST ROWS  BYTES  OPTIMIZER
------------------------------------------------------------------
  4 SELECT STATEMENT                    4   14    700    CHOOSE
  1   HASH JOIN                         4   14    700
  1    TABLE ACCESS BY INDEX     EMP    2   14    448    ANALYZED
  1     INDEX FULL SCAN    EMP_DEPTNO   1   14      0    ANALYZED
  2    TABLE ACCESS FULL        DEPT    1    4     72    ANALYZED

Stored Explain Plan:
                                        TOTAL
POS OPERATION             OBJECT_NAME COST ROWS  BYTES OPTIMIZER
```

Example 12-15. Output from sxpcmp.pl (continued)

```
----------------------------------------------------------------------
3 SELECT STATEMENT                        3    14    700    CHOOSE
1   HASH JOIN                              3    14    700
1     TABLE ACCESS FULL        DEPT        1     4     72    ANALYZED
2     TABLE ACCESS FULL        EMP         1    14    448    ANALYZED
```

Note the following about this output:

1. You can see that the report was run on December 16. One SQL statement had a different execution plan on the day of the report than it did on the previous day, December 15.

2. The execution plan for December 15 demonstrates that the SQL statement joining the EMP and DEPT tables, called by user SCOTT, was employing a full table scan (TABLE ACCESS FULL) on each table.

3. The execution plan for December 16 shows a different execution plan for the same SQL. Rather than scanning the full EMP table, the script uses the index EMP_DEPTNO to identify the rows to include within the join.

4. We deduce that the execution plan change occurred because of the addition of the EMP_DEPTNO index to the EMP table on December 16. Creating this index allowed the Oracle SQL engine to use the index hint in the SQL statement (TABLE ACCESS BY INDEX).

Extending the PDBA Toolkit

In the preceding chapters we've introduced the Perl DBA Toolkit and tried to impress you with all the wonderful ways it can help make Oracle database administration more effective and efficient. But every site, and every DBA, is different. You will undoubtedly find that some of the scripts and supporting modules in the toolkit don't operate quite as you would like them to. You may also find that some of the scripts give you good ideas for other scripts you wish we had included.[*] Here are a few examples of PDBA Toolkit behavior that you may decide you want to modify:

Formatting

You may want to change the way that data is displayed in the *dba_jobsm.pl* script, which reports on the DBA_JOBS view from multiple databases.

Logging

You may want to change the *PDBA::LogFile* module to create a unique file name at each invocation.

Data retrieval

You may want to change the default return type in *PDBA::GQ* from a hash reference to an array reference

Configuration files

You may want to modify the *PDBA::ConfigFile* module to alter the paths where it searches for configuration files.

Security

You may want to use a different form of cryptography in the *PDBA::PWD* module (it currently uses *Crypt::RC4*).

---

[*] Following Vilfredo Pareto's 80-20 rule, most people end up being happy with 80% of a code library written by someone else but discover that the other 20% could stand improvement. The code might fail to fit the way we work, or we might just succumb to a moonlight programming urge and find tweaking irresistible. Tweaking is fine, but the particular way you tweak is quite important. A little forethought and planning can save you a lot of time later on. That's what this chapter is all about.

In writing the software in the toolkit, and in describing the scripts and modules in this book, we've tried to "expose the code"—show you as clearly as possible how we've implemented the logic. One of our goals in developing this toolkit was to provide a ready-to-run set of DBA scripts, of course. But another goal was to supply a framework for you to improve our scripts and to write your own. In this chapter, we'll go a step further with the toolkit. We'll work through two extended examples, showing you some existing scripts and modules and demonstrating how you can change them to suit your specific needs.

The script example
> In this example, we'll look at the problem of checking on scheduled jobs in an Oracle database and providing an easy way to report on those jobs. We'll work through the *dba_jobsm.pl* script in detail, showing our solution, and we'll suggest ways for you to change the script until it suits you.

The module example
> In this example, we'll look at two different modules, *PDBA* and *PDBA::GQ*. For *PDBA*, we'll show how you can add a method. For *PDBA::GQ*, we'll show how you can write code that deals with NULL values returned by Oracle. Both modifications help make processing more efficient.

Modifying a Script in the Toolkit

Let's look at a typical task you'll often perform as part of your Oracle database administration duties: checking on the jobs scheduled via Oracle's built-in scheduling package, DBMS_JOBS. First, we'll see how DBAs typically check on these jobs by examining the DBA_JOBS data dictionary view. Then we'll take a look at a script we've developed to make your checking easier and more efficient. And finally we'll make a few modifications to that script and its supporting files in order to demonstrate how easy it can be to customize and extend the scripts in our toolkit.

The Standard Approach

The Oracle job scheduler is easy to use. You submit a PL/SQL job and Oracle runs it at specified intervals. Here's a short example that illustrates how it works:

1. The ANALYZE_SCOTT procedure will analyze all of SCOTT's objects at 3:00 AM each morning. We create it like this:

```
create or replace procedure analyze_scott
is
begin
   dbms_utility.analyze_schema('SCOTT','COMPUTE');
end;
/
show errors procedure analyze_scott
```

2. Then we submit the job:

```
declare
    jobno integer;
begin
    dbms_job.submit(
        job => jobno
        , what => 'analyze_scott;'
        , next_date => (sysdate + ( 1/1440))        /* Start in 1 min */
        , interval => '(trunc(sysdate) + 1) + (3/24)' /* Then at 3AM */
    );
    commit;
end;
/
```

3. The following SQL on the DBA_JOBS view tells you which jobs are scheduled:

```
select schema_user, job, last_date, next_date, broken,
        interval, failures, what
    from dba_jobs
  order by schema_user, next_date;
```

4. Our newly created procedure appears like this:

```
USER  JOB LAST DATE     NEXT DATE    B INTERVAL     FAILURES  WHAT
----- --- ------------- ------------ - ----------- --------- --------------
SCOTT  42 mar-17 15:50 mar-18 03:00 N (trunc(sys          0  analyze_scott;
                                       date) + 1)
                                       + (3/24)

1 row selected.
```

That's pretty easy. And if you're checking on only a handful of jobs in one or two databases, this approach works just fine. It becomes unwieldy, however, if you need to check a large number of databases on a regular basis.

Checking on Scheduled Jobs with the dba_jobsm.pl Script

We've provided a script in our toolkit that makes checking on scheduled jobs a lot more flexible and efficient. Using the *dba_jobsm.pl* script, you can check on several databases in succession and combine the output into a single report. The script can also email this report to us so we can easily scan it for BROKEN jobs. (A Y in DBA_JOBS's BROKEN column indicates that a job has failed 16 times or has been manually disabled via DBMS_JOB's BROKEN procedure.)

Configuring dba_jobsm.pl

The *dba_jobsm.pl* script is installed automatically when you install the toolkit (see Chapter 9, *Installing the PDBA Toolkit*). You'll find it in Perl's script installation directory. On Unix systems, this is */usr/local/bin/* (or another location, depending on your chosen install configuration). It will also be found in the PDBA installation directory:

PDBA-1.00/routine_tasks/dba_jobsm.pl

On Win32, you'll find the script as *C:\Perl\bin\dba_jobsm.pl*.

There is also a configuration file that stores the parameters for the *dba_jobsm.pl* script (see Example 13-1). On Unix, the *dba_jobs.conf* configuration file is:

PDBA-1.00/routine_tasks/dba_jobs.conf

On Win32 it is:

C:\Perl\site\lib\PDBA\conf\dba_jobs.conf

Example 13-1. dba_jobs.conf

```
package dbajobs;
use vars qw{ $emailAddresses %databases };

$emailAddresses = [qw{yourname@yourdomain.com}];

%databases = ( sherlock => { ts01 => 'system', },
              watson => { ts98 => 'system', ts99 => 'system', } );
1;
```

The configuration file is very straightforward. It contains two hashes: one for the email address to which the final report will be sent, and one for the servers we wish to check, broken down by machine and database.

An example of a final report generated by this script is displayed in Figure 13-1; this particular example was generated with the *-noemail* option specified.

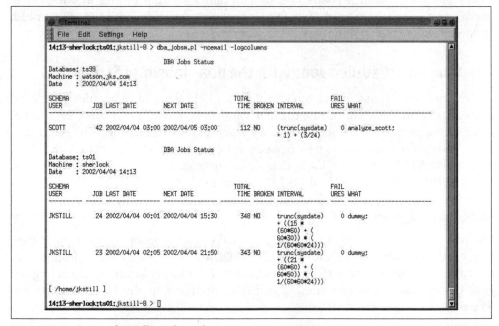

Figure 13-1. Output from dba_jobsm.pl

dba_jobsm.pl: A walkthrough of the main script

The following may look daunting, but we thought we'd walk through at least one complete PDBA Toolkit script in this book, just to show you its low-level wiring. We expect that some readers will find sufficient inspiration in these pages (or frustration with our code) to decide to customize our scripts or create their own. When creating your own scripts, you can treat ours as something of an artist's palette from which you can cut and paste the elements you require.

With that rationalization out of the way, let's plunge into a no-holds-barred familiarization exercise before you embark on your own missions into no-man's-land. We'll focus on one group of lines at a time.

```
01: #!/usr/bin/perl
02:
03: =head1 dba_jobsm.pl
04:
05:  like dba_jobs.pl, but connects to multiple servers
06:  as specified in the configuration file
07:
08: =cut
09:
10: use warnings;
11: use strict;
12: use PDBA;
13: use PDBA::CM;
14: use PDBA::GQ;
15: use PDBA::OPT;
16: use PDBA::ConfigFile;
17: use PDBA::LogFile;
18: use Getopt::Long;
```

Line 1

Informs the command shell that this script runs with the */usr/bin/perl* binary program. The *#!* shebang is recognized by Unix command shells as an identifier indicating which executable to run the script with. This *magic cookie*, as it's sometimes known, must be on line 1. On Win32 the *#!* line is simply treated as just another comment.

Lines 3 to 8

Inline documentation. (The *perldoc FULL_PATH/dba_jobsm.pl* command displays all of the documentation.)*

Lines 10 to 18

Specify the modules needed for this script:

---

* (The *perldoc -f function_name* utility provides online documentation for all of Perl's hundreds of built-in functions.)

use warnings

> Makes Perl detect and flag program warnings as well as errors. Alternatively, use the *-w* flag switch on line 1. (We'll show an example a bit later.)

use strict

> Enforces coding discipline. For instance, you must name package variables explicitly. (See Appendix A, *The Essential Guide to Perl*, for information about variable scoping.)

The next few lines load up the necessary PDBA Toolkit modules; these include the PDBA mother-ship module, the Connection Manager, the Generic Query module, the Options password retriever, the Config File loader, and the Log File creator. (See Chapter 9 for a discussion of all these modules.)

Line 20

> Sets the date format for retrieving date columns from Oracle. (We'll say more about configuring this in a later section.)

Line 22

> Declares our intended use of the *%optctl* hash.

Line 26

> Sets the pass-through option for *Getopt::Long*. We can then specify extra options via the command line to pass through to *PDBA::OPT*. Example 13-2 demonstrates why we need this.

Example 13-2. passthrough.pl

```perl
#!/usr/bin/perl -w

use Getopt::Long;
my %optctl=();

Getopt::Long::Configure(qw{pass_through});

GetOptions( \%optctl, "database=s", "username=s",);

print join(":", @ARGV);
```

The following script call processes the command line options created by *GetOptions*, including *database* and *username*, and leaves the *-pwc_conf* option and its argument in the *@ARGV* program parameters array printed by *passthrough.pl*:

```
$ passthrough.pl -database orcl -username system -pwc_conf test.conf
-pwc_conf:test.conf
```

If you remove the *pass_through* directive, *GetOptions* raises an error, because the *-pwc_conf* flag is unspecified, unlike *database* and *username*.

```
$ passthrough.pl -database orcl -username system -pwc_conf test.conf
Unknown option: pwc_conf
test.conf
```

Let's continue with the next group of lines in *dba_jobsm.pl*:

```
28: GetOptions( \%optctl,
29:    "help!",
30:    "conf=s",
31:    "confpath=s",
32:    "logfile=s",
33:    "logcolumns!",
34:    "email!",
35:    "verbose!",
36:    "debug!",
37: );
```

Lines 28 to 37

Calls the *GetOptions* function from the *Getopt::Long* module, passing the expected command line option names and processing them as they appear on the command line. Those specified with *=s*, such as *conf=s*, require an argument. The following command makes *Getopt::Long* assign the string *-logfile* as the argument to *-conf*. This is because *-conf* explicitly requires an argument:

```
$ dba_jobsm.pl -conf -logfile test.log
Unknown exception from user code:
     Could not load config file -logfile
```

A configured exclamation point following a *GetOptions* parameter, such as *email!*, tells *Getopt::Long* the option is a Boolean switch (1 or 0). These options switch to false with a *no* prefix, as in *dba_jobs.pl -conf dbatest.conf -noemail*. (For much more on *Getopt::Long*, try *perldoc Getopt::Long*.)

```
39: if ( $optctl{help} ) { usage(1) }
```

Line 39

Employs the *usage* subroutine. We'll discuss this in lines 212-229.

Let's move on to the next group of lines:

```
41: # config is required
42: my $configFile = $optctl{conf}
43:    ? $optctl{conf}
44:    : 'dba_jobs.conf';
```

Lines 42 to 44

Determine which configuration file to use. If the expression before *?* is true, the expression following *?* is returned. If the expression before *?* is false, the expression following : is returned. Therefore, if the *-conf* option value fills *$optctl{conf}*, line 43 assigns this value to *$configFile*. Otherwise, line 44 assigns it to a default of *dba_jobs.conf*.

```
46: # load the configuration file
47: unless (
48:    new PDBA::ConfigLoad(
49:       FILE => $configFile,
50:       DEBUG => $optctl{debug},
51:       PATH => $optctl{confpath},
52:    )
```

```
53: ) {
54:   die "could not load config file $configFile\n";
55: }
```

Lines 46 to 55

> Load the configuration file. Lines 48 to 52 invoke *PDBA::ConfigLoad*'s *new* method, passing values for FILE, DEBUG, and PATH. The *PDBA::ConfigLoad* module ignores PATH if it is undefined or if it is an empty string. If the configuration file fails to load, the program exits on line 54 with a *die* command.

```
57: # setup and open the log file
58: my $logFile = $optctl{logfile}
59:   ? $optctl{logfile}
60:   : PDBA->pdbaHome . q{/logs/dba_jobsm.log};
61:
62: my $logFh = new PDBA::LogFile($logFile);
```

Lines 57 to 60

> Determine the name and location of the logfile. As with the configuration file, the name is supplied by the *-logfile* option. The default *dba_jobsm.log* file is placed in *PDBA_HOME/logs* directory. (Note that the forward slash is acceptable to Win32, which uses it internally anyway.)

Line 62

> Creates a *new PDBA::LogFile* object, *$logFh*, and the program writes to this object handle when sending audit messages to the logfile.

```
64: if ( $optctl{debug} ) {
65:
66:   foreach my $machine ( keys %dbajobs::databases ) {
67:     print "machine: $machine\n";
68:     foreach my $database ( keys %{$dbajobs::databases{$machine}} ) {
69:       print "\tdb: $database\n";
70:       print
          "\t\tusername: $dbajobs::databases{$machine}->{$database}\n";
71:     }
72:   }
73:   exit;
74: }
```

Lines 64 to 74

> Execute only if the *-debug* program option is specified. Line 66 sets up a loop which iterates through each *$machine* in the *%dbajobs::databases* hash. This is loaded from the configuration file, with each machine, database, and username being printed to the screen.

```
76: my $instanceName = undef;
77: my $machineName = undef;
78: my $systemDate = undef;
79: my $row = {};
80: my $tmpFile;
```

Lines 76 to 80

> Simply declare some variables for later use.

```
82: if ($optctl{email}) {
83:
84:    use POSIX;
85:
86:    if ( 'unix' eq PDBA->osname ) {
87:       $tmpFile = POSIX::tmpnam();
88:    } else {
89:       $tmpFile = 'C:\TEMP' . POSIX::tmpnam() . 'tmp';
90:    }
91:
92:    print "TMPFILE: $tmpFile\n" if $optctl{verbose};
93:
94:    open(FILE,"> $tmpFile") || die "cannot create $tmpFile\n";
95:    select(FILE);
96:
97:    # reset the format and format_top names, as using select(FILE)
98:    # will cause Perl to look for FILE and FILE_TOP
99:    $~ = 'STDOUT';
100:   $^ = 'STDOUT_TOP';
101:
102: }
```

Line 82

Gatekeeper for the next code body. It only runs if the *-email* flag was set.

Line 84

Loads the *POSIX* module because we need a temporary file for email formatting purposes later on.

Lines 86 to 90

Name this temporary file via the *POSIX::tmpnam* function. On Unix, this defaults to something like */tmp/fileiZZd123*. On Win32, *POSIX::tmpname* returns a *random_value*. string. We want all of our temporary files stored in the same location on Win32, and we ensure this on line 89. If *POSIX::tmpnam* returns a filename of *wpo.*, this is converted into *C:\TEMP\wpo.tmp*.

Line 94

Creates and opens the temporary file.

Line 95

Uses Perl's main *select* operator and sets the default output filehandle to be the temporary file. All *write* and *print* statements without specific filehandle parameters will now go to the temporary file.

Lines 99 to 100

Set the print format names for the *write* operator. The $^ built-in Perl variable sets the name for the header format. The $~ variable sets the equivalent for the body format.

You can avoid using built-in Perl variable names like $~ and $^ if you use the *English* module. This makes all such variables readable to English speakers:

```
use English;
# Use English names so your code won't
# look like an obscure Klingon dialect! :-)
$FORMAT_TOP_NAME = 'STDOUT_TOP';  # $~
$FORMAT_TOP = 'STDOUT';           # $^
```

For more information about such variables, invoke *perldoc perlvar*.

The default names for these are *STDOUT* and *STDOUT_TOP*, which is what our code uses too. The default usually works fine for console output, but when we changed our default filehandle to *FILE* the default formats changed too, into *FILE* and *FILE_TOP*. Because we still want to use *STDOUT* and *STDOUT_TOP*, we need to explicitly reset them both back again.

```
104: foreach my $machine ( keys %dbajobs::databases ) {
105:
106:   foreach my $database ( keys %{$dbajobs::databases{$machine}} ) {
107:
108:     my $username = $dbajobs::databases{$machine}->{$database};
109:
110:     # retrieve the password from the password server
111:     my $password = PDBA::OPT->pwcOptions (
112:       INSTANCE => $database,
113:       MACHINE => $machine,
114:       USERNAME => $username
115:     );
```

Line 104

Begins the loop where the real work begins. As with line 66, this line begins looping through the machines defined in the configuration file.

Line 106

Iterates through each database as defined for each machine.

Line 108

Retrieves the current loop iteration's DBA username.

Lines 111 to 115

Retrieve the password for the username from the password server. (You could modify the *dba_jobsm.pl* script to avoid using the password server, but this would require a fair amount of work and would also necessitate giving up all the security and ease-of-use the server delivers. However, we will demonstrate how this is possible in a later section.)

```
117:     # create a database connection
118:     my $dbh = new PDBA::CM(
119:       DATABASE => $database,
120:       USERNAME => $username,
121:       PASSWORD => $password,
```

```
122:       );
123:
124:       $dbh->do(qq{alter session set nls_date_format = '$nlsDateFormat'});
```

Lines 117 to 122

Create the database connection via *PDBA::CM*'s Connection Manager. One of the advantages of using *PDBA::CM*, rather than DBI, is the use of the *cm.conf* configuration file. This contains a default *ORACLE_HOME* value that sets the *$ENV{ORACLE_HOME}* environment variable, making it unnecessary to set the Oracle environment before running a script.

Line 124

Sets NLS_DATE_FORMAT for your current database session.

```
126:       # get the host and instance name
127:       my $gn = new PDBA::GQ($dbh,'v$instance');
128:       my $gnHash = $gn->next;
129:       $instanceName = $gnHash->{INSTANCE_NAME};
130:       $machineName = $gnHash->{HOST_NAME};
131:       undef $gn;
132:       undef $gnHash;
133:
134:       print "Instance Name: $instanceName\n" if $optctl{verbose};
135:       print "Host Name: $machineName\n" if $optctl{verbose};
136:
137:       # get the system date
138:       $systemDate = PDBA->sysdate($dbh, NLS_DATE_FORMAT => $nlsDateFormat);
139:       print "System Date: $systemDate\n" if $optctl{verbose};
```

Line 127

Uses *PDBA::GQ* to execute a SQL statement of *select * from v$instance*. The *PDBA::GQ* module also prepares the SQL statement. Because we failed to specify any columns, it assumes we want all of them. To select specific columns you can use *PDBA::GQ* like this:

```
my $gn = new PDBA::GQ($dbh,'$v$instance',
    { COLUMNS => [qw(host_name instance_name)] } );
```

Line 128

Retrieves the first row from query object *$gn* via *PDBA::GQ*'s *next* method. Its default return value is a hash reference. On lines 129 and 130 we assign *$instanceName* and *$machineName*. The sharp-eyed among you may be wondering why we haven't followed line 128 with the following:

```
$gn->finish;
```

All open cursors must be finished before database disconnection. Fortunately V$INSTANCE only holds one row, so the *$gn* cursor finished automatically.

Lines 131 to 132

Undefine *$gn* and *$gnHash*, as we're done with them in this particular loop iteration and we should clear them out before the next one.

Line 138

Sets *$systemDate* to the current database SYSDATE value.

```
141:    my $gq = new PDBA::GQ ( $dbh, 'dba_jobs',
142:    {
143:      COLUMNS => [
144:        qw(schema_user job last_date next_date
                interval failures what),
145:        q{round(total_time,2) total_time},
146:        q{decode(broken,'N','NO','Y','YES','UNKNOWN') broken},
147:      ],
148:      ORDER_BY => q{schema_user, next_date}
149:    }
150:    );
```

Line 141

Begins a complex instantiation of a database query via *PDBA::GQ*.

Line 143

Begins specifying the columns to include in the query.

 There is a difference between the *q{}* and *qq{}* operators. They're identical in use to either single quotes (') or double quotes (" ") in Perl. Variables only interpolate within the *qq{}* braces. For instance, let's run the following code:

```
my $str = 'this is Earth calling';
print qq{$str\n};
print q{$str\n};
```

The second printed line remains uninterpolated:

```
this is Earth calling
$str\n
```

The use of these and other quoting functions such as *qw{}* makes Perl code formatting much plainer to the eye. Check out *perldoc perlop* for much more detail.

Lines 145 to 146

Perform column manipulation. We use Oracle's ROUND function to format TOTAL_TIME, and its DECODE function to return YES or NO from the BROKEN column, rather than Y or N (see Figure 13-1).

Line 148

Supplies the ORDER BY clause to the SQL query.

```
152:    # print the column names in the log
153:    my $colHash = $gq->getColumns;
154:    $logFh->printflush(
155:      join('~', (
156:        $machine, $database,
157:        map {$_} sort keys %{$colHash}
158:      )
159:    ) . "\n") if $optctl{logcolumns};
```

Line 153

Uses *PDBA::GQ*'s *getColumns* method to return the SQL query's column names into the hash reference, *$colHash*, in this kind of form:

```
$colHash = { 'BROKEN' => 8,
             'LAST_DATE' => 2,
             'FAILURES' => 5,
             'TOTAL_TIME' => 7,
             'WHAT' => 6,
             'JOB' => 1,
             'INTERVAL' => 4,
             'NEXT_DATE' => 3,
             'SCHEMA_USER' => 0 };
```

Lines 154 to 159

We need to consider these lines together. Line 159 allows the printing of columns only if the *-logcolumns* option was included on the command line. We want these column names printed in the database specified order. That's what line 157 does with the *map* function. The columns retrieved into *$colHash* have no particular order, because hashes lack any guarantee as to the order in which keys are stored (see Appendix A). To get them in the *$gq* query order, we employ a little Perl magic. We *sort* the keys into alphabetical order, we then *map* them to an array, and then *join* all of these elements together with the machine and the database strings to form a ~ delimited superstring. To read about these functions, try the following:

```
$ perldoc -f map
$ perldoc -f sort
$ perldoc -f join
```

```
161:    while ( $row = $gq->next({}) ) {
162:        $logFh->printflush(
163:            join("~", (
164:                $machine ,
165:                $database ,
166:                # the map function is used to place all values from the
167:                # $row hash ref into an array.  The ternary ?: operator
168:                # is used with 'defined()' to avoid warnings on undefined
169:                # values.  These occur when a NULL is returned from a
170:                # SQL statement
171:                map { defined($row->{$_}) ? $row->{$_} : '' }
                        sort keys %$row
172:                )
173:            ) . "\n"
174:        );
175:        write;
176:    }
```

Lines 161 to 185

Retrieve the data from our query object. Line 161 retrieves a row at a time into the hash reference, *$row*.

Lines 162 to 174

Begin the process of retrieving the query data. The column values in the *$row* hash reference are printed to the logfile. Notice the use of Perl's *defined* operator, which traps potential NULLs.

Line 175

Consists of a *write* statement. We'll come back to this at line 231.

```
178:     $dbh->disconnect;
179:
180:     # set number of lines on page left to 0
181:     # forcing a form feed
182:     $- = 0;
183:
184:   }
185: }
```

Line 178

Terminates the connection to this database before the next loop.

Line 182

Issues a form feed via the *$-* built-in Perl variable. This is known as *$FORMAT_ LINES_LEFT*, if you use *English.pm*, and it's the number of lines left on a page of the currently selected output channel.

```
187: if ($optctl{email}) {
188:
189:   #email here
190:   close FILE;
191:   select(STDOUT);
192:
193:   open(FILE, "$tmpFile") ||
            die "cannot open $tmpFile for read - $!\n";
194:   my @msg = <FILE>;
195:   close FILE;
196:   my $msg = join('',@msg);
197:
198:   my $subject = qq{DBA Jobs Report For All Servers};
199:
200:   unless ( PDBA->email($dbajobs::emailAddresses,$msg,$subject) ) {
201:     warn "Error Sending Email\n";
202:   }
203:
204:   unlink $tmpFile;
205:
206:   $logFh->printflush(("report mailed to ",
            @$dbajobs::emailAddresses, "\n"));
207: }
208:
209:
210: ## end of main
```

Line 187

> Follows the main loop exit. If *-email* was set, we execute the following code body.

Lines 190 to 191

> Close the FILE opened earlier and reset STDOUT to be the default output file-handle.

Line 193

> Opens the temporary email file, which has been filled by the *write* function on line 175 (we'll discuss *write* formats later at line 231).

Lines 194 to 196

> Read the entire contents of this temporary file into the *@msg* array before closing the file. Line 196 then creates the scalar *$msg*, from *@msg*, by joining all of its elements together, including their embedded newlines.

Line 198

> Creates the email *$subject* header.

Lines 200 to 202

> Mail the recipients designated in the *dba_jobs.conf* configuration file via the *PDBA* module's *mail* method.

Lines 204 to 206

> Remove the temporary file and write one last audit message, with line 210 marking the end of the main program section.

dba_jobsm.pl: A walkthrough of functions and formats

We've finished looking at the main logic of the script. Now we've reached the script's functions and print formats. Just for orientation, you might like to revisit line 39 in the main program to check its context before looking at the *usage* subroutine:

```
39: if ( $optctl{help} ) { usage(1) }
```

The *usage* routine is called when the *-help* command option is flagged. It accepts one argument, *$exitVal*, read in at line 213. The *usage* subroutine outputs a help message, then exits Perl with *$exitVal* returned to the command shell as the error code:

```
212: sub usage {
213:    my $exitVal = shift;
214:    use File::Basename;
215:    my $basename = basename($0);
216:    print qq/
217: usage: $basename
218:
219:    -help      show help and exit
220:    -conf      configuration file ( needed for email )
221:    -confpath  path to configuration file ( optional )
222:    -logfile   logfile - may include path ( optional )
223:    -logcolumns include column names in logfile
224:    -email     send email to users in config file
```

```
225:    -verbose     verbosity on
226:
227: /;
228:    exit $exitVal;
229: };
```

Lines 214 to 215

Determine the name of the current script with *File::Basename*. Even if the script's name changes, *$basename* remains correct.

Lines 216 to 227

Use Perl's *qq//* operator to print the help information. The use of *qq//* is much neater than a series of *print* statements and much easier to edit.

Line 228

Exits the program.

```
231: no warnings;
232: format STDOUT_TOP =
233:
234:                              DBA Jobs Status
235: Database: @<<<<<<<<<<<<<<
236: $instanceName
237: Machine : @<<<<<<<<<<<<<<
238: $machineName
239: Date    : @<<<<<<<<<<<<<<<<<<<
240: $systemDate
241:
242: SCHEMA                                              TOTAL
     FAIL
243: USER            JOB LAST DATE      NEXT DATE        TIME BROKEN
     INTERVAL        URES WHAT
244: ---------- ----- ---------------- ---------------- --------- ------
     --------------- ---- ------------------------
245:
246: .
247:
248:
249: format STDOUT =
250: @<<<<<<<<< @#### @<<<<<<<<<<<<<<< @<<<<<<<<<<<<<<< @######## @<<<<<
     ^<<<<<<<<<<<<<< @### @<<<<<<<<<<<<<<<<<<<<<<<<<
251: $row->{SCHEMA_USER}, $row->{JOB}, $row->{LAST_DATE},
     $row->{NEXT_DATE}, $row->{TOTAL_TIME}, $row->{BROKEN},
     $row->{INTERVAL}, $row->{FAILURES}, $row->{WHAT}
252: ~~
     ^<<<<<<<<<<<<<<
253:
     $row->{INTERVAL}
254: .
```

Line 231

Begins the print formatting section for the earlier *write* command:

```
175:        write;
```

A *no warnings* call is made at line 231 to prevent Perl from overreacting to acceptable difficulties such as NULL values returning from Oracle.

Lines 232 to 246

    Create the STDOUT_TOP header format, which appears at the top of each page. Perl formats use literal text, variables, and field holders to determine how data will be printed (with much of the original layout borrowed from FORTRAN and the *nroff* program). You can learn more about Perl formats by invoking:

```
$ perldoc perlform
```

Line 235

    Contains the literal text of *'Database: '* followed by a field holder of @<<<<<<<<<. This tells Perl that the print data should be left justified.

Lines 242 to 244

    Print the literal text of the column names.

Line 246

    Terminates the STDOUT_TOP format with a period.

Lines 249 to 253

    Define the STDOUT body of the report.

Line 254

    Terminates the STDOUT format and brings us to the end of the script.

Modifying the dba_jobsm.pl Script

By now you should have a good understanding of the structure and logic of the existing version of the *dba_jobsm.pl* script and its *dba_jobs.conf* configuration file. Now let's talk about how you might want to modify the script and file to provide some code flexibility. In addition to showing specific modifications for this particular case, the following sections should give you the background necessary to be able to examine and modify additional scripts to suit your own requirements.

Configuring parameters

The first change we'll make involves Oracle's NLS_DATE_FORMAT, a setting used within the database to set the default format in which date column data will be returned. This format is currently hard-coded into the script at line 20:

```
20: my $nlsDateFormat = q{yyyy/mm/dd hh24:mi};
```

If we ever want to change this value, we'll have to edit the script each time. It's much better to specify this value as a configurable item in the *dba_jobs.conf* configuration file. So let's comment out line 20 of the script with a # hash character as follows:

```
20: #my $nlsDateFormat = q{yyyy/mm/dd hh24:mi};
```

Now find lines 124 and 138. They look like the following:

```
124:$dbh->do(qq{alter session set nls_date_format = '$nlsDateFormat' });
...
138: $systemDate = PDBA->sysdate($dbh, NLS_DATE_FORMAT => $nlsDateFormat );
```

You need to change these lines to this:

```
124: $dbh->do(qq{alter session set nls_date_format = '$dbajobs::nlsDateFormat' });
...
138: $systemDate = PDBA->sysdate($dbh, NLS_DATE_FORMAT => $dbajobs::nlsDateFormat );
```

Save the *dba_jobsm.pl* file and open *dba_jobs.conf*. Now we'll add an entry for NLS_ DATE_FORMAT. We've displayed the relevant code snippet that adds the *$nlsDateFormat* variable. Notice that this variable name has also been added to the *use vars* statement. Doing so prevents *use warnings* from raising a message about the single use of a variable.

```
package dbajobs;

use vars qw{ $emailAddresses $nlsDateFormat %databases };
$nlsDateFormat = q{yyyy/mm/dd hh24:mi};
$emailAddresses = [qw{yourname@yourdomain.com}];
...
```

Now simply run *dba_jobsm.pl* to test it. Be sure to change the value of the *$nlsDateFormat* variable so you can verify the results.

Adding passwords to the configuration file

Although we encourage you to use the password server, we'll show you how to work around it just in case you're unable to use it for some reason. While putting passwords in configuration files is workable, it is both a security risk and more work to maintain. However, given those caveats, let's begin with the configuration file by creating data constructs that can hold DBA passwords as well as usernames:

```
package dbajobs;
use vars qw{ $emailAddresses $nlsDateFormat %databases };
$nlsDateFormat = q{yyyy/mm/dd hh24:mi};
$emailAddresses = [qw{yourname@yourdomain.com}];

%databases = ( sherlock => { ts01 => [qw{system manager}], },
               watson =>   { ts98 => [qw{system manager}],
                             ts99 => [qw{system manager}], } );
1;
```

The DBA user and its password are placed inside array references. The user is element 0 of each array reference, and the password is element 1.

Now it's time to change the script. Open *dba_jobsm.pl* and locate the following lines:

```
15: use PDBA::OPT;
...
70:     print
```

```
            "\t\tusername: $dbajobs::databases{$machine}->{$database}\n";
...
108:        my $username = $dbajobs::databases{$machine}->{$database};
...
111:        my $password = PDBA::OPT->pwcOptions (
112:          INSTANCE => $database,
113:          MACHINE => $machine,
114:          USERNAME => $username
115:        );
```

Change these lines so they appear like those in Example 13-3:

Example 13-3. Results of changes to dba_jobsm.pl for password usage.

```
15: #use PDBA::OPT;     --- Commented out, array references used below! :-)
...
70:        print
        "\t\tusername: $dbajobs::databases{$machine}->{$database}[0]\n";
...
108:        my $username = $dbajobs::databases{$machine}->{$database}[0];
...
111:        my $password = $dbajobs::databases{$machine}->{$database}[1];
112:        #INSTANCE => $database,
113:        #MACHINE => $machine,
114:        #USERNAME => $username
115:        #);
```

Once again, run the script to validate the changes.

Modifying a Module in the Toolkit

In Chapter 9 we introduced the supporting modules included in the Perl DBA Toolkit and described briefly what they do. Just as you might wish to modify or extend the toolkit's scripts, as we described earlier in this chapter, you might also find a good reason to modify the modules. In an effort to anticipate the kinds of changes you might want to make to these modules, in the following sections we'll provide a quick guide on how to modify the modules in the toolkit. We'll show two examples here and hope you can extrapolate to many more:

Adding a method

We'll add a *usage* method to the *PDBA* module. This will allow us to define a scalar variable containing help screen information, which can then be passed into the *usage* method. This will save us from having to code individual *usage* subroutines in each separate script.

Dealing with NULL columns returned by Oracle

We'll deal with NULLs returned by Oracle when printing output. This is a useful thing to do because NULL values raise *undefined value* errors when included in certain Perl statements.

Modifying the PDBA Module to Add a Method

In this section we'll essentially modify the *PDBA* module in order to add a method that will help us in doing our work. In reality, though, rather than modifying the existing code, we're going to create our own parallel, modified module. We'll explain why we've taken this approach as we work through the example.

We've created a separate downloadable module, called *PDBAx*, for "PDBA Extensions," that contains the code we describe in this section. If you want to do so, you can download and install this code in the same manner as you would the ordinary *PDBA* module. There's no absolute need to download and install *PDBAx*, but you may wish to do so to help follow the rest of this chapter or simply for your own experimentation. You can download *PDBAx-1.00.tar.gz*, or its latest derivative, from our book's page on the O'Reilly site:

> *http://www.oreilly.com/catalog/oracleperl/pdbatoolkit*

Installation is straightforward, as we describe in the following sections.

Installing PDBAx on Unix

Run the following to install *PDBAx* on Unix systems:

```
$ gunzip -c PDBAx-1.00.tar.gz | tar xvf -
$ cd PDBAx-1.00
$ perl Makefile.PL
$ make install
```

There are no tests to run for this module.

Installing PDBAx on Win32

Download the *PDBAx.ppd* PPM file from the web site and save it in a location such as *C:\TEMP*. You probably know the rest of the drill:

```
DOS> ppm
PPM> install --location c:\temp PDBAx
```

Adding a Usage Method

Most of the scripts included in our toolkit employ a *usage* subroutine that is called for various reasons. Perhaps the *-help* option was included on the command line, or perhaps required options were missing. The *usage* routine generally looks something like this:

```
sub usage {
    my $exitVal = shift;
    use File::Basename;
    my $basename = basename($0);
    print qq/
$basename
```

```
usage: $basename
  -machine  database_server
  -database database_instance
  -username account

/;
   exit $exitVal;
};
```

A common *PDBA.pm* method would eliminate the need for this subroutine in other scripts. Writing such a method is one approach to solving your problem. Some suggested code for such a method is shown in Example 13-4.

Example 13-4. The PDBA usage method

```
sub usage {
   my ($exitVal,$helpStrRef) = @_;
   use File::Basename;
   my $basename = basename($0);
   print qq{
usage: $basename

${$helpStrRef}

};
   exit $exitVal;
};
```

Here's how you might use it in a script:

```
use PDBA;

my $help = q{
  -database database to connect to
  -username database account
  -password password for the account
};
...
if ( $optctl{help} ) { PDBA::usage(1,\$help) }
...
```

So now you place your new *usage* method in the *PDBA.pm* file and try it out in a few scripts. And it works great. However, there's one small problem. What happens if you install a newer version of the PDBA Toolkit module library? That's right—your carefully crafted usage method will no longer be in the *PDBA* module, and all of your scripts calling *PDBA::usage* will break. Ouch!

Rather than modifying the *PDBA* module, why not create your own subclassed module? Doing so will allow you to extend the *PDBA* module without fear of breaking scripts that use it in its current incarnation. Creating your own module also eliminates the problems that would occur if you download a new version of the *PDBA* module and it overwrites your carefully crafted extensions.

Perl lets you do this with relative ease, and we'll show you how.* Let's call our new subclassed module *PDBAx*. This module will take the place of *PDBA* in your scripts. The full code for *PDBAx* appears in Example 13-5.

Example 13-5. The entire PDBAx module

```
package PDBAx;

our $VERSION=1.00;

use PDBA;
our @ISA = qw{PDBA};
sub usage {
    my ($exitVal,$helpStrRef) = @_;
    use File::Basename;
    my $basename = basename($0);
    print qq{
usage: $basename

${$helpStrRef}

};
    exit $exitVal;
};
1;
```

You may be surprised at how little code there is in Example 13-5. Yet all the features of the *PDBA* module are available through *PDBAx*. That's because of the magic of the *@ISA* array. The methods and attributes of modules placed in *@ISA* are inherited by calling modules—in this case, *PDBAx*. Try running the code shown in Example 13-6. The *PDBAx osname* method is inherited directly from the *PDBA* module.

Example 13-6. Testing PDBAx

```
#!/usr/bin/perl -w

use warnings;
use strict;

use PDBAx;
print "$PDBA::VERSION\n";

print PDBAx->osname, "\n";

my $help = q{
    -database   database to connect to
    -username   user to connect as
```

---

* We're using the simplest features of Perl's object orientation, as described in Appendix A. For a more definitive description, refer to *Object Oriented Perl*, by Damian Conway (Manning 2000).

Example 13-6. Testing PDBAx (continued)

```
 -password    password for user
};
PDBAx::usage(1,\$help);
```

The benefit of extending PDBA in this way is that when your intrepid authors release the latest version of the PDBA Toolkit, your usage method will be safely encapsulated within its own *PDBAx* module. Even if we come up with similarly named methods, yours will override them. It's a kind of magic.

Modifying the PDBA::GQ Module to Deal with NULL Columns

In the following sections we'll describe how you can modify the *PDBA::GQ* module to deal with Oracle NULL values. First, though, let's take a look at the problems involved in using NULLs.

Oracle and NULL values

When you first start using the Oracle database, NULL values may take a little getting used to. A NULL is never equivalent to any other value, including another NULL. The truth table in Table 13-1 sums up the results of comparing NULL to NULL, with various SQL operators. Note that only one True is returned with the special IS NULL comparison.

Table 13-1. Null truth table

Option	Description
NULL = NULL	False
NULL <> NULL	False
NULL < NULL	False
NULL > NULL	False
NULL IS NOT NULL	False
NULL BETWEEN NULL AND NULL	False
NULL = ''	False
NULL IS NULL	True

One problem you discover when dealing with NULLs in an Oracle database is that Oracle treats empty strings and NULL values the same way. This is different from other databases, and is readily apparent when you use NULLs with Perl. We'll see this in the next section.

Testing the use of NULLs

The *null_test.pl* script in Example 13-7 builds a table, NULL_TEST, and populates it with two rows of data.

Example 13-7. null_test.pl

```
01: #!/usr/bin/perl
02:
03: use warnings;
04: use strict;
05: use PDBA::CM;
06: use PDBA::GQ;
07: use PDBA::DBA;
08:
09: my ( $database, $username, $password ) = qw{ts01 scott tiger};
10:
11: my $dbh = new PDBA::CM(
12:    DATABASE => $database,
13:    USERNAME => $username,
14:    PASSWORD => $password
15: );
16:
17: eval {
18:    local $dbh->{PrintError} = 0;
19:    $dbh->do(q{drop table null_test});
20: };
21:
22: $dbh->do(q{create table null_test
23:    (
24:      first_name varchar2(20) not null,
25:      middle_initial varchar2(1) null,
26:      last_name varchar2(20) not null
27:    )
28: });
29:
30: my $insHandle = $dbh->prepare(q{insert into null_test values(?,?,?)});
31:
32: $insHandle->execute('Alfred','E','Neuman');
33: $insHandle->execute('Peter',undef,'Parker');
34: $insHandle->execute('Clark','','Kent');
35: $dbh->commit;
36:
37: my $gq = new PDBA::GQ ( $dbh, 'null_test');
38:
39: while ( my $row = $gq->next ) {
40:    printf("Last: %-20s First: %-20s MI: %1s\n",
41:      $row->{LAST_NAME},
42:      $row->{FIRST_NAME},
43:      $row->{MIDDLE_INITIAL}
44:    );
45: }
46: $dbh->disconnect;
```

Note the following about this example:

Lines 22 to 28

The CREATE TABLE statement defines two columns, FIRST_NAME and LAST_NAME, which are both required, while the MIDDLE_INITIAL column is nullable.

Line 32

The first row insert places values in all three columns.

Line 33

Only the FIRST_NAME and LAST_NAME columns are populated. The value for the MIDDLE_INITIAL column is defined as *undef*. This causes the MIDDLE_INITIAL value to be NULL.

Line 35

Inserts another row, but this time the MIDDLE_INITIAL column is populated with an empty string.

Using the following SQL, we can now prove that Oracle treats both the empty string and *undef* as NULL values:

```
SQL> select * from null_test where middle_initial is null;

FIRST_NAME           M LAST_NAME
-------------------- - --------------------
Peter                  Parker
Clark                  Kent

2 rows selected.
```

This problem becomes apparent in Perl when a NULL column is retrieved from a database and an attempt is made to reference the value in a statement. You can see this in lines 40 to 44 of Example 13-7, which we reproduce here:

```
40:    printf("Last: %-20s First: %-20s MI: %1s\n",
41:       $row->{LAST_NAME},
42:       $row->{FIRST_NAME},
43:       $row->{MIDDLE_INITIAL}
44:    );
```

Line 40 to 44

Line 40 is the first line of a multi-line *printf* statement. Line 41 references the LAST_NAME, line 42 the FIRST_NAME, and line 43 the MIDDLE_INITIAL. Printing the first row presents no problem, because all three columns are populated. That changes with the second row when the script is executed, as seen here:

```
Last: Neuman             First: Alfred             MI: E
Use of uninitialized value in printf at ./null_test.pl line 40 (#1)
  (W uninitialized) An undefined value was used as if it were already
  defined.  It was interpreted as a "" or a 0, but maybe it was a mistake.
  To suppress this warning assign a defined value to your variables.
  ...
Last: Parker             First: Peter              MI:
```

Whoa! The second row returned a NULL for MIDDLE_INITIAL, which is treated by Perl as an *undef*. This threw out a warning because of the *use warnings* pragma at the top of the script.

Considering changes to the script

The warning output we saw in the previous section could be eliminated by turning off the warning mechanism temporarily as follows:

```
38: no warnings;
39: while ( my $row = $gq->next ) {
40:   printf("Last: %-20s First: %-20s MI: %1s\n",
41:     $row->{LAST_NAME},
42:     $row->{FIRST_NAME},
43:     $row->{MIDDLE_INITIAL}
44:   );
45: }
46: use warnings
```

However, this sweeps potentially difficult problems under the rug, which will almost always re-surface to bite us later. A better solution would ensure that all of the row elements get a guaranteed value before they get pumped into *printf*:

```
39: while ( my $row = $gq->next ) {

      foreach my $key ( keys %$row )
        { $row->{$key} = '' unless defined $row->{$key} }
40:   printf("Last: %-20s First: %-20s MI: %1s\n",
41:     $row->{LAST_NAME},
42:     $row->{FIRST_NAME},
43:     $row->{MIDDLE_INITIAL}
44:   );
45: }
```

The *foreach* loop added between lines 39 and 40 assigns empty strings to any undefined values in the *$row* hash reference, thereby preventing warnings.

Modifying the PDBA::GQ module

An even better solution would extend the *PDBA::GQ* (Generic Query) module so your scripts would automatically deal with NULL column data. However, as we learned earlier, modifying a module presents its own problems. What we need is a modified version of the *PDBA::GQ* module. More specifically, we should modify the *PDBA::GQ->next* method. Example 13-8 shows one way to do this.

Example 13-8. PDBAx::GQ

```
01: package PDBAx::GQ;
02:
03: our $VERSION=1.0;
04:
05: use Carp;
06: use warnings;
07: use strict;
08:
09: use PDBA::GQ;
10: our @ISA = qw{PDBA::GQ};
```

Example 13-8. PDBAx::GQ (continued)

```
11:
12: sub next {
13:     my $self = shift;
14:     my ( $ref ) = @_;
15:     $ref ||= [];
16:
17:     my $refType = ref $ref;
18:
19:     my $data;
20:
21:     $data = $self->SUPER::next($ref);
22:     return unless $data;
23:
24:     # transform NULL columns to a defined value
25:     # to avoid problems with undefined values
26:     if ( 'ARRAY' eq $refType ) {
27:         foreach(@$data){ $_ = '' unless defined }
28:     } elsif ( 'HASH' eq $refType ) {
29:         foreach my $key ( keys %$data )
30:         { $data->{$key} = '' unless defined $data->{$key} }
31:     } else {
32:         croak "invalid ref type of $refType " .
33:             "used to call PDBAx::GQ->next\n"
34:     }
35:     return $data;
36: }
37: 1;
```

Lines 1 to 10

Set up the new module as a subclass of the original *PDBA::GQ* module.

Line 13

Picks up the object's reference in the *$self* variable.

Lines 14 to 17

Here we set up our subclassed *next* method to use an array reference as its default datatype. Line 14 assigns the next argument (if it exists) to the *$ref* variable. Line 15 assigns an empty array to *$ref* if the assignment failed in line 14. (We've also changed this default to an ordinary array reference in this extension, rather than a hash array reference, as with the older *PDBA::GQ*.) Line 17 sets the *$refType* scalar to the type of reference in use. This will be used later when assigning a value to NULL columns. (See Appendix A for more information about references and the related *ref* operator.)

Line 21

Calls the *next* method in the parent class via the *SUPER* pseudoclass. This accesses methods in parent classes and lets you modify the behavior of the base class without rewriting all of its code.

Line 22

Returns if no data was found.

Lines 26 to 31

Here the contents of the returned data are checked for NULL values. We first need to determine if the data is in a hash reference or an array reference. This is done via the *$refType* variable created earlier. If the data is in an array reference, each element is checked to see if it is defined. If it is undefined, an empty string is assigned. This is done in line 27. The same is done for data returned as a hash reference. Lines 29 and 30 assign empty strings to keys with undefined values. Because an empty string is a valid defined value in Perl, we have eliminated our warnings.

We need to change just two of the lines in the *null_test.pl* script we first encountered in Example 13-8:

```
...
06: use PDBAx::GQ;
...
37: my $gq = new PDBAx::GQ ( $dbh, 'null_test');
...
```

All of the functionality of the *PDBA::GQ* module is still available, but your modifications allow you to stop thinking about referencing NULL values.

Taking one more step

The *PDBAx::GQ* extension still has a shortcoming. It assigns an empty string to numeric columns that are NULL, and this may be unsuitable for some purposes. Financial reporting may require that these NULL columns be assigned a numeric zero. While this can be done, the complexity of the code required to do it increases significantly, as we'll see in the code supplied via the downloaded *PDBAx::GQ* module in Example 13-9.

Example 13-9. Assigning zero to NULL numeric columns in PDBAx::GQ

```
01: package PDBAx::GQ;
02:
03: our $VERSION=1.00;
04:
05: use Carp;
06: use warnings;
07: use strict;
08:
09: use PDBA::GQ;
10: our @ISA = qw{PDBA::GQ};
11:
12: my @columnTypes;
13: my %columnTypes;
14:
15: sub new {
```

Example 13-9. Assigning zero to NULL numeric columns in PDBAx::GQ (continued)

```
16:    my $self = shift;
17:    my ( $dbh ) = $_[0];
18:    my $qobj = $self->SUPER::new(@_);
19:
20:    # get column types for array refs
21:    @columnTypes =
           map {scalar $dbh->type_info($_)->{TYPE_NAME}} @{$qobj->{TYPE}};
22:
23:    # get column types for hash refs
24:
25:    # get an array of data type numbers
26:    my @types = @{$qobj->{TYPE}};
27:
28:    # get a hash ref of column names and position
29:    my $nameHash = $qobj->{NAME_uc_hash};
30:
31:    # create a reverse hash with the column number as the key and
32:    # the column name as the value
33:    my %colnumHash = map { $nameHash->{$_} => $_  } keys %$nameHash;
34:
35:    # create an array of the type names ( VARCHAR2, DATE, etc ) from the
36:    # type info method
37:    my @columnTypeNames =
           map { scalar $dbh->type_info($_)->{TYPE_NAME} } @types;
38:
39:    # create a hash with column name as the key and
           data type as the value
40:    %columnTypes =
           map { $colnumHash{$_} =>
                 $columnTypeNames[$_] } 0..$#columnTypeNames;
41:
42:    $qobj->{private_PDBA_DATA_TYPES_ARRAY} = \@columnTypes;
43:    $qobj->{private_PDBA_DATA_TYPES_HASH} = \%columnTypes;
44:    return $qobj;
45: }
46:
47: sub next {
48:    my $self = shift;
49:    my ( $ref ) = @_;
50:    $ref ||= [];
51:
52:    my $refType = ref $ref;
53:
54:    my $data;
55:
56:    $data = $self->SUPER::next($ref);
57:    return unless $data;
58:
59:    # transform NULL columns to a defined value
60:    # to avoid problems with undefined values
61:    if ( 'ARRAY' eq $refType ) {
62:      foreach my $el ( 0..$#{$data} ) {
```

```
63:        unless ( defined $data->[$el] ) {
64:          if ( $self->{private_PDBA_DATA_TYPES_ARRAY}[$el] =~ /CHAR/ ) {
65:            $data->[$el] = '';
66:          } elsif ( $self->{private_PDBA_DATA_TYPES_ARRAY}[$el] =~
                                      /DOUBLE|NUMBER/ ) {
67:            $data->[$el] = 0;
68:          } else { $data->[$el] = '' }
69:        }
70:      }
71:    } elsif ( 'HASH' eq $refType ) {
72:      foreach my $key ( keys %$data ) {
73:        unless (defined $data->{$key} ) {
74:          if ( $self->{private_PDBA_DATA_TYPES_HASH}{$key} =~ /CHAR/ ) {
75:            $data->{$key} = '';
76:          } elsif ( $self->{private_PDBA_DATA_TYPES_HASH}{$key} =~
                                      /DOUBLE|NUMBER/ ) {
77:            $data->{$key} = 0;
78:          } else { $data->{$key} = '' }
79:        }
80:      }
81:    } else {
          croak
          "invalid ref type of $refType used to call PDBAx::GQ->next\n"}
82:
83:    return $data;
84: }
85:
86: 1;
```

In this example we subclass the *new* method of *PDBA::GQ*. We do this so we can determine the datatypes for each column selected in a query.

Line 21

Uses DBI's *type_info* method to retrieve query column datatypes.

Lines 26 to 40

Store the datatypes for each column in both an array and a hash, so we're prepared for whatever the *next* method throws at us.

Lines 42 to 43

Take advantage of a seldom-used Perl DBI feature, the *private_* attributes that may be assigned to a database handle. The DBI documentation states that we're allowed to assign new attributes to a statement handle as long as they begin with the *private_* prefix. These private attributes are used in the *PDBAx::GQ->next* method to determine if the value returned for a column is undefined. If so, it determines the datatype of each of those columns. Once known, a zero is assigned to returned columns with a numeric type, and an empty string to all other undefined columns. This is admittedly more complex than the situation we had before, because of our new requirement to assign zeroes to unassigned numeric columns. However, the added effort is worth it for the convenience of remaining unconcerned about the side effects of NULL columns.

The script in Example 13-10 uses the all-new *PDBAx::GQ* module. Both numeric and character columns are inserted into a test table with NULL values, and then later printed out without any need to check to see if they're undefined. The script is stored in the *PDBAx* distribution as *pdba_ext2.pl*.

Example 13-10. Using the PDBAx:GQ module with numeric and character values

```perl
#!/usr/bin/perl

use warnings;
use strict;
use PDBA::CM;
use PDBAx::GQ;
use PDBA::OPT;
use Getopt::Long;
use PDBAx;

my %optctl=();

my $help=q{
   -machine    database server
   -database   database SID
   -username   account name
   -password   password for account
};

# passthrough allows additional command line options
# to be passed to PDBA::OPT if needed
Getopt::Long::Configure(qw{pass_through});

GetOptions( \%optctl, "help!",      "machine=s",
                      "database=s", "username=s",
                      "password=s", );

if ( $optctl{help} ) { PDBAx::usage(1,\$help) }

# lookup the password if not on the command line
my $password = '';
if ( defined( $optctl{password} ) ) {
   $password = $optctl{password};
} else {

   if (
      ! defined($optctl{machine})
      || ! defined($optctl{database})
      || ! defined($optctl{username})
   ) { PDBAx::usage(1,\$help) }

   $password = PDBA::OPT->pwcOptions (
      INSTANCE => $optctl{database},
```

```
      MACHINE => $optctl{machine},
      USERNAME => $optctl{username}
   );
}
my $dbh = new PDBA::CM( DATABASE => $optctl{database},
                        USERNAME => $optctl{username},
                        PASSWORD => $password, );
# drop test table
eval { $dbh->do(q{drop table star_trek}); };

$dbh->do(q{create table star_trek( title varchar2(50)
                                 , year_released varchar2(4)
                                 , viewings number(4) )} );

my $insHandle = $dbh->prepare(q{ insert into star_trek values(?,?,?) });

$insHandle->execute('Star Trek - The Motion Picture','1979',1);
$insHandle->execute('Star Trek II - The Wrath of Khan','1982',4);
$insHandle->execute('Star Trek III - The Search for Spock','1984',undef);
$insHandle->execute('Star Trek IV - The Voyage Home','1986',8);
$insHandle->execute('Star Trek V - The Final Frontier','1989',1);
$insHandle->execute('Star Trek VI - The Undiscovered Country','1991',3);
$insHandle->execute('Star Trek Generations','1994',1);
$insHandle->execute('Star Trek - First Contact','1996',4);
$insHandle->execute('Star Trek - Insurrection','1998',2);
$insHandle->execute('Star Trek: Nemesis',undef,undef);

$dbh->commit;

my $gq = new PDBAx::GQ($dbh, 'star_trek', {ORDER_BY=>'year_released'});

my $colHash = $gq->getColumns;

while ( my $row = $gq->next ) {
   print "TITLE: $row->[$colHash->{TITLE}]\n";
   print "\tYEAR: $row->[$colHash->{YEAR_RELEASED}]\n";
   print "\tVIEWINGS: $row->[$colHash->{VIEWINGS}]\n";
}
$dbh->disconnect;
```

Previously, printing values returned from NULL columns would have required checking the return values within each script; now, we can safely ignore them:

```
$ pdba_ext2.pl -machine sherlock -database ts01 -username jkstill

TITLE: Star Trek - The Motion Picture
YEAR: 1979
VIEWINGS: 1
TITLE: Star Trek II - The Wrath of Khan
YEAR: 1982
VIEWINGS: 4
TITLE: Star Trek III - The Search for Spock
```

```
YEAR: 1984
VIEWINGS: 0
TITLE: Star Trek IV - The Voyage Home
YEAR: 1986
VIEWINGS: 8
TITLE: Star Trek V - The Final Frontier
YEAR: 1989
VIEWINGS: 1
TITLE: Star Trek VI - The Undiscovered Country
YEAR: 1991
VIEWINGS: 3
TITLE: Star Trek Generations
YEAR: 1994
VIEWINGS: 1
TITLE: Star Trek - First Contact
YFAR: 1996
VIEWINGS: 4
TITLE: Star Trek - Insurrection
YEAR: 1998
VIEWINGS: 2
TITLE: Star Trek: Nemesis
YEAR:
VIEWINGS: 0
```

Notice that one of the entries has a blank year of release, and two of them have zero viewings. These values are actually stored as NULL in the database, but now, because of our implementation of *PDBAx::GQ*, they may be referenced with impunity—without invoking the wrath of Perl and *use warnings*. Revenge is a dish best eaten without undefined values!

Appendixes

This fourth part of the book provides quick references to various aspects of the Perl language. It is designed to supply additional background information for those new to Perl. It consists of the following appendixes:

Appendix A, *The Essential Guide to Perl*, summarizes basic Perl syntax, including object-oriented features.

Appendix B, *The Essential Guide to Perl DBI*, presents the main Perl DBI application programming interface (API) functions.

Appendix C, *The Essential Guide to Regular Expressions*, describes the basics of regular expressions (regexes), patterns of literals and meta-characters used extensively by Perl for pattern matching.

Appendix D, *The Essential Guide to Perl Data Munging*, summarizes the Perl data-munging modules that are helpful in formatting and transforming data for data warehouses and other such Oracle applications; it includes sections on numeric, date, conversion, and XML modules.

The Essential Guide to Perl

In Chapter 1, *Perl Meets Oracle*, we briefly explored the history and culture of Perl without examining the language itself in any detail. In this appendix we'll describe just enough of the language to allow you to understand how Perl DBI works and how you can take advantage of the Oracle applications described in this book. We'll focus on the following:

- Getting information about Perl
- Running Perl scripts
- Variable types
- Program context
- Program and subroutine parameters
- References
- Object orientation

We'll also briefly describe how to get information about Perl and how to invoke it. This will be a roller coaster ride, so hang onto your bitmaps!

Of course, there is much more to learn about Perl. Consult the online and offline references listed in Chapter 1 for additional and much more complete resources.

Obtaining Online Information

Perl is one the most heavily documented languages in the known Universe! This appendix only scratches the surface. Fortunately, there exists a wealth of online information that comes automatically with Perl. To get going, type the following command:

```
$ perldoc perl
```

This will provide you with a complete list of the many available Perl manpages. The most important of these, besides *perldoc perl* itself, are listed in Table A-1.

Table A-1. The main Perl manpage documents

Manpage	Description
perltoc	Table of contents for the manpages
perlsyn	Perl syntax
perldata	Data structures
perlop	Operators and precedence
perlrequick, perlretut, perlre	Regular expressions; see Appendix C
perlvar	Predefined variables
perlsub	Subroutines
perlfunc	Built-in functions
perlreftut, perlref	Perl references
perlmod, perlobj	Modules and objects
perlipc	Inter-process communication
perlrun	Perl execution and options
perldebug, perldiag	Debugging and diagnostics
perlsec	Perl security
perlstyle	The Perl style guide
perltrap	Traps for the unwary

There used to be only a single *perlfaq* page, listing all the Frequently Asked Questions for Perl, but although this page still exists, its original information has been greatly expanded into the nine FAQs detailed in Table A-2. Again, access these with the *perldoc perlfaq* syntax.

Table A-2. The Perl FAQ documents

Manpage	Description
perlfaq	An FAQ overview
perlfaq1	General questions about Perl
perlfaq2	Obtaining and learning about Perl
perlfaq3	Programming tools
perlfaq4	Data manipulation
perlfaq5	Files and formats
perlfaq6	Regular expressions; see Appendix C
perlfaq7	Perl language issues
perlfaq8	System interaction
perlfaq9	Networking

There are also various notes for different operating systems. The main platforms covered are listed in Table A-3.

Table A-3. Operating system documentation

Manpage	Description
perlaix	Notes for AIX
perlsolaris	Notes for Solaris
perlhpux	Notes for HP-UX
perlcygwin	Notes for Cygwin
perlvms	Notes for VMS
perldos	Notes for DOS
perlwin32	Notes for Windows
perlos2	Notes for OS/2
perlos390	Notes for OS/390

Virtually every CPAN module author also provides his or her own self-installing *perldoc* notes for the manpage library. As an example, let's look at the first few rows of the documentation provided for *DBD::Oracle*:

```
$ perldoc DBD::Oracle

NAME
    DBD::Oracle - Oracle database driver for the DBI module

SYNOPSIS
    use DBI;

    $dbh = DBI->connect("dbi:Oracle:$dbname", $user, $passwd);
...
```

Finally, if there's a particular built-in function you're interested in, you can run *perldoc* with the *-f* function switch, to interrogate it:

```
$ perldoc -f printf

printf FILEHANDLE FORMAT, LIST
printf FORMAT, LIST
    Equivalent to "print FILEHANDLE sprintf(FORMAT, LIST)", except
    that "$\" (the output record separator) is not appended. The
    first argument of the list will be interpreted as the "printf"
    format. If "use locale" is in effect, the character used for the
    decimal point in formatted real numbers is affected by the
    LC_NUMERIC locale. See the perllocale manpage.

    Don't fall into the trap of using a "printf" when a simple
    "print" would do. The "print" is more efficient and less error
    prone.
```

For more online information, try *http://www.perl.com* or *http://www.cpan.org*.

Of course, there are also many excellent printed books describing the Perl language for both beginners and advanced developers. See Chapter 1 for some suggestions.

Running Perl Scripts

You can run your Perl scripts in several ways on Unix. For example, you can invoke the *perl* program directly on the command line as follows:

```
$ perl my_unix_perl_script.pl
```

Alternatively, make your script executable and then install a full path call to your chosen version of Perl on the first line of your script. This is done using the *shebang* *#!* syntax familiar to shell programmers:

```
#!/usr/local/bin/perl

use warnings;
use strict;

# Rest of my script ....
```

You can now run the program directly:

```
$ chmod +x my_unix_perl_script.pl
$ ./my_unix_perl_script.pl
```

On most Win32 systems, the *.pl* suffix is usually associated with the Perl interpreter; it should work correctly if you double-click on your script or if you call it directly. Alternatively just call *perl* directly again and specify the script name:

```
C:\> perl my_win32_perl_script.pl
```

Perl Variable Types: Scalars, Arrays, and Hashes

There are three basic variable types in Perl, the last two of which are merely collections of the first arranged in specific patterns. These three variable types are illustrated in Figure A-1; note that we've substituted a Perl camel for any kind of scalar element, such as a string, an integer, or a float.

Scalars

Scalars are single-valued entities—numbers (floats, decimals, hexadecimals, etc.), strings, or references. (We'll describe references later in this appendix.) Scalars, which are prefixed with the dollar sign ($), are the basic building blocks of Perl, the indivisible atom from classical Greek science. Everything in Perl reduces to scalars, which bear names up to 251 characters in length. Because Perl is a weakly typed

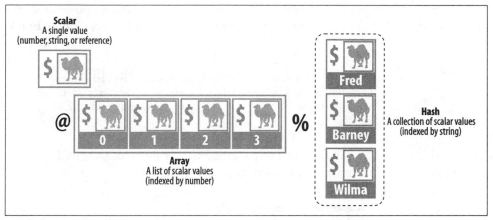

Figure A-1. Perl's three main variable types

language,[*] scalar types also change "automagically" between strings and numbers as you use them:

```
$harpo = "1"; # A previously unmentioned $harpo is
              # set to a string value of "1"

$harpo++; # Perl recognizes that you wish to turn "1" into 1, and
          # then add one on, to get to 2

$harpo = "Groucho";  # The $harpo variable turns dynamically
                     # back into a string, from a numeric 2
```

Arrays

Arrays (or list arrays) are simply lists of scalars indexed by number, starting from zero (the second element is one away from the beginning). A typical array can be set up in the following way:

```
@video_collection =
    ("Day at the Races", "Duck Soup", "A Night at the Opera");
```

The @video_collection array has three string elements. However, an array can consist of any mixture of atomic scalar types:

```
@casablanca_items = ("Rick's", 2, 4000.00, "A Beautiful Friendship");
```

You can think of an array as being like an ice hockey team wearing shirt numbers, but no names. Each player is still an individual, but he or she is accessible within the team (or array) by number. To access an individual array element, we precede the

---

[*] A weakly typed language is one in which variables do not have to have their datatypes strictly defined (as integers, floats, strings, and so on). On the other hand, a strongly typed language is one in which all variables must be predeclared with their datatypes.

array name with a scalar $ symbol, and follow it with the numeric position of the scalar within the array. This position, or shirt number, is held within square brackets.

Whenever you see *[]* square brackets in Perl, outside of regular expressions, you should think immediately in terms of arrays, array slices, anonymous arrays, or lists. There is almost certainly something array-like going on!

To demonstrate scalar notation of array elements, let's introduce a simple *foreach* loop in Perl to iterate through a list, from 0 to 3:

```
foreach $i (0..3) {
    print $i, " ", $casablanca_items[$i], "\n";
}
```

This prints out:

```
0 Rick's
1 2
2 4000
3 A Beautiful Friendship
```

Notice how 4000 printed out, rather than 4000.00. If it can, Perl reduces floats to integers in memory, to save space. It turns them back again as necessary.

There are two ways of finding out the size of an array. The first way is to use the $# notation in front of the array name. This provides the highest array index (the size of the array minus one). The other is to assign an array to a scalar. Perl interprets this in scalar context, and gives us the size of the array. The following code generates the two different types of figures:

```
$highest_index = $#casablanca_items; # Watch out for comment confusion!
$size_of_array = @casablanca_items;

print "highest_index >", $highest_index, "<\n";
print "size_of_array >", $size_of_array, "<\n";
```

This code produces the following:

```
highest_index >3<
size_of_array >4<
```

Some people avoid using the $# syntax for the highest current array index. Because # is also a Perl symbol that is used to begin a comment (which extends to the end of the line), the various # symbols can become confusing within complicated code blocks.

Hashes

Hashes (or associative arrays) are collections of scalars indexed by string names rather than integers. Think of the ice hockey team, in the second period, now wearing shirts displaying only their names, without the numbers. In Figure A-1, the three scalar values are represented by "Fred," "Barney," and "Wilma." Although at first the concept of hashes may seem a bit confusing, you'll find that you'll tend to use it for most things in Perl once you're used to it (especially with object orientation, as we'll see later). A hash can be constructed via the following flat list initialization technique:

```
%middle_earth_leaders =
    ('Saruman', 'Orthanc', 'Sauron', 'Mordor',
     'Bombadil', 'The Old Forest');
```

This pattern goes in a *key=>value* order. To make this visually clearer, we can add some syntactic sugar, indent a little more, and rewrite:

```
%middle_earth_leaders =
    (Saruman => 'Orthanc',
     Sauron => 'Mordor',
     Bombadil => 'The Old Forest');
```

The => aliases as a comma, while making it clear that the left-hand values are key strings, without the need for the now unnecessary quote marks.

The other main difference between ordinary arrays and hash arrays is that you can always work out where the individual scalars are inside an array by knowing their numeric position. Imagine our ice hockey team lining up in a numeric order before the start of the game. Hashes are different. We can never be sure in what order the *key/value* pairs will come out. This time, imagine the entire team mobbing the crucial goal scorer just after the final whistle. There's no predefined order. To access each scalar, we generally iterate the unordered string index names, and then sort them out, before re-accessing the hash:

```
foreach $key (sort keys %middle_earth_leaders) {
    print $key, " => ", $middle_earth_leaders{$key}, "\n";
}
```

Notice again that we use *$* in front of the hash array name to get the scalar value. However, we know we're dealing with hashes because the clue is curly brackets ({ }), which contain the index string name. The above code produces the following output:

```
Bombadil -> The Old Forest
Saruman => Orthanc
Sauron => Mordor
```

Incidentally, this is where we can use our *$_* pronoun for the first time, as a sort of "it." Instead of using the *$key* variable explicitly, we could use the following code:

```
foreach (sort keys %middle_earth_leaders) {
    print $_, " => ", $middle_earth_leaders{$_}, "\n";
}
```

Notice that there is no scalar variable following the *foreach*, in the first line of code, as earlier. However, *$_* is being used in the same position of *$key* inside the loop. What's going on? Perl takes the preceding code and assumes that because *foreach* has no associated scalar, we really *meant* to use the "it" pronoun, *$_*. Perl therefore translates the above code into the following logical snippet before executing it. Notice the assumed first appearance of *$_*:

```
for $_ (sort keys %middle_earth_leaders) {
    print $_, " => ", $middle_earth_leaders{$_}, "\n";
}
```

Revenge of the Mnemonics

Here are some easy ways to remember our Perl definitions:

Scalars

> To remember scalars, think of the *$* dollar sign preceding the variable name—it looks a bit like an "S" for "Scalar."

Arrays

> The simplest way to remember the @ array notation, is that @ has an "A" in the middle, which stands for "Array."

Hashes

> To try to remember the hash symbol, think of the % character, with its slash and two small opposed circular elements, as standing for *key/value*. Imagine that *key* and *value* each represents one circle from the percentage division sign, with the slash dividing them into the *key/value* pair. (OK, it's not great, but this *is* the "Revenge of the Mnemonics"!)

Array and Hash Array Slices

In case you're having trouble imagining arrays and hashes in terms of hockey teams accessed by number or name, try thinking of them in more traditional pie shapes. This can make it easier to imagine array slices, which are discrete collections of scalars. The two different pie types, and slice patterns, are displayed in Figure A-2.

Perl Contexts: Void, Scalar, List, and Boolean

There are three main *lvalue* (left-hand value) contexts in Perl; void context, scalar context, and list context. They typically operate when subroutines are called or when an *lvalue* assignment is made:

```
localtime();                # Step 1: Void context, nothing returned

$this_time = localtime();   # Step 2: Scalar context, scalar returned
print "$this_time \n";
```

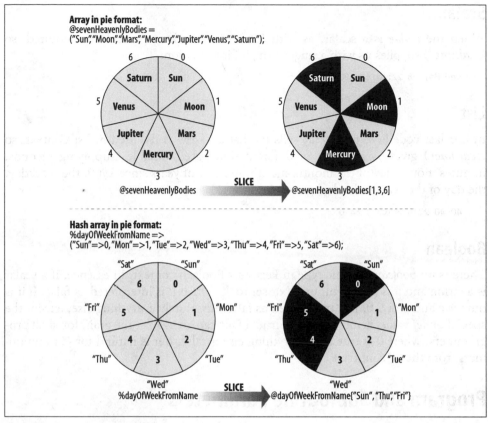

Figure A-2. Array slices in Perl

```
@array_time = localtime(); # Step 3: Array (or list) context, array
print "@array_time \n";     #         returned.
```

This code produces:

```
Wed Mar  6 22:40:40 2002
40 40 22 6 2 102 3 64 0
```

Let's look at the three contexts illustrated here.

Void

In void context the *localtime()* function fails to return anything. Otherwise Perl uses a built-in *wantarray* operator in the background to return whether the function is supposed to return a scalar value or an array list.

Scalar

When the *lvalue* is a scalar, as with *$this_time*, we know a scalar is required, so *localtime()* supplies us with a single string of information:

```
Wed Mar  6 22:40:40 2002
```

List

In our last code line, *wantarray* tells us that an array is required in list context, so *localtime()* gives us an array of different time-based variables supplying seconds, minutes, hours, day of the month, month, number of years since 1900, the weekday, the day of the year, and a daylight savings time flag:

```
40 40 22 6 2 102 3 64 0
```

Boolean

There is no *boolean* variable type in Perl, just Boolean context. In essence, if a scalar is a string and it is either empty "", or set to "0", then it is interpreted as false. If it is numeric and 0 or 0.0, it is interpreted as false. Absolutely everything else, except the special *undef* value, is interpreted as true. (This can go against the grain for shell programmers, where 0 is true and everything else is false, but is natural for C programmers from the ol' country.)

Program and Subroutine Parameters

The main part of any Perl script is sometimes known as *package main*, and just like any Perl package it can have subroutines. Calling these routines is straightforward. An example, displayed in Figure A-3, is broken down as follows:

1. You can deliver any number of parameters directly into a Perl script via the special built-in *@ARGV* array. The script's own file name is stored in another special scalar variable, *$0*. For instance, in Figure A-3, if the script was called *doctor_yes.pl* and had three parameters, we could run it like this:

   ```
   $ perl doctor_yes.pl '007' 'James' 'Bond'
   ```

   In the background, Perl would set the following values for us before the rest of the script was executed:

   ```
   $0 = 'doctor_yes.pl';
   @ARGV = ('007', 'James', 'Bond');
   ```

   We're then free to use these values throughout the rest of the program, as if we're accessing ordinary variables.

2. There is a kind of *mini-@ARGV* for subroutines, and each subroutine gets its own one. This is the *@_* array, which dynamically expands depending on how many parameters we decide to send in. When we call *funcOneTakesTwoParams()*

in Figure A-3, with two parameters Laurel and Hardy, this fills the @_ array, dedicated to *funcOneTakesTwoParams()*, with the two appropriate strings.

3. In *funcTwoTakesSixParams()* the six parameters are sent in here to fill another totally separate @_ array. This has absolutely nothing to do with the totally separate @_ array owned by *funcOneTakesTwoParams()*.

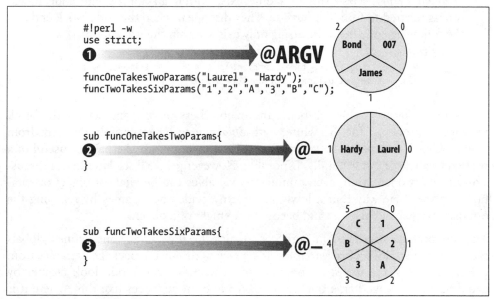

```perl
#!perl -w
use strict;
❶

funcOneTakesTwoParams("Laurel", "Hardy");
funcTwoTakesSixParams("1","2","A","3","B","C");


sub funcOneTakesTwoParams{
❷

}


sub funcTwoTakesSixParams{
❸

}
```

Figure A-3. @ARGV and @_

Environmental Variable Access

A Perl script can also make use of environmental variables. These are stored within the built-in *%ENV* hash:

```perl
$old_oracle_home = $ENV{ORACLE_HOME};   # Store latest ORACLE_HOME
$ENV{ORACLE_HOME} = "C:\ORANT";         # Now set new ORACLE_HOME
```

Variable Types

Production Perl code generally starts off with the following line:

```perl
use strict;
```

This pragma disciplines the naming of Perl's two main types of variable:

Package variables

These are your typical global variables. We've seen how the main Perl script is known as *package main*. When we use other packages, we'll see that each one has an entirely different namespace; in this way, different package variables avoid naming clashes. What *use strict* does is to ensure that we fully qualify these variable names, so *$friendly_variable* in a small script must be used as *$main:: friendly_variable* in a script employing the *use strict* pragma. You can localize package variables, within a code block, by the *local* operator, but only temporarily until the code block ends.

Lexical variables

Prefixed by *my*, these variables only exist within an appropriate code block, unless referred to from the outside. They disappear when the code block ends. In the following code the *$timeString* only exists within the *while* loop:

```
while($flag == 1){
    my $timeString = some_time_function( );          # $timeString my'ed
    $flag = some_validation_function($timeString);
}
```

Think of package variables as being the major chess pieces, one set for the black package and one set for the white, with *$black::king* being entirely different from *$white::king*. Think of the lexical *my* variables as being more like pawns, useful to a particular package but generally disposable. However, as we'll see later in our discussion of object orientation, even humble *my* variables can be vital for object orientation - in the same way that a lowly pawn can decide chess games by reaching the opposite package's back line and becoming a knight or a queen.

The *our* prefix, introduced in Perl 5.6, mimics the *my* syntax, but defines globals rather than lexically scoped variables. It's a way of disguising package variables from the discipline of the *use strict* pragma, often to make your code look cleaner by avoiding full package name qualification. Aside from instances like this, where it is assumed that you know what you're doing, the *use strict* pragma will insist that you employ either fully qualified package variable names or lexically declared variables. Think of *our* as being like a bishop disguised as a pawn. Because it takes other pieces diagonally, a bishop is sometimes used to hold up pawn defenses, but is still a major piece possessing lethal power.*

Taint Mode

As well as *use strict*, you can also run your program with extra warnings to detect syntax ambiguities, unused variables, and that sort of thing. You can turn these warnings on via either the *-w* flag, or (in Perl Version 5.6 onwards) the *use warnings* pragma. For instance, the following code at the top of a program will turn on extra warnings:

```
#!/usr/local/bin/perl -w
use strict;
```

---

* At least one of your authors has forgotten this more than once, and has suffered the consequences when the big pawn thing has turned the game, with an unexpected backwards corner-to-corner diagonal move, to take a queen.

Alternatively, use the more modern form:

```
#!/usr/local/bin/perl
use warnings;
use strict;
```

To go beyond warnings in certain classes of programs, you must use *taint mode*. This mode works on the simple principle that nothing derived from outside your program should be allowed to change anything else held outside your program. All data is checked in taint mode, and the tainted variety usually includes *@ARGV* program parameters, *%ENV* environmental variables, and any file input. Anything else that uses tainted data also becomes tainted. You turn taint mode on with the following -T switch:

```
#!/usr/local/bin/perl -T
```

There are many mechanisms within Perl for laundering tainted data, but they all work on the basic assumption that you know what you're doing before you untaint such data. All CGI scripts should use taint mode, as should any other program being accessed remotely, especially via the Internet. You should also consider taint mode for any kind of daemon, or indeed any other kind of program that deals with external users or sensitive data.

Perl References

The big difference between Perl 4 and Perl 5 was the introduction of references, which made object orientation possible. You can think of references as being a kind of pointers, locators, or remote tracking devices. They are the glue spot trails sticking Perl 5 data structures together. Think of ET pointing the way home, Indiana Jones standing on the X marking the spot in Venice, or James Bond trailing Goldfinger's car with a remote tracking device. The bony finger, the X, or the beeper are all references to remote information. So how does Perl point to its own vital information? In structure, references are simple scalars holding two vital pieces of information:

- What kind of thing am I pointing at?
- Where is the thing I'm pointing at located (in hexadecimal memory)?

These two pieces of information can be seen in Figure A-4, stored under each of our three references. The first refers to a scalar, the second to an array, and the third to a hash. Each reference holds the variable type it's referring to *and* its memory address. We can see this for ourselves if we create three similar references, and then print them out:

```
$camel = "Asimov";
@camel = ("Foundation and Earth", "I, Robot", "Nightfall");
%camel = (Emperor => "Cleon",
          CouncilMan => "Trevize",
```

```
        Robot => "R. Daneel Olivaw");

$scalar_ref = \$camel;   # References created by backslashing
$array_ref = \@camel;    # the original variable.
$hash_ref = \%camel;

print $scalar_ref, " ", $array_ref, " ", $hash_ref, "\n";
```

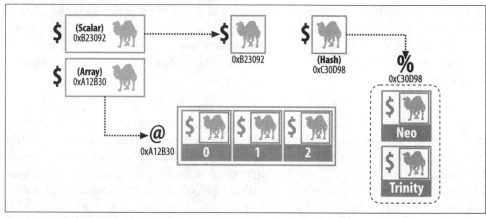

Figure A-4. The glue of Perl references

Notice that each original variable is named *camel*, but this causes absolutely no clash
in Perl because scalars, arrays, and hashes are all different variable types, in the same
way that Homer Simpson, Springfield philosopher, and Homer the Greek, Trojan
chronicler, are different types of people, despite possessing the same name. When
executed, the *print* statement shown above produced memory address traces like
these:

```
SCALAR(0x457c3f4) ARRAY(0x457f420) HASH(0x457f468)
```

We can now take these three references and go back along their arrows, to get the
original information back out again:

```
print "SCALAR: ${$scalar_ref} \n"; # Isolate reference with braces
                                    # then dereference with a $ symbol.

print "ARRAY: @{$array_ref} \n"; # Isolate reference with braces,
                                 # then dereference with a @ symbol.

%copy_camel = %{$hash_ref}; # Isolate reference with braces, and then
                            # dereference with a % to create hash copy.

foreach $key (keys %copy_camel) {
   print "HASH VALUE: $copy_camel{$key} \n"; # Get key, then value.
}
```

This code produces:

```
SCALAR: Asimov
ARRAY: Foundation and Earth I, Robot Nightfall
HASH VALUE: Cleon
HASH VALUE: Trevize
HASH VALUE: R. Daneel Olivaw
```

Arrow Notation

If you work carefully through the above code you'll see how the references are iso-lated by curly braces. The variable symbols, $, @, and %, are then used to derefer-ence the data to the appropriate variable type. If this notation looks a little clumsy, relax, because you're among friends. For hashes and arrays, the arrow operator may ride to the rescue. Let's rewrite that code for the two array types:

```
for $index (0..$#{$array_ref}) {          # Work out size of array

   print "ARRAY $index: $array_ref->[$index] \n"; # Drill down arrow
}

for $key (keys %{$hash_ref}) { # Work out original keys

   print "HASH $key: $hash_ref->{$key} \n"; # Drill down arrow
}
```

The arrow operator can make life easier, because it makes the diagrammatic arrows in Figure A-4 come alive directly within the code:

```
ARRAY 0: Foundation and Earth
ARRAY 1: I, Robot
ARRAY 2: Nightfall
HASH Emperor: Cleon
HASH CouncilMan: Trevize
HASH Robot: R. Daneel Olivaw
```

The ref Operator

References are simply ordinary scalars, meaning that they can be stored in both arrays and hashes. We illustrate this in Figure A-5, where from a single *$binary_tree_root_ref* scalar we spider through a binary tree, made up of anonymous hashes, to quickly find ROWID information.

In dynamic coding like this, however, there is a problem. We're often unaware of what variable types our references are pointing to, which is information required for accurate de-referencing. The solution is then to use the *ref* operator. This returns the type of variable being pointed to. The main values returned by *ref* are detailed in Table A-4.

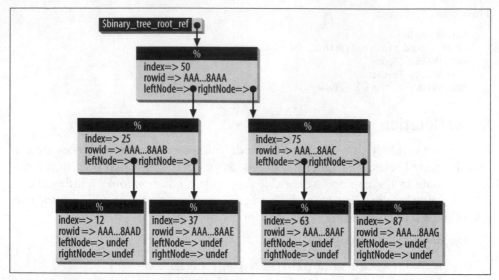

Figure A-5. Binary tree built from hashes

Table A-4. The main return values of ref

Return value	Description
undef	ref was supplied with a non-reference scalar
SCALAR	Points to a scalar
ARRAY	Points to an array
HASH	Points to a hash
CODE	Points to a subroutine
REF	Points to another scalar reference ·

We can now use *ref* to navigate our way around any data structure held together by references, with blocks of code such as the following:

```
if (( ref($this_ref) eq "SCALAR" ) || ( ref($this_ref) eq "REF" )) {

    # This reference is either pointing to an ordinary scalar,
    # or a scalar reference.  Deal with accordingly...

} elsif ( ref($this_ref) eq "ARRAY" ) {

    # This reference is pointing to an array...

} elsif ( ref($this_ref) eq "HASH" ) {

    # Pointing to a hash...
```

```
} elsif ( not ref $this_ref ) {

    # $this_ref is an ordinary scalar...
}
```

Anonymous Arrays and Hashes

In addition to generating named arrays and hashes, we can also generate anonymous arrays and hashes in Perl. Think of an anonymous array as being like an amateur ice hockey team being created spontaneously by a group of friends on a visit to a local ice rink. There's simply no need for a team name. This ability to create unnamed arrays on the fly creates enormous dynamism within our code, and is especially good for the creation of multidimensional arrays (think of a series of wooden Russian dolls opening up to reveal more dolls inside).

Here are the basics of creating anonymous arrays:

1. To create a reference to a named array, we could use the following code:
   ```
   @le_carre = ('Tinker', 'Tailor', 'Soldier', 'Spy');
   $array_ref = \@le_carre;
   ```

2. To refer to an anonymous array, we can just cut out the middleman:
   ```
   $array_ref = ['Tinker', 'Tailor', 'Soldier', 'Spy'];
   ```
   Think of the leading [square bracket as being a scalar array reference in disguise, with everything up to the] square bracket being inside the anonymous array.

3. We can now create multidimensional arrays, extending the basic idea to create an outer array and two inner ones:
   ```
   $chess_ref = [ ["Black King", "Black Queen"],
                  ["White Bishop", "White Knight", "White Rook"]
                ];
   ```

4. We now have a two-dimensional array accessible from the *$chess_ref* scalar reference. For instance, to access *"White Rook"* we'd use:
   ```
   print $chess_ref->[1]->[2]; # 2nd inner array, 3rd element.
   ```
   (Remember that array indexes start from zero.)

5. To dig out *"Black King"*, we'd use the following:
   ```
   print $chess_ref->[0]->[0]; # 1st inner array, 1st element.
   ```

6. We can also use more than two dimensions. So if between Oracle projects you're a part-time professor of astrophysics, specializing in 11-dimensional M-theory, Perl is the language for you.

You can create anonymous hashes in the same basic way:

1. This time we use curly braces:
   ```
   $planets_ref = { Mercury =>
                      { Temp => 'Ridiculously Hot', Position => 1 },
   ```

```
                              Mars =>
                                { Temp => 'Blisteringly Cold', Position => 4 } };
```

2. To get the position of Mars, relative to the sun, we would use:

```
    print $planets_ref->{Mars}->{Position}; # Key Mars, then Key Position.
```

3. The temperature of Mercury would be:

```
    print $planets_ref->{Mercury}->{Temp}; # Key Mercury, then Key Temp
```

You can also mix and match your anonymous hash and array elements.

1. Take a look at the following devil's advocate example:

```
    $stars_ref = { Aldebaran =>
                      [ { LightYears => 60 },
                        { Constellation =>
                            [ 'Taurus', 'Hyades', 'Crab Nebula' ] } ] } ;
```

2. We want to get the third element of interest, under the Constellation flag, for the
   star Aldebaran, home of the Emperor Zurg. Can we find it?:

```
    print $stars_ref->{Aldebaran}->[1]->{Constellation}->[2];
```

3. In the words of Buzz Lightyear, "yes, we can!"

```
    Crab Nebula
```

Perl's Object Orientation

So far, we've covered the whole of basic Perl in fewer than 20 pages (Perl purists will
be horrified at how much we've skipped over!) Now we're ready to engage hyper-
drive and head toward Perl's object orientation zone.

Packages

In order to provide the Holy Grail of code reusability, Perl provides plenty of scope
for the creation of software packages. These packages are generally held in a Perl
module file, such as *MyPackage.pm*, which can be accessed from a main script like
this:

```
    use MyPackage;
```

A basic package skeleton can look as simple as this:

```
    package MyPackage;
    use strict;

    sub doSomeStuff      {  # Some subroutine code here }
    sub doSomeOtherStuff {  # Some other subroutine code here }
```

To create our package, all we needed to do was name it and create some methods.
And that was it.

Bless this Object

To go beyond packages and into object territory, we use the wizardry of the *bless* command. We'll extend our earlier skeleton and make it into a real class by adding a *new* constructor containing this most magical of commands:

```perl
package MyPackage;
use strict;

sub new {
    my($class) = @_;
    my $self = {};          # Anonymous hash! :-)
    bless $self, $class;
    return $self;
}
sub doSomeStuff      { # Some subroutine code here }
sub doSomeOtherStuff { # Some other subroutine code here }
```

There's an awful lot going on within those few lines of code in the *new* method. We've broken it down into 11 life-cycle steps, listed below and illustrated in Figure A-6.

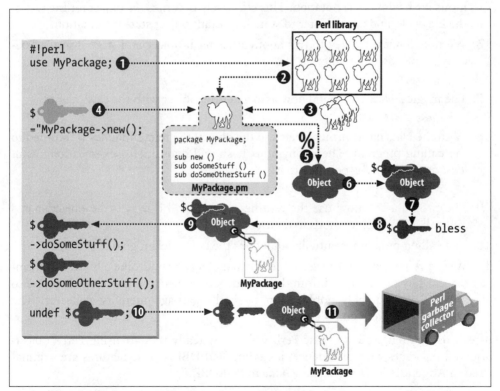

Figure A-6. Object-oriented life cycle in Perl

1. To initiate the life cycle we call the *use MyPackage* command to import the package from the Perl library.

2. The package imports into memory and stands ready for action.

3. If it were a more complex package, *MyPackage* could multiply inherit from other objects in the Perl library.

4. The *new* method is called in the main script, requesting that a key be returned to a brand new object generated by the packaged class constructor:

```
$key = MyPackage->new( );
```

5. As we've seen, this *new* method contains the following code:

```
my($class) = @_;
my $self = {};
bless $self, $class;
return $self
```

When the arrow notation is used with a package name to call a method, such as *new*, the package name gets sent automatically into the method as the first parameter of the special @_ subroutine parameter array. We take this string *'MyPackage'* and assign it to the *$class* scalar variable. We then create an anonymous hash with the *{}* notation. This effectively becomes *the* object for the rest of the life cycle, and is used later to store important object state information.

6. We take a reference key to this anonymous hash object and store it in the lexically scoped *$self* variable:

```
my $self = {};
```

7. The magical *bless* command now associates the object with the class name:

```
bless $self, $class;
```

8. With the class name firmly labeled to the object, the referential key is returned to the calling program. The anonymous hash will continue to exist as long as *at least one* reference is pointing to it:

```
return $self;
```

9. The program can now use the returned key to drill down to the object's class and call its various methods to do useful work.

10. The calling program eventually undefines the key or lets it go out of scope.

11. With a reference count of zero, the original object has become a bubble of memory entirely disconnected from the outside world. Because it's of no more use to anyone, it is quickly gobbled up by Perl's garbage memory collector. The object's life cycle is complete.

After this lightning tour of basic Perl, we're now ready to start using Perl's object-oriented packages with confidence, including Perl DBI (whose features are summarized in Appendix B, *The Essential Guide to Perl DBI*).

The Essential Guide to Perl DBI

In this appendix we'll examine the main elements of the application programming interface (API) for Perl DBI, the Perl module that's responsible for communication between Perl and the Oracle database. Of course, there is much more to learn about Perl DBI. Consult the online and offline references listed in Chapter 1, *Perl Meets Oracle*, for additional and much more complete resources.

As with virtually all CPAN modules, you can generate the full online documentation for both Perl DBI and *DBD::Oracle* (the Oracle-dependent driver for Perl DBI), with the two following commands:

```
$ perldoc DBI
$ perldoc DBD::Oracle
```

DBI Class Methods

Before we connect to Oracle, we must establish a few DBI variable-naming conventions (listed in Table B-1).

Table B-1. Conventional Perl DBI variable names

Name	Description
$dbh	The database handle created on database connection.
$sth	The SQL statement handle.
$drh	The driver handle, mostly used internally by the Perl DBI package.
$h	Can represent any of the three main handles above.
$rc	A general DBI return code, mostly used in a Boolean context.
$rv	A general DBI return value, often used numerically.
@ary	A list of returned scalars, or a row fetched from the database.
$rows	The number of rows processed.
$fh	A file handle, often used to change any default output from *STDOUT*.

Table B-1. Conventional Perl DBI variable names (continued)

Name	Description
undef	Perl's generic undefined value is used in DBI for NULLs.
%attr	A general name for hashes used to store various attributes.

connect

The *connect* Perl DBI constructor method generates our main database handle, *$dbh*:

```
use DBI;
my $data_source = "dbi:Oracle:orcl";
my $user = "scott";
my $password = "tiger";
my %attr = (RaiseError => 0, AutoCommit => 1);
my $dbh = DBI->connect($data_source, $username, $password, \%attr)
        or die $DBI::errstr;
```

Note the following characteristics of the connection string held above in *$data_source*:

- *$data_source* is composed of three elements separated by colons. However if *$data_source* is undefined, the *connect* method will replace it with the environmental variable DBI_DSN, making the following possible:

  ```
  DBI->connect(undef, $username, $password)
  ```

  This becomes interpreted as:

  ```
  DBI->connect($ENV{DBI_DSN}, $username, $password)
  ```

- Sometimes the "Oracle" driver part of the connection string may be missing, as in:

  ```
  DBI->connect("dbi::orcl", $username, $password)
  ```

  In this case, the environmental variable DBI_DRIVER is assumed, as if the code actually looked like this:

  ```
  DBI->connect("dbi:$ENV{DBI_DRIVER}:orcl", $username, $password)
  ```

- Sometimes, the actual target database string, such as *orcl*, may be missing:

  ```
  DBI->connect("dbi:Oracle:", $username, $password)
  ```

  In this case TWO_TASK, or subsequently ORACLE_SID, is assumed:

  ```
  DBI->connect("dbi:Oracle:$ENV{TWO_TASK}", $username, $password)
  ```

Looking inside the $dbh variable

Assuming that everything goes well, we should now have a valid database handle stored in the *$dbh* variable. But what's actually inside this? Let's find out:

```
my $dbh = DBI->connect('dbi:Oracle:orcl', 'scott', 'tiger');
print "dbh >", $dbh, "<\n";
```

Blessed references give us both the class label and an object reference:

```
dbh >DBI::db=HASH(0x466cd40)<
```

What we have in *$dbh* is the key to a *DBI::db* object. However, Perl DBI is unusual in Perl. It operates within a hierarchy of objects rather than just one. As well as having *DBI::db* objects, we later hang SQL statement objects off these objects (like baubles from a Christmas tree). Each database handle gets its own collection of statement handles. This hierarchy can be seen in Figure B-1.

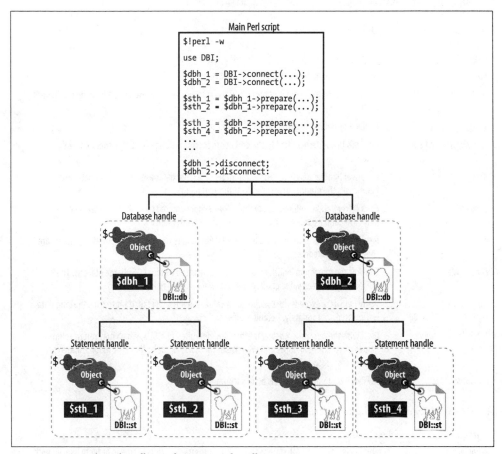

Figure B-1. Database handles and statement handles

Each of these handles can also be assigned its own collection of initial and modifiable attributes. Let's see that connection code again:

```
my %attr = (RaiseError => 0, AutoCommit => 1);
$dbh = DBI->connect($data_source, $username, $password, \%attr );
```

You'll often see variations on this theme, with anonymous hashes used instead:

```
$dbh = DBI->connect($data_source, $username, $password,
                    {RaiseError => 0, AutoCommit => 1} ); # Anon. Hash
```

We cover the main generic handle attributes in Table B-2 (many of these are read-only) and the database handle specific attributes in Table B-3. Reading and occasionally resetting these attributes is straightforward:

```
$old_value = $h->{AttributeName};       # Reading
$h->{AttributeName} = $some_new_value;   # Setting
```

Table B-2. Main generic handle attributes

Attribute	Description
PrintError	Forces errors to generate warnings. Default is on.
RaiseError	Forces errors to make the program die. PrintError runs before RaiseError, if both are on. Default is off.
Warn	Enabled by default to generate useful warnings.
ShowErrorStatement	Appends DBI statement text to the end of other error messages usually generated by the database.
Kids	For driver handles Kids is the current number of related database handles. For database handles it's the number of associated statement handles.
CachedKids	For a driver handle, references database connections created by connect_cached. For database handles, this references prepare_cached statements.
Taint	If switched on, all "fetched" data is tainted if Perl is in taint mode and method arguments are checked for taintedness.
LongReadLen	Controls the maximum length of long fields such as the various LOBs (large objects). The default LongReadLen value of 80 returns undef for all long fields.
LongTruncOk	If any long data exceeds the LongReadLen value, the fetch will fail. If set to true, the long data is truncated appropriately. Default is off.
FetchHashKeyName	Used with the fetchrow_hashref method and defaulted to NAME, which may return column names in a mixture of upper and lowercase. Set to NAME_uc or NAME_lc to force uppercase or lowercase, respectively.
ChopBlanks	For fixed-width fields, controls blanks trimming.

Table B-3. Main database handle attributes

Attribute	Description
AutoCommit	Automatically commits DML statements when set to true. Defaults to true in order to line up with JDBC and ODBC standards. Robust transactions in production code should switch this attribute off and use the eval operator, which fills the $@ variable with relevant information if RaiseError throws the eval statement (if switched on; see earlier). This behavior is used to create try-catch[a] structures:

```
$dbh->{AutoCommit} = 0; # Turn off!  :-)
$dbh->{RaiseError} = 1; # Turn on!  8-)
eval { # try
    do_some_stuff();
    do_some_other_stuff();
```

Table B-3. Main database handle attributes (continued)

Attribute	Description
| | ```
$dbh->commit;
};
if ($@) { # catch
    warn "Transaction failed: $@";
    $dbh->rollback;
    do_some_other_cleanup_stuff();
}
``` |
Driver	Holds the parent driver's handle. Useful for finding the name of the driver on a multi-driver system: ```print $dbh->{Driver}->{Name}, "\n";```
Name	Holds the *TNSNAME* of the database, where *TNSNAME* is part of the connection string, *dbi:Oracle: TNSNAME*.
Statement	Holds the latest prepared or executed statement string.
RowCacheSize	A driver hint for row cache sizes for SELECT statements. Very useful for speeding up DBI.

[a]See Pete Jordan's *Exception.pm* module for more explicit try-catch structures: *http://www.cpan.org/authors/id/P/PJ/PJORDAN/*

Alternative Oracle connection scenarios

There are several alternatives for connecting to Oracle. You can use the first alternative, shown in the following example, if you don't have access to a *tnsnames.ora* file:

```
$dbh = DBI->connect("dbi:Oracle:host=myhost.com;sid=orcl",
                    $username, $password);
```

You can specify the port number in the connection, as shown in the next example. If you don't specify the port number, *DBD::Oracle* will try ports 1526 and 1521 in that order. Other variations, which are particularly appropriate for older SQL*Net systems, can be used if *TWO_TASK* or *ORACLE_SID* have not been set:

```
$dbh = DBI->connect('dbi:Oracle:T:Machine:sid','username','password');
$dbh = DBI->connect('dbi:Oracle:','username@T:Machine:sid','password');
$dbh = DBI->connect('dbi:Oracle:','username@orcl','password');
$dbh = DBI->connect('dbi:Oracle:orcl','username','password');
$dbh = DBI->connect('dbi:Oracle:orcl','username/password','');
$dbh = DBI->connect('dbi:Oracle:host=foobar;sid=orcl;port=1521',
                    'scott/tiger', '');
$dbh = DBI->connect('dbi:Oracle:',
q{scott/tiger@(DESCRIPTION=(ADDRESS=(PROTOCOL=TCP)(HOST=myhost)
(PORT=1521))(CONNECT_DATA=(SID=orcl)))}, "");
```

Oracle-specific connection attributes

You can select three connection attributes especially for Oracle:

ora_session_mode
> Used to connect with SYSDBA or SYSOPER authorization:
> ```
> DBI->connect($data_source, $username, $password,
>     { ora_session_mode => 2 }); # SYSDBA
> ```
```

```
DBI->connect($data_source, $username, $password,
             { ora_session_mode => 4 }); # SYSOPER
```

ora_oratab_orahome

Set this attribute to true when you are using a *DBD::Oracle* version built against Oracle7. Doing so changes *$ENV{ORACLE_HOME}* to the Oracle home directory specified in */etc/oratab*, if the database is listed there:

```
DBI->connect($data_source, $username, $password,
             { ora_oratab_orahome => 1 }); # True
```

ora_module_name

Passed to the SET_MODULE function in the DBMS_APPLICATION_INFO package, which identifies this calling Perl application for monitoring and performance tuning purposes. In the following example, *$0* is the built-in Perl scalar variable holding the name of the Perl script.:

```
DBI->connect($dsn, $user, $passwd, { ora_module_name => $0 } );
```

connect_cached

The *connect_cached* method is virtually identical in appearance to *connect*, described in the previous section:

```
$dbh = DBI->connect_cached($data_source, $username, $password, \%attr);
```

New database handles are cached. Whenever another call is now made to *connect_cached* using identical connection parameters, the cached database handle is returned if it is still available. If the handle is not available, a new one is created, as with *connect*.

available_drivers

The *available_drivers* method lets us know which DBD drivers (such as *DBD::Oracle*) are available on the system:

```
@ary = DBI->available_drivers;
```

data_sources

The *data_sources* method lists the available database targets. This method is useful for populating drop-down CGI or Perl/Tk boxes to choose a target database before connection. If no 'Oracle' parameter is supplied, the environmental variable *DBI_DRIVER* is assumed:

```
@ary = DBI->data_sources('Oracle');
```

(*DBD::Oracle* reads *oratab* and *tnsnames.ora* to get this information.)

trace

The *trace* method lets you set the desired debug trace level. Various debug trace levels (shown in Table B-4) are possible under DBI. The default is to turn off tracing.

Table B-4. Tracing levels

Level	Description
0	Tracing is disabled.
1	Useful for overviews.
2	For more serious debug work.
3, 4, 5...	Ever more complex detail for hard-core developers.

Typical calls might look like this:

```
DBI->trace(0);                        # Turn tracing off.
DBI->trace(1);                        # Turn tracing on, STDERR output.
DBI->trace(2, "my_trace_file.txt");   # Increase trace level, and
                                      # redirect to named file.
```

> You can use another method in conjunction with *trace* for your own debug messages, as shown here:
>
> ```
> DBI->trace_msg( $message ) ;
> DBI->trace_msg( $message, $min_level ) ;
> ```
>
> If the trace level is greater than 0, this will write *$message* to either STDERR or any other nominated trace file, or you can specify the minimum level it should report on.

For further trace ability, Perl DBI also holds the very latest handle information in the following handles:

$DBI::err:
   Holds the Oracle error code from the last method called.

$DBI::errstr:
   Returns the latest Oracle error message.

Let's test this by setting up a piece of code we know will go wrong:

```
$sth = $dbh->prepare('SELECT Should_go_wrong" from dual'); # Quote! :)

print "DBI::err:    >", $DBI::err, "<\n";
print "DBI::errstr: >", $DBI::errstr, "<\n";
```

This produces the following output:

```
DBI->err:    >1740<
DBI->errstr: >ORA-01740: missing double quote in identifier
(DBD ERROR: OCIStmtPrepare)<
```

Database Handles—Preparation

There are two groups of database handle methods. The methods in the first group help prepare SQL statement handles or check that they can be prepared. The methods in the second group work with SQL statement executions or clean up afterward. In this section, we'll work through the first group, those that help prepare the SQL statement handles. Later in this chapter, after covering the statement handles themselves, we'll discuss the second group of database handle methods. Think of these two groups as being like artillery troops and assault troops. They're all wearing the same uniform, but some prepare the ground while others go in and do the real work.

ping

The *ping* method checks to see if the target database server is still running. It is useful for batch programs. If this function fails to return true, there is little point trying to use the handle. You need to reconnect to the database:

```
$rc = $dbh->ping;
```

prepare

The *prepare* method creates and prepares a statement handle for later execution:

```
$sth = $dbh->prepare("SELECT SYSDATE FROM DUAL");
```

prepare_cached

The *prepare_cached* method is similar in concept to *connect_cached*, as described earlier:

```
$sth = $dbh->prepare_cached($statement);
```

If the same parameters are re-sent to *prepare_cached*, it tries to use a cached *$sth* statement handle instead of creating a new one.

quote

The *quote* method provides an excellent utility for preparing DML statements:

```
$quoteString = $dbh->quote("Let's buy O'Reilly books!");  # :-)
print "quoteString >", $quoteString, "<\n";
```

This produces the following output:

```
quoteString >'Let''s buy O''Reilly books!'<
```

Notice the doubled single-quotes which make this string ideal for inserting into an Oracle table. Here's one we created earlier:

```
create table test_table (message_col varchar2(50));
```

The following code is now possible:

```
$dbh->{AutoCommit} = 0; # Turning AutoCommit off! :)
eval {
```

```
    $quoteString = $dbh->quote("Let's buy O'Reilly books!");
    $sth = $dbh->prepare("INSERT INTO test_table
                            VALUES ( $quoteString )");
    $sth->execute;
    $dbh->commit;
};
if ($@) {
    warn "Transaction failed: $@";
    $dbh->rollback;
}
```

The row inserts neatly into the database:

```
SQL> SELECT * from test_table;

MESSAGE_COL
--------------------------------------------------
Let's buy O'Reilly books!

SQL>
```

An undefined value, such as *$dbh->quote($an_undefined_value)*, will be returned as the string NULL (without single quotation marks) to match how NULLs are represented in SQL.

Statement Handle Methods

Before we execute prepared statements, we can bind IN *and* OUT parameters using the methods described in this section.

bind_param

The *bind_param* method binds parameters to SQL statements. Placeholders are numbered from 1 upwards. For example:

```
$sth = $dbh->prepare("SELECT * FROM emp
                        WHERE ename LIKE ? OR ename LIKE ?");

$sth->bind_param(1, "MILLER");
$sth->bind_param(2, "K%");

$sth->execute;
```

You can also use named parameters, described at the end of the next section.

bind_param_inout

The *bind_param_inout* method, available under *DBD::Oracle*, helps us with PL/SQL. This method allows us to call procedures with OUT parameters. Let's see how it works.

1. First of all, let's create a simple Oracle procedure:

```
CREATE OR REPLACE PROCEDURE oracle_power (in_base IN NUMBER,
                                          in_power IN NUMBER,
                                          out_result OUT NUMBER) IS
BEGIN
   out_result := POWER(in_base, in_power);
END;
```

2. Avoiding Perl's own *9**4* notation, we can now run the following code to work out 9 to the power of 4:

```
$sth = $dbh->prepare("BEGIN oracle_power(?, ?, ?); END;");

$sth->bind_param(1, 9); # 1st parameter, value 9
$sth->bind_param(2, 4); # 2nd parameter, value 4

$sth->bind_param_inout( 3, \$got_the_power, 50); # Notice reference! :)
$sth->execute;

print "got_the_power >", $got_the_power, "<\n";
```

We must supply *bind_param_inout* with an extra parameter, in this case 50, which is the maximum length of data we're expecting to receive back. If in doubt, opt for an XXL size here, as long as you have sufficient memory. The Perl code shown above returns the following result:

```
got_the_power >6561<
```

As an alternative to using question marks, you can also use named bound parameters with *DBD::Oracle*. In the following example, the procedure has been predefined like this:

```
CREATE OR REPLACE PROCEDURE
    squarer ( in_number IN NUMBER, inout_result IN OUT NUMBER ) IS
BEGIN
    inout_result := POWER(in_number, 2);
END;
```

Perl DBI code to use this procedure would look something like this:

```
my $in_number = 3;
my $inout_result;

$sth = $db->prepare(q{
  BEGIN
      squarer(:in_number, :inout_result);
  END;
                    });

# We bind here, then execute the call.

$sth->bind_param(":in_number", $in_number);
$sth->bind_param_inout(":inout_result", \$inout_result, 1);

$sth->execute;
print $inout_result;
```

execute

We've already strewn the *execute* method liberally throughout this chapter. It's used to execute prepared statements. It returns an *undef* on failure, or the number of rows affected if this information can be determined. Otherwise, it returns -1.

```
$rv = $sth->execute;
```

If bind variables are being used, we can send these in as an array, rather than binding them all explicitly with separate *bind_param* calls:

```
$rv = $sth->execute( @bound_values );
```

fetchrow_array

The *fetchrow_array* method fetches rows from an array. A popular FETCH command is illustrated in Figure B-2.

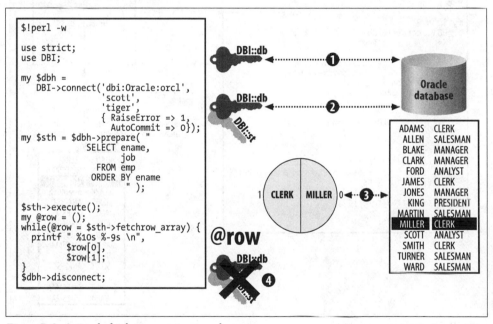

Figure B-2. A simple fetchrow_array example

Let's see what's going on here.

1. Working through Figure B-2, we first create our object with the *connect* method. (The diagram displays internal objects, but we never need to concern ourselves with these in our coding work.)

2. Next we prepare our statement handle.

3. We're then able to loop around the statement handle object using the *fetchrow_array* method, which creates a copy of each data row selected.

4. We finally *disconnect* the database handle, which leads to the destruction of associated DBI objects by the garbage memory collector.

fetchrow_arrayref

Going a step beyond *fetchrow_array*, the *fetchrow_arrayref* method is more efficient because instead of copying data rows into a local array, it provides a reference to the row of data already stored within the driver. It's a fairly straightforward operation to drill down from the reference into this remote array, as shown in Figure B-3.

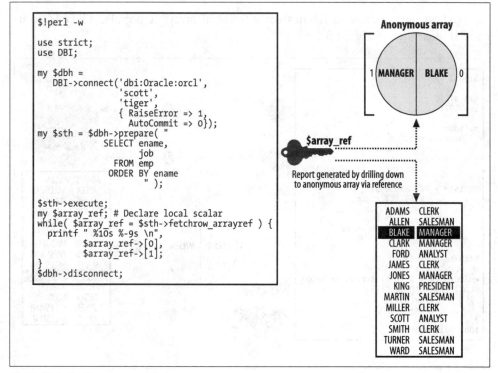

Figure B-3. fetchrow_arrayref

fetchrow_hashref

In a similar manner, the *fetchrow_hashref* method (shown in Figure B-4) returns a reference to an anonymous hash for each row. This time the data is keyed on column name, rather than numeric index. It's best to give this method an optional string parameter of either *NAME_uc* or *NAME_lc* to ensure that column names are always in a preferred case; otherwise, they may be in mixed case, especially if you're using Perl DBI in a portable manner across different database types.

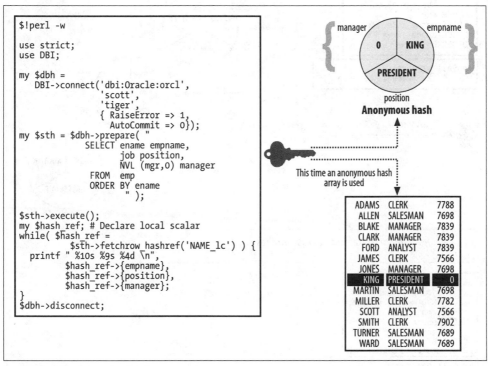

```
$!perl -w

use strict;
use DBI;

my $dbh =
    DBI->connect('dbi:Oracle:orcl',
                 'scott',
                 'tiger',
                 { RaiseError => 1,
                   AutoCommit => 0});
my $sth = $dbh->prepare( "
            SELECT ename empname,
                   job position,
                   NVL (mgr,0) manager
            FROM   emp
            ORDER BY ename
                   " );

$sth->execute();
my $hash_ref; # Declare local scalar
while( $hash_ref =
          $sth->fetchrow_hashref('NAME_lc') ) {
  printf " %10s %9s %4d \n",
         $hash_ref->{empname},
         $hash_ref->{position},
         $hash_ref->{manager};
}
$dbh->disconnect;
```

Figure B-4. fetchrow_hashref

fetchall_arrayref

Instead of accessing data one row at a time, you can get a single reference to access all of the data in one go (if you have the available memory). Use the *fetchall_arrayref* method, as shown in Figure B-5, which demonstrates the default use of *fetchall_arrayref*. A single key accesses a first-level array composed of reference keys to second-level arrays. There is one of these for each row of data found by the SELECT statement.

Figure B-6 demonstrates a variation on this theme. An optional hash marks out the various column names required. This transforms the second-level arrays into hashes, accessed by column name rather than numeric index.

fetchall_hashref

The *fetchall_hashref* method can only be used with SELECT statements containing unique key data combinations, such as single-column primary keys. This method

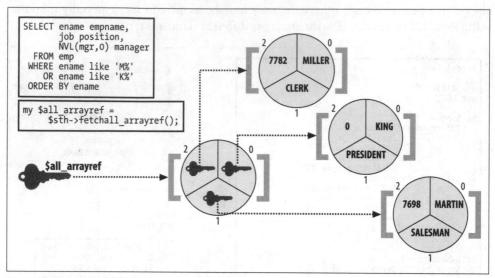

```
SELECT ename empname,
       job position,
       NVL(mgr,0) manager
  FROM emp
 WHERE ename like 'M%'
    OR ename like 'K%'
 ORDER BY ename
```

```
my $all_arrayref =
    $sth->fetchall_arrayref();
```

Figure B-5. fetchall_arrayref with array batches

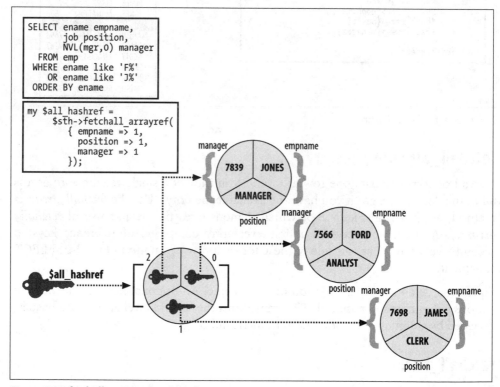

```
SELECT ename empname,
       job position,
       NVL(mgr,0) manager
  FROM emp
 WHERE ename like 'F%'
    OR ename like 'J%'
 ORDER BY ename
```

```
my $all_hashref =
    $sth->fetchall_arrayref(
        { empname => 1,
          position => 1,
          manager => 1
        });
```

Figure B-6. fetchall_arrayref with hashes

creates a first-level hash possessing as many index keys as there are uniquely keyed rows. We can then drill down from this hash into second-level hashes, which contain all of the row data by column name. Figure B-7 illustrates the use of this method.

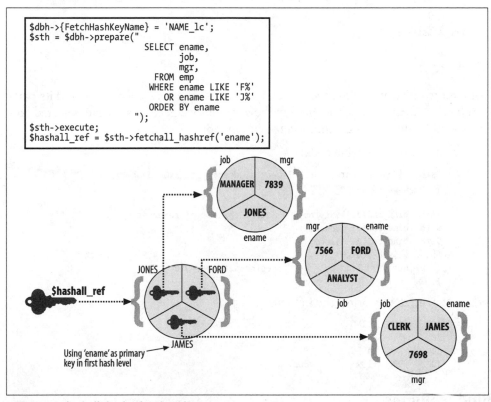

```
$dbh->{FetchHashKeyName} = 'NAME_lc';
$sth = $dbh->prepare("
                    SELECT ename,
                           job,
                           mgr,
                      FROM emp
                     WHERE ename LIKE 'F%'
                        OR ename LIKE 'J%'
                     ORDER BY ename
                    ");
$sth->execute;
$hashall_ref = $sth->fetchall_hashref('ename');
```

Figure B-7. fetchall_hashref with its key requirement

finish

The *finish* method deactivates an active SELECT statement handle, thus causing any pending unfetched data to be discarded. This can free up resources in the server, especially for large GROUP BY or ORDER BY queries. It is rarely used, however, because statement handles deactivate anyway after a last row is fetched. Nevertheless, you may want to use this method if you're only fetching a fixed number of rows from a statement (see the *selectrow_array* method mentioned later). You should also *finish* active statements before disconnecting from a database:

```
$rc = $sth->finish;
```

rows

The *rows* method holds the number of rows processed by the statement; it returns -1 if it is unable to determine a figure. When you use this method with a SELECT statement, wait until all of the rows have been fetched before calling it, to get accurate results:

```
$rv = $sth->rows;
```

bind_col

For a more efficient way to access data, you can use the *bind_col* method and its partner, *bind_columns*. We simply bind in the variables we need to associate selected columns with, before calling a simple *fetch* command:

Let's examine the following code:

```
$sth = $dbh->prepare(" SELECT deptno, dname, loc FROM dept ");
$sth->execute;

$sth->bind_col(1, \$deptno); # Notice the use of referencing! :)
$sth->bind_col(2, \$dname);
$sth->bind_col(3, \$loc);
while ( $sth->fetch ) {                          # Simple fetch
    printf "%2d %14s %13s \n", $deptno, $dname, $loc;
}
```

When executed, this prints the following:

```
10      ACCOUNTING      NEW YORK
20        RESEARCH        DALLAS
30           SALES       CHICAGO
40      OPERATIONS        BOSTON
```

bind_columns

Using the *bind_columns* method, you can shrink those three *bind_col* lines into a single *bind_columns* call. Simply ensure that you have the same number of variables in the *bind_columns* call as there are fields to be selected, and also make sure you then get them in the right order. For example:

```
$sth->bind_columns(\$deptno, \$dname, \$loc);   # List of references
```

dump_results

This prototyping method fetches all the selected rows out from a statement, as comma-separated values, and prints them to STDOUT:

```
$sth->dump_results;
```

Database Handles—SQL and Cleanup

To save coding, we often combine database and statement handles using the methods described in this section. When we are finished executing SQL statements, we clean up with a database disconnection, also described in this section.

do

The *do* method is typically used to *prepare* and *execute* DML statements in one call. We can also use it in combination with bind parameters, as shown in the following example:

```
$dbh->{AutoCommit} = 0; # Turn it off! :)

$sth = $dbh->do("DELETE FROM test_table");  # Binds unnecessary
$dbh->commit;

$sth =
    $dbh->do("INSERT INTO test_table values (?)",
            undef,                        # <= Can be Attributes
            "It's worse than that Jim");   # Binding this 1st value
$dbh->commit;
```

Let's just check that:

```
SQL> select * from test_table;

MESSAGE_COL
--------------------------------------------------
It's worse than that Jim

SQL>
```

If the statement will be executed several times, it is often more efficient to carry out a single *prepare*, followed by many *execute* commands, to avoid constantly re-preparing the same DML statement.

selectrow_array

The *selectrow_array* method is a super-method that combines the *prepare*, *execute*, and *fetchrow_array* entries—all in one go. It generates an array consisting of the first row found:

```
@row_ary = $dbh->selectrow_array($statement);
```

selectall_arrayref

The *selectall_arrayref* alternative method uses *fetchall_arrayref* and thereby generates a reference to a first-level array containing references to however many second-level arrays are necessary to hold every row returned by the SELECT statement. It's a head twister—but in a good way. Here's an example; see the earlier Figure B-5 for more details.

```
$ary_ref = $dbh->selectall_arrayref($statement);
```

selectall_hashref

We use the *fetchall_hashref* method, this time as the final link in the selection chain, with *selectall_hashref*. You must supply a column key, as illustrated in the following example. See the earlier Figure B-7 for more details.

```
$hash_ref = $dbh->selectall_hashref($statement, $key); # Use key! :)
```

selectcol_arrayref

The *selectcol_arrayref* method returns a reference to an array containing the first field from each row:

```
$ary_ref = $dbh->selectcol_arrayref($statement);
```

Other columns can be pushed into the array via the *Columns* attribute. Groovy!

```
$ary_ref =
    $dbh->selectcol_arrayref($select_statement, { Columns => [1,2] });
```

commit

The *commit* method commits transactions when *AutoCommit* is set to false:

```
$rc = $dbh->commit;
```

rollback

The *rollback* method rolls back transactions:

```
$rc = $dbh->rollback;
```

begin_work

This method switches *AutoCommit* off until either a *commit* or a *rollback* is encountered, thus completing a single explicit transaction. The *AutoCommit* behavior then reverts back to what it was previously.

disconnect

The *disconnect* method is typically seen just before the end of a program. It neatly closes down the database connection.

```
$rc = $dbh->disconnect or warn $dbh->errstr;
```

If you're using transactions, it is good practice to explicitly call either *commit* or *rollback* before disconnecting in order to keep your code clean and reliable.

Metadata

There are several metadata-related method calls associated with the main database handle. These are summarized in Table B-5. (There will be an increasing amount of metadata in future versions of DBI. Check *perldoc DBI* for the latest details.)

Table B-5. Database handle metadata methods

Method	Description
table_info	Lists schemas, tables, and other object metadata.
tables	A simpler interface to the *tables_info* method.
primary_key_info	Provides primary key metadata.
primary_key	A simpler interface to the *primary_key_info* method.
type_info_all	Returns a reference to a read-only array used to drill down on all type information in the database.
type_info	Returns information on a particular data type.
foreign_key_info	Returns foreign key information.
column_info	Returns column information.

Statement Handle Metadata

There are many read-only attributes you can access via the statement handle. Rather than describe all of them individually, we've provided the following piece of code as a good guide to the main ones used. Note that some are straightforward string values, whereas others are array references to columnar information:

```
use DBI;

my $dbh = DBI->connect('dbi:Oracle:orcl', 'scott', 'tiger',
                       {RaiseError => 1, AutoCommit => 0} );

my $sth = $dbh->prepare("SELECT empno, hiredate
                         FROM emp
                         WHERE ename = ? ");

$sth->bind_param(1, 'MILLER');  # SQL uses 1 bound parameter
$sth->execute;

print "Number of Fields : ", $sth->{NUM_OF_FIELDS}, "\n";
print "Bound parameters : ", $sth->{NUM_OF_PARAMS}, "\n\n";

for $column (0..($sth->{NUM_OF_FIELDS} - 1)) {  # Columns, 0 - N
```

```
    print "Column Name      : ", $sth->{NAME}->[$column], "\n",
          "SQL Data Type    : ", $sth->{TYPE}->[$column], "\n",
          "Precision        : ", $sth->{PRECISION}->[$column], "\n",
          "Scale            : ", $sth->{SCALE}->[$column], "\n",
          "Nullable? (1=yes): ", $sth->{NULLABLE}->[$column], "\n\n";
}
print "SQL Statement     : ", $sth->{Statement}, "\n";
```

When the above code is run, it generates the following listing:

```
Number of Fields : 2
Bound parameters : 1

Column Name      : EMPNO
SQL Data Type    : 3
Precision        : 4
Scale            : 0
Nullable? (1=yes):

Column Name      : HIREDATE
SQL Data Type    : 9
Precision        : 75
Scale            : 0
Nullable? (1=yes): 1

SQL Statement     : SELECT empno, hiredate
                          FROM emp
                          WHERE ename = ?
```

You can see that some figures included above are unreliable when used with irrelevant data types, such as 75 for the *Precision* of the HIREDATE column.

Oracle-Specific Methods

There are a number of special Perl DBI methods that support the use of DBD::Oracle and its handling of particular Oracle datatypes and operations.

DBMS_OUTPUT Methods

Four additional functions, available within *DBD::Oracle*, are provided for use in accessing Oracle's DBMS_OUTPUT built-in package; they are listed in Table B-6.

Table B-6. DBD::Oracle's private methods for Perl DBI

DBD::Oracle function	Description
plsql_errstr	Provides debug text from potential PL/SQL compilation errors
dbms_output_enable	Enables the DBMS_OUTPUT package for use with Perl
dbms_output_get	Provides access to the DBMS_OUTPUT.GET_LINE function
dbms_output_put	Provides access to the DBMS_OUTPUT.PUT_LINE function

The following code illustrates the use of some of these private methods:

```perl
#! perl -w
use strict;
use DBI;

# Step 1: Connect to orcacle database, orcl.

my $dbh = DBI->connect('dbi:Oracle:orcl', 'scott', 'tiger'),
                        {RaiseError => 1, AutoCommit => 0} );

# Step 2: Enable the later collection of DBMS_OUTPUT information.

$dbh->func( 1_000_000, 'dbms_output_enable');

# Step 3: Prepare and run some anonymous PL/SQL containing some
# output from DBMS_OUTPUT.

my $sth = $dbh->prepare(q{
    DECLARE
        hello_string VARCHAR2(50);
    BEGIN
        SELECT 'Hello ' || USER || '! :-)'
          INTO hello_string
          FROM DUAL;
        dbms_output.put_line( hello_string );
    END;
                            });
$sth->execute;

# Step 4: Get the output and print it out.

print $dbh->func( 'dbms_output_get' ), "\n";

$dbh->disconnect;
```

Let's see what's going on here.

1. First of all, set up the connection to the target database.

2. Now we use our private *dbms_output_enable* method to adjust the memory necessary to pick up DBMS_OUTPUT.PUT_LINE calls later.

3. We prepare a very simple piece of anonymous PL/SQL to print out a message from our sponsor.

4. Now we use a second private method, *dbms_output_get*, to pick up the relevant message via *DBD::Oracle* so we can print it out:

```
$ perl hello_dbd.pl
Hello SCOTT! :-)
```

Handling LOBs

When *DBD::Oracle* fetches LOBs (large objects), they are treated as LONGs and are subject to the *LongReadLen* and *LongTruncOk* handle attributes described earlier. Note that at the time of this writing, only single-row LOB updates were supported, and the ability to pass LOBS to PL/SQL blocks was not available. Consider the following examples:

- To insert or update a large LOB, *DBD::Oracle* has to know about this operation in advance. To do this in Oracle8 you need to set the *ora_type* attribute—for example:

  ```
  $sth->bind_param($field_num, $lob_value, { ora_type => ORA_CLOB });
  ```

- The ORA_CLOB or alternative ORA_BLOB constants are imported with:

  ```
  use DBD::Oracle qw(:ora_types);
  ```

- To make scripts work for both Oracle7 and Oracle8 (and later), Oracle7's *DBD:: Oracle* treats the LOBs as LONGs without error. Specify them as ORA_CLOB or ORA_BLOB, as above, and DBI will be able to handle the LOBs properly.

- In inserts or update, where there are multiple LOB fields of the same type in a particular table, you must tell *DBD::Oracle* which field the LOB parameter relates to:

  ```
  $sth->bind_param(1, $myLobValue,
                     { ora_type => ORA_CLOB, ora_field= > 'my_column1' });
  ```

- At the time of this writing there is no direct way to write LOBs in chunks via *DBD::Oracle*. The official back-door workaround is to use DBMS_LOB.WRITE-APPEND or, with some earlier versions of Perl DBI, the undocumented feature *blob_read*. Note, though, that it is always better to stick with documented DBI functions to remain on the safe side. (See Chapter 7, *Invoking the Oracle Call Interface with Oracle::OCI*, for mention of a possible future solution to this LOB problem via *Oracle::OCI*.)

Binding Cursors

DBD::Oracle returns cursors from PL/SQL blocks as shown here:

```
use DBI;
use DBD::Oracle qw(:ora_types);

my $dbh = DBI->connect('dbi:Oracle:orcl', 'scott', 'tiger'),
                        {RaiseError => 1, AutoCommit => 0} );

my $sth = $dbh->prepare(q{
   BEGIN OPEN :cursor FOR
      SELECT deptno, dname, loc
         FROM dept
         FROM user_tables WHERE loc = :loc;
   END; });
```

```
$sth->bind_param(":loc", "BOSTON");

my $sth_curs;
$sth->bind_param_inout(":cursor", \$sth_curs, 0,
                       { ora_type => ORA_RSET } );
$sth->execute;

# $sth_curs can now be used like any other statement handle...

while ( @row = $sth_curs->fetchrow_array ) {
...
```

Notice how *ora_type* is set to ORA_SET; this is mandatory. See the *curref.pl* script in the *Oracle.ex* directory in *DBD::Oracle*'s source distribution for more examples.

The Essential Guide
to Regular Expressions

The concept of regular expressions (or *regexes* as they're often known) is central to the Perl language. Regular expressions have been available for a long time in Unix tools such as *grep*, *sed*, *awk*, and *egrep*, and they have also made their way into Java and Python. But they are most closely associated with Perl where they are used extensively for pattern matching. They are also very important for data munging, as we describe in Appendix D, *The Essential Guide to Perl Data Munging*.

Regular expressions are patterns of literals and metacharacters that match target combinations of characters embedded within input data. Although the simplest regular expression can be very simple indeed (it's simply a literal string), regexes can also be very complex. They can provide amazing efficiency, but can also lead to great frustration. We have found that unless you live in the same universe as Spock or Data, where regexes compete with music and chess for sublime mathematical resonance, they most likely mean pain, bashed foreheads, and late-night viewings of *Casablanca* and *The Matrix* to calm the nerves. It's only really by writing a million and one regexes that most people do eventually figure out what the heck is going on—and even then, there's more to learn.

In this appendix, we'll look at the origins of regular expressions and the main concepts underlying their use. We'll also examine Perl's built-in string-handling functions, which often supply enough functionality that you won't need to use regexes at all. We'll discuss the basics of constructing regular expressions and will pay special attention to the use of metacharacters and suffixes. *Metacharacters* are special characters such as the asterisk (*) that can be used to drive fuzzy nonliteral matching. *Suffixes* are special switches at the end of matches and substitutions that change their exact operation—for example, by making them replace strings globally across an entire input, rather than just substituting the first one.

Obviously, in this short appendix we can only scratch the surface of regular expressions. We strongly recommend that you consult the definitive reference on regular expressions, Jeffrey Friedl's excellent *Mastering Regular Expressions* (O'Reilly & Associates); because of its cover design, it's known as the Owl Book. You can also generate the full online documentation for Perl regular expressions with the following command:

```
$ perldoc perlre
```

The Origins of Regular Expressions

Where did regular expressions come from and why the funny name? Rather interestingly, they grew from original research work on artificial intelligence, dating back nearly 60 years and preceding the era of computing.

The Early History

In the 1940s, Warren McCulloch and Walter Pitts modeled neuron-like finite state machines to mimic the human nervous system in an effort to help build a Turing machine. After being introduced to this research by John von Neumann, mathematician Stephen Kleene later described these models in a notation that he called *regular sets*. The actual term *regular expression* made its initial debut in Kleene's 1951 paper, from the University of Wisconsin at Madison, titled "Representation of events in nerve nets and finite automata."

Regexes supplemented Kleene's Princeton University doctoral work, dating from the 1930s, on recursive algorithms,* a fundamental contribution which helped make electronic computing directly possible in the first place. Kleene's work also complemented related work by the more famous British scientist Alan Turing, who like Kleene was a doctoral student (1936–1938) of Professor Alonzo Church, the enigmatic head of Princeton's mathematics department. Church himself had extended the earlier recursive work of Vienna's Gödel, who'd briefly lectured Kleene at Princeton in 1934 before returning to Austria. Gödel later escaped from Hitler's Germany and came back to Princeton in 1940, via Russia and Japan, after World War II broke out. After Turing completed his own doctorate, and some hurried studies on ciphers, he returned to England in 1938 to successfully crack the Nazi's ENIGMA code via the use of repetitive symbolic manipulations. In these various ways, an early form of regular expressions grew from the mathematical culture dish of Princeton.

After the war ended, research continued towards regular expressions proper and the creation of their backbone components. The most famous of these is the asterisk wildcard, still technically known as the *Kleene Star*, which was heavily adopted by many different computing applications. From these beginnings, Kleene's regular expressions gradually made their way into a wide range of programming languages, helping develop many other different technologies along the way.

---

* There's a good joke on recursion: You can only learn how it works if you understand it already. (You'll be pleased to hear that's all we're going to say about recursion.)

qed, ed, and vi

Jumping ahead a number of decades, MIT's Ken Thompson incorporated Kleene's regular sets notation into Butler Lampson and Peter Deutsch's original Berkeley *qed* editor program. This was the distant ancestor of Thompson's *ed* and Bill Joy's personal interpretation of *vi*. With the help of Dennis Ritchie, regexes were also popularized via the Unix *grep* program, and from this historical point, regexes inveigled their way into *sed*, *lex*, *awk*, *nawk*, *gawk*, and a host of other programs, including the venerable *CHANGE* command line editor within SQL*Plus.

Enter Perl

When Perl bubbled spontaneously from its primeval soup in 1987, consisting mainly of amino acids stripped from *sed* and *awk*, the rest was pure biological determinism, swimming along in the moonlight with the general tide of Unix. If you add Larry Wall's linguistic origins to this tidal churn, the strong relationship between Perl and regexes was an almost inevitable development (or a successful pre-adaptation, as Darwinist Stephen J. Gould might have put it). And the relationship with regexes has remained central to Perl ever since, as Figure C-1 illustrates.

Perl vs. grep

Regular expressions are found within many Unix tools to pattern-match groups of characters within input data. Such data usually comes in through files, though it can be any kind of data held within a scalar zvariable. Although many such tools exist— for example, *grep* and *awk**—for finding patterns of characters, it's within Perl that pattern matching has been most strongly developed. Perl contains the greatest range of operators and metacharacters for finding and substituting patterns into something else. Compared to *grep*, regexes in Perl have three major advantages:

1. They pulsate strongly within the beating heart of the Perl core engine. You can therefore program far more complex regular expressions in Perl than you could ever imagine doing with *grep*, and you can then immediately wrap them within programming constructs.

2. Regexes in Perl can deal with binary data, without turning your *xterm* screen into a mass of Klingon ideographs. This can all too easily happen when you do an ordinary *grep* on a binary file.

3. Because Perl is available on virtually every operating system, regexes written in Perl can be equally widespread. This is especially comforting for sysadmins

---

* *grep* itself stands for *Global Regular Expression Print*. *awk* is named after the surnames of its creators, Alfred V. *Aho*, Peter J. *Weinberger*, and Brian W. *Kernighan*. (Alfred Aho also invented *egrep*. The roots of regexes go deep.)

operating across an entire range of OS quadrants. And because Perl works seamlessly on Win32, you therefore get regexes there too.

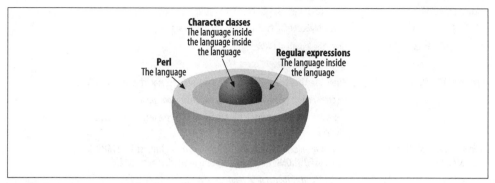

Figure C-1. Languages within languages

Built-in String Handling Functions

Lending the power of regular expressions to some simple data-handling operations is a bit like giving a Kalashnikov to a small fish. It's simply overkill. To prevent ourselves from getting carried away and throwing away potential speed, we'll summarize the more useful of Perl's built-in string handling functions in Table C-1. Repeat after us:

> We're only allowed to use regular expressions if the built-in functions won't hack it.

In this table, the Perl function is shown in lowercase (e.g., *index*) and its replaceable parameters in uppercase (e.g., *STRING*). As with most things in Perl, many of the functions in Table C-1 use *$_* as a default *EXPRESSION* value, if no *EXPRESSION* value is supplied.

Table C-1. Built-in Perl string-handling functions

Function	Description
index STRING, SUBSTRING [,OFFSET]	Returns the position of the first *SUBSTRING* in *STRING*, where the first position is zero. If *OFFSET* is given, it tells *index* how many characters to skip before searching: *index('Toad of Toad Hall', 'Toad')* gives 0 *index('Toad of Toad Hall', 'Toad', 1)* gives 8 (-1 is returned if no match is found)
join EXPRESSION, LIST	Joins a *LIST* of strings into a single string, each separated by *EXPRESSION* (which can be an empty string, ""): *join ":", "Badger", "Ratty", "Mole"* gives *Badger:Ratty:Mole*
lc EXPRESSION	Lowercases *EXPRESSION*: *lc "The Stoats took the Hall"* gives *the stoats took the hall*

Table C-1. Built-in Perl string-handling functions (continued)

Function	Description
lcfirst EXPRESSION	Lowercases the first letter of *EXPRESSION*: *lcfirst "MyBeautifulMind"* gives *myBeautifulMind*
length EXPRESSION	Gives the length of *EXPRESSION*: *length "Washerwoman"* gives *11*
reverse EXPRESSION	When used in a scalar context and with a single scalar, this reverses *EXPRESSION*: *reverse "Poop poop, said Toad"* gives *daoT dias ,poop pooP* (*reverse* is also often used in a list context to reverse arrays, hashes, and other listy type things.)
rindex STRING, SUBSTRING [,POSITION]	Similar to *index*, this returns the position of the rightmost *SUBSTRING* in *STRING*. The optional *POSITION* is the rightmost position which is acceptable: *rindex "Toad of Toad Hall", "Toad"* gives *8* *rindex "Toad of Toad Hall", "Toad", 7* gives *0* (-1 is returned if no match is found.)
split /PATTERN/, EXPRESSION, LIMIT	This function is the black sheep of the built-in string handling world, because it rather naughtily uses regular expressions to process the */PATTERN/* match, to split *EXPRESSION* strings into lists. After we've covered regular expressions proper, we'll come back to *split*, one of the most useful of the Perl munge operators.
sprintf FORMAT, LIST	Returns a formatted string in the manner of the ubiquitous *printf* conventions from the C programming language. The main *sprintf* Perl formatters are described in Table C-2. This is highly useful for reports.

substr EXPRESSION, OFFSET [,LENGTH] [,REPLACEMENT]	Extracts a substring out of *EXPRESSION*, starting at *OFFSET*, where the first position is zero: *substr "Messing about in boats", 8* gives *about in boats*
	If *OFFSET* is negative, the count starts from the right-hand side of the string: *substr "Messing about in boats", -8* gives *in boats*
	If *LENGTH* is omitted, everything to the end of the string is returned. Otherwise, *LENGTH* determines the length of the string returned: *substr "Messing about in boats", 8, 5* gives *about*
	If *LENGTH* is negative, this is how many characters are left off the end of the substring: *substr "Messing about in boats", 8, -5* gives *about in*
	The optional *REPLACEMENT* will replace the substring it finds in *EXPRESSION*:
	
	`$stoat1 = "Messing about in boats";`
	`$stoat2 = substr $stoat1, 0, 16, "Wonderful";`
	`print $stoat1, "\n";`
	`print $stoat2, "\n";`
	
	This produces:
	
	`Wonderful boats`
	`Messing about in`
	
	An alternative to using *REPLACEMENT* is to use *substr* on the left-hand side of an assignment operation:
	
	`$stoat = "Messing about in boats";`
	`substr ($stoat, 0, 16) = "Wonderful";`
	`print $stoat, "\n";`

Table C-1. Built-in Perl string-handling functions (continued)

Function	Description
	This produces: Wonderful boats
uc EXPRESSION	Uppercases EXPRESSION: uc "canal barge" gives CANAL BARGE
ucfirst EXPRESSION	Uppercases the first character of EXPRESSION: ucfirst "railway engine" gives Railway engine

Table C-2. Perl formats for sprintf

Formatter	Description
%c	A character with the given number
%s	A string
%d	A signed integer, in decimal
%u	An unsigned integer, in decimal
%o	An unsigned integer, in octal
%x	An unsigned integer, in hexadecimal
%e	A floating-point number, in scientific notation (e.g., 1.00e+09 for 1 billion)
%f	A floating-point number, in fixed decimal notation
%g	A floating-point number, in either %e or %f notation
%X	Like %x, but using upper-case letters
%E	Like %e, but using an upper-case "E" (e.g., 1.00E+09)
%G	Like %g, but with an upper-case "E" (if applicable)
%b	An unsigned integer, in binary
%p	A pointer (outputs the Perl value's address in hexadecimal)
%n	This is a special formatter which stores the number of characters output so far into the next variable in the parameter list
%%	An ordinary percent sign

Regular Expression Concepts

As we mentioned earlier, regular expressions are patterns of literals and metacharacters that match target combinations of characters embedded within input data:

Literal character

A plain honest-to-goodness character, which mostly means no harm to anyone and which goes about under the motto, "What you see is what you get". So when you see the letter *n* by itself, without a mischievous backslash nearby, it means "please match the letter *n* at this position, and nothing else".

Metacharacter

A nonalphabetic keyboard character, such as ^, *, $, and so on, which either has a special meaning or can give special meaning to surrounding characters. For instance, the \ metacharacter backslash gives a special meaning to the letter *n*, making it into the newline character, \n.

Matching, Substitution, and Translation

There are three main types of regular expression. All three work only on scalars, usually strings:

m// is for match

At the basic level, *m//* simply tells you whether the required regular expression is matched, or exists, within the input data. Because matching is so ubiquitous within Perl, just the simple use of // will indicate to Perl that you're performing a match. If you change the delimiters, however, you do need to explicitly use the *m* prefix, as in *m%my match%*. (We'll say more about delimiters shortly.)

s/// is for substitute

If you want to replace the located matches with something else, you call up the substitution operator. You always need to use the *s* prefix.

tr/// is for translate

Although St. Peter at the Perly gates would fail to recognize *tr///* as a *definitive* regular expression operator, it's so close in form and function that we can usually get away with fudging the issue. The translate operator takes a range of characters on its left side, and replaces them with another range of specified characters on its right side. Its typical use is to capitalize a passage of text, or shift some number ranges. To keep old *sed* users happy, *tr///* also possesses a synonym, the *y///* operator, which behaves in an identical fashion. A typical translation program to uppercase every line of an input file would look like this:

```
while(<>){
    tr/a-z/A-Z/;
    print;
}
```

Regular expression input

A special double character is used to indicate the scalar value the regex should work on. This is the =~ pattern binding operator. Although this looks a lot like an = assignment operator, try to think of it being more like the word "contains":*

```
print "I have found a match" if $target_string =~ /corleone/;
```

---

* The =~ operator originates from the ~ and !~ regex operators in *awk*.

This translates into English, as follows:

> Print out the phrase, 'I have found a match' if the variable *$target_string contains* the matching word 'corleone'.

As with *awk*, the good angel of =~ has a naughty devil partner-in-crime for negative assertions, *!~*:

```
print "I have failed to find a match" if $target_string !~ /michael/;
```

This translates to:

> Print out the phrase 'I have failed to find a match' if *$target_string fails to contain* the word 'michael'.

> You can use any nonalphanumeric or non-space character as a delimiter within Perl regexes. This is particularly useful when you're matching strings that contain / Unix slash characters, which you need to otherwise escape with a \ backslash character. A typically required match pattern string might be *"/etc/passwd"*. When using the standard match syntax, this would become */\etc\/passwd/*, a process known as *toothpicking*. You can avoid this unsightly use by changing the delimiter character directly following from the now compulsory match function character, *m*, thus *m#/etc/passwd#*. No more fangs!
>
> You can also use four sets of brackets, *m<...>, m{...}, m(...),* and *m[...]*. The first two are usually preferred because their bracket characters are less frequently used within regexes. You can also mix and match brackets for substitutions, *s{...}<...>*, though you may still prefer *s(...)(...)* or even *s#...#...#*. As a rule of thumb, use delimiters that aren't going to appear in your regex to keep everything clean. For example *s<><>* is a good one if you're not dealing with XML or HTML.

The implicit use of $_

As with many other places in Perl, if no scalar variable is supplied to our regular expression via the =~ or *!~* constructs, it's assumed that the scalar value under consideration is the *$_* default value. The good angel of =~ is also assumed:

```
$_ = "Who is greater, Von Mises or Hayek?";
print if /greater/;
```

The *print* statement here could be fully expanded to:

```
print $_ if $_ =~ m/greater/;
```

Either of the two preceding print statements would translate to:

> Print the full contents of the *$_* variable, if *$_ contains* a match for the word 'greater'.

The Implicit Left-to-Right Assumption

Some rules are so implicit in Perl (and in regular expressions in general) that it's hard to spot them as assumptions as opposed to incontrovertible facts of life. The important one to watch out for is that regular expressions work in a *left-to-right* fashion. This may seem obvious to native English speakers, but if you're a fluent writer of *right-to-left* Arabic or Hebrew script, or you're trying to match *right-to-left* Unicode data, the importance of this assumption becomes more significant. If there are two or more matches on a single line, it is the left-most one that is matched first. Without the special /g global suffix, which we'll talk about later, it is only this first match that is either then validated, recorded, or substituted. (As with all computer languages that ultimately originate from the English language, Perl goes left-to-right, following the left-to-right convention of Latin, which followed the left-to-right tradition of fourth century BC classical Greek.)

Let's run our first regular expression to take a look at this concept. Try to keep an open mind on the following syntactical details, just for the moment; we promise to get to the meaty details of regular bracketing, curly bracketing, list context, and so on, a bit later. All we need to know for now is that we're looking for a seven-character phrase, in the supplied text, starting with the word "Bag," and we're going to store this in the *$seven_letter_Bag_phrase* variable. As we'll also cover later, the . *{4}* notation picks up any four characters, except \n newlines:

```perl
#!/usr/bin/perl

use strict;

my $party_text =
    "When Mr. Bilbo Baggins of Bag End announced that " .
    "he would shortly be celebrating his eleventy-first " .
    "birthday with a party of special magnificence, there " .
    "was much talk and excitement in Hobbiton.";

my ($seven_letter_Bag_phrase) = ($party_text =~ m/(Bag.{4})/);
```

So what got stored inside the *$seven_letter_Bag_phrase* variable?:

```perl
print "Seven Letter Bag Phrase: >", $seven_letter_Bag_phrase, "<\n";
```

This provides an output of:

```
Seven Letter Bag Phrase: >Baggins<
```

This may be a surprise. Our clever plan was to get you to guess "Bag End," as this may seem at first glance the slightly more obvious match within the supplied *$party_text* variable. However using our left-to-right rule, the first match found was in fact "Baggins." As soon as we'd matched this, it was game over. To get the actual word "Bag," followed by a space and then a three-letter word, we'd have to tune our regular expression accordingly. For instance, we could re-tune our original code like this, to make sure there is an \s for space character after the word "Bag":

```
my ($seven_letter_Bag_phrase) = ($party_text =~ m/(Bag\s.{3})/);

print "Seven Letter Bag Phrase: >", $seven_letter_Bag_phrase, "<\n";
```

This produces:

```
Seven Letter Bag Phrase: >Bag End<
```

(We'll also explain more about \s later.)

Planning regular expressions is like planning killer attack moves in chess. It's easy to go forward with all bishops blazing, but we've got to leave ourselves covered at the back. Let's summarize the rules we followed here:

1. In the first case, we were after "Bag End," so we played a quick *Bag.{4}* move to go and grab it.

2. We then got punished for our hastiness, because this matched the more left "Baggins," too.

3. By replaying the move with *Bag\s.{3}*, we got the desired result.

4. Our regex opponent had to concede to us the "Bag End" phrase we were after originally. Fantastic!

Regular expressions can also be likened to the perfect jury. They must always get the guilty party (or match), and must always release the innocent bystander (or fail to match an unwanted pattern). Of course in the real world, perfect juries are uncommon, and we therefore tend to err on the side of letting the odd guilty person go (or miss the odd match), in order to make sure innocent bystanders (or false matches) are never wrongly convicted. Getting regular expressions to match exact requirements can be equally troublesome. It is only through fine-tuning and the constant honing of regex common law that we're able to achieve ultimate grand regex mastery.

Regular Expression Architectures

There are two major regular expression engine types.

The DFA (Deterministic Finite Automaton)
> With a name taking us back to Kleene's 1951 paper on neural nerve nets, the DFA engine powers many regex tools, including most versions of Alfred Aho's *egrep*, and *awk*, as well as *lex* and *flex*. Basically, while the DFA filters the input text, it simultaneously holds every single possible combination of text the regex could be searching for. Think of a police cell filling with the usual suspects, until the guilty party is recognized or the match found. The DFA engine therefore provides fast, consistent matches.

The NFA (Nondeterministic Finite Automaton)
> The alternative backtracker NFA engine drives Perl, *sed*, *vi*, and most versions of *grep*. It is controlled much more by the actual regex. It works by bumping and

```
```

grinding through the input text one character at a time. If it goes up a blind alley, it backtracks to the last position that still makes sense (the saved state), and then begins working through the regex again, bumping and grinding once more through the text. It's a bit like a mad genius film editor, checking out a film sequence one frame at a time, and then cutting backwards and forwards until the Holy Grail's final cut is discovered. The NFA approach is illustrated in Figure C-2, where the Witch King of Angmar has crafted a regex to try to find Baggins.

Although the NFA is logically slower than the DFA engine at finding matches, it has two major advantages which often overcome this speed gap:

- Its backtracking architecture allows the NFA to save and store marked snippets of information as it works through the text. Think of Theseus trying to locate the Cretan Minotaur in the labyrinth at Knossos. He could use Ariadne's ball of silken thread to retrace his way out from blind alleys and dead ends, until in the end he found and slaughtered the Minotaur (or got his match). He could then get out of the maze, once again using the thread, bringing with him his life and his sword. The DFA would approach the situation differently. If there were 99 blind alleys, it would send in 100 gladiators, only one of which would find and kill the Minotaur (or get the match). Then all 100 gladiators would stay where they were (99 stuck up blind alleys, 1 in the central chamber), all incapable of going anywhere except forwards into the nearest wall. The task would be achieved, and the Minotaur would be dead, but no gladiators would be able to re-emerge into the light. This is illustrated in Figure C-3.

- The other disadvantage of the DFA engine is that its swordsmen slaves would never benefit from a map. Their orders are always to just keep piling into the Labyrinth, like the Roman soldiers in *The Life of Brian*, until every possible cubby-hole, including the central chamber, is covered. In other words whatever regex you provide, as long as it's logically similar to another regex looking for the same match, it makes no speed difference to the match. The same 100 gladiators will always end up in the same 100 locations, one of which will *happen* to be the final match in the central chamber. NFA regexes, on the other hand, are very different. If you become skilled at regexes (or skilled at solving mazes), you can begin directing the route of Theseus beforehand by drawing him a map (or a better regex). And the better your map-drawing or predictive skills become, the fewer blind alleys Theseus will hit, the less backtracking he'll have to do, and the quicker he'll find the Minotaur. Because you can craft your regex in this way to speed up the game, the NFA appeals to code crafters and Perl hackers everywhere.

m/Baggins/

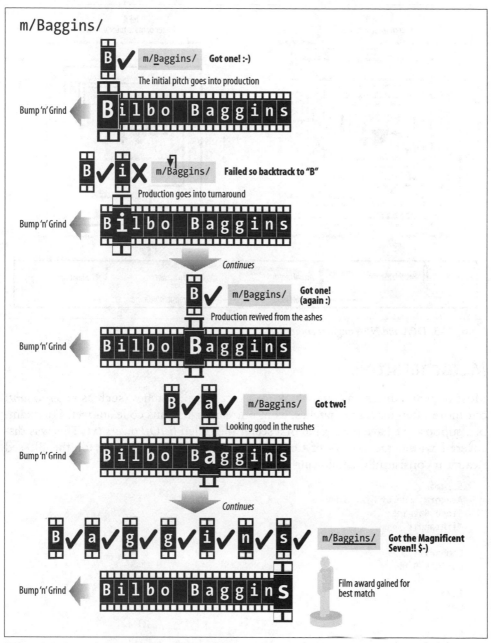

Figure C-2. Bump 'n' grind backtrack matching

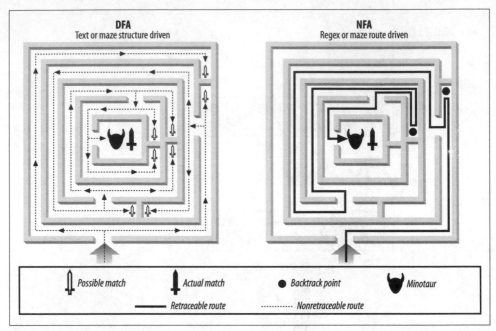

Figure C-3. DFA and NFA engines compared

Metacharacters

Most regular expressions rarely look for exact literal matches (such as *m/Saruman/*) but more often for *fuzzy* matches, as in our earlier Baggins code snippet. For example, suppose we have possession of a secret file called *listOfPowers.txt*. This was discovered within the bowels of Orthanc by Gandalf before he left for the Blessed Realm. It consists of the following names:

```
Saruman
Aragorn, son of Arathorn
Frodo Baggins
Mithrandir
Sauron
Bombadill
Durin's Bane
Smaug
Elrond
Galadriel
Witch-King
Celeborn
Radagast
Dain Ironfoot
Denethor
```

We'd like to find all the Powers known to have existed within Middle-Earth in the Third Age, whose names begin with an "*S*" and end with an "*n.*" Example C-1 is the program we use.

Example C-1. Using regex metacharacters—findTheBaddies.pl

```perl
#!perl

while(<>){
   print if /S.*n/;
}
```

Notice the use of two special metacharacters, the . (dot) and the * (Kleene Star), within our main match expression. Before we explain how these are being used, let's see what we get:

```
$ perl findTheBaddies.pl listOfPowers.txt

Saruman
Sauron
```

The results seem appropriate, but notice how we failed to pick up *Smaug* or anything else that *nearly* matches. So how are these two metacharacters combining? Before we answer this question, let's examine all of Perl's main regex metacharacters in Table C-3.

Table C-3. Perl's main regular expression metacharacters

Metacharacter	Description
\...	The backslash giveth and the backslash taketh away. If the next character is special (for example, a $, *, or even another \), the backslash character takes away its specialness and makes it just another character (so \\ means "match a single backslash"). If the backslashed character is ordinary (e.g., a straightforward "n", "b", or "w" keyboard letter), \ usually gives it special meaning (\n for a newline character).
...|...	This is used for alternation, matching either one expression or the other, as in: *m/Merry|Pippin/* for a match that contains either "Merry" or "Pippin."
(...)	This has two concurrent meanings: It can group various matches, usually in combination with the alternation just shown, as in *m/(Sam|Frodo|Gollum) bore the ring in Mordor/.* At the same time, it will store or return whatever is found within the brackets, usually into backreference variables, so we can make use of this information elsewhere in the program (we'll say more about this later).
[...]	The character class brackets allow you to provide a range of match characters, so *[abc]fg* can match *afg, bfg* or *cfg.* You can also use a character class range, so that *[0-9]* is equivalent to *[0123456789].*
[^...]	A slight variation on *[...].* If the first character encountered within a character class is a ∧ (caret), it negates the whole thing. So *[^abc]fg* will match *dfg, efg,* and every character in the known Unicode universe preceding the *fg* string, *except* an "*a*" or a "*b*" or a "*c.*"
*	The Kleene Star—match the preceding item zero or more times, up to infinity. See the Kleene Star and the other regex multipliers at work in Figure C-4.
+	Match the preceding item one or more times.

Table C-3. Perl's main regular expression metacharacters (continued)

Metacharacter	Description
?	Match the preceding item zero times or once only.
{Exact Count}	Match the preceding item an exact number of times. For instance, *a{4}* means "Find exactly four *"a"* characters within the pattern, so they look like *aaaa."*
{Min,}	(Note the comma.) Find at least the specified number of the previous item, up to infinity. For example, *a{3,}* greedily matches *aaa, aaaa, aaaaa,* and so on. (We'll say more about "greediness" shortly.) Incidentally *{0,}* is exactly equivalent to *, the Kleene Star shorthand version, and *{1,}* is exactly equivalent to +.
{Min, Max}	Match an exact range of the preceding item. For instance, *a{4,5}* fails to match *a, aa, aaa,* but will completely match *aaaa* and *aaaaa.* Under greedy conditions, it will match the first five characters of *aaaaaa, aaaaaaa,* and so on. The *{0,1}* construct is exactly equivalent to the *?* metacharacter above, as you can see in Figure C-4.
^	Anchors the beginning of a string, and sometimes follows the *\n* newline character depending on the */m* match suffix discussed later. This means that *m/^Angmar/* will match "Angmar was of old the realm of the Witch-King" but fails to match "The Witch-King of Angmar."
$	Anchors the end of a string before any *\n* newline, if there is one. It can occasionally precede other embedded *\n* newlines, depending on suffixes (described later). This means that *m/Minas Morgul$/* will match "Dreadful was the vale of Minas Morgul," but refuses to match "Minas Morgul was once the fair moonlit valley of Minas Ithil."
.	The dot character matches any character except the *\n* newline, although this behavior can be modified slightly with the */s* suffix, as we'll see later.

To answer our original question, we can now see how the */S.*n/* match worked its magic on the *listOfPowers.txt* file:

1. It looked for a capital *"S."* (No prizes so far.)
2. The . dot character then meant it looked for any character, except *\n* newlines, and the * meant it looked for zero or more of them.
3. The regex then looked for an *"n"* to terminate the name, which ensured that *Smaug* was pulled at the last hurdle because it didn't comply with this condition.
4. Only *Saruman* and *Sauron* matched all three of these requirements in full, with *aruma* and *auro* matching the *.** multiplier.

In the following sections, we'll examine how we can further refine such munge requirements to search for other fuzzy data, while keeping track of what falls within our fuzzy requirements and what falls outside them.

Character Class Shortcuts

If you've ever used character class ranges with an older version of *grep*, you may have used a command like the following one to find words of at least one character in length:

```
$ grep '[a-zA-Z0-9][a-zA-Z0-9]*' myFile.txt
```

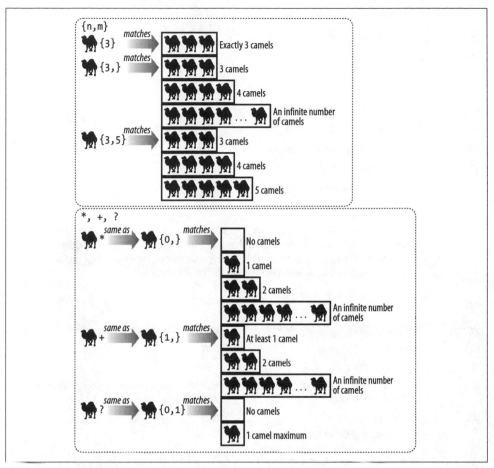

Figure C-4. Variable numeric character requirements

This seems reasonable enough, and the ranges are nice because they've cut out the typing in of many alphabetical characters. But this is still too much work for a Perl-head; a similar match in Perl would involve just three keystrokes:

```
\w+
```

There are many other such regex shortcuts in Perl for other character class ranges. To illustrate these, including \w, we'll first detail some double-quotish characters which are recognized within Perl regexes, in Table C-4. Table C-5 will then display some of the best-known character class shortcuts. (Fortunately, many of these have now made their way into more modern versions of *grep* and *egrep*, too.)

Table C-4. Escaped characters

Escape	Description
\0	Null character
\a	Alarm (often producing an OS bell ring)

Table C-4. Escaped characters (continued)

Escape	Description
\e	Escape character
\f	Form feed
\n	Newline
\r	Return
\t	Tab
\cX	Control character, where Control-C is \cC
\N{NAME}	Named character, such as \N{greek:Alpha}
\x{abcd}	Hexadecimal character, where \x{263a} is a smiley face

 The . (dot) character is normally used to represent any character, except \n newline. However, it has no such special meaning within character classes. Therefore [.]+ literally means one or more . dot characters, such as full-stops, periods, or decimal points.

Table C-5. Character class shortcuts

Symbol	Description	Fully expanded version
\d	Any digit.	[0–9]
\D	Anything except a digit.	[^0–9]
\s	Whitespace, including spaces, tabs, line feeds, form feeds and newlines.	[\t\n\r\f] (Note that the first character in this range is a single ordinary spacebar character.)
\S	Non-whitespace.	[^ \t\n\r\f]
	(You have to be careful when using shortcuts such as \s and \S. They can easily look like each other within large code blocks, or even within small ones.)	
\w	A word, or alphanumeric character (includes underscores, typically found in file names).	[a–zA–Z0–9_] (Note that this also depends upon your locale settings—for example, ö in a German locale is matched by \w; see *perldoc perllocale* for more details.)
\W	Non-word character.	[^a–zA–Z0–9_]
	(The ends and beginnings of strings, as marked by the ^ and $ string anchors, are often honorary \W characters for the devilish purposes of regexes.)	

Boundaries

In addition to the ^ (caret) and $ (dollar) string anchors, there are two other special boundary assertions commonly used in Perl regexes. These are described in Table C-6.

Table C-6. Positions and boundaries

Symbol	Description
\b	This matches any boundary between a \w word character, and a \W non-word character, in either the \w\W or \W\w order. It is a zero-width assertion and can be seen matching various word boundaries in Figure C-5. For the purposes of \b boundary matches, the ^ and $ anchors count as honorary \W non-word characters.
\B	Simply the opposite of \b. This is the boundary between either a \w\w or \W\W pairing.
\A	This is like a strict ^. It matches at the beginning of the string. We'll see later in this appendix how ^ can also match just after embedded \n characters, if it is used with the /m match suffix. However, \A only matches right at the start of the string, come what may.
\z	Again, this is like a super-strict $. The \z symbol only matches at the end of a string, with or without \n new-lines, and with or without the /m match suffix (described later).
\Z	This usually means the same as $—that is, it comes either before the \n newline at the end of a string, (if there is one) or right at the end (if there isn't). With the /m match suffix, the $ character can then come before \n characters embedded within the string, whereas \Z cannot.

Beware of punctuation within words such as *"Let's"*, as in Figure C-5. Remember that \w is both for alphanumerics and the underscore, but it never covers punctuation marks, such as apostrophes. Sometimes it's better to use matches, such as the following, to pick up words containing punctuation:

    m/\s+\S+\s+/

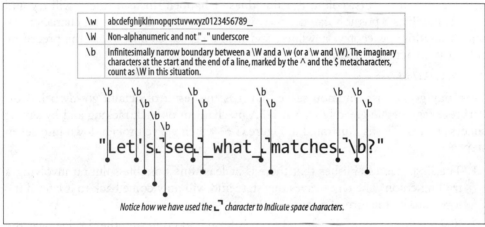

Figure C-5. Word boundaries

This means: "Some spaces, followed by some nonspaces, followed by some more spaces." The sequential non-space characters can be a word containing apostrophes. Notice how it may also be difficult, at first glance, to pick out the difference between the \s and the \S shortcuts.

Greediness

If the first great principle of Perl regexes is the left-most match wins, the second great principle is that by default any match will try to take as much text as it can. More specifically, the mass character quantifiers will always try to grab the maximal possible match. These quantifiers include:

* (or {0,})
+ (or {1,})
? (or {0,1})
{Min,}
{Exact Count}(see Table C-7 for the special case created by this quantifier)
{Min,Max}

Particularly when they're used in combination with the . (dot) character, they will always try to eat as much as they can, unless we tell them otherwise. For instance, let's take a typical line out of an */etc/passwd* file line:

andyd:fruitbat:/home/andyd:dba,apache,users:/bin/ksh

You might expect the substitution *s/.*:/jkstill:/* to produce the following:

jkstill:fruitbat:/home/andyd:dba,apache,users:/bin/ksh

You might have thought the .* would only take the *andyd*, and allow the colon character to match the first colon. But this doesn't happen. Instead, the .* will try and grab as much as it possibly can get away with. Remember that the . dot character can match anything, except \n newlines, and that includes colons. What the preceding substitution actually produces is:

    jkstill:/bin/ksh

This may go against common sense, but it is the result of default *greedy* behavior. Perl regexes operate greedily via the NFA mechanism of backtracking and by saving success states. This is illustrated in Figure C-6, which we've broken down into seven steps:.

1. The first step establishes that there is at least one possible solution involving a trailing colon. The regex saves this state and will only come back to it later if it's forced to by the turn of events.

2. Being greedy, the regex decides to march on and go for another bridge over the river into the enemy's territory. It assigns the colon it has just found to being part of the .* match and moves on until it can (if it's lucky) find a second save state and another colon.

3. Continuing the greedy pattern, the regex has another go to see if it can feed yet more bridge-head territory into the .* multiplier. It finds a third save state.

4. Once again, the regex moves on to greedily acquire a fourth save state. This is the last one it will successfully find, but it has yet to learn this.

5. The regex goes for glory and attempts to acquire a fifth save state, but crashes and burns instead, running out of text and failing to find a fifth colon to complete its target match. It has gone a colon too far.

6. Using the NFA architecture, the regex can now backtrack to the latest save state.

7. It hands this save state result onto the rest of the substitution program, which will then go on to complete the operation by replacing *andyd:fruitbat:/home/ andyd:dba,apache,users:* with *jkstill:*. Mission accomplished.

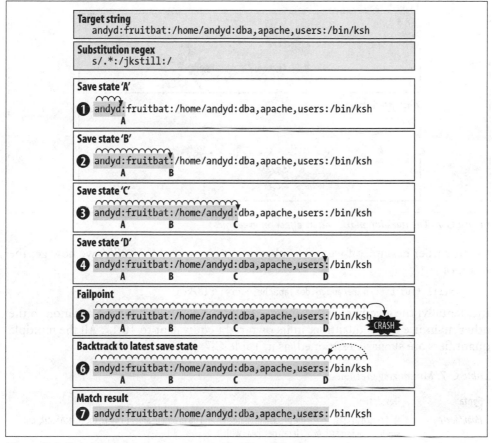

Figure C-6. Greedy matching, save states and backtracking

When you're munging large quantities of data, be sure to take this greedy behavior into account when crafting your regular expressions.

Now that we know how the NFA works on greediness, we can think about the regex pathways that will take up the least amount of work. However, sometimes we would rather avoid this maximally greedy behavior—perhaps we want just the bare minimum. In the case under consideration, all we really wanted to do was to replace *andyd:* with *jkstill:*. So how do we do this? With the multiply useful ? (question mark character), summarized in Figure C-7. What we have in the top portion of Figure C-7 is a maximally greedy regex, which eats *as much* it can, while still ultimately producing the match. In the bottom half, the regex has been limited by the shackles of the extra question mark suffix. It is now a minimalist regex, and will match *as little* as it can to find a successful match. It may be less than happy about this, but what can it do?

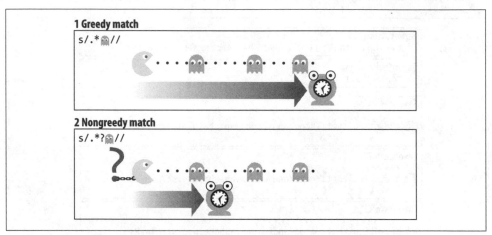

Figure C-7. The question mark and its effect on greediness

In our earlier example, if we use a substitution regex of *s/.*?:/jkstill:/*, we now get the result of:

```
jkstill:fruitbat:/home/andyd:dba,apache,users:/bin/ksh
```

Incidentally, the greediness-restraining ? (question mark) suffix is, in addition to the other main use of ?, a quantifier in its own right equivalent to {0,1}. All the multiple quantifiers are similarly restrained, as in Table C-7.

Table C-7. Minimizing greediness

Syntax	Description
{Min,Max}?	Will match at least *Min* of the preceding character, and up to *Max* in order to make the match work, but will try to only match *Min* if it can get away with it.
{Min,}?	Will match at least *Min* of the preceding character, and up to infinity of them in order to make the match work, but again will try to only match *Min*.
{Exact Count}?	Although minimization is logically available here, this match always has to get an *Exact Count* anyway, regardless of whether it's greedy or otherwise. There may be processing implications by making this non-greedy, but these constantly vary depending on whatever else you're doing.
*?	From zero to infinity of the preceding character, and as close as possible to zero, to make the match work.

Table C-7. Minimizing greediness (continued)

Syntax	Description
+?	From one to infinity of the preceding characters, and as close as possible to one, to make the match work.
??	This match will try to find zero to one of the preceding character, but will prefer to find zero characters, if that will make the match work.

Interpolated Strings

Variables found within Perl regexes behave similarly to interpolated strings within print statements. This is because of two levels of parsing:

1. The first parse interpolates, or expands, any possible variables.

2. The second parse works out the actual regular expression, and how to process it.

For instance:

```
$orginal_Gandalf = "Olorin";

$wizard_String = "Olorin or Mithrandir? ";

if ($wizard_String =~ m/$original_Gandalf/)
{
    print "Wizard found! <|:-))))"
}
```

This interpolates the *$original_Gandalf* variable inside the match, which expands to *Olorin* and then processes the regex on the *$wizard_String* input data to see if it contains *Olorin*. The resultant output is:

```
Wizard found! <|:-))))
```

However, although regexes can generally be treated in the same way double-quoted interpolated strings are treated, this varies slightly with the special use of metacharacters. For instance, Example C-2 will fail.

Example C-2. almostInterpolated.pl—Checking interpolation in regexes

```
#!perl -w

use strict;

my $regex_pattern = "[*Casablanca";

my $input_film = "[*Casablanca";

if ($input_film =~ m/$regex_pattern/)
{
    print "Is the Maltese Falcon just as good?\n";
}
```

If we run *almostInterpolated.pl*, we get a rude awakening:

```
$ perl almostInterpolated.pl
Unmatched [ before HERE mark in regex m/[ << HERE *Casablanca/ at almostInterpolated.
pl line 10.
```

This is because [is a special regex metacharacter for character classes, as described in Table C-3, which needs a matching] dancing partner. Because we're looking for the [square bracket opener as an actual literal within the string, we need to backslash it to escape its special meaning. Fortunately, we can avoid pasting backslashes everywhere into our pattern. We can use the *quotemeta( )* built-in function instead. What this does is return the input string value with all nonalphanumeric characters, including the underscore, backslashed for our convenience:

```
my $regex_pattern = quotemeta('[*Casablanca');

my $input_film = "[*Casablanca";

if ($input_film =~ m/$regex_pattern/)
{
    print "Is the Maltese Falcon just as good?\n";
}
```

Now we get:

```
$ perl almostInterpolated.pl

Is the Maltese Falcon just as good?
```

Scalar or List Context Results

A match in a scalar setting will generally produce either a 1 for true (if it finds a match) or an empty string "" for false (if it fails to find the required match):

```
# Scalar context on the LHS, left hand side.

$my_string = "Galadriel and Celeborn";

# Note below how the =~ symbol takes precedence over the = symbol.
# What happens in the following, is that the $my_string =~ m/Galad/
# operation takes place, and then the $result = (match operation)
# comes second.

$result = $my_string =~ m/Galad/;

print "Expecting 1: result: >", $result, "<\n";

$result = $my_string =~ /Legolas and Gimli/;

print "Expecting Empty String: result: >", $result, "<\n";
```

Fingers crossed, we get the results we're after:

```
Expecting 1: result: >1<
Expecting Empty String: result: ><
```

Excellent. This behavior of returning 1 or "" differs if Perl detects that a list array is required on the left-hand side of the equation (i.e., whether it is in scalar context or list context). In this case, if anything within a match is marked for storage with parentheses, these values are copied across into the list array elements on the left-hand side. If no valid match is found, these array elements are left empty:

```
# Array context on the LHS

$my_string = "Galadriel and Celeborn";

# Once again, the =~ operation takes precedence over the = operation,
# and the wantarray() function detects that a list is required on the
# left-hand side.

($queen, $king) = $my_string =~ m/(Galad\w+)\s+\w+\s+(\w+)/;

# Valid results expected

print "Value Expected, Queen: >", $queen, "<\n";
print "Value Expected, King: >", $king, "<\n";

($queen, $king) = $my_string =~ m/(Legolas\w+)\s+\w+\s+(\w+)/;

print "Empty String Expected, Queen: >", $queen, "<\n";
print "Empty String Expected, King: >", $king, "<\n";
```

When executed, this provides:

```
Value Expected, Queen: >Galadriel<
Value Expected, King: >Celeborn<
Empty String Expected, Queen: ><
Empty String Expected, King: ><
```

This is a bit fiddly, but if you work through a few examples of your own, it should begin to make sense.

Alternation and Memory

We promised earlier, when we were discussing list contexts and the internal use of the *wantarray()* function, that we'd cover backreferences. So what's the mechanism behind backreference memory storage?

Capturing backreferences

As we explained earlier, backreferences are made possible by the architecture of the NFA engine, which always leaves a ball of string back into the labyrinth. Think of the bracketing as paired knots in the string, which tell the regular expression what to retrieve. We can see this in action in Figure C-8, where we're using backreferences to store the noted values in special built-in variables, rather than returning them as part of a list. Note also the use of the /i regex suffix in Figure C-8, which ignores the alphabetic case of the target string under scrutiny.

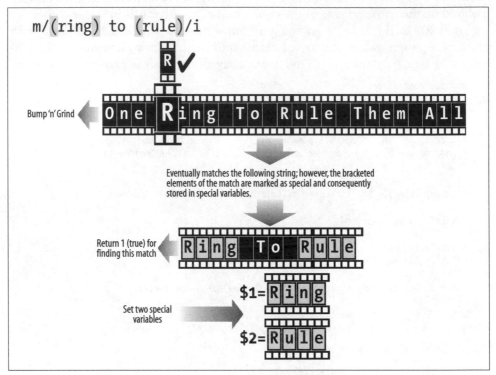

Figure C-8. Capturing backreferences and ignoring case

Note the following:

- These special built-in variables start from $1, and move up to $n, depending on how many bracketed elements you have (which always start from the left).

- This is why we are prohibited from starting the name of a normal Perl scalar value with a number. Such names are reserved for built-in regex backreferences.

- A value, like $1, will continue to exist within your program until another regular expression is executed that successfully matches. (Such values are dynamically scoped until the end of the innermost block, until the end of the current file, until the *eval* statement, or until the next successful match, whichever comes first.)

- You can nest your brackets as much as you dare.

Let's run through Example C-3, with a range from $1 to $12.

Example C-3. Capturing multi-bracketed values—roundDozen.pl

```perl
#!perl -w

# Start with a large match, involving twelve captures

$_ = "abcdefghijklmnopqrstuvwxyz";

# a b c d e f g h i j k l m n o p q r s t u v w x y z

m/(.(.(.(.(.(.(.(.(.(.(.(.)).).).).).).).).).).).)/;
# 1 2 3 4 5 6 7 8 9 t e w w e t 9 8 7 6 5 4 3 2 1  backreferences

# t = ten, e = eleven, w = twelve

print '$1  :', $1,  "\n";
print '$2  :', $2,  "\n";
print '$3  :', $3,  "\n";
print '$4  :', $4,  "\n";
print '$5  :', $5,  "\n";
print '$6  :', $6,  "\n";
print '$7  :', $7,  "\n";
print '$8  :', $8,  "\n";
print '$9  :', $9,  "\n";
print '$10 :', $10, "\n";
print '$11 :', $11, "\n";
print '$12 :', $12, "\n";

# Now let's go for a small match, which only fills
# up $1, $2 and $3

$_ = "1234567890";

# 1 2 3 4 5 6 7 8 9 0

m/(.(.(.).).)/;
# 1 2 3 3 2 1 backreferences

print '$1  :', $1,  "\n";
print '$2  :', $2,  "\n";
print '$3  :', $3,  "\n";
print '$4  :', $4,  "\n";
print '$5  :', $5,  "\n";
print '$6  :', $6,  "\n";
print '$7  :', $7,  "\n";
print '$8  :', $8,  "\n";
print '$9  :', $9,  "\n";
print '$10 :', $10, "\n";
print '$11 :', $11, "\n";
print '$12 :', $12, "\n";
```

Running this script produces the following results:

```
$ perl roundDozen.pl
$1  :abcdefghijklmnopqrstuvw
```

```
$2  :bcdefghijklmnopqrstuv
$3  :cdefghijklmnopqrstu
$4  :defghijklmnopqrst
$5  :efghijklmnopqrs
$6  :fghijklmnopqr
$7  :ghijklmnopq
$8  :hijklmnop
$9  :ijklmno
$10 :jklmn
$11 :klm
$12 :l
$1  :12345
$2  :234
$3  :3
Use of uninitialized value in print at roundDozen.pl line 32.
$4  :
Use of uninitialized value in print at roundDozen.pl line 33.
$5  :
Use of uninitialized value in print at roundDozen.pl line 34.
$6  :
Use of uninitialized value in print at roundDozen.pl line 35.
$7  :
Use of uninitialized value in print at roundDozen.pl line 36.
$8  :
Use of uninitialized value in print at roundDozen.pl line 37.
$9  :
Use of uninitialized value in print at roundDozen.pl line 38.
$10 :
Use of uninitialized value in print at roundDozen.pl line 39.
$11 :
Use of uninitialized value in print at roundDozen.pl line 40.
$12 :
```

Note the following:

- On the first set of printouts, we got $1 to $12 printed out neatly, following the left-to-right bracketing rule.

- However, on the second print run, after the second regular expression the values, $1, $2, and $3 printed out OK, but $4 to $12 are now completely undefined.

- You may have expected $4 to $12 to remain the same as they were after the first regex, but to keep a logically consistent picture, the entire board is swept clean if a successful match is found. As soon as you run another matching regex, the whole $1 to $n shooting match begins again, all the way up to infinity.

You can also use backreferences within the actual matches. The rule is that if these are used on the left side of the substitution or within an ordinary match, you must use the \1 style notation (instead of $1). On the other hand, on the right-hand side of the substitution you can use the straight *$1* notation. For instance, you might be trying to replace all double-word typos in a piece of text with equivalent single words:

```
#!perl -w

# Our input string has two double-word typos,
# "work work", and "was was".  We'd like to remove both of them.

$_ = "Ludwig von Mises greatest work work was Human Action, " .
    "and F.A. Hayek's greatest work was was the Road to Serfdom.";

# On the left side of the substitution, to pick up
# the double-word, we have to use \1 in the match,
# and on the right side substitution we use $1 to replace
# both instances of the same word with a single string value.

s#\b(\w+)\b\s+\1\b#$1#g; # Substitute double-word typos

print;
```

Note the following:

- We've used the # character to delineate the substitution, to prevent eye-strain among all those shooting-star slashes.
- We've also used the global suffix, g, which we'll talk about shortly, to ensure that we substitute the first match found, *work work*, and the second one too, *was was*.
- The use of the \b word boundary ensures that we're only picking up real individual words, and avoiding phrase combinations such as:

      the theocracy
      lathe the
      bathe their

Our solution code produces the following output text:

```
Ludwig von Mises greatest work was Human Action, and F.A. Hayek's
greatest work was the Road to Serfdom.
```

Match Suffixes

We'll complete this appendix by looking at how we can alter the operation of regexes with the various suffixes listed in Table C-8, including /g used in the double-word substitution in the previous section.

Table C-8. Match and substitution suffix modifiers

Suffix	Description
/i	Matches ignore alphabetic case, so m/http/i will pick up *http, Http, HTTp,* and *HTTP,* as well as every other possible combination of these letters.
/g	Matches: Used in matches for globally parsing strings into sub-units.
	Substitutions: Used within substitutions for globally replacing all matches found, as well as the first one found in the left-most position.

Table C-8. Match and substitution suffix modifiers (continued)

Suffix	Description
/s	Most often used with data that contains embedded \n newline characters. The /s suffix allows the . (dot) character to match \n newlines in addition to everything else. All input therefore effectively becomes a single line. (Use this suffix with care, especially in combination with greedy multipliers.)
/m	Often used in combination with /s. The /m suffix modifies the behavior of the ^ and $ end anchors. Instead of being fixed to the ends of the match, /m allows these anchors to occur wrapped around \n newlines, with $ coming just before \n, and ^ coming just after \n. This allows a single-line data entry to be treated as multiple lines. An extended example of this, in combination with /s, can be found in Figure C-9.
/o	There are usually two parse operations associated with each regular expression. The first expands any embedded variables that may make up the matches and replacements. The second then computes the actual regular expression. Both of these operations possess a processing hit, which you may wish to avoid on a regex within a million-row loop. To compile a regex only once, the first time it is used you can use the /o suffix.
/e	Only used within substitutions. This evaluates the replacement on the right-hand side, as if it were an ordinary code expression.
/x	Used to make regexes clearer. This suffix ignores most whitespace, allowing indentation, and also allows comments within the match pattern.

/i—Ignore Case

The /i suffix simply makes the match ignore the alphabetic case on the match side of the equation. Consider the following example.

We have the following file to process:

```
http
Http
HTtp
HTTp
HTTP
hTTP
htTP
httP
```

We'll work this through following code snippet, which has yet to use the /i suffix:

```
while(<>){

    print if /http/;    # No /i suffix

}
```

This processes the file to produce:

```
http
```

Now we'll change the code snippet to include the /i suffix:

```
while(<>){

    print if /http/i;   # /i suffix in place

}
```

The code now totally ignores case, and prints the following list:

```
http
Http
HTtp
HTTp
HTTP
hTTP
htTP
httP
```

/g—Global Matching

When used with the match operator, the global suffix /g will gradually break down a string into parsed components, as shown in Example C-4.

Example C-4. Global matching—parseGlobal.pl

```
#!perl -w

$_ = "/usr/local/apache/conf/httpd.conf";

while (m#/([\w.]+)#g){

    print $1, "\n";

}
```

When executed, *parseGlobal.pl* breaks down the input string into its wordy components:

```
$ perl parser.pl
usr
local
apache
conf
httpd.conf
```

Let's look at some examples of global replacements:

- The global suffix is more often used with substitution, as with its *sed* program ancestor, to replace *all* matches found. This usually occurs in the following way:

  ```
  s/$match/$replacement/g
  ```

- The following code snippet has yet to use the global suffix to deal with the two major fortresses of Morgoth, Sauron's old master, in the First Age of Middle-Earth:

  ```
  $_ = "Angband Angband Angband";

  s/Angband/Utumno/;

  print;
  ```

- When executed, this returns:

  Utumno Angband Angband

- The following code is identical, except for the addition of the /g suffix:

```
$_ = "Angband Angband Angband";

s/Angband/Utumno/g;

print;
```

- This returns:

  Utumno Utumno Utumno

/s & /m—Single- and Multiple-Line Matching

The /s and /m suffixes are often used in combination, especially when many lines of data have been packed into a single scalar variable. Their combined use can best be seen in Figure C-9.

/o—Compile Only Once

To avoid recompiling regexes unnecessarily, you can use the /o suffix. A typical usage of /o is shown in the following example:

1. We have the following constantly changing diary file:

```
Wed: Mow Lawn
Mon: Sell Donuts
Sun: Meet President
Sat: Save World
Tue: This must be Belgium
Thu: Shred Evidence
Sun: Change Oil on Car
Fri: Buy Monkey Nuts
```

2. Every day we run the following program to work out our daily routine. This had been taking three nanoseconds too long, so we added the /o suffix to get the regex compile time down a bit, as the regex needs compiling only once within the loop:

```
#!perl -w

@time_array = localtime;
@day_array = ('Sun', 'Mon', 'Tue', 'Wed', 'Thu', 'Fri', 'Sat');

$today_match = $day_array[ $time_array[6] ];

print "Appointments for ", $today_match, "day\n\n";

while(<>){
```

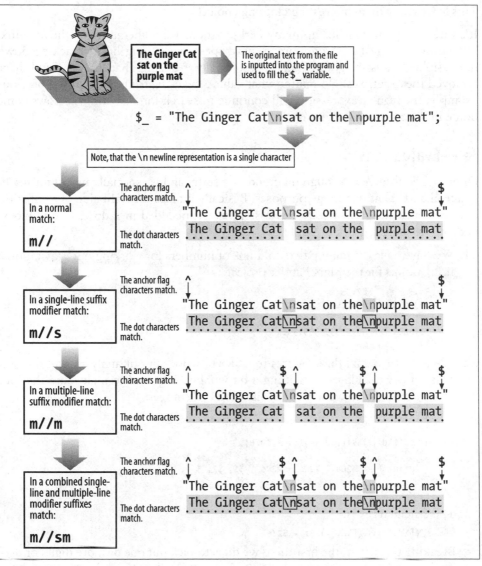

Figure C-9. Single- and multiple-line suffixes

```
        print if /$today_match/o;

    }
```

3. Today happens to be Sunday, so let's find out what we'll be doing later by executing the program on the appointments file:

```
Appointments for Sunday

Sun: Meet President
Sun: Change Oil on Car
```

This leaves us with an interesting clothing choice!

It's often tempting to spice up many Perl programs via a liberal use of the /o suffix, but beware. Many Perl programmers have spent many long hours tracking down impossible "I-must-be-going-mad" bugs, finally realizing that they should have removed the /o suffixes. No matter what value *$today_match* goes to in the previous example, the regular expression will continue to search for *Sun* until the cows come home in the twenty-third century.

/e—Evaluations

Often overlooked, /e is a rough diamond of a suffix and is especially useful for mathematical and scientific munge purposes. Basically it takes the right side of a substitution and evaluates it as a code expression, as if embedded in a do{...} code block. Let's run through a quick example:

1. We have a file containing two columns of numbers for working out gravitational firing points for the Mars Lander project:

   ```
   34.5        87.33
   99300.3002  459020
   17777.3     2
   32.880993   999999999999.3314
   13.4        26.42140
   ```

2. We need to add all these figures together to work out our analysis, and the buttons on our calculator are getting a bit wobbly. We need to make sure that our results are right, so we write the following Perl snippet:

   ```
   while(<>){

       s/([\d.]+)\s+([\d.]+)/$1 + $2/e;

       printf("-> %20s + %20s = %20s", $1, $2, $_);

   }
   ```

3. The crucial regex is:

   ```
   s/([\d.]+)\s+([\d.]+)/$1 + $2/e
   ```

   Breaking this down, the first thing we do is to pick out one or more digits or decimal points, and save these into *$1* via the use of backreference brackets:[*]

   ```
   ([\d.]+)
   ```

   We then look for one or more spaces, so we can throw them away:

   ```
   \s+
   ```

---

[*] Remember that . (dot) characters within class ranges lose their specialness, and become mere full-stops or decimal points.

We now look for a second number, which may contain a decimal point. We save this into *$2*:

```
([\d.]+)
```

The */e* suffix then wraps a *do{...}* block around the *$1 + $2* expression. Logically, the expression now looks like this:

```
s/([\d.]+)\s+([\d.]+)/ do { $1 + $2 } /e
```

4. The expression can now be evaluated. We substitute the sum into the *$_* variable, which previously consisted of the two numbers separated by spaces. Running the code snippet over the file, we get the following results.

```
->          34.5 +           87.33 =          121.83
->     99300.3002 +          459020 =     558320.3002
->        17777.3 +               2 =         17779.3
->      32.880993 + 999999999999.3314 = 1000000000032.21
->           13.4 +         26.42140 =         39.8214
```

We can now begin our Mars Lander rocket firing pattern analysis with confidence.

You may think */e* is pretty clever, but it gets better. You can wrap unending amounts of *eval{...}* commands around the original *do{...}* code block by adding an extra evaluation command to the suffix, */ee*. This will take whatever the first expression evaluation gives you, and then evaluate it, so that the following two lines are equivalent:

```
s/PATTERN/CODE/ee
s/PATTERN/eval(CODE)/e
```

Let's work through another example to cover it:

1. This time we have the following three-column file:

```
134.5  + 87.33
99.3   - 45.3
17.3   + 2
100.03 - 4.12
100    + 9
```

2. Notice that the mathematical operation we wish to use on the two numbers is the second column within the file. Unfortunately, we only find out what each one is when we're actually processing the line. We therefore have to select this operator out from the file, build up the code string, and then evaluate its outcome before printing the formatted results. We do this via the following code snippet:

```
while(<>){

    s/([\d.]+)\s+([+-])\s+([\d.]+)/"\$result = $1 $2 $3"/ee;

    printf("-> %8s %1s %-8s = %9s\n", $1, $2, $3, $result);

}
```

3. Let's break down the regular expression:

```
s/([\d.]+)\s+([+-])\s+([\d.]+)/"\$result = $1 $2 $3"/ee
```

On the left side, we once again store the first number into *$1*:

```
([\d.]+)
```

We then throw away some spaces on either side of the mathematical operation we wish to perform.* The calculation will either be an addition or a subtraction, and will be stored in *$2*:

```
\s+([+-])\s+
```

We then pick up the second number and store it into *$3*:

```
([\d.]+)
```

4. On the right-hand side of the regex, we build up a string that will perform the required operation upon our two numbers, and then store the calculated number into the *$result* variable. We've backslashed *$result* to prevent it from being interpreted as an empty string, within the string evaluation:

```
"\$result = $1 $2 $3"
```

This code is then evaluated via the *eval{...}* double-e suffix:

```
/ee
```

5. The results can now be printed out:

```
->     134.5 + 87.33   =     221.83
->      99.3 - 45.3    =         54
->      17.3 + 2       =       19.3
->    100.03 - 4.12    =      95.91
->       100 + 9       =        109
```

/x—The Expressive Modifier

You may have noticed that some of the regexes we've talked about were starting to get rather long and trickier to follow until we broke them down across several lines. This is where /x steps out from behind the curtain.

Some years ago, Jeffrey Friedl, author of *Mastering Regular Expressions*, was replying to a regex question on *comp.lang.perl.misc* when he pretty-printed a very large regular expression to make it easier to read. Larry Wall saw the post and liked it so much that he immediately added the /x suffix to Perl. This made it possible for everyone to create indented regexes containing embedded comments.

Essentially, within /x regexes you can use any amount of whitespace, and the regex will ignore it. You can also put comments within the regex, prefixed by the usual Perl # hash comment character. If you do want to include spaces or # hashes within the

---

* Notice how we have the hyphen, indicating the minus sign, as the second character inside the class range *[+-]*. This prevents Perl from marking it as some kind of a class range.

actual regex, you merely backslash them, or use the \s escape for spaces. Let's work through a regex problem and see how we can help solve it more clearly with the assistance of /x:

We have an Oracle PL/SQL program file, *mars_rocket.sql*, which has some C-style comments within it which we wish to remove. There is a reason for this, but it's classified:

```
/*
|| Create this procedure to fire the positioning rockets when
|| we approach the Martian surface.
*/
CREATE OR REPLACE PROCEDURE mars_rocket (v_thrust_in IN NUMBER)
AS
    v_momentum NUMBER; /* Adjustment factor */
    v_twist NUMBER;    /* Rotational factor */
BEGIN
    /*
    || Loop and then fire.
    */
    LOOP
        EXIT WHEN v_thrust_in = 0;
        v_twist := v_thrust_in + mars_env.gravi_bind;    /* Newton :-) */
        v_momentum := v_thrust_in + mars_env.mass_emc; /* Einstein :-) */

        mars_env.fire_retros(v_twist, v_momentum); /* Fire in the hole */

    END LOOP;

    /* Fired and forgotten. */

END mars_rocket;
/
```

Example C-5 shows our program to remove these comments, making use of the /x suffix.

Example C-5. Removing C-style comments with the /x suffix—xErase.pl

```perl
#!perl -w

# Open the target file, and the target.

open(MARS_IN, $ARGV[0]) or die "Could not read $ARGV[0]";
open(MARS_OUT, ">$ARGV[1]")
    or die "Could not open $ARGV[1], to write to";

# Slurp the entire file

$/ = undef; # Houston, - Undefining the input record separator.
```

```
$_ = <MARS_IN>; # Entire file slurped into
                # the single default $_ variable.

# The main substitution begins:
s{
                        # The search pattern brackets are {},
                        # and the replacement brackets are [].
                        # We're removing all C-style comments, so
                        # the replacement is completely empty.
    /\*                 # We're looking for the C-style comment
                        # start marker.  We have to escape the
                        # Kleene Star, to make it a normal asterisk.
    .*?                 # We're then looking for any character,
                        # including the \n newline, though we're
                        # doing this minimally, to avoid stripping
                        # out everything between the first comment
                        # and the last.
    \*/                 # We then find the first C-style comment
                        # terminator.  Once again, we've had to
                        # backslash the asterisk.
}
[]gsx;
# The gsx suffixes mean:
#
# g: We're replacing every match we find within the file.
# s: Because we've slurped the entire file into a single variable,
#    including \n newlines, we need to treat the entire thing as a
#    single line, so . dot will match \n newlines, and catch comments
#    which spread over more than one line.
# x: The "expressive" syntax means we can break down a potentially
#    confusing regex, over many lines, and use comments :-)

# Now print out the new file without C-style comments and close down.

print MARS_OUT $_;

close(MARS_IN);
close(MARS_OUT);
```

Because of the /x suffix within the program, we can now fully expand the match pattern with white space, and pepper it with plenty of comments. This will help our *Marsonauts* figure out what our regex is trying to do when they come to maintain the script halfway through on the trip out.

Now we test run the program, to create the *mars_bar.sql* output file:

```
$ perl xErase.pl mars_rocket.sql mars_bar.sql
```

The *mars.bar.sql* output file has now had all of its C-style comments removed:

```
CREATE OR REPLACE PROCEDURE mars_rocket (v_thrust_in IN NUMBER)
AS
    v_momentum NUMBER;
    v_twist NUMBER;
BEGIN

    LOOP
        EXIT WHEN v_thrust_in = 0;
        v_twist := v_thrust_in + mars_env.gravi_bind;
        v_momentum := v_thrust_in + mars_env.mass_emc;

        mars_env.fire_retros(v_twist, v_momentum);

    END LOOP;


END mars_rocket;
/
```

We can almost see Tom Hanks, getting excited about this in the follow-up movie.

Splitting Up is Easy To Do

As promised, we need to dissect the *split* operator, which basically splits up strings into array lists with the following differing input patterns:

```
split /PATTERN/, EXPRESSION, LIMIT
split /PATTERN/, EXPRESSION
split /PATTERN/
split
```

The operator takes a regex */PATTERN/*, and then splits the *EXPRESSION* string value by it into a list (usually an array). If *LIMIT* is specified, the maximum size of the list will be this value; otherwise, the list will be as long as it needs to be. For instance:

```
@a = split /:/, "andyd:banana:/bin/ksh:dba";
print scalar @a, "\n"; # Size of array
print "@a", "\n";      # Prints interpolated array
```

This splits on the *:* (colon) character, and will produce the following output:

```
4
andyd banana /bin/ksh dba
```

On the other hand, with *LIMIT* defined, the following keeps the split down to just three elements:

```
@a = split /:/, "andyd:banana:/bin/ksh:dba", 3;
print scalar @a, "\n"; # Size of array
print "@a", "\n";      # Prints interpolated array
```

Notice how the *LIMIT* value of *3* above changes the output below, retaining the : colon within the third and last element:

```
3
andyd banana /bin/ksh:dba
```

If *EXPRESSION* is omitted, the current value contained within *$_* is used. If */PAT-TERN/* itself is omitted, the regex split pattern assumed is /\s+/, for a split on any amount of white space. This is particularly useful for splitting up columnar output:

```
$_ = "-rw-r--r--   1 jkstill 766  22:49 sqlnet.log";
@a = split;              # => split /\s+/, $_;
print scalar @a, "\n"; # Size of array
print "@a", "\n";       # Prints interpolated array
```

This produces the following interpolated output, showing the size of the new *@a* array and then its six discrete elements:

```
6
-rw-r--r-- 1 jkstill 766 22:49 sqlnet.log
```

This appendix barely touches upon Perl's regular expression capabilities. There is much more to discover. (The Camel and Owl books are good places to start, as is the online *perldoc perlre* command.) Nobody ever stops learning about regexes. Just when you think you possess a complete knowledge, another little wrinkle turns up. This is especially true today with the growing use of Unicode. But hey, where would life be if every day were utterly predictable? As Mithrandir said to Sam, Merry, and Pippin at the Grey Havens, on the last day of Middle-Earth's Third Age:

> Well, here at last, dear friends, on the shores of the Sea comes the end of our fellowship in Middle-Earth. Go in peace! I will not say: do not weep; for not all regexes are an evil.

The Essential Guide to Perl Data Munging

Oracle DBAs spend a great deal of time handling data that for one reason or another needs to be cleaned, transformed, and/or formatted. They need to fill Oracle data warehouses with customer data from multiple sources, import data into Oracle databases from non-Oracle data streams, and convert and format source material of all kinds. Whether it's an XML stream from a web page, a SQL*Loader feed from a telecom switch, or a snapshot transfer from another database, DBAs must ensure that these data transfers are clean, accurate, and timely. Unfortunately, the raw data they're given to work with is often dirty, inaccurate, behind schedule, and unfit for SQL*Loader. This is a job for Perl and its wonderful world of data munging!

Data munging, the process of transforming data as it is transferred from one place to another, is a topic that is increasingly important for Oracle DBAs to understand. It is also an operation that Perl is particularly good at. Perl DBI's innate ability to deal with multiple database types simultaneously also makes the transfer of data from one database to another as simple as lining up dominoes!

This appendix presents the basics of data munging and illustrates a typical data-munging operation—importing a MySQL data stream into an Oracle database, transforming it as necessary. We'll also describe the many Perl data-munging modules that you can download from CPAN and use in conjunction with Oracle databases. We'll examine these modules in several major categories:

Numeric modules

> The modules in this category deal with numeric data and handle mathematical operations used in data munging. We'll pay special attention to the very useful *Number::Format* module.

Date modules

> The modules in this category deal with the special requirements of dates and their formatting and conversion. Because speed is often important in data munging, we'll focus on the very efficient C-based *Date::Calc* module.

Conversion modules

> The modules in this category perform conversions of data from one text format to another. We'll take a special look at *Convert::Recode*, a popular Perl data conversion module that can convert between many different kinds of character sets—for example, between ASCII and EBCDIC mainframe formats.

Perl XML modules

> The modules in this category use XML in performing data munging. We'll focus on the *XML::XMLtoDBMS* module, part of the XML-DBMS middleware project, which is especially effective at transferring variable data between XML documents and relational databases.

What Is Data Munging?

Data munging means taking data that's stored in one format and changing it into another format. The term "data munging" has an ironically mixed etymological origin. The following definition is taken from version 4.3.0 of the Jargon file:[*]

> **munge** /muhnj/ vt.
>
> 1. [derogatory] To imperfectly transform information. 2. A comprehensive rewrite of a routine, data structure or the whole program. 3. To modify data in some way the speaker doesn't need to go into right now or cannot describe succinctly (compare *mumble*). 4. To add *spamblock* to an email address.
>
> This term is often confused with *mung*, which probably was derived from it. However, it also appears the word 'munge' was in common use in Scotland in the 1940s, and in Yorkshire in the 1950s, as a verb, meaning to munch up into a masticated mess, and as a noun, meaning the result of munging something up (the parallel with the *kluge/ kludge* pair is amusing). The OED[†] reports 'munge' as an archaic verb meaning "to wipe (a person's nose)".

Perl, with its excellent text-processing capabilities and high performance, is ideally suited to the task of data munging. In this chapter we'll focus on those munging capabilities most relevant to processing Oracle data. If you want to learn more, we recommend the book, *Data Munging With Perl*, by David Cross (Manning, 2001), which we've found to be invaluable in our own data-munging efforts:

How Data Munging Works

Figure D-1 illustrates graphically how data munging works. As shown in the figure, there are several distinct components and steps involved in a data-munging operation:

---

[*] See *http://www.tuxedo.org/~esr/jargon/html/entry/munge.html*.Used with permission. Available in print, as *The New Hacker's Dictionary*, edited by Eric S. Raymond, 3rd ed. (MIT Press, 1996), *http://www-mitpress. mit.edu*.

[†] Oxford English Dictionary: *http://www.oed.com*

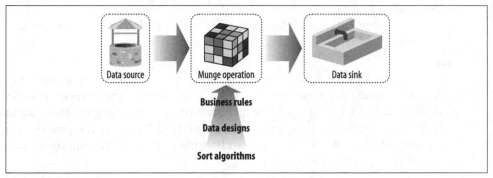

Figure D-1. Basic data-munging principles

The data source

On one side of the munging equation is our data source, or initial wellspring of data. This can be anything from a raw binary file to a stream of digital output from a remote MySQL database. Because Perl was designed from the start to be one of the fastest text-processing languages available, it is able to process and transform data at a very high speed. For this reason, Perl is an ideal language for data munging.

The munge operation

Once the source data is extracted, we begin our munge operation. This operation can be any kind of transformation. We can reverse data, expand data, and recombine data. We can munge it through regular expressions or *sprintf* style commands, as in Appendix C, *The Essential Guide to Regular Expressions*, or we can parse it through complex data trees. Although Perl abounds with such techniques, there are three controlling paradigms:

Sort algorithms

Some of the world's brightest mathematicians have created sort algorithms, and all of these algorithms can be programmed in Perl. The language is also packed with built-in commands, such as *sort* and *map*, and Perl-specific sort techniques, such as the Schwartzian transform.[*]

Data structure and design

The central munge operation must be able to represent the data structures for both the source and the sink (which is essentially the destination), no matter how complex. It must also be able to transform data from one structure into the other. Because Perl's referenced structures are virtually unbounded in extent, Perl is a perfect language for handling such transformations.

---

[*] *http://www.perlfaq.com/cgi-bin/view?view_by_category=sorting*

Business rules

> We can easily encapsulate business rules within Perl modules, and can thus provide reusable, business-specific data transformations.

The data sink

> Our transformed data is finally deposited within a chosen data sink. A data sink works conceptually the same way as a "heat sink" does in engineering; it sucks away the final output from a processing operation. In data munging, this output is the final data generated, rather than the unwanted "heat" in the process. (In engineering, the heat would be generated by a piece of electrical equipment such as a satellite or a laptop computer.)[*]

The Art of Algorithms

There are legions of algorithms used with data munging. The most venerable source for all of them is Donald Knuth's *The Art of Computer Programming,* volumes 1–3 (Addison-Wesley, 1998). Professor Knuth began writing this *magnum opus* in 1962, and it is divided into several volumes as follows:

> *Volume 1: Fundamental Algorithms*
> *Volume 2: Seminumerical Algorithms*
> *Volume 3: Sorting and Searching*

We make use of his *Soundex* algorithm, from volume 3, later in this appendix, and you can check out Professor Knuth's own home page here:

> *http://www-cs-faculty.stanford.edu/~knuth*

Those who already have volumes 1 through 3 will be happy to know that Professor Knuth is also aiming to complete the following volumes:

> *Volume 4: Combinatorial Algorithms*
> *Volume 5: Syntactic Algorithms*

For a more Perl-based approach, check out the following excellent book, written by several of the main authors behind *perldoc*:

> *Mastering Algorithms with Perl,* by Jon Orwant, John Macdonald, and Jarkko Hietaniemi (O'Reilly & Associates, 1999)[†]

Enter the Real World

You may have spotted a problem with Figure D-1. Yes, it's just *too* spotless and clean for the real world. One data source, one munge operation, and one data sink. How

---

[*] Another analogy is that of sinking a putt in golf. Getting the data in the right hole is the final process destination in our data-munging operation.

[†] *http://www.oreilly.com/catalog/maperl*

---

convenient. If you've ever carried out telecom call transfers, share deal transfers, or any other major corporate data transfer, you'll know that data-munging operations often tend to look a bit more like Figure D-2.

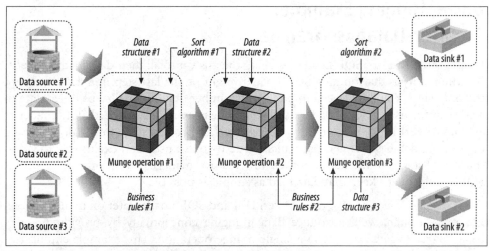

Figure D-2. A real-world data-munging operation

But this is no problem for Perl. Although Figure D-2 is complex, that's just fine, because Perl is also designed to be complex. That allows it to map itself to the real world's necessary complexity. Or, in the words of Mr. Wall himself:[*]

> You have a deep desire to turn the complex into the simple, and Perl is just another tool to help you do that—just as I am using English right now to try to simplify reality. I can use English for that because English is a mess.
>
> This is important, and a little hard to understand. English is useful *because* it's a mess. Since English is a mess, it maps well onto the problem space, which is also a mess, which we call reality. Similarly, Perl was designed to be a mess (though in the nicest of possible ways).
>
> This is counterintuitive, so let me explain. If you've been educated as any kind of an engineer, it has been pounded into your skull that great engineering is simple engineering. We are taught to admire suspension bridges more than railroad trestles. We are taught to value simplicity and beauty. That's nice. I like circles too.
>
> However, complexity is not always the enemy. What's important is not simplicity or complexity, but how you bridge the two.

In the next section, we'll take a look at a real-world Oracle data transfer and illustrate how Perl can help munge the data. We'll later point you towards the many Perl

---

[*] Second State of the Onion address, from the 1998 Perl Conference, *http://www.perl.com/pub/a/1998/08/show/onion.html*

modules that you can use to invoke the specific conversion or formatting operations you need in order to transform your data appropriately.

Data-Munging Example: An Inter-Database Transfer

People often think of SQL*Loader as being the answer to all their data loading needs. But the reality is that running SQL*Loader might be the last step in a data load, not the only step. You might need to perform a number of additional steps to get data in a state fit for use by SQL*Loader. And sometimes you might not need SQL*Loader at all; often, Perl DBI works equally well as the last process stage for finally inserting data into a database. This is particularly true if you've used Perl exclusively to get to that last stage. Why add another process to manage, even one as good as SQL*Loader? Let's keep that data load as simple as possible.

We'll discuss the respective roles of Perl DBI and SQL*Loader later on in more detail. For now though, we'll introduce data munging conceptually by providing a very basic *source-to-sink* example in a single munge operation. This example emphasizes Perl DBI's ability to munge data across from one database type to another within a single Perl script. In this example, MySQL is the source and Oracle is the sink. We're going to munge the data from one datatype (MySQL) into another (Oracle), plus do a little date format munging on the side.

The MySQL Source

We'll assume in this example that the data you are loading into an Oracle database comes from a MySQL database. You can find out more about MySQL at the following sites:

> *http://www.mysql.com*
> *http://sourceforge.net/projects/mysql*

You might also like to check out Jochen Wiedmann's *DBD::mysql* driver; this driver is the interface that allows Perl programs to connect to MySQL databases via Perl DBI:

> *http://www.cpan.org/authors/id/JWIED*

Assuming that a MySQL *test* database has already been created, let's go ahead and create the source data and prepare to transfer it to our Oracle database, *orcl*. These are the steps we followed:

1. We entered MySQL, and switched to the *test* database:

```
$ mysql --user=irish --password=lion
...
mysql> use test;
Database changed
```

2. We then created a new clone EMP table, *emp_store*:

```
mysql> create table emp_store (
    ->    empno numeric(4) not null,
    ->    ename varchar(10),
    ->    job varchar(9),
    ->    mgr numeric(4),
    ->    hiredate date,
    ->    sal numeric(7,2),
    ->    comm numeric(7,2),
    ->    deptno numeric(2) );
Query OK, 0 rows affected (0.02 sec)

mysql> describe emp_store;
+----------+--------------+------+-----+---------+-------+
| Field    | Type         | Null | Key | Default | Extra |
+----------+--------------+------+-----+---------+-------+
| empno    | decimal(4,0) |      |     | 0       |       |
| ename    | varchar(10)  | YES  |     | NULL    |       |
| job      | varchar(9)   | YES  |     | NULL    |       |
| mgr      | decimal(4,0) | YES  |     | NULL    |       |
| hiredate | date         | YES  |     | NULL    |       |
| sal      | decimal(7,2) | YES  |     | NULL    |       |
| comm     | decimal(7,2) | YES  |     | NULL    |       |
| deptno   | decimal(2,0) | YES  |     | NULL    |       |
+----------+--------------+------+-----+---------+-------+
8 rows in set (0.00 sec)
```

3. Three test rows were inserted into our MySQL table, using the MySQL default date format of *YYYY-MM-DD*. (This is going to be the extra thing we'll have to munge, later, to smoothly transfer data from one database type to another.):

```
mysql> insert into emp_store
    -> values (1001, 'Groucho', 'Professor', 1,
    ->          '2001-01-01', 100, 10, 10);
Query OK, 1 row affected (0.00 sec)

mysql> insert into emp_store
    -> values (1002, 'Chico', 'Minister', 2,
    ->          '2001-01-02', 200, 20, 20);
Query OK, 1 row affected (0.00 sec)

mysql> insert into emp_store
    -> values (1003, 'Harpo', 'Stowaway', 3,
    ->          '2001-01-03', 300, 30, 30);
Query OK, 1 row affected (0.00 sec)

mysql> select * from emp_store;
+------+---------+-----------+-----+------------+--------+-------+--------+
| empno| ename   | job       | mgr | hiredate   | sal    | comm  | deptno |
+------+---------+-----------+-----+------------+--------+-------+--------+
| 1001 | Groucho | Professor |   1 | 2001-01-01 | 100.00 | 10.00 |     10 |
| 1002 | Chico   | Minister  |   2 | 2001-01-02 | 200.00 | 20.00 |     20 |
| 1003 | Harpo   | Stowaway  |   3 | 2001-01-03 | 300.00 | 30.00 |     30 |
+------+---------+-----------+-----+------------+--------+-------+--------+
3 rows in set (0.00 sec)
```

4. Finally, we quit out of MySQL:

```
mysql> quit
Bye
```

The Oracle Sink

We'd like to transfer these three rows across to the EMP table under Oracle's *orcl* database. We'll do this via the munge script in Example D-1.

Example D-1. Inter-database transfers into Oracle—mySQLtoOracle.pl

```perl
#!perl -w

use strict;
use DBI;

# Step 1: Establish a MySQL source database handle, and
# an Oracle sink database handle.  Notice we can connect to two
# different databases, and database types, at the same time,
# in one Perl script.  Code Simplicities 'R' Us! :-)

my $mysql_dbh = DBI->connect('DBI:mysql:database=test;host=localhost',
                             'irish', 'lion')
                or die "Couldn't connect to MySQL database: " .
                       DBI->errstr;

my $oracle_dbh = DBI->connect('DBI:Oracle:orcl', 'scott', 'tiger',
                              { RaiseError=>1, AutoCommit=>0 } );

# Step 2: Prepare and execute the selection statement taking
# data from our MySQL source.  Bind the columns, for efficiency.

my $select_sql = qq { SELECT empno,    ename,
                             job,      mgr,
                             hiredate, sal,
                             comm,     deptno
                      FROM emp_store };

my $mysql_sth = $mysql_dbh->prepare( $select_sql )
                or die "Couldn't prepare selection statement: " .
                       $mysql_dbh->errstr;
$mysql_sth->execute;

# Create the munge bind variables
my ($empno, $ename, $job, $mgr, $hiredate, $sal, $comm, $deptno );
$mysql_sth->bind_columns( \$empno,    \$ename,
                          \$job,      \$mgr,
                          \$hiredate, \$sal,
                          \$comm,     \$deptno );
# Step 3: Prepare our Oracle insert statement.

my $insert_sql =
```

```
      qq{ INSERT
          INTO emp ( empno,    ename,
                     job,      mgr,
                     hiredate, sal,
                     comm,     deptno )
          VALUES ( ?, ?,
                   ?, ?,
                   to_date( ? , 'YYYY-MM-DD'), ?,
                   ?, ?) };

my $oracle_sth = $oracle_dbh->prepare( $insert_sql );

# Step 4: Select from MySQL and fill bound array, before populating
# Oracle EMP table.

while ($mysql_sth->fetch) {

  $oracle_sth->bind_param(1, $empno);
  $oracle_sth->bind_param(2, $ename);
  $oracle_sth->bind_param(3, $job);
  $oracle_sth->bind_param(4, $mgr);
  $oracle_sth->bind_param(5, $hiredate);
  $oracle_sth->bind_param(6, $sal);
  $oracle_sth->bind_param(7, $comm);
  $oracle_sth->bind_param(8, $deptno);

  # Insert!
  $oracle_sth->execute;
}

# Step 5: Clean up, commit the transaction, and finish.

$oracle_dbh->commit();

$mysql_dbh->disconnect();
$oracle_dbh->disconnect();
```

Let's see what's going on in this code:

1. We create our two database handles, one to draw data from the MySQL source and the other to pour the munged data into the Oracle sink.

2. We prepare the main selection statement to draw information from the source. This will fill our first known data structure.

3. Next, we prepare the matching Oracle INSERT statement, using our second data structure, which will push the data into the sink. Notice the *to_date()* function for munging the *hiredate* column. As we're mixing Perl and Oracle, we're unconcerned as to who does the munging, as long as the job gets done.

   Note that there are several other ways we could have performed this date column munge operation in Perl. For instance, the following code could have been adapted to produce an "Oracle-friendly" date string that could be inserted directly into the database:

```
@date_array = reverse split /-/, '2001-01-02';
$date_array[1] =
    ('JAN', 'FEB', 'MAR', 'APR', 'MAY', 'JUN',
     'JUL', 'AUG', 'SEP', 'OCT', 'NOV', 'DEC')[$date_array[1]-1];
$oracle_insert_date = join '-', @date_array;
print 'oracle_insert_date: >', $oracle_insert_date, "\n";
```

This code snippet would produce:

```
Oracle_insert_date: >02-JAN-2001<
```

However, we're not zealots. The munge problem Perl is helping us overcome here is the transformation of MySQL data into Oracle data. Because it's easier to let the Oracle database engine do the extra date column munge work in this particular case, that's the route we'll choose here. (Note that the *join* and *split* functions are mentioned in Appendix C; for more on these functions, try *perldoc -f join* and *perldoc -f split*. You can also try *perldoc -f reverse* for an explanation of this other built-in Perl function.)

4. Once everything's set, we begin the munge. As each row is drawn from the MySQL source, we pump it straight down into the Oracle sink, using the *$oracle_sth->execute* statement and the *to_date()* data transformation.

5. When the task is finished, we clean up and shut down the munge.

Running the script itself is straightforward:

```
$ perl mySQLtoOracle.pl
```

We can then check the *orcl* database. Notice that our earlier *to_date()* operation has given us the dates in the more usual Oracle-style *DD-MON-YY* format:

```
$ sqlplus scott/tiger@orcl

ORCL> select * from emp where empno < 2000;

    EMPNO ENAME      JOB       MGR HIREDATE     SAL   COMM DEPTNO
--------- ---------- --------- --- --------- ------ ------ ---------
     1001 Groucho    Professor   1 01-JAN-01    100     10        10
     1002 Chico      Minister    2 02-JAN-01    200     20        20
     1003 Harpo      Stowaway    3 03-JAN-01    300     30        30

3 rows selected.

ORCL>
```

That concludes our simple example—but wait a minute! There seems to be precious little in the way of actual data transformation going on except for the date munge. The main transformation here was from MySQL data to Oracle data, and the fact is that this transformation is extraordinarily simple to do in Perl. Nevertheless, the reality is that very few other languages could have managed this transformation so trivially, in so few lines of code.

We can add onto this simple example by layering on additional data-munging operations, depending on specific processing requirements. For instance, we could pull information from other databases to get hold of department descriptions, drag in other personnel information from remote HR databases, aggregate the salaries, substitute some of the data to match agreed-upon business rules, and so on. And all of this is easily done in Perl. For many more data-munging examples, refer to the more detailed sources mentioned at the beginning of this chapter.

The use of Perl for data munging gives us something else in addition to the excellent resources of Perl DBI. We also get the ability to use the 200-plus built-in operators, such as *split*, *join*, and *reverse*, binary-capable functions such as *read*, regular expressions (covered in Appendix C), and the 2000-plus object-oriented Perl modules available from *www.cpan.org* (or *www.activestate.com*). We can make use of all of these resources, in conjunction with Perl DBI, to carry out a wide range of the most difficult data-munging operations. In the rest of this appendix, we'll summarize what we consider to be the best of these 2000-plus data-munging modules. Whether you're regularly filling data warehouses with difficult-to-extrapolate aggregated data, managing the ever-increasing complexity of XML information transfer, or just moving small pieces of fiddly DBA data from one place to another, Perl is a comprehensive one-stop shop full of data-munging functionality.

Numeric Modules

Many Perl data-munging modules are available on CPAN that you can use to convert and otherwise manipulate numeric data, analogous to Oracle functions such as TO_NUMBER or TO_CHAR, but often going beyond these with increased specialization (an example is *Number::Latin*). Those we consider to be the most useful in pre-handling Oracle database data are summarized in Table D-1.

You can obtain these modules and many others from both the CPAN (for Unix) and ActiveState (for Win32) archives. You can check for the latest status of PPM packages at:

http://aspn.activestate.com/ASPN/Downloads/ActivePerl/PPM/Packages

Table D-1. Numeric modules

CPAN module	Description/CPAN address
Number::Encode	Written by Luis Muñoz; converts bit strings into numeric strings, in a similar manner to Oracle's BIN_TO_NUM.
	http://www.cpan.org/authors/id/L/LU/LUISMUNOZ/
Number::Format	Written by William R. Ward; a popular number formatting package, which performs a variety of numeric operations and is described in the next section.
	http://www.cpan.org/authors/id/WRW/

Table D-1. Numeric modules (continued)

CPAN module	Description/CPAN address
Number::Latin	Written by Sean M. Burke and going beyond Oracle function capabilities, this module converts numbers to and from the W3C Latin numbering system. This system uses the *'a'..'z'*, *'aa'..'az'*, *'ba'..'zz'* notation, often seen in spreadsheets.
	http://www.cpan.org/authors/id/S/SB/SBURKE/
Number::Phone::US	Written by Hugh Kennedy; validates US telephone numbers.
	http://www.cpan.org/authors/id/K/KE/KENNEDYH/
Number::Spice	Written by Wim Verhaegen; reformats to the *Spice* notation for integrated circuit design[a] —for example, 225 *picofarads* becomes *225p.*
	http://www.cpan.org/authors/id/W/WI/WIMV/
Number::Spell	Written by Les Howard; spells out integers in words—for example, *print(spell_number(777))* outputs *seven hundred seventy seven.*
	http://www.cpan.org/authors/id/L/LH/LHOWARD/

[a]The Simulation Program for Integrated Circuits Emphasis. Check out the classic Berkeley Spice circuit design tool at *http://freshmeat.net/projects/berkeleyspice/*

Let's take a look at one of these modules, *Number::Format*, and how you might use it to format Oracle database data.

Number::Format

Number::Format is a very useful Perl module that offers a variety of useful conversion methods, which produce results similar to Oracle's built-in TO_NUMBER and TO_CHAR functions. *Number::Format* also adds a few features that aren't available in the Oracle functions, such as the wide range of negative number formats you can adopt. We illustrate a typical usage of *Number::Format*'s *format_number*, *format_price*, and *format_bytes* in Example D-2. (This particular example deals with the Altairian Dollar currency favored by recent Galactic President, Zaphod Beeblebrox.)

Example D-2. The Number::Format module—numberFormat.pl

```
#!perl -w
use strict;

use Number::Format;
# The neg_account key uses an "x" to represent the number, and then
# whatever other formatting you require.

my $Altarian =
   new Number::Format( -thousands_sep => ',',
                       -decimal_point => '.',
                       -int_curr_symbol => 'ALT',
                       -decimal_digits => 4,
                       -decimal_fill => 2,
                       -neg_format => '(x)',     # Accounting Style Negs
```

Example D-2. The Number::Format module—numberFormat.pl (continued)

```
                    -kilo_suffix => ' KiloAlt',
                    -mega_suffix => ' MegaAlt',
                    -giga_suffix => ' PanGalacticGargle' );

my $finiteProbability = 6666666666.66;

# We've used a negative currency amount for format_price( ) to
# demonstrate the regular collapses of the Altairian Dollar! :-)
print $Altarian->format_number( $finiteProbability ),     "\n",
    $Altarian->format_price (-$finiteProbability, 3 ), "\n",
    $Altarian->format_bytes ( $finiteProbability );
```

Running the *numberFormat.pl* script produces the following output. Notice that the accounting-style *neg_format* method has enclosed our negative figure in brackets:

```
$ perl numberFormat.pl
6,666,666,666.6600
(ALT 6,666,666,666.660)
6.2088 PanGalacticGargle
```

You can download the *Number::Format* tarball from:

http://www.cpan.org/authors/id/WRW

You can install the Win32 ActivePerl package as follows:

```
C:\>ppm
PPM> install Number-Format
```

Mathematics Modules

There are four mathematical modules bundled with Perl (summarized in Table D-2) that you can use to handle most of the mathematical data-munging operations you are likely to perform. For less common operations, check CPAN; you will find many unbundled modules there that provide mathematical support for data-munging operations on data ranging from Fibonaci[*] numbers through financial annuities.

Table D-2. Mathematics modules bundled with Perl

Module	Description
Mark::BigFloat	Written by Mark Biggar; used for operations on arbitrary-length floating-point numbers.
Math::BigInt	Also written by Mark Biggar; a related module used for operations on integers of any length.

---

[*] The Fibonaci numbers are an inductive sequence of numbers in which each term is generated by the two previous terms. The first two terms are both assigned the value of 1 and all other terms are created by adding the last two numbers together. The first few terms of the sequence is 1, 1, 2, 3, 5, 8, 13, 21, 34, 55. This number pattern is often useful for mathematical and financial analysis, and is also used within Mother Nature to determine many different growth patterns. For instance, we may have five fingers, and vine leaves may have five fronds, because both are using the Fibonaci number sequence.

Table D-2. Mathematics modules bundled with Perl (continued)

Module	Description
Math::Complex	Written by Raphael Manfredi and Jarkko Hietaniemi; used for operations on complex numbers.
Math::Trig	Also written by Manfredi and Hietaniemi; used to provide trigonometric support, including a definition of the *pi* constant (π).

Date Modules

There are a large number of Perl modules that you can use to format and convert data that represents dates. Date handling has traditionally been a challenge for Oracle DBAs and developers. The fact is that dates are, well, confusing. After 100,000 years of Neolithic Sky watching, with some heavy input from the Babylonians, dates have become more twisted in their logic than a boat full of lawyers arguing over a politician's expense account. Although Oracle provides a number of built-in functions for date handling (TO_DATE, TO_CHAR, etc.), you may find these functions cumbersome or inefficient. This is particularly true if you're working with time intervals (NUMTODSINTERVAL, NUMTOYMINTERVAL, TO_DSINTERVAL etc.). The Perl data modules described in this section provide easier ways to handle data conversion. You will also find them helpful if you simply want to pre-clean data in Perl before overloading the Oracle SQL engine with calls to Oracle's own date functions.

The date-related modules listed in Table D-3 are available on both CPAN (for Unix) and ActiveState (for Win32). Some of them are dependent on each other, so we've listed them out in the appropriate installation order (least dependent first). Some also require additional modules, which are listed in Table D-3 (also in installation order wherever possible).

Table D-3. Date-based modules

CPAN module	Description/CPAN address
Date::Business	Written by Richard DeSimine; calculates business dates.
	http://www.cpan.org/authors/id/D/DE/DESIMINER
Date::Calc	Written by Steffen Beyer; a C-based date formatting masterpiece, described in detail in the following section.
	http://www.cpan.org/authors/id/STBEY
Date::Pcalc	Written by J. David Eisenberg; a pure Perl version of *Date::Calc*.
	http://www.cpan.org/authors/id/STBEY
Date::Christmas	Written by Elaine M. Ashton; returns Christmas day for any Gregorian year following 1600 AD — for example, *christmasday(2002) => Wednesday*.
	http://www.cpan.org/authors/id/H/HF/HFB

Table D-3. Date-based modules (continued)

CPAN module	Description/CPAN address
Date::Decade	Written by Michael Diekmann; provides decade-based date calculations; relies on either *Date::Calc* or *Date::Pcalc*. *http://www.cpan.org/authors/id/M/MI/MIDI*
Date::Easter	Written by Rich Bowen; requires several extra modules, listed in Table D-4. Date::Easter provides both Gregorian and Orthodox Easter information. *http://www.cpan.org/authors/id/RBOW*
Date::Handler	Written by Benoit Beausejour; handles time zones and locales. *http://www.cpan.org/authors/id/B/BB/BBEAUSEJ*
Date::Japanese::Era	Written by Tatsuhiko Miyagawa; converts dates between the Japanese Era and Gregorian calendar; requires two modules, listed in Table D-4. *http://www.cpan.org/authors/id/M/MI/MIYAGAWA*
Date::Simple	Written by John Tobey; this speed-driven module validates dates, calculates date-time intervals, performs day-of-week arithmetic, and much more. *http://www.cpan.org/authors/id/JTOBEY*
Date::Range	Written by Tony Bowden; calculates date ranges and analyzes date patterns; relies on *Date::Simple* and *Test::Simple* (see Table D-4). *http://www.cpan.org/authors/id/T/TM/TMTM*
Date::Manip	Written by Sullivan Beck; a pure-Perl module for dates and times, which is recommended when the faster *Date::Calc* fails to provide the required options or when you need some really clever date string parsing. *Date::Manip* is the Daisy-Cutter date module in the Perl world; when all else fails, you can rely on *Date::Manip* to provide that extra bit of functionality. *http://www.cpan.org/authors/id/SBECK*
DateTime::Precise	Written by Blair Zajac; this object-oriented module deals with the usual date and time suspects, plus GPS operations and fractional seconds. *http://www.cpan.org/authors/id/B/BZ/BZAJAC*

Table D-4. Required modules for date-based formatting

CPAN module	Reliant module	Description/CPAN address
Mime::Base64	Date::Japanese::Era	Written by Gisle Aas; used for Base64 strings. *http://www.cpan.org/authors/id/GAAS*
Jcode	Date::Japanese::Era	Written by Dan Kogai; code for the Japanese character set. *http://www.cpan.org/authors/id/D/DA/DANKOGAI*
Devel::CoreStack	Date::Easter	Written by Alligator Descartes; used for debuggers. *http://www.cpan.org/authors/id/ADESC*
Test::Harness	Date::Easter	Written by Michael G. Schwern; a test harness for Perl modules. *http://www.cpan.org/authors/id/MSCHWERN*
Test::Simple	Date::Easter, Date::Range	Also written by Michael G. Schwern; provides basic utilities for writing Perl tests. *http://www.cpan.org/authors/id/MSCHWERN*

In the following sections we'll look at *Date::Calc*, the module we consider the most powerful in the Perl date munging world because of its high speed.

Date::Calc and Date::Calendar

Perl's most useful and efficient date formatting module is Steffen Beyer's *Date::Calc*. Although this module offers fewer methods than does the *Date::Manip* module, *Date::Calc*'s C library greatly enhances its munge processing speed. You can obtain this module from:

> *http://www.cpan.org/authors/id/STBEY*

We'll also look at *Date::Calendar*, which comes with *Date::Calc* and provides some handy methods for dealing with business calendars. To use *Date::Calendar*, you may have to install the *Bit::Vector* module, also available from Steffen Beyer's CPAN site.

For Win32 users, the latest *Bit::Vector* and *Date::Calc* versions are available from ActiveState (although *Date::Calc* is already pre-installed with ActivePerl):

```
C:\>ppm
PPM> install Bit-Vector
PPM> install Date-Calc      # To get the latest version! :-)
```

The Date-Calc-5.0 API

In the following list we've described every nondeprecated method in the *Date::Calc* 5.0 API:

Days_in_Year
> The days in the year, up to the supplied month (1..12), in the given year:
> ```
> $days = Days_in_Year($year, $month);
> ```

Days_in_Month
> The number of days in a month for a given year. The year is required, although it's logically only necessary for February's leap-year variations:
> ```
> $days = Days_in_Month($year, $month);
> ```

Weeks_in_Year
> Fetches the number of weeks in a given year (either 52 or 53) (see Figure D-3):
> ```
> $weeks = Weeks_in_Year($year);
> ```

eap_year
> Returns 1 for true, in a leap year, otherwise 0 for false:
> ```
> $leap_year_flag = leap_year($year);
> ```

check_date
> Returns 1 if the year, month, day combination is a real date, otherwise 0:
> ```
> $valid_date_flag = check_date($year, $month, $day);
> ```

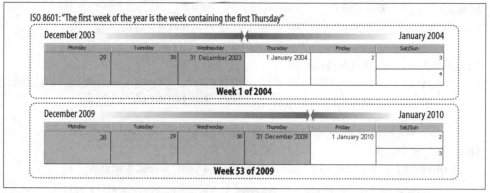

Figure D-3. ISO 8601—Which year owns which week?

check_time

Returns 1 if the hour, minute, second combination is valid, otherwise 0:

```
$valid_time_flag = check_time($hour, $min, $sec);  # 24 hour clock! :-)
```

check_business_date

Returns 1, for valid business dates (e.g., Year 2002, Week 47, Day 3), otherwise 0:

```
$valid_business_flag = check_business_date($year, $week, $day_of_week);
```

Day_of_Year

Returns the year day from 1...366 (with 366 for leap years):

```
$day_of_year = Day_of_Year($year, $month, $day);
```

Date_to_Days

Starting from 1 Jan 1 AD, which is day one,[*] returns the number of days since that date, such that *Date_to_Days(1, 1, 1)* returns 1:

```
$days = Date_to_Days($year, $month, $day);
```

Day_of_Week

Returns the weekday of the supplied date (*1 = Monday, .., 7 = Sunday*):

```
$weekday = Day_of_Week($year, $month, $day);  # Returns 1..7
```

Week_Number

Returns the year's week number; *Week_Number(2002, 12, 25)* gives 52:

```
$week = Week_Number($year, $month, $day);
```

Week_of_Year

Using ISO 8601, decides which year owns a week split over a New Year cusp by calculating which year has the Thursday. The first week containing it (and therefore four days) is the first week in any year:

```
($week, $year) = Week_of_Year($year, $month, $day);
```

---

[*] The Gregorian calendar goes from 31 Dec 1 BC, to 1 Jan 1 AD. There's no year zero.

Monday_of_Week

Generates the date on the first day of the given year's week:

```
($year, $month, $day) = Monday_of_Week($week, $year);
```

Nth_Weekday_of_Month_Year

For recurring dates. You can calculate the third Tuesday's date in May, using *Nth_Weekday_of_Month_Year(2003, 5, 2, 3)* to return *(2003, 5, 20)*:

```
($year, $month, $day) =
    Nth_Weekday_of_Month_Year($year,$month,$day_of_week,$nth_weekday);
```

Standard_to_Business

Converts a given date to a business format of year, week, and day:

```
($year,$week,$day_of_week) = Standard_to_Business($year,$month,$day);
```

Business_to_Standard

The dark half of *Standard_to_Business*. This performs a reverse operation:

```
($year,$month,$day) = Business_to_Standard($year,$week,$day_of_week);
```

Delta_Days

The number of days between dates. A greater second date makes this positive:

```
$diff_days = Delta_Days($year1,$month1,$day1,$year2,$month2,$day2);
```

Delta_DHMS

The days, hours, minutes, and seconds difference between two date-times:

```
($diff_days, $diff_hours, $diff_mins, $diff_sec) =
    Delta_DHMS($year1, $month1, $day1, $hour1, $min1, $sec1,
                $year2, $month2, $day2, $hour2, $min2, $sec2);
```

Add_Delta_DHMS

Performs complex date and time addition in many permutations, the most usual of which is to take a date and time, add on some differences, and then see what new date and time is generated:

```
($year, $month, $day, $hour, $min, $sec) =
    Add_Delta_DHMS($year, $month, $day, $hour, $min, $sec,
                    $diff_day, $diff_hour, $diff_min, $diff_sec);
```

Delta_YMD

Creates an array: *($year2—$year1,$mnth2—$mnth1,$day2—$day1)*:

```
($diff_year, $diff_mnth, $diff_day) =
    Delta_YMD($year1, $mnth1, $day1, $year2, $mnth2, $day2);
```

Delta_YMDHMS

Similar to *Delta_YMD*, but with the extra time element:

```
($diff_year,$diff_month,$diff_day,$diff_hour,$diff_min,$diff_sec) =
    Delta_YMDHMS($year1, $month1, $day1, $hour1, $min1, $sec1,
                  $year2, $month2, $day2, $hour2, $min2, $sec2);
```

Normalize_DHMS

Takes four different time elements, days, hours, minutes, and seconds, negative or positive relative to right now. It then combines them into a smoothed-out figure:

```
use Date::Calc qw ( Normalize_DHMS ) ;

# Take away 3 days from right now, add on 120 hours, take away
# 750 minutes, and add on 3645 seconds.  We should end up
# with 1 day, 12 hours, 30 minutes and 45 seconds as the
# smoothed out computed result, in relation to right now.

($diff_day, $diff_hour, $diff_min, $diff_sec) =
    Normalize_DHMS(-3, +120, -750, +3645);  # days, hours, mins, secs

# We're expecting 1 day, 12 minutes, 30 minutes and 45 seconds! :-)
print "$diff_day day, $diff_hour hrs, $diff_min min $diff_sec sec\n";
```

Executing this code produces the following result:

```
$ perl normalizeDHMS.pl
1 day, 12 hrs, 30 min, 45 sec
```

Add_Delta_Days

Answers questions such as "What's the date 30 days from today?":

```
($year, $month, $day) = Add_Delta_Days($year, $month, $day, $diff_day);
```

Add_Delta_DHMS

Answers questions like "What's the date-time if we add on 30 hours?":

```
($year, $month, $day, $hour, $min, $sec) =
    Add_Delta_DHMS($year, $month, $day, $hour, $min, $sec,
                   $diff_day, $diff_hour, $diff_min, $diff_sec);
```

Add_Delta_YM

Returns the date, when provided with a date, plus a year and month offset:

```
($year, $month, $day) =
    Add_Delta_YM($year, $month, $day, $diff_year, $diff_month);
```

Add_Delta_YMD

Extends *Add_Delta_YM* by allowing the addition of an offset days figure:

```
($year, $month, $day) =
    Add_Delta_YMD($year,$month,$day,$diff_year,$diff_month,$diff_days);
```

Add_Delta_YMDHMS

Another extension to *Add_Delta_YMD*, this time allowing a time offset:

```
($year, $month, $day, $hour, $min, $sec) = Add_Delta_YMDHMS(
    $year,$month,$day,$hour,$min,$sec,
    $diff_year,$diff_month,$diff_day,$diff_hour,$diff_min,$diff_sec);
```

System_Clock

Returns the list of values displayed in Table D-5, with *localtime()* being used by default. An optional true flag calls *gmtime()* instead, to get the GMT

(Greenwich Mean Time) or UTC (Universal Time Coordinated), depending on your system:[*]

```
($year, $month, $day, $hour, $min, $sec, $Julian_day_of_year,
    $day_of_week, $daylight_savings) = System_Clock([$gmt_flag]);
```

Table D-5. Figures provided by Date::Calc's system_clock

Figure type	Range	Comments
Year	1970..2038+	Your OS determines the maximum value
Month	1..12	January = 1, .., December = 12
Day of month	1..31	Notice that this is not 0..n format, as with hours below
Hour	0..23	The 24-hour clock is used
Minute	0..59	Notice that this is not 1..60
Second	0..59	Range may be 0..61, to cope with leap seconds
Day of year	1..366	The 366 figure is for leap years
Day of week	1..7	Monday = 1, .., Sunday = 7
Daylight Savings	-1..1	-1 = daylight savings info unavailable, 0 = daylight savings currently out of use, 1 = daylight savings in use

Leap seconds slip into the calendar every 500 days or so at the end of December or June. Our globe spins 2 milliseconds a day slower than it did in 1900 because of the moon's tidal braking effect. Therefore, GMT gradually diverges from the atomic clocks measuring UTC. Leap seconds bring everything together again.

Note that tidal braking has already stopped the moon's face rotating relative to the Earth, giving rise to Pink Floyd's album, *The Dark Side of the Moon*. One day, a single face of the Earth will oppose a more distant Moon. However, by then the Sun will have expanded, giving us something even more interesting to experience—a Floyd album called *Jolly Red Giant* perhaps?

For more information (not about Pink Floyd, promise), see: *http://www.npl.co.uk/npl/ctm/leap_second.html*.

Today

Returns a subset from *System_Clock*: the year, month and day:

```
($year, $month, $day) = Today([$gmt]);
```

Now

Another *System_Clock* subset returns the current hour, minute, and second:

```
($hour, $min, $sec) = Now([$gmt_flag]);
```

---

[*] For a discussion of Julian dates and Julian days, try the following web page: *http://aa.usno.navy.mil/data/docs/JulianDate.html*

Today_and_Now

Returns the current year, month, day, hour, minute, and second:

```
($year, $month, $day, $hour, $min, $sec) = Today_and_Now([$gmt]);
```

This_Year

Returns the current year:

```
$year = This_Year([$gmt_flag]);
```

Gmtime

Returns the GMT values displayed in Table D-6 according to the optional parameter, the number of seconds since midnight, 1 Jan 1970. This is the start of the Unix epoch. If absent, the current *time()* value is used:

```
($year, $month, $day, $hour, $min, $sec, $doy, $dow, $dst) =
    Gmtime([$time_in_seconds_since_1970]);
```

Localtime

The local time equivalent to *Gmtime*:

```
($year,$mnth,$day,$hour,$min,$sec,$doy,$dow,$dst) = Localtime([$time]);
```

Mktime

Generates the number of seconds since the 1970 epoch:

```
$time = Mktime($year, $month, $day, $hour, $min, $sec);
```

Timezone

Generates differential time offsets between local time and GMT. Those to the east of Greenwich, England receive positive offsets. Those to the west receive negative ones. A daylight savings flag is also returned:

```
($diff_year, $diff_month, $diff_day,
    $diff_hour, $diff_min, $diff_sec, $dst) = Timezone([$time]);
```

Date_to_Time

This is similar to *Mktime*, but faster because it avoids system calls:

```
$time = Date_to_Time($year, $month, $day, $hour, $min, $sec);
```

Time_to_Date

Returns the GMT date-time values when supplied with the appropriate number of seconds since 1970. Uses the built-in *time()* function as the default:

```
($year, $month, $day, $hour, $min, $sec) = Time_to_Date([$time]);
```

Easter_Sunday

Calculates the Gregorian Easter Sunday date for the years 1583 to 2299, via the Gauss algorithm. The original Easter was agreed to by the early Christians in 325 AD. This held firm until 1582 AD when the Gregorian Easter, which now differs from the Orthodox one, became the first Sunday following the first full moon preceding a Sunday after the Spring equinox:

```
($year, $month, $day) = Easter_Sunday($year);
```

For Orthodox functionality, try the *Date::Easter* module in Table D-3.

Decode_Month

Requires a string to uniquely identify a month in the current *Date::Calc* language. For example, the parameters '*N*', '*nov*', and '*November*' all return 11. Zero is returned if *Decode_Month* fails to work out the month:

```
$month = Decode_Month($string);
```

Decode_Day_of_Week

As with *Decode_Month*, a string able to identify a day will return 1 to 7:

```
$day_of_week = Decode_Day_of_Week($string);
```

Decode_Language

Returns *Date::Calc*'s internal ID for a supported language, if uniquely identified from a string. Otherwise, zero is returned. Eleven languages come automatically with *Date::Calc*, as detailed in Table D-6. Others can be added by following the instructions in *INSTALL.txt*:

```
$lang = Decode_Language($string);
```

Table D-6. Languages supplied with Date::Calc 5.0

Internal ID	Language	Comments/English translation
1	English	Default language for *Date::Calc*
2	Français	French
3	Deutsch	German
4	Español	Spanish
5	Português	Portuguese
6	Nederlands	Dutch
7	Italiano	Italian
8	Norsk	Norwegian
9	Svenska	Swedish
10	Dansk	Danish
11	Suomi	Finnish

Decode_Date_EU

One of the cleverest Perl functions we've ever seen. Feed it a string, with some kind of embedded date, and if *Decode_Date_EU* can identify three lucky numbers inside it, in the European date order of day, month, and year, it returns this list. An empty list is returned if no date can be found.

```
($year,$month,$day) = Decode_Date_EU($string);
```

Decode_Date_US

Behaves identically to *Decode_Date_EU* above, except it tries to find a valid date in the North American date format of month, day, year:

```
($year,$month,$day) = Decode_Date_US($string);
```

Fixed_Window

Takes a two-digit number and turns it into a four-digit year, dependent on a fixed window centered around 1970. All numbers from 70 to 99 are converted in the range 1970 to 1999. All numbers below 70 are converted upwards. For example, 69 goes to *2069*:

```
$year = Fixed_Window($non_negative_number_less_than_100);
```

Moving_Window

Imposes a 100-year window, cross-haired upon today's date, to go back 50 years and forward 50 years. The two-digit entry is initially mapped to the current century. If more than 50 years ago, 100 years are added to the total. If 50 years or more into the future, 100 years are taken off:

```
$year = Moving_Window($non_negative_number_less_than_100);
```

Date_to_Text

Translates year, month, and day into a short piece of text, dependent on the currently selected language. For example, with the English default language, *Date_to_Text(2002, 12, 25)* creates *Wed 25-Dec-2002*:

```
$string = Date_to_Text($year,$month,$day);
```

Date_to_Text_Long

Provides a longer date-string, dependent on language; *Date_to_Text_Long(2002,12,25)* creates *Wednesday, December 25th 2002*:

```
$string = Date_to_Text_Long($year,$month,$day);
```

English_Ordinal

Takes a cardinal number and turns it into an English ordinal abbreviation, so *English_Ordinal(101)* produces *101st*:

```
$string = English_Ordinal($number);
```

Calendar

Produces a calendar string:

```
$string = Calendar($year,$month[,$orthodox]);
```

The optional *$orthodox* flag, if set to true, returns a calendar starting on a Sunday, rather than a Monday, so *Calendar(2002, 12, 1)* produces:

```
    December 2002
Sun Mon Tue Wed Thu Fri Sat
  1   2   3   4   5   6   7
  8   9  10  11  12  13  14
 15  16  17  18  19  20  21
 22  23  24  25  26  27  28
 29  30  31
```

Month_to_Text

Provides the full month name, in the current language, when supplied with a number in the range 1 to 12. *Month_to_Text(11)* outputs *November*:

```
$string = Month_to_Text($month);
```

Day_of_Week_to_Text

>With a day range of *1..7*, *Day_of_Week_to_Text(2)* returns *Tuesday*:

```
$string = Day_of_Week_to_Text($day_of_week);
```

Day_of_Week_Abbreviation

>Returns day of the week abbreviations, such as *Mon* for *1*:

```
$abbrev_string = Day_of_Week_Abbreviation($day_of_week);
```

Language_to_Text

>When given a valid internal ID, returns the name of the language:

```
$string = Language_to_Text($lang);
```

Language

>Works out the internal ID for the current language, or changes it:

```
$lang = Language();
Language($lang);
$oldlang = Language($newlang);
```

Languages

>Returns the total number of languages *Date::Calc* is currently supporting:

```
$max_lang = Languages();
```

Parse_Date

>Does its best to parse a date string for you:

```
($year, $month, $day) = Parse_Date($string);
```

ISO_LC

>Returns a string in which all ISO-Latin-1 characters are lower-cased:

```
$lower = ISO_LC($string);
```

ISO_UC

>Returns a string in which all ISO-Latin-1 characters are upper-cased:

```
$upper = ISO_UC($string);
```

Version

>And finally, this one provides the current version of *Date::Calc*—for example, *5.0*:

```
$string = Date::Calc::Version();
```

Conversion Modules

Perl provides a variety of modules that you can use to convert from one data format to another. In Table D-7 we list what we think are the most useful conversion modules available from CPAN. All of them should also be available via ActivePerl's PPM, except possibly *Convert::Recode*, which requires the use of the GNU *recode* program; we'll describe that one shortly.

Table D-7. Perl conversion modules

CPAN module	Description/CPAN Address
Convert::EBCDIC	Written by Chris Leach; converts between EBCDIC and ASCII format.
	http://www.cpan.org/authors/id/CXL
Convert::Recode	Written by Ed Avis, built upon work from Gisle Aas; creates a Perl front end to the GNU *recode* library (described in the next section).
	http://www.cpan.org/authors/id/E/ED/EDAVIS
Convert::SciEng	Written by Colin Kuskie; converts numbers with scientific- and engineering-style suffixes.
	http://www.cpan.org/authors/id/COLINK
Convert::Translit	Written by Genji Schmeder; converts between 8-bit character sets.
	http://www.cpan.org/authors/id/GENJISCH
Convert::Units	Written by Robert Rothenberg; converts unit measurements, such as *meters*, to other units, such as *inches*.
	http://www.cpan.org/authors/id/R/RR/RRWO
Convert::UU	Written by Andreas J. König; used for *uuencode* and *uudecode* work.
	http://www.cpan.org/authors/id/ANDK

Convert::Recode and GNU recode

The *Convert::Recode* module provides a front end to the GNU *recode* library, which is a powerhouse of conversion operations. You can download this library, which was written by François Pinard, from:

> *http://www.gnu.org/software/recode/recode.html*
> *ftp://ftp.gnu.org/gnu/recode*

The *recode* library converts between more than 300 different character sets, depending on what's possible upon your operating system. The following command tells you what sets you have access to, once you've installed *recode*:

```
$ recode -l
```

On SuSE 7.3 Linux, we had 281 character sets, from *arabic7* to *MacGreek*.

You can install this library as follows:

1. Once you have the tarball downloaded, unpack as follows:

   ```
   $ gzip -d recode-3.6.tar.gz
   $ tar xvf recode-3.6.tar
   $ cd recode-3.6
   ```

2. Before configuring, take a look at the *INSTALL* file:

   ```
   $ vi README INSTALL
   $ ./configure
   $ make
   ```

3. Instead of *make test*, as with Perl modules, use *make check* instead:

   ```
   $ make check
   ...
   ```

```
==============================
All 95 tests were successful
==============================
...
```

4. Now we can install:

```
$ make install
```

5. Once the *recode* install completes, we're ready to install Perl's *Convert::Recode*
   module, which is a standard Perl install.

Convert::Recode is unusual in that you roll your own methods directly from it. Simply identify the two character sets you wish to convert between, such as *ascii* and *ebcdic*, and then decide the conversion direction. Once you've decided, just add a _ *to_* string between the two character set names and then import the final method via Convert::Recode. For example:

```
use Convert::Recode qw(ascii_to_ebcdic);
```

or:

```
use Convert::Recode qw(ebcdic_to_ ascii);
```

We've created two short programs; *recodeAscEbc.pl* in Example D-3, and *recodeEbcAsc.pl* in Example D-4. We're going to use these to:

- Convert *feedRecode.txt* into an EBCDIC equivalent, *ebcdicRecode.txt*
- Then re-convert this back into an ASCII file called *outRecode.txt*

Example D-3. ASCII to EBCDIC—recodeAscEbc.pl

```perl
#!perl -w

use Convert::Recode qw(ascii_to_ebcdic);

while (<>) {
   print ascii_to_ebcdic($_);
}
```

Example D-4. EBCDIC to ASCII—recodeEbcAsc.pl

```perl
#!perl -w

use Convert::Recode qw(ebcdic_to_ascii);

while (<>) {
   print ebcdic_to_ascii($_);
}
```

The original *feedRecode.txt* file looks like this:

```
To sit in solemn silence,
In a dull dank dock,
In a pestilential prison,
With a life long lock,
```

```
Awaiting the sensation of a short sharp shock,
From a cheap and chippy chopper,
On a big black block
```

The execution run, which converts this file from ASCII into EBCDIC and then back again, looks like this:

```
$ perl recodeAscEbc.pl feedRecode.txt > ebcdicRecode.txt
$ perl recodeEbcAsc.pl ebcdicRecode.txt > outRecode.txt
```

This conversion run is displayed in the ASCII-based *vi* editor in Figure D-4.

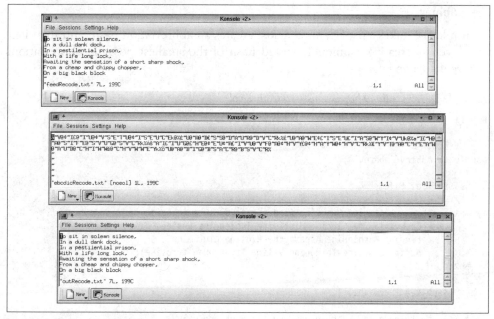

Figure D-4. Convert::Recode at work

Text Conversion Modules

Perl comes with a number of text-based conversion modules bundled into it. These are listed in Table D-8.

Table D-8. Perl-bundled text processing modules

Module	Description
Text::Abbrev	Written by the Perl 5 porters; when supplied with an array, *Text::Abbrev* returns a hash of keyed abbreviations and original string values (see Example D-5).
Text::ParseWords	Written by Hal Pomeranz; parses text into token arrays or arrays of arrays (see Example D-6).
Text::Soundex	Written by Mike Stok; a Perl implementation of Donald Knuth's *Soundex* algorithm (see Example D-7).

Table D-8. Perl-bundled text processing modules (continued)

Module	Description
Text::Tabs	Written by David Muir Sharnoff; does what the Unix utilities *expand( )* and *unexpand( )* do. Given a line with tabs, *expand* replaces them with a specified number of spaces. The *unexpand* method adds tabs to a line when it can save bytes by doing so.
Text::Wrap	Written by David Muir Sharnoff; this line wrapper forms simple paragraphs from munged lines.

Let's take a look at some of these modules in action.

Text::Abbrev

Example D-5 takes a list of amino acids, creates an abbreviation hash, and then iterates over it, creating a uniquely sorted hash of the smallest possible abbreviations before displaying it.

Example D-5. Text list abbreviations—textAbbrev.pl

```perl
#!perl -w

use strict;
use Text::Abbrev('abbrev');

# The Stuff of Life

my %h1 = abbrev qw(Alanine Cysteine Aspartic_Acid Glutamic_Acid
            Phenylalanine Glycine Histidine Isoleucine Lysine
            Leucine Methionine Asparagine Proline Glutamine
            Arginine Serine Threonine Valine Tryptophan Tyrosine);
my %h2;

for my $abb_key (keys %h1) {

   # Iterate through the hash, producing all keys and values.
   # Build up a 2nd hash, with the smallest possible abbreviations.

   # Have we started filling the 2nd hash yet, with reversed data?

   if (defined ($h2{ $h1{$abb_key} } )){

      # Yes, we already have an abbreviation.  Is the current one
      # longer than the new one?  If so, replace it.

      if (length($h2{ $h1{$abb_key} } ) > length($abb_key)){

         # This abbreviation is shorter, so we replace.

         $h2{ $h1{$abb_key} } = $abb_key;
      }

   } else {
```

```perl
      # Provide our first value, for hash 2. Reverse the sense
      # of the hash. The value becomes key, the key becomes the value.

      $h2{ $h1{$abb_key} } = $abb_key;
   }
}

# Now we've built up our reduced hash, print it out.

for my $min_key (sort keys %h2) {
   printf("%15s : %15s\n", $min_key, $h2{$min_key});
}
```

The results are as follows:

```
$ perl textAbbrev.pl
       Alanine :              Al
      Arginine :              Ar
    Asparagine :          Aspara
 Aspartic_Acid :          Aspart
      Cysteine :               C
 Glutamic_Acid :         Glutamic
     Glutamine :         Glutamin
       Glycine :             Gly
     Histidine :               H
    Isoleucine :               I
       Leucine :              Le
        Lysine :              Ly
    Methionine :               M
 Phenylalanine :              Ph
       Proline :              Pr
        Serine :               S
     Threonine :              Th
    Tryptophan :              Tr
      Tyrosine :              Ty
        Valine :               V
```

Text::ParseWords

This time, in Example D-6, we'll split a list of words into separate elements via a regular expression splitting on white space. You may sometimes want to include spaces inside the strings, and we can do this with either quote characters or backslash escapes. We'll then create a tagged list of values, in XML format, to send them further down a potential munge chain.

Example D-6. Text list parsing—textParseWords.pl

```perl
#!perl -w

use strict;
use Text::ParseWords('quotewords');
```

Example D-6. Text list parsing—textParseWords.pl (continued)

```perl
# We want to keep the spaces within Aspartic Acid, and Glutamic acid.
# We can do this in two ways, either by using non-escaped quote marks,
# or escaped space characters.  To cut things down a bit, we'll only
# use amino acids beginning with "A" or "G".

my @amino_acids =
   quotewords('\s+', # Regular Expression to split on white space
             0,
             q{   Alanine "Aspartic Acid"   Glutamic\ Acid
                  Glycine        Asparagine   Glutamine Arginine} );

print '<?xml version="1.0"?>', "\n";
print '<!DOCTYPE Genetics SYSTEM "genetics.dtd">', "\n";

for my $array_element (sort @amino_acids) {
   printf("<Amino_Acid>%s</Amino_Acid>\n", $array_element);
}
```

This produces the following XML-style output. All the spaces have gone, except the ones we wanted to keep. Mission accomplished:

```
$ perl textParseWords.pl
<?xml version="1.0"?>
<!DOCTYPE Genetics SYSTEM "genetics.dtd">
<Amino_Acid>Alanine</Amino_Acid>
<Amino_Acid>Arginine</Amino_Acid>
<Amino_Acid>Asparagine</Amino_Acid>
<Amino_Acid>Aspartic Acid</Amino_Acid>
<Amino_Acid>Glutamic Acid</Amino_Acid>
<Amino_Acid>Glutamine</Amino_Acid>
<Amino_Acid>Glycine</Amino_Acid>
```

Text::Soundex

In Example D-7 we want to find all the sound-alike amino acids. This is so we can put checks into a later munge process and avoid word confusion, as in John le Carré's spy novel, *Tinker, Tailor, Soldier, Spy*, where "Tinker," "Tailor," "Soldier," and "Poor Man" (for George Smiley) were used as codes for possible traitorous moles. This avoided "Tailor" getting confused with the more usual "Sailor." (You may notice the similarity between *Text::Soundex*, and Oracle's SOUNDEX function which is based on exactly the same Knuthian algorithm—see the first part of this appendix for more on such algorithms.)

Example D-7. Identifying soundalikes—textSoundex.pl

```perl
#!perl -w

use strict;
use Text::Soundex('soundex');

# Yet More Stuff of Life.  We want to find out the amino acids
```

```perl
# which sound the same.

my @amino_array =
     ('Alanine', 'Cysteine', 'Aspartic Acid', 'Glutamic Acid',
      'Phenylalanine', 'Glycine', 'Histidine', 'Isoleucine', 'Lysine',
      'Leucine', 'Methionine', 'Asparagine', 'Proline', 'Glutamine',
      'Arginine', 'Serine', 'Threonine', 'Valine', 'Tryptophan',
      'Tyrosine'
     );

# Build up all the Soundex codes, for the array above.

my @soundex_codes = soundex @amino_array;

# Now we want to build up a hash of amino acids that sound
# like each other.  We'll do this by going through the Sortex codes,
# and add up counters on a temporary hash.

my %soundex_count_hash;

for my $soundex_element (sort @soundex_codes) {
   $soundex_count_hash{$soundex_element}++;
}

# Now if anything in the @soundex_codes list, has at least a double,
# it is going to have a value of at least 2, in the %soundex_count_hash
# variable. So now we can go through that, and when we find the double+
# values, we'll whizz through the @amino_array, and add to our new
# %doubles_hash.

my %doubles_hash;

for my $soundex_key (keys %soundex_count_hash) {

   if ($soundex_count_hash{$soundex_key} > 1) {

       # Ah, we've found a code that had at least 2 ++ operations
       # performed on it, earlier.  Find the amino acids, which
       # produced this code, and add them to the final hash.

       for my $amino_element (@amino_array) {

          # Regenerate the code for the amino acid and compare.

          if ($soundex_key eq soundex $amino_element) {

             # The soundex codes are the same.  Hurrah! :-)

             $doubles_hash{$amino_element} = $soundex_key;
          }
```

Example D-7. Identifying soundalikes—textSoundex.pl (continued)

```
      }
    }
}

# Finally, print out the soundalike list, with soundex codes first.

for my $amino_element (sort keys %doubles_hash) {
    printf("%10s : %s\n",$doubles_hash{$amino_element},$amino_element);
}
```

Here are the results:

```
$ perl textSoundex.pl
      A216 : Asparagine
      A216 : Aspartic Acid
      G435 : Glutamic Acid
      G435 : Glutamine
      L250 : Leucine
      L250 : Lysine
```

XML Modules

XML (eXtensible Markup Language) is becoming increasingly important in the Oracle world. The language most associated with XML is Java, but there's plenty of XML-related Perl functionality as well, and we'll explore that in the context of data munging in this section.

Perl's XML facilities are surprisingly powerful. Some would even claim they go beyond Java, with more than 300 CPAN modules, SAX2 support, DOM support, and machine facilities allowing the pipelining of XML and XSLT transformations.

Good Perl XML resources include:

http://www.xml.com/pub/q/perlxml:
   Main *xml.com* portal page for articles on Perl and XML.

http://www.perlxml.net:
   One of the central Perl XML portals.

http://www.xmlproj.com/perl-xml-faq.dkb:
   Main Perl XML FAQ.

http://xmlxslt.sourceforge.net:
   XML::XSLT home page.

http://perl.apache.org:
   Main Perl Apache portal, mostly related to *mod_perl*.

http://xml.sergeant.org:
   For the latest razor-sharp detail, go to Matt Sergeant's place.

http://sourceforge.net/projects/expat:
> James Clark's *expat* XML parser C library, as accessed by the venerable *XML::Parser* module written by Larry Wall and Clark Cooper.

http://www.xmlsoft.org:
> Home of the *libxml2* XML C library, used by the *XML::LibXML* parser.

http://www.cpan.org/modules/by-module/XML:
> The main CPAN page, for Perl XML projects.

http://sourceforge.net/projects/perl-xml:
> The main SourceForge site, for Perl XML projects.

Many different XML modules are also on ActiveState. Most of those covered in this section also have a complementary ActivePerl package:

> *http://www.activestate.com*

We'll concentrate in this chapter on the Unix side of life, because this is where we need the more detailed installation instructions. The actual scripts and XML file outputs should be identical for ActivePerl PPM loads.

General Perl XML Parsers

There are two main XML parsers employed by the majority of Perl XML users:

XML::Parser
> This was the first major Perl XML parser, and it relies upon *expat*. As XML has matured, many supplementary modules have been created for it to deal with DOM and SAX issues. *XML::Parser* comes automatically with ActiveState, and we'll be installing it shortly on Unix.

XML::LibXML
> Created by Matt Sergeant and Christian Glahn, this is Perl's interface to Daniel Velliard's *libxml2* XML C library. Unlike *XML::Parser*, this was written after most of the major XML standards had become settled. At the time of writing, there was no ActiveState binary available for *XML::LibXML*; however, one is sure to come soon. We'll also demonstrate installing this system on Unix, as we need it for the *XML::XMLtoDBMS* munge described at the end of this section.

XML::Parser

You can obtain the latest *XML::Parser* from the following CPAN address:

> *http://www.cpan.org/authors/id/C/CO/COOPERCL*

You may also want to pre-install Gisle Aas's LWP World Wide Web library bundle, *libwww-perl*, and URI module, to provide *XML::Parser*'s *make test* step with extra tests. See Chapter 5, *Embedding Perl into Apache with mod_perl*, for the required LWP installation details.

The *expat* C program download is also available from:

http://sourceforge.net/projects/expat

Follow these steps:

1. We start with the *expat* tarball:

```
$ gzip -d expat-1.95.2.tar.gz
$ tar xvf expat-1.95.2.tar
$ cd expat-1.95.2
```

2. The *README* file is the best place to go next:

```
$ vi README
```

3. Useful help for the configuration is available via the following command:

```
$ ./configure -help
```

4. The default installation directories and files are as follows:

```
/usr/local/lib/libexpat
/usr/local/include/expat.h
/usr/local/bin/xmlwf
```

If you'd like to change these, do the following:

```
$ ./configure --prefix=/home/oracle/xml
```

This will create:

```
/home/oracle/xml/lib/libexpat
/home/oracle/xml/include/expat.h
/home/oracle/xml/bin/xmlwf
```

5. We were happy with the default:

```
$ ./configure
```

6. Now we can build and install *expat*:

```
$ make
$ make install
```

7. In a triumphant burst of heroic action glory, we install *XML::Parser*:

```
$ gzip -d XML-Parser.2.30.tar.gz
$ tar xvf XML-Parser.2.30.tar
$ cd XML-Parser.2.30
$ vi README
```

With a clean *expat* install, the following should be straightforward:

```
$ perl Makefile.PL
$ make
```

You may get some messages about the absence of LWP and URI—you can safely ignore these if you left them out deliberately.

```
$ make test
...
All tests successful.
Files=13,Tests=113,6 wallclock secs (2.93 cusr + 0.24 csys = 3.17 CPU)

$ make install
```

XML::Parser is now well and truly on board. Next up is *XML::LibXML*.

XML::LibXML

The latest *XML::LibXML* download is available from CPAN. We also need the *XML::SAX* module from the same place:

> *http://www.cpan.org/modules/by-module/XML*

XML::LibXML is based on the *libxml2* C library, which is available from:

> *http://www.xmlsoft.org*

Follow these steps:

1. We start with the *libxml2* tarball:

   ```
   $ gzip -d libxml2-2.4.10.tar.gz
   $ tar xvf libxml2-2.4.10.tar
   $ cd libxml2-2.4.10
   $ vi README INSTALL
   ```

   You'll find much fuller documentation online at *http://xmlsoft.org*.

2. The actual installation should be very similar to *expat* as described in the previous section. Configuration help can also be found via the following command:

   ```
   $ ./configure --help
   ```

   We were happy with the defaults and went for the simplest route:

   ```
   $ ./configure
   $ make
   $ make install
   ```

3. Once installation completes, you can run a large test suite, which deviates slightly from our usual Perl pattern by coming *after* the installation:

   ```
   $ make tests
   ...
   Testing catal
   Add and del operations on XML Catalogs
   ```

   Some of these regression tests may fail because of a tiny number of platform incompatibilities. If the warnings look acceptable, move on.

4. We can now come to grips with the actual *XML::LibXML* Perl module. Before we install this, though (come on, you *knew* there'd be a catch), we have to install Matt Sergeant's *XML::SAX* module. This is a straightforward typical Perl installation.

5. The same goes for XML::LibXML. Just unpack the tarball and install with the usual *perl Makefile.PL* installation run.

XML::LibXSLT

If you are interested in XSLT (Extensible Stylesheet Language Transformations), the Gemini twin of *XML::LibXML* is *XML::LibXSLT*, and now's a good time to install it, because it relies on *XML::LibXML*. We'll require Daniel Veillard's *libxslt* C library. For more information try the following:

> *http://www.w3.org/TR/xslt*
> *http://xmlsoft.org/XSLT*

To get hold of *XML::LibXSLT* and *libxslt* go here:

> *http://www.cpan.org/authors/id/M/MS/MSERGEANT*
> *http://xmlsoft.org/XSLT/downloads.html*

Follow these steps:

1. The installation follows the usual pattern. First, *libxslt*:

```
$ gzip -d libxslt-1.0.9.tar.gz
$ tar xvf libxslt-1.0.9.tar
$ cd libxslt-1.0.9
$ ./configure
$ make
$ make install
```

2. Next, unpack *XML::LibXSLT* and run through its *perl Makefile.PL* steps.

Do you need *XML::LibXSLT*? Not really, but if you're a completist as we are, you'll feel that it's nice to be fully loaded with *XML::LibXSLT*. The ability to transform data with XSLT enables us to cope with XML files that fail to match our exact requirements. This way, we can feed XML through a transformation operation, as in Figure D-5, to make it fit our munging needs.

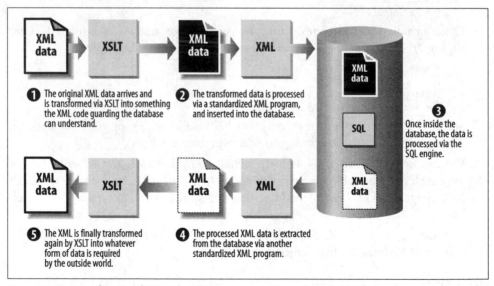

Figure D-5. Transforming data with XSLT

Let's see what's going on here.

1. Suppose that we wish to pump out XML-ized news data from our corporate public relations database. This news could include the following data file, *horsefeather.xml*:

```
<?xml version="1.0"?>
<news>
 <item>
  <title>Hackenbush Speaks Out</title>
  <publication>Horsefeather Gazette</publication>
  <url>http://www.horse.feather</url>
  <date>20021225</date>
  <quote>"That's no Lady.  That's my Wife."</quote>
 </item>
</news>
```

2. For web browsers, we need to transform this presentation slightly with the XSLT code in Example D-8, stored in *horsefeather.xsl*. Notice, particularly, the date transformation code, which can take a string like *20021225* and turn it into the corresponding *25 December 2002:* string.

Example D-8. XSLT code—horsefeather.xsl

```
<?xml version="1.0"?>
<xsl:stylesheet xmlns:xsl="http://www.w3.org/1999/XSL/Transform" version="1.0">
<xsl:output method="html"/>
 <xsl:template match="/">
  <HTML>
  <HEAD>
  <TITLE>Horsefeather News - World Latest</TITLE>
  </HEAD>
  <BODY>
  <xsl:apply-templates select="//item">
  <xsl:sort order="descending" data-type="text" select="date"/>
  </xsl:apply-templates>
  </BODY>
  </HTML>
</xsl:template>

<xsl:template match="item">
 <P><STRONG>
 <CITE><xsl:value-of select="publication"/></CITE>,
 <xsl:apply-templates select="date"/>
 "<a href="{url}"><xsl:value-of select="title"/></a>"
 </STRONG></P>
 <BLOCKQUOTE>
 <xsl:value-of select="comment"/>
 <EM><xsl:value-of select="quote"/></EM>
 </BLOCKQUOTE>
</xsl:template>

<xsl:template match="date">
```

Example D-8. XSLT code—horsefeather.xsl (continued)

```
  <xsl:param name="date" select="."/>
  <xsl:variable name="day" select="number(substring($date,7,2))"/>
  <xsl:variable name="month" select="number(substring($date,5,2))"/>
  <xsl:variable name="year" select="number(substring($date,1,4))"/>

  <xsl:if test="$day>0">
   <xsl:value-of select="$day" />
   <xsl:text> </xsl:text>
  </xsl:if>

  <xsl:choose>
   <xsl:when test="$month= 1">January</xsl:when>
   <xsl:when test="$month= 2">February</xsl:when>
   <xsl:when test="$month= 3">March</xsl:when>
   <xsl:when test="$month= 4">April</xsl:when>
   <xsl:when test="$month= 5">May</xsl:when>
   <xsl:when test="$month= 6">June</xsl:when>
   <xsl:when test="$month= 7">July</xsl:when>
   <xsl:when test="$month= 8">August</xsl:when>
   <xsl:when test="$month= 9">September</xsl:when>
   <xsl:when test="$month=10">October</xsl:when>
   <xsl:when test="$month=11">November</xsl:when>
   <xsl:when test="$month=12">December</xsl:when>
  </xsl:choose>
  <xsl:if test="$year>0">
   <xsl:text> </xsl:text>
   <xsl:value-of select="$year" />
   <xsl:text>: </xsl:text>
  </xsl:if>
 </xsl:template>
</xsl:stylesheet>
```

3. We then need the Perl code in Example D-9 to transform our original XML into viewable HTML.

Example D-9. Transforming news output—xmlLibXSLT.pl

```perl
#!perl -w

use strict;

use XML::LibXSLT;
use XML::LibXML;

my $parser = XML::LibXML->new( );
my $xslt = XML::LibXSLT->new( );

my $source = $parser->parse_file('horsefeather.xml');
my $style_doc = $parser->parse_file('horsefeather.xsl');

my $stylesheet = $xslt->parse_stylesheet($style_doc);
```

Example D-9. Transforming news output—xmlLibXSLT.pl (continued)

```
my $results = $stylesheet->transform($source);

print $stylesheet->output_string($results);
```

4. We simulate the online running of *xmlLibXSLT.pl* with this command:

```
$ perl xmlLibXSLT.pl > horsefeather.html
```

5. The resultant *horsefeather.html* file now pops out of the transformation:

```
<HTML>
<HEAD>
<meta content="text/html; charset=UTF-8" http-equiv="Content-Type">
<TITLE>Horsefeather News - World Latest</TITLE>
</HEAD>
<BODY>
<P><STRONG><CITE>Horsefeather Gazette</CITE>,
  25 December 2002:
  &quot;
  <a href="http://www.horse.feather">Hackenbush Speaks Out</a>&quot;
  </STRONG></P>
<BLOCKQUOTE>
<EM>&quot;That's no Lady.  That's my Wife.&quot;</EM>
</BLOCKQUOTE>
</BODY>
</HTML>
```

This can be viewed in Figure D-6.

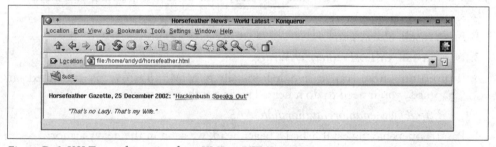

Figure D-6. XSLT transformation from XML to HTML

XML Database Facilities

Now that we have our parsers loaded, we can start racking up our XML weapon toolset prior to battle. In the following sections we'll look at the following Perl XML modules:

> *XML::Generator::DBI*
> *XML::XPath*
> *XML::XMLtoDBMS*

In addition to these, there are many other Perl XML modules available from CPAN. If you have XML needs that these modules don't satisfy, just visit *cpan.org*, and type in "XML" via the search page. Prepare to be bombarded by 1001 different XML responses. The same goes for the XML-based PPM packages on *ActiveState.com*. It seems that all the world has been writing XML modules for Perl. Enjoy!

XML::Generator::DBI

XML::Generator::DBI, written by Matt Sergeant, transforms database calls to XML SAX events. It is useful for quickly generating XML files directly from SQL statements. It's also the replacement for the earlier *DBIx::XML_RDB*, another module from the prolific Mr. Sergeant. Check it out at:

> *http://www.cpan.org/authors/id/M/MS/MSERGEANT*

For testing purposes, and general usage, we also require the services of Michael Koehne's *XML::Handler::YAWriter* (Yet Another Writer, for Perl SAX):

> *http://www.cpan.org/authors/id/K/KR/KRAEHE*

This, in turn, requires the talents of Ken MacLeod's *XML::Parser::PerlSAX*, which comes as part of his *libxml-perl* package. It consists of a general cornucopia of productivity tools, designed originally for use with *XML::Parser*::

> *http://www.cpan.org/authors/id/KMACLEOD*

Then it's time for that ol' Potomac two-step, with bundle unpacking and *Makefile. PL*:

1. First, install *libxml-perl*.
2. Now install *XML::Handler::YAWriter*:
3. If up until now you've avoided installing *MIME::Base64*, as described in Chapter 5, you'll need to do it here. This is another prerequisite module:

   > *http://www.cpan.org/authors/id/GAAS*

4. Paratroopers having established a beachhead, we send in the heavy armor:

   ```
   $ gzip -d XML-Generator-DBI-0.01.tar.gz
   $ tar xvf XML-Generator-DBI-0.01.tar
   $ cd XML-Generator-DBI-0.01
   ```

5. Before building and testing *XML::Generator::DBI*, we need to edit the *PWD* file, which comes with the tarball. The *PWD* information is needed to verify *make test* investigations. Our *PWD* file looked like this:

   ```
   # user name
   UID=scott
   # password
   PWD=tiger
   # Driver to use (as in dbi:Driver)
   DRIVER=Oracle
   # Extra stuff (as in dbi:Driver:extra_stuff)
   ```

```
EXTRA=ORCL.WORLD
# Query to use - Get Groucho! :-)
QUERY=SELECT ename, hiredate FROM EMP WHERE empno = 1001
```

6. Once *PWD* is ready, restart the dance band:

```
$ perl Makefile.PL
$ make
```

7. The *make test* step uses the *PWD* information to generate quite a bit of test information. We're expecting to see *hiredate* data on *Groucho* from the test rows we originally loaded into EMP:

```
$ make test
...
  <select query="SELECT ename, hiredate FROM EMP WHERE empno = 1001">
   <row>
    <ENAME>Groucho</ENAME>
    <HIREDATE>01-JAN-01</HIREDATE>
   </row>
  </select>
...
t/01yawriter....ok
All tests successful.
Files=2, Tests=7, 1 wallclock secs (0.49 cusr + 0.03 csys = 0.52 CPU)
```

8. Once the tests look good, install:

```
$ make install
```

We're now ready to run our XML script to produce *ducksoup.xml* in Example D-10.

Example D-10. First attempt linking XML to DBI—xmlGenDBI.pl

```perl
#!perl -w

use XML::Generator::DBI;
use XML::Handler::YAWriter;
use DBI;

my $writer = XML::Handler::YAWriter->new(AsFile => "ducksoup.xml");

my $dbh = DBI->connect("dbi:Oracle:ORCL.WORLD", "scott", "tiger");

my $xml_generator = XML::Generator::DBI->new( Handler => $writer,
                                              dbh => $dbh );

$xml_generator->execute('select * from emp where empno < 2000');
$dbh->disconnect;
```

What Example D-10 should do, in a mere handful of lines, is to take a SELECT statement, and turn it into an XML file. You might recall the data we added to the EMP table earlier in this chapter:

```
SQL> select * from EMP where empno < 2000;
    EMPNO ENAME      JOB        MGR HIREDATE    SAL    COMM DEPTNO
---------- ---------- --------- ------ --------- ------ ------- ------
```

```
1001  Groucho      Professor      1 01-JAN-01   100      10      10
1002  Chico        Minister       2 02-JAN-01   200      20      20
1003  Harpo        Stowaway       3 03-JAN-01   300      30      30
```

Let's run the script and see what happens:

```
$ perl xmlGenDBI.pl
```

We've taken just the first *<row>* output from our generated *ducksoup.xml* file:

```
<?xml version="1.0" encoding="UTF-8"?><database>
 <select query="select * from emp where empno &lt; 2000">
  <row>
   <EMPNO>1001</EMPNO>
   <ENAME>Groucho</ENAME>
   <JOB>Professor</JOB>
   <MGR>1</MGR>
   <HIREDATE>01-JAN-01</HIREDATE>
   <SAL>100</SAL>
   <COMM>10</COMM>
   <DEPTNO>10</DEPTNO>
  </row>
  ...
 </select>
</database>
```

We can now munge data out of an Oracle database, into XML format, but what about going the other way? This is where *XML::XPath* comes in.

XML::XPath

The *XML::Xpath* module follows all of the XPath standards you may have seen with other XML toolsets. This XML package is also from:

> *http://www.cpan.org/modules/by-module/XML*

You can learn more about XPath at:

> *http://www.w3.org/TR/xpath*

We're going to use *XML::XPath* to read XML file data and then pump it into the database to reverse the munge direction from *XML::Generator::DBI*. There are other ways of doing this—with XLST transformations for example—but we'll use *XML::XPath* because of its flexibility, its appropriateness for munge-style operations, and its simplicity.

Follow these steps:

1. *XML::XPath* requires *XML::Parser*, as installed earlier, but nothing else:

```
$ gzip -d XML-XPath-1.12.tar.gz
$ tar xvf XML-XPath-1.12.tar
$ cd XML-XPath-1.12
$ perl Makefile.PL
$ make
```

2. You'll get lots of output, from 187 tests (we counted 'em) in version 1.12:

```
$ make test
$ make install
```

You may recall that there were two other Marx brothers in addition to the main three: Zeppo, who appeared in most of the earlier films, and Gummo, who quit the act while it was still on Broadway. However, we do rather coincidentally have their information stored in an XML file, in Example D-11, *nightopera.xml*. We'll show how we feed XML into Oracle here.

Example D-11. Feeding XML into Oracle—nightopera.xml

```
<?xml version="1.0" encoding="UTF-8"?>
<database>
 <select>
  <row>
   <EMPNO>1004</EMPNO>
   <ENAME>Zeppo</ENAME>
   <JOB>President</JOB>
   <MGR>1</MGR>
   <HIREDATE>04-JAN-01</HIREDATE>
   <SAL>400</SAL>
   <COMM>40</COMM>
   <DEPTNO>20</DEPTNO>
  </row>
  <row>
   <EMPNO>1005</EMPNO>
   <ENAME>Gummo</ENAME>
   <JOB>Tenor</JOB>
   <MGR>1</MGR>
   <HIREDATE>05-JAN-01</HIREDATE>
   <SAL>500</SAL>
   <COMM>50</COMM>
   <DEPTNO>10</DEPTNO>
  </row>
 </select>
</database>
```

We uploaded it to EMP with the *XML::XPath* script in Example D-12. We've worked through this script immediately following the example:

Example D-12. Feeding XML into Oracle—dbiXPATH.pl

```perl
#!perl -w
use strict;
use DBI;
use XML::XPath;
# Step 1: Connect up to the sink database.
my $dbh = DBI->connect('dbi:Oracle:ORCL.WORLD', 'scott', 'tiger') ||
          die $DBI::errstr;

# Step 2: Locate the source XML data.
```

Example D-12. Feeding XML into Oracle—dbiXPATH.pl (continued)

```perl
my $xpath = XML::XPath->new(filename => 'nightopera.xml');

# Step 3: Prepare the insertion DML.
my $insert_dml =    qq{ INSERT
        INTO emp ( empno,     ename,
                   job,       mgr,
                   hiredate, sal,
                   comm,      deptno )
           VALUES ( to_number( ? ),              ?,
                    ?,                           to_number ( ? ),
                    to_date( ? , 'DD-MON-YY'), to_number ( ? ),
                    to_number ( ? ),            to_number ( ? ) ) };

my $sth = $dbh->prepare( $insert_dml );

# Step 4: Extract the XML records one by one, through the loop,
# and insert into database.
for my $row ($xpath->findnodes('/database/select/row')) {
    # Line sucked from the source.
    my $empno = $row->find('EMPNO')->string_value;
    my $ename = $row->find('ENAME')->string_value;
    my $job = $row->find('JOB')->string_value;
    my $mgr = $row->find('MGR')->string_value;
    my $hiredate = $row->find('HIREDATE')->string_value;
    my $sal = $row->find('SAL')->string_value;
    my $comm = $row->find('COMM')->string_value;
    my $deptno = $row->find('DEPTNO')->string_value;
    # Line inserted into the sink.

    $sth->execute( $empno,
                   $ename,
                   $job,
                   $mgr,
                   $hiredate,
                   $sal,
                   $comm,
                   $deptno ) || die $DBI::errstr;
}

# Step 5: Clean up, and disconnect.
$dbh->disconnect;
```

Let's see what's going on here.

1. There are two parallel pathways moving through this script. The first is DBI-based, and our first step with it is to open up a database connection.

2. In our second path, we locate the XML source input file, *nightopera.xml*.

3. Getting back to the first track, we prepare an INSERT statement.

4. The XML process then uses the *findnodes()* and *find()* methods, to whizz through *nightopera.xml*, sucking out the relevant information before plugging it straight down into the data sink.

5. Once through the loop, we disconnect and clean up (as per union rules).

We can see the results here, from the SCOTT.EMP table.

```
SQL> select * from emp where empno in (1004, 1005);

   EMPNO ENAME      JOB          MGR HIREDATE      SAL   COMM DEPTNO
--------- ---------- --------- ------ --------- ------ -------- ------
    1004 Zeppo      President     1 04-JAN-32    400     40     20
    1005 Gummo      Tenor         1 05-JAN-33    500     50     10
```

A combination of *XML::Generator::DBI* and *XML::XPath* may be all you require to carry out whatever munging operations you require, both to and from the Oracle database, especially if you want access to all the other Perl modules at the same time. However, as with all things in Perl, there is another way to do it.

XML::XMLtoDBMS

Let's suppose that we want to extract data from our database into an XML file. We'd like to then beam this across the galaxy to Betelgeuse, via the local StarGate at Vega, and load it there into a Betelgeusian database. We'd like to do all this with a single Perl module. Step forward *XML::XMLtoDBMS*, a module specially blended with DBI to provide an all-purpose alternative. This module springs directly from its XML-DBMS middleware parent project, which also provides a Java-based alternative. Assuming that we've loaded every XML module discussed so far, except the optional *XML::LibXSLT*, we have everything we need except for one last module, Graham Barr's *TimeDate* bundle:

> *http://www.cpan.org/authors/id/GBARR/*

Once installed, we also have *Date::Format* and *Date::Parse* on board; these came with *TimeDate*. We're now ready for the green light.

The parent project, XML-DBMS, is Ronald Bourret's Java-based middleware for transferring data between XML documents and relational databases. It deals with many of the coding inconveniences in-between and is ideal for data munging purposes. Check it out at:

> *http://www.rpbourret.com/xmldbms/index.htm*

From here you'll be directed to the Perl download of *XML::XMLtoDBMS*, by Nick Semenov. This is ported directly from Ronald Bourret's XML-DBMS software, which is itself written in Java. Before we install *XML::XMLtoDBMS*, however, let's run through a quick checklist of everything we need:

> *expat*
> *XML::Parser*

XML::Parser::PerlSAX (via *libxml-perl*)
libxml2
XML::SAX
XML::LibXML
Date::Format (via *TimeDate*)
Date::Parse (via *TimeDate*)

Once you have these modules and the *XML::XMLtoDBMS* tarball, it's time for that new dance, the Chesapeake bay whirl:

```
$ gzip -d perl-xml-dbms-1.03.tgz
$ tar xvf perl-xml-dbms-1.03.tar
$ cd XML-DBMS
$ vi README
```

We really ought to read the *README* file this time, as *XML::XMLtoDBMS* can be challenging to understand. But once we've got our head round it, the actual installation is straightforward. However, we do need one small adjustment.

To cope with the standard Oracle date format, *DD-MON-YY*, we're going to introduce a one-line adjustment to the *XMLtoDBMS.pm* module for the 1.03 version, which is an open source product under constant development. (This may very well have been amended in later versions.) Add the marked line to the *convertFormat* subroutine. We need this line because it will be difficult to re-insert XML date information back into Oracle, via *XML::XMLtoDBMS*, if the data is not in *DD-MON-YY* format:

```
sub convertFormat
{
        my $formatString = shift;

        $formatString =~ s/YYYY/%Y/g;
        $formatString =~ s/YY/%y/g;
        $formatString =~ s/MM/%m/g;
        $formatString =~ s/MON/%b/g; # Typical Oracle month format.
        $formatString =~ s/DD/%d/g;
        $formatString =~ s/hh/%H/g;
        $formatString =~ s/mm/%M/g;
        $formatString =~ s/ss/%S/g;
        return $formatString;
}
```

A small aside, for those who may think that the fact that this module expects a different date format points out a conceptual weakness of open source software. We disagree. This, we believe, is its greatest strength. If you find that something fails to work *exactly* the way you expect, you can fix the source code directly, to *make* it do what you want.

Once we've made this small adjustment, installation is routine:

```
$ perl Makefile.PL
$ make
```

```
$ make test
$ make install
```

Take a look at the eventual results in Figure D-7.

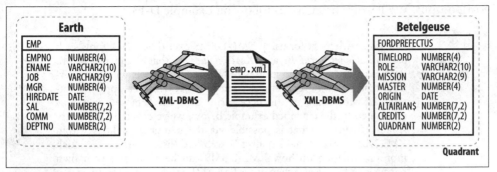

Figure D-7. One Perl XML module to munge them all

The target data-sink table, on Betelgeuse, was created many centuries ago with the following statement:

```
SQL> create table FordPrefectus
  2  ( TimeLord   number(4) not null,
  3    Role       varchar2(10),
  4    Mission    varchar2(9),
  5    Master     number(4),
  6    Origin     date,
  7    Altairian$ number(7,2),
  8    Credits    number(7,2),
  9    Quadrant   number(2) );

Table created.
```

OK, it *is* rather remarkable that they have Oracle-type databases on Betelgeuse, but Professor Hawking tells us it's something to do with the infinite pathway effect of those quantum-type particles which make black holes evaporate. The eagle-eyed among you may have also noted that the FORDPREFECTUS table on Betelgeuse is *remarkably* similar to SCOTT's EMP table back here on Earth. This too is mere quantum coincidence.

Even more fortuitously, the most popular entertainment stars on Betelgeuse are the Marx Brothers, as televised transmissions of their films have only started reaching the Betelgeusian quadrant in the last five years. They would therefore like more information on these black-and-white magicians of the silver screen. As a consequence, we recently received an XML-encoded 3-D message cube, asking us to send the requisite details.

Source mapping

We have agreed upon an XML mapping with the Betelgeusians to facilitate the requested information transfer. At our end, we need a mapping file to construct the XML output. We'll work through this following Example D-13.

The primary benefit for using XML-DBMS over other XML tools such as *XML::Generator::DBI* and *XML::XPath*, is that it can treat XML data as arbitrarily nested groups of tables. Other tools with less overhead tend to treat everything as a single table, which can provide bottlenecks with some of the necessarily complex data sets you may encounter. In the extended example below, we've covered only a very small segment of what is possible via the mapping facilities within XML-DBMS. See Ronald Bourret's web site (listed earlier) for much more information on how XML-DBMS can help to solve your own particular XML needs when other Perl XML modules are insufficient.

Example D-13. Source mapping for XML::XMLtoDBMS—emp.map

```
<?xml version="1.0" ?>
<XMLToDBMS Version="1.0">
   <Options>
      <DateTimeFormats><Patterns Date="DD-MON-YY"/>
      </DateTimeFormats>
   </Options>
   <Maps>
      <IgnoreRoot>
         <ElementType Name="employees"/>
         <PseudoRoot>
            <ElementType Name="emp"/>
            <CandidateKey Generate="No"><Column Name="empno"/>
            </CandidateKey>
         </PseudoRoot>
      </IgnoreRoot>
         <ClassMap>
         <ElementType Name="emp"/>
         <ToClassTable><Table Name="emp"/>
         </ToClassTable>
         <PropertyMap>
            <ElementType Name="empno"/>
            <ToColumn><Column Name="empno"/>
            </ToColumn>
         </PropertyMap>
         <PropertyMap>
            <ElementType Name="ename"/>
            <ToColumn><Column Name="ename"/>
            </ToColumn>
         </PropertyMap>
         <PropertyMap>
            <ElementType Name="job"/>
            <ToColumn><Column Name="job"/>
            </ToColumn>
```

```
        </PropertyMap>
        <PropertyMap>
            <ElementType Name="mgr"/>
            <ToColumn><Column Name="mgr"/>
            </ToColumn>
        </PropertyMap>
        <PropertyMap>
            <ElementType Name="hiredate"/>
            <ToColumn><Column Name="hiredate"/>
            </ToColumn>
        </PropertyMap>
        <PropertyMap>
            <ElementType Name="sal"/>
            <ToColumn><Column Name="sal"/>
            </ToColumn>
        </PropertyMap>
        <PropertyMap>
            <ElementType Name="comm"/>
            <ToColumn><Column Name="comm"/>
            </ToColumn>
        </PropertyMap>
        <PropertyMap>
            <ElementType Name="deptno"/>
            <ToColumn><Column Name="deptno"/>
            </ToColumn>
        </PropertyMap>
    </ClassMap>
  </Maps>
</XMLToDBMS>
```

Let's see what's happening here:

1. There are four particularly interesting nodes within the *emp.map* XML file. The first is the *<Options>* node, which details the date format we're going to use, *DD-MON-YY*, which is possible after our earlier code adjustment.

2. The second is the *<IgnoreRoot>* node, containing two important elements:

    a. The first is the initial *<ElementType>*, which sets the conceptual name for the whole XML-ised *blob* of information as *employees*.

    b. The second, is the *<CandidateKey>* node, which tells us that the primary key for *emp* is the *<Column>* value, *empno*.

3. The next important node grouping is the one marked by *<ToClassTable>*, which contains the *<Table>* node, confirming to us that our table name is indeed *emp*. This may seem to be duplication, but it's important, as we'll see later. Also notice the *<ClassMap>* and *<ElementType>* mapping just above. The point here is that we've chosen to map some elements to tables, with *<ClassMap>*, and some other elements to columns, with *<PropertyMap>*.

4. The next node group, under *<PropertyMap>*, is significant. It gives us a conceptual name for each column, under *<ElementType>*, but supplies us with an actual column name, under the *<Column>* node.

There are far more complex things possible with the mappings available in *XML:: XMLtoDBMS*—for example, table pairs with different primary and foreign key constraints, varying numbers of columns, date and time format differences, and much more. You name it, it's probably in the mapping language. As you can see from Example D-13, however, even a relatively simple exchange of data can generate a large mapping file. But once you've got the basic structure, the rest is just plugging in the numbers.

You might wish to examine the DTD file, *xmldbms.dtd,* which comes with the download, as well as visit the web pages:

Source output

Now that we have the mapping, we can generate the XML in Example D-14.

Example D-14. Creating our source data—outXMLDBMS.pl

```
#!perl -w

use strict;
use DBI;
use XML::XMLtoDBMS;

# Step 1: Connect to Oracle, as usual.
# Then use the database handle to feed XML::XMLtoDBMS.

my $dbh = DBI->connect('dbi:Oracle:ORCL.WORLD', 'scott', 'tiger') ||
            die $DBI::errstr;

my $xmlToDbms = new XML::XMLtoDBMS($dbh);

$xmlToDbms->setMap('emp.map');

# Step 2:  Get hold of the data.  Use the primary keys of our
# required rows, to isolate them.

my $xmlOut = $xmlToDbms->retrieveDocument(
                'emp',
                [['1001'],['1002'],['1003'],['1004'],['1005']] );
# Step 3: Output the data to XML.

open (XML, ">emp.xml");
# Prettify printing with format 1 line break
print XML $xmlOut->toString(1);
close XML;
# Step 4: It's important to clean up the acquired DOM memory,
# as well as disconnecting from the Oracle server.
```

Example D-14. Creating our source data—outXMLDBMS.pl (continued)

```
$xmlToDbms->destroy;
$dbh->disconnect;
```

Let's work through the code.

1. We acquire a database connection via DBI. Once this is done, we can forget about DBI entirely, as *XML::XMLtoDBMS* takes the database handle and does all the work, based on the *emp.map* instructions created earlier.

2. Once we have the appropriate handles in place, we retrieve the required data from the SCOTT.EMP table using *retrieveDocument()*. Notice the use of the EMPNO primary keys to get the five rows required. There are several other filter techniques also available.

3. The next step is simple. We produce the *emp.xml* file we'll be sending through the Vegan StarGate.

4. Once we're done, we clean up, both destroying the memory used to create the XML file and disconnecting from the database.

Let's run the script:

```
$ perl outXMLDBMS.pl
```

A snippet of the resultant output file, *emp.xml*, is displayed here, with one of the *<emp>* records:

```
<?xml version="1.0" encoding="UTF-8"?>
<employees>
  <emp>
    <mgr>1</mgr>
    <sal>100</sal>
    <ename>Groucho</ename>
    <job>Professor</job>
    <empno>1001</empno>
    <deptno>10</deptno>
    <comm>10</comm>
    <hiredate>01-Jan-01</hiredate>
  </emp>
  ...
</employees>
```

Notice that we have *Groucho* embedded, like a nugget of gold, within the XML.

Sink mapping

Once *emp.xml* is beamed across to Betelgeuse by hyperwave-relay, we're going to need another mapping file. This one will cope with the different column names in FORDPREFECTUS. We've detailed this mapping in Example D-15.

Example D-15. Mapping the data into the sink—timelord.map

```xml
<?xml version="1.0" ?><XMLToDBMS Version="1.0">
    <Options>
        <DateTimeFormats><Patterns Date="DD-MON-YY"/>
        </DateTimeFormats>
    </Options>
    <Maps>
        <IgnoreRoot>
            <ElementType Name="employees"/>
            <PseudoRoot>
                <ElementType Name="emp"/>
                <CandidateKey Generate="No"><Column Name="timelord"/>
                </CandidateKey>
            </PseudoRoot>
        </IgnoreRoot>
        <ClassMap>
        <ElementType Name="emp"/>
        <ToClassTable><Table Name="fordprefectus"/>
        </ToClassTable>
        <PropertyMap>
            <ElementType Name="empno"/>
            <ToColumn><Column Name="timelord"/>
            </ToColumn>
        </PropertyMap>
        <PropertyMap>
            <ElementType Name="ename"/>
            <ToColumn><Column Name="role"/>
            </ToColumn>
        </PropertyMap>
        <PropertyMap>
            <ElementType Name="job"/>
            <ToColumn><Column Name="mission"/>
            </ToColumn>
        </PropertyMap>
        <PropertyMap>
            <ElementType Name="mgr"/>
            <ToColumn><Column Name="master"/>
            </ToColumn>
        </PropertyMap>
        <PropertyMap>
            <ElementType Name="hiredate"/>
            <ToColumn><Column Name="origin"/>
            </ToColumn>
        </PropertyMap>
        <PropertyMap>
            <ElementType Name="sal"/>
            <ToColumn><Column Name="altairian$"/>
            </ToColumn>
        </PropertyMap>
        <PropertyMap>
            <ElementType Name="comm"/>
            <ToColumn><Column Name="credits"/>
            </ToColumn>
```

```
          </PropertyMap>
          <PropertyMap>
            <ElementType Name="deptno"/>
            <ToColumn><Column Name="quadrant"/>
            </ToColumn>
          </PropertyMap>
      </ClassMap>
    </Maps>
</XMLToDBMS>
```

Let's see what's going on in this example.

1. Notice the date format in the *<Options>* node near the start of the file.

2. Notice also that the *<CandidateKey>* column name for the primary key is *timelord*.

3. The *<ToClassTable>* mapping also varies slightly. We have all the *emp* data mapped to the table *fordprefectus*.

4. Within each *<PropertyMap>* node, we also have each *<ElementType>*, such as *empno*, being mapped across to a new *<Column>* name value, such as *timelord*. This pattern repeats throughout the mapping file.

Sink input

Meanwhile on Betelgeuse, the XML from Earth has arrived and our friends have the requisite mapping file. All that needs to be done, in Example D-16, is to run a universal Perloid script, operating on the galactic standard Traalix operating system and load it up into the database. Let's go.

Example D-16. Inputting into the sink—inXMLDBMS.pl

```perl
#!perl -w

use strict;
use DBI;
use XML::XMLtoDBMS;

# Step 1: Connect to our remote Oracle database on Betelgeuse :-)
# Use the connection acquired to create our XML::XMLtoDBMS object.

my $dbh = DBI->connect('dbi:Oracle:BETELGEUSE.WORLD',
                       'zaphod', 'h33b13br0x') || die $DBI::errstr;

my $xmlToDbms = new XML::XMLtoDBMS($dbh);

$xmlToDbms->setMap('timelord.map');

# Step 2:  Acquire the XML file, and then store it in the datasink.

my $xmlIn =
```

Example D-16. Inputting into the sink—inXMLDBMS.pl (continued)

```
$xmlToDbms->storeDocument( Source => {File => "emp.xml"} );

# Step 3: Disconnect and clean up memory.

$xmlToDbms->destroy;
$dbh->disconnect;
```

Here's what's happening:

1. We open the database connection and use it to prime *XML::XMLtoDBMS* before setting the configuration via *timelord.map*.

2. Using *storeDocument( )*, we pump the *emp.xml* file into the data sink.

3. Finally, we wrap up the memory, disconnect, and exit.

Results

The table data folds neatly into FORDPREFECTUS. Mission accomplished:

```
SQL> select * from FordPrefectus ;

TIMELORD ROLE    MISSION   MASTER ORIGIN    ALTAIRIAN$ CREDITS QUADRANT
-------- ------- --------- ------ --------- ---------- ------- --------
    1001 Groucho Professor      1 01-JAN-01        100      10       10
    1002 Chico   Minister       2 02-JAN-01        200      20       20
    1003 Harpo   Stowaway       3 03-JAN-01        300      30       30
    1004 Zeppo   President      1 04-JAN-01        400      40       20
    1005 Gummo   Tenor          1 05-JAN-01        500      50       10
```

What's Coming in XML::DBMS?

Features coming in Version 2.0 of XML-DBMS include the following:

- Updates and deletes, as well as further selection filters
- Heterogeneous joins
- Additional mapping language features, such as per-column formatting and limited transformation
- The generation of map files from the database
- Support for database-generated keys

Index

Symbols

<% . . . %> (angle brackets-percent signs),
   Perl in Embperl template, 174
[! . . . !] (square brackets-exclamation points),
   Perl in Embperl template, 166
[- . . . -] (square brackets-hyphens), Perl in
   Embperl template, 166
[+ . . . +] (square brackets-plus signs), Perl in
   Embperl template, 166
-> (arrow notation), Perl, 453
* (asterisk), Perl regex metacharacter, 495, 500
*? (asterisk-question mark), Perl regex
   metacharacter, 502
@ (at sign), Perl variable notation, 453
^ (caret sign), Perl regex metacharacter, 496
$ (dollar sign)
  Perl hashes, 445
  Perl regex metacharacter, 496
  Perl scalars, 442
  Perl variable notation, 453
$# (dollar sign-number sign) Perl syntax, 444
$_ (dollar sign-underscore)
  implicit use in regexes, 489
  pronoun in Perl hashes, 445
. (dot character), Perl regex
   metacharacter, 496, 498
=~ (equal sign-tilde), Perl pattern-binding
   operator, 488
!~ (exclamation point-tilde), Perl
   pattern-binding operator, 489
% (percent sign)
  Perl in Mason template, 174
  Perl variable notation, 453

+ (plus sign), Perl regex metacharacter, 495,
   500
+? (plus sign-question mark), Perl regex
   metacharacter, 503
? (question mark), Perl regex
   metacharacter, 496, 500
?? (question mark-question mark), Perl regex
   metacharacter, 503
| (vertical bar), Perl regex metacharacter, 495
<> (angle brackets)
  mucr8.pl file, 292
  spdrvr.pl, 390
{} (curly braces)
  Embperl, 167
  idxr.pl, 304
() (parentheses), Perl regex
   metacharacter, 495
[] (square brackets), 167
  Perl arrays, 444
  Perl regex metacharacter, 495
[^] (square brackets-caret sign), Perl regex
   metacharacter, 495
/ (backslash), Perl regex metacharacter, 495

A

accounts
  creating multiuser with mucr8.pl, 230,
   290–295
  creating single user
   with create_user.pl, 282–288
   with dup_user.pl, 288–290
   with PDBA::DBA, 234
  dropping, 230, 280, 296

We'd like to hear your suggestions for improving our indexes. Send email to *index@oreilly.com*.

accounts (*continued*)
    duplicating with PDBA Toolkit
        scripts, 230
    granting privileges while creating, 283
    managing, 229
        with PDBA Toolkit scripts, 280–296
    reports on users, 387
    setting quotas while creating, 283
    specifying tablespaces, 286
Active Server Pages (see ASP)
ActivePerl, 28
    CGI scripts, 116
    downloading latest build of, 36
    installing Perl on Win32 and, 36
    loading DBD::Chart for, 104
    package for DDL::Oracle, 88
ActiveState, 28
    date-related modules on, 534
AIX, installing Perl from prebuilt package, 31
alarmTime parameter (chkalert.pl), 333
alert log, 328
    filename, 329
    Karma email error notification, 133
    location of, 329
    monitoring, 230
        with chkalert.pl, 329
        PDBA Toolkit scripts, 230
        with PDBA Toolkit scripts, 328–342
alertLevel parameter (dbup.conf), 358
alert_orcl.log, 329
algorithms
    compression, lossless vs. lossy, 100
    data munging, resources, 524
all method (PDBA::GQ), 245
    retrieving all rows simultaneously, 246
ALTER INDEX REBUILD statement
        (Oracle), 300
ANALYZE command (Oracle), 382
angle brackets (<>)
    mucr8.pl file, 292
    spdrvr.pl, 390
angle brackets-percent signs (<% . . . %>),
        Perl in Embperl template, 174
angle brackets-percent signs (<%perl> . . .
        </%perl>), 175
Apache, 111–118
    building with Perl, 113
    CGI scripts
        ActivePerl and, 116
        directory for, 114
    configuring Mason for, 172–177

    downloading, 112
        Unix version, 112
        Win32 version, 114
    embedding Perl into (see mod_perl)
    Embperl and, 162, 164
    installing
        on Unix, 112–114
        on Win32, 114
    interface with Storable.pm, 163
    mod_perl modules, table of, 145
    ORACLE_HOME variable and, 149
    Perl and, 111
        (see also mod_perl)
    Perl modules, 144–151
    running httpd servers as root, 113
    server functions, rewriting CGI scripts
        into, 144
    using DBD::Chart with, 116–118
    web resource for, 111
Apache AutoConf Interface (APACI), 113
Apache Run Time Configuration Directives,
        web resource, 112
Apache Software Foundation (ASF), 112
APACHE variable, installing Mason, 170
Apache::AuthDBI, 148
Apache::DBI, 137, 145, 147–149
    Apache::OWA and, 157
    downloading, 148
Apache::OWA, 137, 155–160
    Apache::DBI and, 157
    configuring, 158–160
    downloading, 158
    installing
        on Unix, 157
        on Win32, 158
    web resources for, 156
Apache::Registry, 136, 144, 145–147
    "my" variables and, 146
Apache::Request, 157
Apache::Session, 163
    Embperl and, 168
Apache::SessionX, 163
APACI (Apache AutoConf Interface), 113
applications
    data warehouse, limiting resource
        consumption, 305
    described in this book, download sites, 17
    Perl
        open source, 15
        servicing users/requests, 180
arguments, parsing command-line, 348

arrays
    anonymous, in Perl, 455
    fetching rows from, 469
    generating, 475
    generating references to, 475
    Perl, 443
        determining size of, 444
arrow notation (->), Perl, 453
ASF (Apache Software Foundation), 112
ASP (Active Server Pages), 7, 161
associative arrays (see hashes)
asterisk (*), Perl regex metacharacter, 495, 500
asterisk-question mark (*?), Perl regex
        metacharacter, 502
at sign (@), Perl variable notation, 453
@ARGV array (Perl), 448
@_ array (Perl), 448
@emailAddresses parameter
        (maxext.conf), 315
attributes
    in mucr8.msg file, 293
    Perl DBI database handle, 462
@video_collection array (Perl), 443
Authen::ACE, 223
authentication, 252
AutoCommit attribute, connecting to Oracle
        databases via PDBA::CM, 234
AUTOEXEC.BAT file, Orac and, 83
available_drivers method (Perl DBI), 464
AxKit, 176

B

backreferences, capturing, 505–509
backslash (/), Perl regex metacharacter, 495
bandwidth, Perl and, 7
baseline.pl, 231
    command-line options, table of, 374
    example output, 375
batch processor, DDL::Oracle as, 88
begin_work method (Perl DBI), 476
binary data, extracting with sqlunldr.pl, 320
binary large objects (BLOBs), fine-grained
        access to, 181
bind_col method (Perl DBI), 474
bind_columns method (Perl DBI), 474
bind_param method (Perl DBI), 467
bind_param_inout method
        (DBD::Oracle), 467
Bit::Vector, 536
bless command (Perl), 457
BLOBs (binary large objects), fine-grained
        access to, 181

Blowfish, 123
boolean variable type, Perl and, 448
./boot test compilation errors, 188

C

C language
    embedding Perl in, 203
    files, scanning for constructs, 186
    Oracle::OCI vs., 181
C libraries
    connecting with, 184
    Perl and, 202
caret sign (^), Perl regex metacharacter, 496
carriage return/line feed (see CR/LF)
case sensitivity
    inline Perl in Mason, 175
    Perl string-handling functions, 487
    suffix for enabling regex match to
            ignore, 510
CBO (cost-based optimizer), 382
CGI (Common Gateway Interface), 110
    scripts (see CGI scripts)
CGI environment variables, Apache::Registry
            and, 147
CGI scripts, 110
    with ActivePerl on Apache, 116
    disadvantages of, 136
    improving performance of, 136
        (see also Apache::Registry)
    managing (see Apache::Registry;
            Apache::DBI)
    mod_perl and, 137
    Oracletool and, 111
    rewriting into Apache server
            functions, 144
    web resources for, 138
cgi.pm resource, 111
character large objects (CLOBs), 317
charts, for performance statistics
            (see DBD::Chart)
checksums, PDBA Toolkit scripts and, 397
chkalert.conf, 331–334
chkalert_NT.pl, 230
    command-line options, table of, 342
    installing on Win32, 337–342
    Oracle_SID_AlertLogMon, testing, 340
    starting monitoring service, 339
chkalert.pl, 230, 329
    command-line option, table of, 337
    configuring on Unix, 331–336
    features of, 330
    installing on Unix, 331–336

chkalert.pl (*continued*)
  -kill option, 336
  modifying configuration parameters, 333
  on Win32 (see chkalert_NT.pl)
  running, 334
  testing, 336
  Unix/Win32 versions, 331
chkalert_service.pl, 230
  command-line options, 338
CLOBs (character large objects), 317
cm.conf, 266
  overriding ignoring of by PDBA::CM, 267
column_diff_rpt, reporting changes to table
      columns, 383, 386
column_info method (Perl DBI), 477
column_rpt, reporting on table columns, 386
command line, scanning for options intended
      for password server, 250
  (see also PDBA::OPT/PDBA::PWC)
command-line arguments, parsing, 348
commit method (Perl DBI), 476
Common Gateway Interface (see CGI)
Comprehensive Perl Archive Network
      (see CPAN)
compression algorithms, lossless vs. lossy, 100
configuration files
  adding passwords to, 420
  creating for PDBA password client, 276
  driving scripts, changing, 235
  PDBA Unix, installing, 261
configuration variables, referring to by
      package name, 240
configuring
  Apache::OWA, 158–160
  chkalert.pl on Unix, 331–336
  dba_jobsm.pl, 405
  dbup.pl on Unix, 354
  dbup.pl/dbup_NT.pl, 353–361
    setting DBA on call, 360
    setting pager and email addresses, 359
    upDays/upHours parameters, 358
    uptime requirements, 357
  Karma
    on Unix, 130–133
    on Win32, 134
  kss.pl, 310
  Mason for Apache, 172–177
  mod_perl on Win32, 152
  PDBA Toolkit, 265–278
    password client, 275–278
    password server, 268–275
    PDBA module, 265
    PDBA::CM, 266

connect method (Perl DBI), 460–464
connect PDBA role, 296
connect_cached method (Perl DBI), 464
connectInterval parameter (dbup.conf), 356
Connection Manager (see PDBA::CM)
conversion data-munging modules, 544–552
Convert::Recode, 545
cost-based optimizer (CBO), 382
CPAN (Comprehensive Perl Archive
      Network), 6
  data-munging modules
    conversion, 544–552
    date, 534–544
    mathematics, 533
    numeric, 531–533
    text conversion, 547–552
    XML, 552–574
  downloading source from, 34
CPAN module
  installing Perl modules, 39–42
    from command line, 41
    interactive CPAN shell, 40
  unreliability of, 42, 138
CPAN packages, LWP.pm and, 139
create method (PDBA::DBA), 235
create_user.conf, 283–286
create_user.pl, 230, 281–287
  command-line options, table of, 286
creating
  charts for performance statistics
        (see DBD::Chart)
  GUI-driven applications in Perl
        (see Perl/Tk)
  Internet Perl clients with LWP.pm, 138
  log files, 248
  multiuser accounts with
        mucr8.pl, 290–295
  objects, 235
    with PDBA Toolkit, 229
  oracle user from command line, 230
  PROFILEs, 306
  single user accounts
    with create_user.pl, 281–287
    with dup_user.pl, 288–290
  statement handles, 466
  tablespaces, PDBA repository
        installation, 369
  user accounts
    with PDBA::DBA, 234
    tablespaces and, 286
creating Internet Perl clients, 138
CR/LF (carriage return/line feed), 118
  configuring dbup.pl/dbup_NT.pl, 354

Crypt::Beowulf, 223
Crypt::Blowfish, 123
Crypt::IDEA, 123
Crypt::RC4, 258, 264
   PDBA password server and, 270
Crypt::SSLeay, 139
Crypt::Twofish2, 223
C::Scan, required by Oracle::OCI, 186
curly braces ({ })
   Embperl, 167
   idxr.pl, 304
cursors, binding, 480
Cygwin, 28, 51
   downloading, 52
   installing DBD::Oracle under, 57–61
      accessing Oracle client libraries, 57, 60
   installing Perl DBI under, 56
   installing Perl under, 52–56
      packages required, 54
   security and, 56
   web resource for, 52
CYGWIN variable, 56

D

DAD (Database Access Descriptor), 158
Data Definition Language (see DDL)
data dictionary, Oracle
   loading baseline data into PDBA
      repository, 374–376
   PDBA repository and, 366
Data Manipulation Language (DML), 180
data munging, 522
   components of, 523
   conversion methods, 532
   CPAN modules
      conversion, 544–552
      date, 534–544
      mathematic, 533
      numeric, 531–533
      text conversion, 547–552
      XML, 552–574
   guide to, 521–574
   how it works, 522
   inter-database transfer
      MySQL source, 526–528
      Oracle target, 528–531
   regexes and, 501
   resource for further information, 522
data warehouse applications, limiting
      resource consumption, 305

Database Access Descriptor (DAD), 158
database connectivity
   monitoring with dbup.pl/dbup_
      NT.pl, 343–365
      %uptime hash parameters, 357
   monitoring with PDBA Toolkit
      scripts, 342–365
   polling, 343
Database Driver for Oracle (see DBD::Oracle)
database handles
   attributes, Perl DBI, 462
   Perl DBI
      SQL and cleanup, 475–477
      statement handle methods, 465–474
database repository, building with DBA
      Toolkit, 366–402
database server, checking on, 466
databases
   administering
      cutting/pasting scripts, avoiding
         (see DDL::Oracle)
      with PDBA Toolkit scripts
         (see PDBA Toolkit scripts)
      Unix system administration and
         (see StatsView)
      (see also Oracletool)
   automating administration tasks, 244
   checking availability of, 230
   connections
      closing down, 476
      pooling, 137
      (see also Apache::DBI;
         database connectivity)
   monitoring, 111
      with Oracletool, 125
      with PDBA Toolkit scripts, 328–365
      (see also Karma)
   Oracle
      limiting resource
         consumption, 305–308
      NULL values and, 425
      space problems on, 297–300
   Oracle DDL from Oracle8i,
      reverse-engineering
      (see DDL::Oracle)
   relational, operations of (see OCI,
      relational functions)
   reporting status of jobs in, 231
   schemas
      comparing, 231
      dumping, 318

databases, schemas (*continued*)
    examining/saving
        (see SchemaView-Plus)
        (see also SchemaDiff; sqlunldr.pl)
    targets, retrieving list of, 464
    tracking changes to (see PDBA repository;
        reports, of database changes)
    transfering among
        example of data munging, 526–531
        MySQL source, 526–528
        Oracle target, 528–531
Data::Dumper, required by Mason, 170
Data::Flow, required by Oracle::OCI, 186
data_sources method (Perl DBI), 464
datatypes, cookie manipulation, 157
Date::Calc, 536
    Date-Calc 5.0 API
        languages supplied with, 542
        methods in, 536
    system_clock method, figures provided
        by, 540
Date::Calendar, 536
-dateformat option (sqlunldr.pl), 318
Date::Format, XML::XMLtoDBMS and, 565
Date::Manip, 344
    installing
        on Unix, 344
        on Win32, 344–347
    Manip.cnf, 344–347
Date::Parse, XML::XMLtoDBMS and, 565
date/time information
    -dateformat option, 318
    leap seconds in calendar, 540
    modules, 534–544
    Oracle date format, XML::XMLtoDBMS
        and, 566
    parsing, 258, 264, 344
    PDBA repository reports, changing in, 373
date/time utilities, 156
dbaAddresses parameter (chkalert.pl), 333
dba_jobs.conf, 406
dba_jobsm.pl, 231, 405–419
    configuring, 405
    example report generated by, 406
    functions/formats description, 417–419
    modifying, 419–421
        adding passwords to config file, 420
        configuring parameters, 419
    script description, 407–417
dba_jobs.pl, 231
DB_BLOCK_BUFFERS parameter
    (Oracle), 379

DBD drivers, retrieving list of, 464
DBD::Chart, 66, 95–104
    downloading, 98
    installing
        on Unix, 98–103
        on Win32, 103
    libraries required, 99
    loading for ActivePerl, 104
    modules required, 98
    preparing, 98
    Unix downloads required, 99
    using Apache with, 116–118
    using Perl/Tk applications with, 102
dbdimp.c file, patching DBD::Oracle, 215
DBD::mysql driver, 526
DBD::Oracle, 11–13
    architecture compared to Oracle::OCI, 179
    cursors, binding, 480
    documentation provided for, 441
    downloading, 47, 56
    extproc_perl and, 212–217
    handling LOBs, 480
    installing, 44–46
        under Cygwin, 57–61
        environment variables, 44
        error hit list, 45
    limitation of, 50
    methods for Perl DBI, 478
    online documentation for, 459
    patch provided with extproc_perl
        download, 211, 214
    patching, 214–216
        setting variables, 215
    PDBA repository and, 374
    Perl DBI and, 459
        coding with Oracle::OCI, 194
    relationship to Oracle::OCI, 181
    versions of, xi, 58
    (see also Perl DBI)
DBD::Proxy, 50
dbgextp.sql file, debugging external
        procedure setup, 209
$dbh variable (Perl DBI), 460–463
dbignore.pl, 230
dbiproxy daemon, 44
    running Perl DBI by proxy, 50
DBI::ProxyServer, 50
    packages required, 51
dbish/dbishell programs, 96
DBMS_OUTPUT package, 478
dbms_output_enable method
        (DBD::Oracle), 478

dbms_output_get method
        (DBD::Oracle), 478
dbms_output_put method
        DBD::Oracle), 478
dbup.conf, 354
    DBA on-call schedule, 360
    email addresses, 359
    operational parameters, 355
    test configuration, 362–365
dbup_NT.pl, 230
dbup.pl, 230
dbup.pl/dbup_NT.pl, 343–365
    command-line options, table of, 365
    configuring, 353–361
        setting DBA on call, 360
        setting pager and email addresses, 359
        upDays/upHours parameters, 358
        uptime requirements, 357
    Date::Manip and, 344
    password server and, 348
    testing monitor, 362–365
dbup_service.pl, 230, 354
DDL (Data Definition Language)
    extracting, 315–327
        with ddl_oracle.pl, 323–327
    generating, 229
    Oracle and, 85
    time boundaries and, 231
DDL::Oracle, 65, 84–90, 325
    as batch and list processor, 88
    download example scripts, table of, 88
    downloading, 84
    installing
        on Win32, 88
        on Unix, 85
    mailing list, 85
    using as batch and list processor,
        defrag.pl, 89
    using Orac with, 85–88
        example program, 86
ddl_oracle.pl, 229, 323–327
    command-line options, table of, 325
    scripts generated by, table of, 326
DEBUG_EXTPROC package, 210
debugging
    external procedure listeners, 209
    gdb program and, 210
    installing Oracle::OCI on Unix, 189
    Perl GUI debuggers, 108
    Perl GUI tools for, download sites, 21
    Perl scripts, 109
    setting tracing level, 464

defrag.pl command, 89
    parameters, files created by, 90
    scripts created by, 89
Deterministic Finite Automaton (DFA), 491
developer PDBA role, 296
DFA (Deterministic Finite Automaton), 491
Digest::MD5, 139
directory paths
    alert log, 329
    create_user.conf, 283
    creating to log files, 248
    dba_jobsm.pl, 405
    installing Perl on Unix, 29
    for PDBA Toolkit
        with configuration files on Win32, 262
        scripts, 279
        supporting modules/scripts on
            Unix, 259
    Win32 CGI scripts, 116
disconnect method (Perl DBI), 476
DJ Deloric's GNU Programming Platform
        (DJGPP), 61
DJGPP (DJ Delorie's GNU Programming
        Platform), 61
DML (Data Manipulation Language), 180
DML statements, preparing, 466
do . . . until loops, Embperl syntax, 167
do method (Perl DBI), 475
dollar sign ($)
    Perl hashes, 445
    Perl regex metacharacter, 496
    Perl scalars, 442
    Perl variable notation, 453
dollar sign-number sign ($#) Perl syntax, 444
dollar sign-underscore ($_)
    implicit use in regexes, 489
    pronoun in Perl, 445
dot character (.), Perl regex
        metacharacter, 496, 498
downloading
    ActivePerl, latest build, 36
    Apache, 112
        Unix version, 112
        Win32 version, 114
    Apache::DBI, 148
    Apache::OWA, 158
    Apache::Request, 157
    Apache::Session, 163
    Apache::SessionX, 163
    Bit::Vector, 536
    Crypt::Blowfish, 123
    Crypt::IDEA, 123

downloading (*continued*)
  Crypt::RC4, 258
  C::Scan, 186
  Cygwin, 52
  Cygwin packages, 53
  Data::Flow, 186
  Date::Calc, 536
  Date::Calendar, 536
  Date::Manip, 344
  DBD::Chart, 98
  DBD::Oracle, 47, 56
  DDL::Oracle, 84
  expat program, 553
  extproc_perl, 207
  FreezeThaw, 170
  Karma, 128
  libapreq, 157
  libnet library, 130
  libxml2, 555
  libxslt, 555
  LWP.pm, 138
  Mail::Sendmail, 258
  Mason, 169
  MIME::Base64, 560
  MLDBM, 169
  mod_perl, 140
  Number::Format, 533
  Open Perl IDE, 107
  Orac, 82
  ora_explain.PL, 73
  Params::Validate, 170
  PDBA Toolkit, 259
  PDBA.ppd, 262
  PDBAx, 422
  Perl, 28
    source from CPAN, 34
  Perl DBI, 47, 56
  Perl/Tk, 67
  PNG, 77
  recode library, 545
  SchemaDiff, 90
  Senora, 92
  StatsView, 75–80
    gnuplot installation, 79
    PNG installation, 77–79
    PNG, need for, 76
    zlib installation, 76
  Storable, 163, 170
  TimeDate, 258
  Time::HiRes, 169
  Tk::GBARR, 75

  Win32::Daemon, 264
  XML::Dumper, 106
  XML::LibXML, 555
  XML::LibXSLT, 555
  XML::Parser, 553
  XML::SAX, 555
  XML::XMLtoDBMS, 565
  XML::XPath, 562
  zlib, 76
drop method (PDBA::DBA), 235
drop_user.pl, 230, 296
-dryrun option (mucr8.pl), 295
dump_results method (Perl DBI), 474
dup_user.pl, 230, 288–290
dynamic SQL utilities, 156

E

ebugDBA parameter (chkalert.pl), 333
ed program, regular expressions and, 484
email
  in Karma via MailTools.pm, 130
    error notification, 132
  Perl and, 201
  sending from Perl scripts, 254, 256
email method (PDBA module), 254, 256
emailHome parameter (dbup.conf), 360
emailWork parameter (dbup.conf), 360
embedded web scripting, 161–177
  web resources for, 176
  (see also Embperl; Mason)
Embperl, 162–169
  Apache and, 162
  Apache::Session and, 168
  deploying, 164–165
  forms handling, 168
  installing
    on Unix, 162
    on Win32, 163
  latest release of, 162
  modules required by, 162
  syntax, 166–168
    controlling template-driven program
      flow, 166
    embedding Perl in Embperl
      templates, 166
    variable naming, 168
  web resources for, 162
EMBPERL_DEBUG variable, 164
encryption
  Oracletool security levels, 122
  passwords (see password encryption)

PDBA password server and, 270
Perl and, 201
%encryption data structure (pwd.conf), 270
<<END_DATE_PK>> tag (spdrvr.pl), 390
%ENV hash (Perl), 449
environment variables
  cm.conf and, 266
  Oracle
    DBD::Oracle and, 44
    predefining, 232
  Perl scripts and, 449
  specifying, 149
  Win32
    PPM and, 47
    web resource for, 47
equal sign-tilde (=~), Perl pattern-binding
    operator, 488
error conditions, PDBA Toolkit monitoring
    scripts, 230
errorList parameter (chkalert.pl), 334
errors
  ./boot test compilation, avoiding when
    installing Oracle::OCI, 188
  insufficient privileges on underlying
    objects and sxp.pl, 396
  no password available and sxp.pl, 396
  ORACLE not available, 188
  unique constraint error and sxp.pl, 395
exclamation point-tilde (!~), Perl
    pattern-binding operator, 489
execute method
  PDBA::GQ, 246
  Perl DBI, 469
expat program, 553
exp_exclude.conf, 324
Export utility (Oracle), 316
extensibility, Senora vs. SQL*Plus, 93
Extensible Markup Language (see XML)
Extensible Stylesheet Language
    Transformations (XSLT), 556
extents
  allocating in LMTs, 312
  dictionary-managed, 230
  managing usage of, 229, 312–315
  (see also LMTs)
external procedures, 202
  Oracle, resources, 204
  setting up, 207–209
EXTPROC listener
  PL/SQL broadcasts to, 206
  restrictive privileges for, 208
  tnsnames.ora entry for, 208

EXTPROC program, 204
  case sensitivity when referring to, 209
  directory for, 209
  security alerts about, 205
extproc_perl, 204, 206–209
  building Perl
    new Perl, 210–212
    (see also oracle user, building Perl for)
  connecting to host database, 216
  DBD::Oracle patch provided with, 211,
    214
  debugging external procedure listeners, 209
  deploying, 220
  destroying Perl interpreter and Perl
    data, 220
  downloading, 207
  functions, 220
  installing, 217–220
    linking header files, 219
    ora_perl_boot.pl, 217–219
  obtaining version of, 220
  Perl and DBD::Oracle, patching
    DBD::Oracle, 214–216
  Perl DBI and DBD::Oracle, 212–217
    OCIExtProcContext, 213
  setting up external procedures, 207–209
  testing, 221
  Win32 and, 206
extproc_plsql, connecting with, 184
ExtProc.pm, 204
extracting
  binary data with sqlunldr.pl, 320
  data with sqlunldr.pl, 316–323
  DDL and data with PDBA Toolkit
    scripts, 315–327
  DDL with ddl_oracle.pl, 323–327
ExtUtils::Embed, 202

F

%fdat variable, 169
fetchall_arrayref method (Perl), 246
fetchall_arrayref method (Perl DBI), 471
fetchall_hashref method (Perl DBI), 471
fetchrow_array method (Perl DBI), 469
fetchrow_arrayref method (Perl DBI), 470
fetchrow_hashref method (Perl), 246
fctchrow_hashref method (Perl DBI), 470
Fibonaci numbers, 533
files
  C language, scanning for constructs, 186
  parameter, created by defrag.pl
    command, 90

finish method (Perl DBI), 473
_flush function (extproc_perl), 220
FORCE_CONFIG attribute, overriding
     ignoring of cm.conf, 267
foreach loops, Embperl syntax, 167
foreign_key_info method (Perl DBI), 477
FreeType, 101
FreezeThaw, required by Mason, 170
FreshMeat.net, Perl open source resource, 90
fromAddress parameter (dbup.conf), 356
function calls
    extracting DDL from (see ddl_oracle.pl)
    validating parameters, 170
functions
    cookie manipulation, 157
    OCI, 183–185
        categories of, 184
        one-to-one mapping with
            Oracle::OCI, 183

G

gathering statistics (see StatsView)
gcc compiler, Cygwin and, 52
gd library, DBD::Chart and, 100
gdb program, 210
GD.pm, DBD::Chart and, 98, 100
getColumns method (PDBA::GQ), 245
Getopt::Long, 348
    configuring for pass-through mode, 351
getptrdef.h, 188
GNU recode library, 545
gnuplot program
    gd and, 79
    graphics formats and, 76
    installing, 79
    PATH variable and, 80
    Statsview and, 74
    web resources for, 79
grep program, Perl regexes and, 484
GUI extensions to Perl, 65–109
guides to
    Perl, 439–458
    Perl data munging, 521–574
    Perl DBI, 459–481
    regular expressions, 482–520

H

%Hash data structure (pwd.pl), attributes
    of, 275
hash reference, retrieving, 245

hashes, 445
    anonymous, 455
        returning references to, 470
Hello World example, Perl DBI script, 48
hoursToPageImmediate parameter
    (dbup.conf), 356
HP-UX, installing Perl from from prebuilt
    package, 32
HTF package, 156
HTML
    generating via HTP, 156
    image maps, manipulating, 156
    utilities, 156
HTML::Mason (see Mason)
HTML::Parser, 139
HTML-SimpleParse, 139
HTML::Tagset, 139
HTML::Template, 176
HTP package, 156
httpd.conf, 143
    Apache::DBI and, 148
    Apache::Registry and, 146
    configuring Apache::OWA, 158
    configuring Mason for Apache, 173
    configuring mod_perl on Win32, 152
    environment variables, specifying, 149
HTTP_proxy/HTTP_proxy_* variables, PPM
    and, 47

I

%idat variable, 169
IDE (integrated development
    environment), 107
IDEA algorithm, 123
IDLE_TIME (Oracle), 305
idxr.conf
    command-line options, table of, 303
    fragmentation and, 302
    parameters, 301
idxr.pl, 230, 300–304
    testing, 303
    tracking, 304
image maps
    manipulating, 156
    for statistics (see DBD::Chart)
Import utility (Oracle), 316
index function (Perl), 485
index_column_diff_rpt, reporting changes to
    index columns, 386
index_column_rpt, reporting changes to
    index columns, 386

indexes
    analyzing via ANALYZE command, 382
    checking/rebuilding, 230
    determining whether rebuild required, 303
    maintaining, 229
        with PDBA Toolkit scripts, 297–304
    rebuilding with idxr.pl, 300–304
    tracking changes to (see PDBA repository;
        reports, of database changes)
index_rpt, reporting on indexes, 386
info method (PDBA::DBA), 235
installing
    Apache
        on Unix, 112–114
        on Win32, 114
    Apache::OWA
        on Unix, 157
        on Win32, 158
    chkalert_NT.pl on Win32, 337–342
    chkalert.pl on Unix, 331–336
    Date::Manip
        on Unix, 344
        on Win32, 344–347
    DBD::Chart
        on Unix, 98–103
        on Win32, 103
    DBD::Oracle, 44–46
        under Cygwin, 57–61
        environment variables, 44
        error hit list, 45
    DDL::Oracle, 325
        on Win32, 88
        on Unix, 85
    Embperl
        on Unix, 162
        on Win32, 163
    extproc_perl, 217–220
        linking header files, 219
        ora_perl_boot.pl, 217–219
    gnuplot, 79
    Karma
        on Unix, 128–130
        on Win32, 133
    kss_NT.pl, 309
    kss.pl, 308
    MailTools.pm, 130
    Mason
        on Unix, 169–171
        on Win32, 171
    mod_perl
        on Unix, 138–144
        on Win32, 151

modules
    via CPAN, 39–42
    methods for, 38–43
    traditional method for, 38, 42
modules on Win32, web resource for, 46
Open Perl IDE, 107
Orac, 82
Oracle::OCI
    on Unix, 186–189
    on Win32, 185
Oracletool
    on Unix, 119
    on Win32, 120
PDBA repository, 369–374
    access to
        V$PARAMETER/V$INSTANCE
        parameters, 372
    copying pdbarepq.conf, 373
    editing pdba_tbs8i.sql, 369
    tablespace creation, 369
PDBA Toolkit
    on Unix, 257–261
    on Win32, 261–265
PDBA Toolkit scripts, 229
PDBA Unix configuration files, 261
PDBAx, 422
Perl, 28–38
    under Cygwin, 52–56
    on Unix, 29–36
    on Win32, 36
Perl DBI, 38–47
    under Cygwin, 56
    on Unix, 43–46
    on Win32, 46–47
Perl/Tk
    on Unix, 67
    on Win32, 68
PNG, 77–79
recode library, 545
SchemaDiff, 90
SchemaView-Plus
    on Unix, 105
    on Win32, 106
Senora, 92
StatsView, 80–82
    sv program, 80
TermReadKey.pm, 129
Tk::GBARR, 75
XML::Dumper, 106
XML::Generator::DBI on Unix, 560
XML::LibXML on Unix, 555
XML::LibXSLT, 555

installing (*continued*)
    XML::Parser, 553
    XML::XMLtoDBMS on Unix, 566
    zlib, 76
%instanceAuth data structure (pwd.conf), 271
integrated development environment
        (IDE), 107
Internet, connecting to, Perl and, 201
Internet Perl clients, creating, 138
IO::Socket::SSL, 140
IRIX, installing Perl from from prebuilt
        package, 32

J

Java
    Perl and, 7
    Perl port of XML-DBMS from, 23
Java Server Pages (JSP), 161
JOB_QUEUE_PROCESSES parameter
        (Oracle), 379
join function (Perl), 485
Joint Photographic Experts Group (see JPEG)
JPEG (Joint Photographic Experts Group), 76
    DBD::Chart and, 99
JSP (Java Server Pages), 161

K

Kake Pad (Perl IDE), 108
Karma, 127–135
    configuring
        on Unix, 130–133
        on Win32, 134
    downloading, 128
    installing
        on Unix, 128–130
        on Win32, 133
    modules required by, 128
    OS monitor agent, 131
    running on Win32, 135
        Perl modules, extra, 135
    web resources for, 128
karmad program (see Win32, installing Karma)
KARMA_HOME variable, 129
-kill option (chkalert.pl), 336
Komodo (Perl IDE), 108
kss.conf, 310
kss_NT.pl, 230
    installing, 309
kss.pl, 230
    avoiding running on databases using
        MTS, 307
    command-line options, table of, 309

configuring, 310
    installing, 308
    on Win32 (see kss_NT.pl)
    running as owner of Oracle processes, 309
kss_service.pl, 230

L

large objects (LOBs), handling, 480
lc function (Perl), 485
lcfirst function (Perl), 486
LD_LIBRARY_PATH variable
    DBD::Chart and, 101
    Karma and, 129
    running Perl scripts on Unix, 49
Lempel Ziv Welch (LZW) algorithm, 78
length function (Perl), 486
lexical variables, Perl, 450
libapreq library, 157
libnet library, 128
    downloading, 130
    modules in, 130
libnet module, 139
liboci.a file, installing DBD::Oracle under
        Cygwin, 59
libperl, shared, determining whether running
        Perl distribution with, 210
libperl.a archive, 203
libraries
    C, Perl and, 202
    gd, 100
    GNU recode, 545
    libxml2, 553
    libxslt, 555
    mod_perl Apache, specifying, 142–144
    PERL_LIB, 220
libwww-perl, XML::Parser and, 553
libxml2 library
    downloading, 555
    interface to, 553
libxslt library, 555
line endings, 118
    (see also CR/LF)
Linux
    installing Perl from from prebuilt
        package, 32
    installing StatsView on
        Solaris ps -ef command, 80
        (see also StatsView, installing)
    Red Hat Linux (see Red Hat Linux,
        installing Apache::OWA)
    (see also Unix)
Linux Red Hat 6, x

Linux SuSE 7.3, x
    character sets, 545
    installing Oracle::OCI on, ORACLE not
        available errors with Oracle9i, 188
    Oracletool connection options, 120
list processor, DDL::Oracle as, 88
    defrag.pl, 89
lists in Perl, 448
LMTs (locally managed tablespaces), 312
    advantages of, 369
LOBs (large objects), handling, 480
locally managed tablespaces (see LMTs)
locks, locking strategies, 156
log files
    automating reading of, 244
    creating, 248
        independent of platforms, 249
    creating path to, 248
    peforming buffered/nonbuffered prints
        to, 248
logfile parameter (dbup.conf), 357
logFile parameter (idxr.conf), 302
logging by PDBA Toolkit scripts, 248
lossless vs. lossy compression, 100
ls option (Senora DataDictionary plug-in), 94
ls( ) subroutine, as example of security
        risk, 219
LWP Library for WWW access in Perl
        (see LWP.pm)
LWP.pm, 138
    CPAN packages used with, 139
    Embperl and, 163
    modules required by, 139
    optional SSL modules used with, 139
    required for mod_perl installation, 138
    running make test in mod_perl
        installation, 141
LZW (Lempel Ziv Welch) algorithm, 78

M

machine parameter (dbup.conf), 357
Mail::Sendmail, 258, 264
mailServer parameter (dbup.conf), 355
MailTools.pm, 128
    error notification in Karma, 132
    installing, 130
makepath method (PDBA::LogFile), 248
Manip.cnf, obtaining/configuring, 344–347
Mason, 161, 169–177
    configuring for Apache, 172–177
    downloading, 169

embedding Perl in template, 174
error browser reporting, 175
features, table of, 173
inline use of Perl, example program, 174
installing
    on Unix, 169–171
    on Win32, 171
modules required by, 169
performance of, 170
master_priv_rpt, reporting on database
        privilege grants, 386
matching regular expressions, 488
mathematic operations, 533
maxConnectRetries parameter
        (dbup.conf), 356
maxext.conf, 314
maxext.pl, 230, 313–315
    command-line options, table of, 315
    results from, 315
maxLogLines parameter (chkalert.pl), 333
maxRunTime parameter (idxr.conf), 301
%mdat variable, 169
metacharacters, 482, 488
    regexes, 494–509
        boundaries, 498
        character class shortcuts, 496
        escaped characters, 497
methods
    accessing DBMS_OUTPUT package, 478
    adding to PDBA module, 422–425
        usage method, 422–425
    PDBA module, 254–257
    PDBA::LogFile, 248
    Perl built-in string-handling, 485
    Perl DBI, 459–465
        metadata-related, 477
        Oracle-specific, 478–481
    used by PDBA Toolkit, 234
MIME::Base64, 139, 560
minExtentsCanExtend parameter
        (maxext.conf), 314
minPctBlocksUnused parameter
        (maxext.conf), 315
MLDBM (Multi-Level DBM), required by
        Mason, 169
modifying
    PDBA module, 422–425
        adding usage method, 422–425
    PDBA Toolkit modules, 421–435
    PDBA Toolkit scripts, 404–421
        dba_jobsm.pl, 419–421
    PDBA::GQ, 428–435

mod_perl, 137–155
  Apache mod_perl modules, table of, 145
  build options, 140
  CGI scripts and, 137
  configuring on Win32, 152
  downloading, 140
  Embperl and, 162
  independent distribution of, 151
  installing
    on Unix, 138–144
    on Win32, 151
  PL/SQL Web Toolkit and, 137
  specifying mod_perl Apache
      library, 142–144
  testing on Win32, 152
  web resources for, 137
  writing modules, 153–155
modules
  adding, 29
  Apache mod_perl, table of, 145
  Apache Perl, 144–151
  combining with PDBA Toolkit, 227
  CPAN
    conversion, 544–552
    date, 534–544
    mathematics, 533
    numeric, 531–533
    text conversion, 547–552
    XML, 552–574
  for data munging, 521
  described in this book, download sites, 17
  evolution of, 6
  installing
    via CPAN, 39–42
    methods for, 38–43
    traditional method for, 38, 42
    on Win32, web resource for, 46
  in libnet library, 130
  LWP.pm, required for mod_perl
      installation, 138
  PDBA Toolkit, 228, 231, 232–257
    modifying, 421–435
    password control, 250
    PDBA module, 254–257
    PDBA::CM, 232–234
    PDBA::ConfigFile, 235–237
    PDBA::ConfigLoad, 237–240
    PDBA::Daemon, 240–245
    PDBA::DBA, 234
    PDBA::GQ, 245–248
    PDBA::LogFile, 248–250
    PDBA::OPT, 250

    PDBA::PidFile, 251
    PDBA::PWC, 254
    PDBA::PWD, 252–254
    PDBA::PWDNT, 254
    Win32::Daemon, 240–245
  required by DBD::Chart, 98
  required by Embperl, 162
  required by Karma, 128
  required by LWP.pm, 139
  required by Mason, 169
  required by Oracle::OCI, 186
  required by SchemaView-Plus, 105
  required by XML::XMLtoDBMS, 565
  required for PDBA Toolkit, 258
  as tools for DBAs, 15
  Tuning.pm, 95
  upgrading, 29
  writing Win32 Perl Apache, 153–155
mostRecentlyAnalyzed parameter
      (idxr.conf), 301
MSI Microsoft Windows installer, 36
MTS (Multi-Threaded Server), avoiding
      running kss.pl on databases
      using, 307
mucr7.msg, 292
mucr8.conf, privileges in, 293
mucr8.msg, attributes, 293
mucr8.pl, 230, 290–295
  command-line options, table of, 294
Multi-Level DBM (see MLDBM)
multilevel hashes, serializing, 169
Multi-Threaded Server (see MTS)
"my" variables, Apache::Registry and, 146
my_script.pl, 230
MySQL
  transfering data from, 526–528
  web resources for, 526

N

Net8 listener process, 204
Net::Daemon, 51
Net::SSLeay, 139
new method
  PDBA::DBA, 235
  PDBA::GQ, 245
  PDBA::LogFile, 248
next method (PDBA::GQ), 245
  Perl fetchrow_hashref method and, 246
NFA (Nondeterministic Finite
      Automaton), 491
NLS_DATE_FORMAT parameter (dba_
      jobsm.pl), modifying, 419

Nondeterministic Finite Automaton
  (NFA), 491
NULL values
  Oracle databases and, 425
  testing use of, 425
null_test.pl, 231, 425
Number::Format, 532
numberFormat.pl, code example, 532
numeric operations, 531–533

O

object orientation, in Perl, 456–458
objects
  creating, 235
    with PDBA Toolkit script, 229
  dropping, 235
  examining space of with
    maxext.pl, 313–315
  gathering information about, 235
  monitoring size/number of extents in, 230
OCI (Oracle Call Interface), 13–15, 180
  datatype mapping functions, 185
  DML capabilities in, 180
  features, 180
  functions, 183–185
    categories of, 184
    one-to-one mapping with
      Oracle::OCI, 183
    table of, 14
  installing Perl DBI and, 38
  invoking with Oracle::OCI, 178–200
  navigational functions, 184
  Oracle::PLSQL, future availability, 198
  Perl DBI and, code example illustrating
    integration of, 195–198
  procedure functions, 184
  relational functions, 184
  type functions, 184
  Version 8.1 demonstration programs,
    table of, 200
  web resources for, 183
OCIExtProcContext, 213
  using Perl DBI for host callbacks, 216
Open Perl IDE, 107
OpenBSD, installing Perl from from prebuilt
    package, 32
OpenSSL program, 139
operating system commands, Perl and, 201
operating systems, x
operating systems documentation, regarding
    Perl, 441
OPS$ Oracle accounts, security of, 252

OptiPerl (Perl IDE), 108
.ora files, configuration of, setting up external
    procedures, 208
Orac, 65, 82–84
  directories for storing personal options, 83
  downloading, 82
  installing, 82
  personalizing, 83
  running, 83
  user options, table of, 84
  using DDL::Oracle with, 85–88
    example program, 86
orac_dba.pl program icon, 83
Oracle
  client libraries, Cygwin installation under
      DBD::Oracle installation, 57, 60
  data dictionary
    PDBA repository and, 366
    tables in PDBA repository, 367
  database server, connecting to (see OCI)
  databases
    limiting resource
      consumption, 305–308
    NULL values and, 425
    space problems on, 297–300
    transfering data to, 528–531
  date format, XML::XMLtoDBMS and, 566
  DDL and, 85
  embedding Perl into, 204–223
  environment variables
    DBD::Oracle and, 44
    predefining, 232
  external procedures, resources, 204
  schemas, comparing (see SchemaDiff)
  server, parallel server management
      (see OCI)
  user privileges, Oracletool selection
      reports, 122
  versions of, x
  XML and, 552
Oracle Call Interface (see OCI)
Oracle DDL from Oracle8i databases,
    reverse-engineering
    (see DDL::Oracle)
Oracle Enterprise database server
  mapping datatypes (see OCI, datatype
      mapping functions)
  navigating between objects supplied by
      (see OCI, navigational functions)
ORACLE not available errors, on Linux
    SuSE 7.73 with Oracle9i, 188
Oracle Technology Network (OTN), 182

oracle user
    building Perl for, 211
        resetting PATH variable, 212
    creating from command line, 230
    HOME directory, 211
Oracle8, data dictionary tables, PDBA
        repository and, 367
Oracle8i
    editing pdba_tbs8i.sql, 369
    LMTs in, 312
Oracle9i
    installing Oracle::OCI on
        ./boot test compilation errors, 188
    installing Oracle::OCI on Linux
        SuSE 7.73, ORACLE not available
        errors, 188
    Oracletool connection options, 120
    patching DBD::Oracle, 215
    setting up external procedures with
        PLExtProc, 209
Oracle9i Application HTTP Server (iAS), web
        resource, 112
ORACLE_BASE variable, cm.conf and, 266
ORACLE_HOME variable
    Apache and, 149
    cm.conf and, 266
    DBD::Oracle and, 215
    Karma and, 129
    Orac and, 83
    Oracletool and, 120, 121
    PDBA Toolkit and, 258
    Perl DBI Hello World example, 49
    SchemaView-Plus and, 106
    setting up external procedures, 209
OracleNet, 204
Oracle::OCI, 179
    architecture compared to Perl
        DBD::Oracle, 179
    C language vs., 181
    coding with, 190–198
        mixing modules, code
            example, 195–198
        Perl DBI and DBD::Oracle code
            example, 194
        pure Oracle::OCI code
            example, 190–194
        requirement, 179
    future of, 198–200
    installation directories, 189
    installing
        on Unix, 186–189
        on Win32, 185

invoking OCI with, 178–200
mail archive, 189
relationship to Perl DBD::Oracle, 181
resources for further information, 189
setting environment, 186
troubleshooting installation, 189
versions of, 187
Oracle::OCI Project, contributing to, 199
Oracle/Perl
    architecture, 10–15
    tools for DBAs, 15–24
Oracle::PLSQL, future availability, 198
ORACLE_SID variable
    DBD::Oracle and, 215
    Oracle::OCI and, 187
    PDBA Toolkit and, 258
Oracle_SID_AlertLogMon, testing, 340
Oracletool, 118–127
    adding SQL scripts to, 125
    connection options, 120
    initialization parameters, 121
    installing
        on Unix, 119
        on Win32, 120
    monitoring databases with, 125
    Preferences/privileges, 122
    security, 122–123
    selection reports, Oracle user
        privileges, 122
    v2.0 features, 124–127
    web resource for, 119, 123
ORACLE_USERID variable
    DBD::Oracle and, 45, 215
    Oracle::OCI and, 187
    PDBA Toolkit installation, 260
OraExplain, 65, 72
ora_explain.PL, 73
ora_module_name attribute (Perl DBI), 464
oramon account, PDBA Toolkit
        installation, 260
ora_oratab_orahome attribute (Perl DBI), 464
ora_perl_boot.pl bootstrap file, 204, 217–219
    using after installation, 219
ora_session_mode attribute (Perl DBI), 463
oratabFile parameter (chkalert.pl), 333
orclALRT.log, 329
osname method (PDBA module), 254
OTN (Oracle Technology Network), 182
OWA package, 156
OWA_COOKIE package, 157
OWA_IMAGE package, 157
OWA_OPT_LOCK package, 156

OWA_PATTERN package, 157
OWA_TEXT package, 157
OWA_UTIL package, 156

P

package variables, Perl, 449
packages
   ActivePerl for DDL::Oracle, 88
   extracting DDL from (see ddl_oracle.pl)
     Perl, 456
   PPM ActivePerl, advantages of, 46
   prebuilt, installing Perl on Unix from, 31
   .gz suffix and, 32
   required by Cygwin, 54
   downloading, 53
pager parameter (dbup.conf), 360
parameter files, created by defrag.pl
     command, 90
parameter_diff_rpt
   example output, 379
   reporting changes to initialization
     parameters, 386
parameter_rpt, reporting on initialization
     parameters, 386
parameters
   binding to SQL statements, 467
   configuring, 419
   initialization, reporting changes to, 386
   reporting changes to, 378–380
Params::Validate
   installing on Win32, 171
   Mason and, 170, 171
parentheses (()), Perl regex
     metacharacter, 495
password encryption
   via TCP socket, pwd.pl, 229
password server, 348–351
   client module communicating with, 254
   installing as Unix daemon or Win32
     service, 229
   installing kss_NT.pl, 309
   loading parameters, 353
   PDBA repository and, 375
   PDBA (see PDBA password server)
   scanning command line for options
     intended for, 250
passwords
   batch, problems with, 253
   encrypted, retrieving, 229
   encrypting
     PDBA Toolkit scripts, 229
     (see also password encryption)

generating in PDBA::DBA, 287
   inherent problems with, 253
   Karma security, TermReadKey.pm, 129
   managing via pwd.pl, 252
   Oracletool security levels, 122
   PDBA Toolkit password-control
     modules, 250
   security of, 253
PATH variable
   gnuplot and, 80
   installing Perl and, 30
   resetting when building Perl for oracle
     user, 212
   separator in, determining, 254
pathsep method (PDBA module), 254
PDBA Extensions (PDBAx), 422
PDBA module, 254–257
   adding usage method to, 422–425
   configuring, 265
   methods, 254–257
PDBA password client
   configuring, 275–278
     creating configuration file for, 276
PDBA password server
   configuring, 268–275
     encrypting passwords, 270
     securing pwd.conf, 272
     setting passwords, 268
     setting TCP port, 268
     setting up password server users, 270
     setting up per-account
       authorization, 271
   running on Unix, 273
   running on Win32, 273–275
     Windows NT 4.0/2000, 275
PDBA repository, 228
   allotting storage space for, 370
   changing date format in reports, 373
   creating baseline for, 231
   DBD::Oracle and, 374
   installing, 369–374
     access to
       V$PARAMETER/V$INSTANCE
       parameters, 372
     copying pdbarepq.conf, 373
     editing pdba_tbs8i.sql, 369
     tablespace creation, 369
   loading with data, 374–376
   Oracle data dictionary and, 366
     tables in, 367
   overhead, 366
   password server and, 375

PDBA repository (*continued*)
    specialized tables in, 368
    table structure, 367–369
    viewing data, 376
    (see also reports, of database changes)
PDBA Toolkit (Perl DBA Toolkit), 228–232
    building database repository
        with, 366–402
        (see also PDBA repository)
    configuring, 265–278
        password client, 275–278
        password server, 268–275
        PDBA module, 265
        PDBA::CM, 266
    connection manager, 232
    downloading, 259
    example behaviors to modify, 403
    extending, 231, 403–435
        (see also PDBA::OPT; PDBA::PWC)
    installing
        on Unix, 257–261
        on Win32, 261–265
    methods (see PDBA::DBA)
    modules, 228, 231, 232–257
        modifying, 421–435
        PDBA module, 254–257
        PDBA::CM, 232–234
        PDBA::ConfigFile, 235–237
        PDBA::ConfigLoad, 237–240
        PDBA::Daemon, 240–245
        PDBA::DBA, 234
        PDBA::GQ, 245–248
        PDBA::LogFile, 248–250
        PDBA::OPT, 250
        PDBA::PidFile, 251
        PDBA::PWC, 254
        PDBA::PWD, 252–254
        PDBA::PWDNT, 254
        Win32::Daemon, 240–245
    password client for NT (see
        PDBA::PWDNT)
    password client (see PDBA::PWC)
    passwords, managing (see PDBA::PWD)
    programs in, 228
    repository (see PDBA repository)
    required modules, directory for
        on Unix, 259
    security, script installation order, 229
    utilities logging (see PDBA::LogFile)
    utilities (see PDBA module)

PDBA Toolkit scripts, 227, 228–231
    baseline.pl, collecting baseline data
        dictionary data, 374
    checksums and, 397
    chkalert.pl, monitoring alert log with, 329
    create_user.pl, 281–287
    database administration, 229
    dba_jobsm.pl, 405–419
        configuring, 405
        functions/formats description, 417–419
        modifying, 419–421
        script description, 407–417
    dbup.pl/dbup_NT.pl
        monitoring database
            connections, 343–365
        testing monitor, 362–365
    ddl_oracle.pl, 323–327
    directory for on Unix, 259
    directory paths for, 279
    dropping user accounts, 296
    dup_user.pl, 288–290
    extending toolkit, 231
    extracting DDL and data, 315–327
    functions/formats, line-by-line description
        of, 417–419
    idxr.pl, rebuilding indexes, 300–304
    installing, 229
    killing sniped sessions, 305–311
    kss.pl
        installing on Unix, 308
        installing on Win32, 309
        line-by-line description of, 407–417
    logging by, 248
    maintaining indexes, 297–304
    managing extent usage, 312–315
    managing user accounts, 280–296
    maxext.pl, 313–315
    modifying, 404–421
    monitoring, 230
    monitoring alert log with, 328–342
    monitoring database connections, 342–365
    monitoring databases, 328–365
    mucr8.pl, 290–295
    password encryption, 229
    pdba_tbs8i.sql, 369
    repository, 231
    spdrvr.pl
        command-line options, 387–389
        implementation of, 384–392
        options and tags, 390–392

parameters, 379
   PDBA-generated SQL used with, 380
   predefined reports, 385–387
   reporting parameter changes, 378–380
   viewing repository data, 376
sqlunldr.pl, 316–323
SXP, 393
sxpcmp.pl, 400
   example output, 401
sxp.pl, 394–396
   command-line options, 395
   password/privilege messages, 396
   unique constraint error, 395
sxprpt.pl, 396
tablespace creation, 369
PDBA::CM, 232–234
   configuration file (see cm.conf)
   configuring, 266
   RaiseError/AutoCommit, 234
   SYSDBA/SYSOPER, login cases for, 233
pdba.conf, 265
PDBA::ConfigFile, 235–237
   simplifying configuration, 235–237
PDBA::ConfigLoad, 237–240
   loading script configuration files, 239
   referring to config variables by package
      name, 240
PDBA::Daemon, 240–245
   creating Unix daemon in Perl, 240–242
   using Unix daemons in Perl, 244
PDBA::DBA, 234
   creating user accounts, 234
   generating passwords in, 287
PDBA::GQ, 245–248
   modifying, 428–435
pdbaHome method (PDBA module), 254
   code example, 255
PDBA_HOME variable
   PDBA Toolkit and, 257
      default on Unix, 256
      installing on Win32, 261
      Unix configuration files, 261
   retrieving value of, 254
      code example, 255
   setting from command line, 257
PDBA::LogFile, 248–250
   methods, 248
   PERMS attribute, 250
PDBA::OPT, 230, 250, 347–353
   command-line overrides for, 353
   password server and, 348–351
PDBA::PidFile, 251

PDBA.ppd, 262
PDBA::PWC, 254, 347–353
   password server and, 348–351
   using in Perl scripts, 278
   on Win32 (see PDBA::PWDNT)
PDBA::PWD, 252–254
   PDBA password server and, 270
PDBA::PWDNT, 254
pdbarep_create.log, 373
pdbarep_create.sql, 372
pdbarepq.conf, 373, 380
pdba_tbs8i.sql, 369
PDBAx (PDBA Extensions), 422
percent sign (%)
   Perl in Mason template, 174
   Perl variable notation, 453
performance
   Apache::DBI and, 147
   Apache::Registry and, 146
   CGI scripts, 136
      (see also Apache::Registry)
   limiting resource consumption, 305
   Mason and, 170
   Perl and, 202
   perl_mod, 136
   sniped sessions and, 230, 305
   statistics, reporting via DBD::Chart, 95
Perl, 4
   advantages of, 7–10
   Apache and, 111
      (see also mod_perl)
   applications, servicing users/requests, 180
   arrays, 443
      determining size of, 444
   boolean variable type and, 448
   built-in functions, 441
   built-in string-handling functions, 485
   communicating with PL/SQL, 202
   connectivity with PL/SQL, 198
   contexts, 446
      list, 448
      scalar, 448
      void, 447
   corporate world and, 7
   creating Unix daemon, 240–242
   creating Win32 daemon, 242–244, 264
   data munging (see data munging)
   data parsing (see SchemaView-Plus)
   data structures, converting to/from
      strings, 170
   debuggers, 108

Perl (*continued*)
    distribution with shared libperl,
        determining whether running, 210
    documentation
        perldoc command, 439
        resources, 24–26
    downloading, 28
        from CPAN, 34
    driver for SQL*Plus, 231
    embedding into
        Apache (see mod_perl)
        C, 203
        Embperl templates, 166
        Mason template, 174
        Oracle, 204–223
        PL/SQL, 201–223
    FAQ documents, 440
    finding installation of, 30
    GUI extensions, 65–109
    guide to, 439–458
        (see also Perl scripts,
            program/subroutine parameters)
    hash structures, saving in
        platform-independent files, 170
    hashes, 445
    installing, 28–38
        under Cygwin, 52–56
        on Unix, 29–36
        on Win32, 36
    limitations of, 384
    manpage documents, 440
    modules (see modules)
    object orientation in, 456–458
    obtaining online information, 439–442
    operating system documentation, 441
    origins of, 4
    references, 451–456
        anonymous arrays/hashes, 455
        arrow notation, 453
        ref operator, 453
    regexes
        alternation/memory, 505–509
        delimiters in, 489
        greediness of, 500–502
        grep vs., 484
        history of, 484
        interpolated strings, 503
        metacharacters, 495
        scalar/list context results, 504
        string-handling functions and, 485
        (see also regular expressions)
    resources for futher information, 24
    scalars, 442

    scripts (see Perl scripts)
    security, web resource for modules, 223
    source, installing Perl on Unix
        from, 33–36
    storing data structures in, 162
    tools for DBAs, 15–24
        connectivity tools, 16
        modules and applications, 15
        scripts, 16
        table of, 17–24
    upgrading, 30
    "use strict" line in, 449
    using Unix daemons, 244
    using Win32 services, 244
    versions of, x
    web access in (see LWP.pm)
    web extensions, 110–135
    on Win32, 6
    writing ad hoc SQL reports, 384
    XML and, 552
        XML parsers, 553–559
<%perl> . . . </%perl> (angle
        brackets-percent signs), 175
Perl C library, calling, 203
Perl Database Interface (see Perl DBI)
Perl DBA Toolkit (see PDBA Toolkit)
Perl DBI (Database Interface), 11–13
    API, 12
    class methods, 459–465
    combining with Perl/Tk, 68–72
    connecting to
        Oracle, 460–464
        as SYSDBA/SYSOPER, 233
    database handles
        SQL and cleanup, 475–477
        statement handle methods, 465–474
    DBD::Oracle and, 459
        coding with Oracle::OCI, 194
    documentation, 26
    downloading, 47, 56
    extproc_perl and, 212–217
    functions, table of, 12
    guide to, 459–481
    installing, 38–47
        under Cygwin, 56
        on Unix, 43–46
        on Win32, 46–47
    limitations of, 178
    methods
        metadata-related, 477
        Oracle-specific, 478–481
    OCI and, code example illustrating
        integration of, 195–198

OCIExtProcContext and, 216
online documentation for, 459
origins of, 11
running
    Hello World example, 48
    by proxy, 50
using in loop-back mode, 212
variable naming conventions, 459
versions of, xi
Perl IDEs (integrated development
        environments), web resources
        for, 108
Perl integrated development environments
        (IDEs), web resources for, 108
Perl Interactive Query Tool (PIQT), 96
perl -MCPAN command
    interactive CPAN shell, 40
    loading LWP-related modules, 138
    loading mod_perl and related
        modules, 138
    PDBA Toolkit, installing modules
        required by, 259
perl orac_dbal.pl command, 83
Perl Package Description (see PPD)
Perl Package Manager (see PPM)
Perl scripts
    calling subroutines, 448
    debugging, 109
    environment variables, 449
        lexical, 450
        package, 449
    package main, 448
    PDBA Toolkit and, 259
    program/subroutine parameters, 448–451
    running, 442
        on Unix, 49
        on Win32, 50
    sending email from, 254, 256
    taint mode, 450
    using PDBA::PWC in, 278
perl -v command, 30
perldbgui program, 109
perldoc command, accessing Perl
        documentation, 439
perldoc ExtUtils::MakeMaker
        command, 260
PerlFreshRestart option, 143
PERL_LIB library, creating during cxtproc_
        perl deployment, 220
Perl/Oracle
    architecture, 10–15
    use by DBAs, 15–24

Perl/Oracle architecture, 10–15
    DBD::Oracle, 11–13
    OCI, 13–15
        functions, table of, 14
    Perl DBI, 11–13
Perl/Tk, 66–72
    combining with Perl DBI, 68–72
    downloading, 67
    example programs, 68, 71
    installing
        on Unix, 67
        on Win32, 68
    programs, basic structure of, 69
    resources for further information, 66
PERMS attribute (PDBA::LogFile), 250
persistent connections, 148
pie charts, for performance statistics
        (see DBD::Chart)
ping method (Perl DBI), 466
PIQT (Perl Interactive Query Tool), 96
PIRPC package, 51
platforms
    Apache runs on, 111
    creating log files independent of, 249
    for Perl/Oracle, x
    porting Unix applications to Win32
        (see Cygwin)
    retrieving types of, 254
PLSExtProc
    alternative use of for database context, 217
    patching DBD::Oracle, 215
PL/SQL
    advantages of Perl, 201
    communicating with Perl, 202
    connectivity with Perl, 198
    embedding Perl into, 201–223
    features, 201
    limitations of, 201
    (see also Perl, embedding into PL/SQL)
PL/SQL Runtime Engine, 204
PL/SQL Server Pages (PSPs), 162
PL/SQL Web Toolkit
    mod_perl and, 137
    packages in, 156
    (see also Apache::OWA)
plsql_errstr method (DBD::Oracle), 478
PluginMgr register command (Senora), 95
plug-ins, Senora
    DataDictionary, ls option, 94
    SQL*Plus vs., 93
    table of, 94

plus sign (+), Perl regex metacharacter, 495, 500

plus sign-question mark (+?), Perl regex metacharacter, 503

PNG (Portable Network Graphics), 76
   DBD::Chart and, 99
   installing, 77–79
   StatsView and, 76

$port data structure (pwd.conf), 268

portability, exporting/importing objects into Oracle databases, 316

Portable Network Graphics (see PNG)

POSIX commands, Mason and, 169

PPD (Perl Package Description), 46
   obtaining latest files, 47

ppm command, 47

PPM (Perl Package Manager), 46
   Perl DBI and, 46
   running, 46

ppm utility, 46
   (see also PPM)

prepare method
   PDBA::GQ, 246
   Perl DBI, 466

prepare_cached method (Perl DBI), 466

primary_key method (Perl DBI), 477

primary_key_info method (Perl DBI), 477

print method (PDBA::LogFile), 248

printflush method (PDBA::LogFile), 248, 250

printif method (PDBA::LogFile), 250

privileges
   developer account, 285
   granting while creating user accounts, 283
   in mucr8.conf file, 293
   reporting on database privilege grants, 386
   system, reporting on changes to, 386

procedures
   calling with OUT parameters, 467
   cookie manipulation, 157
   extracting DDL from (see ddl_oracle.pl)

profile_rpt, reporting on profiles, 386

PROFILEs
   creating, 306
   setting RESOURCE_LIMIT parameter (Oracle), 308

PROFILEs (Oracle), 305

programs
   background (see PDBA::Daemon; Win32::Daemon)
   concurrent, preventing running of, 251
   Perl scripts, 448–451

PSPs (PL/SQL Server Pages), 162

ptkdb program, 109

pwc.pl, 229, 254
   command-line options for, 276
   (see also PDBA password client)

%pwd data structure (pwd.conf), 268

pwd.conf
   data structures, 268
   securing, 272
   (see also PDBA password server)

pwd.pl, 229
   password management in, 252

pwd_service.pl, 229
   locating on Win32, 274

Q

qed program, regular expressions and, 484

queries, generic (see PDBA::GQ)

question mark (?), Perl regex metacharacter, 496, 500

question mark-question mark (??), Perl regex metacharacter, 503

quotas, setting while creating user accounts, 283

quote method (Perl DBI), 466

R

RaiseError attribute, connecting to Oracle databases via PDBA::CM, 234

recode library, 545

Red Hat Linux, installing Apache::OWA, 157

ref operator in Perl, 453
   main return values of, 454

regexes (see regular expressions)

registry, PDBA settings, 262

regular expressions, 156, 482
   altering operation of, 509–520
   architectures, 491–492
   capturing backreferences, 505–509
   concepts, 487–492
   data munging and, 501
   guide to, 482–520
   history of, 483–485
   implicit use of $_, 489
   input, 488
   left-to-right assumption, 490–491
   match suffixes, 509–520
   matching/substituting/translating, 488
   metacharacters, 494–509
      boundaries, 498
      character class shortcuts, 496
      escaped characters, 497

Perl and, 202
PL/SQL Web Toolkit, 202
qed/ed/vi, 484
resource for further information, 482
split operator, 519
-report_list option (spdrvr.pl), 389
reports
    comparing SQL execution plans, 397–402
    of database changes, 377–392
        predefined in spdrvr.pl, 385–387
    performance statistics via DBD::Chart, 95
    writing SQL, comparing Perl and
        SQL*Plus, 385
-rep_report parameter_diff_rpt
        command, 378
-rep_start_date/-rep_end_date switches, 378
reverse function (Perl), 486
rindex (Perl), 486
role_privs_diff_rpt, reporting on changes to
        privileges, 386
role_privs_rpt, reporting on privileges, 386
role_rpt, reporting on roles, 386
roles, reports on, 386
rollback method (Perl DBI), 476
rows
    fetching from arrays, 469
    retrieving, 245
rows method (Perl DBI), 474
RPC::PlClient, 51
RPC::PlServer, 51

S

scalability, mod_perl, 137
scalar values, in Perl, 442, 448
scheduled jobs, checking on, 405–419
SchemaDiff, 66, 90–92
    downloading, 90
    installing, 90
    running, 91
schemas
    comparing/generating
        (see also SchemaDiff)
    , 231
    dumping, example of, 318
        (see also sqlunldr.pl)
    examining/saving (see SchemaView-Plus)
    tracking changes to (see PDBA repository;
        reports, of database changes)
SchemaView-Plus, 66, 104–106
    installing on Unix, 105
    installing on Win32, 106

scripts
    CGI (see CGI scripts)
    configuration files
        changing (see PDBA::ConfigLoad;
            PDBA::ConfigFile)
        loading, 237, 239
        locating, 237
    created by defrag.pl command, 89
    for DBA tasks, avoiding cutting/pasting
        (see DDL::Oracle)
    PDBA Toolkit (see PDBA Toolkit scripts)
    Perl (see Perl scripts)
    web (see embedded web scripting)
Secure Sockets Layer (SSL), modules used
        with LWP.pm, 139
security
    batch job passwords and, 253
    Cygwin and, 56
    EXTPROC and, 205
    ls( ) subroutine as example of risk, 219
    OPS$ Oracle accounts, 252
    Oracletool, 119, 122–123
    passwords and, 253
    PDBA password server and, 270
    PDBA Toolkit, script installation order, 229
    Perl, web resource for security
        modules, 223
    pwd.conf, 272
        %instanceAuth data structure, 271
    (see also passwords)
SELECT statements (Oracle), 471
selectall_arrayref method (Perl DBI), 475
selectall_hashref method (Perl DBI), 476
selectcol_arrayref method (Perl DBI), 476
selectrow_array method (Perl DBI), 475
Senora, 66, 92–95
    DataDictionary plug-in, ls option, 94
    downloading, 92
    flexibility of, 94
    installing, 92
    options, Unix-style, 93
    plug-ins, table of, 94
    running, 94–95
    SQL*Plus and, 93
sequence_rpt, reporting on sequences, 386
serverName parameter (chkalert.pl), 334
sessions
    limiting resource consumption, 305
    sniped, killing, 230
    with PDBA Toolkit scripts, 305–311
SHARED_POOL_SIZE parameter
        (Oracle), 379

sleepTime parameter (kss.conf), 310
Solaris
    installing Perl from prebuilt package, 31
    installing StatsView on, ps -ef
        command, 80
        (see also StatsView, installing)
Solaris 8, x
    installing Apache::OWA, 157
SourceForge.net, Perl open source resource, 90
spdrvr.pl, 231
    command-line options, 387–389
        date options, 390
        options and tags, 390–392
        -report_list option, 389
        report-specific options, 388
        text options, 391
    implementation of, 384–392
    parameters, 379
    PDBA-generated SQL used with, example
        of, 380
    predefined reports, 385–387
    reporting parameter changes, 378–380
    viewing repository data, 376
split function (Perl), 486
split operator (regex), 519
sprintf function (Perl), 486
    formats for, 487
SPX report, comparing execution
        plans, 397–402
SQL
    cache, warning about excursions into, 395
    collecting for PDBA repository, 394–396
    execution plans (see SQL execution plans)
    execution, troubleshooting
        slowdown, 368, 393
    scripts (see SQL scripts)
    statements (see SQL statements)
    tracking in V$SQLTEXT data dictionary
        view, 368, 393
SQL execution plans
    and cache examination (see OraExplain)
    comparing, 231
    reporting on, 231, 392–402
SQL explain plan (see SXP)
SQL Query Tool, 96
SQL scripts
    adding to Oracletool, 125
    created by defrag.pl command, 90
    repository of (see Orac)
SQL statements
    binding parameters to, 467
    collecting/storing from data dictionary, 231

examining, 231, 393
    generating XML files from, 560–562
    number of rows processed by, 474
SQL*Loader, 180
SQL*Net, 204
SQL*Plus
    alternative to (see Senora)
    dropping user accounts, limitations of, 296
    Perl compared to, 384
    Perl DBI tools, 96
    Perl driver for, 231
    Senora and, 93
    writing ad hoc SQL reports, 384
SQL*Plus Driver (see spdrvr.pl)
sqlunldr.pl, 229, 316–323
    command-line options, table of, 317
    features of, 316
square brackets ([]), 167
    Perl, 444
    Perl regex metacharacter, 495
square brackets-caret sign ([^]), Perl regex
        metacharacter, 495
square brackets-exclamation points ([! . . . !]),
        Perl in Embperl template, 166
square brackets-hyphens ([- . . . -]), Perl in
        Embperl template, 166
square brackets-plus signs ([+ . . . +]), Perl in
        Embperl template, 166
SSL (Secure Sockets Layer), modules used
        with LWP.pm, 139
<<START_DATE_PK>> tag (spdrvr.pl), 390
STARTUP_EXTPROC_AGENT, debugging
        external procedures setup, 210
statement handle metadata, Perl DBI, 477
statement handles, creating, 466
statistics, gathering (see StatsView)
StatsView, 65, 74–82
    downloading, 75–80
        gnuplot installation, 79
        PNG installation, 77–79
        PNG, need for, 76
        zlib installation, 76
    installing, 80–82
        ps -ef command, 80
        sv program, 80
    installing Tk::GBARR, 75
Storable
    downloading, 163
Storable package, 51, 139
    required by Mason, 170

Storable.pm
    Embperl on Unix, storing data structures
        in Perl, 162
    interface with Apache, 163
strings
    functions for handling in Perl, 485
    interpolated in Perl regexes, 503
subroutines, Perl scripts, 448–451
substitution operator, regexes, 488
substr function (Perl), 486
suffixes of regexes, 482
sv program (StatsView), 80
svplus program, 106
SXP (SQL explain plan)
    repository tables, 369
    scripts, 393
sxpcmp.pl, 231, 393, 400
    example output, 401
sxp.pl, 231, 393, 394–396
    command-line options, 395
    password/privilege messages, 396
    unique constraint error, 395
sxprpt.pl, 231, 393, 396
SYSDBA/SYSOPER, login cases for with
        PDBA::CM, 233
sys_privs_diff_rpt, reporting on changes to
        system privileges, 386
sys_privs_rpt, system privileges, 386

T

table_info method (Perl DBI), 477
table_privs_diff_rpt, reporting changes to
        table privileges, 384, 386
table_privs_rpt, reporting on table
        privileges, 387
table_rpt, reporting on tables, 382, 387
tables
    analyzing via ANALYZE command, 382
    dumping several (see sqlunldr.pl)
    indexes on (see indexes)
    in PDBA repository, structure of, 367–369
        Oracle data dictionary tables, 367
    reporting on, 382, 387
        (see also reports, of database changes)
    SXP repository, 369
    tracking changes to (see PDBA repository)
tables method (Perl DBI), 477
tablespace_rpt, reporting on tablespaces, 387
tablespaces, 286
    creating, PDBA repository installation, 369
    locally managed, 312
    reporting on, 387

taint mode in Perl scripts, 450
Template Toolkit, 176
templating (see embedded web scripting)
TermReadKey.pm, 128
    installing, 129
testing
    extproc_perl, 221
    mod_perl on Win32, 152
text processing, modules for, 547–552
Text::Abbrev, 548
Text::ParseWords, 549
Text::Soundex, 550
throttleDelaySeconds parameter
        (chkalert.pl), 334
time/date information
    -dateformat option, 318
    leap seconds in calendar, 540
    modules, 534–544
    parsing, 258, 264, 344
    PDBA repository reports, changing
        in, 373
TimeDate module, 258, 264
    XML::XMLtoDBMS and, 565
time/date utilities, 156
Time::HiRes, required by Mason, 169
Tk::GBARR, installing, 75
Tk::JPEG
    DBD::Chart installation, 103
    using Perl/Tk canvas applications with, 99
Tk::PNG, DBD::Chart installation, 103
TNS_ADMIN variable
    cm.conf and, 266
    Oracletool and, 120, 121
    PDBA Toolkit and, 258
tnsnames.ora, setting up external
        procedures, 208
trace method (Perl DBI), 464
tracing levels, table of, 464
translate operator, regular expressions, 488
troubleshooting
    developer PDBA role/connect PDBA
        role, 296
    SQL execution slowdown, 368
    (see also debugging)
Tuning.pm module, 95
TWO_TASK variable
    Oracle::OCI and, 188
    PDBA Toolkit and, 258
type_info method (Perl DBI), 477
type_info_all method (Perl DBI), 477
TZ variable, Date::Manip and, 344–347

U

uc/ucfirst functions (Perl), 487
%udat variable, 169
UltraEdit (Perl IDE), 108
Unix
administering (see StatsView)
alert log on, 329
background programs, 240
configuring chkalert.pl on, 331–336
configuring dbup.pl on, 354
configuring Karma on, 130–133
Karma OS monitor agent, 131
daemons
creating in Perl, 240–242
resource for further information, 241
using in Perl, 244
directory for PDBA Toolkit scripts, 279
installing Apache on, 112–114
APACI installation, 113
directory for CGI scripts, 114
installing Apache::OWA on, 157
installing chkalert.pl on, 331–336
locating/updating
chkalert.conf, 331–334
installing Date::Manip on, 344
installing DBD::Chart on, 98–103
gd library and, 100
GD.pm, 101
JPEG and, 99
required downloads, 99
required libraries, 99
required modules, 98
Tk::JPEG, 103
Tk::PNG, 103
installing DDL::Oracle on, 85, 325
installing Embperl on, 162
LWP.pm installation, 163
modules required, 162
installing Karma on, 128–130
MailTools.pm installation, 130
TermReadKey.pm installation, 129
installing kss.pl on, 308
installing Mason on, 169–171
modules required, 169
installing mod_perl on, 138–144
build options, 140
include paths, 140
LWP.pm, 138
modules required by LWP.pm, 139
optional SSL modules, 139

preinstallation security measure, 140
specifying mod_perl Apache
library, 142–144
installing Oracle::OCI on, 186–189
errors in build, troubleshooting, 189
installing Oracletool on, 119
installing password server as daemon, 229
installing PDBA Toolkit on, 257–261
account to install from, 258
Perl modules/scripts
installation, 258–261
setting PDBA environment, 257
installing PDBAx on, 422
installing Perl DBI on, 43–46
installing Perl on, 29–36
from prebuilt package, 31
from source, 33–36
installing Perl/Tk on, 67
X Windows server access, 68
installing SchemaView-Plus on, 105
installing XML::Generator::DBI on, 560
installing XML::LibXML on, 555
installing XML::Parser on, 553
installing XML::XMLtoDBMS on, 566
running PDBA password server on, 273
running Perl scripts on, 49
shared objects, 202
upDays parameter (dbup.conf), 357
upHours parameter (dbup.conf), 358
URI module, 139
XML::Parser and, 553
"use strict" line in Perl code, 449
user accounts (see accounts)
username parameter (dbup.conf), 358
user_rpt, reporting on users, 387
%users data structure (pwd.conf), 270
utilities
development (see Oracletool)
in PDBA Toolkit (see PDBA module)

V

variables
CGI environment, Apache::Registry
and, 147
config, referring to by package name, 240
naming, Embperl syntax, 168
Perl DBI naming conventions, 459
Perl hash, 168
uninitialized lexical, Apache::Registry
and, 146

version control system, reporting database
    changes and, 378
_version function (extproc_perl), 220
vertical bar (|), Perl regex metacharacter, 495
vi program, regular expressions and, 484
V$INSTANCE parameter (pdbarep_
    grants.sql), 372
V$PARAMETER parameter (pdbarep_
    grants.sql), 372
V$SQLTEXT data dictionary table, tracking
    SQL in, 368

W

wantarray function (Perl), 505
watchdogLength/Time parameter
    (chkalert.pl), 334
web data, storing persistent, 163
web extensions to Perl, 110–135
web forms
    handling via Embperl, 168
    storing data associated with, 169
web servers (see Apache)
web sites for downloading Perl, modules,
    tarballs, and items related to this
    book (see downloading)
while loops, Embperl syntax, 167
Win32
    alert log on, 329
    background programs, 240
    CGI scripts, 116
    configuring dbup_NT.pl on, 354
    configuring Karma on, 134
    configuring mod_perl on, 152
    creating daemon in Perl, 242–244, 264
    DDLs, 202
    directory for PDBA Toolkit scripts, 279
    environment variables
        PPM and, 47
        web resource for, 47
    extproc_perl and, 206
    installing Apache on, 114
        directory for CGI scripts, 115
        running Apache as console
            application, 115
    installing Apache::OWA on, 158
    installing chkalert_NT.pl on, 337–342
    installing Date::Manip on, 344–347
        TZ variable, 344–347
    installing DBD::Chart on, 103
        loading DBD::Chart for
            ActivePerl, 104
    installing DDL::Oracle on, 88

installing Embperl on, 163
installing Karma on, 133
installing kss_NT.pl on, 309
installing Mason on, 171
installing mod_perl on, 151
installing Number::Format on, 533
installing Oracle::OCI on, 185
    ORACLE not available errors on Linux
        SuSE 7.3, 188
    precursor modules required, 186
installing Oracletool on, 120
    securing oracletool.pl, 121
installing password server as service, 229
installing PDBA Toolkit on, 261–265
    additional Perl modules
        installation, 263–265
    registry settings, 262
installing PDBAx on, 422
installing Perl DBI on, 46–47
installing Perl on, 36
    local drives, 37
installing Perl/Tk on, 68
installing SchemaView-Plus on, 106
Perl and, 6
Perl Apache modules, writing, 153–155
porting Unix applications to (see Cygwin)
running Karma on, 135
    Perl modules, extra, 135
running PDBA password server, 273–275
running PDBA password server on
    Windows NT 4.0/2000, 275
running Perl on, Cygwin and, 52
running Perl scripts on, 50
service control application, Perl
    services, 242
sniped sessions, killing, 230
testing mod_perl on, 152
using services in Perl, 244
web resource for Apache, 112
Win32::Daemon, 240–245, 264
    chkalert_NT.pl and, 337
    creating Win32 daemon in Perl, 242–244
    PDBA password server and, 273
    using Win32 services in Perl, 244
Windows 2000, x
    installing kss_NT.pl on, 309
    PDBA password server on, 275
    starting alert log monitoring service, 339
    starting kill sniped session service on, 309
Windows 95/98
    MSI Microsoft Windows program
        installer, 37

Windows NT
MSI Microsoft Windows program
installer, 37
starting alert log monitoring service, 339
starting kill sniped session service, 309
Windows NT 4.0, x
PDBA password server, 275

X

X PixMap (XPM), support for, 101
X Windows server, Perl/Tk Unix installation
and, 68
XML (Extensible Markup Language)
data parsing (see SchemaView-Plus)
database facilities, 559–574
modules, 552–574
database facilities, 559–574
parsers, 553–559
XML::XMLtoDBMS (see
XML::XMLtoDBMS)
XML-DBMS Version 2.0, forthcoming
features, 574
XML::Dumper
downloading, 106
installing, 106

xmlGenDBI.pl, 561
XML::Generator::DBI, 560–562
installing on Unix, 560
XML::Handler::YAWriter, 560
XML::LibXML, 553
installing on Unix, 555
XML::LibXSLT, 555
XML::Parser, 553
XML::Parser::PerlSAX, 560
XML::XMLtoDBMS, 565–574
installing on Unix, 566
modules required by, 565
Oracle date format and, 566
XML sink input, 573
XML sink mapping, 571
XML source mapping, 568–570
XML source output, 570
XML::XPath, 562–565
XPM (X PixMap), support for, 101
XSLT (Extensible Stylesheet Language
Transformations), 556

Z

zlib program, 76
DBD::Chart and, 99

About the Authors

Andy Duncan is the coauthor of *Oracle & Open Source* (O'Reilly, 2001), as well as *Perl for Oracle DBAs* (O'Reilly, 2002). The first book arose after Andy's creation, in 1998, of the Orac Perl/Tk tool for Oracle DBAs. Since then, he has worked mainly as an independent development and DBA consultant, and has counted both Oracle Corporation and Sun Microsystems among his long-term clients. In addition to performing Oracle, Perl, and Java consultancy work, Andy teaches as a senior instructor for Learning Tree International, covering both introductory and advanced Perl courses. He lives in Oxfordshire, England, and can be reached via *andy_j_duncan@yahoo.com*.

Jared Still has been an Oracle DBA in health insurance and manufacturing environments since 1994 (and version 7.0.13 of Oracle). He first began dabbling with Perl in 1993 and it was love at first sight. Perl became an integral part of his Oracle toolkit when it was used to rapidly prototype and implement complex reporting based on data in Oracle databases. Jared has been working with databases of various ilks since 1988, and along the way has also worked as a Unix system administrator. When not riding herd on the databases at the OK Corral, he likes to spend time tinkering on his car, fly fishing, or sitting on the deck in the backyard at his home doing absolutely nothing. He can be reached at *jkstill@cybcon.com*.

Colophon

Our look is the result of reader comments, our own experimentation, and feedback from distribution channels. Distinctive covers complement our distinctive approach to technical topics, breathing personality and life into potentially dry subjects.

The animals on the cover of *Perl for Oracle DBAs* are thread-winged lacewings. Lacewings can be found all over the world, primarily in warmer climates. They live mostly in sheltered, sandy areas such as wooded dunes, forest floors, and riverbanks, until they reach adult form, at which time their wings enable them to roam more freely.

In their larvae state, lacewings prey voraciously on such unsuspecting victims as aphids, mites, and scale insects. They hide under pieces of wood or debris, wait for insects to pass, then attack with their pincer-like mandibles.

Lacewings undergo full metamorphosis throughout their lives. The adult form is characterized by two sets of wings, a long, slender abdomen, and clubbed antennae. Lacewings are one type of many nerve-winged insects because of the intricate pattern of lines (nerves) running through their transparent wings.

Darren Kelly was the production editor for *Perl for Oracle DBAs*. Nancy Crumpton provided production services and wrote the index. Jan Fehler was the copyeditor. Tatiana Apandi Diaz and Claire Cloutier provided quality control.

ɔy designed the cover of this book, based on a series design by Edie The cover image is a 19th-century engraving from *The Riverside Natural* ɔlume 2. Emma Colby produced the cover layout with QuarkXPress 4.1 ɔe's ITC Garamond font.

David ɔato designed the interior layout. This book was converted to FrameMaker 5.5.6 with a format conversion tool created by Erik Ray, Jason McIntosh, Neil Walls, and Mike Sierra that uses Perl and XML technologies. The text font is Linotype Birka; the heading font is Adobe Myriad Condensed; and the code font is Lucas-Font's TheSans Mono Condensed. The illustrations that appear in the book were produced by Robert Romano and Jessamyn Read using Macromedia FreeHand 9 and Adobe Photoshop 6. The tip and warning icons were drawn by Christopher Bing. This colophon was written by Linley Dolby.

More Titles from O'Reilly

Oracle Books for DBAs

Oracle SQL*Plus: The Definitive Guide

By Jonathan Gennick
1st Edition March 1999
526 pages, ISBN 1-56592-578-5

This book is the definitive guide to SQL*Plus, Oracle's interactive query tool. Despite the wide availability and usage of SQL*Plus, few developers and DBAs know how powerful it really is. This book introduces SQL*Plus, provides a syntax quick reference, and describes how to write and execute script files, generate ad hoc reports, extract data from the database, query the data dictionary tables, use the SQL*Plus administrative features (new in Oracle8i), and much more.

Oracle Essentials: Oracle9i, Oracle8i & Oracle8

By Rick Greenwald, Robert Stackowiak & Jonathan Stern
2nd Edition June 2001
381 pages, ISBN 0-596-00179-7

Updated for Oracle's latest release, Oracle9i, Oracle Essentials is a concise and readable technical introduction to Oracle features and technologies, including the Oracle architecture, data structures, configuration, networking, tuning, and data warehousing. It introduces such major Oracle9i features as Real Application clusters, flashback queries, clickstream intelligence, Oracle Database and Web Cache, XML integration, the Oracle9i Application Server, Oracle9i Portal, and much more.

Oracle Database Administration: The Essential Reference

By David Kreines & Brian Laskey
1st Edition April 1999
580 pages, ISBN 1-56592-516-5

This book provides a concise reference to the enormous store of information Oracle8 or Oracle7 DBAs need every day. It covers DBA tasks (e.g., installation, tuning, backups, networking, auditing, query optimization) and provides quick references to initialization parameters, SQL statements, data dictionary tables, system privileges, roles, and syntax for SQL*Plus, Export, Import, and SQL*Loader.

Oracle DBA Checklists Pocket Reference

By Quest Software
1st Edition April 2001
80 pages, ISBN 0-596-00122-3

In a series of easy-to-use checklists, the Oracle DBA Checklists Pocket Reference summarizes the enormous number of tasks an Oracle DBA must perform. Each section takes the stress out of DBA problem solving with a step-by-step "cookbook" approach to presenting DBA quick-reference material, making it easy to find the information you need—and find it fast.

Unix for Oracle DBAs Pocket Reference

By Donald K. Burleson
1st Edition January 2001
110 pages, ISBN 0-596-00066-9

If you are an Oracle DBA moving to Unix from another environment such as Windows NT or IBM Mainframe, you know that the commands you need to learn are far different from those covered in most beginning Unix books. In this handy pocket-sized book, Don Burleson introduces those Unix commands that you as an Oracle DBA most need to know.

Oracle RMAN Pocket Reference

Darl Kuhn & Scott Schulze
1st Edition November 2001
126 pages, ISBN 0-596-00233-5

Oracle RMAN Pocket Reference is ideal for DBAs who require a concise reference to common RMAN tasks. The first portion of the book presents commands for such tasks as taking a full database backup, recovering from loss of data file, and cloning a database. The second portion offers a very concise RMAN syntax reference. This book will save DBAs time when performing tasks that are infrequent, yet extremely vital.

O'REILLY®

TO ORDER: 800-998-9938 • order@oreilly.com • www.oreilly.com
ONLINE EDITIONS OF MOST O'REILLY TITLES ARE AVAILABLE BY SUBSCRIPTION AT safari.oreilly.com
ALSO AVAILABLE AT MOST RETAIL AND ONLINE BOOKSTORES

Perl

Learning Perl, 3rd Edition

By Randal Schwartz & Tom Phoenix
3rd Edition July 2001
330 pages, ISBN 0-596-00132-0

Learning Perl is the quintessential tutorial for the Perl programming language. The third edition has not only been updated to Perl Version 5.6, but has also been rewritten from the ground up to reflect the needs of programmers learning Perl today. Other books may teach you to program in Perl, but this book will turn you into a Perl programmer.

Mastering Regular Expressions

By Jeffrey E. F. Friedl
1st Edition January 1997
368 pages, ISBN 1-56592-257-3

Regular expressions, a powerful tool for manipulating text and data, are found in scripting languages, editors, programming environments, and specialized tools. In this book, author Jeffrey Friedl leads you through the steps of crafting a regular expression that gets the job done. He examines a variety of tools and uses them in an extensive array of examples, with a major focus on Perl.

Learning Perl on Win32 Systems

By Randal L. Schwartz, Erik Olson & Tom Christiansen
1st Edition August 1997
306 pages, ISBN 1-56592-324-3

In this carefully paced course, leading Perl trainers and a Windows NT practitioner teach you to program in the language that promises to emerge as the scripting language of choice on NT. Based on the "llama" book, this book features tips for PC users and new NT-specific examples, along with a foreword by Larry Wall, the creator of Perl, and Dick Hardt, the creator of Perl for Win32.

Perl/Tk Pocket Reference

By Stephen Lidie
1st Edition November 1998
103 pages, ISBN 1-56592-517-3

The *Perl/Tk Pocket Reference* is a companion volume to *Learning Perl/Tk*. This handy reference book describes every Perl/Tk graphical element, including general widget and variable information, callbacks, geometry management, bindings, events, and window management, as well as composite widget, font, and image creation and manipulation commands.

Mastering Perl/Tk

By Steve Lidie & Nancy Walsh
1st Edition January 2002
768 pages, ISBN 1-56592-716-8

Beginners and seasoned Perl/Tk programmers alike will find *Mastering Perl/Tk* to be the definitive book on creating graphical user interfaces with Perl/Tk. After a fast-moving tutorial, the book goes into detail on creating custom widgets, working with bindings and callbacks, IPC techniques, and examples using many of the nonstandard add-on widgets for Perl/Tk (including Tix widgets). Every Perl/Tk programmer will need this book.

Perl Cookbook

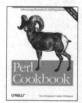

By Tom Christiansen & Nathan Torkington
1st Edition August 1998
794 pages, ISBN 1-56592-243-3

The *Perl Cookbook* is a comprehensive collection of problems, solutions, and practical examples for anyone programming in Perl. You'll find hundreds of rigorously reviewed Perl "recipes" for manipulating strings, numbers, dates, arrays, and hashes; pattern matching and text substitutions; references, data structures, objects, and classes; signals and exceptions; and much more.

o stay in touch with O'Reilly

inning web site

reilly.com/

Web"—PC Magazine
Business 50 Awards

Our web site is a library of comprehensive product
information (including book excerpts and tables of
contents), downloadable software, background articles,
interviews with technology leaders, links to relevant sites,
book cover art, and more. File us in your bookmarks or
favorites!

2. Join our email mailing lists

Sign up to get email announcements of new books and
conferences, special offers, and O'Reilly Network technology newsletters at:

> *http://www.elists.oreilly.com*

It's easy to customize your free elists subscription so
you'll get exactly the O'Reilly news you want.

3. Get examples from our books

To find example files for a book, go to:

> *http://www.oreilly.com/catalog*

select the book, and follow the "Examples" link.

4. Work with us

Check out our web site for current employment
opportunites:

> *http://jobs.oreilly.com/*

5. Register your book

Register your book at:

> *http://register.oreilly.com*

6. Contact us

O'Reilly & Associates, Inc.
1005 Gravenstein Hwy North
Sebastopol, CA 95472 USA
TEL: 707-827-7000 or 800-998-9938
(6am to 5pm PST)
FAX: 707-829-0104

order@oreilly.com
For answers to problems regarding your order or
our products. To place a book order online visit:
http://www.oreilly.com/order_new/

catalog@oreilly.com
To request a copy of our latest catalog.

booktech@oreilly.com
For book content technical questions or corrections.

proposals@oreilly.com
To submit new book proposals to our editors and
product managers.

international@oreilly.com
For information about our international distributors
or translation queries. For a list of our distributors
outside of North America check out:
http://international.oreilly.com/distributors.html

O'REILLY®

TO ORDER: **800-998-9938** • **order@oreilly.com** • **www.oreilly.com**
ONLINE EDITIONS OF MOST O'REILLY TITLES ARE AVAILABLE BY SUBSCRIPTION AT **safari.oreilly.com**
ALSO AVAILABLE AT MOST RETAIL AND ONLINE BOOKSTORES